The War Lords
Military Commanders of the Twentieth Century

Edited by

Field Marshal Sir Michael Carver

LITTLE, BROWN AND COMPANY   BOSTON · TORONTO

FIRST AMERICAN EDITION

T 10/76

LIBRARY OF CONGRESS CATALOGING IN PUBLICATION DATA

Main entry under title:

The War lords.

Includes index.
1. Military biography. 2. Military history, Modern —
20th century. I. Carver, Michael, Sir, 1915-
U51.W32 1976   355.3′31′0922 [B]   76-14402
ISBN 0-316-13060-5

PRINTED IN THE UNITED STATES OF AMERICA

CONTENTS

Contents

Contents

ACKNOWLEDGEMENTS

Acknowledgement is due to Richard Barry for his translation of the chapters on Marshal Joffre, Marshal Foch, Field-Marshal von Rundstedt and Marshal Juin.

INTRODUCTION

Field-Marshal Sir Michael Carver,
General Editor

The twentieth century has brought new dimensions to war. This book sets out to show how the major military figures in the two world wars of the first half of the century attempted to direct war in conditions which, certainly as far as the First World War was concerned, were unfamiliar. The pace of change was fast and the military profession tends to be conservative between wars for lack of opportunity to test itself in changing conditions. In war change is so rapid that it is difficult for anybody to adapt himself to it; but adapt themselves the participants must and do.

Wars greatly accelerate the pace of technical development, but new weapons and developments are usually superimposed on the old, leading to a considerable period of overlap. A new weapon produces its own counter-weapon and the older ones continue to exist side by side with it. The motor vehicle and the aeroplane were both in use in 1914; but even at the end of the Second World War the bulk of transport of both the German and Russian armies was horsed. Even in the age of the nuclear weapon, the rifle and the bayonet, derivative of the pike, are still in service and the former at least in many ways more relevant to the conflicts of the second half of the century than almost all the other weapons that have been added to the soldier's armoury in the three-quarters of the twentieth century that have passed.

The figures described here are the commanders: not, with some exceptions, the high staff officers who from their desks and in constant struggle with their political masters directed policy. Not that these Chiefs of Staff are not worthy of study, but their actions and reactions were so intimately entwined with the political history of the wars that it is unreal to attempt to deal with them as characters in isolation, fascinating as some of them and their relations with the politicians were. Some of them appear in these pages, having started as commanders in the field or at sea and progressed from there to the council table.

As late as the Franco-Prussian War of 1870, kings and princes took the field as commanders and the direction of land operations at least was still regarded, except in Britain and America, as a field in which royalty could properly exercise its authority. When Winston Churchill was at his lowest ebb in July 1942, it was seriously suggested in a motion in the House of Commons that the Duke of Gloucester should assume supreme command. Prince Rupprecht of Bavaria, who was in command of a German army group in 1918, was the last relic of a system of command which had been accepted for centuries. Mountbatten in the Second World War gained his place purely on his professional ability, not on account of his royal connection.

The optimum balance between political direction and military command of operations can hardly be said to have been satisfactorily found in the First World War at any stage. Accepting a misinterpretation of Clausewitz, which implied that once war had been declared the soldiers and sailors took over direction, and the politicians took a back seat until victory (or defeat) was achieved, the tendency for the first few years was for the politicians meekly to accept that the demands of the military men must be met and all shoulders put to the wheel to achieve them. When things went badly they muttered and fussed, but took no real political initiative and sought no other way out of the apparent impasse into which the military machine had ground itself, like a driver continuing to spin his wheels deeper and deeper into the bog.

Only when the sacrifices were becoming intolerable, and no end appeared to be in sight, did men like Clemenceau and Lloyd George begin to take a real grip of affairs. Even then they did it in a roundabout way. By 1914 governments were only just beginning to concern themselves with the direction of industrial, commercial and financial affairs. The volume and the detail of work which the direction of a major war involved, and the short time scale within which it had to be tackled, were totally unfamiliar to the political and governmental machines of 1914. It is little wonder that in all the participating nations the direction of a war involving such vast resources was haphazard and inefficient. The attempt to solve the myriad problems greatly increased the degree of governmental involvement in national life, and had a profound effect on events both during and after the war in all countries.

Railways and the telegraph had affected the American Civil War and Bismarck's Prussian wars of the late nineteenth century. The Russo-Japanese War in the first years of the twentieth century had given significant pointers to the influence of the industrial processes of the rapidly developing engineering industry based on steel; but the full impact of the Industrial Revolution on warfare was not to be seen until the First World War. Tactics, and strategy too, were still in 1914 based on Napoleonic concepts, which in the event it was found impossible to apply. The result on land was the development of a mutual mass mincing-machine into which bodies, weapons and ammunition were poured in the hope that the other side would be exhausted first, as in the end it was; but at a cost to European civilisation far outweighing the trivial causes for which the opponents had plunged into war.

Although the military figures of the First World War loomed large in the public eye at the time, and have been the subject of much controversy since, their positive contribution either to the actual outcome of operations or to the art of war was small. Even Allenby, who seemed to restore mobility and sense to war in Palestine towards the end, served in retrospect only to preserve for several decades the existence of horsed cavalry long after its ability to influence events on the battlefield had been rendered nugatory by modern weapons combined with man-made obstacles. Foch, perhaps the most intellectual and theoretical of all those described here, made his mark as much by sheer enthusiasm and the knowledge that he had the powerful political backing of both Clemenceau and Lloyd George as by the acuteness of his perception or the originality of his decisions.

That the conditions of warfare in the First World War overwhelmed the participants is not surprising. The means of transport available, and the short distance between base and front line, permitted the deployment of hordes of men and mountains of material. Not only was the latter available in large quantities (although never enough to satisfy the consumers), but it included entirely novel developments: the motor car and all its variants up to and including the tank; the aeroplane; radio-telephony; the submarine – all in use for the first time in Europe. The machine gun, the mine, gas, greatly improved explosives: all these added complications not only to the direction of operations, but also to their logistic support and to the problems of industrial production and the labour required for it.

Little wonder therefore that the senior military figures did not immediately grasp the correct potentialities of these new weapons, not always as great as their inventors or enthusiastic supporters claimed.

If there is one characteristic which stands out in the battles of 1914–18, it is the almost total lack of control once the battle had started. Communication invariably broke down. Very few commanders at any level had the faintest idea about what had happened or what was happening on their own side, let alone 'on the other side of the hill'. Even if they had reserves which could physically be moved in time to influence the battle, they hardly ever had good enough information on which to do so. The result often was just to pour more meat into the mincing-machine, reinforcing loss, there being no success to exploit.

All these melancholy facts of life were well known to the generals and admirals of the Second World War, all of whom had had direct experience of the first. Only the air marshals were operating in an almost totally new environment, so great had been the developments in aircraft and air warfare between 1918 and 1939. Nevertheless there were factors that made the Second World War very different from its predecessor. The most significant differences were in the field of radio communications, notably the development of radar; of automotive vehicles, especially the tank and many other forms of tracked and wheeled cross-country vehicle; and above all of air power, which had a far more revolutionary effect on naval warfare than it did on land or as a form of warfare in its own right. Nevertheless its effect on land warfare, although often exaggerated, had continually to be taken into account and particularly on movement to the battlefield by sea, land and air. As a very rough generalisation it can be said that the Germans had adapted themselves best to these new developments in land warfare, the British in air warfare and the United States in naval warfare.

In the Second World War, political control of military operations was exercised much more closely and directly, in spite of the fact that the battle-fields were farther-flung. Churchill, Hitler and Stalin were supreme war lords and intervened (generals, admirals and air marshals would say interfered) in considerable detail. Chiang Kai-shek exercised the same direct control, although not very effectively. Roosevelt, although titular Commander-in-Chief, was less inclined to involve himself in the detail of military operations or to override the advice of his Chiefs of Staff; Admiral Leahy playing as significant a role with him as paramilitary *éminence grise*, as General Ismay did with Churchill.

The First World War was not truly a world war. It was really a European war, although its ripples spread widely. In contrast number two was, when Japan entered the lists at the end of 1941, truly a world war. However, if one is to bring it into focus and study it objectively, one must divide it into separate campaigns. First the western European land war: 1940 saw it break fitfully into full development and then die, until revived in 1944 with the invasion of Normandy. Second, the Mediterranean land-air-sea war: this began with entry of Italy into the lists as France fell; saw the ebb and flow of the war in Greece and North Africa; and finished with the slogging match in Italy. Third, the submarine war in the Atlantic. Fourth, the air war over western Europe. Fifth, the Russo-German conflict. Sixth, the China-Japan-South-East-Asia land-air-sea war; and finally the Americo-Japanese sea-air-island war.

These were basically separate wars, but inevitably interrelated, the connecting link being the resources with which they were fought: the men, the material and the means of moving both about. The war in the Mediterranean did not assume any great importance to the Germans until it threatened, and then led to, the collapse of the Italians. From 1941 onwards the Russian front was far and away the greatest German commitment, and it remained so to the end, even after the Anglo-American entry into France added a *coup de grâce*.

The war against Japan was in essence a continuation and development of Japan's invasion of China, following on that of Manchuria in the 1930s. After Pearl Harbor the Pacific war became a major preoccupation of the United States, and involved them in support of Chiang Kai-shek, with implications that have lasted well into the second half of the century. The Japanese advance into South-East Asia had dramatic short- and long-term effects on the British Empire east of Suez, and on the whole concept of imperial defence that had been enshrined in British military textbooks since the formation of the Committee of Imperial Defence early in the century. This man was totally unrelated, as far as the Japanese were concerned, to the war being fought by the other members of the Axis west of Suez, although this had very significant effects on the resources which their opponents could deploy.

So much for the wars which included all three elements. In addition to these, there were two single-service wars waged almost independently of the others: the submarine war, fought principally in the Atlantic between the German and British and later also the American navies with air force participation; and the air-bombing war, first the Germans against Britain, parried by RAF Fighter Command and the army's Anti-Aircraft Command; and then, in retaliation, Bomber Command, later joined by their USAF colleagues, against Germany, with other targets rather reluctantly added.

The submarine war was a matter of life and death. It was Germany's one hope of bringing the British war effort to an end before America could develop and deploy its strength in Europe. No other campaign had such a direct importance to Britain and its war effort. In contrast the air-bombing war, although highly unpleasant to those who lived where the bombs fell, had only a marginal effect. Airmen and others will argue for ever about its value: whether or not, if differently conducted, it could have been more effective; the amount of war effort it involved or diverted. It was not able, as its most fervent advocates had predicted, to replace the pressures of land warfare or of naval blockade. It probably hardened rather than softened the morale of the enemy population. Whatever its value, it is indisputable that between the evacuation from Dunkirk in 1940 and the return to France on D-Day 1944, Britain had to find some way of fighting Germany. Running up and down the desert coast of North Africa was not enough. The bombing campaign was a necessity for national morale if for nothing else.

The entry of the air force as a third element in war greatly complicated the difficulty of directing and controlling military operations at the strategic level. It had been difficult enough in the First World War to resolve the conflicting demands of sailors and soldiers, especially with eccentrics like Admiral of the Fleet Sir John Fisher around. In the Second World War it was infinitely more complicated and difficult. Nowhere was it really satisfactorily achieved. The British devotion to a committee system survived for a long time, but under American pressure gave way to the concept of the supreme commander overlording land, air and, to a certain but rather limited degree, naval forces (unless he were himself an admiral, as Nimitz was). This did not solve all the problems and conflicts by any means, particularly if Montgomery was one of the subordinates, but it at least produced one point of decision and access. In fact successive army commanders-in-chief in the Middle East – Wavell, Auchinleck and Alexander – acted and were treated by Churchill and the Chiefs of Staff as if they were supreme commanders.

Much play has been made of the dangers of the German system, by which the OKW, the supreme joint command, overlorded the OKH, the supreme army command, taking decisions which it was alleged were unrealistic and divorced from reality. There is no doubt that, particularly as far as the Russian front was concerned, there was confusion as to where the point of decision lay; but this was due as much if not more to Hitler's deliberate system of not allowing any individual commander or headquarters to exercise too much independence than to defects in the organisation. Since 1945 all major military nations, including our own, have adopted the supreme commander concept for command in the field or its equivalent, and have instituted a chairman or chief of defence staff to preside over their single-service chiefs of staff. It was the lack of direct representation of the single-service staffs in the OKW which, apart from the idiosyncrasies of Hitler's methods of command, was its fatal flaw.

Disagreements, arguments, conflicts of interest and requirements between the three services were a continuing theme in all the warring nations. Overlying these were the differences between allies on both sides, each wanting a lion's share of the resources available, each keeping its eye open for its own postwar interests and each seeking the limelight and the glory. The Allies had more trouble on this score than the Axis, reduced as it was virtually to two, although Italy was a constant source of annoyance and liability to Germany.

The war lords of the Second World War described here are principally British, German and American. Russia contributes two and Japan only one, not because they did not play a major part in the military operations of the war, but because of the difficulties of finding enough material to provide a balanced picture of them. France, so prominent in the First World War, was virtually a non-combatant until the final phases, as the United States was in the first, and none of its military commanders then exercised influence on military operations on a truly major scale. De Gaulle did so in the political sphere as did Pétain, and fleetingly Darlan; but in this book we are not directly concerned with that scene.

With few exceptions the admirals, generals and air marshals of the Second World War shared one motive, a determination that their operations should not resemble those of their predecessors. Their reaction took different forms. The admirals, particularly in the submarine war, had the greatest difficulty in escaping from the old pattern; but in the US Navy the aircraft-carrier had become the battleship and the Pacific its perfect sphere of action. Some generals, inspired by Lawrence and Liddell Hart, put their trust in mobility, dispersion, deception and special forces. Wavell and Auchinleck were of this school; they and their desert generals were unfortunate to be faced, in Rommel, with one who had mastered it better than they. Patton later had more luck. Others were more traditional and sought the answer in a more efficient and cautious application of First World War methods, aided by all the additions, especially to fire power, that modern invention could provide. They, coming later when material was in greater abundance, were more fortunate. Alexander, Montgomery and Freyberg were of this school, as were Eisenhower and his principal lieutenants. Slim combined the best of both.

The air marshals had originally hoped that the power they exercised would make the war a short affair and avoid the need both for long-drawn-out land campaigns, with their long casualty lists and limitless logistic demands, and for extended naval campaigns of attrition as well as fleet actions. Although the influence of air power on both land and sea operations was greater than the generals and admirals had been prepared to envisage, the airmen were sadly disappointed, and saw with horror the danger that they might be forced to revert to the fate from which Smuts and Trenchard had helped them to escape, that of being merely the servants of the navy and the army. They soon found that they had sorely underestimated the strength they needed to make an impact either on the enemy's economy or on his fighting potential, and that the defence, in the form of the fighter and the anti-aircraft gun, constantly threatened to stultify the attack, on which their strategy fundamentally depended. This was particularly so once radar was introduced and as electronic warfare developed.

Amphibious and seaborne operations played a larger part than in any previous war. The Americans became masters of the art in the Pacific, while as Chief of Combined Operations Mountbatten laid the foundations for the major operations undertaken by British and American forces first in the Mediterranean and then across the Channel. It was ironic that, having been appointed Supreme Commander South-East Asia Command, he was denied the resources to apply his expertise. He had to be content with supervising a jungle war in which air supply played a significant role, and with exercising his diplomatic talents in attempting to co-ordinate operations with Stilwell, who was nominally also subordinate to Chiang Kai-shek, but continually quarrelled with him and with General Wedemeyer, the American air commander, as well as with almost everybody else.

The war lords of the First World War never overcame the environment in which they fought, and were dominated by it. Those of the Second World War, with stronger and more determined political support, did better. It is possible to imagine the first war ending, say, in 1916 or 1917 and Europe and its component nations being no worse off, even better off, than they were when it actually finished towards the end of 1918.

If the Second World War had ended at any period before Hitler and his regime had been clearly and totally defeated, Europe and the world would have become a very different place. Given the state of military preparedness of the British, French, Russians and Americans in 1939, it is difficult to see how victory could have been achieved much sooner or at much less cost than it was, certainly once Japan had entered the lists. For this economy of effort the war lords of the Second World War, in comparison with those of the first, deserve some credit.

The choice of figures to be portrayed in this gallery has not been an easy task. It is open to criticism and has already been subjected to it. My first short list included a hundred names, a number clearly beyond the limit of a manageable volume. I had therefore to impose criteria to narrow the field, and chose to exclude those who were perhaps more truly 'war lords' in that they directed policy at the highest level. The principal criterion was that the man should have exercised command of a considerable force – land, sea or air – in an important campaign: a secondary one was to see that as many different campaigns as possible of the two world wars were covered; that duplication was avoided and that the subjects themselves were of interest. Pressure of space forced me to concentrate on the two world wars and to exclude such important operations as the Russo-Japanese and Sino-Japanese wars, and the guerrilla and anti-terrorist campaigns of the second half of the century.

These criteria have therefore excluded Lawrence, Wingate, Tito, Mao Tse-tung, as they have Alanbrooke, Portal, Pound, Marshall, King, Arnold and Chiang Kai-shek.

Even after the application of this strict self-discipline, the space left for the authors to describe the character and achievements of a military figure of major importance is very limited. The authors' task has therefore been a particularly difficult one. It will be found that different authors have chosen different ways of meeting the problem: uniformity of approach has not been demanded. I am grateful to them all for the pains they have taken to meet the severity of the limits imposed upon them and for the skill and ingenuity they have employed.

Admiral of the Fleet The Earl Jellicoe

A. Temple Patterson

When John Rushworth Jellicoe became the first British admiral to hold supreme command at sea in modern war, the problems that faced him were enormous. Long generations of supremacy at sea had been followed by a hundred years which saw on the one hand virtually no major sea battles and on the other a naval revolution involving the introduction of steam, steel, long-range guns, mines, torpedoes, wireless, submarines and even the first aircraft. The weapons and in many cases the methods that had brought victory in the past were obsolete, but the traditions and popular mythology of the triumphant age of sail lingered on. A nation and a navy bred to believe themselves invincible at sea looked to him to repeat the glories of the past. Yet he himself understood better than most some of the great difficulties that stood in the way. Rodney, Howe and Nelson had after all worked with factors known and familiar. Those with which a twentieth-century admiral had to cope were still largely imponderables, menacing uncertainties on which the recent Russo-Japanese War could throw little light.

Moreover Jellicoe knew the rapid progress and technical efficiency of the German navy, unhampered by ancient habits and traditions, and at least suspected its superiority in several important respects – better armour protection, completer watertight subdivision of its capital ships and the penetrative power of its shells. War was to reveal that its submarines had a greater radius of operation and its torpedoes and mines were better than the British. Even in gunnery, on which together with the unromantic advantage of numerical supremacy Jellicoe relied for victory, the German director pointer gave an advantage in poor visibility, and Jutland showed up other German superiorities, in night-fighting practice and signalling.

In part at least, British inferiority in technical matters stemmed from the inferior status then accorded to engineers and technicians in the Royal Navy. Although its German opponents were more alive to the effects of the technological revolution of the late nineteenth and early twentieth centuries – indeed the material superiority of the German navy may be considered a reflection of Germany's lead over Britain in this 'Second Industrial Revolution' – the British Sea Lords and higher command continued to be drawn exclusively from the executive or seaman branch of the service until after the Second World War.

Jellicoe's difficulties were even greater than he himself realised, for with all his talents he was a prisoner of his time and training, freer than many others from inherited fetishes and obsessions but still not wholly free. Nevertheless he grasped the realities of the situation well enough for his sense of the vastness of his responsibilities to impose on him a ceaseless strain. Furthermore the time required for even an able man marked out for advancement to climb the ladder of promotion brought these responsibilities upon him at a time when his powers were perhaps beginning to pass their peak, and the result was a burden that might well have bent the shoulders of an Atlas.

Born at Southampton in 1859, the son of a liner captain who became commodore of the Royal Mail Company's fleet and a local doctor's daughter whose relatives included several naval officers, Jellicoe had set his heart on a naval career from early boyhood. Entering the training ship *Britannia* at the age of twelve, he earned the reputation of being 'one of the cleverest cadets the ship has ever had'. As a young lieutenant he developed a passion for gunnery, then a sadly neglected branch of the service, and during his course at Whale Island gunnery school his abilities caught the eye of its captain, the formidable reformer 'Jacky' Fisher. Appointed to the staff of the school, he became Fisher's most prized protégé; but although Fisher played a great part in moulding his career he was never regarded in the navy as having owed his advancement merely to favouritism. His ability, industry, pleasant personality and powers of leadership were widely recognised, and Fisher was by no means the only senior officer who soon appreciated his outstanding potentialities.

Thenceforward his career alternated between service at sea and in the Admiralty. In 1904 Fisher became First Sea Lord, and his reforms opened a new era in the navy's history, of which he became the presiding genius, while Jellicoe developed into his right-hand man. In 1908 he was appointed Controller, in which post he was responsible for superintending the departments that built, fitted out and repaired ships. He soon realised and sought to make others realise that the German dreadnoughts then being built were probably superior to their British rivals. It was true that they were less heavily gunned, but, as Jellicoe repeatedly emphasised, if in ships of equal displacement the British put more weight into gun armament the German ships must have advantages in some other directions. These he had deduced were the better armour protection and the completer watertight subdivision below water already referred to. Their greater beam facilitated these advantages, for whereas British vessels were limited by the width of our existing docks, the Germans were building their docks to take their ships and not their ships to fit their docks. Jellicoe, however, at least managed to secure approval for the construction of two floating docks capable of taking the largest battleships for repair purposes.

He was also uneasy about the relative ineffectiveness at long range and therefore oblique impact of the shells fired by the heavy guns of the British. Trials he arranged in 1910 showed that in many cases the shells burst on impact without penetrating the target's armour. He therefore asked the Ordnance Board to produce an armour-piercing shell that would be more adequate to the long ranges at which future sea battles would be fought, but unhappily his term as Controller ended soon afterwards and his successor let the matter drop, nor did Jellicoe revive it when he became Commander-in-Chief of the Grand Fleet, until the battle of Jutland belatedly and tragically underlined its importance.

The Controllership was followed by two years in command of the Atlantic Fleet. By now Fisher had decided that here was the man to lead Britain's battlefleet in the war with Germany he was convinced must come, and was describing Jellicoe in his correspondence as the future Nelson. His next step forward, in 1911, was the command of the 2nd Division of the Home Fleet under Sir George Callaghan. The importance of this appointment to Fisher's mind was that it would almost automatically make Jellicoe Callaghan's successor as C-in-C of this fleet. Thus he would be where Fisher wanted him in time for the clash with Germany and the great sea battle he expected, to which he was now alluding apocalyptically as Armageddon. Though no longer First Sea Lord, he was acting as unofficial adviser to the new First Lord, Winston Churchill, whom he had persuaded to promote Jellicoe (at that moment twenty-first on the list of twenty-two vice-admirals) over the heads of all those senior to him to the command in question.

Already, however, while commanding the Atlantic Fleet in combined exercises, Jellicoe had written with distaste of a night action which had been included: 'The difficulty of distinguishing friend from foe and the exceeding uncertainty of the result confirmed the opinion I had long held that a night action was a pure lottery, more particularly if destroyers took part in it.' To this judgement may doubtless be traced his omission when C-in-C to train the Grand Fleet in night action.

On the other hand at this time he was by no means wedded to the single line-ahead formation which was then the navy's basic principle of battle, nor opposed either to independent action by squadrons such as Admiral Sir William May and his flag-captain Herbert Richmond were advocating and May even tried out in manoeuvres, or to the creation of special fast squadrons. On one occasion during the 1912 manoeuvres under Callaghan's command he departed without orders from the line-ahead and took successful action with his squadron against the 'enemy's' rear, his chief subsequently approving. Again, in the secret War Orders and Dispositions he drew up for the flag-officers and captains under his own command, he definitely envisaged the employment of fast divisions, placed if possible on either wing during the approach to battle, to make separate attacks if circumstances were favourable.

In the 1913 manoeuvres he gave a brilliant performance as commander of the Red Fleet representing a hostile force convoying and clearing the way for an invading army. Outmanoeuvring Admiral Callaghan who commanded the defending Blue Fleet, he landed the troops he was escorting in the Humber and on the north-east coast, with the result that the manoeuvres were hurriedly ended lest they should give information and encouragement to Germany. It seems likely, indeed, that he was then at the peak of his powers, not yet worn down as he was to be later by long-continued strain and anxieties. Nevertheless his inclination to caution and in particular his strong sense of the dangers to be feared from submarines in modern naval warfare must have been intensified soon afterwards by a memorandum on these dangers which Fisher sent him. Although his mind was very far from being a mere *tabula rasa* for the reception of Fisher's ideas, it is probable that his anxieties and eventual pessimism on this subject owed something to his mentor's views.

When war broke out in 1914 he duly took over from Callaghan the command of what was renamed the Grand Fleet. Fifty-four years of age, he was a small, spare, wiry, alert and vigorous man, a dedicated worker with great technical knowledge and a first-class administrator who might have been a superlative one but for his excessive concern for details and the difficulty he found in delegating responsibilty. Moreover throughout his career he had been occupied more with the *matériel* and administrative sides of his profession than with strategy and tactics; and, though he was gifted in these too, his approach to them was rather empirical since he was not well read in naval history. Though capable of bold actions he inclined instinctively to orthodoxy and tradition, and his tendency to caution was henceforth reinforced by an oppressive sense of the vital importance of his task. But he inspired affection and trust in officers and men alike, endearing himself to the lower deck by his care for their welfare and kindling in his senior officers reliance on his leadership and often personal devotion.

Public opinion in Britain, and on the whole naval opinion also, had expected a major sea battle to be fought almost at once and result in a great British victory. But the German High Seas Fleet did not come out and Fisher's Armageddon was not fought. Instead the Germans preferred to keep their fleet in harbour or in the Baltic, ready to sally forth at any favourable moment. Among the advantages of this strategy of a 'fleet in being' was that while Jellicoe had always to keep as many as possible of his ships in a state of readiness in case the enemy left harbour, for his German opponent this was necessary only when he intended to come out. Since the Grand Fleet was liable at any time to have at least a dozen vessels refitting and others temporarily disabled or detached, the possibility that the Germans might have equality or even superiority at their 'selected moment' caused Jellicoe constant anxiety. Moreover the enemy could hope, while waiting for their 'day', to whittle down the British preponderance in capital ships by mining and submarine attacks and perhaps by catching some part of the Grand Fleet at a disadvantage.

On the other hand Britain's geographical position and overall numerical superiority seemed at first sufficient to gain without battle her main strategic aims at sea – the economic blockade of Germany, the security of her own seaborne commerce, and safety from invasion on any dangerous scale. It was true that on Jellicoe's advice all idea of a close blockade of the enemy's ports had been abandoned on the very eve of the war; but it was unnecessary to bottle up the High Seas Fleet in its harbours provided that its surface ships at least could be confined to the North Sea and kept from doing any considerable damage there. What in fact had to be achieved was a blockade, not of the German harbours, but of the North Sea. The means employed were the holding of its two exits, the Dover Straits by a mine barrage and a patrol with the Channel Fleet to back them, and the wider passage between the Shetlands and the Norwegian coast by a patrolling squadron of cruisers with the Grand Fleet available in case of a major German venture. This meant that the enemy had a considerable but precarious freedom of movement within the North Sea, but that in at least its northern waters Jellicoe could make sweeps in the hope of catching the High Seas Fleet or some part of it at sea – as his dashing subordinate Vice-Admiral Beatty did, though with incomplete success, in the battlecruiser fight off the Dogger Bank. Only after the Germans realised and began to exploit the potentialities of the submarine did a different and almost reversed situation emerge, with a new and highly dangerous form of counter-blockade operating against Britain.

As yet Jellicoe did not see the threat which submarines could pose to our seaborne trade, and his concern about them and about mines was limited to the damage he feared they could do to the battlefleet. This concern, and a resultant reaction towards cautious orthodoxy, appeared in the battle orders he drew up in the first weeks of the war. He still laid down that squadron commanders had discretionary powers to act independently in certain circumstances, but the use of separate fast divisions he had formerly proposed was ruled out for the time being, though the idea of a detachable division reappeared before Jutland with the creation of the fast Fifth Battle Squadron; and he pronounced that 'generally speaking, so long as the action is being fought on approximately parallel courses, the whole fleet should form one line of battle'. A few weeks later he took care to make plain, first in a letter to Churchill and then more explicitly in a memorandum to the Admiralty, the cautious strategy and tactics he intended to follow in order to shun or guard against any danger that threatened to reduce or destroy the superiority in numbers that was his chief asset. In the part of the memorandum dealing with his proposed battle tactics he wrote:

If . . . the enemy battlefleet were to turn away . . . I should assume that the intention was to lead us over mines and submarines, and should decline to be so drawn . . . This . . . may be deemed a refusal of battle, and indeed might result in failure to bring the enemy to action as soon as is expected and hoped . . . but with new and untried methods of warfare new tactics must be devised to meet them; [though] I feel that such tactics, if not understood, may bring odium upon me.

To this declaration, with its prophetic closing words, both Churchill and the Board replied in terms of full approval.

There followed twenty months of waiting and watching, gunnery practice, fleet exercises and multifarious anxieties, during which Jellicoe's health began to deteriorate somewhat. By the spring of 1916, though confidence in him was still widespread in the navy, discontent with his seemingly unenter- prising strategy was growing in certain quarters outside the service and could even be found within it. The mounting pressure for more offensive moves led to two attempts to lure the High Seas Fleet out by seaplane raids on a Zeppe- lin base in Schleswig with covering forces supported by the battlecruisers and more remotely by the Grand Fleet. In these Jellicoe had little faith, pointing out that even after a dawn raid it was very unlikely that the German battle- fleet would be contacted before 5 pm or later, much too late for any decision to be reached.

Meanwhile on the German side a new and more enterprising C-in-C, Vice- Admiral Reinhard Scheer, had begun a series of cautious sorties in which he sought to trap and destroy a part of the British fleet and so achieve the long- desired parity of forces. On 31 May one of these led to the battle of Jutland. On the previous day one of his signals had been intercepted and decoded, enabling the Admiralty to warn Jellicoe that the High Seas Fleet would probably put to sea early on the morrow. Thus he was able to leave harbour that night, giving Beatty, who for some time had been stationed at Rosyth with his battlecruisers and the Fifth Battle Squadron, his expected position at 2 pm on the 31st and instructing him to be 69 miles SSE of it at that hour.

Shortly before, Jellicoe had issued revised battle orders based on three dominant conceptions: subordination of the offensive spirit to defensive pre- cautions, especially against torpedoes; the single line of battle; and centralised command. In considering the first it must be realised that his wariness about torpedoes, mines and submarines was still common to practically the whole navy, and that although the war was to show that the submarine's limitations prevented it from being used effectively with a battlefleet, this was not yet evident in 1916. He was in fact unaware that the Germans had never practised using submarines in co-operation with the High Seas Fleet in action and still considered that the possibility of their retreating and attempting to lead him over a trap of mines and submarines must always be guarded against. This manoeuvre he believed that they would cover by a smokescreen and a tor- pedo attack by destroyers to which the counter would be to turn temporarily away from the enemy. Both this and the alternative turn towards a torpedo attack, relying on 'combing' the torpedoes by individual ships steering so that they passed between them, had been practised before the war; but though the latter prevented losing touch with the enemy the turn-away was considered safer.

The return to the orthodox single line-ahead battle formation rested on the considerations that manoeuvring in separate squadrons with the aim of concentrating on a part of the enemy's line and overwhelming it involved the risk that a squadron operating independently might itself be overwhelmed by a concentrated enemy; that the high speeds and increased battle ranges of modern ships would make it practically impossible for a C-in-C to keep control of squadrons operating separately; and that these increased ranges had made it possible to achieve the desired concentration of fire on a part of the enemy while maintaining the single line-ahead. This was particularly the case if the manoeuvre of 'crossing the T', or placing a fleet in single line athwart the enemy's line of advance, could be executed. Since the line-ahead formation implied reliance on the big gun for victory and tactics were then largely dominated by gunnery officers like Jellicoe himself, it is scarcely surprising that it won general approval.

The third dominant idea, centralised control, was closely linked with the single line-ahead, which it was claimed was the only safe way of ensuring it. By the beginning of the twentieth century it was being carried to extremes and the subsequent introduction of wireless telegraphy strengthened it further, at the cost of stifling the initiative of subordinates. Jellicoe still laid down that his divisional commanders had discretionary powers in certain circumstances, but the very fact that he described these carefully may have caused them to be regarded as the only cases in which individual action was justified. Moreover most of his subordinates had been too much schooled in the prevailing tradition of 'orders are orders' to be able to take advantage of such decentralisation as was offered them.

To quote the distinguished American naval historian Professor Marder:

[Jellicoe] would seek a decision through a formal, long-range, heavy-gun duel on parallel lines in broad daylight. As he would have been the first to admit, the plan of battle and the subsidiary tactics were conservative and cautious . . . Yet, given the stakes and the dangers of new and sinister underwater weapons, who can say without drawing on knowledge not available to Jellicoe that they were excessively cautious? . . . They represented after all the tactical ideas of the time and were based largely on academic peacetime exercises and manoeuvres . . . It needed the gruelling test of battle experience to suggest modifications.

Jellicoe's plan of battle, however, was based on the assumption that the Germans either wanted to stand and fight or could be compelled to do so. This meant that if they did not, and could not be compelled, time and sea-room would be needed to achieve victory by the orthodox methods, and neither was available on 31 May.

Throughout the battle he also suffered disastrously from signalling short-comings, at the hands of both the Admiralty and most of his subordinates. These began with an egregious blunder by the Director of Naval Operations, who sent him a signal on the morning of the 31st that the German flagship was still in port. Besides causing Jellicoe to slacken speed in order to econo-mise destroyer fuel and so reducing further the limited daylight he would have for fighting, this shook his faith, after the High Seas Fleet was encoun-tered well out to sea not very long afterwards, in any subsequent information passed to him by the Admiralty, at least when it conflicted with what he had from other sources.

The next major signalling failure occurred after the battlecruiser action which formed the first phase of the battle. Although Beatty despite his early losses had gallantly managed to lead the German fleet on to Jellicoe's guns without its becoming aware that the whole Grand Fleet was at sea, he had not kept his chief accurately informed of the enemy's position, formation and strength, partly because his flagship's wireless gear was shot away. Thus, when Jellicoe sighted Scheer almost at the last moment, he was still in his cruising formation of six columns in line-ahead disposed abeam, with only a minute in which to decide on the form and direction of his deployment. Nevertheless his instantaneous decision to deploy on his port column, though it increased the range and delayed the crunch of the battle when already only two or three hours of daylight remained, gave him three cardinal advantages: crossing Scheer's 'T', gaining the better visibility and getting between Scheer and his bases with the prospect of a whole morrow's battle if no decision was reached that evening. It has therefore received general retrospective approval, including that of Lord Cunningham, the greatest British seaman of the Second World War.

There followed two brief main-fleet encounters, in each of which the posi-tion Jellicoe had seized subjected Scheer to a heavy and accurate fire to which he could make little reply. He extricated himself from both, however, by the simultaneous sixteen-point turns-about which the High Seas Fleet had previously practised, covering himself each time by a destroyer attack and a smokescreen. This smoke and the prevailing mist prevented Jellicoe both times from grasping immediately what had happened; but when after a few minutes in each case he realised that the enemy had made some sort of turn-away, he knew that this could hardly be intended to lead him over mines or submarines, since he had established contact by surprise and they could therefore have had no time to prepare a minefield or a submarine trap. Nevertheless one of his two alternatives, a turn to follow them, was still virtually ruled out by the general acceptance of the view that immediate pursuit of a retreating foe (in fact the classic 'stern chase') was practically pre-cluded by the danger from torpedoes. The other alternative was to keep between the enemy and their bases; and this, after a temporary turn-away to avoid the destroyers' torpedoes, was what he did. As Beatty's flag-captain

Chatfield, who was no partisan of Jellicoe's, wrote later: 'Most experienced commanders would probably have acted as he did. His was a weapon on which the world depended, and . . . he was not prepared to take immeasurable risks with it.' Churchill put it more pithily: 'He could have lost the war in an afternoon.'

Determined to avoid his *bête noire* of a night action for which the Grand Fleet was neither equipped nor trained, Jellicoe intended to remain between the enemy and their ports till morning enabled him to renew the action. But three things, only one of which can be laid to his charge, frustrated him. First, though the least important since without the other two it would hardly have mattered, he misjudged the route Scheer would take home, guarding the two which seemed most likely and discounting that via Horns Reef. Secondly the Admiralty, after intercepting and decoding three signals from Scheer one of which made his intention obvious by asking for airship reconnaissance off Horns Reef next morning, sent Jellicoe a summary of the three which omitted this vital fact. Even then it would have sufficed, if the course it reported Scheer to be taking had been plotted from his known position at dark, to tell Jellicoe his objective, had not the C-in-C's confidence in Admiralty signals been shaken by its morning message and another subsequent piece of mis-information. Lastly there was the most fatal of the signalling failures, when in the night Scheer forced his way home past the British rear in a series of short though violent clashes involving only light forces on the British side. Amazingly, neither these nor several capital ships which had an inkling of what was happening managed to report it to Jellicoe. As a result Scheer got clear away. Not he alone but the stars in their courses had fought against Jellicoe.

Tactically the battle was indecisive, since neither side dealt the other a crippling blow. But though the High Seas Fleet had earned considerable credit, it had not achieved its objective of obtaining parity or near-parity of forces by trapping and destroying part of the British fleet. On the contrary Scheer's faith in further sorties was diminished and he became convinced that only by unrestricted submarine warfare could victory be won. Unhappily the British public, which had been encouraged by the press to expect another Trafalgar from Jellicoe, were neither inclined nor well enough informed to take such a sober and balanced view. Instead they vented much of their disappointment on the modest and unassuming admiral, who had no great talent for self-justification. Even when most of them gradually came round to realising that an important strategic success had been won, they could not regard it with enthusiasm.

A more positive aftermath of Jutland was the reorganisation of the fleet, to which Jellicoe instantly applied himself so successfully that his true greatness as a fleet commander has been said to lie in his capitalisation of the lessons of the battle. In August, however, when another sortie by Scheer gave him a second chance, the same combination of caution and bad luck frustrated it.

As he converged on the unsuspecting Scheer one of his light cruisers was torpedoed by an unseen submarine and believed at first to have been mined. Fearing that he might be leading the fleet into a minefield, he turned back until the situation was clarified, losing four hours during which Scheer was warned of his proximity and fled.

By now the escalating German submarine campaign had become the crux of the war at sea, and Jellicoe realised that what mattered was no longer victory over the High Seas Fleet but over the submarine menace. In November he was transferred to the Admiralty as First Sea Lord to cope with this, Beatty succeeding him in command of the Grand Fleet. He had however little to add to the methods hitherto employed against the U-boats – patrolling dangerous areas with small craft and arming and strictly routeing merchantmen. Convoy was not resorted to except for troopships and some other specially important vessels, and Jellicoe shared the view of the bulk of the navy's higher command that it could not be extended. Their arguments were that it would be impossible to find the necessary escort ships, and that merchantmen could not keep station in the way needed for convoy (which later experience showed to be untrue). It was argued too that a convoy system would involve loss of carrying power since vessels would make fewer voyages, and would create delays since convoys would have to travel below the speed of their slowest ships to leave a margin for station-keeping, and also because sudden influxes into our ports of masses of shipping at one time would mean congestion and slower turns-around.

In March 1917 however the Admiralty realised that its belief that escorts could not be provided had arisen partly from a gross miscalculation of the number of voyages needing protection in the ocean trades. In hopes of discouraging the enemy the totals of arrivals and departures of ships in its weekly statements had included the repeated calls of all coasters and short sea traders of over 300 tons, so that they appeared to average about 2500 a week each way. The Admiralty, in fact, had been hoist with its own propaganda. But when some sceptics among its junior personnel investigated these figures, the actual arrivals and departures in the ocean trades emerged as between 120 and 140 a week. In April, moreover, the entry of the United States into the war opened a prospect of more escort vessels, though as yet the American navy had not many of these. The Prime Minister, Lloyd George, had been convinced for some time that convoy was the sole remedy for what was now a critical situation, but when he pressed for it at a War Cabinet meeting on 23 April to which Jellicoe had been summoned, the latter replied that the obstacle was still shortage of destroyers, despite the possibility of American aid. On the 25th another War Cabinet to which he had not been called discussed the question again and decided that the Prime Minister should visit the Admiralty on the 30th to investigate further. But meanwhile Admiral Duff, the Director of the Anti-Submarine Division, had announced to Jellicoe his conversion to convoy and been instructed to draw up a minute recommending it, which he submitted on the 26th. Jellicoe approved it next day and a trial of it was immediately arranged, leaving Lloyd George little to do on the 30th but make himself pleasant. To his dying day Duff denied that the threat of the Prime Minister's descent on the Admiralty had led to this rather abrupt decision to adopt convoy, insisting that he had been influenced only by the rising shipping losses. Jellicoe too, in his *The Submarine Peril*, published in 1934 as an attempted counterblast to some parts of Lloyd George's *War Memoirs*, rejected all suggestions that in approving Duff's minute he had been swayed by outside pressure. But it is just possible that despite making that statement in all good faith seventeen years later he may in fact have been influenced, if only subconsciously, to accelerate a step already under consideration by his knowledge (which Duff did not possess) of the Prime Minister's intentions.

The adoption of convoy, however, did not transform the situation immediately, since the problem of finding sufficient escort vessels continued well into 1918, so that cause for anxiety and strain persisted till the end of Jellicoe's tenure of office and took further toll of his health. To this may be traced in part the growing pessimism – or what to an optimist like Lloyd George seemed to be pessimism – which he now displayed. The Premier, eupeptic, intensely vital, indomitable and ruthless, was losing patience with a tired, over-conscientious man who could not delegate business, constantly overworked and always saw the black side of things too clearly. But his first reaction was to try to relieve Jellicoe of as much detail as possible by appointing Sir Eric Geddes, a railway tycoon who had been successfully organising transport behind the British lines in France, to take supreme charge of all naval and mercantile shipbuilding. Jellicoe however remained pessimistic, even about the convoy system, and at a War Cabinet in June declared that Britain could not continue the war in 1918 unless the Flanders offensive then being planned could capture the U-boat bases on the Belgian coast. This alarmist note caused Lloyd George to consider replacing him, but since he was not on good terms with the high command of the army he hesitated to take a step that might prejudice his relations with the navy too. Instead he made Geddes First Lord in place of Jellicoe's friend and backer Sir Edward Carson and created the post of Deputy First Sea Lord for the popular and imperturbable Admiral Sir Rosslyn Wemyss, probably as a preliminary to putting him in Jellicoe's place if opportunity offered. Jellicoe liked Wemyss, but his constitutional inability to delegate authority hamstrung the latter's friendly efforts to help him, while his relations with Geddes steadily deteriorated owing to the new First Lord's brusque manners and ignorance of naval courtesies and customs. On Christmas Eve Geddes, having obtained Wemyss's reluctant consent to take over, suddenly dismissed him, denying afterwards that he had been influenced by Lloyd George. While it is hard to escape the conclusion that Jellicoe was no longer fitted to continue as First Sea Lord, it is equally hard not to regard the manner of his removal as shabby.

Several attempts were made during the rest of the war to find him employment, the most respectable being a proposal which fell through, that he should be made Allied Naval C-in-C in the Mediterranean. After the war he was given the important mission of touring the Empire to advise on the development of the Dominion navies, and in his report drew attention to Japan as the country from which future danger might arise. Afterwards he spent a happy and successful term as Governor-General of New Zealand, on his return from which the viscountcy he had received after his dismissal from the First Sea Lordship was converted into an earldom; and the last years of his life until his death in 1935 were divided between peaceful domesticity, dabbling in Conservative politics and the presidency of the British Legion in succession to Earl Haig.

Jutland had been the apex of his career. All that went before had led up to those few seconds of swift decision when, at the opening of the main battle, he had seized the advantage over Scheer. That was his greatest moment; the rest a long, slow anti-climax. There was a touch of Hamlet in him, and certainly for the British navy the times were out of joint. But the task which fell to him, not of setting them right but of adapting it to them, was in part beyond his powers. It would be going too far to ascribe to him – though he contributed to it – that continued over-reliance on the battleship and the big gun and renewed failure to appreciate the submarine threat to our seaborne trade which marked the higher command of the navy between the wars. That was due partly to over-confidence in Asdic as a defence against underwater attack; and in the 1930s it was Chatfield, Beatty's man and never Jellicoe's, who headed the 'battleship school'. Nevertheless much of this failure stemmed from the lingering memory of Jutland. In repeated attempts to explain why the Grand Fleet had not succeeded in blowing its numerically weaker opponent out of the water the battle was refought again and again in the Tactical School and the Naval College, and fleet exercises at sea were still designed to bring about the great gun duel as their climax; while the study of the U-boat war against shipping and its lessons was neglected. The results were the staggering merchant-ship losses of the Second World War.

MARSHAL JOSEPH JOFFRE

General André Beaufre

After the Battle of the Marne General Joffre enjoyed unparalleled prestige and popularity. He had saved France and the country's gratitude to him was frenetic. Later, as position warfare, punctuated by unproductive offensives, dragged on and Joffre's attitude to the government became increasingly authoritarian, he became the target of much criticism and his star waned until eventually he was relieved of command of the armies on the transparent pretext of his elevation to Marshal of France. After the war, though growing in stature in some people's eyes, Joffre's personality and the part he had played in the Battle of the Marne were subjects of public discussion. Several books, such as Pierrefite's *GQG Secteur I*, the *Carnets de Gallieni* and Liddell Hart's *Reputations*, definitely placed a question mark against Marshal Joffre's prestige. Liddell Hart in particular, with a certain bias it must be admitted, could find no more to say in praise of Joffre than that he had been 'a national nerve sedative' at a crucial moment.

Today, when histories of the Battle of the Marne have been published, after Joffre himself has given an extremely detailed account in his memoirs,* Joffre's precise role in the course of operations in France at the outset of the First World War can be restored to its proper place. As a result due tribute can now be paid to a man who played a vital part in the development of Europe's history. There can in fact be no doubt that at a moment when most factors seemed to point towards the defeat of France, Joffre's strategic ability and Joffre's conduct contributed decisively to the change in the country's destiny. It is this role, played in so masterly a fashion at a particularly critical moment, that has earned him the undisputed fame accorded to him today by all who have given thought to this period of French history.

Joseph Jacques Césaire Joffre, born at Rivesaltes on 12 January 1852, came of a humble family. Being intelligent by nature and a hard worker he obtained a scholarship from the Perpignan Lycée enabling him to go to Paris to study for the École Polytechnique, into which he passed fourteenth in 1869 at the

---

* *The Memoirs of Marshal Joffre*, translated by Colonel T. Bentley Mott, Geoffrey Bles, London 1932.

age of seventeen. During the war of 1870 he served as an Engineer second-lieutenant in one of the Paris forts. After the war he returned to the Polytechnique to finish his course and from there joined the Engineers. As a result of his wife's death in 1885 he asked to be posted overseas. He took part in the Formosa and Upper Tongking campaigns and returned to France in 1888, being posted first to a railway regiment and then as instructor to the Artillery School in Fontainebleau.

He first made his mark in 1892. He was responsible for building a railway in Senegal and was placed in command of a column which was to reinforce that of Colonel Bonnier. Bonnier was taken by surprise by the Touareg and his column cut to pieces. Joffre caught up with the remnants but instead of withdrawing took on Bonnier's task; he pushed forward, captured Timbuktu, challenged the Touareg and pacified the area, all this taking place 500 miles from any French base. He was promoted lieutenant-colonel, awarded the Legion of Honour and returned to France. Then he departed for Madagascar, where he fortified the Diego Suarez naval base under the orders of Gallieni. In 1900 he returned to France, was promoted brigadier-general and appointed Director of Engineers in the War Ministry. After this he commanded a division and then an army corps; in 1910 he was appointed to the *Conseil supérieur de la Guerre* (War Council) as Director of Rearward Services. He was then aged fifty-eight.

This was the moment when a palace intrigue led to the resignation of General Michel, Vice-President of the Council and overall Commander-in-Chief designate. He did not share the novel ideas of the General Staff on the absolute primacy of offensive action. General Gallieni, who had apparently masterminded this manoeuvre, refused to take General Michel's place on the score of age but warmly recommended Joffre since, being younger, he would have time to exert a decisive influence on the army's development. It should be added that Joffre was considered a 'good republican', in other words reliable from the civil power's point of view. He was appointed Chief of the General Staff, this bringing the General Staff – for the first time – under the authority of the Commander-in-Chief designate.

Joffre's achievements during his time in this post from 1911 to 1914 were considerable; their value was to be proved on the outbreak of war, but they are nevertheless still little recognised. He had to make good deficiencies in the arms programme, work out and disseminate strategic and tactical doctrine, prepare commanders and staffs for their assignments, ensure that the French army was better able to match the German by a change of plan and the introduction of three years military service and, to cap it all, work out a fresh operational plan, known as Plan XVII. Three years was certainly not too much for a task of this magnitude.

Numerically French forces equalled those of the Germans, but they were inferior in that French allocations of funds for equipment were only approximately half those of the Germans. From the armaments point of view much remained to be done; though adequate numbers of the 75mm field gun were available, for instance, there were only 1250 rounds per gun and there was no heavy field artillery at all. Joffre favoured heavy artillery, which the Germans possessed in great quantity. He managed to have some 105mm, 120mm and 155mm guns produced and initiated a study of long-range naval guns. Budgetary considerations unfortunately did not permit development of this heavy artillery. Nevertheless the production of prototypes and formation of experimental units did enable French firepower to be increased rapidly later in the war.

The inferiority of the French regular forces at the start of mobilisation meant that frontier security was a precarious business. An increase in peacetime strength was essential both to reinforce the covering troops and provide adequate regular forces in reserve. This was the primary object of the introduction of three years' military service in 1913, a major step in putting the French army in a position to defend the country. Joffre played an essential part in this decision. As a result the strength of the French army was increased by 210,000 men, bringing it to around 700,000 as against 800,000 in the German army.

The availability of these regular forces, together with the additional troops provided by mobilisation, justified preparation of a fresh plan. Plan XVI, which was in force in 1911, was a defensive-offensive plan to counter a German invasion in the direction of Metz, Toul and Verdun. It assumed that Belgian neutrality would be respected, but alternative provision was made for location of the reserve army in the north – no more than an inadequate palliative. Revision of the plan had to be based on a number of political assumptions: the support of a British expeditionary force, Italian neutrality, the probability of intervention in Belgium, the support provided by a Russian offensive. The attitude to be adopted by French forces had to be decided: was it to be defensive, defensive-offensive or offensive?

Plan XVII, which Joffre was destined both to prepare and execute, has been the object of much misappreciation. Based on the action resulting from it, it has generally been held to be an operational plan laid down in advance, similar to the Schlieffen Plan on the German side; its main feature has been thought of as a general offensive with the main effort in the Ardennes. This was the concept that, in the event, was put into practice, but there was nothing preconceived about it; Plan XVII was actually only a plan for concentration with a number of alternatives depending on the assumptions made regarding enemy action. Joffre's main idea was to give himself the possibility of carrying out various manoeuvres – the plan amounted to adoption of an 'on guard' position before the start of fencing rather than a scenario arranged in advance. Anyone following the preparation and execution of this plan must inevitably be struck by its pragmatic character and the fact that its essence was manoeuvre. Herein lay its strength and it was this that opened the way to the recovery of the Marne after the initial setbacks.

Inevitably the battle of manoeuvre which Joffre was preparing himself to conduct was bound to be fought in that atmosphere of dynamism produced by the French determination to be permanently on the offensive. The plan was designed to counter any defensive reactions stemming from previous plans and make the enemy feel the weight of French action all along the front in order to immobilise and paralyse him. Here again subsequent and undoubtedly justified criticism of the crazy ideas about the *tactical* offensive prevalent in 1914 must not lead us to misjudge the advantages in terms of *strategy* and *morale* presented by this desire for dynamic action. Bad tactics were due to lack of recent battle experience and false lessons drawn from the Manchurian campaign. From the overall point of view, however, the fact that the French army, though beaten on the frontiers, was eventually able to impose its will on the enemy was due to this much-criticised predilection for the offensive.

It has often been said that being placed at the head of affairs in 1911 Joffre was inadequately prepared for the part he had to play and that in fact he succumbed to the influence of the 'young Turks' on the General Staff, including Colonel de Grandmaison. In fact, although Joffre brought a breath of fresh air into the French army, he retained a jealous and strict control over all major decisions. His day-to-day actions from 1911 onwards and during the battle are a model of rational reaction to constantly recurring difficulties. It should be added that he made careful preparation for this battle of manoeuvre by means of numerous exercises without troops, large-scale annual manoeuvres with troops and the issue of a new directive on 'tactical employment of formations'. His labours in this field were to prove decisive, as was his series of visits to the Russian army.

Such as it was, Plan XVII constituted a considerable advance on Plan XVI. Facing the anticipated seventy-three divisions Plan XVI provided for only thirty-eight French regular divisions plus sixteen reserve divisions assigned to secondary tasks. Plan XVII provided for twenty-one regular corps, three independent divisions, ten cavalry divisions and fourteen reserve divisions totalling some 580 regular battalions, 332 squadrons and 653 batteries against the German 600 regular battalions, 350 squadrons, 500 horse-drawn batteries and 100 heavy batteries. Taking account of a probable six infantry divisions and one cavalry division from Britain and four divisions from Belgium, the French could count on a certain degree of superiority. It is also worth noting that France, with 1,300,000 men in the field, was providing the main effort against Germany – Russia provided only 7–800,000 men. The balance had been re-established in the nick of time.

On 25 July 1914 severance of relations between Serbia and Austria heralded the probability of war, but the French government was hesitant to take the necessary measures in the absence of the President of the Republic and the Prime Minister, who were on their way back from Russia by sea. When they returned on 29 July people were still hoping that peace could be preserved. Joffre had to press hard to ensure that France was prepared for the worst. On the 30th the government would agree only to certain half-measures, not including the recall of reservists. Not until the 31st, armed with intelligence on the German army, could Joffre obtain agreement to mobilisation of the covering forces; he was forced to wait until 1 August before a decision was taken for general mobilisation on the 2nd.

As we have seen, Plan XVII was only a plan for concentration with various alternatives. The form of the French manoeuvre was dependent on the line which the enemy was found to be taking. On 2 August it was not known where he would make his main effort – against Verdun, farther north or in Belgium. Should it prove to be Belgium, the most likely hypothesis, it was equally not known how wide the German move would be. The mistaken notion that the Germans would not use their reserve divisions in the front line led people to think that the German right would not extend north of the Sambre and Meuse valleys. But this still required confirmation. So Joffre was to be seen preparing his battle step by step and then manoeuvring in accordance with information as it reached him. There was no *a priori* action as in the case of the Schlieffen Plan; it was a genuine battle of manoeuvre directed by Joffre from beginning to end.

On 2 August came the news of the violation of Belgian neutrality and the invasion of Luxembourg. Joffre decided to move the concentration of his reserve army, the Fifth, farther to his left, along the Meuse from Stenay to Givet. On 3 August he warned army commanders of the possibility that they would be required to take the offensive in Lorraine and Alsace in order to tie the enemy down and bring the French right wing up to the Rhine. On the 4th he gave orders for the planned offensive to be launched in Upper Alsace and on the 5th sent cavalry forward into Belgium. When he heard on the 7th that the Belgians were facing six army corps, he despatched the Cavalry Corps together with some infantry to hold the crossings of the Meuse south of Namur. At this point he was envisaging envelopment of the German right flank based on the line Liège-Namur-Dinant. On the right, in Alsace, Alt-kirch was captured, but on the 8th the French offensive was driven back. On the 9th Joffre reorganised the command structure of his right flank, forming an Army of Alsace under General Pau. Since the British, who had not mobilised until the 5th, were behind schedule, he decided to move into Belgium in force without waiting for them, seeing that Liège was still holding out. He then confirmed to the First and Second Army the order for a holding offensive in Lorraine to be launched on 14 August. It was to be synchronised with the Russian move into East Prussia.

On the 14th, when the offensive opened in Lorraine, the situation in Belgium was still obscure. The main German forces were thought to be behind the Ourthe and their main effort was still expected to come south of the

Meuse. General Lanrezac, commanding Fifth Army, feared an outflanking move west of the Meuse, but Joffre was still doubtful. On the 15th however the likelihood of this was confirmed by large-scale German crossings of the Meuse north-east of Namur. Joffre ordered Fifth Army to prepare to move north. He asked for the First Military Region (Lille) to be placed under his orders and formed a group of reserve divisions to cover this area. Nevertheless information was still contradictory; 1 French Corps was attacked at Dinant and it looked as if the main German effort was being made in the Belgian Ardennes north of Givet. That evening Joffre ordered Fifth Army to move up to the Sambre and on the 17th widened the movement by sending the Cavalry Corps north of the Sambre.

The German manoeuvre began to become clearer only on the 18th. If their main effort was found to be south of Namur, a converging attack by Fifth, Fourth and Third Army was planned. The British were not due to move until the 21st. Should the main German effort develop north of Namur, however, it would be essential to reinforce the left flank. The IX Corps was taken from Second Army and plans prepared to move Maunoury's Army of Lorraine to the left flank. On the 19th the second hypothesis proved to be correct; the Belgians reported that four German corps were moving on Brussels and the north-west and that they themselves were withdrawing on Antwerp. Thereupon Joffre, based on a faulty order of battle of the German army, deduced that the enemy centre in the Ardennes was thin. By the morning of the 20th French forces in Lorraine had made considerable progress and Fifth Army had reached the Sambre. At 4 pm however it was learnt that Second Army had been heavily repulsed in Lorraine, that First Army had been brought to a halt and that the German right wing in Belgium consisted of five army corps. On 21 August therefore orders were issued to stop the Germans in the north and for Third and Fourth Army to attack them in the centre through the Ardennes.

On 21 August the Germans reached Roubaix and faced south. The French were therefore going to have to fight facing north. In Lorraine Second Army was withdrawing and Joffre halted it in front of Nancy. The fighting in Belgium on 22, 23 and 24 August ended in a general defeat for the French, but Joffre did not really grasp the fact since his estimate of the strength ratio of the two sides was inaccurate. On 24 August, however, when his planned manoeuvre had clearly been put out of court, Joffre decided on a general withdrawal with the idea of holding on until the effect of Russian action was felt. General Instruction No. 2 was accordingly issued on 25 August; it prescribed withdrawal to the line Amiens-Reims with the right resting on Verdun and a defensive attitude in Lorraine and on the Meuse heights. On 26 August, while the British were withdrawing on Noyon towards the rear of Fifth Army, Joffre formed a fresh army, the Sixth, in the west under Maunoury with troops taken from Lorraine and Alsace. On 27 August however the British were hustled out of Le Cateau. Joffre ordered Fifth

Army to counter-attack north-west in order to extricate them. On 28 August, since touch was apparently being lost between Fourth and Fifth Army, he formed an army detachment under Foch to reinforce the centre. On 29 August he visited Fifth Army in order to launch the Guise counter-offensive and then went to see General French.

The Sixth Army, however, which was detraining in the Amiens area, was already threatened by the German advance. Joffre directed it towards the fortified camp of Paris. The operation that he had momentarily planned between the Somme and Verdun had become impossible. He had to gain some elbow room and withdraw to the Aube and the Seine where he might be able to resume his outflanking manoeuvre. On 1 September von Kluck was reported moving south but to the east of Paris. Reinforcement of the left flank was in progress when news arrived of the Russian defeat in East Prussia. This was the point at which Joffre signed his General Instruction No. 4, setting out the operation destined to be the Battle of the Marne. At this stage there were divided opinions among Joffre's staff, some questioning whether it would not be better to revert to an offensive in the centre launched from west of Verdun; the problem of date was also raised – whether it was better to wait and withdraw farther or seize what might be a fleeting opportunity. Joffre opted for envelopment from the west and in principle the deepest possible withdrawal back to the Seine.

On 2 and 3 September it was confirmed that von Kluck was moving south, contrary, moreover, to von Moltke's orders which had been intercepted over the radio, Gallieni was placed under the orders of GHQ and asked for instructions. Joffre indicated that he should move in the direction of Meaux when the moment arrived. On 4 September von Kluck was reported moving south-south-east. The situation envisaged in General Instruction No. 4 was in process of becoming fact. Against Berthelot's advice Joffre held that the great moment had arrived. At 10 am moreover Gallieni telephoned proposing that he attack eastwards. Joffre, who was still thinking of an operation south of the Marne, asked for the views of Franchet d'Esperey (who had taken the place of Lanrezac) and of Foch. Meanwhile Gallieni had gone to see French who was in favour of a general offensive. d'Esperey's and Foch's replies, when they arrived, were entirely favourable and they suggested that Maunoury take action north of the Marne. Accordingly at 10 pm Joffre took the decision to fight the decisive battle on 6 September and signed his famous order of the day.

The genesis of the Battle of the Marne has been described in some detail in order to show the true nature of this gigantic battle of manoeuvre, undoubtedly conducted with consummate skill by Joffre. We have seen how the ideas that gave birth to successive operations were formed and how the plan which was eventually that of the Battle of the Marne was built up progressively. Due note will have been taken of the commander's pragmatism and imperturbability, of his indefatigable activity and his ability to maintain continuous contact with the armies.

All this illustrates the indisputable superiority of the French high command. Though defeated on the frontiers and forced to admit that all his initial illusions lay in ruins, Joffre had the strength of character to take the brave decisions to disengage in good time and to plan the counter-manoeuvre which was to re-establish the position. His superhuman calm in face of the storm stands out in contrast to the nervousness of, for instance, Moltke, Bülow or even von Kluck, whose independent decisions were so catastrophic. The main characteristic of this great battle, however, was that it was nothing less than a gigantic war game, in which the generals of the period, who had no experience of major war, played according to known rules, considering themselves beaten when the situation seemed to them abnormal.

This is the explanation of the victory of the Marne; it sprang from an error by von Kluck and a good manoeuvre by Joffre. To recover himself von Kluck opened a yawning gap in the German line between his First Army and his neighbour von Bülow and into it Franchet d'Esperey and the French advanced without however really realising the opportunity that was being offered them. Of course we may lament today that the Franco-British manoeuvre was not carried out to perfection, that Maunoury did not make his appearance on 5 September, that his turning movement was not wider, that the British and French did not plunge more resolutely into the gap which faced them, that Joffre did not really realise that the gap existed. But these are the imponderables of war, when everyone is forced to act in the light of developments which he cannot completely fathom. Overall, however, the French made fewer mistakes than the Germans. From this disparity victory emerged and so it was that France was saved.

Seldom in fact has a battle had more far-reaching consequences. In 1914 the world was moving towards an eruption by Wilhelmine Germany, a second-hand creation of Bismarck's. Economically Germany had advanced at an increasing rate. Militarily her power, both on land and sea, was considerable. In face of this France had only been able to redress the balance by allying herself with Russia and Britain; for her own defence she could only put into the field forces which, though large by her own standards, were still definitely inferior to those of Germany. Moreover the French appreciation of German strength was a poor one. The French deployed on too narrow a front and so were wide open to an enveloping move, for which the German plan provided; they thought that their riposte to this could be an attempt to break the German centre. This was proof of complete misinterpretation of the tactical possibilities offered by modern fire power. So France was apparently heading inevitably for defeat. Here, it seemed, was a watershed of history.

But it did not happen. From these conditions, almost all of them unfavourable, Joffre succeeded in extracting the essentials for recovery. The

French recovery, a truly miraculous one, demonstrates the decisive importance of human will-power in the unfolding of history – if Joffre had been commanding the German army and Moltke the French, Germany would have won the war in 1914. The whole of modern history would have changed. The victory of the Marne sounded the death-knell of German domination. Though it brought salvation, it was incomplete and four long years of effort were necessary in order to perfect it. But this great event, the work of a few men, fundamentally deflected the portended evolution of history. A definitive halt had been called to the German war machine in the west.

The sequel was equally remarkable. Defeat on the frontiers had been a surprise; the victory of the Marne was another surprise. Yet a third surprise now awaited the battered but victorious French army – after withdrawing to the Aisne, the Germans dug in and so ushered in trench warfare.

Once more Joffre's reply was to manoeuvre; he in his turn tried to outflank this fortified front from the west. Thus began what has been called the 'race to the sea', co-ordinated by Foch. The result was a series of battles that proved the bankruptcy of outflanking action when faced with a vigorous and determined enemy. The rapid victory upon which the Schlieffen Plan and Plan XVII had both reckoned so gaily was proved to be no more than a mirage. After a fearful passage of arms, during which each side was forced to discover the realities of the new type of warfare, the armies took root opposite each other, dug into the ground. They were to remain there for four long years.

Joffre now had to solve the novel problem set him by trench warfare. His action over this period of two years covering 1915 and 1916 has been the object of much criticism. Naturally he was groping his way in his efforts to find new solutions. It should be recognised however that he was the man who laid down the main lines for modernisation of that French army that was eventually to be victorious in 1918. He was the man who set up the programmes for the weapons, artillery, ammunition and the aircraft and tanks as well which were to come forward in such quantity from 1917 onwards. Administratively therefore what he did was beneficial.

As regards inter-Allied strategy his influence grew until by the time he was promoted Marshal of France (a thin pretext for his dismissal from command of the French armies), his was the dominant voice.

His fall from grace was due to the apparently unsatisfactory results of two years of war and also to his continuous struggle with the politicians to preserve the high command's freedom of military action. It did not do justice to his considerable achievements; he had rebuilt a modern army, an army of the industrial era; he had worked out fresh doctrines; he had won new-style battles such as Verdun and the Somme. By the time he was relieved by Nivelle early in 1917 he had worn down two great enemy commanders, Moltke and Falkenhayn. Hindenburg, their successor, would have been forced to make a large-scale withdrawal in France as a precaution against the offensive that Joffre was preparing for the spring of 1917. His balance sheet cannot record victory, but it is very definitely weighted on the credit side; above all it includes the fact that the seeds of future victory were sown. So Joffre served his country well.

In addition however he left his successors certain great lessons: the value of fearless character, of a flexible pragmatic mind, of impeccable operational ability on the strategic level. With his strong personality he was able to offset all the unfavourable factors that loomed so large over the future of France in 1914; he illustrated how decisive is the commander's role in those events of which the web of history is woven. He was not merely a 'national nerve sedative' during a crucial phase, as Liddell Hart maintains in the passage quoted above. He was largely responsible for deciding the destiny of France at a moment when it hung in the balance; in doing so he set the First World War firmly on a new course.

FIELD-MARSHAL THE EARL HAIG

John Terraine

Field-Marshal The Earl Haig of Bemersyde was born in 1861; he entered the army in 1885; in August 1914 he commanded 1 Corps of the British Expeditionary Force; in December 1915 he was appointed Commander-in-Chief of that force, which, by 11 November 1918, had risen to a total strength of 1,968,682 officers and men; he held this command until April 1919; he died in 1928. Controversy had already attached itself to the name of Haig before his death, and has continued ever since, despite the fact that the close of his active career was marked by nine successive victories of a character unparalleled in British military history.

Douglas Haig was born in Edinburgh, educated at Clifton College and Brasenose College, Oxford. His three years at Oxford shaped his character for professional life in an atmosphere of wider intellectual scope than that enjoyed by most young officers, so that when he entered the army, age as well as education would set him apart. When he went up to Brasenose he already possessed comfortable private means; he joined the best clubs, moved in aristocratic and fashionable circles; he took up polo, with sufficient skill to carry him later to international standard. He was popular; he was good looking. But he was also Scottish, with a practical, thoughtful strain from his Border ancestors which saved him from becoming a charming nobody. 'Douglas Haig', wrote General Sir Ian Hamilton, 'was not born into the world with a silver spoon in his mouth; but possibly with a silver pencil in his hand ready to start his calculations.'

Haig did not, in the end, take an Oxford degree; he passed his examinations, but having missed a term through illness he lacked the full residential qualification. He decided against making up the lost university term; it was time to begin his chosen career, the army. So he spent the autumn of 1883 at a crammer, and entered the Royal Military College in February 1884. It was at Sandhurst, says one of his biographers, Duff Cooper, 'that the legend of Haig, as of a man who must one day rise to the highest command, originated'. In December 1884 he passed out first in order of merit, with the Anson Memorial Sword.

In 1885 Haig received his commission in the 7th Hussars; three years later the industry and application already displayed at Sandhurst brought him the appointment of adjutant of the regiment. In 1893 he presented himself for the Staff College examination. To his disgust he failed on two counts: his mathematics paper fell short by eighteen marks – which was something that hard work could put right; what could not be altered was the surprising discovery that he was colour-blind. Haig, however, was undeterred; during the next two years he reported on cavalry manoeuvres in France and Germany, completed the new *Cavalry Drill Book* and performed staff duties, his work so impressing Sir Evelyn Wood, the Quartermaster-General, that in 1896 he was able to enter the Staff College by nomination. In a vintage year the chief instructor, Colonel G. F. R. Henderson, said of him to a fellow student: 'There is a fellow in your batch who one of these days will be Commander-in-Chief.'

Haig's denigrators have made much of the benefits he is supposed to have derived, professionally, from wealth, family influence or royal favour; all of which make it a little difficult to explain why he was still a captain at thirty-six. But there is no mystery about what made him the army's youngest major-general at forty-two; the answer is simple – active service. The life of a regimental officer in the last decades of the nineteenth century could become very stagnant, passing from one imperial garrison routine to another. Active service was the only cure for this, and Haig's swift promotions show that he firmly seized the opportunities presented to him by the Nile Expedition of 1897 and the South African War in 1899.

Haig was a cavalryman, and in both campaigns his chief service was with that arm. But there are cavalrymen and cavalrymen. The word by itself is not very helpful; to understand what it meant with reference to Haig, we need to see what duties he carried out with the cavalry in the field. His first duty in Egypt was to train a squadron and lead it in the early skirmishes; this he did quite satisfactorily, as his contemporaries were in the habit of doing. Where he departed from most of them was in becoming, as the main campaign developed, staff officer to Colonel Broadwood, commanding the whole of the Egyptian cavalry. It was now that he justified his psc (passed staff college) and since Broadwood belonged distinctly to the 'Have at them!' school, on at least one important occasion it fell to Haig to give direction and cohesion to the brigade while its commander was wielding his sabre with the front rank.

It was in the Sudan that Haig became a marked man; a reputation began to gather round him. When war broke out in South Africa, and the decision was taken to send out an army corps including a cavalry division, it was Haig who accompanied the cavalry commander, Major-General J. D. P. French, as chief staff officer. It was in that capacity that he served French throughout the important Colesberg operations which covered Cape Colony during the period of British defeat early in the war. French's reputation was greatly –

and deservedly – enhanced at Colesberg, but he was the first to recognise how much depended on his Chief of Staff.

Although nominally superseded by a superior officer, it was Haig who signed the cavalry divisional orders for the advance to Kimberley in February 1900, which has been called 'French's finest hour', and was certainly the highlight of the achievement of British cavalry in that war. Against an entirely mounted enemy, British operations generally had an air of clumsiness and slowness; on this occasion that image was dispelled. French had under him three cavalry brigades and two mounted infantry brigades, a total of 8500 men. The manoeuvre that followed is generally known as the 'dash to Kimberley', and if the experience of it left a strong mark on all who took part, the picture of it has been unwarrantably printed on 'cavalry thinking' thereafter. Here is Haig's description of the key moment, when the advancing cavalry found the enemy positioned on both flanks:

> There seemed only one thing to be done if we were to get to Kimberley before the Boers barred our path, namely charge through the gap between the two positions ... The 9th and 16th Lancers were then ordered to charge ... Our Lancers caught several Boers and rode down many others in the open plain, and really suffered little from the very hot rifle fire – about 20 casualties I fancy and we passed within 1000 yards of the Boer position!

It was a dramatic moment and undoubtedly a highly misleading one. In later years Haig would be accused of endlessly trying to find the mythical 'Gee in Gap' through which the cavalry would charge home. If excuses required to be made, the brilliant success of the dash to Kimberley might provide them, but in fact they do not. Haig learnt other lessons, not only affecting cavalry, from his observation of the South African War: the need 'to improve our cavalry in dismounted action'; the need to 'pay more attention to this class of work in time of peace. Musketry training and field firing to be made more practical. Tactical schemes for cavalry in *all* kinds of country.' Turning to the artillery he found that 'many have over-estimated the power of shrapnel fire'; in the infantry, 'troops seem to be posted too thickly upon a defensive position'. In all this there is a perception of future conditions which shows the commander as well as the highly trained staff officer at work. It was precisely dismounted action and good shooting that distinguished the British cavalry in 1914; it was precisely over-emphasis on shrapnel at the expense of high explosive that weakened the British artillery in 1914–15; and it was too-dense infantry formations that repeatedly caused heavy casualties in the New Armies when they took the field.

Haig spent the last part of the South African War commanding a group of columns in Cape Colony, engaged in the educative but frustrating pursuit of a Boer commando under Jan Smuts. Patience, perseverance and attention to detail were the virtues chiefly exhibited in this work. These Haig possessed;

what he did not possess was a formula for defeating the finest mounted infantry in the world with half-trained men and horses. So it was chiefly as a staff officer that Haig distinguished himself in South Africa, and it is no coincidence that when he gave evidence to the Royal Commission on the war, their first and most searching questions to him were about staff organisation and staff duties.

Emerging from the South African War with the substantive rank of lieutenant-colonel, Haig commanded a cavalry regiment, the 17th Lancers, for one year after the war. At the end of 1903 he was appointed Inspector-General of Cavalry in India, with the substantive rank of colonel and the local rank of major-general. For the next nine years staff duties were his preoccupation. As Inspector-General his work followed two lines: first, increasing the efficiency of the cavalry in India, which was the object of inspection itself. As carried out by Haig, and described by one of his own staff officers, this was 'a ruthless testing out of every phase of the life of the unit'. Secondly there was a higher education for war, inculcated in staff rides, which a later generation would call 'tactical exercises without troops'. The proceedings and lessons of these rides were later collected in his one and only book, *Cavalry Studies*. Its quality ranges from an axiom founded upon the glowing memory of the 'dash to Kimberley', 'the bullet from [the small-bore rifle] has little stopping power against the horse', to an utterance of prophetic significance in his own later career: 'the whole question of co-operation with an ally is fraught with difficulties and danger. When the theatre of operation lies in the country of the ally, these difficulties increase. . . .' 'Haig was in no doubt that the 'ally' in question would be France, that the 'theatre of operation' would also be France, and that the enemy would be Germany.

Such thoughts were confined to very few at that time. King Edward VII paid his famous visit to Paris in the year that Haig went to India; the following year, 1904, was the year of the Entente Cordiale; in 1905 Russia, France's ally since 1891, was defeated by Japan and swept by revolution – a combination that greatly diminished her as a European power factor; Germany's attempt to exploit this circumstance produced the Tangier Crisis, which brought the states of Europe very close to war. The year 1905 was also the year of the landslide Liberal victory in the British election that brought Mr Haldane to the War Office, so inaugurating the army reforms that finally fashioned the General Staff, reorganised the Home Army as an expeditionary force, and prepared the mobilisation of the nation by the creation of the Territorial Army. The year 1906 was the year in which staff talks between Britain and France began. These were momentous times, but very few understood their drift; in the government and its party, all too few.

Like Haig, Richard Burdon Haldane was a Scotsman, born, in fact, in Edinburgh only a few doors away from the Haigs. He had the Scottish bent for general principles, for going to the roots of matters. From the first his intention was to imbue the army with a new practicality, an up-to-date realism that would wipe out the bad memories of South Africa. He needed helpers, men who could share his vision and pursue it with energy; many years later he recalled: 'After surveying the whole Army, I took upon myself to ask Lord Haig, who was then in India, to come over to this country and to think for us. From all I could discover even then, he seemed to be the most highly equipped thinker in the British Army.' Haldane was not alone in this opinion.

It is impossible to form a correct assessment of Haig's career in the First World War without an understanding of his role in preparing the army for that war between 1906 and 1909. This work, in close collaboration with Haldane, gave him a more intimate sense of the nature of the army that fought the war than that of any other senior officer. It was also during this period that he formed lasting impressions of individuals, for better or for worse. General Kiggell, for example, who later became his Chief of Staff to the wonderment of many, was his Assistant Director of Staff Duties at the War Office in 1908, and succeeded him as Director; Haig learned to appreciate him as an 'educated soldier'. A number of loyalties were forged at this time, as well as some less happy sentiments.

At the War Office Haig held the posts of, first, Director of Military Training, then Director of Staff Duties, the latter reorganised to take in some of the functions of the former. His contribution lies in two fields, both fundamental. In September 1906, very soon after his arrival, he wrote to Sir Gerald Ellison, Haldane's Military Private Secretary:

Our object in my opinion should be to start a system of finance suited to the 'supposed situation', i.e. a great war requiring the whole resources of the nation to bring it to a successful end. Even if the proposed system costs more in peace, it should be inaugurated provided that it is more practical in war. The Swiss system seems to me to be exactly what is wanted 'to root the army in the people' . . .

And in the following month we find Lord Esher writing to Haldane that Haig 'wants to be able, as I understand, at the end of 12 months to place an Army of 900,000 men in the field, and keep it there for five years'.

It is impossible to overstate the visionary, indeed revolutionary, quality of such ideas at that time: a war 'requiring the whole resources of the nation' – unheard of; a system 'to root the army in the people' – unknown since the Middle Ages; '900,000 men in the field' – also unheard of; 'for five years' – unthinkable! It was with this in mind that Haig argued for a Territorial Army of twenty-eight divisions, and urged against much so-called expert opinion that it should be complete and self-contained in all respects. In the event, fourteen divisions were all that finance permitted, yet these were the beginnings of the citizen army that ultimately fought the war. No one had an earlier or better understanding of the citizen army than Haig.

His second contribution was in a narrower but equally vital matter: providing the whole army (and Dominion contingents) with a unified, up-to-date method of organisation and control. This was embodied in *Field Service Regulations Part II*, worked out by Haig and Kiggell, and tested in a staff ride in 1908. Haig's respect for *Field Service Regulations* (both parts) never wavered.

Haig returned to India in 1909 as Chief of Staff, and in 1912 he took command of the army corps at Aldershot which, in the event of war, would at once become 1 Corps in the Expeditionary Force, the only one already formed in peacetime. In both these posts he continued to prepare himself and all those under him for the war that was visibly approaching. In India he carried out a series of staff rides, each one 'devoted to a definite phase of fighting against a European enemy', in the words of his staff officer, John Charteris. It was in India that he evolved his concept of the phases of a war, based on his study of military history, from which he never departed; they would be, said Haig:

1. The manoeuvre for position.
2. The clash of battle.
3. The wearing-out fight of varying duration.
4. The eventual decisive blow.

Posterity, understandably, has dwelt much upon the third phase, which in the war that was coming lasted three whole years, and this being the twentieth century required the wearing-out, not just of armies, but of the nations behind them.

At Aldershot Haig worked to perfect a particular instrument of war, large by British standards, very small by those of the Continent. How well he succeeded is shown by the achievement of 1 Corps at the First Battle of Ypres. He undoubtedly inculcated a fine *esprit de corps*, based on proficiency, which filled the formation with confidence in itself and in him. The Kaiser himself, in 1915, told an American correspondent that he considered 1 Corps under Haig 'the best in the world'. On hearing this, Haig commented that it was 'a compliment to Aldershot methods and Aldershot training, rather than to my own command in battle'.

What kind of an officer, then, do we find commanding Britain's only large army formation on the eve of war? First let it be noted that this post alone placed him in a very select circle of future commanders: Sir Horace Smith-Dorrien, a full general, and Sir John French, a field-marshal. Haig was now a lieutenant-general, fifty-three years old, in a prime of life that found him physically the equal of many much younger men, and morally assured. He was as 'educated' an officer as the army possessed: a careful student of military history, with staff and command experience in two campaigns, and a rare awareness of the working of army affairs at their very centre. He was rightly conscious of possessing high professional qualifications. He was very sure of himself, which is an asset in a commander, but not always an unlimited asset. On the debit side of his account we must list an uneven capacity for picking men (his two divisional commanders were both well up to their jobs, some members of his personal staff were not); a detachment from politics (internal), which is strange and limiting in one aspiring to high office, but which proved a strength when the army was split by politics in March 1914; and an alarming inarticulateness that made it difficult for him to communicate except with those who knew him well, and laid him open to serious misjudgement. But there were very few among his contemporaries who would not be expecting Douglas Haig to distinguish himself in the field.

Until the Industrial Revolution placed its brand on nations, the styles and weapons of war changed slowly, in step with the slow changes of technology itself. The Tower musket ('Brown Bess') served the British infantry from the days of William III to the Crimean War; HMS *Victory* was already forty-nine years old at the Battle of Trafalgar, with another twenty years' service ahead of her. The Industrial Revolution changed everything and made change itself a constant. The deployment of masses by railway and the development of modern fire power were innovations of the American Civil War (there were many others); smokeless powder and the magazine rifle created the empty battlefields of the South African War – and with them the necessity for a new kind of soldier; the Russo-Japanese War rubbed in the lesson of artillery fire power and demonstrated the combination of barbed wire and machine guns. The First World War presented all these novelties in a concentrated form, and added to them a wide new range of its own: war in the air, submarine warfare, the application of the internal combustion engine to war in many forms, poison gas, liquid flame, wireless telegraphy – the list is long. The mass production and the inventiveness of modern industry made this war of the mass armies drawn from mass populations like no previous human experience. It was into this unceasing ferment of lethal change that Haig and all his contemporaries, friends or foes, marched off in August 1914, and it is in that context that they require to be judged.

Haig himself did not march off happily. From close personal acquaintance he had grave doubts about the capacity of Commander-in-Chief Field-Marshal Sir John French: 'In my own heart, I know that French is quite unfit for this great command at a time of crisis in our Nation's history.' He was equally dubious of the plan of campaign to which the army and the country now found themselves fettered, thanks to the industrious efforts of Sir Henry Wilson as DMO, and the lofty detachment of the Liberal government from questions of national strategy. Haig wrote to Haldane on 4 August:

This war will last many months, possibly years, so I venture to hope that our only bolt (and that not a very big one) may not suddenly be shot on a project of which the success seems to be quite doubtful – I mean the checking of the German advance into France. Would it not be better to begin at once to enlarge our Expeditionary Force by amalgamating less regular forces with it?

The next day he had an opportunity of expanding these thoughts at the great Council of War called at No. 10 Downing Street – an occasion as revealing as it was extraordinary. Haig's contribution was, first, to help to dispose of a sudden desire on the part of Sir John French to have the Expeditionary Force conveyed to Antwerp, despite the fact that its approaches lay through Dutch waters, and Holland was neutral. Later, Haig made some further points:

> Great Britain and Germany would be fighting for their existence. Therefore the war was bound to be a long war, and neither would acknowledge defeat after a short struggle . . . I held that we must organize our resources for a war of several years.
>
> 2nd. Great Britain must at once take in hand the creating of an Army. I mentioned one million as the number to aim at immediately . . .
>
> 3rd . . . I urged that a considerable proportion of officers and N.C.O.s should be withdrawn forthwith from the Expeditionary Force . . .

It was odd that a corps commander should be present at all at such a gathering; it was odder still that it should be a corps commander who put forward this long view of the war. It is important to remember that Haig's eye was always fixed – until August 1918 – on a distant horizon. This was liable to make those who sought elixirs of quick victory impatient with him; ironically, when the quick victory did come in sight, it was he who perceived it first. Meanwhile on 5 August 1914 at Downing Street, at least one man fortunately agreed with Haig's unfashionable ideas: the new Secretary of State for War, Lord Kitchener, who two days later issued his call for 'the first hundred thousand'.

The war very soon fulfilled all Haig's misgivings and more besides. He had fully accepted that it was the function of the British Expeditionary Force (BEF) to fight beside the French army and conform to French plans, since it would at most comprise six infantry divisions, compared with France's sixty-two. What came as very startling news, on 13 August, was the revelation by Sir John French that the concentration point would not be, as most supposed, Amiens, but Maubeuge, close to the Belgian frontier. Haig commented:

> We are to detrain . . . some 60 or 70 miles to the east of Amiens! In view of the ignorance still existing regarding the enemy's movements, the rate of his advance into Belgium, and his intentions, it seems to some of us somewhat risky to begin our concentration so close to the enemy . . . I have an uneasy feeling lest we may be committed to some great general action before we have had time to absorb our reservists. Any precipitate engage-

ment of our little force may lose us the inestimable value which our highly trained divisions do possess not only as a unit in battle, but also as a leaven for raising the morale of the great National Army which the Govt. is now proceeding to organize.

The truth, familiar to us but still hidden from soldiers even of Haig's seniority, was that the BEF was now caught in the toils of a French plan of rare absurdity: a headlong offensive into Germany. What now seems incredible is that there had been no critical examination of the French plan by the British General Staff at the time when mobilisation arrangements were being made. The BEF – and the nation – would now pay the price of that negligence, because the French plan collapsed at the first breath of reality. As Haig feared, the BEF *was* committed too soon and too far forward. Instead of a great advance it found itself making a great retreat, which was particularly hard on the 60 per cent of reservists in its ranks. Fortunately his own corps got off very lightly, but II Corps suffered losses that affected its morale and fighting value for the rest of the year. And I Corps was only temporarily spared: at Ypres in October it too would pass through the fires of terrible battle, so that by the end of 1914 little would be left of that 'leaven' for the national army that Haig desired.

Until the First Battle of Ypres, Haig's part in the war displayed him as a competent corps commander, but no particular distinction had come his way. On 28 August, as the retiring I Corps approached La Fère, Haig learned from an aerial report that large German forces were passing across his front, and that of his right-hand neighbour, General Lanrezac's French Fifth Army. Haig made immediate plans to co-operate with the French in a counter-attack, only to be flatly forbidden to do so by GHQ, with the result that Lanrezac attacked alone next day and won the first French victory of the war while his allies rested. In the advance from the Marne to the Aisne, I Corps took the lead, but by now the offensive spirit of the BEF was somewhat blunted. Haig fretted at the slowness of the cavalry which held up his own divisions, but could not prevent the Germans just beating him to the important Chemin des Dames ridge, overlooking the Aisne valley. On that escarpment I Corps made its first acquaintance with trench warfare and its weapons:

Our troops are certainly fighting at a great disadvantage in not having
(a) large bomb throwers (Minen Werfer)
(b) small effective hand bombs with mechanical safety catch arrangements.

Haig at once ordered the Royal Engineers to experiment with grenades and mortars, and a few weeks later was lending some of these extemporised weapons to other corps. But he soon realised that the nature of the war itself was changing fundamentally: 'In front of this Corps, and for many miles on either side, affairs have reached a deadlock, and no decision seems possible in this area.'

There followed what is generally, but erroneously, called 'the race to the sea'. In fact, in the words of General Foch, 'it was an attempt to exploit the last vestige of our victory on the Marne', to escape the deadlock on the Aisne and turn the German right. Unfortunately as another French general said, the Allies were 'always twenty-four hours and an army corps behind the enemy'. So, mile by mile, the two sides edged towards the coast, the final encounter taking place along the lines, Armentières, Ypres, Dixmude, known in British history as the First Battle of Ypres.

On the Allied side the battle was fought under the overall direction of General Foch, and at all times it was the French who bore the brunt of it. From 20 October it was increasingly I Corps that bore the brunt of the British fighting, and Haig who controlled it. By the time the battle reached its final climax, he was not only giving orders to his own two divisions, but to the 7th Division (belonging to IV Corps), parts of II Corps and the Cavalry Corps. In what was always, in 'blind country', very much a soldiers', regimental officers', brigadiers' battle, Haig's functions were threefold: first, to reinterpret realistically the absurdly optimistic directives of GHQ, where Sir John French spoke of the Germans 'playing their last card', and looked forward to 'a decisive result'. Secondly, when the facts of great German numerical superiority and overwhelming artillery superiority were being dinned in, it fell to Haig to shuffle and reshuffle the few cards in the British pack: the remains of a brigade to plug this gap, some cavalry to paper over another, a request for support from the French, relief for units worn down beyond belief. This work did not become any easier when both the I Corps divisional commanders and seven of their staff officers were knocked out by a single German shell on 31 October.

And finally Haig had to keep up the morale of soldiers who were enduring an intensity of fire power never before experienced, whose weariness was almost indescribable, and whose losses were by now disastrous. According to Charteris very few officers from GHQ were ever seen farther forward than corps HQ: 'D.H. himself errs, I think, in the other extreme. He is constantly in extreme danger of being hit; he goes everywhere on horseback. I do not know what would happen if he were knocked out.' It was on 31 October, when news came in that the British line was broken, that Haig made his famous ride up the Menin Road. The official history says: 'his appearance, moving up at a slow trot with part of his staff behind him as at an inspection, doing much to restore confidence'. Certainly, to all who saw him, he conveyed an unforgettable impression of authority and calm.

The final crisis of 'First Ypres' came on 11 November; it was a miracle that the BEF came through it. Sir John French paid a generous tribute to the work of I Corps and its commander: 'The success of this great defence . . . was due in the first place to the quick grasp of the situation by Sir Douglas Haig, who so skilfully handled the scanty forces at his disposal, and economised his few reserves with such soldierlike foresight.'

Haig was promoted to full general, coming out of this ordeal of battle better than his C-in-C, about whom grave doubts were now growing at home, while the early misgivings in Haig's own mind about him had grown with the experience of war. This was not a good omen for the BEF as the year drew to its end. But the misfortune of First Ypres went much deeper than that: British casualties during the battle amounted to fifty-eight thousand officers and men, bringing the total for the war to eighty-nine thousand. These were almost all regulars; it meant that, in the words of the official history: 'The old British Army was gone past recall, leaving but a remnant to carry on the training of the New Armies.' That was the special tragedy of Ypres.

'The year 1915,' wrote Winston Churchill, 'was disastrous to the cause of the Allies and to the whole world. By the mistakes of this year the opportunity was lost of confining the conflagration within limits which though enormous were not uncontrolled . . . in January 1915,' he still insisted, years afterwards, 'the terrific affair was still not unmanageable.' He missed a daunting, but fundamental, truth: that Germany had seized in 1914 a strategic initiative that had not, as some supposed, been wrested from her at the Battle of the Marne, that would not, in fact, be wrested from her until her last strategic reserve was expended in July 1918. During all the intervening time, enjoying the advantage of the interior lines, and with her armies firmly planted on French soil, she was able to compel the Allies to dance to her tune. For the British there would be a double bondage: their actions would have to conform not only to the intentions of the Germans, their enemies, but to those of the French, the 'senior partners'. Haig, still holding a relatively low command, was one of the few who grasped these truths.

The BEF had by now expanded to six army corps, and was duly reorganised as two armies, the First under Haig, the Second under General Smith-Dorrien. It was now that the Ypres sector passed into the keeping of the Second Army, whose main effort of the year was the defensive Second Battle of Ypres, chiefly remembered as the first use of poison gas during the war. The British contribution to the Allied offensives of 1915 was made by the First Army; patterns that were to become all too familiar now emerged, the blueprints of an increasingly destructive future.

By March 1915 Haig had formulated the central thought about the war from which he never departed – a great simplicity that eluded many subtle minds: 'We cannot hope to win until we have defeated the German Army.' There were those who, at different times, would advocate almost anything but this, who would urge the advantages of defeating the Austrian army, the Turkish army, the Bulgarian army, or the possibility of defeating Germany herself while her army remained undefeated. To Haig all such notions were departures from the first principles of war, principles succinctly summed up by Sir William Robertson, soon to become CIGS:

> An essential condition of success in war being the concentration of effort
> on the 'decisive front', or place where the main issue will probably be
> fought out, it follows that soldiers and statesmen charged with the direc-
> tion of military operations should be agreed amongst themselves as to
> where that front is . . . In the Great War the decisive front was fixed for us
> by the deployment of the enemy's masses in France and Belgium . . .

The persistent refusal of many statesmen and some soldiers to accept this fact
has been aptly called by Major-General J. F. C. Fuller 'the strategy of evasion'. The alternative to it was, of course, the strategy of attrition, cause of
the anger and argument that has attached to Haig's name ever since.

In March 1915 the First Army conducted a dress rehearsal for many future
occasions at Neuve Chapelle. In three days' fighting it succeeded only in
capturing its first objective, at a cost of some thirteen thousand officers and
men, the Germans losing about the same number. This result was disappointing, but in retrospect, considering how poorly equipped the whole army was
at this stage, how weak in heavy artillery, how poorly supplied with ammunition by comparison with later occasions, the surprise is that it did so well.
Certainly Neuve Chapelle did not convey any sense of an insuperable problem;
the real hazards of trench warfare – the extreme difficulty of controlling a
battle once launched, the problem of communication, the problem of reinforcement and supply through congested trench systems, the problem of
maintaining any momentum at all after the break-in – had yet to emerge in
the later gloomy battles of the year: Aubers Ridge, Festubert, Loos.

Because every attack ended in loss and frustration it is too easy to think of
them as mere repetitive futilities; this is to miss the most important quality
of 1915, which was a year of unprecedented innovation. We have noted the
use of gas at Ypres; liquid fire made its appearance not long afterwards; when
a reasonable flow of trench mortars began to reach the army it became possible to experiment with smoke; the field telephone and wireless transformed
communication, and at the same time extended intelligence and counter-
intelligence; aerial observation by aeroplane or balloon poured into every
headquarters, requiring to be translated and disseminated at high speed in
the form of maps; artillery barrages with their timetables became ever more
sophisticated. It was all new, all requiring more careful and detailed staff
work. The 'General Staff war' was emerging, and First Army headquarters
had the reputation of being better than most at this kind of thing. GHQ of
the BEF, under Field-Marshal Sir John French, did not have such a reputation.

Confidence in Sir John French's qualities as Commander-in-Chief received
a rude shock – for those very few who knew the facts – as early as the beginning of September 1914. During the retreat from Mons he had announced his
intention of pulling the BEF right out of the Allied line of battle, and retiring
behind the Seine to rest for about eight days, leaving the French to fill the

gap and get on with the war. This extraordinary proposal had brought Lord Kitchener to GHQ to overrule him in person. Doubts about the C-in-C in government circles were never entirely removed after this; as early as January 1915 one informed observer was speaking of the possibility of French being replaced by Haig. The 'shell scandal' in May, when French appeared to be using the press as a stick with which to beat the government, did him more harm. By June the King, once his loyal supporter, was telling Lord Esher that French should be superseded. In July both the King and Lord Kitchener were asking Haig to write to them privately about 'the situation and doings of the Army'.

In September the issue came to a head: the occasion was the ill-fated Battle of Loos, the First Army's last offensive effort of 1915. Neither French nor Haig wanted to fight a battle in this industrial wasteland; it was General Joffre, the French Commander-in-Chief, who insisted that they should do so, as part of his own Artois offensive. Well aware of the strength of the German position, Haig now pinned his faith on careful artillery preparation instead of the surprise rush of Neuve Chapelle, hoping that an element of surprise would nevertheless be provided by the use of poison gas. If the German line was to be broken however, not just dented, everything would depend on the judicious use of reserves, and Haig noted with dismay that out of three reserve divisions allocated to him, two were New Army divisions that had just arrived in France, completely untested in battle. Worse still, all three reserve divisions were held much too far back, and released to First Army only when it was too late for them to be effective. The resulting débâcle after the usual opening half-success destroyed the last shreds of support for French on the part of his government superiors at home and his chief subordinate in the field. On 19 December Haig became Commander-in-Chief of the BEF.

It was during the next two years that the shadows gathered around Haig's name and reputation; the shadows are called 'The Somme', 'Arras' and 'Passchendaele'. It was these three great battles (actually falling within a period of eighteen months) with their total of eight hundred thousand British casualties, that constituted together what Haig called 'the wearing-out fight' and what history has called 'the war of attrition' on the western front. The narrative of those battles, their torments, their hardships, the endurance, the courage, the skills – yes, skills – displayed in them have been described often enough. All we need be concerned with now is their projection in the mind of the Commander-in-Chief who ordered them. Why? Why did he go on with them in often adverse circumstances? How did he justify himself? Can his justification be justified?

We have seen that it was already Haig's fixed belief that only the defeat of the German army could win (and thus end) the war. His objective throughout was to end the war. This was also, needless to say, the objective of the Allied governments, and in December 1915 their authorised representatives met at Chantilly and agreed the following:

... that the decisions of the war can only be obtained in the principal theatres, that is to say in those in which the enemy has maintained the greater part of his forces ... The decision should be obtained by co-ordinated offensives on these fronts.

The year 1916, hard though it may be to believe, was the *first time* the Allies had actually planned co-ordinated offensives on the western front, the eastern front and the Italian front. Both Joffre and Haig fought hard, throughout the year, to keep the plan alive.

With a clear idea of his objective (much clearer than that of his various political masters) Haig's problem was really one of ways and means. At the very centre of these considerations was the French alliance, about which he had also arrived at two firm conclusions. The first of these was embodied in a statement that he made on 1 January 1916 to the head of the French Mission at GHQ, General des Vallières:

I showed him the instructions which I have received from the S. of S. for War containing the orders of the Govt. to me. I pointed out that I am *not under* General Joffre's orders, but that would make no difference, as my intention was to do my utmost to carry out General Joffre's wishes on strategical matters, as if they were orders.

It had to be so. Yet few people perceived it at the time, and to this day British strategy in the First World War is written about as though it existed in isolation, independent of the needs and wishes of Britain's allies.

The second of Haig's conclusions about the alliance also embodies a fact often ignored. Until 1916 France had borne incomparably the larger burden of the war in the west; by the beginning of that year her casualties amounted to 2,385,000 – compared with British casualties totalling just under 375,000. This was not only bad for Anglo-French relations – 'perfidious Albion' was a concept deeply planted in many French minds – but also, of course, disastrous for France herself. On 14 January Haig noted:

I think the French man-power situation is serious as they are not likely to stand another winter's war. There is no doubt to my mind but that the war must be won by the force of the British Empire.

It was to this already tragic situation that German initiative added, in February 1916, the Battle of Verdun, whose avowed object was to bleed the forces of France to death.

To the very end of the war Haig suffered this double oppression: a sense of unalterable subordination (in 1918 Marshal Foch became Allied generalissimo, and France had 102 divisions in the field compared with the British Empire's 60), and a sense of his ally's increasing weakness. As the Battle of Verdun developed and French losses grew, the pressures on Haig to intervene were naturally intense. With the New Army divisions now pouring into France,

Haig was only too well aware of the unfitness of his army for a great battle: 'I have not got an Army in France really, but a collection of divisions untrained for the Field. The actual fighting Army will be evolved from them.' With this thought in mind he resisted demands for immediate British action. But he could not resist extending his front to provide the French with some reserves; he could not resist accepting 1 July as the opening date for the great offensive, though he would have preferred August; he could not blink the fact that his own army, not the French, would now have to play the leading role in it; and he could not alter the chosen locale. He would have preferred to make his attack in Flanders, where there were tempting strategic prizes; Joffre insisted on the Somme.

It is against this background of strategic compulsion that the battles of 1916 and 1917 have to be viewed – a compulsion, it must be added, made more absolute by the material conditions of the war. The war of masses required a mass of matériel: between 9 August 1914 and 10 November 1918 $25\frac{1}{2}$ million tons of miscellaneous stores were shipped to the BEF in France. It is impossible to form a visual image of such an amount; it is equally impossible to form an image of the $5\frac{1}{4}$ million tons of ammunition included in that total by the requirements of an artillery war. It hardly helps, but does indicate a scale of magnitude, to point out that in the first fortnight of the Battle of the Somme, the British artillery fired 3,526,000 rounds (75,000 tons); that the preliminary bombardment alone at Arras used 2,687,653 rounds, and at the Third Battle of Ypres, 4,283,550 rounds. In November 1918 the number of motor lorries or tractors with the BEF was 31,770 – a very large increase over the 1100 or so in 1914, but a ludicrously small number by comparison with, say, the 970,000 vehicles that served General Eisenhower between D-Day in 1944 and VE-Day 1945. The point being, quite simply, this: the 1914–18 war, in terms of transportation, was from beginning to end chiefly a railway war, a horse-drawn war, a manpower war. And that meant that once the vast masses of stores required for a battle were accumulated by immense effort in the required position, it amounted virtually to a defeat in the field if they were not put to the use intended.

These, then, were the pressures under which Haig and his armies fought the war of attrition; it was a hard, grim business. It always *is* a hard, grim business. The British were now doing what the French had been doing for two years, and what the Russians would have to do in the Second World War. The experience of all three shows that it is no easy matter to 'defeat the German Army'. And the experience of the eastern front in the Second World War shows that the price is no less high in a war of movement than in the static war of trenches.* Nevertheless the quest for movement, the desire to

---

* Operation Barbarossa was launched on 22 June 1941; by the end of the year German losses alone exceeded those of the French and Germans combined in the ten-month 'blood-bath' at Verdun in 1916. Between 1941 and 1945 the military *dead* of the Soviet Union equalled the military dead of all combatants in the whole of the First World War.

break the deadlock of the trenches, was both understandable and legitimate. It was in 1916 that the means of doing so appeared, and perhaps more rubbish has been uttered about Haig in this connection than in any other.

The first use of tanks in war was on 15 September 1916; out of forty-nine available, thirty-two actually went into action, and thanks to them a striking local success was obtained near the village of Flers. The decision to use the only weapon that seemed able to defy the lethal combination of barbed wire and machine guns for such a small result has been resoundingly condemned. 'So the great secret was sold for the battered ruin of a little hamlet on the Somme, which was not worth capturing,' wrote Lloyd George; he was only one of many who held this view – and who should have known better.

The attack launched on 15 September was not merely one more stage in the British 'push' on the Somme. The French Sixth Army, on the right of the British, had already begun a major offensive on 3 September, which it resumed on 12 September. On that day also the Allied forces at Salonika passed to the offensive, and the Russians, whose offensive under General Brusilov had achieved great results already, now made yet another effort, in conjunction with the Rumanians who had just entered the war. On 15 September the Italians attacked on the river Isonzo. It was the first – indeed, the only – time in the war that the Allies succeeded in co-ordinating their efforts in this way. The object of this great combined endeavour was not the capture of 'a little hamlet on the Somme'; it was the defeat of Germany. In such an endeavour it was unthinkable that the British should not play their part, and equally unthinkable that they should hold anything back.

Hindsight, with all its accuracy, informs us that the great Allied offensive failed. Many people thought that the tanks had also failed; out of the thirty-two that went into action on the 15th, nine broke down mechanically and five became ditched, so that in the end only eighteen out of the original forty-nine took part in the battle, and very few of these were fit for action on 16 September. The Mark I tank of 1916 was certainly no war-winner; it was, however, despite its critics, a very useful adjunct to battle. Haig had no doubts about this, and on 18 September he sent his Deputy CGS to London to ask for a thousand tanks. He never got them: for Arras, in April 1917, forty-eight were available; for Third Ypres in July, 136; at Cambrai, fourteen months after the début on the Somme, there were 476, and for Amiens in August 1918 the largest number ever in one British action, 534. But Haig never lost faith, and the improved tanks of 1918 rewarded him by playing a large part in his victories.

Meanwhile the battles of attrition continued. The German Chief of Staff, General von Falkenhayn, was dismissed in August 1916; his successors, Field-Marshal von Hindenburg and General Ludendorff, took one look at the Somme battle and decided that if this went on: 'Our defeat seemed inevitable. ... Accordingly, the construction had been begun as early as September of powerful rear positions in the West ...' At a terrible price Haig and his raw armies had imposed their will on the enemy and made great strides with that destruction of the German field army which, by the end of the next year, had transformed it from the most professional force in the world to what Ludendorff called 'more nearly a militia'.

When the Germans withdrew to their 'powerful rear positions', which the British have persisted in calling 'The Hindenburg Line' in February 1917, they gravely disrupted the offensive plans of the new French C-in-C, General Nivelle. The result was that the Battle of Arras, originally conceived as a British diversionary attack, while the French offensive in Champagne won the war in forty-eight hours according to General Nivelle's prescription, turned instead into a battle of attrition in its own right. The disappointment and the fresh loss resulting from Nivelle's offensive at last brought about a state of affairs that Haig had long feared: a substantial part of the French army was for a time in a state of mutiny, and it became impossible for France to continue shouldering the burden of the war. In 1917 the process begun on the Somme in July 1916 came to its fruition: onto the British armies under Haig now fell the task of waging the war on the western front, while their allies collapsed all around them – the French in May, the Russians (finally) in October, the Italians in that same month. It is against this sombre backcloth that the British experience in the Third Battle of Ypres has to be assessed. The battle's quarter of a million casualties, the revolting conditions in which it was fought, everything that is contained in the hated word 'Passchendaele', make it one of the most emotive, controversial facts in Haig's whole career. Here it must suffice simply to ask whether, if the British army had not made the effort and sacrifice that it did, the German situation would have looked as it did to Ludendorff:

> The Army had come victoriously through 1917; but it had become apparent that the holding of the Western Front purely by a defensive could no longer be counted on ... The enormous material resources of the enemy had given his attack a considerable preponderance over our defence ... Against the weight of the enemy's material the troops no longer displayed their old stubbornness; they thought with horror of fresh defensive battles and longed for a war of movement ...

'We cannot hope to win until we have defeated the German Army': it was hard going, but it was being done.

Unfortunately this fact was very difficult to perceive at the time. The very small advances at Ypres set beside its long casualty lists, the dejection when the brilliant opening success at Cambrai in November was cancelled out by the German counter-stroke, brought to a head the mistrust and misunderstanding between Haig and his political masters that had been building up throughout the year. In dealing with a politician as silver-tongued and volatile as Mr Lloyd George, now Prime Minister, Haig's inarticulateness was more than ever a drawback. 'Lucidity of speech,' wrote Lloyd George, referring to

Haig, 'is unquestionably one of the surest tests of mental precision . . . In my experience a confused talker is never a clear thinker.' Lloyd George had long been convinced that Haig was a fool, and Third Ypres seemed to be the final sickening proof he was right.

For the BEF, in 1918, this clash of temperament between Prime Minister and C-in-C was almost fatal. Reluctantly Lloyd George concluded that he could not dismiss Haig, though he no longer had confidence in him. What he *could* do, though, was deprive him of all chances of another Third Ypres: he could withhold reinforcements from the BEF. And so we see, in January and February 1918, the amazing spectacle of the BEF having to disband 141 infantry battalions, while the Germans were bringing to the western front some 500,000 new troops made available by the collapse of Russia. And it was on the British sector that the weight of this reinforcement would be felt: against the extended fronts of the British Fifth and Third armies, Ludendorff massed no less than sixty-two divisions and nearly six thousand guns. 'In the West,' he wrote, 'the Army pined for the offensive'; the date appointed was 21 March 1918.

Whatever else the 'March Offensive' may have shown, it clearly displayed the folly of the idea that – except in freak conditions – the offensive was more costly than the defensive during the First World War. The German offensive in Picardy in March was almost immediately followed by another attack in Flanders. The two together lasted 41 days, and cost the British Army 239,793 casualties; the 105 days of Third Ypres had cost 244,897. Because of the appalling losses, because whole units just vanished, because hundreds of guns were captured, and the Fifth Army was forced to make a long retreat, a misleading air of disaster has hung about these battles ever since. The truth is, that while the Germans certainly scored some spectacular tactical successes, particularly at the outset, they also suffered some grave tactical reverses and complete strategic defeat.

The most important strategic prize available to the Germans was the separation of the French and British armies, and their defeat in detail. By 24 March this prize was definitely within reach; that it was never seized was chiefly due to two men: Ludendorff and Haig. In this battle, intended to be the decisive battle of the war, Ludendorff displayed his most serious failings as a commander: irresponsible opportunism and irresolution. 'I forbid myself to use the word "strategy",' he announced – and not surprisingly he failed to give strategic direction to the battle; he missed his moment.* Haig on the other hand was the first to perceive the full danger to the Allied cause, after a fateful meeting with General Pétain, the French Commander-in-Chief. He was also the first to perceive what the remedy must be. There was only one way to make sure that Pétain did not carry out his declared intention of retiring

---

* Incredible though it may seem, for this all-out offensive Ludendorff provided no arm of exploitation at all; only once did the Germans have as many as thirteen tanks in action; there were no armoured cars, no motorcycle machine gunners, no cavalry.

away from the British flank: Haig telegraphed to the CIGS, asking him and the Secretary of State for War to come at once 'to arrange that General Foch or some other determined general, who would fight, should be given supreme control of the operations in France'. When this was done, on 26 March, the chances of Ludendorff splitting the Allied front, already fading, vanished completely. The consolation prizes, the great rail centres of Amiens and Hazebrouck, also eluded him. German losses were high; the Americans were coming in at last; it was a bad beginning for Germany.

However there was no doubt about one thing: thanks in no small part to the British government's reluctance to reinforce its army, the BEF was now in a very weak condition. Out of fifty British divisions no less than ten were considered to be 'exhausted', of which five were earmarked to be broken up. At the end of May there was further misfortune, when four weak British divisions, resting on a 'quiet' French sector, were caught up in the next German offensive and decimated once again. All through May, June and July Haig's chief preoccupation was nursing his army, rebuilding its strength to face the resumption of the Flanders attack, which he confidently expected and which Ludendorff confidently intended. It was Foch's counterstroke on 18 July (the Second Battle of the Marne, mainly a French battle, but with British, Italians and Americans also present) that put an end to Germany's offensive power; from this moment the Allies held the initiative. And now, despite all the losses of the battles of attrition, despite the fearful hammering of March and April, despite the government's continuing lukewarmness, it was Haig's armies that became the spearhead of that initiative.

The first act of Haig's victorious 'Hundred Days' in 1918, the first and most striking of his nine successive victories, was the Battle of Amiens, launched on 8 August. In this action the British used over five hundred tanks, over two thousand guns and the Allies concentrated nineteen hundred aircraft; the signs of things to come were becoming clear. Brilliant staff work, complete secrecy, and the favour of a friendly mist (as the Germans had been favoured on 21 March) made this a triumphant occasion. The German official monograph wrote: 'As the sun set on the battlefield on 8 August the greatest defeat which the German Army had suffered since the beginning of the war was an accomplished fact.' Ludendorff called this 'the black day of the German Army in the history of the war. This was the worst experience I had to go through . . .' Three days later, at a conference at German Supreme Headquarters, the Kaiser said: 'I see that we must strike a balance. We have nearly reached the limit of our powers of resistance. The war must be ended.'

It took three months of hard fighting and heavy losses to give the Kaiser's utterance effect. During all that time Haig's armies continued to set the pace of the Allied offensive. 'Risks which a month ago would have been criminal to incur, ought now to be incurred as a duty,' he told his army commanders on 22 August; victory was really in sight at last, and he was the first to perceive it. For reasons that run deep into the recesses of British psychology, the names of the nine great battles by which the British army ensured victory in 1918 are scarcely known; no streets, no squares, no parks or public buildings are named after them. Yet they do have names:

The Battle of Amiens, 8–13 August
The Battle of Bapaume, 21 August–1 September
The Battle of the Scarpe, 26 August–3 September
The Battle of Havrincourt and Epéhy, 12–18 September
The Battle of Cambrai and the Hindenburg Line, 27 September–5 October
The Battle of Flanders, 28 September–14 October
The Battle of Le Cateau, 6–12 October
The Battle of the Selle, 17–25 October
The Battle of the Sambre, 1–11 November.

Never at any time in history [said Marshal Foch] has the British Army achieved greater results in attack than in this unbroken offensive . . . The victory was indeed complete, thanks to the excellence of the Commanders of Armies, Corps and Divisions, thanks above all to the unselfishness, to the wise, loyal and energetic policy of their Commander-in-Chief, who made easy a great combination, and sanctioned a prolonged and gigantic effort.

In the hundred days of victory Haig's armies captured 188,700 prisoners and 2,840 guns; all the other Allies in the west together captured 196,700 prisoners and 3,775 guns. This then was Haig's achievement; it seems to be a far cry from the miseries of the battles of attrition – but not in Haig's eyes. In his final despatch he wrote:

If the operations of the past 4½ years are regarded as a single continuous campaign, there can be recognized in them the same general features and the same necessary stages which between forces of approximately equal strength have marked all the conclusive battles of history . . .
    If the whole operations of the present war are regarded in correct perspective, the victories af the summer and autumn of 1918 will be seen to be . . . directly dependant upon the two years of stubborn fighting that preceded them.

Haig deeply regretted the heavy losses and great suffering of his soldiers (and dedicated the rest of his life to their service as founder of the British Legion), but he never accepted that their great endeavour required apology:

In the stage of the wearing-out struggle losses will necessarily be heavy on both sides, for in it the price of victory is paid. If the opposing forces are approximately equal in numbers, in courage, in morale and in equipment, there is no way of avoiding payment of the price or of eliminating this phase of the struggle.

In short:

> To direct attention to any single phase of that stupendous and incessant struggle and seek in it the explanation of success, to the exclusion or neglect of other phases possibly less striking in their immediate or obvious consequences, is in my opinion to risk the formation of unsound doctrine regarding the character and requirements of modern war.

Misled by false prophets the next generation ignored this warning to its grave peril and confusion; those upon whom it fell once more to defeat the German army would confirm the truth of Haig's words.

FIELD-MARSHAL PAUL VON HINDENBURG

Norman Stone

Public opinion from 1914 to 1918 demanded heroes, in the grand manner of previous wars. The war itself demanded technicians, committees, the bureaucracy for whom it was, in Max Weber's phrase, 'a triumphal march'; it became too complex to be controlled by a single will, especially one brought up in the outdated nineteenth-century ideas with which European armies went to war. The gap between illusion and reality was never greater than in 1914–18. All European armies produced commanders who commanded only in name. They enjoyed vast public esteem – Kitchener, Grand Duke Nicholas, Hindenburg being the most obvious cases – but they often spent their time playing patience while other men made the decisions. Hindenburg seems to have spent inordinate time in having his portrait painted.

Hindenburg, who commanded Germany's eastern front until 1916, and then took over command of all the fronts, in the Kaiser's name, was such a 'wooden Titan'. The public believed in him, sometimes hysterically. His legend, in the last twenty years of his life, was if anything greater than Bismarck's. Huge wooden statues of him were erected in German towns; the public were allowed, in exchange for contributions to the war-chest, to hammer nails into them. In 1916–18 German militarism went so far that Hindenburg took charge of vital areas of the economy, and dictated diplomatic policy to the Foreign Office. The legend survived defeat, indeed thrived on defeat; Hindenburg became President of the Weimar Republic in 1925 and held the office until his death in 1934. He had virtually taken the place of the monarchy: a German for whom all Germans could feel affinity, whatever their party allegiance. It was characteristic of him that before being elected, partly on Communist votes, he should have asked his Kaiser's permission to stand.

His was a legend that survived everything, except posterity. In his last years he was involved with Hitler's coming to power: in the end it was through his presidential authority that Hitler, on 30 January 1933, became Chancellor of the Reich. His failure to arrest this fatal development is now of course held typical of the general failure of the conservative elements in Germany to stop National Socialism.

No one now believes that Hindenburg was a great man in the nineteenth-century manner. The great acts with which he used to be credited were the work of a team: Ludendorff, Hoffman, Groener, Haeften, Wetzell, Geyer during the First World War. Hindenburg is really a code name for a committee, one dominated during the First World War by Ludendorff. Similarly, in his years as President of the Weimar Republic, he was guided all along by a small circle of men – latterly, Schleicher, Papen, and his son Oskar, with their Junker contacts. It seems that his great talent was to identify in advance in which direction opinions were tending, to formulate them and support them, so much so that finding Hindenburg expressing with great authority their own opinions, people agreed in praising him for perspicacity. He may not have been a great commander, but he was unquestionably a great chairman.

There was certainly nothing novel in Hindenburg for the bulk of his long life. He was born in 1847 in Prussian-ruled Poznania, scion of a well-established Junker family whose members had served the kings of Prussia and the tsars of Russia in traditional Baltic-noble fashion. He inherited, and never challenged, the stock views of his class: an upright but narrow-minded code. As he said, 'Discipline and hard work were, for me, the highest good, to be placed above cosmopolitan fantasies.' He devoted his life to the service of Prussia and her kings; and after the mid-nineteenth century this devotion seemed to be more important than ever before. 'Against increasing inclinations towards parliamentarianism, against the parties and the special interests, there seemed to be, in the modern constitutional state, only two institutions that unreservedly maintained the unity of the state, even at the cost of their lives: the sovereign and his officers' corps.' The Prussian army, for which Hindenburg was destined from his earliest youth, asserted these values to the full. It was not an army with wide horizons. It had no great empire to hold down, like the British, Russian, Austrian or French armies; its officers would have been surprised, and perhaps insulted, to learn that theirs was a 'civilising mission'. Prussian officers were well known for their narrowness of view, their inability to compromise; to the end of the Bismarckian empire the Prussian upper class failed to learn the English lesson, that flexibility and openness could achieve much more for an upper class than stiffness and insistence on traditional rights. In these circumstances 'service of the state' had for the Prussian upper class the obvious reciprocation, that the state should also serve its supposed servants and defend them against their enemies. Hindenburg and his like may have started from the standpoint that the state must be above the class battle; in practice they used the state relentlessly in pursuit of their own class interest, narrowly conceived at that. The Prussian officers' corps remained more exclusively upper class than any other officers' corps in Europe. The vast bulk of posts in the General Staff went to Junkers' sons; Jews were an extreme rarity in the officers' corps; and it was even with some reluctance that the corps accepted middle-class people at all, despite their great wealth. In the Europe of 1900 this was becoming an anachronism peculiar to Germany, for in other countries men of the lower orders had no such difficulties in making their way up through the officers' corps – even in supposedly reactionary Austria–Hungary a third of the officers' corps was recruited from men of lower middle-class or even peasant stock; and in Russia the proportion was even rather higher.

In this army Hindenburg advanced steadily enough. He served as subaltern in the Austro-Prussian War of 1866, and then in the Franco-Prussian War of 1870–1. His career was promising enough for him to receive a rare distinction, of being present at the proclamation, in Versailles, of the German Empire, at his King's invitation. Thereafter he moved steadily up the military ladder, acquiring valuable contacts at court, and serving in the General Staff in Berlin under Schlieffen. He was responsible for studies of the Russians' likely plans in wartime, and his work was favourably noticed by the famous Chief of the German General Staff, Count Schlieffen, who gave Hindenburg what was, for him, the highest praise: 'I consider him capable of conducting operations.' Hindenburg eventually came to command a corps district (Magdeburg), and was among those generals likely to command one or other of the eight armies that Germany planned to put up in wartime. But in 1910 he reached the age of retirement, and went to live in Hanover. He was told to hold himself ready, in 1914, to take command of an army; but the posts were all filled up, either by generals more senior than Hindenburg, or by royal figures whose claims naturally came before his. It was not until disaster struck one of the armies, Eighth, in East Prussia, that the call came for Hindenburg.

It was the start of a remarkable military career. After being appointed, on 22 August 1914, to command Eighth Army, Hindenburg rose to command all the German forces on the eastern front in November 1914, and after a run of victories that brought headlines throughout the world, became virtual Commander-in-Chief of the German army in August 1916. He held this post to the end of the war, and beyond it. To the public, Hindenburg was the great hero. To colleagues, and men generally in the know, he was merely a figurehead.

The driving figure in Hindenburg's entourage was Erich Ludendorff, his Chief of Staff in Eighth Army, and latterly effective Chief of Staff* of the whole field army (1916–18). The ideas were usually Ludendorff's; the authority Hindenburg's. No doubt Hindenburg's role was more positive than Ludendorff and others subsequently made out. Groener, Ludendorff's rival, at first regarded Hindenburg as 'a totem-pole'; but when, as head of the *Kriegsamt* that ran the war economy, he saw the two men together, he recognised that there was more to Hindenburg than a simple 'trade-name for Ludendorff'. The difference was, a staff officer suggested, that Hindenburg was respected, while Ludendorff was admired. At all events the final responsibility was

* Hindenburg was theoretically Chief of the General Staff under the Kaiser's command; Ludendorff was First Quartermaster General. In Germany, quartermaster-generals, despite their title, were directors of military operations.

Hindenburg's, and to his credit he never shrank from discharging it, whereas Ludendorff cut and ran when the ship went down.

Hindenburg's military reputation rested particularly on Tannenberg, and the run of victories won by the Germans against Russia in 1914–15. At Tannenberg, 26–30 August 1914, a Russian army was destroyed – four hundred guns and one hundred thousand prisoners being taken. The Russian invasion of Germany, which could if successful have brought early ruin to the German cause, was stopped in its tracks. This feat appeared to be miraculous: a sort of Thermopylae and Cannae rolled into one. Thirteen German divisions had been given the task of holding off nearly thirty Russian ones. By confusing his opponents Hindenburg had been able to isolate half of the Russian forces and defeat them before the other half could become effective. By 30 August 1914 the Russian Second Army had been destroyed; by 14 September the Russian First Army had been driven out of East Prussia as well. This began a process by which the Russians, despite what the public on both sides were told was overwhelming superiority of numbers, were driven out of Poland (summer 1915) and confined to the marsh and steppe of White Russia and the western Ukraine. Their attempts to break out in 1916 (the Brusilov offensive) failed, in the end; the intervention of Rumania on their side (autumn 1916) ended in German occupation of Rumania by early 1917. The Russian Revolution took Russia out of the war by the end of the year, and Germany was able to dictate her will. She allowed the separate nationalities of Russia – Ukrainians, Baltic peoples, Lithuanians, Poles – to create nation states, although their independence was of course restricted to a pro-German stance. Tannenberg seemed therefore to be the initiation of a *Drang nach Osten*; Hindenburg's laurels were in the east. Walter Hubatsch writes: '[Tannenberg] was a truly decisive battle of the western world . . . If Finland to-day is independent, it is a long-range consequence of Hindenburg's strategy.'

It is rather characteristic of the Hindenburg legend that Tannenberg itself was not at all, in reality, the outstanding piece of perspicacity and brilliant manoeuvre that it was cracked up to be. In the first place the Russian army never brought its full strength to bear. There were nearly thirty infantry divisions earmarked for the front against Germany. But the Russian commanders decided that they (unlike the Germans) would not use their reserve divisions in the field; instead these divisions were left as fortress guards in Kovno, Grodno, Novogeorgievsk, Warsaw. Another six divisions, including the Guard Corps, were placed in Warsaw to form a new army, improvised at the last minute. This left the Russian First Army with five and a half infantry divisions, the Russian Second Army with thirteen. These latter were further reduced, to nine, by an arbitrary exercise in superfluous flank coverage. In this way the Russian armies were, in infantry, only barely superior to the German Eighth Army when the forces actually met on the field. A further Russian miscalculation affected things badly for the Russian commanders: their supreme belief in cavalry.

The Russian planners had based everything on a supposition that waves of cavalry could charge into East Prussia, sweeping all before them. First Army, invading from the east, had six and a half cavalry divisions; Second Army, invading from the south, had three. The German Eighth Army had only one. Maybe this belief in cavalry would have made sense if war had been waged on Russian territory, where roads and railways were less frequent than on German soil, and where infantry would, correspondingly, have been less mobile. But in East Prussia cavalry raids could hardly be very effective. The cavalry divisions, under fierce Cossack commanders, wandered off in bewildered and exasperated search for the enemy. They lost touch with each other, and separate groups of each division lost touch with divisional commanders. The handful of small field-pieces they had were no match for well-handled German territorial units, and there was one cavalry reverse after another. Even for purposes of reconnaissance, cavalry was not particularly useful to the Russians, for isolated groups of horsemen could only state that they had seen isolated groups of infantry, and it took as much as a day for their message to reach army headquarters. There had been talk, before 1914, of a Russian wave of Huns sweeping into East Prussia. But the nearest that Russian cavalry came to a Hun was the aged Khan of Nakhichevan, who broke down in despair a few miles west of the border, losing touch with his units, weeping in a tent, and suffering so badly from piles that he could not even get on his horse. Furthermore these cavalry units spoiled the pattern of Russian mobilisation. Ferrying and supplying a cavalry division took as much rolling stock as the transport of an infantry division which, with fifty-four guns to the cavalry division's twelve, and sixteen thousand rifles to a cavalry division's four thousand, was a much more formidable opponent for the Germans. Russian mobility was reduced, not improved, by reliance on cavalry. Tannenberg was not so much a restatement of Roncesvalles as another exercise in the Charge of the Light Brigade.

Moreover the Russian forces were split. First Army had been attacked not long after crossing the border (16–20 August). It had defeated German attempts to destroy it. It now supposed that the Germans were withdrawing to the west, and faulty intelligence displayed that two of the four German corps were retiring towards the fortress of Königsberg. This army supposed that its task must be to follow the German retreat. and until the end of August its commander, Rennenkampf, ordered preparations to be undertaken for the siege of Königsberg (which was in reality defended only by a small territorial group). With this an entire Russian army was subtracted until the end of August. The other Russian army, Second (Samsonov), came up from the south in a bedraggled condition. It was told that the Germans were retreating, that there would only be some frontier cordon or other, and that the centre and right of the army should advance as fast as possible, while the left maintained a guard. Advancing in this way the centre (two and a half army corps) encountered a German group, and was involved in action from 24 August that effectively prevented it from doing anything else. The right, moving through broken country, fell into disorganisation. One corps was detached to help First Army if need be. The other, on its left, split in two groups and wandered forward through the lake-and-forest country south of Lötzen. The left-hand corps was told not to cross the border at all, but to maintain station as a flank guard just south of it. All of this made sense only in terms of a German retreat.

The first commander of the German Eighth Army, Prittwitz, had directed an attack on the Russian First Army and had been defeated in frontal battles (Gumbinnen, 20 August). He had panicked, considered retreat beyond the Vistula, and telephoned the high command to say that all was lost. He was then superseded by Hindenburg, who picked up plans he found Prittwitz's staff had put together. It was here that the Hindenburg legend began. According to it he and Ludendorff stopped all ideas of retreat, and instead planned a great coup. Three divisions would be moved west from the Gumbinnen theatre by rail, to attack the Russian Second Army left wing. The centre would hold the Russian centre. The other two corps left in the Gumbinnen theatre would march south-west to catch the right wing of the Russian Second Army, and there would be an envelopment battle like Cannae: the flank props would be knocked away, the Russian centre isolated, surrounded. So indeed it happened, particularly since the Russian First Army continued to be mesmerised by Königsberg.

But the reality was different. The chief planned movement was that of the three divisions to attack the left wing of Samsonov's army. This movement had been planned long before 1914, and was foreseen by the Russians – hence their immobilising a single corps south of the border to face it. The movement succeeded, but mainly by a series of accidents. In the first place, transport did not end until 25 August; the Russians were therefore given false security. Then, the attack did not open until 26 August, and even 27 August for most of the German troops. Consequently the Russian troops in extended order, who fancied that they had won a battle, were suddenly struck by forces whose presence they did not suspect. Not surprisingly the Russian flank guard retired some way in confusion, and the three German divisions were able to move due east, into the rear of the Russian centre.

This occurred as much despite Hindenburg's plans as because of them. Similarly, the Russian centre became involved in confusion mainly because of engagements in which it was victorious, despite what Hindenburg wanted. Heavy, frontal fighting was prescribed in the centre for both sides, and the Russians had the better part. But the successes led them to being enmeshed in an area of low visibility, where communications broke down. Finally the Russian right was also seized more or less by accident. Hindenburg had ordered the remaining two corps of the Gumbinnen theatre to march south-west. He did not know that there were Russian troops there; and his orders merely indicated that these two corps should join the beleaguered centre,

near Allenstein. They would no doubt have been moved west by rail had there
been any trains available; but evacuation of the other troops meant that
there were not. They marched south-west along a single high road, and then
had to cross the same area of lakes and forests in which the right-hand corps
of Samsonov's army found itself. In doing so they encountered first one, then
another Russian division – to very considerable bewilderment. The Germans'
superior weight told, and the Russian divisions retired south of the border
(Bischofsburg-Lautenburg, 26–27 August). Then the two German corps tried
to rejoin their centre. But there was only one usable road, and only one corps
at a time could use it. Hindenburg told the corps of lesser quality (1st Reserve)
to take it first. Then, on 28 August, he woke up to the true position: his own
right-hand group had penetrated the rear of the Russian centre, and his left-
hand group was in position to close the ring. The other corps of this group
was therefore told to move west, rather than north-west; and in due course it
encountered German troops from the other wing. On 29 August the Russian
central group began to surrender. This coup had been the decisive element;
and it was a by-product of a disciplined manoeuvre of retreat, not an expression of a will to attack.

All in all Tannenberg was of course a respectable feat of arms. The German
divisions, in a difficult situation, had held together. Their commanders had
acted sensibly. But it was Russian blundering that changed Tannenberg into
an epic victory for the Germans – faulty intelligence, the wrong weapons, ill-
co-ordinated movements, breakdowns of supply and communications. Hindenburg deserved about as much credit for the battle as Joffre got for the
Marne. He kept his nerve, and a great victory happened almost by itself. It
was small wonder that commanders such as these supposed that God had put
an ace up their sleeves, and that repetition of 'the method' would bring
greater results still.

The virtues of Hindenburg's command were similarly exaggerated throughout the war on the eastern front. There was always sense, vigour, discipline.
German commanders – at least for most of the time – did not indulge in fantastic illusions of the type that Russian commanders allowed themselves, as
to the effectiveness of cavalry. The fact, too, that Germany could not afford
great casualties generally influenced the eastern commanders' conduct for
the better: Hindenburg knew, on the whole, where to stop. Of course he, like
the western generals, ran into frontal battles that cost his armies a great deal.
Throughout December 1914, for instance, he drove his troops (Ninth Army)
into a series of frontal assaults on Russian lines in Poland (the Bzura-Rawka
lines) that cost one hundred thousand casualties for little return. But on the
whole Hindenburg learnt the lessons of such campaigns quicker than generals
did in the west; he broke off such battles and preferred to rely on manoeuvre
along the enemy flank, wherever this was possible. This moderating touch
was probably Hindenburg's, rather than Ludendorff's, contribution; and it
was Germany's misfortune that successes stemming essentially from discip-

line, knowing where to stop, were ascribed to some supposed genius of Ludendorff's. By 1918 Ludendorff himself had clearly come to suppose that outrageously misplaced schemes were the key to victory; and used the campaigns of 1914–15 in the east as evidence for his opinion.

The eastern fighting generated many legends. Most pervasive of all was the idea that the German commanders were taking on an overwhelming superiority. The Russian army was thought to have countless millions of men at its beck and call, as the Austro-Hungarian commander, Conrad von Hötzendorff, said, 'We are holding the door against half of Asia.' This was simply not true. The Central Powers in 1914–15 were barely inferior to the Russian forces; and because these were some way beyond their railheads, the balance of forces was probably equal for most of the time. There were some eighty-four German and Austro-Hungarian divisions to ninety-nine Russian ones for most of the first two years of war. The reason for this lay in faulty Russian conscription arrangements. The Russian War Ministry had never thought that it would have to call up all young Russian males for military service; in 1900, 320,000 per annum had been thought sufficient, and only just before the war was a figure of 585,000 arrived at. In any case Russia could not afford to supply millions of men in her army: as it was, food and clothing alone took up three-quarters of her military budget in 1913–14. Exemptions were lavishly granted, and many of the soldiers formally called up were in reality 'sent on permanent leave' as soon as they had done some desultory kicking round the barracks. The high casualties of 1914–15 caused a supply crisis in manpower, and it was not made up until the winter of 1915–16, when less strange arrangements were made.

The Germans also enjoyed a well-documented material superiority in the east. For much of 1915 Russian shell shortage acted as a crippling drag on operations. Russia ordered fourteen million shells from western Europe and America by December 1914, but almost none of them arrived until September 1915. Because of this reliance on foreign goods, she failed to develop her own industry for war purposes until the late summer of 1915; until then she fought on stocks of shell assembled before 1914, and a home production not exceeding, in the first five months of 1915, two rounds per gun per day. This was further complicated by confusions in the transporting of shell, the stockpiling of huge quantities in fortresses, in which – as with cavalry – there was a singular faith, and which fell to the Germans without much ado in the course of the summer. Finally Russian artillery tended to let its infantry down, particularly the reserve divisions. In the early stages of the battle of Lodz, for instance, between 11 and 14 November, the Russian right wing was stove in because guns failed to support infantry. A Siberian corps lost twenty thousand men in prisoners, but only four guns. In circumstances like this Hindenburg could achieve what appeared to be miracles.

Moreover the war in the east remained a war of manoeuvre in ways altogether different from those of the west. There was at most one rifle for two yards on the eastern front. In the west, there were six rifles per yard. Besides, in eastern conditions reserves could not be shuttled around as they could in the west. Railways and roads were lacking; and where present were inefficiently used. It took the Russian army in October 1914 four weeks to transport ten army corps from western Galicia to the middle Vistula – a distance not much above 200 miles. It took the whole of May 1915 to assemble a Russian army in the Bukovina, and supply problems made it retreat even after it had launched a successful offensive. By contrast the French assembled twelve divisions to defend Amiens between 24 and 27 March 1918; the Germans assembled eight divisions at Gorlice-Tarnów within a week in May 1915, and thirty divisions within two weeks to fend off the danger of Rumanian intervention and a renewed Russian offensive. A Russian calculation was that it took two weeks to move a single army corps of two divisions from the northern to the southern part of the eastern front.

It was possible, in circumstances such as these, for the Germans to assemble troops quite speedily and to break through. The attackers would then spread out to north and south of the breakthrough point, capturing a respectable 'bag' of Russian soldiers (in the end, two million). Russian reserves would not arrive until all lines of defence had been overrun. The result was that Hindenburg could usually arrive at tactical successes going far beyond the dreams of generals in the west, their horizons limited to hillocks and villages, Lodz in November 1914, the Masurian Lakes in February 1915, Courland in April–May 1915, the Kovno campaign of August and the Vilna campaign of September 1915 – all fell into this category. The Masurian Lakes battle was typical. On 7 February two armies were launched from East Prussia in a pincer movement through the snows. The Russian Tenth Army was driven back. The central element of it, xx Corps, could not escape because the roads were choked with other units moving back. It got stuck in the forest of Agustów and began to disintegrate. Reserves were supposed to go to a new army, Twelfth, forming on the Germans' southern flank. They did not get there in time, and the army could only feebly move forward. The isolated corps was forced to surrender. The Germans then advanced east, lengthening their flank. Then the threat of Twelfth Army became real, and Hindenburg, his flanks threatened, withdrew again to East Prussia after an unsuccessful attempt on the Russian fortress of Osowiec. This was a tactical success, with a captured Russian corps commander and one hundred thousand prisoners. It made headlines.

But these engagements were not in themselves decisive. The war could be won only in the west; so long as France held out even victories of some scale against Russia were of little use, and, in so far as they cost valuable lives, were even harmful to the cause overall. It was not at all easy to overthrow Russia; indeed the task was really beyond the Germans. In the summer of 1915 they inflicted a huge defeat on Russia and moved through Poland. Then they encountered the same problems as the Russians had faced – trackless swamp, dusty steppe, no railways, little water for horses, disease. On the whole they did better than the Russians in overcoming these. Even so German offensives after September 1915 were costly failures. Troops could move forward, even at the best of times, only 2½ miles in a day, and the front settled down in trench warfare. Russia could not really be overthrown by main force, as Falkenhayn, virtual Commander-in-Chief 1914–16, always insisted. Hindenburg's schemes for an ambitious double envelopment of the Russians from both north and south of the eastern front were bound to fail, since there was never sufficient mobility for them. Until lorries and trains became general in Russia, there could be no alternative to the plodding infantryman – effective, maybe, in the limited terrain of France, but certainly ineffective against the Russian plains. Indeed the Germans would quite possibly have inflicted a sharper defeat on Russia if they had stayed put along their own borders, where conditions were more favourable to flexible offensives. Russia was overthrown in the end because of revolution – a revolution partly brought about no doubt because the tsarist regime was discredited by German victories, but much more by the simple effects of the war economy: inflation, shortages, class war. In so far as Hindenburg's campaigns had anything to do with it, they may even have postponed the revolution. The cry: 'the enemy is at the gates' was the most powerful weapon in the Tsar's hands. On the whole, Falkenhayn, who asserted throughout 1915 that vast extensions of territory in the east were pointless, was right. It was Hindenburg and Ludendorff, with their dreams of empire, who were fighting an old-fashioned war.

Falkenhayn fumbled his strategic opening in the first half of 1916. He led off in an offensive against France – Verdun – and allowed it to develop into a blind slogging match which it had not been supposed to be. He used up huge amounts of ammunition (fourteen million rounds per month, when Germany's production was less than seven million) and threw away five hundred thousand men. In consequence of this he was discredited and replaced by Hindenburg at the end of August 1916. The German people were now expectant that the hero of Tannenberg would rescue them from what seemed to be an impossible position. The time was ripe for extreme measures; and Ludendorff began to dominate the partnership with Hindenburg. The strategic behaviour of the German supreme command in 1916–18 is therefore more fittingly discussed under the heading Ludendorff, since it was mainly his behaviour. Hindenburg was clearly 'a totem-pole'; it is characteristic that just before the March offensive of 1918, on which the fate of Germany was to depend, he should have written to his wife to announce that Ludendorff was hard at work on his offensive, that he himself had acquired a copy of *Faust* and a history of German literature 'for there will be time on my hands in the days to come'.

What Hindenburg specifically contributed to German development in this period was a dosage of common sense. Although the German public reached paroxysms of enthusiasm for the national cause, Hindenburg always sensed the limitations. For instance he – unlike Ludendorff – stood at a considerable distance from the extreme imperialists. 'Many of them are simply fit for an asylum; they go on demanding annexation of Ceylon by Brunswick, conscription of the Mona Lisa for the Berlin Museum.' The foot on the brake, demonstrably there in the eastern campaigns of 1914–15, was probably Hindenburg's, with his strong sense of the possible. On the other hand he was, with all his apparent massiveness, a trimmer: he gave way to prevailing opinions, as he did in the end to the extreme nationalists in 1916–18, again to the moderates in November 1918, and finally to Hitler in 1933. He was in other words 'a good German': fittingly a halfway house between Bismarck and Hitler.

Marshal Philippe Pétain

Alistair Horne

In the ancient tradition of the French Academy a newly elected 'immortal' delivers an *éloge* in the memory of his predecessor. None can have been more difficult to phrase than that which fell the lot of Ambassador André François Poncet. It was he who, in 1953, filled the vacancy left by Philippe Pétain, dead after spending his last years in a fortress prison, and stripped of every honour collected during a long life as France's most venerated soldier. François Poncet rose brilliantly to an occasion of exceptional delicacy. Marshal Pétain, he said: '. . . has traced in our history pages some of which remain luminous while others give rise to interpretations that still conflict and arouse lively passions. We must celebrate the first. We cannot ignore the second.' Those 'lively passions' still make it hard for most Frenchmen to evaluate rationally Pétain's military contributions, and for anyone to do so it is easier to consider him as having terminated his career by 1936; the date by which the influence of the old marshal (already eighty) had been largely removed from French councils of war.

Pétain was born on 24 April 1856, at a modest farmhouse near Arras. His family came of solid Artois peasant stock, with no military background. He seems to have been inspired to join the army by the anecdotes of a nonagenarian great-uncle, the Abbé Lefèvre, who had served under Napoleon. In many ways Pétain was the odd man out in the First World War military hierarchy of both sides. Whereas Joffre, Foch and de Castelnau were all Pyreneeans, Pétain was a typical, hard-headed northerner; the exact antithesis of Foch, the passionate meridional. In not belonging to an officer caste he contrasted with those like his future opponent, von Falkenhayn, who more closely resembled the norm of the era; and this was a factor limiting an advancement painfully slow even by comparison with Falkenhayn's. Unlike the Polytechnicians, Foch and Joffre, Pétain worked his way through the Spartan school of St Cyr. He graduated in 1878 in a 'promotion' that was nicknamed 'Plevna', after the famous siege of the previous year where an isolated Turkish force had held off the Russians for many months at a heavy cost to the attackers. It seemed almost an act of predestination that Pétain was to gain his fame at Verdun, the modern Plevna, as the foremost proponent of defensive warfare. On receiving his commission he opted for the newly formed *Chasseurs Alpins*, five years' service with whom doubtless accounted in part for his splendid physique. He then transferred to the infantry, and from here onwards – although he was extremely industrious – promotion followed at discouragingly long intervals; five years a *sous-lieutenant*, seven a subaltern, ten a captain, he was forty-four before getting his battalion – or three years older than Falkenhayn.

During the bout of anti-clericalism that had afflicted the pre-war French army under the aegis of Prime Minister Combes and General André, devoted Catholics like Foch and de Castelnau had suffered temporary checks to their careers. But confession could not be said to have been a factor in the slowness of Pétain's promotion; indeed he boasted of not having been to Mass for thirty years! Much more relevant was the fact that in an age where friends-at-court were vital to military progress, Pétain the peasant from Artois had none. Nor did he ever exert himself to cultivate any. He had a chronic contempt for what he considered any form of intrigue – and this extended to embrace most politicians. Even as a subaltern, when most of his contemporaries – mindful of where lay the springs of promotion under the Third Republic – were actively courting the politicians, Pétain was bold enough to place a reservist deputy under arrest for some minor military infringement. He seemed to have had no respect or fear for any political figure; to Poincaré he remarked acidly during the war that 'nobody was better placed than the President himself to be aware that France was neither led nor governed'. In 1939 he would refuse to be a candidate for the presidency, describing it as an office only 'suitable for defeated marshals'. The antipathy became mutual; in 1917, after Pétain was to lay a share of blame for the French army mutinies at the door of the politicians, one of the more impressive deputies of the epoch, Abel Ferry, wrote in his diary: 'Pétain is a bastard. He has command, but he is closed to everything which is not exclusively pertaining to military order. He sees only the defects of parliamentary collaboration . . .' This sourness in Pétain's relations with politics and politicians remained to the end of his life, and it proved detrimental to his own career as well as to the conduct of the First World War.

In contradistinction to most of his contemporaries, the young Pétain seemed unambitious almost to the point of self-extinction. He refused the post of commandant at the Rifle School on the grounds that it would have brought him promotion over the heads of more senior officers. What told most against him, however, was that while the fiery Foch and most of the other leading intellects in the French army all swam with the prevailing current of the *attaque à outrance* doctrine, he alone stood against the tide. During the critical years leading up to 1914, the French army had come to interpret its defeat in the Franco-Prussian War of 1870 as deriving – broadly speaking – from a lack of offensive spirit. There was much talk about the posture of attack being best suited to the national temperament; the *furia francese* was evoked from as far off as the Battle of Pavia in 1525; and the new mood was well matched to the Bergsonian philosophy (then all the rage in France) of the *élan vital*. As the years moved further away from the actual experience of combat over Europe's long spell of peace, so in France the idea of the offensive strayed ever further from reality.

The *attaque à outrance* gospel found its ultimate prophet in Colonel de Grandmaison, Chief of the *Troisième Bureau* (Operations) of the General Staff, who in 1911 engineered the appointment of General Joffre, a sapper regarded as being malleable to de Grandmaison's theories. From top to bottom the army became impregnated with de Grandmaison's extravagant, semi-mystical notions:

> In the offensive, impudence is the best of assurances . . . Let us go even to excess, and that perhaps will not be far enough . . . For the attack only two things are necessary; to know where the enemy is and to decide what to do. What the enemy intends to do is of no consequence.

Harking back to the grim memories of the physical invasion of France in 1870, de Grandmaison also inculcated into the French army the rigid dogma that should the scorned enemy dare to seize the initiative even for a moment every inch of terrain must be defended to the death, and if lost regained by an immediate riposte, however inopportune. Altogether de Grandmaison's doctrine was to cost France the lives of hundreds of thousands of her best men; including that of the prophet himself, when fallen from grace.

Even the sparkling intellect of Foch was swept along by the de Grandmaison current, and while his contemporaries were obsessed by the science of the offensive, Pétain was pragmatically studying recent campaigns where the defence had given such a good account of itself; such as the Boer War, the Russo-Japanese War of 1905 – and, of course, Plevna. As early as 1884 Pétain is recorded as opposing army regulations prescribing that the infantry could advance under the heaviest fire against well-defended trenches. Equally he criticised the new regulations of ten years later, which ordained that the infantry should assault in waves, 'elbow to elbow', and accompanied by the regimental music; though not by close-support artillery. Pétain did not ignore the potentialities of such new weapons as the machine gun and the heavy howitzer – which the de Grandmaison school contemptuously dismissed from its armoury – and even the humble rifle in its modern form (he was himself a distinguished shot). The nucleus of his studies was simply that 'fire power kills'. Carried to its logical conclusion this meant that (if he were right) a well-organised defence could break up the *attaque à outrance* long before it reached the enemy. This was rank heresy, and for a long time it barred the way ahead to Pétain. It was not until 1906 that a posting as instructor at the École de Guerre gave him the platform he required.

His lectures there seemed singularly unglamorous alongside those of the dashing and flamboyant Foch (already an international figure for at least a decade) and of Colonel de Maud'huy, who was alleged to make his sons pray each evening to become as 'brave as Bayard'. Ever glacial and impassive, Pétain was nicknamed *précis-le-sec*; nevertheless the hall was always packed and by his lucidity and cold common sense he dominated his audience, stuffed to excess elsewhere by nonsense about the total ascendancy of the moral over the material. (One of his converts in these days was a thoughtful, gangly young man called Charles de Gaulle, who was so impressed by Pétain's teachings that on leaving St Cyr he applied to join the regiment then under his command, the 33rd.) The essence of Pétain's doctrine was, and remained, that the all-out offensive should only be undertaken once the defence had been decisively weakened; not by attritive, and costly, infantry pinpricks, but by an overwhelming concentration of artillery fire power. This in turn presupposed a close liaison between artillery and infantry, something unheard of in those days, and for which Pétain was to strive all through his First World War career. It was all not very dissimilar to the Montgomery technique of a war later. The persuasiveness of Pétain's arguments produced a measure of (temporary) success; under their influence the army regulations of 1904 prescribed more supple and flexible infantry formations in the attack, incorporating sensible elements of fire and cover. But then the de Grandmaison school reached its zenith, and – alas for France – by 1914 army infantry regulations had reverted to far more rigid and less pragmatic principles.

At the summer manoeuvres of 1913 in which Colonel Pétain's 33rd Regiment took part, the infantry attacked in close line abreast, at the double with bayonets fixed, without any artillery preparation – and wonderful targets in their scarlet *pantalons*. It was just how the French army would enter the war the following August, transforming the frontier stubble fields into bright carpets of red and blue. After the manoeuvres Pétain is recorded as having summed up in the presence of his commanding general, and with the unrestrained sarcasm he seemed to reserve for his superiors: 'I am sure that General le Gallet intended, the better to impress you, to present a synthesis of all the faults that a modern army should not commit.' Was it any wonder that when the curtain fell Pétain at fifty-eight was still only a colonel; a bachelor who had never served abroad, with imminent retirement ahead, in anticipation of which he had already bought a small house on the outskirts of St Omer? But over a brief space of eighteen months he was then to rise from command of a brigade of a few thousand men to be an army commander.

At the time of leaving for the wars Pétain was a man of commendable vigour for his age. After the war it was said that a doctor who gave him a check-up (incredibly enough without recognising him) remarked: 'One can see that you weren't in the war.' (Alas, but for such robustness, the final degradation might have been spared Pétain.) With the commanding posture that was the unmistakable and indelible mark of St Cyr, there was no more impressive sight on a French parade ground. To see him and General de Castlenau together one might well have assumed that Pétain was the born aristocrat, the squat and rather swarthy *capucin botté* (or 'Fighting Friar') the peasant; instead of the reverse. Jean de Pierrefeu describes Pétain arriving at GHQ to assume the supreme command:

I had the impression of a marble statue, of a Roman senator in a museum. Big vigorous, of imposing figure, impassive face and pale complexion, with a direct and thoughtful glance . . .

and François Poncet (in his *éloge*) writes of

. . . a majestic carriage, naturally noble . . . his blue eyes contained a certain mystery. One would think they were made of ice . . . from his whole personality emanated an air of sovereignty . . . Whenever he appears, he imposes . . . Whoever once saw this figure, will never forget it.

Certainly women never did. Even to the twilight of his life, Pétain was seldom without a mistress. In one of his earliest love affairs a well-brought-up girl from the Midi had given herself spontaneously to him, but – apparently through fear of sacrificing his independence – he had rejected her, and she had married a painter instead. That he should have remained a bachelor until so late in life appears to have been due largely to allowing his one great love, Annie Hardon, to slip through his hands and marry a rival. (In a Barbara Cartland kind of happy ending, she divorced and finally married Pétain; but not till 1920.) His easy success with women often led him into precarious adventures. On the eve of his appointment to take over command of the wilting forces at Verdun in 1916, one of the most critical moments in French history, Pétain had disappeared off the face of the earth. Only an ADC with a knowledge of his habits was able to track him down to a love-nest in the Gare du Nord hotel; as it was, no doubt partly in consequence of his nocturnal exertions at an advanced age, Pétain was subsequently to spend the first crucial days of his new command in bed with double pneumonia! In the following year French intelligence intercepted a cable from the German Ambassador in Madrid reporting to Berlin that he had found a *maja* for the new French Commander-in-Chief, for the modest fee of 12,000 pesetas a month.

Throughout his life Pétain retained many of his peasant characteristics. One of these was simplicity – which he shared with Joffre, and it was about all they had in common. He was early to rise and late to bed, and in rare moments of leisure liked to potter around the garden; declaring that once he retired he would take up farming. Of an evening his favourite pastime was to leaf through historical picture books, studying the men who had left their mark during the past half-century. Seldom going to bed before midnight, he was often fond of reading Corneille – his favourite author – till 2 am. In contrast to Foch, he so hated being photographed that most of the contemporary photographs show him characteristically glaring at the camera, and at his trial in 1945 he insisted on appearing in the simplest uniform of a Marshal of France, his only decoration the *Médaille Militaire*, which was awarded to all ranks alike. Another attribute of Pétain's peasant background, one noted only by those who knew him well, was a certain timidity in the presence of the grand; often well disguised, it may well have laid at the root of his abrasiveness with the arrogance of politicians. The general's character, in fact, says the admiring, but observant Pierrefeu:

> ... was one of excessive humility beneath a cold reserve ... Pétain's scornfulness, though natural to him, was enhanced by his shyness. Whenever he felt this paralysing shyness overtake him, he would charge forward with his eyes shut, and lash his interlocutor with cruel words.

Pierrefeu also noted, with extraordinary relevance to the sad, final phase of Pétain's career, that the 'guiding principle of his mind' was

> ... *a noble fatalism** ... There was a belief in the power of human will, certainly, and in the virtue of effort, but on condition that both are in conformity with those great movements whose issue cannot be influenced and must be followed lest one be crushed by them.

In August 1914, though he still retained his rank of colonel, Pétain was given command of a brigade in the Fifth Army of the unhappy General Lanrezac, who – facing the Belgian Ardennes at the north end of the French line – was to bear the full weight of the Schlieffen thrust. In the retreat from the frontiers Pétain showed severity in the forced marches he imposed on his men, laden down with their regulation 55-pound packs; at the same time, the stone-wall defence and the deadly, concentrated fire power of his formations impressed friend and foe alike. At the end of August he was promoted to brigadier on the field; so suddenly that the elderly lady on whom he was billeted had to furnish him with stars unsewn from her father's uniform. The following day he fought his first offensive action, at the Battle of Guise. It was a small but useful delaying action, and once again Pétain's units excelled themselves in their use of fire power and movement. The disastrous failure of France's Plan XVII was followed by Joffre's ruthless and wholesale *limogeage* of inept generals, resulting in rapid promotion for those who had shone, with Pétain foremost among these. On 2 September he assumed command of the 6th Division, the morale of which was in a poor state. Shortly before the Marne, when some of its men broke column to despoil plum trees along the line of march, Pétain angrily rode among them, firing his revolver in the air. His mixture of stern discipline and competent leadership in combat rapidly restored morale, and on the Marne the 6th played a leading part in the battle; once again distinguished by the weight of concentrated and

* Author's italics.

methodic fire power that Pétain's divisional artillery was able to bring to bear.

Fresh promotion followed swiftly; in October Pétain was given command of XXXIII Corps. As the first miserable winter in the trenches set in he demonstrated that – as well as being a tough disciplinarian – he was outstandingly concerned to alleviate the living conditions of his troops. He arranged special leave, and organised the first army theatre; but most important of all he called a halt to the repeated minor attacks, conducted at a heavy cost in lives, that some commanders – under the influence still of the de Grandmaison doctrines – felt they had to launch in order to retake a few yards of terrain. In May 1915 Foch led a full-scale offensive in Artois with eighteen divisions. After a characteristically skilful artillery preparation, Pétain's XXXIII Corps smashed the German line at Arras, penetrating to a depth of $2\frac{1}{2}$ miles along a 7-mile front. For a moment it looked as if a major breakthrough had been achieved. But the corps on either side of Pétain were repulsed with heavy losses, and no reinforcements were to reach Pétain in time for him to exploit his success. Nevertheless under Joffre's orders Foch kept 'nibbling away' long after Pétain felt the offensive failed, and the French lost 102,500 men. From the lessons of the abortive Artois campaign, Pétain drafted a memorandum to the high command that was both farsighted and at the same time revealingly tinged with his 'fatalism': 'The present war has taken the form of a war of attrition. There is no longer the "decisive battle" as formerly. Success will come in the final analysis to the side which has the last man.' With this in mind, continued Pétain, manpower should be husbanded to the limit so as to save it for the decisive moment when the Germans had made their last effort. It was a theme to which he remained faithful right through to 1918.

In July Pétain was promoted yet again to take over the Second Army – just in time to prepare it for Joffre's new push, in Champagne in the autumn. Pétain was not at all happy about Joffre's plans, pointing out that since May the Germans had now constructed a second line behind the whole front, far enough back to be out of the range of most of the French guns. While insisting that the Germans were too strong for a breakthrough to succeed, he pleaded for a systematic, step-by-step movement that would be economical in lives. This was rejected by Joffre and de Castelnau (then in command of the whole operation) who hoped to crash through the enemy front in one single *attaque brusquée*. Much as Pétain predicted, the Champagne offensive was halted bloodily on the Germans' virtually untouched second line; another 242,000 were added to the year's casualty lists, against 141,000 Germans. Even Pétain experienced one of his few failures here; his intense preliminary bombardment was just too prolonged, sacrificing the vital element of surprise, and about all he had to show for his efforts was the capture of one cemetery. But at least, unlike most of his fellow commanders, he knew when to stop – instead of trying to redeem failure fruitlessly, and at a frightful cost in lives.

All the time Pétain was learning with an almost unique rapidity, and with an adaptability unusual at his age. Says Spears: 'at every stage of the war he was just a little ahead of practice, theory and thought of the moment'. In an era when the various arms existed in virtual ignorance of each other's function, Pétain the St Cyrien infantryman had learned more about the use of artillery than many gunners would ever know. At Artois it was said that he had laid every gun himself. By the end of 1915 an army commander widely respected by the army elite,* though still little known outside, Pétain had developed his life-long theories on fire power into a series of pithy axioms: 'The offensive is the fire which advances; the defensive the fire which stops . . . Cannon conquers, infantry occupies . . .'

After the abortive autumn offensives, and as Joffre was drawing his plans for the next year's 'Big Push' on the Somme, Pétain wrote a barely disguised criticism of the high command's bull-headed striving for a *percée*. Stressing the continued Allied inadequacy in heavy artillery, he declared that it was impossible to

> . . . carry with the same *élan* the successive positions of the enemy . . . one does not seek, in fact, to produce a breakthrough. In this first offensive act, what one wants is to inflict such casualties on the enemy that it will be possible later on to attack in depth, at certain chosen points, with superiority.

Although he too was essentially a disciple of attrition, it was in a quite different sense from Joffre and Haig with their supremely simple calculations that the Germans could be defeated eventually through losing man for man, by virtue of the Allied superiority in numbers. 'One does not fight with men against matériel,' was another of Pétain's favourite maxims; attrition had to be effected by guns, not unprotected infantrymen. His technique was that of a series of minutely planned, economical offensives with limited objectives, acting like the picador breaking down the bull's neck muscle – until the critical moment of exhaustion arrived when the final sword-thrust could be risked. 'Audacity is the art of knowing how not to be too audacious,' declared Pétain; a tenet that lay at the roots of his later reputation as the over-cautious general. But this reputation was not founded purely on cold reasoning. The esteem in which he was held by the *poilus* was already legendary; because, unique among French commanders, he was looked on as *the* leader who really cared for his men. It had been widely noted that at the Marne when the infantry quailed under German shellfire, Pétain had moved up into the front line with them; unlike some other generals who had led their troops, Plaza-Toro-like, from the various chateaux of France. Later he told a decimated regiment: 'You went into the assault singing the *Marseillaise*; it was magnificent. But next time you will not need to sing the *Marseillaise*. There will be a sufficient number of guns to ensure your attack is a success. . . .'

He was as good as his word. By the end of 1915 his troops had acquired faith

---

* Even Haig commented in his diary: 'I found him businesslike, knowledgeable, and brief in speech. The latter is, I find, a rare quality in Frenchmen!'

that if Pétain called for an attack there must be some point to it, that it would not be a senseless sacrifice to gain recognition for an over-ambitious general from the conquest of a few yards of enemy trench. His long years in junior command had given him an intimacy with the *poilu* denied to most of the other French chiefs, and – unlike Haig and Joffre, or Falkenhayn – he knew very well what wounded men looked like. Despite his rapid rise to stardom he still retained a measure of the paternalism of the good CO, and neglect of the fighting soldier would throw Pétain into a searing rage. 'What an idiot!' he exclaimed of a battalion commander at Verdun, who having received the order of alert just as the rations arrived had ordered his men to move at once on empty stomachs; 'He doesn't deserve to be a corporal.'

It was the tragic irony of fate that at Verdun this unusually humanitarian general would be called upon to subject the men under his command to what was shortly to become the most inhuman conflict of the whole war.

On 21 February 1916, when Falkenhayn launched his 'bleeding-white' experiment against Verdun, Pétain was still commanding the Second Army, then at rest behind the lines, after the hard autumn battles. Within three days of fighting, the force of the German onslaught and the devastating non-stop artillery barrages had all but swamped the French secondary defences. On the 25th, the lynch-pin of Fort Douaumont, hitherto considered impregnable, fell to a handful of Germans, and there seemed to be nothing to stem the flood before Verdun itself. The previous night Joffre, aroused from his habitual imperturbability, dispatched de Castelnau – currently his second-in-command – to Verdun on a salvage mission. De Castelnau's immediate decision was: 'Send for Pétain!'

Hustled from the arms of his mistress, early on the morning of 25 February Pétain found 'the panic was at its peak' at GHQ. Verdun was expected to fall momentarily, 'and everybody was saying that General Herr [the local commander] should be shot'. On reaching the threatened sector Pétain was greeted by de Castelnau, who tore out a sheet from his notebook and scribbled on it the historic order that – in the true Foch–de Grandmaison tradition – Verdun must be defended *at all costs*. Pétain demurred on the grounds that he was not yet *au fait* with the situation. But de Castelnau was adamant; thus from the beginning Pétain's hands were tied. It seems probable that left to act on his principles Pétain might then have conducted a fighting withdrawal, exacting the maximum toll on the attackers while economising his own losses, even at the risk of abandoning the Verdun citadel – and regardless of its moral significance. As he had written after the Artois offensive the previous spring: 'It is always prejudicial to cede ground to the enemy. But these inconveniences cannot be related to ... a loss ... of several thousands of men.' The next day Pétain was stricken with double pneumonia, and for the ensuing critical days – like Marshal Saxe at Fontenoy – he directed the battle from his sickbed. Miraculously his illness was concealed from the French public, already deeply discouraged by the news from Verdun.

Though shaking with fever, Pétain gathered the threads of the battle into his hands with astonishing rapidity. He realised that – at least tactically – the situation was not quite as desperate as it had seemed at first sight. Only one bastion of prime importance had been lost so far – Fort Douaumont. One of the elite formations of the French army, General Balfourier's 'Iron' xx Corps, had now reached the front; two further corps were on their way, and a third standing by. In Pétain's opinion, 'the fact that Verdun still remained in our hands on February 25th constituted a real success', and if it could hold out another two or three days, it would be safe. But, 'our façade, so rudely shaken, could crumble from one moment to another'. In fact, for reasons of which Pétain could not be aware (see Falkenhayn chapter), the initial German impetus was bogging down; the parsimonious Falkenhayn was holding back reserves urgently needed for pressing the attack, and the artillery was encountering difficulty in moving forward over terrain which their own pounding had turned into a lunar morass.

True to form, de Castelnau had issued an order for the immediate recapture of Douaumont, but after one suicidal failure Pétain immediately rescinded it. 'Conserve your strength,' he told his commanders: 'the counter-offensive will follow.' Meanwhile a *'position de barrage'* was to be established, backed by powerful artillery reinforcements. It was here, his old passion, that Pétain really made his influence felt at Verdun. He virtually took over control of the artillery, asking his commanders each morning: 'What have your batteries been doing? Leave the other details till later.' Repeatedly he insisted that the artillery must 'give the infantry the impression that it is supporting them and that it is not dominated'. Next to the artillery the most important initial measure taken by Pétain was to assure communications with the menaced salient. Only the most precarious of lifelines connected Verdun with the hinterland, and the railway links had been cut by German long-range guns. Pétain now devoted top priority to developing a road artery that could safely supply an army of half a million men. He succeeded, and the famous road was to become sanctified in French history books as the *Voie Sacrée*. During the critical first week of March alone, over 25,000 tons of supplies and 190,000 men were funnelled through it to Verdun. Along the *Voie Sacrée* was to pass two-thirds of the whole army, and it was to achieve for Verdun the precedent of being the first major battle to be supplied almost exclusively by motor transport.

Pétain's artillery brought up onto the left bank of the Meuse began to have an immediate effect; from this moment, wrote the German *Reichs Archives*, 'began the flanking fire on the ravines and roads north of Douaumont that was to cause us such severe casualties'. To halt this flanking fire, Falkenhayn was now – with utmost reluctance – persuaded to widen the front of the attack to the Mort Homme, and then to Côte 304, on the left bank. For two terrible months the battle see-sawed back and forth over these two small ridges, bringing some of the worst suffering in the entire war; and also, despite the heroic defence put up by Pétain's men, bringing the Germans each day a few yards closer to Verdun. By the end of May French losses equalled the German total at Stalingrad in the Second World War – and still the battle ground on. Pétain himself was becoming increasingly affected by what he saw. In a moving passage in his memoirs he wrote: 'my heart leapt as I saw our youths of twenty going into the furnace of Verdun, reflecting that with the light-heartedness of their age they would pass too rapidly from the enthusiasm of the first engagement to the lassitude provoked by suffering . . .' On returning from the line, 'their postures betrayed a total dejection, they sagged beneath the weight of horrifying memories.'

Towards the end of March President Poincaré had visited Verdun and was shocked to note, 'Pétain has in his eyes a nervous tic, which betrays a certain fatigue.' He was even more shocked when Pétain remarked, 'I do not know if I will be obliged to abandon Verdun but if the measure appeared necessary to me I would not hesitate to consider it.' Poincaré replied, 'Don't think of it, General. It would be a parliamentary catastrophe.' Shared between both the government and GHQ, the feeling grew that Verdun was proving too much for Pétain.

In order to contain the demoralisation of the troops that he saw there, Pétain had persuaded Joffre to accept the *noria* system (named after the perpetually rotating water wheels of French North Africa), whereby units sent into this particularly atrocious battle would be relieved after the shortest possible time. Thus, while only a relatively small proportion of the German army went through Verdun, almost the whole French army was to be conditioned by its horrors. At the same time Joffre watched in alarm as effectives earmarked for the 'Big Push' on the Somme were being steadily consumed at Verdun. And, despite this deployment of manpower, Pétain had not yet once assumed the offensive at Verdun.

So in May Pétain was 'sacked upwards' to become an army group commander, and to make way for two more ruthless generals: Nivelle* and Mangin, nicknamed 'the Butcher'. On 22 May an attempt by Mangin to recapture Fort Douaumont ended in costly failure, and encouraged the Germans to resume their offensive. Attacking in June with even greater concentration than that of February, the Germans captured Fort Vaux. But just as Vaux was falling, Russian General Brusilov unleashed the first of the co-ordinated Allied offensives planned the previous December. Although this signified the relief of Verdun, the Germans attacked yet again; this brought them to the glacis of Fort Souville, located on the last ridge before Verdun. A few days later Haig and Foch attacked on the Somme. Verdun was now definitively relieved. The French had held to the end, but in the last weeks there had been ominous signs of morale cracking, with units refusing to return to the line. It was a sinister preview of what was to happen on a far greater scale, also under Nivelle, the following year.

* It was he, not Pétain, who gave birth to the immortal slogan: *'Ils ne passeront pas!'*

In his handling of the defensive Battle of Verdun, Pétain became the great soldier-hero of France. With his gaze riveted to that narrow, grim front he may have lacked the overall vision of the war that was accessible to de Castelnau or Joffre; but in terms of human intangibles what he saw at Verdun the mutinies of 1917 proved he saw with far greater clairvoyance than either of his seniors. The cost of saving Verdun had been perhaps just too great for the heroic and hard-tried *poilu* to bear.

In the autumn of 1916 Nivelle and Mangin – under the more remote but nevertheless restraining influence of Pétain as army group commander – launched the successful counter-strokes that recaptured Fort Douaumont as well as most of the terrain which the Germans had taken at such appalling cost over the preceding ten months. Out of it Nivelle suddenly emerged as France's new ideal of the aggressive general. Joffre, for whom the stalemate on the Somme compounded with the early blunders at Verdun, was *limogé* and replaced as C-in-C by Nivelle; who, like Pétain, had been a mere colonel in 1914. Nivelle exuded great charm, and inordinate self-confidence, but at least part of the reason for his being promoted (disastrously for France) over the head of Pétain stemmed from the politicians' understandable apprehension at having a C-in-C with such manifest contempt of themselves. Although Nivelle's successes at Verdun had been no more than limited operations with specific tactical objectives, of the very kind that Pétain himself had long been espousing, from them he drew disproportionately grandiose conclusions. 'We have the formula,' he declared triumphantly as he left Verdun; 'Our method has proved itself. Victory is certain . . .' With his 'method', the creeping barrage he had perfected, gunner Nivelle set to work planning the great spring offensive for 1917, which was to end the war in one swift blow 'of violence, brutality and rapidity'. The long ridge of the Chemin des Dames overlooking the river Aisne, and one of the most important bulwarks of the German line, was the chosen sector.

In the meantime however the new German high command under Hindenburg/Ludendorff were shortening their whole front, pulling back to immensely strong positions on the Hindenburg Line. French security was worse than usual, and the massive weight of Nivelle's artillery preparation simply came down like a haymaker swung into thin air. When on 16 April 1917 the French infantry left their trenches exhilarated by Nivelle's promises, they advanced half a mile into a vacuum; then came up against thousands of intact machine guns. Where Nivelle had predicted 10,000 wounded, there were something like 120,000 casualties. Demoralised troops flooded towards the rear, and news of the massacre on the Chemin des Dames spread like wildfire. Nivelle had broken the French army.

Regiments sent up to reinforce the line bleated in macabre imitation of sheep on their way to the *abattoir*. There were cries of 'Down with the War!', and officers were set upon. On 3 May mutiny proper broke out. Ordered into the battle, the 21st Division (which had experienced some of the worst fighting at Verdun the previous year) refused to a man. The ringleaders were summarily shot, or sent to Devil's Island, but unit after unit – among them the finest in the French army – followed suit. By June half the entire army was reckoned to have become contaminated, and at one point it was said that there was not one single reliable division between Soissons and Paris. The truly remarkable aspect about the mutinies was that – through the exceptional secrecy maintained by the French – nothing leaked out until order was re-established, and to this day details of them remain veiled in mystery. Yet, had German intelligence been alerted and had Ludendorff been able to attack then with even a portion of the force he mustered in March 1918, the consequences for France must have been catastrophic.

As it was, this was France's darkest hour in the First World War. Once again (and not for the last time) she called for Pétain. The choice to replace the disgraced Nivelle fell between himself and Foch, and Spears who knew both well remarks: 'I could only pray that the choice of the Government would fall on Pétain.' Of Foch as a commander, he added '. . . that he had immense moral courage, but that his reserves were invariably badly placed.'

As of that grim spring of 1917, however, it was neither courage nor strategic grasp that was of paramount importance. At that moment General Pétain, not Foch, was the one leader in whom the French fighting soldier had *moral* confidence, and as the *médécin de l'armée* he now made probably his greatest contribution to France. On 15 May 1917 Pétain took over as C-in-C, with Foch as Chief of the General Staff. Energetically he set to attacking the deep malaise in the French army on a variety of fronts. First he concentrated his attention on the civilian sources of defeatist and left-wing pacifist propaganda that from the rear had been progressively demoralising the troops, some of it blatantly financed by German funds. Foremost was the *Bonnet Rouge* journal, run by two shadowy figures – Miguel Almereyda and Emile Duval. Here Pétain found an invaluable ally among the despised politicians; the vitriolic 'Tiger', Clemenceau, who was to become Prime Minister that November. With Clemenceau leading the attack in the Senate, *Bonnet Rouge* was suppressed; Duval and another proven traitor in German pay, Bolo Pasha, were shot while Almereyda died mysteriously in prison; Malvy, the wilfully over-permissive Minister of the Interior, was forced to resign. By the autumn of 1917 the Augean Stable behind the lines was cleansed.

In restoring health to the army itself, Pétain employed a judicious blend of stick and carrot. By no means a gentle man as a disciplinarian, he did not now shirk from the execution of the mutineer ringleaders. But justice was carried out swiftly – and restrainedly. In a secret report written by Pétain and revealed by Spears many years later, Pétain states that only fifty-five executions were carried out, of which no more than thirty were of men actually guilty of 'collective disobedience'. Hand in hand with this, Pétain introduced a mass of reforms designed to improve the basic living conditions of the *poilu*.

Many of these related to seemingly minor issues, but they stemmed from deep-seated grievances that had been flagrantly neglected year after year. Regular leave was properly organised at last, station canteens (comparable to the long-established British YMCA) and reliable leave trains were introduced; rest camps well behind the front and out of the sound of gunfire were instituted; while at the front the building of proper lavatories, showers and sleeping quarters was accelerated. Finally (a source of discontent patently close to the French heart), inept army cooks were sent off on culinary courses, and both the quality and flow of the precious *pinard** was improved.

But above all, Monty-like, Pétain made a point of visiting in person almost every division of the French army, exposing to view both himself and his intentions. Though cold and never displaying familiarity, Pétain's presence was invariably magical. In these days, Pierrefeu speaks of him as being:

> ... calm and imposing, a true commander-in-chief wielding sovereign authority. He spoke as man to men, dominating them with his prestige, without trying to put himself on a lower level ... But there was such sincerity and seriousness in his tone, he seemed so absolutely honest, just and human, that nobody doubted his word. The General derived all his strength, in fact, from his humanity. He loathed sentimentality, but he was never able to meet an ambulance without emotion.

His solemn promise was that there would be no more offensives *à la Nivelle*, repeatedly declaring, 'We must wait for the Americans and the tanks.' The troops were made to feel what his Second Army had felt while he commanded it at Verdun; that here was a leader that would not squander their lives vainly.

Already by the end of the summer, Pétain felt confident enough to embark on a series of limited offensives; partly as therapeutic morale-raisers; partly to use up German reserves that were beginning to accumulate menacingly on the western front, following the collapse of Russia. These offensives were models of Pétain's long-developed technique. In late August General Guillaumat attacked at Verdun, taking several thousand prisoners and a substantial strip of terrain. But the moment serious German resistance was encountered, Pétain halted and prepared to attack elsewhere. In October General Maistre's Sixth Army was thrown in at Malmaison to execute a more ambitious operation. Again typical of Pétain, all was concentrated at one vital point, with a density of one gun for every six yards of front firing off two million 75mm shells and 850,000 'heavies' in the course of the artillery preparation. The result was that the whole Chemin des Dames position, which Nivelle had fought so disastrously to gain in April, fell into Pétain's hands; the defenders suffered some 40,000 casualties including 11,500 prisoners, 200 cannon and 720 machine guns – all for a total French loss of 14,700. (Meanwhile, with far

* The French army's rough red wine ration.

more discouraging results and disproportionate losses, the British at Passchendaele had been bearing the greater part of the burden on the western front
while the French army recuperated.)

The fruits of Pétain's limited offensives did restore French army morale to a
quite remarkable degree, and by the end of the year it was ready to face the
dangers of 1918; or, at least, as ready as it could be. But it was fairly clear that
no amount of Malmaisons was likely to achieve a decisive victory in the
foreseeable future; and in the meantime Ludendorff was preparing his all-out
last-throw bid for victory. At dawn on 21 March the sledgehammer blow fell
on General Gough's British Fifth Army, breaking its defences wide open.
Ludendorff's aim was to split the Allied forces, and roll the British contingent
back to the Channel, and it came within close measure of succeeding. Already
at the beginning of the year there had been a fundamental disagreement
between Pétain and Foch on how to meet the anticipated German onslaught.
With each arguing along lines true to form, Foch advised meeting it with a
powerful Allied counter-offensive; Pétain, with an elastic defence in depth.
The old de Grandmaison tenet that it was prejudicial to yield an inch of
ground still died hard, and Pétain's thesis met with resistance; but undoubtedly if Foch's had been accepted the slender Allied reserves would have
been squandered prematurely before the full weight of the German impetus
had been committed. As it was, the Allied strategy was largely decided by
events.

By 25 March Pétain had managed to deploy some twenty French divisions
to help out Haig – in itself a notable testimony to the extent to which his
'cure' of the army had succeeded the previous year. The following day the
Doullens Conference took place, an important milestone in the conduct of
the war, at which it was agreed that Foch should assume the role of 'supremo'
co-ordinating all the Allied armies. During the conference Pétain had given
a bleak appreciation, and (in agreement with Clemenceau) made it plain that
if the choice were to be imposed on him the French forces would have to
withdraw southwards to cover Paris – even at the risk of opening a dangerous
gap between them and Haig. Haig remarked (in his diaries) that '. . . Pétain
had a terrible look. He had the appearance of a commander who was in a
funk.'

It was an aspect of Pétain's character that he would on occasions display
extreme glumness when dealing with politicians, or his military superiors and
equals – while at the same time maintaining a show of greater assurance and
self-confidence to his subordinates. But it does seem that at this stage in the
war inherent *fatalism*, or pessimism, had taken a strong hold over him.
Pétain's own turn to bear the brunt came in May, when Ludendorff struck a
new blow on the Aisne, smashing through once again to the Marne in a matter
of four days. Here French intelligence was taken by surprise, and the whole
French hierarchy from Pétain downwards seems to have been at fault. The
final German surge carried them perilously close to Paris; but for the first

time American divisions were there to plug the gap – the Americans that Pétain had been counting on for so long.

By the end of May Pétain had largely recovered his nerve, and is recorded as predicting – with notable accuracy: 'If we can hold on until the end of June, our situation will be excellent. In July we can resume the offensive; after that, victory will be ours.' Although the organising of the crucial defensive stages of the 1918 battles had been very largely Pétain's work, during the final months of the war his was the lesser role. This was partly because the overall strategic direction of the offensives was in Foch's hands as Allied Supremo, and partly because the major effort (from August onwards) was executed by the British and the Americans. So often previously at odds with each other, in these months Pétain and Foch – with his triumphant *'tout le monde à la bataille'* at last vindicated – worked together as an indispensable, complementary tandem.

It might well be said that without Foch and his spirit of *l'attaque*, the war would not have been won in 1918; on the other hand without Pétain in 1917 it would almost certainly have been lost. As a war lord Pétain in the First World War should perhaps be evaluated more as an organiser than as a battle commander. Says Liddell Hart, 'for want of opportunity history may not rate him among the great strategists; . . . he was more an inventor of tactical methods than an executive tactician.' On two scores – his pessimism and his espousal of the technique of the limited offensive – Pétain bears comparison with his opponent, von Falkenhayn. But the difference was that in Falkenhayn pessimism was conditioned less by humanitarian principles than cold reasoning. Secondly, whereas for the French (after 1916) the policy of the limited offensive meant that they could not *lose* the war, because they could afford to 'wait for the Americans and the tanks', for the Germans it meant that *they could only lose* it – because time (from 1915 onwards) was always against them. As Liddell Hart suggests, Pétain may have had no strikingly original strategic views on how the First World War should be fought; however, he knew better than most of the other war lords on either side how it should *not* be fought.

After the armistice Pétain (promoted marshal) enjoyed unparalleled prestige and affection throughout the French army. With old age soon removing Foch from the public arena, a still virile Pétain remained the principal arbiter of military thought for the best part of another generation. In 1922 he was appointed inspector-general, which post he held until his retirement in 1931 aged seventy-five. In 1934 he was brought back again into harness as Minister of War under the Doumergue government. Pétain's influence over the French army in these inter-war years was, in turn, deeply affected by his own First World War experiences; particularly at Verdun. Never again, he promised, should the youth of France be forced to accept such hideous sacrifices, harking back repeatedly to one of his favourite maxims: 'One does not fight with men against material; it is with material served by men that one makes war.' In an annex to his book, *La Bataille de Verdun*, Pétain noted pointedly:

> If from the beginning we had had confidence in the skill of our military engineers, the struggle before Verdun would have taken a different course. Fort Douaumont, occupied as it ought to have been, would not have been taken . . . Fortification, what little there was of it, played a very large role in the victory . . .

From here it was but a logical step to the conception of the Maginot Line, a more or less continuous chain of super Douaumonts, guarding France's eastern frontier.

Years after the First World War Pétain wrote of the French soldier at Verdun that '. . . the constant vision of death had penetrated him with a resignation which bordered on fatalism'. For Pétain himself that quality of fatalism was, by 1940, to be renamed 'defeatism'. Yet, in the animosity engendered after France's intolerable defeat then, too much of the blame for the disastrous state of her army has been heaped upon Pétain's head. To begin with it is quite unjust to suggest that he singlehanded laced the army into a kind of intellectual straitjacket; the French army mentality of the day donned it all too willingly. Secondly it is at most only a half-truth to identify Pétain – as he has been – as the arch apostle of static, stagnant, archaic warfare. From earliest days he was deeply conscious of the importance of the new air weapon; probably more so than de Gaulle, who came to be regarded as *the* French prophet-without-honour of the modern blitzkrieg. Pétain fought hard for a unified high command, motivated by the exigencies of air warfare; and he urged the creation by France of an offensive, 'deterrent' air force, pleading (unsuccessfully) for priority to be given to the construction of bombers rather than fighters. True, he erred seriously in regarding the tank as being principally an adjunct to the infantry, and did not support the conception of the self-contained armoured division. He was not alone in this error. On the other hand it was not Pétain's policy to keep the major bulk of the army locked up in *his* Maginot Line, always stressing the necessity of keeping free a powerful *masse de manoeuvre** well behind the line to meet the eventuality of any German breakthrough.

Speaking at the École de Guerre in 1935 about the impact of air power and armour on the warfare of the future, Pétain prophesied: '. . . victory will belong to him who is the first to exploit to the maximum the properties of modern engines and to combine their action, on whatever level, to destroy the adversary's means of carrying on the struggle . . .' And at St Quentin the following year – the year of Hitler's re-entry into the Rhineland – he declared:

> The concept of the defensive army which has had priority in France since the Treaty of Versailles has had its day . . . we must direct our

---

* Such as Gamelin failed dismally to have at hand in the critical days of May 1940.

activity so that we have on the ground and in the air powerful forces for immediate unleashing . . . for the modern offensive techniques are alone capable of effectively collaborating with an ally in peril . . .

How many other generals of eighty would have been quite so 'with it'? What is most important, however, as far as Pétain's reputation is concerned, is that the really irreparable damage to the French military machine was done from 1936 to 1940 – after Pétain had retired from the scene.

General Erich Ludendorff

Norman Stone

'We'll just blow a hole in the middle. The rest will follow of its own accord': it was thus that General Erich Ludendorff announced to one of his army group commanders the essentials of his military philosophy, before embarking on the great offensive of March 1918, the last hope of the German Empire. Ludendorff was later accused by military writers of putting tactics above strategy, of failing to develop any large-scale scheme of things, and of simply following his nose, whatever the confusions that resulted. It was a criticism that had much foundation; but, at bottom, Ludendorff was only expressing what almost all great commanders have said at one time or another – as with Cromwell, who went furthest when he did not know where he was going, or Hitler, 'the sleep-walker'. Ludendorff belonged in much the same mould as the late Napoleon, or Charles XII of Sweden: heroically fighting a hopeless cause, knowing that the odds were impossible, yet always waiting for some final twist, a *deus ex machina*, to save him and his cause. It was an attitude very close to madness; and modern writers sometimes wonder if Ludendorff's mental instability had not gone so far, by summer 1918, as to constitute a kind of madness.

Certainly, Ludendorff's later life (he died in 1937) showed an unmistakable insanity. He fled to Sweden, to refuge offered by a friend, to escape the German Revolution of November 1918, but returned to Germany shortly after and was involved in extreme right-wing politics. In 1923 he joined Hitler in the Munich Putsch, being left to advance, unarmed and alone, against the victorious police. He stood for President of the Reich in 1925, with derisory results. Thereafter he established himself as a writer of scurrilous right-wing pamphlets, denouncing the Roman Catholic Church, the Jews, the Freemasons; he broke with all of his old colleagues in the Imperial Army, and was the object of libel actions from some of them. Relations with Field-Marshal Hindenburg became strained, and finally broke completely. He was left in his own world of Teutonic fantasy, which gave him, after 1933, a position of resistance to the Nazi regime on the grounds that it was not Nazi enough. Of his last years Malcolm Muggeridge writes:

Ludendorff's opposition to the Nazi regime was of a different order [to

Niemöller's]: lunacy's privilege rather than faith's responsibility. In his fortnightly magazine, *At the Fount of German Power*, mixed up with anti-semitic fury, astrological predictions and other occult matter, appeared criticism of the Third Reich when everywhere else it had been suppressed. Later the magazine, suddenly popular as the single remaining opposition organ, was also subjected to the *Gleichschaltung* process, and lapsed back into its original obscurity; and Hitler and Ludendorff, ceremonially but not very cordially, met and conversed together. After this ceremonial meeting, Ludendorff continued undisturbed with his pagan rites, occasionally to be seen wearing horned head-pieces and other Wagnerian accoutrements. When he died he was given a State funeral, though at subsequent private obsequies his remains were consigned to Valhalla to the accompaniment of ancient German chants and ritual, strange figures, presumably friends and retainers, appearing in suitable costumes, and making strange moan.

A fanaticism of this, almost insane, variety suited the mood of Germany in the First World War. 'The German people has no choice. Either we win in this offensive, or we go down for ever,' was Ludendorff's view of things early in 1918, and virtually all Germans either consciously or subconsciously agreed with him. On the face of things it was a crazy judgement. The German army in the west had only a trivial superiority in terms of divisions – 194½ to 170 – and an actual inferiority (11,500 to 18,500) in terms of artillery, quite apart from their almost total absence of tanks and the Allies' domination of the air. There was not much chance of getting troops for the west from elsewhere. In Russia there were still, in March 1918, some forty infantry divisions, but most of them were made up of forty-year-olds, underfed and mutinous; they had also been stripped of their horses and most of their guns, so that they were immobile. The Austro-Hungarian army, Germany's only serious ally, already had its hands full in fighting Italy and holding down the Balkans, and not much could be expected from there. Some heavy artillery was sent; and in August 1918 two Austro-Hungarian divisions came to the western front, but in such condition that the German town-major in Rethel had to issue them with boots. Even if the Germans did break through, they could not move nearly as fast as the Allies could, and so could hardly exploit their breakthrough. There were under thirty thousand lorries on the German side, and supplies of petrol were too limited for full use to be made of them. Moreover they had almost no stocks of rubber to rely on; the standard tyre of a German lorry was made of wood, sometimes with bits of iron attached, and although synthetic rubber could, by 1918, be produced, it was in no great quantity nor was it of high quality. These lorries churned up the roads of northern France, travelling at 5 miles per hour, and made the roads sometimes unusable for horse transport.

The Western powers suffered from no such embarrassments – they had over 100,000 lorries, with unlimited supplies of rubber and petrol. The Allies' movement of reserves was correspondingly more flexible than the Germans'. Even if Ludendorff won a great tactical victory – as he did in March 1918 – he would be unable to follow it up as fast as the Allies closed the gap. Thus in March 1918 Ludendorff destroyed most of the fourteen infantry divisions of the British Fifth Army, almost at a stroke, between 21 and 24 March. But by 26 March twelve French divisions either had arrived, or were arriving, to take their places – one-third by train, the rest by autobus or lorry. By the end of March the German offensive slackened and died down, costing the Allies and the Germans alike something over 300,000 men.

The German position was, in other words, one where an offensive was virtually bound to fail. On the other hand Germany had advantages that Ludendorff threw away by his behaviour. Had he refrained from his offensives of 1918, he would have forced the Western powers to do the attacking if they intended to win the war. Neither the French nor the British, with experience behind them of the attrition of 1915, the Somme, and the Third Battle of Ypres (Passchendaele), relished renewed offensives. The American armies were due to arrive in 1918; but they were not yet trained, and their capacity for an offensive could legitimately be questioned. The German army would have been in a good position to wage defensive warfare, based on the well-planned trench lines of France and Flanders; and the Western powers, with, of course, great disagreements of their own, might well have fallen apart if faced by a stubborn defensive action rather than an offensive that pushed them all together again. Such, clearly, would have been Ludendorff's most sensible course. Instead he chose the offensive and threw away Germany's cards in a gamble for complete *Siegfrieden*. It was Napoleonic, grandiose. It was also disastrous.

The fact is that discussion of 'might-have-beens' in a situation such as Germany found herself in 1917–18 is pointless. The men in charge of Germany's destiny could not contemplate anything other than complete victory; limited strategy, such as had been practised by Erich von Falkenhayn in the first two years of the war, no longer had any appeal for most of them; and this accounts for their choice of Ludendorff to take Falkenhayn's place at the end of August 1916. It would no doubt be too much of an over-simplification to say that it was a class question; but that was its essence. The Prussian upper class came under pressure during the war years more than ever before. Before 1914 they had managed to hold Prussia in a tight grip. Their political parties – the Conservatives and Free Conservatives – were able to survive in an age of universal suffrage because they could rely on a mass of loyal rural votes, from the peasants of Junker estates. They could also play a nationalist card – the defence of German culture against the 'hordes' of Catholic Poles then immigrating to Prussia, lowering wages and at the same time acquiring land from bankrupt Germans. The Conservatives survived brilliantly in Prussia itself where – unlike Germany as a whole – the state parliament was elected by a fancy franchise that gave a few hundred thousand wealthy men much the same representation as millions of urban workers. Two-thirds of its seats were filled by Conservatives of one stamp or another. On this basis the Junkers literally ran Prussia – awarding jobs in the state's service (and of course the army) to themselves, their brothers, their cousins and their uncles. The taxation machinery of East Prussia was singularly ineffective, since the tax returns and death duties of Junker families were ultimately supervised by a functionary who was related to them. The Dohna-Schlobitten family, with an income of 400,000 marks, paid in taxes in 1904 less than 400 marks. A variety of interesting devices and political intrigues promoted the Junker cause at the expense of Social Democrats and free-thinking Liberals. But after 1914 popular pressure came as never before. The charmed world of Junker families was challenged from below; by 1916 the German working class, and even some of the peasantry, were restive, feeling that they were being sacrificed in a 'bosses' war'.

There were increasing manifestations of this discontent. Of course few people doubted that the workers were essentially patriotic. Just the same a price would have to be paid for their patriotism; and it was this that Junker Prussia resented having to meet. When the Russian Revolution broke out in March 1917, the example was contagious: there were sudden strikes in Berlin, Leipzig, the Ruhr; even a mutiny in the fleet. War weariness abounded, and there was constant talk from Vienna of a separate peace with the Entente. The German Social Democrats, who had hitherto supported the war effort, began to feel that their supporters were slipping farther off to the left, to the newly founded, independent, Social Democratic party and the ultra-left *Spartakusbund* of Rosa Luxemburg and Karl Liebknecht. Their leaders (Ebert and Scheidemann) demanded concessions with which to win back their followers – among them a grant of equal franchise in Prussia. This would have meant domination of the Prussian state by the Social Democrats and their allies; it put a great fright into the Conservatives. Just the same the Kaiser and his Chancellor, Theobald von Bethmann Hollweg, felt that the concession must be made; and at Easter 1917 the Kaiser announced his intention of altering the Prussian franchise – a firm promise being made early in July.

It was typical of the position of the military in German public life that they intervened to prevent equalisation of the franchise. Hindenburg grumbled to his Conservative friends (Plessen and Berg) in the Kaiser's entourage; and Ludendorff staged a coup against the Chancellor. He fomented pessimism as to the war's outcome among deputies of the Reichstag. These got together to demand a compromise peace. Ludendorff then turned round to the Kaiser, indicating that Bethmann Hollweg had lost control of the Reichstag. He and Hindenburg said that they would resign, since the survival of Bethmann Hollweg merely prejudiced the war effort, ruining the morale of the army. The Kaiser thereupon dismissed Bethmann Hollweg.

The generals were left with a Reichstag resolution for compromise peace on their hands. The promoters of this resolution patriotically asked the generals' advice as to its effect on army morale. The generals then rewrote the text; indeed Ludendorff made last-minute alterations in it just before giving it to a 'tame' Socialist, Südekum, to take to the Wolff-Bureau for announcement to the world. Then the generals were consulted as to the next Chancellor. They would have preferred Admiral Tirpitz, then discharging patriotic enthusiasms from the safety of retirement. The politicians would not accept him, and as a compromise a faceless, aged and almost wholly deaf civil servant, Michaelis, emerged, to act more or less self-confessedly as a tool of the generals. The Prussian franchise question, which had started off the crisis, was finally submitted to the Prussian Parliament in November 1917. It was voted out almost at once; a commission dominated by Conservatives saw to it that a completely harmless, though also extremely complicated, system would be substituted for the existing arrangements.

The German high command was in effect fighting a class war as well as a war against France and Great Britain. The generals knew that they had to win the European war to win their war at home, and despite the evidence continued to believe that they could win both. They also took the lead in demanding vast war aims, which sensible people knew were never likely to be realised. Ludendorff took a chief role in demanding great sacrifices of Russia. The non-Russian parts of the Tsar's empire would be cut off – the Ukraine, the Baltic countries, Poland and Lithuania in the first instance, the Caucasus peoples thereafter. Germany would annex part of Poland, including valuable mines and forests, and maybe part of Lithuania as well. By Ludendorff's own prescriptions the Baltic peoples would be annexed to the German crown and ruled by a small minority of local German landowners, the Manteuffel-Zoeges, von der Ropps, Ungern-Sternbergs and Thiesenhausens who formed the most brutally *Herrenvolk*-conscious group in all Europe. Tame Germanophil rulers would be named for the truncated Polish kingdom and the Ukraine; there was even a scheme for annexing the Crimea, where local Germans – with some effort – had been discovered, and which was to be in Ludendorff's words 'the German Riviera'. Later on, as Russia collapsed completely, German agents went off into the Caucasus in search of the oil of Baku. One of them, Wesendonck, recorded his opinion that 'even the idea of a German land-route to China is not to be ruled out altogether'. The policy inside Germany had in other words its counterpart outside Germany, in the areas conquered by the German army. Ludendorff and his colleagues wanted to keep it all.

If Ludendorff's strategy was an out-and-out *'jusqu'au boutiste'* one, the causes were therefore much wider than Ludendorff's own outlook. The German ruling class could not face defeat; for defeat would, they felt, be followed by a revolution in which Junker Prussia would be irretrievably destroyed. Even a compromise peace was impossible in terms of these people's outlook. It was not until October 1918 that they began to see things in a different light; not until the very end of the war that they announced unreservedly that Belgium would be evacuated. No doubt Allied statesmen also wanted to pursue the war to a victorious conclusion. But German behaviour ensured that they would have every reason to pursue this course: the most peaceable, moderate English liberal could not fail to support the war so long as Belgian neutrality was not guaranteed by Germany. Ludendorff was therefore involved in a vicious circle. He had to demand vast war aims to make the war effort seem worth it in the German people's eyes; and yet each heightening of war aims only meant that the war would have to be yet more brutally waged. In this way compromise, which in 1917 seemed at the least not impossible, was completely ruled out by the turn of 1917–18. The only way out appeared to be Ludendorff's *Siegfried* offensives.

No doubt all of this was, seen from the outside, crazy. On the other hand Germany had been in seemingly impossible situations before, and something had always turned up: indeed this was the pattern of Ludendorff's own career as a general. In 1914 the Marne had been compensated by Tannenberg, and thereafter victories in the east (Lodz, the Masurian Lakes, Gorlice-Tarnów and the conquest of Poland in summer 1915, the overthrow of Serbia in autumn 1915) had made up for successive reverses in France, for the Dardanelles menace, for the intervention of Italy. In 1916 this pattern went on, since failure at Verdun was answered by an Allied failure on the Somme, and in the autumn the overthrow of Rumania; and in 1917 the intervention of the United States was balanced out by the fall of Russia. Always the *deus ex machina* helped Germany, and it is not surprising to find, for instance, a writer in the German equivalent of *The Church Times* recording his view early in 1918, 'that if there are still sincere Christians in England, they must surely now plea for mercy, and see that the Lord is fighting for Germany'. Just as, according to legend, Frederick the Great had been saved during the Seven Years' War when the anti-Prussian Tsaritsa died, and her successor, the pro-Prussian Peter, reversed her policy, so Germany in the First World War seemed to have profited greatly from the fortuitous decease of assorted tsarissas. It was with faith in Germany's destiny, a faith increasingly buttressed by astrologists and quack prophets, that Ludendorff launched his great offensive.

The situation was altogether similar to that of Germany in the latter part of the Second World War, when again a German leader fought his wars with batteries of quack doctors and star gazers. There is also a similarity in so far as the military machine itself was remarkably efficient to the end, despite the crackpot notions of its high command. Ludendorff may not have been much of a long-term strategist, may have been unable to distinguish between the accidental, the short-term, the fortuitous on the one side, and the great long-term factors on the other. But he, and the army as a whole, none the less had remarkable military gifts that did much to overcome the long-term factors counting against Germany. No doubt this was, in part at least, a consequence of the situation in which Germany found herself. She could not afford to be as prodigal with her soldiers' lives as the Western powers and Russia could, for her population of 65 million could not stand comparison with the populations of England, France and Russia combined (265 million). As a consequence it was German soldiers rather than Western ones who hit on tactical innovations, new methods of strategy, that came close to overcoming the material deficiencies; and Germany lost absolutely less men than did France in 1914–18, despite her having to fight on several fronts.

Scarcity was, in the First World War, the mother of invention. Blockaded Germany could not rely on imports of Chilean saltpetre for her explosives. She developed a whole range of new processes: the Franck-Caro and Haber-Bosch processes enabled her to use nitrogen in the air itself and turn it into explosive substances. Again the fact that the blockade made it impossible for Germany to export on the same scale as before 1914 meant that a great 'shake-out' of resources from exports to munitions work could take place. Men thrown out of traditional employment by the blockade could simply be turned to producing munitions, and German shell production was actually quicker off the mark than the English, French or Russian. By the autumn of 1916 Germany was producing almost eight million rounds per month, a figure somewhat higher than the French, and twice as great as the British. Later on ways were found of overcoming the deficiencies in rubber and other vital raw materials: as George Orwell later said, blockades in future would hardly be effective, since we lived in a civilisation in which nylon stockings or explosives could be produced from milk. Arms output in Germany came literally to depend on the atmosphere and on coal gas; and in the end even petrol was produced from coal gas.

In much the same way Ludendorff and his team hit on a variety of tactical and strategic devices that did much to overcome the natural problems of outnumbered and besieged Germany. It was Germans who first appreciated new methods of defence late in 1916, and Germans again who pioneered new techniques of offensive action. Virtually all of the European armies were outstandingly slow in their response to the novel problems of 1914. They fought the war they had imagined, not the one they encountered. Before 1914 they had thought that the mass infantry attack would be the key to victory. This led them to make fundamental errors in matters of artillery. They all laid in stocks of shrapnel, not high-explosive shell: naturally shrapnel bursting over the heads of a mass infantry attack would be more effective than high-explosive shell, the weapon designed against fortifications. In the same way, they laid in flat-trajectory artillery, not high-trajectory guns that could make short work of enemy fortifications. Only the Germans had made serious preparations for high-trajectory guns that could lob high-explosive shells: and even they did this for the wrong reason, namely, in order to deal with fortresses. No one thought that the war would last more than a few months, because trade and commerce could not stand disruption for any longer. It was thus with a wholly misleading picture of the war that generals began the campaign; and if the first campaign in the west was one of manoeuvre, it was partly because of a coincidence of gross error on both sides.

As soon as the first trenches were dug, late in September 1914, reality pushed its way through. Mass infantry attacks against a hidden enemy ended in bloody reverses. Soil offered a much better defence than concrete. Cavalry was useless. The war seemed to promise to last for ever. The blockade was not effective. Trade and industry, far from suffering hopeless disruption, often profited from wartime conditions, and profits rose as never before. There was no naval engagement of any decisiveness. In other words all of the rules had been stood on their heads. In these circumstances generals in all countries supposed that the only answer to the new conditions was to lay in huge stocks of shell. The guns would be increased in number, and they would simply fire off huge numbers of shells until the enemy was pulverised. This did not turn out to be much of an answer in 1915. In western conditions the guns might well pulverise an enemy front line, and there would literally be nothing – animal or vegetable – left alive in it. Then the attacker would push his troops through the hole. They would stumble forward on foot. The defender would bring up reserves by rail – and strengthen his artillery at the sides of the hole. The attackers would run into a salient, fired on from three sides by enemy guns and stopped in front by enemy reserves.

This happened to the French and British in spring 1915 in Artois and Champagne, and again in September. The Western powers reacted by demanding yet greater quantities of shell, and the way was open for their huge matériel battles – the Somme in the latter half of 1916, Third Ypres in the latter half of 1917. Bombardments that used up in a few days four million shells were the order of the day. 'Artillery conquers, infantry occupies', was the slogan behind these battles. No doubt these methods were not simply a consequence of military thinking; they were also a reflection of the generals' opinion of their own men. The men, especially those in the British army, had been scraped together hurriedly, given perfunctory training and placed under officers whose nearest experience to war was maybe a boy-scout camp. Traditional professional soldiers did not believe such men to be capable of much other than walking forward, their officers in front, their sergeants behind (with a pistol), and their fellows in a long line dressing to the left. Provided the guns could destroy everything living in front, then maybe such formations would move forward relatively unchecked. Hence the belief in shell that gave the battles of 1916–17 their nightmare quality, that led to such terrible slaughter in campaigns that left their mark for generations of British thinking. For even these huge quantities of shell turned out to be counter-productive. The attackers' progress was impeded by the terrain smashed up by so much shell. The defenders could construct huge dugouts, sometimes sixty feet deep, to withstand all but the heaviest shell; and the infantry formations used by the British were so clumsy that a dedicated machine gunner could do dreadful damage. But it was characteristic of British military thinking that many army staffs could not see any other answer. Nor were they forced towards one until late in 1917, because the reserves of manpower and matériel, especially after promise of American intervention, seemed inexhaustible.

The German army, after Ludendorff took over effective direction in August 1916, produced a much more flexible response. In the first place defence was no longer based on the outdated prescription of 1915–16. Ludendorff promoted highly intelligent and flexible directors of specialist arms – Geyer, an infantry captain, was promoted from the trenches to examine the tactical manuals; Bruchmüller similarly rewrote the terms of co-operation between infantry and artillery; and a whole range of new commanders appeared who understood the importance of new techniques in defence and attack. These men had originally caught Ludendorff's notice in the eastern campaigns of 1914–15, and were often promoted from regimental commands to corps, army and in the end army group commands – Hutier, Below, Kathen, Watter, Berrer (killed at Caporetto), Kühne were simply shuttled around from front to front, from the Baltic to Galicia, to Italy and then to France and Flanders, to take over units specially created for them. The result was a flexibility in defence and attack that went far beyond what other armies, except in 1917 the French, were able to achieve.

In the first place Ludendorff broke altogether with the principle that ground should be held, whatever the cost. He recognised that a powerful bombardment would knock out virtually anything holding the front line: therefore troops should be moved back as far as possible, out of range of all but the enemy's biggest pieces. In the latter part of 1916 German methods involved abandonment of useless ground; Geyer's pamphlet on tactics appeared at this time. When the enemy appeared beyond the front line, he would be counter-attacked; and there would be a mass of strongpoints, machine-gun nests, stitched across the ground to catch him from all sides as the counter-attack was launched. It was a principle that put the utmost reliance on the quality of troops: if cut off they must continue to fight following their own initiative until the relieving counter-attack came; they must not lose their heads even if their artillery seemed to desert them. In so far as any tactical system is ultimately a verdict on the quality of one's own men, Ludendorff both expressed and received that of the German soldier. In the early part of 1917 he carried this new system to its logical extent and evacuated the exposed part of the German salient in northern France, thus at a stroke making nugatory French preparations of offensive action in the spring (Nivelle offensive, April 1917). It was a sign that German tactical thinking had progressed beyond that of Germany's opponents.

This new system worked quite well throughout 1917, and the Western powers were driven to adopt it quite soon, though always reluctantly and always with much clumsiness. However it was not complete without a new system of offensive warfare; and this too was primarily a German creation. In the latter half of 1917 pioneers of tactical thought had worked with success to find a 'method'; one by which quantities of shell could be used, but which did not thereby rule out either surprise or mobility, as the shell-dominated offensives of the Somme, Verdun and Third Ypres had done. Bombardments would be short, but extremely intense: the week's bombardment of the Somme, Third Ypres, or Verdun had no repetition in Ludendorff's great offensives of 1918, with the result that the ground was not churned up into a morass, and surprise was not immediately forfeited. In March and again in April and May 1918 the successive German offensives on the St Quentin-La Fère, Lys and Vesle sectors were preceded by a mere three or four hours' bombardment. Gas shells formed a quarter of the shell used, as the accent was laid on paralysing enemy communications and morale rather than physically destroying him. Infantry and artillery worked very closely – an ideal towards which all armies had striven, but which in the German army came closest to realisation. Attackers were pushed forward, not in long lines, but in small, irregular formations, which were given the task of pressing as far ahead as possible, regardless of obstacles to right or left, in an effort at paralysing enemy command and communications. In the weeks before the offensives there was no obvious preparation; the troops were moved up only just before the attack.

These methods brought astonishing results in March 1918 and in subsequent months. The British Fifth Army, for instance, was subjected to these methods quite by surprise, since it had expected a repeat version, in reverse, of its own tactics on the Somme and in Flanders. The French under Duchêne on 27 May also reeled far back, even beyond the Marne, sacrificing thousands of men and hundreds of guns. It was evidence of what could be achieved, in this war, by a commander who was prepared to think things out instead of being mesmerised by matériel in the Western powers' style.

Ludendorff came to grief because his tactical innovations were not matched by deep strategic thinking. True to his watchword, he blew a hole in the enemy line and let the rest look after itself. Indeed he fell into a particular trap of not-quite-great commanders, and supposed that success would come because he was himself, which after all had been his pattern throughout the war and even before it. He did break through the Allied lines three times – 21 March, 9 April and 27 May. His troops forged far forward. Then he encountered the problem that had bedevilled every breakthrough operation since 1915: reserves arrived fast on the enemy side; his own troops were caught in great salients, which were not prepared for occupation by troops, and which permitted threefold enfilading of the occupant. As it turned out there was an answer to this problem, one pioneered by the Russian, Brusilov, in 1916: to attack on wide fronts one after another, not bothering to exploit any breakthrough. Brusilov had done wonders against the Austro-Hungarians with this method, though maybe he did not himself see the reasons for his success. Ludendorff's mistake was to push his troops through the hole made by the operation: it would have been much better to stop, and to attack somewhere else, thus bringing the enemy reserves to a state of confusion.

It was by these methods that Ludendorff was ultimately defeated. His troops were defeated in their exposed salients, from which Ludendorff had not had the courage to withdraw. Even when they fell back on the prepared lines, they could still be broken through. But Foch and Haig had learned the lessons of 1917–18: they did not pursue particularly once the breakthrough was made. Rather to Ludendorff's contempt, they neglected to exploit their breakthroughs, and just began somewhere else. This was the sense of Foch's *tout le monde à la bataille*: French in the centre, at Villers-Cotterêts on 18 July and in subsequent days; British at Amiens on 8 August; British at Cambrai late in August; Americans at St Mihiel in September, and the Argonne a few days later; British in the Hindenburg Line; French, British and Belgians in Flanders early in October. These hammer blows had German reserves scurrying to and fro on the lateral railway lines, arriving unprepared and exhausted; more important still, they had Ludendorff in a state of nervous collapse. By the end of September, even before Bulgaria dropped out of the war, Ludendorff's nerve had broken. For four days he did not even conduct affairs; merely stared helplessly at his table, until at last he nerved himself to say that an armistice must be made. A few weeks later he had resigned and had fled in disguise to Sweden, leaving Hindenburg to clear up the mess.

Ultimately genius is knowing where to stop. Ludendorff did not have this quality in 1918; indeed he would have despised it, for he himself thought, as did the later Napoleon, that his success came from some magic touch and not just hard work and self-discipline. He had always been a man of outstanding competence. His rise in the army before 1914 had been very fast: although quite young (he was born in 1865) he had risen to dominate the General Staff up to 1912, and it was only his energetic reforming spirit that resulted in a temporary setback. His capacity for overall knowledge of things German was astonishing: in the end he was arbiter of the German economy, German foreign policy, internal policy as well as of military affairs. The *Oberste Heeresleitung* was Germany's collective Lloyd George: it represented the kind of populist conservatism that won wars in this century. But power went to Ludendorff's head. He rejected compromise, just as he rejected, in the summer of 1918, the widespread retreat that might have saved things. Later on he contributed nothing but hatred and spite; up to his death in 1937 he destroyed all his old friendships, his marriage, and even his legend. Ludendorff was typical of the German Second Empire: enormous energy, extreme narrow-mindedness; and, in the end, a legacy of the might-have-been, laced with spite.

GENERAL SIR IAN HAMILTON

Robert Rhodes James

Few modern commanders have evoked estimates that are so varied as Sir Ian Hamilton. 'I can't look upon him as a very big man,' one of his Gallipoli corps commanders wrote, 'as he is really *shallow* by nature.' 'The salient fact,' wrote a senior member of his staff, 'is that he was *no use*.' Yet to Winston Churchill, 'his mind is built upon a big scale, being broad and strong, capable of thinking in army corps and if necessary in continents and working always with serene smoothness undisturbed alike by responsibility or danger.' Lord Roberts described him as 'quite the most brilliant commander I have serving under me'. There are few judgements available to us that enter into the middle ground between devoted admiration and contemptuous dismissal. Even now, sixty years after he was relieved of his command at Gallipoli and entered into his long retirement, and less than thirty years after his death, the ancient controversies still flare and flicker.

Hamilton was a career professional soldier. Recognised in the 1880s by Roberts as an outstanding officer, he transformed the musketry of the Indian Army, and demonstrated outstanding administrative ability in Burma and Chitral. Possessed of exceptional courage, he was recommended three times for the Victoria Cross, and rose swiftly. In the South African War he was Kitchener's Chief of Staff at the age of forty-eight and the young Churchill, already a warm admirer of this brave, articulate and charming soldier, echoed a general opinion when he wrote, 'It is evident that here is a man who in the years to come will have much to do with the administration of the British Army in times of peace and its direction in the field.'

This prediction was not, however, fulfilled. Hamilton had one of the most acute intellects in the British army, and a formidable gift of expression. His conclusions about the South African War were sensible and original, and included the development of mobile heavy artillery, revised infantry tactics, the construction of 'steel shields on wheels' to protect advancing infantry, and the reduction of the role of cavalry. These proposals and others were included in his book *The Fighting of the Future*, which demonstrated both his prescience and his unorthodox independence. His most remarkable work at this time was *A Staff Officer's Scrap Book*, published in two volumes between

1905 and 1907, and which is the standard work on the Russo-Japanese fighting in Manchuria, where he was the official British observer. The controversies that these activities aroused did not assist his career, nor did his unwise intervention in the burning issue of compulsory service in 1910, when he was on the other side to Roberts. The latter, indignant at the action of his protégé, published a sharp retort entitled *Fallacies and Facts*, and the other proponents of compulsory service were equally incensed. As they included several influential officers, the effect on Hamilton's career was unfortunate.

In his early portrait Churchill wrote of him that 'he takes a very independent view on all subjects, sometimes with a slight bias towards or affection for their radical and democratic aspects'. This was also part of the problem. Hamilton was not alone in having important political friends, but unusual in the prewar British army in that they were usually Liberals, Churchill being among the most prominent. At a time of unparalleled rancour in British party politics, this did Hamilton no good at all.

Between 1905 and 1910 Hamilton was GOC Southern Command, and subsequently in the Mediterranean Command. His most important supporter in the army was Kitchener, but whose influence at that time did not extend far outside Egypt. By 1914 Ian Hamilton was sixty-two, aide-de-camp general to the King, his career apparently over. But at this point, in the flurry of the opening of the war, Kitchener became Secretary of State for War, and Hamilton was immediately appointed to command the Central Force in England. His association with Kitchener was very close. 'Every day, almost, I used to run in and burst into a sweat from the two blazing fires and the antics of that poor untamed bull in the china shop,' as he subsequently related. At one point Kitchener seriously considered appointing Hamilton to replace Sir John French in France, but the word reached French, and Kitchener had to disclaim the notion. But it was a significant indication of Kitchener's regard for his former Chief of Staff.

In appearance Ian Hamilton was slight, alert and eager. The fingers of his left hand were shrivelled, the result of a serious injury suffered at Majuba Hill in 1881, when he had been recommended for his first VC. His left leg had been badly injured in the Tirah Campaign and hurriedly set, with the result that it was slightly shorter than the other. His charm was formidable, and it was not for nothing that his men had called him 'old full compliments and half rations', and it had the capacity to arouse mistrust as well as affection. But his record of active service and administrative experience was without comparison among the active serving officers of the army, and it was evident that his opportunity must come. It came, under very strange and ominous circumstances, on 12 March 1915. Hamilton subsequently described the occasion, when he was summoned to Kitchener's office.

Opening the door I bade him good morning and walked up to his desk where he went on writing like a graven image. After a moment, he looked up and said in a matter-of-fact tone, 'We are sending a military force to support the Fleet now at the Dardanelles, and you are to have Command.'

Hamilton had written in *A Staff Officer's Scrap Book:*

> Are not the best moments in life those in which it is borne in to a poor mortal that some immortal has clearly designated the field of action, wherein he has only to be true to his convictions and himself, and advance confidently by word of command to the accomplishment of some pre-destined end?

It was in a spirit of exultation that Hamilton, with a hastily collected staff whom he hardly knew, left London on the evening of Friday 13 March to proceed to the Dardanelles. 'A sense of boyish enthusiasm for adventure was in the air,' one of the staff officers later recalled. They were seen off by Winston Churchill and 'a few dazed wives', and Ian Hamilton proceeded as swiftly as train and destoyer could take him to the place of battle and his destiny.

It is not possible to describe in detail the complex and controversial series of events that had initiated the naval assault on the Dardanelles. By the time that Hamilton and his eager but inexperienced staff reached the area, Admiral Carden had collapsed from exhaustion, and his successor, Vice-Admiral de Robeck, was about to launch his major assault on the Dardanelles defences.

Hamilton was a witness of that celebrated attack on 18 March. It opened propitiously, but then a series of disasters impelled de Robeck to withdraw, at the cost of three battleships sunk and three crippled. The sailors were prepared to try again, but Lieutenant-General Birdwood, commanding the Australian and New Zealand Army Corps (Anzac) who had been at the Dardanelles for several weeks, had never been confident of the chances of a naval attack alone, and Hamilton endorsed his view. On the following day he informed Kitchener:

> I am most reluctantly driven to the conclusion that the Straits are not likely to be forced by battleships as at one time seemed probable and that, if my troops are to take part, it will not take the subsidiary form antici-pated. The Army's part will not be a case of landing parties, for the destruction of forts, but rather a case of a deliberate and progressive military operation carried out in force to make good a passage for the Navy.

Kitchener replied at once:

> You know my views – that the passage of the Dardanelles must be forced, and that if large military operations on the Gallipoli Peninsula by your troops are necessary to clear the way, these operations must be undertaken

after careful consideration of the local defences, and they must be carried through.

Hamilton later described this cable as 'a peremptory instruction that he was to take the Peninsula'.

De Robeck meanwhile was shaken by the losses of 18 March and unsure of their cause. In fact the Allied ships had blundered onto an unchartered row of mines (although one, the French battleship *Bouvet*, was probably sunk by a shell in the main magazine), but this was not known at the time. Thus when Hamilton and de Robeck met on the *Queen Elizabeth* on 22 March, the soldiers were very willing to undertake a joint operation, and de Robeck's relief was manifest. In London Churchill vainly urged the resumption of the naval attack, but the decision had in fact been taken by the men on the spot. 'No formal decision to make a land attack was even recorded in the records of the Cabinet on the War Council,' as Churchill has written: '. . . the silent plunge into this vast military venture must be regarded as an extraordinary episode'.

Hamilton's problems were very formidable. As he himself said, his knowledge of the Turkish forces and the Dardanelles area was 'nil'. The forces at his disposal were scattered around the area in spectacular confusion. His one regular army division, the 29th, arrived from England hopelessly ill equipped, and detached from virtually all its matériel and supplies. The task of converting Mudros into the expedition's base was a nightmare. The administrative headquarters staff did not arrive until 11 April, there were no engineers apart from the divisional field companies, no headquarters signal company, no trench equipment of any kind, and a severe shortage of artillery and ammunition. Somehow, through desperate improvisation, some order was brought to the chaos, but the Mediterranean Expeditionary Force was a conspicuously ill prepared one for the task it confronted. On top of all this, security was non-existent. As the official Australian correspondent tartly wrote: 'The attack was heralded as few have ever been. No condition designed to proclaim it seems to have been omitted.'

Meanwhile there were strong disagreements between Hamilton's three senior commanders – Birdwood (Anzac), Sir Aylmer Hunter-Weston (29th Division), and General Paris (Royal Naval Division) – about strategy. Hamilton and his staff favoured landings at Suvla Bay and the southern tip of the Gallipoli Peninsula, near Cape Helles. Birdwood favoured landing on the Asiatic shore of the Dardanelles, and agreed with General Maxwell (GOC Egypt) that 'Gallipoli gives us no liberty of manoeuvre, you are cramped and liable to be held up and have a sort of miniature Flanders to fight.' The more Hunter-Weston considered the Helles plan, with the few small beaches available, the less he liked it. Others considered Bulair, the neck of the peninsula, to be the obvious place to attack. The answer to this argument, of course, was that it was also obvious to the Turks, and to their able German commander, Liman von Sanders.

These discussions were characterised by a sharpness that augured ill for the force. Hamilton, citing Kitchener's instructions, refused to consider the Asiatic landing and clung tenaciously to his plan to 'take a good run at the Peninsula and jump plump on – both feet together'. In the end the strategy bore tribute to Hamilton's intelligence and imagination, but also demonstrated serious weaknesses in his ability as a commander.

A major feint, by the Royal Naval Division, was to be made at Bulair to tie down Turkish forces for the first, vital, twenty-four hours. The French were to land on the Asiatic shore at Kum Kale, remain for twenty-four hours and then withdraw. Meanwhile Birdwood's Anzacs were to land on the peninsula just south of Suvla Bay and push across to Mal Tepe, a commanding hill to the north-west of Maidos, thereby cutting off the Turkish troops in the south. The main landing was to be by the 29th Division in the Helles area, on five small beaches.

This was a very ambitious plan indeed, and as events were to prove, far beyond the capacities of very brave but inexperienced troops. The essential logistical support was meagre, and Birdwood was not the only person who was perturbed by Hamilton's attitude towards these matters. Subsequently Hamilton wrote, '. . . in my mind the crux was to get my army ashore . . . Once ashore, I could hardly think Great Britain and France would not in the long run defeat Turkey . . . the problem as it presented itself to us was *how to get ashore!*'

It should be remembered that at that time no one had any indication of the quality of the Turkish soldier when well led. The experience of the Balkan wars and of certain incidents in the war before April 1915 gave rise to the assumption that the Turks would not provide serious resistance. Thus Hamilton's preoccupation with 'getting ashore' and the complete absence of plans for action after that event was not as foolish as it now appears. But the assumption of Turkish ineptitude and lack of fighting spirit was catastrophically wrong. Liman von Sanders's plans were flexible. Against the urgings of his Turkish commanders – notably an unknown young colonel, Mustafa Kemal – he decided not to establish his main efforts at the beaches, but to concentrate inland, until the British had disclosed their strategy. Von Sanders, like the British, overestimated the effects of heavy naval bombardments, and he was subsequently severely criticised by the Turks for not 'driving the British into the sea' on the first day. In the light of what happened, and the narrowness by which the British did not suffer a total defeat in the first twelve hours of the campaign, these criticisms of von Sanders's strategy seem sound. But von Sanders, like Hamilton, was operating in new military territory, and he, too, was unsure of the quality of his army.

The Gallipoli landings of 25 April have been described so often that a brief summary is sufficient. Birdwood's fiery Anzacs landed more than a mile to the north of their intended position in very wild and difficult country. For several hours there was little organised resistance and some parties moved well inland. By the afternoon however the situation had completely changed. Kemal threw in every unit he could find, and the Turks fought with a fury that was wholly unexpected. By the evening the exhausted Anzacs were clinging to fragments of cliff and gully, and Birdwood was agitatedly advising evacuation.

In the south, three of the five landings were virtually uncontested. At another – W Beach – resistance was much stronger, but eventually overcome. But at V Beach, the principal landing place, the British were bloodily repulsed.

Throughout this tumultuous day Hamilton exercised no command, in spite of the advantage of being on the *Queen Elizabeth* and being in a uniquely good position to discover what the situation was. In fact to the staff officers on the battleship it was extremely difficult to discover what was going on. But it was not Hamilton's way to intervene. Not until the evening, when he ordered Birdwood to hold on at Anzac, did he make any decisive move – and that only in response to a direct request. The British and Dominion forces had suffered undreamed-of casualties, were exhausted and bewildered, and the situation on both fronts was critical.

Somehow, by an extraordinary and indeed epic performance by the troops, the two precarious positions were established and enlarged in the following two weeks – but at heavy cost. The arrangements for handling the wounded completely broke down, and much unnecessary suffering and loss of lives resulted. The lack of attention given to logistics in the planning was now exacting a heavy toll, and the inaccuracy of the few maps that the British possessed was only too evident. None the less they were determined to advance. It was only after the failure of what was subsequently called the First Battle of Krithia that even Hamilton's confidence began to falter, and he asked Kitchener for reinforcements. By this time the British and Anzacs had suffered more than eight thousand casualties, and the soldiers were, temporarily, spent. Kitchener ordered the 42nd (East Lancashire) Territorial Division from Egypt, but it was evident that the main burden would continue to be borne by the 29th Division in the Helles area and by the Anzacs in their besieged eyrie in the north.

The glowing expectations of a swift and easy victory had vanished. Trench warfare began. Inexorably Gallipoli became the second major theatre of war for the Allies. The calls for more men, more ammunition, more guns, more equipment became increasingly insistent. With reluctance, the government had to respond. The weather became remorselessly hotter. Dysentery broke out in the army. In spite of several pitched battles on the Helles front in May and June, at heavy cost for both sides, no real progress was made. The Turkish shelling from Asia became gradually more serious. The arrival of a single German submarine and the sinking of three British warships – the *Triumph, Majestic* and *Goliath* – cleared the seas of the navy, to the consternation of the Allied troops and the joy of the Turks. It was a bitter, gruelling battle in a confined area.

Hamilton had established his headquarters on the island of Imbros, a physical separation which was – unreasonably – resented, but which detached him from the kind of overall command that he should have exercised and never did. Hunter-Weston's brutal and futile setpiece assaults at Helles were his own decisions, and were contrary to Kitchener's orders to Hamilton to wait for the new, promised reinforcements. Hamilton agreed. Writing to Kitchener on 7 June he said, 'anything like a general advance and general attack cannot be entertained at present, as, apart from munitions, the men are not equal to it'. This was only too true, but the attacks continued throughout June and July in appalling heat. The troops spoke bitterly of 'Imbros, Mudros, and Chaos'. General Cox, commanding the Indian Brigade, wrote, 'G.H.Q. became out of touch with the Army . . . The Army on the spot knew quite well that the ideas and hopes of its Commanders as expressed to them in addresses, orders, etc, were not in accordance with the facts that were being faced by them at the Front.' But until he collapsed from strain, Hunter-Weston battered away at heavy cost with unquenchable optimism, while Hamilton reluctantly acquiesced.

But by the end of June new elements had entered his calculations. Substantial reinforcements from England were on their way. And at Anzac, now secure after one of the most remarkable performances in the annals of war, daring reconnaissance to the north had ascertained that there were passable and virtually undefended routes to the Sari Bair summits. The Suvla Bay area was also very lightly defended. Gradually the attention of GHQ was drawn to this area, until its potentialities for a brilliant and decisive master stroke dominated everything.

It is still, after all these years, intensely dispiriting to relate the history of this tragically bungled operation of war. The basic idea, which emerged from Birdwood's staff, was absolutely feasible. But it was constantly expanded until it was far too large and far too ambitious, even for fresh and fit soldiers. By July the Anzacs were neither. Their spirit was indomitable, but the majority were exhausted, tense, and ill. In one week alone over one thousand cases of acute dysentery were reported at Anzac, but figures give no true indication of the extent of the epidemic. Virtually no one escaped it, and the official Australian historian has recorded how 'the great frames which had impressed beholders in Egypt now stood out gauntly'. And these troops were now expected to undertake a most complex night march, over very difficult terrain, the difficulties of which were much more severe than was realised.

It was clearly impossible to increase the Anzac garrison by more than one division, and the question arose of what was to be done with the new army corps coming from England. It was out of this problem that the plan for a landing at Suvla arose, and this project was, from the very outset, an appendage to the original plan. So, also, were other attacks at Helles and at Anzac. As in April, ambitions and optimism had outstripped resources. It was another theoretically brilliant but practically deeply flawed project.

Once again the command was divided. The Suvla landing was to be commanded by the elderly Sir Frederick Stopford, aged sixty-one, in poor health, with no experience whatever of command in the field. His instructions from Hamilton were significant:

> Your primary objective will be to secure Suvla Bay as a base for all the forces operating in the northern zone. Owing to the difficult nature of the terrain, it is possible that the attainment of this objective will, in the first instance, require the use of the whole of the troops at your disposal. Should, however, you find it possible to achieve this object with only a portion of your force, your next step will be to give as much assistance as is in your power to the G.O.C. Anzac.

Stopford himself was doubtful whether he could help Birdwood, and told Hamilton so clearly, but Hamilton did not react. For, in Hamilton's own words, 'Anzac was to deliver the knock-out blow. Helles and Suvla were complementary operations.' Security, after the lesson of April, was so rigidly enforced that very few people indeed knew of the forthcoming operations, or their objectives. Stopford had good cause for subsequent complaint about the aloof manner in which he and his staff were treated. The senior officers concerned were not briefed until 30 July, a week before a massive and deeply complicated operation. Once again the vital 'Q' staff was kept at arms' length until almost the last moment. Once again the command was divided. Once again there was no overall command. Once again the objectives were vague and grandiose. Once again communications were neglected. All the April errors were faithfully repeated, and some new ones were added for good measure.

Hamilton must bear the full responsibility for the subsequent disaster. He was showing his years, and was suffering, like everyone else, from the heat and 'the prevalent condition'. But the August plan, although not of his conception, in its final form bore all the marks of his deficiencies as a commander. The adage that in war one cannot guarantee success, one can only deserve it, holds very true in this battle. The British, again principally as the result of the valour and determination of the troops and the errors of von Sanders, very nearly won a brilliant victory. But their commanders did not deserve success, and, in the event, they did not get it.

The night march from Anzac very nearly succeeded. The diversionary assault at Lone Pine in the Anzac sector very nearly broke through the Turkish lines. The Suvla landing was almost uncontested, and while the battle raged in the hills to their right, the British clung to the shore and wilted in the fierce heat. GHQ in Imbros, its attention concentrated on Anzac, was unconcerned about Suvla. It was not until thirty-six hours after the landing that Hamilton intervened to urge Stopford forward. It was too late. The great opportunity had been lost. The Turks flung the British and New Zealanders off Sari Bair in a charge led by Kemal personally, and threw back the British advance across the Suvla Plain. By 10 August the great August offensive had failed, at dreadful cost. All that remained was aftermath.

The feeling that Hamilton had had his chance and had lost it was now pervasive in his staff and began to grow ominously in London. His constant optimism now grated on his army and the government. On 14 October he was relieved of his command and replaced by General Sir Charles Monro. Hamilton returned to England intent upon restoring his lost reputation. It was to remain his obsession for the rest of his long life.

Ian Hamilton was one of the few British commanders in the First World War for whom it is possible to feel real affection and sympathy. He was evidently a most attractive, intelligent and sensitive man. One is not at all surprised to learn that in spite of everything his armies felt deep affection and regard for him. Nor has the historian any difficulty in comprehending the emotions of his family and friends that he was a tragic victim of other people's follies and inadequacies. Many commanders have been saved by their subordinates; there is no doubt that Hamilton was often badly let down by his.

But the more one looks at the evidence, and the more one analyses his conduct of the Gallipoli campaign, the more one is struck by his fundamental inadequacies. In his letters and telegrams to Kitchener and Asquith he was notably, and fatally, inconsistent. On the one day everything is proceeding magnificently; on the next, urgent reinforcements are required for survival; and then on the third all is well again. He certainly had much to complain of in his military and political leaders; but they, too, had much to complain of in him. In the final analysis one can only conclude that he lacked that element in a commander which is so difficult to define with exactitude – that inner confidence, that basic common sense, that understanding of reality, however unpleasant it might be, and that mental and moral toughness, which separates a Slim from a Hamilton.

It is difficult to fault the judgement of the official British historian of this tragic campaign:

> The enthusiasm, self confidence, and personal courage demanded of the military commander-in-chief he possessed in full measure. But he lacked the iron will and dominating personality of a truly great commander . . . Hamilton's optimism, too, inclined him to over-confidence in battle. He left too much to his subordinates and hesitated to override their plans, even when in his opinion they were missing opportunities.

To the end he never doubted that history would vindicate him. But he was never offered another command in the field, despite many appeals. He became lieutenant of the Tower of London, was elected rector of Edinburgh

University, and wrote more books, of which *Gallipoli Diary* – not a diary at all, but subsequent recollections – was the most notable and revealing. He, died at the age of ninety-four in 1947. It had been a full and remarkable life, but the final judgement of history, that cold and unrelenting commentator, must be that given a supreme opportunity he was inadequate to its demands. It is a harsh and cold wreath to lay on the tomb of a gallant, good and brave man. But the truth is often thus.

General Mustafa Kemal (Atatürk)

Lord Kinross

Mustafa Kemal, like Alexander the Great, was a Macedonian. Unlike that other great war lord, he came of a modest middle-class family, being the son of a Turkish Customs official. Born in the cosmopolitan city of Salonika, he grew to maturity through the last disturbed decades of the declining Ottoman Empire, whose ultimate fall he was to see and indeed to precipitate.

As a twelve-year-old boy Mustafa, who already had a will of his own, insisted on being sent to a modern military secondary school, thus choosing for himself the best education available to a young Ottoman Turk at this time. Striking a heroic pose he declared to his mother: 'I was born as a soldier. I shall die as a soldier.' He might, with equal truth, have prophesied, 'I was born as a soldier. I shall die as a statesman.' For he had embarked on a career that might equally lead him into politics. At this period of turbulent change, at the turn of the century, it was the power of the army alone that could overthrow, in the name of democracy, the autocratic rule of the tyrannical Sultan Abdul Hamid.

Such was the objective of Mustafa Kemal's officer colleagues in Salonika, who had formed with revolutionary intent a Liberal Committee of Union and Progress, and became generally known as the 'Young Turks'. In 1908, under the leadership of a young major, Enver Bey, they enforced, through a *coup d'état* against Abdul Hamid, the re-establishment of a constitution for the empire, which he had abolished some thirty years earlier. Mustafa Kemal played only a minor role in the coup and in the counsels of the Young Turk administration. His revolutionary views were too advanced for Enver and his colleagues; his realistic expression of them was overbearing and brash. To get rid of him they continually posted him out of the way, to such remote stations as Tripoli in North Africa. But with the outbreak of a counter-revolution, staged by the Sultan in Istanbul, he had a chance to show his military capacities as divisional Chief of Staff in the 'Army of Liberation', which marched to the city and deposed the Sultan once and for all.

This earned for him sufficient status in the army to make his political views generally heard – if not indeed heeded. In a forthright speech to the annual party congress of the Committee of Union and Progress, he condemned the association of the army with politics. Army officers, he insisted, should be called upon to decide whether to remain in the party and resign from the army, or to remain in the army and resign from the party. Such realistic views proved unacceptable to the bulk of the delegates. But Mustafa Kemal suited his actions to his principles by withdrawing from politics and immersing himself in his military duties.

As a staff officer attached to the training command of the Third Army, he was serving a government committed to a policy of army reform. For this purpose it had called in German officers to train, re-equip and generally to renew the outdated Turkish forces. Kemal had to co-operate with these German colleagues, reluctant at first in his patriotic pride to do so, but able with his professional conscience to respect soldiery as a science, whether practised by friends or by enemies, and coming as a true soldier to respect the worth of a German Military Mission to the Turkish Army of Tomorrow.

He soon proved himself an adept instructor in infantry training, lucid and ruthless in analysis as he expounded the replacement of an old by a new tactical system. The practice of army manoeuvres in open country, discontinued by Abdul Hamid, was now revived, and these he came to plan and to lead in person, earning the praise of the German Marshal von der Göltz. Mustafa Kemal thus built up for himself a military reputation quite out of proportion to his adjutant-major's rank.

With his juniors he was strict, reprimanding them for those minor mistakes and omissions that can lead to major disasters in warfare, but inspiring in them the will to excel and consistently winning their loyal admiration. With his Turkish seniors he was often impatient, submitting to them outspoken reports in criticism of staff work and military exercises. Inclined to dismiss him as a mere theorist, who might in practice fail when it came to handling troops in battle, they removed him from his staff post and placed him in command of an infantry regiment. But he proved himself just as able to command troops in the field as to instruct officers at headquarters.

The approach of the First World War found Mustafa Kemal languishing on the fringe of it as military attaché in Bulgaria, where Enver had sent him. In August 1914 a secret alliance, aimed against Russia, was signed between Turkey and Germany. In Sofia and in letters to his comrades in Istanbul Kemal strongly opposed Turkey's entry into the war on the German side. Not merely had he a personal mistrust of the Germans, but, as a military analyst with a shrewd grasp of strategy, he doubted their professional capacity to win. If they won, they would make a mere satellite of Turkey; if they lost, Turkey would lose everything. He saw clearly that the war would be a long one. Turkey should thus for the present remain neutral, gaining time to re-establish the strength of her army, which had lately suffered severe losses in two successive Balkan wars. But if the war were to spread to the point at which Turkish involvement became inevitable, she should enter into it against

Germany and the Central Powers. In a well-reasoned official despatch to Enver, now Minister of War, he counselled in this context a possible invasion of Bulgaria which, in alliance with Austria, might otherwise expand eastwards at Turkey's expense.

But Enver was impatient for a short, sharp war leading to victory for his country and fame for himself at the side of his German confederates. Without consulting his ministerial colleagues he launched it late in October 1914, with a gratuitous naval attack upon the Russian Black Sea fleet. This provoked a declaration of war by the three Allied powers. Impulsively Enver followed this up, against German advice, with a disastrous land invasion aimed against Russia in the Caucasus, which lost him an entire army in the Asiatic winter snows. On his return he embarked on another spectacular but equally abortive offensive against the Suez Canal.

At this crucial moment in the military history of the Ottoman Empire, which called for a watchful defensive strategy, Enver emerged as no true professional commander, but a man of hot-headed illusions and dreams. Meanwhile the cool-headed professional, Mustafa Kemal, remained fretting in Sofia, a young highly trained lieutenant-colonel without a command. Though Kemal had opposed the war and regarded the Germans as his natural enemies, he was impatient as a patriot to make common cause with them as his military allies.

Eventually, early in 1915, he was appointed commander of the 19th Division, now forming with the Fifth Army at Maidos in the Gallipoli Peninsula, where an Allied offensive was seen to be imminent. His army commander was General Liman von Sanders who now headed the German Military Mission. In his initial inspection of the area to be defended, von Sanders found the Turkish forces scattered in small coastal units around the Dardanelles, 'like the frontier detachments of the good old days'. These provided means of immediate resistance to an enemy landing on the shores of the peninsula, but allowed for no reserves to check a strong and energetic advance inland. Von Sanders thus withdrew his defence force to points of danger inland, leaving only 'the most indispensable security detachments' to defend the coast itself.

This principle of holding the vertebral ridges of the peninsula and obliging the enemy to storm them on landing was one of which Kemal himself approved. But the German general, in his opinion, had carried it to hazardous lengths. He had concentrated his 19th Division in the centre of the peninsula, thence to contain any landing on the west coast in the area of Gaba Tepe, to prevent an advance across the plain to the east coast, and generally to act as a reserve, moving in any direction where the main attack might fall. This confined Kemal's defence of the coast itself to inadequate outposts, failing to allow for its peculiar features and for the vulnerability of troops landing on small beaches, even against the smallest of well-entrenched forces.

But his protest against this deficiency, jointly with that of his neighbouring divisional commander, was rejected by von Sanders. Furthermore von Sanders had so dispersed his army as to place two divisions on the Asiatic side of the straits and two more at Bulair, on the narrow neck of land to the north, leaving only two for the defence of the main peninsula, where the enemy was in fact to land. Mustafa Kemal, from his careful study of the terrain, was convinced that he would do so on the beaches around two main points – Gaba Tepe and Cape Helles, commanding the tip of the peninsula to the south of it.

Sure enough, soon after dawn on 25 April 1915 he was awoken by the sound of gunfire from the direction of Gaba Tepe, beyond the central Sari Bair ridge which was the key to the defence of the peninsula. He at once mustered his divisional forces. Informed on the telephone by his corps commander that an enemy force had climbed the heights of Ari Burnu, north of Gaba Tepe, he was ordered to send a battalion against it. This instantly awakened in Kemal the intuition of the born military commander. Here, as he sensed the situation, was no minor attack to be met by a mere battalion, but the enemy's major offensive, from the expected direction, against the key defensive ridge of the peninsula. It would call for nothing less than the engagement of his entire division. Exceeding his orders he thus marched the whole of his best infantry regiment up to the highest crest of the ridge, at Khoja Chemen Tepe. Leaving his men to rest, he walked southwards to the adjoining crest of Chunuk Bair. Here suddenly he encountered a detachment of Turkish troops fleeing back towards the crest.

'Why are you running away?' he asked them. 'Sir, the enemy,' they replied. They pointed to the hillside below, where a line of Anzac skirmishers now advanced unopposed from the beach where they had landed. When he protested: 'You cannot run away from the enemy,' they replied that they had no more ammunition. He ordered them to fix bayonets and lie down on the ground. At this the enemy too lay down. Kemal had thus gained a moment of time, which enabled him to call up at the double the men of his regiment. It was a moment that may well have been crucial to the entire Gallipoli campaign.

Kemal sent the regiment into action with an order of the day: 'I don't order you to attack, I order you to die.' As they died, he ordered up a second regiment, still on his own responsibility, to replace them. Then, now with the authority of his corps commander, he called up the remainder of his 19th Division for an all-out offensive along the entire Sari Bair front. In a day of ferocious fighting the Anzacs were slowly driven back, if not right to the sea, then at least to the confined strip of coastal spurs and ridges they had first occupied. The Turks firmly held the heights above them, which commanded the peninsula.

Mustafa Kemal, with his intuitive, cool-headed judgement, his sense of urgency and his insistent, rousing leadership had, at the start of an invasion on the lines he had predicted, saved the Turks from a defeat that might well have opened the road to Istanbul. Seeing him at his headquarters, a fellow divisional commander, the German Colonel Kannengiesser, was impressed by this 'clear-thinking, active, quiet man, who knew what he wanted. He weighed and decided everything for himself, without looking elsewhere for support or agreement to his opinions . . . His stubborn energy gave him apparently complete control, both of his troops and of himself.'

Following this and the synchronised landings around Cape Helles, three months were to elapse before the enemy, now landing strong reinforcements, launched a further offensive inland. When Kemal's corps commander consulted him as to the enemy's probable objective, he expressed the conviction that as before he would make for the Sari Bair ridge, which he still saw as the key to the peninsula. From the crest of Chunuk Bair Kemal showed him the two valleys up which the attack would most probably come. But the corps commander, with a smile, scorned such an approach as impossible. Consenting none the less to strengthen the garrison at the head of the shortest valley, he still left it, in Kemal's words, 'the most important point in our defences and the most inadequately manned'. Meanwhile, much as before, Liman von Sanders had dispersed the forces of his army over other such areas of possible attack as Bulair, the Asiatic shore and Cape Helles.

For the second time in the campaign Kemal was right where his superiors were wrong. The main objective of the British forces proved indeed to be the Sari Bair ridge. On 6 August they launched a frontal night assault up the predicted valleys and occupied the two crests of Chunuk Bair and Khoja Chemen. Though the undefended Turkish outposts were soon occupied by the Anzacs, they failed with the dawn to achieve their main objectives. This gave valuable time to Liman von Sanders, who now grasped that this was the main attack, to call up reinforcements from the outlying areas to the central front. Meanwhile a new force of some fifteen thousand British troops, mostly of Kitchener's New Army, were landing on the beaches of Suvla Bay. Meeting with little effective resistance from a mere three under-armed Turkish battalions, they advanced in a north-easterly direction to the Anafarta range farther north.

Until reinforcements could arrive the situation on the Sari Bair ridge, as Kemal saw it, was precarious. This was more especially due to divisions of command. There was confusion over Chunuk Bair, which was outside his personal authority, but on which he kept an anxious eye – now in the hands of the enemy, now partially in those of the Turks or under continuous Turkish attack. Confusion reigned everywhere on his right flank, where two divisional commanders were killed in quick succession and no command in effect existed.

Kemal, through the new group commander from Bulair, drew the attention of von Sanders, now on Anafarta, to the critical situation that thus threatened the Sari Bair ridge and to the consequent need for a unified command. To von Sanders's Chief of Staff he insisted: 'The only remedy is to put all the available troops under my command.' In reply to the ironic question, 'Won't that be too many?' Kemal replied, 'It will be too few.' In the evening the group commander informed von Sanders that his troops from Bulair were not ready to go into action that night at Anafarta as promised. Von Sanders promptly relieved him of his command, afterwards noting: 'That evening I gave the command of all the troops in the Anafarta section to Colonel Mustafa Kemal Bey, commander of the 19th Division . . . He was a leader that delighted in responsibility . . . I had full confidence in his energy.'

Kemal was thus now in control of the whole main Gallipoli front. Though he was taking over a battle already half lost through the errors and muddles of others, he was exhilarated by responsibility and determined on victory, free now to take action, knowing what action to take and fully realising the need, after too long a delay in the despatch of reinforcements, to take it quickly. He ordered an immediate attack at first light.

Success depended on a preliminary race between the Turks and their enemies for the Anafarta ridge and its summit of Tekke Tepe. Sir Ian Hamilton, the British commander, making up for time lost at Suvla, aimed at forestalling the Turks through its occupation by daybreak – even if only by a single battalion. As dawn broke it was only a single British company that arrived on the summit – to be met by a detachment of Turks pouring over it from the opposite side. The British had lost the race by a mere half-hour. As the Turks, pouring forth volleys of fire, swarmed down the hillside, the men of Kitchener's Army broke with the cry, 'The Turks are on us!' In his diary a young British officer, compared his fellow troops to 'a crowd streaming away from a football-match'. Kemal, directing the battle from a point of vantage, had routed a far stronger enemy with a single incomplete division – since his second was operating far to the left, where von Sanders had expected the main British attack. He attributed his victory to the factor of surprise. The enemy, advancing in small groups, had expected only slight skirmishes. But his own Turkish skirmishers, well co-ordinated and superior in marksmanship, had by their downhill momentum broken the enemy's morale.

So the British had been driven from the Anafarta ridge. But Sir Ian Hamilton could still gaze up in hope towards the ridge of Sari Bair. Here the crest of Chunuk Bair, tenaciously held by the Anzacs, was to Kemal still the pivot of the whole campaign. Now given a free hand by von Sanders, he transferred his two best regiments to reinforce the 18th Division in a frontal assault on it that night. This he planned to direct from the front line in person. Despite misgivings expressed by his divisional commander and other officers, he adhered to the conclusion that under a 'cool and courageous command' he could defeat the enemy by means of a sudden, surprise assault. He was embarking on a desperate gamble – a frontal attack against machine guns, artillery, and well-entrenched troops such as had hitherto generally failed. If it now failed the British forces would be in a position to occupy the whole of the Sari Bair ridge from the summit of Chunuk Bair, hence to dominate the peninsula and achieve final victory. None the less, rather than delay and thus give greater advantage to the enemy, he had to take this risk.

The initial attack, still in the dark, was to be swift but totally silent, without gunfire. Only the bayonet was to be used. The fate of the battle could depend on the surprise of the first few minutes. The hour of the attack was 4.30 am, just before it was light and his troops would be visible. As he wrote afterwards:

> Should the enemy infantry open fire with his machine-guns and should the land and naval guns open fire on our troops in our close packed formation I didn't doubt the impossibility of the attack. I ran forward at once. I encountered the Divisional Commander. Together and with those accompanying us we passed in front of the assault lines. I greeted the men and addressed them: 'Soldiers! There is no doubt that we shall defeat the enemy opposing us. But don't you hurry, let me get in front first. When you see me raise my whip all of you rush forward together!'

He raised his whip. Dense masses of Turkish soldiers with fixed bayonets and officers with drawn swords poured over the skyline 'like lions'. The British soldiers had no time even to raise their rifles. They were overwhelmed in their trenches. All thousand of them on the summit were annihilated. Sir Ian Hamilton's front line was broken. Kemal's gamble had succeeded triumphantly. Nothing could now save the Sari Bair ridge for the Anzacs.

Such was the ebb tide of the Gallipoli campaign, which led to the evacuation from the peninsula of the Allied forces.

> Seldom in history [wrote the British official historian] can the exertions of a single divisional commander have exercised, on three separate occasions, so profound an influence not only on the course of a battle, but, perhaps, on the fate of a campaign and even the destiny of a nation.

Supremely confident in his own capacities, Mustafa Kemal had never been afraid to take hazardous risks or to act regardless of orders. Competent in organisation and scrupulous in his attention to military detail, he had shown a comprehensive mastery of terrain and a keen grasp of tactical essentials. With his swift intuitive convictions as to how an enemy would act and how best to act against him, he was a commander of outstanding vision.

This extended, in human terms, to a true understanding of the men he commanded. He knew the psychology of the Turk and the dogged, fanatical fighting spirit of which he was capable once his blood was roused; and he knew how to rouse it. With the incomplete reform and all too slow modernisation of the Ottoman army, the unchanging Turkish soldier of this empire in decline, primitive still in education and training but hardy in physique and brave in spirit, had for too long been denied the inspiration of vigorous leadership. But here now in the hero of Gallipoli he had a commander of true calibre, invested with some of the magical quality of legend, for whom he was eager to fight and to die. For his men Kemal was the bearer of a charmed life, endowed with the high military virtues of skill and courage and, above all things, the divine blessing of luck.

Thanks largely to Enver's distrust of all rivals, no hero's welcome awaited the victor of Gallipoli on his return to Istanbul. Mustafa Kemal remained relatively unknown to the Turkish people. But to an increasing few among the young generation his legend gradually spread. Meanwhile Enver saw no reason to expedite his merited promotion to general or to reward him with a responsible army command. As a corps commander he was despatched out of the way to the eastern front, there to help retrieve some of the debris of Enver's own disastrous Caucasian campaign and the subsequent Russian offensive. Here, more than a year after the Gallipoli campaign, General Mustafa Kemal Pasha was given his first army command. But in March 1917 came the Russian Revolution and as the tsarist armies crumbled to pieces the Russian front was no more. Mustafa Kemal was transferred to the Syrian front to command the important Seventh Army, now forming in Aleppo

In August 1918, after a year of major Turkish losses and staff disagreements, his army was one of the three grouped to confront a final Allied offensive commanded by Allenby. This was to be a 'strategic masterpiece' in which, after a feint in the centre, he would break through the Turkish front line on the left with his infantry, then, in a series of swift encircling movements, strike with his cavalry to the rear of it. Breaking through with his main assault against the Eighth Army on the coast and achieving total surprise, his infantry drove the Turks swarming northwards in disarray, while his cavalry wheeled to cut off their retreat. In the centre the right wing of Kemal's Seventh Army was cut to pieces. But he held the remainder together and retreated eastwards towards the Jordan, seeing the vital necessity of preventing his enemy from crossing the river and thus cutting the only line of retreat for the Turkish Fourth Army on the Arab front beyond it. After a week of hazards and hardships he crossed it, thus freeing his army from the enemy's net. Thence he marched northwards, first to Damascus, which von Sanders had been forced to abandon, then north again to Rayak.

Here it became clear to Kemal that there no longer existed any authority on any front or in any unit. Only a further retreat on a major scale could save what remained of the Turkish forces. The moment had come once more to exceed his instructions. He ordered the retreat and communicated the order for his information to Liman von Sanders. He approved it and then agreed to move all surviving Turkish forces a further 120 miles northwards to Aleppo, close to the frontier between Syria and Turkey, and here to reorganise. It was now in effect Mustafa Kemal who took over the unified command of the three Turkish armies.

Thus Allenby's lightning offensive was temporarily halted, while Kemal gained a respite to collect his scattered forces and prepare for a last defence of Turkish territory. When Aleppo came under attack he withdrew from it, fighting a series of rearguard actions in which his troops were repeatedly attacked but never defeated, as he withdrew to the heights above the city, defending not Syrian territory but the soil of Turkey itself. He was still defending it when news was received of an armistice signed between Turkey and Britain on the island of Mudros. At the end of the war he remained the sole Turkish military commander without a defeat to his name.

For Mustafa Kemal this was no end but a new beginning. Undefeated in battle, he was more than ever undefeated in spirit. The soldier in him soldiered on. At Adana he formally took over from von Sanders the command of all the troops in southern Turkey, reassembled and regrouped his units, dispersed forces to stations in the interior, transferred arms and ammunition to possible centres of resistance elsewhere. Enjoining loyal officers to 'get ready, in groups, for guerrilla fighting', he sowed the idea of the recruitment of a new 'national force' after the army group's dissolution. Then he returned to Istanbul.

Here, with a group of loyal officers around him, he resolved to fight the armistice and the Allied plans for the total subjection and partition of Turkey through a movement of national resistance in Anatolia, the historic heartland of the Turkish people. Here there had been, since the armistice, a spontaneous germination of local nationalist groups and organisations. Faced with the problem of how to get there himself, he was once again blessed with 'indescribable luck'. The Allies, concerned at the breakdown of law and order in the unoccupied parts of Anatolia, which they could not control, sought the co-operation of the Turkish authorities. Their proposed solution was the despatch of an energetic young officer, with the status of inspector, to combine the civil and military elements into an organisation strong enough to restore the position. Their choice fell on Mustafa Kemal, who contrived so to draft his own instructions as to give him the command of two army corps, with direct authority over five provinces and indirect authority over five more, to which a further two were added later. Feeling 'as if a cage had been opened and as if I were a bird ready to open my wings and fly through the sky', Kemal left for Anatolia.

Just before sailing he had news that at the instance of the Supreme Council of the Peace Conference in Paris, a substantial Greek force had occupied Smyrna and its hinterland. Inflaming Turkish patriotism afresh, this gave a sudden new spark of reality to Kemal's nationalist movement. He landed at Samsun, on the Black Sea coast, on 19 May 1919, thus crossing the threshold of what has been aptly called 'a twilight zone between diplomacy, planned popular rising, guerrilla and open warfare'.

So the Kemalist Revolution was born. In the political dimension its 'Declaration of Independence' was signed up in the mountains at Amasya. A congress at Erzurum, the 'capital' of eastern Turkey, drafted a National Pact, which insisted, in terms of those principles of self-determination laid down by the peace conference, on the preservation, if necessary by force, of Turkey's existing ethnological frontiers. Its acceptance by a further congress at Sivas was followed by the formation of a representative committee, which became in effect the first revolutionary 'government'. In its name Kemal now broke off relations with the Sultan's government, which after some hesitation resigned. This led to the election of a new parliament, in Istanbul, in which Kemalist delegates formed a majority. But it was to survive for a bare two months. The Allies, carrying out a strict military occupation of Istanbul, stormed into the building where it was sitting and forced its dissolution. Immediately Mustafa Kemal, following elections, established his own parliament in Angora, the first Grand National Assembly, which under his presidency was to serve henceforward as the supreme source of political authority for the national liberation of Turkey.

Now the military dimension prevailed once again. First the Sultan, with a 'Caliph's Army' of irregulars, launched a civil war against the nationalist forces. Waged in the name of Islam in the reactionary interests of belligerent local chieftains, it amounted in effect to a widespread series of internal revolts. Their subjection was no task for regular forces, reluctant to fight their own countrymen. Thus Kemal and his fellow commanders had to recruit their own irregular bands, pitting the forces of one group of bandits against another, while seeking to ensure that even their own chosen allies did not grow powerful enough to become a threat to themselves.

But now, on top of the civil war, the nationalists were confronted with a major foreign invasion. The Supreme Council of the Allies announced the terms of the Treaty of Sèvres. These amounted to a complete break-up of the Ottoman Empire, with Turkey serving as a mere rump of an inland state, encircled by a string of foreign states and spheres of interest. They authorised the Greek forces to advance inland from Smyrna. The Turkish War of Independence began in earnest. Greatly superior in numbers and modern equipment, the Greeks hoped for a swift defeat of the sparse, ill-equipped Turkish forces in battle.

But Kemal was too shrewd a strategist to give them any such chance. 'The Greek columns', as Winston Churchill described the offensive, 'trailed along the country roads passing safely through many ugly defiles, and at their approach the Turks, under strong and sagacious leadership, vanished into the recesses of Anatolia.' In a great strategic retreat Kemal, with the military courage of the realist, first sacrificed the holy city and former Ottoman capital of Bursa. Thence his main forces retreated up a valley right to the edge of the Anatolian plateau at the railway junction of Eskishehir, there to regroup in anticipation of a further offensive in the autumn. It was launched in the direction of the railway, with some initial success. But the French and Italians took alarm at the prospect of a Greek conquest of all Anatolia and persuaded the Supreme Council that the moment had come to impose restraint. Thus the Greeks were instructed to advance no farther. Kemal, meanwhile, by his swift retreat had gained time to suppress the last of the three major irregular revolts and so to bring the civil war to a virtual end.

Now, with the Greek forces dug in over a wide area, he had a further respite in which to build up his regular army to the point at which it would be strong enough to drive the Greeks back to the coast. To obtain arms, ammunition and supplies he switched into the diplomatic dimension, with the despatch of an official mission to Soviet Russia. But as the price of such aid the Russians demanded important frontier concessions in their Armenian provinces. Firmly rejecting this demand, Kemal ordered his loyal commander in the east to march with his army into Armenia. Here in a brief campaign he recaptured Kars and Ardahan, thus restoring Turkey's original eastern frontiers. This opened the way in March 1921 for the Treaty of Moscow, in which those two notable realists, Kemal and Stalin, settled their mutual frontiers along a line that survives undisputed today. As a result Russian gold and supplies started to flow into Turkey, to the especial benefit of the new regular army that Kemal was now forming with the staunch co-operation of Ismet, a former comrade in arms who was now Chief of his General Staff.

Meanwhile the Greeks, no longer subjected to Allied restraint, united their forces for a further advance up to the plateau. It took the form of a reconnaissance in force from Bursa. They were surprised to encounter in a valley at Inönü a resolute and disciplined force, commanded by Ismet, inferior in numbers and equipment but not in leadership and fighting spirit to their own, which stubbornly defended its own territory and at the end of the day forced a Greek retreat. Here for the Greeks was the foretaste of a reviving Turkish military power, with which they would be obliged to contend henceforward.

In the summer the Greek forces – now under the command of King Constantine, the first Christian monarch to set foot in Anatolia since the Crusades – resumed their offensive. This time they planned to take Eskishehir, not by a frontal attack from the west, but by a flank attack from the south, which soon threatened to encircle the city and cut its communications with Angora. Hurrying down from Angora, Kemal at once decided to evacuate the city and ordered a general retreat. As Churchill summed up the situation: 'The Greeks had gained a strategic and tactical success; they had gained possession of the railway for the further advance; but they had not destroyed the Turkish army or any part of it.' That army was soon trekking across the long weary wastes of the Anatolian plateau until it reached a point within 50 miles of Angora, behind a great bend in the Sakarya river where Kemal had decided to stand.

Given supreme powers by his General Assembly, he made drastic requisitions throughout Anatolia to obtain equipment for his forces. He ordered the public to hand in all arms and ammunition suitable for military purposes. He commandeered from them 40 per cent of all stocks of cloth, leather, foodstuffs, oil and other specified commodities. He confiscated 10 per cent of their horse and ox carts and 20 per cent of their riding and draught animals. He made a census of all smithies and workshops and improvised others, turning them over to the forging of daggers and bayonets, and establishing a maintenance service so that no weapon should go unrepaired. Here, as Kemal saw it ahead of its time, was total war. For this effort the entire population was mobilised, including the women. Arms and supplies from every corner of Anatolia were loaded on to the long peasant ox carts, beneath loads of hay for the oxen, and were driven to the front over mountain and plateau for hundreds of miles.

The Turks had a bare three weeks in which to complete their preparations for the crucial Battle of the Sakarya, which was to last for twenty-two days and nights – by one day the longest, so Kemal claimed, in history. He had chosen a strong defensive position some forty miles before Angora at a loop in the great river, flanked by two tributaries, with an accessible railway and well enough watered country behind. The Greeks had ahead of them a ten-day trek across the Asiatic steppe in the stifling heat before encountering their enemy. Abandoning a plan to outflank the Turkish position with a detour over the plateau to the south, they turned northwards to throw bridges across the river and launch a frontal attack near the centre, where in fact the main Turkish forces were concentrated. Their positions were established on a series of hilltops, which the Greeks had to storm and occupy one after the other, against that stubborn defence at which the Turkish soldiers excelled. They changed hands several times over, often at a cost which Kemal could ill afford, since the reserves at his disposal, by contrast with those at Gallipoli, were limited, while the forces of his enemy outnumbered his own.

The climax of the battle was the fall to the Greeks, after a four-day engagement, of the key ridge of Chal Dag, enabling them to occupy positions in the lower ground beyond it. But both sides had momentarily fought themselves to a standstill. It was the Turks who held on longest and the Greeks who retreated. Their force was spent. They dug themselves in at various points, still east of the river. Would they face the hazards of a last defensive battle? Or would the retreat, covered by their artillery, become general? The answer came from Athens, which ordered a final retreat. Soon the Greek army was trailing wearily back to the rim of the plateau, evading the pursuit of the Turks, who were too exhausted to press their advantage. King Constantine, with a rash disregard of geography, had attempted for political motives a task beyond his military powers. Thanks to 'the warrior chief who led the Turks' (in Churchill's phrase), always a master of tactics and now proving himself equally a master of strategy, the Greeks, perhaps for the last time in history, had failed to found for themselves an empire in Asia.

A year was now to pass while Kemal prepared systematically for a final offensive to drive the Greeks into the sea. The fight could be renewed only when his new regular army had been strengthened and armed to the point at which he felt certain of victory. Time was on his side, for the troops were defending their own homeland in a national cause under the leadership of an inspired commander. The Greek troops on the other hand were fighting in a foreign land, under divided leadership, in a cause for which they had no great enthusiasm.

Moreover Mustafa Kemal now had allies to sustain him. Following his victory France signed with him a separate treaty of peace, handing over to the nationalists large stocks of arms, including Creusot guns, munitions and other war materials, with the implication that more might be available. Italy, who in her antagonism to Greece had from the start sold arms to the nationalists and connived with gunrunners to avoid the Allied control points, now completed the withdrawal of her forces from Anatolia to sign a similar agreement to that of the French. No regular supply of arms came from Russia as initially hoped, but consignments of roubles in sufficient quantity to finance their further purchase in Italy and elsewhere.

Meanwhile the snows melted in the mountains, the crops sprouted on the plateau and the sun hardened the ground to a point at which a successful advance by the new nationalist army became a practical venture. It was in fact hastened by a last gamble on the part of the Greeks, who transferred two divisions from Asia Minor to the Chatalja lines before Istanbul in an unsuccessful threat to occupy the city. These troop movements equalised the Turkish and Greek forces in Anatolia. Thus Kemal at once put forward the planned date of his offensive.

The keynote of his plan was surprise, first strategical, then tactical. Always ready to profit from the methods of a redoubtable enemy, he followed the example of Allenby in the Palestine campaign by first deluding the enemy as to his main point of attack. This was not to be Eskishehir to the north of their front (as Greek intelligence predicted) but Afyon, to the south, which commanded the railway to the coast at Smyrna. Over a period of a month, with the greatest possible secrecy, he moved his required forces by night from north to south, leaving only a small force before Eskishehir itself, but ordering camp fires to be lit every night to suggest a concentration of several divisions. Having thus achieved strategical surprise, his tactical plan was a dual attack on the main Greek positions with his infantry and artillery, then a cavalry sweep westwards, with a swift enveloping movement to cut the retreat of the Greek armies, just as Allenby had cut that of the Turkish armies in Palestine.

As zero hour approached he issued a battle order: 'Soldiers, your goal is the Mediterranean.' From the hilltop of Koja Tepe, early in the morning of 26 August 1922 he watched the sun rise above the horizon of the Anatolian plateau, then turned westwards, where a thunderous artillery barrage preceded his attack. Ahead of him was a broad amphitheatre of steeper and rockier hilltops, each fortified by the Greeks, each the objective of a Turkish division, to be stormed till the summit was reached. All, thanks to the achievement of surprise, were in Turkish hands by 9.30 that morning. Meanwhile the Turkish cavalry swept round to the Greek rear, harrying the enemy troops from the west and cutting the railway at a point to be known henceforward as Yildirim – otherwise Lightning – Kemal. For it had indeed been a lightning offensive. Only at two key points did the Turks meet with an effective resistance. But both were captured later in the day.

The first lines of their defence thus swiftly broken, the Greeks barely had time to man the second and third lines beyond the hills, which thus fell to the Turks in quick succession. They had evacuated Afyon with hardly a shot fired. The Turkish forces moved on, reaching the road through the valley towards Smyrna at Dumlupinar – which was to give the battle its name – while their cavalry and mobile infantry wheeled round farther to the west of them to close the line of retreat. Presently, the Greeks were surrounded but for a single escape route.

Thus within four days of the initial attack half the Greek army was annihilated or captured, with the loss of all its war material. In a retreat lasting for a week the other half, no longer a fighting force, was in headlong flight to the coast, burning villages and crops, slaughtering civilians as it fled. For this, according to the soldiers' orders, was a 'war of extermination'. Kemal entered Smyrna as a conquering hero. The first major offensive of a nation committed for a decade past to defence, had ended in triumph, the fruit of meticulous planning and a masterly concept of strategical and tactical surprise. The 'Verdun' of the Greeks had crumbled before an overwhelming force, directed unexpectedly at a single point, and to a swift exploitation of its undefended flank. Kemal had won his battle in fifteen days. 'Forgive me,' he afterwards remarked, 'one can sometimes make mathematical errors. I was one day out in my estimate.'

The conqueror had no intention of halting his operations in Smyrna. His final objective was Istanbul and the former Turkish capital of Edirne (Adrianople) in eastern Thrace. He moved his troops up the Asiatic coast of the Dardanelles towards Chanak, the frontier of the Neutral Zone, confronting the Allies with the choice between resisting and placating the nationalists. The French and the Italians withdrew. The British stood firm. Quick to exploit Allied differences Kemal made a show of force against Britain by sending a detachment of cavalry into the zone. Both Turks and British were given orders not to fire unless fired upon. There followed a game of bluff on both sides. But a divided British Cabinet took a belligerent line, drawing up an ultimatum for delivery by the British to the Turkish commander, which threatened war unless the Kemalists withdrew.

Here however was one of those occasions in history where the politicians were the warmongers and the generals the peacemongers. British General Sir Charles Harington pocketed the ultimatum and delayed its delivery, giving just the time needed at this eleventh hour for peace. Kemal accepted, in the name of his Grand National Assembly, an Allied invitation to a conference at Mundanya, on the Sea of Marmara, to discuss preliminary peace terms. An agreement was reached and signed by all parties. The Turkish War of Independence was over. Later, in the Treaty of Lausanne, the new Turkey obtained from the Allies those frontiers on which Mustafa Kemal, in his National Pact, had insisted. He had achieved the only peace settlement signed after the First World War in which one of the Central Powers gained her own terms from the Allies – moreover the only such settlement to survive the Second World War as an instrument of peace for the future.

Mustafa Kemal, a soldier and politician of genius, had through an added talent for diplomacy saved and regenerated his country. Now the statesman thus born in him was to make of it a new country, the Turkish Republic of today. By future generations of Turks he was to be justly revered and immortalised as Atatürk, Father of the Turks.

FIELD-MARSHAL ERICH VON FALKENHAYN

Alistair Horne

In contrast to the Zhukovs and Mansteins, the Macarthurs, Guderians and Montgomerys, it often seems that all too little talent was thrown up by the First World War – in comparison with the Second World War – that could claim parity with, let alone mastery over, the march of events. All too tragically frequent in 1914–18 were the instances where success seemed balanced on a razor blade and nerve failed; when a hard-won advantage would be thrown away by a lack of audacity or vision, an excess of indecision. With pitifully few exceptions one feels that the war lords of 1914–18 translated to 1939–45 (or, for that matter, to the Napoleonic Wars) would not have made the First Eleven; on the other hand there were a number of leaders of high competence who would have starred in a Second Eleven. Many of these, however – and again in sharp contrast with the Second World War – owed their ascendancy more to factors of caste than genius. In such a category, where Pétain might have been the exception, Erich von Falkenhayn was the rule. Although he came to incorporate more power than any other commander of the era during the brief period in which he was both Minister of War and Chief of the General Staff, his earlier career was neither unconventional nor even particularly interesting. Falkenhayn was born in 1861, of Junker stock. Contrary to the image sometimes held abroad, far from being wealthy, feudal landowners, the Junkers were often impoverished smallholders whose sole common asset was an aristocratic lineage leading back to the medieval Teutonic Knights. The hardship of scraping a livelihood from the poor, sandy soil of bleak eastern Germany traditionally orientated Junker sons towards a military career; while at the same time fostering the spartan habits so inherent in the Prussian army. Typically the Falkenhayns' family home was a modest farmhouse near Thorn, now deep in Polish territory, but they proudly traced their military ancestry back to the twelfth century. One among the many Falkenhayn soldiers had been a general under Frederick the Great, winning the *Pour le Mérite** at the Battle of Liegnitz.

Thus it was hardly unexpected that both Erich and his elder brother chose

---

* Prussia's highest decoration, instituted by Frederick who preferred a French title as he despised his mother tongue.

the army as their profession. Aged eleven he was already a member of the school cadet force, and eight years later he received a commission into the 91st Oldenburg Infantry regiment. At twenty-five he married, and this is about all that is known of his private life. The next year he entered the War Academy. His final report read: '. . . shows a fresh mind and clear deliberation . . . great boldness and a capacity for decisions . . .' These two last characteristics, however, were to be found notably lacking in Falkenhayn at the supreme moments in his career when they were most needed by Germany. His most sympathetic biographer finds no evidence of an above-average intellect; nor indeed of any 'lively urge' for the study of advanced military theory – a characteristic shared with both Haig and Joffre. At thirty-two Falkenhayn was promoted captain on the General Staff, and in 1896 he was posted to the German Military Mission to China. The manifest aim of the mission was to convert China into a useful military ally, like Turkey, but under protest from the nervous Russians it collapsed before it could start work. Already in China, Falkenhayn was transferred to be chief instructor at the Hankow Military School, where – says his critic Liddell Hart – instead of imposing German military ideas on his students 'he allowed the Chinese doctrine of war to gain a hold on himself'. The Boxer Rebellion broke out, and Falkenhayn was appointed to the provisional government in Tientsin. Here he displayed ruthless efficiency to restore order; demolishing part of the ancient, sacred wall of Peking to improve communications with the International Relief Force.

It was Falkenhayn's perceptive reports from China that first caught the eye of the All-Highest. In 1902 he returned to command a line battalion – at the already advanced age of forty-one and still only a major. His future hardly seemed full of promise. Then in 1906 he was appointed Chief of Staff to General von Prittwitz. Commanding an army corps at Metz, von Prittwitz was an incompetent, panicky officer who in the first days of the war was to bring the German forces in East Prussia close to total disaster. Falkenhayn saw his chance and took the running of this key corps increasingly into his own hands, leaving outsiders in no doubt as to the general's dependence on his Chief of Staff. It was at this time that Falkenhayn began to study fortress warfare and his thoughts dwelt, doubtless for the first time, upon Verdun, so close across the post-1870 frontier, which twenty years later was to provide both the apogee and ruin of his career. During the important spring manoeuvres in Alsace-Lorraine, Falkenhayn's mastery of the situation made its decisive mark on the Kaiser, with whom the key to all advancement then lay. Henceforth his rise was meteoric. By 1911 Falkenhayn, a line officer, had achieved what was as improbable as in the British army of that day – the command of a Guards regiment. The following year he was promoted major-general, again a chief of staff, and again at odds with his superior. On the verge of applying for a transfer in 1913, he received notice of his appointment as the Kaiser's Minister of War. With the possible exception of the brother officers he had leapfrogged, no one was more surprised than Falkenhayn.

He filled the post efficiently, pressed a recalcitrant Parliament hard for the creation of three new army corps before the avalanche descended, and stood up for the ritual of duelling as vital to the 'honour of the army'. His administration undoubtedly contributed to the excellence of the German war machine as it entered the war in 1914. In the early war days, well before the Marne, Falkenhayn was one of the rare officers on either side to foresee a long war, predicting to his staff: '. . . a struggle for life or death . . . will last at least one-and-a-half years.' By the end of August he was already expressing serious doubts at the way the offensive in France was being conducted; noting especially the fatal tampering with the Schlieffen Plan that had weakened the right wing. After visiting the battlefields on 2 September, three days before Joffre's historic turn-about on the Marne, he commented with pessimistic insight: 'This is not a won battle, it is a withdrawal according to plan. Show me the booty or the prisoners.' The following day his diary entry reads: 'Impressed again on Moltke . . . the necessity of occupying the north coast and also of halting for rest on the Marne.' Here again Falkenhayn showed commendable strategic foresight. In those chaotic early autumn weeks before the western front stabilised, the British had evacuated the Channel ports as far west as Le Havre. Their seizure then would have presented no great difficulty to the Germans, and might have decisively affected the future conduct of the war.

The French counter-attacked on the Marne. The Schlieffen Plan had failed, and so had the nerve of its executor, von Moltke. A new Chief of Staff had to be found. Hindenburg, hammer of the Russians, was the popular choice; but it would have taken several days for him to arrive at GHQ from the east. Falkenhayn was on the spot, and always close to the ear of the Kaiser. So on 14 September 1914 the ultimate plum fell in Falkenhayn's lap. For nearly six crucial months he also retained his old post; which by 1939–45 standards was as remarkable as if Alanbrooke had combined the offices of CIGS and Minister of War, as well as most of the functions of Minister of Defence. Although the Kaiser still involved himself in the running of the war to a greater extent than would be permitted under the Hindenburg-Ludendorff regime, Falkenhayn thus held far wider executive powers than any Allied leader, encompassing more than just the conduct of war by land. Yet his experience of command and actual battle conditions was even more remote than Joffre's. At the time of his appointment he was a mere fifty-three, younger than all his subordinate army commanders (save the hereditary Crown Prince) and junior to most of the corps commanders; a fact that was to multiply the number of enemies of a man who in any case cultivated few enough friends.

For Falkenhayn was an exceptionally cold and withdrawn personality, one of the most inscrutable of the whole war and about whom less is known than of any other commander. One of his (German) biographers dubbed him 'The

Lonely Warlord'; he had no intimates, no confidantes, no coterie and none of the popular appeal of Hindenburg, so that when at last his influence over the Kaiser began to wane, he was finished. He seldom revealed his true intentions to anyone, and even wrote his memoirs in an icily impersonal third person, infused with a certain amount of *ex post facto* fudging; all of which renders the more difficult any evaluation of his quality as a supreme war lord. If he shared his thoughts with, or consulted, anyone, it was probably the obstinate and slow-thinking Chief of Operations, Colonel Tappen, whose biting sarcasm matched Falkenhayn's and of whom a colleague wrote 'seldom was an officer so hated by his subordinates as he'. Falkenhayn's own capacity for hard work was exceptional. At his desk early each morning, by the daily 11 am conference with the Kaiser he had already received and analysed the reports of the army commanders and various other authorities. Following his session with the Kaiser, he lunched; eating and drinking with utmost frugality, invariably at a *Stammtisch* with the same clique of GHQ staff officers (including Tappen). The same was repeated in the evening, after which Falkenhayn – one of those fortunate beings able to exist on little sleep – worked late into the night, in sharp contrast to the habits of his opposite number, the portly and never-to-be-disturbed-at-night Joffre. He would frequently telephone corps commanders in the small hours, and – as a consequence of his innate misprision of his fellows – habitually took too much detail upon his own shoulders.

The great Moltke once commented: 'There are war lords who need no counsel, who evaluate things themselves and decide . . . But these are stars of the first order, which are barely produced once in a hundred years . . .' Falkenhayn was certainly not such a 'star', and his reluctance to delegate was a failing that, in the view of even his least censorious biographer, was to erode his powers of resistance when a time of serious crisis arrived. It may also have been a contributory factor in a much more fundamental, and disastrous, weakness: his inability to concentrate wholeheartedly on a single objective, about which more will be said later.

Falkenhayn's aversion to exposure led to there being few portraits or photographs of him. But those that do exist reveal, at first sight, the typical Prussian general; close-cropped hair, well-bred nose, features vigorous and stern, eyes that flash with a hard intelligence and imply a capacity for ruthlessness. But the mouth, though partly concealed under the aggressive military moustache, and the sensitive, dimpled chin alter the picture. They are those not of a determined leader, a man of action, but of an indecisive, introversive man of thought. Here lay the vital key to Falkenhayn's character. The ruthlessness was there all right; it was he who was to sanction the first use of gas at Ypres, and to propose unrestricted submarine warfare and promiscuous bombing in reprisal for Allied air raids. He had a Junker's contempt for the press, Parliament, and the 'masses', and casualty lists moved him even less than either Haig or Joffre. Yet his ruthlessness lacked the tenacious singlemindedness of a Ludendorff; too often indecision and excessive prudence were to turn his successes into only half-successes. The disgraced Moltke had assessed perceptively the flaws in his successor's character, writing to the Kaiser in January 1915 that Falkenhayn posed 'a serious danger for the Fatherland . . . Despite an apparently strong will . . . [he] does not possess the inner forces of spirit and soul to draft and carry through operations of great scope . . .' By then however the All-Highest was thoroughly under the Falkenhayn spell, and Moltke received the coldest of imperial rebuffs.

The two salient characteristics of Falkenhayn – indecision and an almost pathological secretiveness – were to bring heartbreaking tragedy to both France and Germany at Verdun and eventually to play a vital part in losing the war for the Central Powers.

The hand Falkenhayn inherited from the younger Moltke comprised a General Staff badly shaken by the collapse of its sacred blueprint, the Schlieffen Plan (for which no alternative contingency had ever been considered), but at the same time an army undefeated, tired but still lusting for offensive action, and baffled as to why it had been put into reverse on the Marne. He had little time to evolve a new strategy. By the autumn of 1914 the Allied war machine, however, after Hindenburg's triumph at Tannenberg and France's appalling casualties of nine hundred thousand in the Battle of the Frontiers, with a British mass army to replace them still a distant mirage, was in far worse shape. A German Napoleon might have been tempted to follow up with one sledgehammer blow to knock out one or other adversary, either to east or west. Falkenhayn however decided upon a more prudent policy of assuring the security of all fronts by means of disconnected, limited offensives. He attacked first at Ypres in October – after Germany had lost her chance of an easy grab of the Channel ports, the 'race for the sea' had ended in a draw, and the western front had ossified. The German protagonists of the offensive *à outrance* criticise Falkenhayn for not throwing into the Ypres battle tough, seasoned troops that could have been switched from the stagnant Lorraine front; instead he deployed largely raw units, suffered heavy losses, and then halted when the British were within an inch of breaking. He struck again at Ypres in spring 1915, this time using chlorine for the first time. But even once the shock of the gas cloud had torn a great hole in the British line, Falkenhayn was not prepared to risk a follow-up, thereby squandering the surprise value of a hideous but novel 'secret weapon'.

Falkenhayn was a dedicated 'westerner'; meaning that like Haig and Joffre he was convinced the war could be decided only on the western front. He considered that even if Russia were knocked out of the war, the Western Allies would never give up the struggle. But he did not believe – and this is where he came into sharp disagreement with Hindenburg/Ludendorff – that Russia *could* be defeated in one brutal campaign. Instead he saw the Central Powers, like Napoleon (whose campaigns he was fond of citing, though he seems to have been more impressed by Napoleon's failures than his successes), getting fatally bogged down in the vastness of Russia. Like Napoleon, also, he fixedly regarded Britain as Germany's most dangerous enemy. Yet for all his conviction of the priority of the western front, paradoxically it was in the east that he attacked throughout 1915, standing on the defensive (with the exception of the Second Ypres) in France. The reason for this lay in the powerful combination of pressures exerted on him by the Austro-Hungarian high command, under Field-Marshal Conrad von Hötzendorf, and Hindenburg/Ludendorff in command of the German *Oberost*.

Most immediate, in the autumn of 1914, was the plight of the Austrians who had been hammered back deep into Galicia by the Russians. Ugly rumours circulated about an Austrian withdrawal behind the Danube, and going so far as to suggest the possibility of a separate peace. At the same time *Oberost* was stressing the continued Russian threat to German territory in East Prussia, and begging for a pre-emptive winter offensive to hamstring the Russian hordes. Falkenhayn claims not to have been over-impressed by the Austrian alarums, yet the fact that he yielded – against his better judgement – to theirs and *Oberost*'s clamour seems to suggest a certain lack of will.

So, halfheartedly, Falkenhayn agreed to attack south-eastwards on Lodz starting in November, followed a couple of months later by a thrust north-eastwards from the Carpathians by Conrad's Austrians, bolstered by German divisions; the whole operation to be under the supreme command of Hindenburg. The immediate consequence was to draw four army corps from the west at a time when success at Ypres may have been a hairsbreadth away; while Ludendorff was left grumbling that Falkenhayn dribbled him forces inadequate for anything more than a local, tactical victory. Thus Germany – for whom time was always on the other side – gained only a half decision on both fronts, a pattern that was to repeat itself throughout 1915. The one supreme advantage of the Central Powers – interior lines of communication – was squandered and abused by Falkenhayn's policy of shuttling troops back and forth from east and west, not to concentrate for an all-out superiority, but for an unco-ordinated jab here and there.

The Hindenburg/Ludendorff blueprint for victory in the east was a gigantic Cannae-style operation that would slice deep into the great enemy bulge in Poland, trapping and annihilating the Russian armies there. Once again, acceding to joint pressure from *Oberost* and the Austrians a reluctant Falkenhayn committed himself to a fresh eastern offensive in May 1915 – but, again, restricting it to limited objectives. Attacking to a plan drafted by Major-General von Seeckt, the genius who was to reconstruct the post-1918 *Reichswehr*, Mackensen's Austro-German force smashed through the Russian lines at Gorlice-Tarnów. In a few days two Russian armies had been shattered, and there began a rout rather than a withdrawal that came close to total disaster. But by early June Falkenhayn was already contemplating a halt to the triumphant offensive, because of aggressive Allied noiscs in the west. He allowed it to continue into August, however; then dropped the guillotine so as to be able to open up yet another sideshow against Serbia and meet the impending French offensive in Champagne-Artois.*

All year Ludendorff had been chafing to launch his deep, deciding thrust through Vilna in the north; in the autumn of 1915 his wish was granted, but only as an independent, limited operation. Thus (so claim the 'easterner' disciples of Hindenburg/Ludendorff) the battered bulk of the Russian armies was enabled to escape through the jaws of the trap. By December the balance for the year in the east comprised the conquest of all Poland, an amazing advance by First World War standards, and a million and a half casualties inflicted by September alone. The Russian steamroller would never again seriously threaten the Germans, and the revolution of 1917 was brought a large stride closer; yet militarily by his half-measures Falkenhayn had 'scotch'd the snake, not killed it'. There was one fight left in the Russian army, and this would provide the undoing of Falkenhayn's greatest ambition, at Verdun the following year.

Out of all the wrangles between 'westerners' and 'easterners' during 1915, one factor was to emerge with a disastrous bearing on the future of the war for the Central Powers. This was the rooted antipathy between the Austrian and German Chiefs of Staff, for which Falkenhayn must take a large share of the blame. Theirs was the fundamental incompatibility of the northern and southern German. Conrad, 'small and elegant, almost girlish in figure', was typical of the Austrian aristocracy of the period. He had been fourteen at the time of the catastrophic defeat of Sadowa at the hands of Bismarck's Prussia in 1866, and that humiliation never ceased to rankle; Falkenhayn, in his whole bearing, was a constant reminder of it; he had once been heard through closed doors, pounding the table and shouting at the Archduke Karl, the Habsburg heir: 'What is your Imperial Highness thinking of? Whom do you think you have in front of you? I am an experienced *Prussian* General!' This was perhaps hardly the best way of getting results from a touchy ally, and even Falkenhayn's own entourage warned him from time to time that he ought to adopt a more conciliatory attitude towards the Austrian commanders. He merely replied, 'One must be tough with the Austrians if one wishes to prevail,' and made little effort to hide his low opinion of the military prowess of their forces. This was particularly intolerable to Conrad who – one of the rare instances in the First World War where a war lord was actually *better* than the troops he commanded – was probably a superior strategist to the Prussian. It was certainly his vision, not Falkenhayn's, that had proved right over the Gorlice–Tarnów offensive of 1915. In his dislike of Conrad and

---

* When the French blow fell, hard a test as it was for German defensive endurance, it had never any prospect of a breakthrough; and, even if it had, it would have regained nothing more than a few miles of French soil without endangering the basic security of the German position in the west. But this was a risk Falkenhayn was never prepared to take.

his exaggerated instinct for secrecy, Falkenhayn took increasingly to hiding his intentions from the Austrian; while Conrad retaliated by sullenly and silently going ahead with his own plans. Without a 'supremo', any joint council of war, or even the degree of co-operation the bickering Allies achieved under Joffre, the lack of liaison between the Central Powers seemed as disaster-prone as it was incredible.

The final, fateful rift occurred in the autumn of 1915 when Falkenhayn launched a fresh campaign to finish off Serbia and secure the land route to Germany's new Turkish ally. The Austrians had been fighting ineptly against the Serbs since the beginning of the war, and characteristically Falkenhayn now insisted that all their forces there should be placed under a German, von Mackensen. When Conrad attempted to exert some influence over operations, he was coldly informed that Mackensen could receive orders only from Falkenhayn. As soon as Serbia was subjected, Conrad announced tersely that he was going on alone to liquidate Montenegro, removing the Austrian Third Army from under Mackensen for that purpose. There were doubtless territorial as well as strategic motives behind the Austrian move, and – livid with rage – Falkenhayn accused Conrad of 'a breach of solemn promises', breaking off all personal relations with him. After an efficient conquest of Montenegro's mountain fortress, Conrad wrote Falkenhayn a conciliatory letter. He received no acknowledgement. He also wrote proposing a co-ordinated blow to knock out Italy in 1916; this received a cold, almost insulting, reply. Meanwhile Falkenhayn was drafting his own plans for Verdun – incredibly enough without breathing any word to his major ally about what was to be Germany's principal effort for 1916.

With 1915 ended perhaps the most successful year of the war for German arms, and the least for the Allies. The costly Allied failures in the west had been matched by even worse disasters in the east. Serbia had been crushed; the link with Turkey and Bulgaria assured; Italy sealed off south of the Alps; and British naval power thwarted at Gallipoli. Falkenhayn's achievements in reorganising Germany's war machine after the Marne had been prodigious, and in preparing it for a long war of attrition he had laid the basis for her war programme to continue long after his own departure. He pushed forward vigorously the supply of raw materials and munitions, multiplied the network of military railways, and developed field entrenchment to the highest level of any combatant. He had kept the enemy from the door everywhere, making Germany secure on all her fronts and creating a veritable '*Festung Europa*'. But, in the words of Frederick the Great, 'He who tries to defend everything defends nothing!' Never again would the prospects seem so bright for Germany; in declining to accept the risk of an all-out offensive in 1915 Falkenhayn had perhaps thrown away one of her best hopes of winning the war. For it was all very well to create a solid defensive position, but in the long run time was bound to run against Germany. Like Japan in 1941, or today's Israel, she had to grab a short, sharp victory, or face ultimate defeat.

Falkenhayn unquestioningly appreciated the dangers, and in order to pursue the decisive victory Germany required he now produced a novel solution – a third way to the established alternatives of breakthrough or attrition; it was to be called 'bleeding-white'. By December 1915 he at least felt secure enough to plan his long-cherished onslaught in the west. In a lengthy memorandum to the Kaiser he began by admitting that 'the Russian armies have not been completely overthrown', but that an advance deeper into Russia led nowhere. France had been 'weakened almost to the limits of endurance'; Britain however remained untouched – and untouchable – and, as in the Napoleonic Wars, she would be able to mount successive coalitions against Germany until their superiority of manpower finally crushed her. Britain was therefore the principal enemy, but how could she be got at? First of all, declared Falkenhayn, there must be unrestricted submarine warfare in 1916, regardless of the danger of bringing America into the war. But, principally, the objective for 1916 was to have 'England's best sword knocked out of her hand' on the Continent. This 'best sword' was the French army, and to break it, Falkenhayn continued:

> . . . the uncertain method of a mass breakthrough, in any case beyond our means, is unnecessary. We can probable do enough for our purposes *with limited resources*.* Within our reach behind the French sector of the Western front there are objectives for the retention of which the French General Staff would be compelled to throw in every man they have. If they do so *the forces of France will bleed to death** – as there can be no question of a voluntary withdrawal – whether we reach our goal or not . . .

The 'objective' selected by Falkenhayn was Verdun, which after the Marne had been left precariously perched at the tip of a long salient, just 150 miles east of Paris. His memorandum made military history, for never before had a war lord proposed to vanquish an enemy by gradually bleeding him to death, and typical of Falkenhayn was his aspiration to achieve this 'with limited resources'. The Kaiser was swiftly won over to the project; not least because of the fact that Falkenhayn had chosen the Fifth Army commanded by his heir, the Crown Prince, for the victorious operation.

Just as Falkenhayn never informed Conrad about the coming Verdun offensive, so also he deliberately concealed from the Crown Prince and Chief of Staff von Knobelsdorf that it was not his intention actually to capture Verdun. Thus the Fifth Army embarked on the fearful operation always in the firm belief that its objective was to seize the prize of the world's most powerful fortress. Though there may have been considerations of the assault troops' morale involved, it was nevertheless an extraordinary act of deception. A second point of discord between Falkenhayn and the Fifth Army leaders arose over the frontage of the attack; they wanted to strike along both banks of the Meuse simultaneously, but Falkenhayn limited the offensive to the

* Author's italics.

right bank only, with a modest outlay of no more than nine divisions, while keeping reserves strictly under his own control. This was yet another disastrous half-measure, which would cost the Germans dear. The attacking divisions would, however, be backed by the most powerful concentration of artillery ever assembled; 1220 guns, most of them heavies and super-heavies, and deployed along a front of only 8 miles. Thus the French infantry, as they moved up to defend the threatened salient, would be ground to pieces from three sides – or literally – 'bled white'.

The German preparations moved with remarkable speed and (Falkenhayn's forte) secrecy, and the attack began on 21 February 1916. The French defences were devastated by the intensity of the shelling; an intensity that would continue with little let-up for the ten months that the battle continued, bringing Verdun the evil reputation as war's most hellish battlefield. Although on paper it was the world's strongest fortress, in fact Verdun had been resting on its laurels far too long; it was defended by a paucity of first-rate troops and its powerful forts denuded of most of their guns. Falkenhayn (and indeed the whole world) overrated its actual strength, and an early collapse at Verdun was probably prevented only by bad weather causing a week's postponement of the German attack. As it was, by the fifth day of the onslaught, with the fall of the supposedly impregnable Fort Douaumont, the way to Verdun seemed wide open. The French high command was in despair. But at the crucial moment of success Falkenhayn held back essential reserves from the Crown Prince. The German push began to bog down, with casualties soaring as a result of French artillery flanking fire from the left bank. Very reluctantly Falkenhayn was persuaded (too late) to mount a clearing operation there. The deadly escalation of Verdun now began.

By the beginning of April, the French had lost 90,000 men, but the attackers had also lost 82,000; by 1 May respective totals had reached 133,000 and 120,000 and the parity was growing. The 'limited' operation had got out of hand, with the Germans being 'bled-white' almost as fast as the French. By May the Crown Prince favoured calling a halt, and Falkenhayn – prey to his habitual indecision – was already wavering, with only Knobelsdorf determined to continue to the bitter end. Though any strategic significance had long since passed out of sight, still the battle ground on, seeming to assume a kind of demonic will of its own. A torrid June brought the deadliest phase so far, with the German tide lapping over Fort Vaux. There were signs that the French might be on the verge of breaking when suddenly relief came – from the least expected quarter, the Russian army, briefly recovered from its terrible mauling of the previous year.

On 4 June General Brusilov, Russia's ablest commander, launched a forty-division attack against the Austrians in Galicia, at the weakest point of the line. Taken by surprise the Austrian front collapsed like the walls of Jericho, and a furious Falkenhayn was forced to transfer troops badly needed at Verdun to shore up his sagging ally. But the Austrian débâcle was largely

Falkenhayn's own fault, the fruit of his bad relations with Conrad, and, specifically, the consequence of his keeping him in the dark over Verdun. For in retaliation Conrad had thinned out the defences opposite Brusilov – without telling Fàlkenhayn – so as to mount his own offensive against the Italians on the Asiago.

On 1 July the Franco-British push on the Somme began, and Verdun was definitively saved; although the high-water mark, at Fort Souville within sight of the city, was not in fact reached until 11 July, with the aid of phosgene gas. From that date the German tide ebbed rapidly; the French had lost over 275,000 men, the attackers close on a quarter of a million.

At Verdun there also died Germany's last good chance of outright victory. Prince Max of Baden writes: '. . . the campaign of 1916 ended in bitter disillusionment all round . . . The word deadlock was on every lip.' Falkenhayn's 'bleeding-white' experiment had proved a disastrous and heartbreaking failure. Yet given Germany's endemic inferiority in manpower, the strategic concept of Verdun was not totally misconceived; if only Falkenhayn had made a wholehearted effort there and not just another of his 'limited objectives'. Had the Crown Prince been given the reserves he required, at the right moment, and been allowed to attack simultaneously on both banks, it was quite possible that he might have carried Verdun on the first – or at least the second – rush, thereby inflicting a psychological defeat of major proportions. But beyond this it would have forced the French high command, if it were to remain true to its diehard principle of never ceding an inch of territory, to throw in reserves (under much worse circumstances) to regain the key fortress. That might have made the grim 'bleeding-white' process all the easier, and less costly, for the Germans.

As a fundamental error, Falkenhayn's holding back of the reserve divisions, to meet some undefined contingency elsewhere, has been likened to Moltke's fatal tampering with the Schlieffen Plan. In Falkenhayn's defence, however, it could be said that Verdun *did* 'bleed white' the French army, as was to be demonstrated by the mutinies of the following year; on the other hand it bled almost equally the German army, which in the long run could not afford this kind of attrition. It could also be said that Verdun materially lessened the shock of the Franco-British 'Big Push' on the Somme. But this was at best a defensive success, whereas the capture of Verdun any time between February and July 1916 would have far outweighed any realistic French victory on the Somme. On the other hand, claims Max of Baden: '. . . the capture of St. Petersburg would have been an easy task compared with our efforts before Verdun. It would have . . . knocked our eastern enemies out of the fight.'

On 27 August Rumania declared war. With his failure at Verdun, coupled with his inability now to frighten Rumania from joining in the war, Falkenhayn's favour had at last run out with the Kaiser. The following day Hindenburg was summoned to GHQ and Falkenhayn tendered his resignation. Few, either in Vienna or before Verdun, mourned his departure. Declining the consolation prize of the ambassadorship in Constantinople, Falkenhayn was given command of the Ninth Army in Rumania. It was his first battle command and he acquitted himself with distinction. In terms of equipment and fighting ability it has to be admitted that the Rumanians were no match for seasoned German troops; their geography was against them and they had missed the boat by delaying their entry into the war. Nevertheless they possessed a three-to-one superiority in men, and the campaign that routed them was a masterly one. Prepared by Falkenhayn before his fall, it was developed and executed by Hindenburg/Ludendorff, while Falkenhayn led its most successful component.

The Rumanians opened the war by pushing westwards through the Carpathian Mountains to seize the enticingly rich plains of Transylvania. But once their main forces were committed there, Mackensen fell upon the Rumanian rear on the Danube front, thrusting eastward into the Dodrudja. The Rumanians were forced to rush units south from Transylvania, where they were then vigorously attacked by Falkenhayn at Hermannstadt and Kronstadt at the beginning of October. They fell back resolutely into the mountains, however, and it looked as if they might be able to hold the key passes until these were blocked by snow. By skilful marching and counter-marching Falkenhayn probed one pass after another, and finally concentrated all on forcing the Vulkan Pass just before the snows would have necessitated a spring campaign. On 5 December he entered Bucharest and the war was over shortly thereafter. If the Rumanian campaign (one of the most neglected of the First World War) was to prove anything, it was that with ingenious leadership a war of movement was still possible even with First World War limitations; it also proved that on a second-rank front Falkenhayn was a first-rate commander!

After Rumania, Falkenhayn was despatched to Turkey – a country that had long commanded his fancy – to reorganise its army and, specifically, to recapture Baghdad. But he seems already to have been a spent man. After Verdun his hair had turned white, and the plight of the Turks by the summer of 1917 was extreme. An extensive reconnaissance persuaded Falkenhayn that the Turks had not the capacity for a renewed offensive in Mesopotamia. Instead he turned his eyes towards Palestine, arriving as Allenby opened his triumphant march on Jerusalem. Falkenhayn's growing pessimism is reflected in a letter of 27 August: 'If only I knew how I could get away from here decently, ie. without damaging Germany's interests, I should long ago have headed for home.'

Army Group F was notably lacking in harmony, and Falkenhayn seems to have failed to understand local conditions or the psychology of the Turkish soldier. He was deceived and out-manoeuvred by Allenby at Beersheba, so that when the decisive British blow fell on 6 November he had no reserves left to meet it. Jerusalem was captured, and after an ill-conceived effort to retake it Falkenhayn was replaced by Liman von Sanders. He ended the war in an unimportant garrison post in revolutionary Russia. His health deteriorated, he was afflicted by constant insomnia, and in April 1922 he died near Potsdam aged only sixty-one.

His subordinate at Verdun and staunch protagonist, General von Zwehl, says in his summing up of Falkenhayn: 'Only a star of the very first order, a warlord and statesman united in one person . . . could have saved Germany.' He admits that Falkenhayn was not such a star. Yet, especially as an organiser, he rendered Germany inestimable services in 1915. At his best, as was shown during the Rumanian campaign, he was a highly competent battle commander. He had the rare insight, at an early stage, to prepare Germany for a long war, and the realism to comprehend her weakness in it. It was a realism with serious flaws in it, however; it did not enable Falkenhayn to grasp the essential fact that Germany was bound to lose a protracted defensive war; at the same time, up to the day of his death, he continued to deceive himself (and the German people) as to the true ratio of the losses at Verdun.

The consequences of Falkenhayn's most fatal defects, his secretiveness and indecision, have been amply traced. In the words of Colonel Bauer: '. . . his decisions were half measures and he wavered even over these. He would probably have made a great statesman, diplomat or parliamentarian and was least of all qualified to command in the field . . .' This last was perhaps unduly harsh; for Bauer was an out-and-out Ludendorff man. Perhaps the fairest summing up of the man who for over a key period held in his hands such a vast combination of powers comes from Liddell Hart: 'Like Napoleon's opponents he saw "too many things at once", and above all saw the enemy's strength too clearly . . . [he] ruined his country by a refusal to take calculated risks. Limitation of risks led to liquidation.'

Marshal Ferdinand Foch

General André Beaufre

Marshal Foch, indisputable victor of the Battle of France in 1918, had been an efficient operator during successive battles on the western front from 1914 onwards. In 1918 he reached a well-deserved apotheosis: Supreme Commander-in-Chief of the Allied armies, Marshal of France and of Poland, British Field-Marshal and voted by the French Parliament to have 'deserved well of his country'.

Since then his outstanding reputation has become somewhat blurred, first because the frightful memories of the First World War have faded and secondly as a result of the controversy concerning the conduct of the war by the French high command and even the nature of the victory of 1918. Today more than fifty years after the great drama, a fairer appreciation can be made of events which for a time governed the destiny of Europe, also of the men who conducted this gigantic struggle. In the process justice will surely be done to that generation of remarkable leaders, Ferdinand Foch among them, who had to resolve the problem with which they were faced through an unforeseen evolution in the art of warfare and its accompanying surprises. In 1914 their evaluation of this evolution was largely faulty despite profound and intense study of the problem, as illustrated by the fact that Foch's prewar writings were considerable. The generals made mistakes, due largely to inexperience of war with modern weapons but also to an exaggerated reverence for Napoleonic tradition and the theories of Clausewitz. But their mistakes were no greater than those which the Germans were to make.

The two sides who were about to confront each other with doctrines generally similar and therefore equally mistaken, both had to invent recipes to meet the new conditions. Four years of struggle and groping were necessary to find solutions that worked. Step by step the two sides made the essential progress. At one moment in 1918 it looked as if Ludendorff had found the answer. But his prescription was still imperfect. At this crucial moment it was left to Foch to foresee and to conduct the type of battle best suited to the requirements of the time. Here lies his indisputable and glorious achievement. It was the culmination of a lifetime's study and thought, of four years of fighting during which his exceptional strength of character was formed. My purpose in this chapter is to bring to life this slow progress to maturity leading up to the final triumph.

Foch was born in Tarbes in 1851; by tradition his family were civil servants. He went to the Jesuit College in St Étienne, where he worked hard. His bent was towards mathematics and so he was entered for the École Polytechnique, going to the Jesuit College in Metz to study for it. Here he was overtaken by the Franco-Prussian War of 1870. He enlisted in the infantry and, when the armistice was signed, returned to his college in Metz, now in occupied France and soon to be annexed to the new German Reich. In 1871 however he was accepted by the Polytechnique, but was posted to the artillery before the end of his two-year course owing to the shortage of junior officers resulting from the war. Seven years later he had become captain in a regiment in Rennes and married Mlle Bienvenue, who brought with her an old country house in Brittany where he spent every holiday for the rest of his life. In 1885, at the age of thirty-four, he entered the Staff College, emerging very high on the list two years later. As a result in 1895, at the age of forty-four, he was posted to the Staff College as instructor.

This stage of his career was decisive both for him and for France. Foch emerged as the most original military thinker of his generation and his influence grew as time went on. As Liddell Hart says in his book *Reputations*, after 1870 all French military writers were searching for the secret of Napoleon's victories as if it were the philosopher's stone. Hitherto all had concentrated on the material aspects – the science of movement, geometric formations or geography. Foch on the other hand, temperamentally constituted as he was, perceived the overriding importance of the psychological side. War, he said, was a terrifying gripping drama and the issue would be decided by psychological factors; the object of battle was not the physical destruction of the enemy's army; the true target was his morale; the side better equipped with moral courage would not yield to any idea of defeat and would impose defeat on a less determined enemy – 'a battle won is a battle we will not acknowledge to be lost'. He used striking phrases: 'war is a trial of moral strength'; 'victory always comes to those who merit it by their greater strength of will and intelligence'; 'victory resides in the will'.

Foch's most original and fundamental contribution to military thinking was this doctrine based on 'will' and psychology. But this was not the limit of his thinking. In fact he used his six years as instructor at the Staff College to study the problem of modern war.

This is a problem faced by every generation, for the evolution of warfare is continuous as new weapons, organisation and equipment make their impact; recognition of this evolution however must remain a matter of conjecture until confirmed by experience. In 1895 twenty-five years had passed since the French army had been defeated because it had had no doctrine of war adapted to the realities of life; the great problem was to work out what the right doctrine should be in the light of introduction of the quick-firing 75mm gun using smokeless powder, the development of the machine gun, use of rail transport and the advent of long-distance electrical communications.

'During six years of intense labour', to use his own expression, Foch immersed himself in study of this problem. The results were summarised in two books, *The Conduct of War* and *The Principles of War*. All the time his object was to discover and to comprehend the basic principles of tactics and of battle. From history and from minute study of concrete instances he drew a whole series of practical lessons – the requirement for information in order to penetrate the fog of war, hence the necessity for reconnaissance, for the ability to act in security under cover of an overall advanced guard, finally the necessity for action to be based on accurate information, not on preconceived ideas, From study of the 1870 battles he deduced that Moltke had won only because of the French generals' inactivity and that they had been paralysed by a mistaken defensive doctrine. The French defeat, he said, had been due not to some superior strategy by the Prussian General Staff but to the initiative and offensive spirit of lower-level commanders who had brought victory by making good the strategic errors of the higher command.

True battle, Foch maintained, was the battle of manoeuvre prepared, initiated and conducted by the commander and culminating in the decisive attack which was an expression of his will-power and which alone could bring victory. As the supreme act in warfare, a battle must be fought to the limit, with no looking over the shoulder. Every man must play his part in it with all his might and all his resources. Whatever strategic calculations may be made with a view to economy of force, it must be recognised that a moment of crisis will inevitably arise when forces will apparently be stretched to breaking point and when, in the midst of appalling danger, the obstacles to be overcome will appear insuperable. At that point the commander must be imbued with the conviction that 'mind is always stronger than matter'; however overwhelming the situation may seem, the moral factor will always prove stronger than the material.

Indomitable determination to win, however, and confidence in victory on the part of the commander would be of no avail, Foch considered, unless all his men were imbued with the same ideas to the very roots of their being. Let there be no mistake – 'generals, not soldiers, win battles and a beaten general is disgraced for ever' – 'the whole art of war is to learn the enemy's situation, to think matters out and to will'.

In this theory, current in the 1890s, one is inevitably struck by the decisive influence exerted by certain German writers, Clausewitz in particular, on the doctrine peculiar to the German Staff College. This was the romanticist concept of war with everything directed towards battle, the sanguinary drama, the struggle of giants with no holds barred. It was a concept based on dynamism and psychology, heralding the doctrine that was to be prevalent in the

French army on the eve of 1914. By frenzied heroism victory could be snatched from the jaws of defeat. Owing to its disregard of the realities of fire power this doctrine brought France more than once to the verge of defeat.

At this point it is worth pausing for a moment to consider the phenomenon of these two great continental armies at the turn of the century. Industrial techniques were transforming national armies into vast organisations able, thanks to the railway, to exist and fight almost anywhere; owing to the increase in fire power visible targets were fast disappearing from the battle-field and the defence was acquiring a crushing superiority over the offensive. Yet at this moment military theorists were placing greater and greater faith in the value of the offensive. Though increasingly difficult to execute, the offensive had apparently become *essential*; it accordingly demanded greater and greater will-power, self-sacrifice and heroism. Instinctively therefore the theorists, the most enlightened of whom was Foch, laid emphasis on moral strength. But was this enough?

On the German side the 1870 battles and the later lessons drawn from the Russo-Japanese War produced two complementary trains of thought, the defensive-offensive preached by Clausewitz and the enveloping manoeuvre around an open flank. The result was the famous Schlieffen Plan of 1905, in which the outflanking manoeuvre was clearly regarded as the be-all and end-all of operational strategy. The idea seemed to be a good one. On the French side, however, though the idea of an outflanking move was not abandoned, priority was apparently still given to the breakthrough battle. This was the result of the cult of the offensive, which obviously led people to dream about decisive attacks. A passage in one of Foch's books, admittedly written later, illustrates the current concept of the offensive: 'The enemy's defeat . . . should at once be magnified and exploited by mobile action in strength sufficient to take advantage of the confusion already produced in the enemy's formations.' In other words a deep, sustained offensive was visualised. Here again the outline of Plan XVII, implemented in 1914, becomes visible.

It will be observed that these ideas, which were germinating early in the century on the German side as well as the French, were the result of thinking by men without war experience. They made superhuman efforts to foresee what the next military conflict would be like, but the background of prag-matism, which only experience can provide, was not available to exercise its sobering influence upon their imagination. Schlieffen dreamt of a vast out-flanking movement and thought that he could rival Hannibal at the Battle of Cannae. He did not realise that the difference in scale of the outflanking manoeuvre (a few hundred yards at Cannae, two hundred miles in 1914) had totally changed the nature of the phenomenon – he would need weeks to out-flank an enemy who was no less mobile than his own outflanking wing. Pro-vided the enemy was not stupid, therefore, he would be able to disengage by withdrawing. And so it turned out in the event. Foch dreamt of spreading disorganisation by means of a deep breakthrough; he did not realise that this breakthrough was feasible only if no account were taken of the effect of defensive fire, now a formidable factor. Each side disregarded certain basic realities and on each side millions of men prepared for war on mistaken assumptions that no one could verify at the time.

This highlights the dramatic aspect of preparation for war, that gigantic conundrum with which the military intelligentsia is always faced. Everyone knows that war evolves, that tomorrow's procedures will be very different from yesterday's. But how to guess what they will be? As the memory of past experience fades, imaginations run riot and become further divorced from reality. Doctrines become accepted, in some respects increasingly mistaken, but how can anyone tell in advance? The public, which is not well informed, does not generally understand that the military art is always evolving (some-times very rapidly as it is today), but that it can be tried out in practice only during a war, in other words at more or less lengthy intervals. When that happens everyone can see not only the enormity of the mistakes made in peacetime appreciations, but the magnitude of the problems still to be resolved if operations are to result in victory. War therefore becomes a process of experimental and usually groping research; amid setbacks and dangers the necessary adjustments are made. Sometimes the evolution required is too fundamental or too difficult to grasp. In that case war sinks into a morass of indecisive operations. It becomes protracted and ruinous. The people become exhausted. The finger is then pointed at the incompetence of commanders or the rigidity of doctrines until some new 'inventor' of genius discovers and implements some new solution.

It was to be Foch's remarkable fate to play the decisive role of 'inventor'.

In 1901 Ferdinand Foch was posted to a regiment. This was an unhappy period for the French army owing to the divorce between church and state – and Foch's brother was a Jesuit. He took advantage of his posting however to continue his work. In 1903 he was promoted colonel and took over com-mand of the 35th Artillery Regiment in Vannes. At the end of his period of command in 1905 he became Chief of Staff to v Corps in Orléans. In 1907, at the age of fifty-six, he was promoted brigadier-general and posted to the Army General Staff. While in this appointment command of the Staff College fell vacant and this was thought to be a suitable post for Foch. He had an interview with Clemenceau, the Prime Minister, and the following conversa-tion is said to have taken place:

'I am offering you command of the Staff College.'

'I am grateful to you, Monsieur le Président, but I am sure you know that one of my brothers is a Jesuit.'

'I know and I don't care a damn; you will turn out good officers for us and nothing else counts.'

There is no knowing whether this little incident has been accurately recorded, but it is of significance when one remembers that it was Clemenceau who selected Foch instead of Pétain in 1918.

Foch was accordingly in charge of the Staff College until 1911 when he became commander of the 13th Division in Chaumont. In 1912 he took command of VIII Corps and in 1913 that of XX Corps in Nancy. It was in this appointment that Foch was overtaken by the war.

The point to note about this *curriculum vitae* is that although Foch's promotion was slow (he became a brigadier-general at fifty-six and a corps commander at sixty-three) his merit was acknowledged in every post that he occupied; towards the end of this period his promotion became more rapid, until he was eventually given command of the Nancy Army Corps, marking him out for the most senior appointments. War confirmed the validity of this decision.

XX Corps formed part of Second Army commanded by General de Castelnau; it was deployed along the frontier facing Metz. On 14 August it took the offensive. Though suffering severe casualties, it captured the hills along the frontier, where the Germans were firmly established. The enemy moved back some 10 miles to the line Sarrebourg-Morhange where he occupied a fresh position. The corps attacked towards Morhange, suffering further severe casualties – it was discovering the effects of the machine gun and heavy artillery; its morale remained high however. Unfortunately XV Corps on its right was driven back by a German counter-offensive; XX Corps was forced to withdraw rapidly, but although exhausted and depleted, not only did it cover Nancy and the Charmes Gap but carried out a successful counter-attack against the Germans advancing towards the Gap. Nancy was saved and the Germans did not succeed in crossing the Meurthe.

In this his first battle Foch was admittedly commanding a crack corps, but he had given immediate proof of his capacity as a leader; he combined flexibility in manoeuvre with determination; his drive had been such that, despite its casualties and the shock to morale inherent in the surprises of actual fighting, his corps had played the primary role in re-establishing the situation in Lorraine. So the theorist was also a man of action. Foch's seniors reached the same conclusion and as a result he was selected to command Ninth Army, then in process of forming in the centre as the French withdrew from Belgium towards the Marne and the Seine.

It was in this post that Foch was to show his true mettle as an army commander. In the first place, with everyone in full retreat, he had to form this still non-existent army and he had only a few staff officers to do it with, though admittedly they included Weygand as Chief of Staff. Foch was allotted three corps and four divisions. They had to be concentrated, resupplied with food, ammunition and equipment and formed into a homogeneous entity. He was given his command in general headquarters on 29 August; on 5 September, only a week later, he was forced to fight a defensive battle on a

20-mile front covering Sézanne, Fère-Champenoise and Arcis-sur-Aube. At this point the Germans were planning to break through the French centre and so it fell to Foch to hold the main enemy effort. On 6 September he succeeded in bringing the Germans to a halt, but had to employ all his available forces to do so. On 7 September he was ordered to support an offensive by Fifth Army on his left. Despite all his efforts his left was pinned to the ground, while on his right and in the centre he was only just able to hold the German attacks. On the 8th his army's situation seemed critical; on the right XI Corps gave way, losing Fère-Champenoise; in the centre IX Corps was taken in rear by the Prussian Guards and forced to withdraw; if it lost Mondemont Ninth Army was in danger of being cut in two.

This was the situation at midday when Foch reported to GHQ: 'I am hard pressed on my right; my centre is giving way; situation excellent; I am attacking.' This was not mere braggadocio: it stemmed from Foch's conviction that, in what he called the battle of manoeuvre, after the confrontation phase must come the decisive attack. This was the concept he had worked out in 1898 and he was putting it into practice sixteen years later. He let loose his crack division, the 42nd. The enemy was taken by surprise, gave up some ground and halted. Foch then asked Fifth Army to reinforce him next day and General Franchet d'Esperey gave him X Corps and the 51st Division. Foch relieved the 42nd Division and moved X Corps against the flank of the German X Corps. On the morning of the 8th however the enemy resumed his attack, held up X Corps and pushed XI Corps back several miles. By the evening the situation was still critical, particularly around the Saint-Gond marshes. Foch accordingly moved the 42nd Division up to counter-attack on the 9th although it had had only twenty-four hours' rest. It was not ready to attack until 6 pm. The order to do so was issued at once. Once more the enemy was taken by surprise and thrown off balance; he dug in. The attack was resumed at 5 am on the 10th and found the enemy in full retreat. This was the victory of the Marne; the main action had taken place elsewhere, but Foch with his Ninth Army had formed the central pivot in a very hard-fought battle; the morale of his men and the determination of their commander had been decisive. The pursuit carried Ninth Army north of Reims. There, the enemy reorganised and on the French side resources were not available for another major offensive. So a halt was called.

Now however the decisive area had moved farther west, each side trying to outflank the other. Foch's success during the Battle of the Marne had been such that on 4 October he was appointed Deputy Commander-in-Chief and given the task of co-ordinating the operations of the northern group of armies. He left at once by car in the middle of the night and almost alone. He first went to see General de Castelnau, commanding Second Army, at Breteuil, where he breakfasted. He left again at 6 am and at 9 am arrived at Aubigny, where were the headquarters of General de Maud'huy, commanding Tenth Army. So he had come to grips with his new problem at once. His purpose was to prevent the French forces being outflanked by forming a tenuous line on the left. At this point the northernmost French detachments were near Lille and they were not being attacked. Along the front however the Germans had reconcentrated their forces and were again attacking furiously. On 10 October Foch set up his headquarters in Doullens. His primary task was to accelerate the moving of reinforcements in men and equipment and ensure that they arrived in time in the crucial areas. Everything had to be improvised; it was a gymnastic exercise on the part of the staff. Once again however it was Foch who imparted the drive, for in a fluid situation like this maintenance of confidence was essential. Moreover he now showed for the first time his ability to influence his allies. Troops of the BEF were detraining in the Lille area and Foch had to co-ordinate their movement with the rest. On the same day the Belgian army evacuated Antwerp and fell back to the Yser. Foch was already covering the British detraining areas with Conneau's cavalry corps and he now despatched the French Marine Brigade by rail to Ghent to cover the right of the Belgian army; meanwhile two French territorial divisions dug in round Ypres. The defences here were reinforced by a British division intended for the defence of Antwerp but despatched too late. In the space of two days a defence line from the Oise to the sea had been organised.

On 13 October four German corps launched an all-out attack along the Yser front, now firmly occupied from Dixmude to the sea. Though the Germans suffered heavy casualties, the battle raged until 19 October. The British were now deployed at Ypres and south of it, however, and the French had formed a fresh army under General d'Urbal in the Ypres-Dixmude area. Nevertheless the Germans reinforced and continued to hammer away; by 21 October they were threatening to break through the front at Dixmude and force a crossing of the Yser. Foch hurried to the area and ordered the dykes to be opened. The resulting floods together with the heroism of the Belgians finally stopped the German army on the Yser on 30 October.

The Germans now transferred their effort to the Dixmude area held by the British, where the defence was crumbling. Foch hurried to St Omer to see General French and promised him reinforcements. By 31 October however the British were exhausted, their last reserves had been used and they were falling back on Gheluvelt and Hooge. The situation was critical. Foch was at Vlamertinghe, General d'Urbal's headquarters, when General French happened to pass through by car. After a dramatic discussion Foch persuaded French to postpone his order for withdrawal, promising that XVI and XXXII French Corps would arrive within twenty-four hours. On 2 November however the enemy increased his pressure between Dixmude and the Lys. On 3 November he launched a furious attack on Ypres and XX French Corps was rushed up by road to reinforce the defence. The following week was one of slaughter, the Germans finally exhausting themselves. By 15 November it was all over. The enemy had been definitely held.

This had been a defensive victory; Foch did not have the resources to win a positive victory ending in the enemy's defeat. Nevertheless it was a vitally important victory, for the German advance on the western front was now definitely blocked. The enemy had put eleven army corps into action and had lost some three hundred thousand men, but he had been able neither to outflank the Allied left nor break through their defences, hurriedly constituted though they were. By ceaseless activity, sound intuition, tireless energy and moral ascendancy General Foch had succeeded in co-ordinating the action of the Allied armies under the most difficult circumstances. It was a brilliant achievement setting a definitive seal upon the results of the Battle of the Marne.

Mobile warfare was over; operations stagnated into position warfare, an entirely new experience for the Allies. The problem now was to understand this form of warfare and find the tactical and strategical answers that would lead to victory. It was a difficult puzzle to unravel; the process was to take four long years and Foch was to play a vital role in it, first as experimenter, then as inventor. Though he had his difficult moments, his ability was such that he became the inevitable choice as the man who would lead the Allied armies to victory.

From December 1914 to August 1916 Foch commanded the northern group of armies. He was accordingly in the forefront of inter-Allied problems, an experience he was to find valuable later, and he served his apprenticeship in the trench warfare which was the result of the superiority of the defensive over the offensive. This superiority was admittedly only of a tactical nature, but it seemed to destroy the foundations of any strategy based on the superiority of the offensive. During this first phase, when he was commanding a group of armies, Foch was trying to discover a *tactical* solution to the problem, some means of restoring the power of the attack.

The offensive in Artois, between Neuville St Vaast and Notre-Dame-de-Lorette in May 1915, was his first experiment. Foch's attack was based on use of heavy artillery, but resources did not allow him to move on a front of more than six miles. After heavy fighting he had scored only a partial success. The recipe therefore required revision; Foch decided that he must extend the front of attack, which meant using more guns, and somehow pin down the enemy reserves.

Though neither of these conditions was fulfilled, it was decided to attack again in September to relieve pressure on the Russians who had suffered a series of defeats. Despite help from the British, this attack too was a partial failure. So preparations were made for a very large-scale offensive in 1916, from which victory was expected. It was to take place on the Somme, employing large British and French forces; Foch was to be in charge of it. On 21 February however the Germans attacked at Verdun, drawing in some of the French reserves; Foch was left with only twenty-six French divisions instead of forty though the shortfall was partially made good by raising the

British contribution from twenty divisions to twenty-six. The offensive moved off on 1 July after heavy artillery preparation. The battle lasted into September and certain valuable local results were achieved, but British casualties were too high. Admittedly forty German divisions had been ground to pieces and the Germans had been forced to abandon their Verdun offensive, but the recipe was still too ponderous. Clearly, as had been seen at Verdun, superiority in artillery did not produce a decisive breakthrough. The end result was a battle of attrition. Foch went on thinking and dreaming of his battle of manoeuvre.

At this point Foch reached the age limit. At the same time however there occurred the great upheaval in senior posts that preceded and followed the dismissal of Joffre, now held to be out of date.

Fortunately for France Foch was appointed head of the Study Bureau for inter-Allied Questions and in May 1917 was nominated Army Chief of Staff in Paris. In this capacity he was able to intervene in Italy and alleviate the grave consequences of the Italian defeat. He was then appointed French representative on the Supreme Inter-Allied War Council and chairman of the executive committee of the Supreme War Council. An inter-Allied reserve was placed under the orders of this executive committee, but Commanders-in-Chief Pétain for the French and Haig for the British viewed this encroachment upon their resources with a jaundiced eye and the size of the reserve was reduced on 3 March.

Then, on 21 March, the first German offensive opened against the British front. A breakthrough was made in twenty-four hours and a 50-mile-wide gap opened between the British and the left of the French Sixth Army. The situation appeared so menacing that at a meeting in Doullens on 26 March the British government proposed that General Foch be commissioned to co-ordinate the operations of the Allied armies. On 14 April actual command of the Allied armies was substituted for co-ordination of operations. Admittedly five days earlier the Germans had again broken through the British front, this time on the Lys.

The first part of the Battle of France, the defensive phase, was the more spectacular. The enemy launched a series of offensives and on each occasion, in a single day, broke through a front hitherto considered impregnable. He scored four successes in a row. So the Germans had found the recipe for breaking through fortified fronts; it consisted of: complete surprise, a short but violent artillery preparation with the object of neutralising rather than destroying, flexible exploitation by infantry advancing rapidly and attempting to infiltrate to the greatest possible depth. This was not unlike the tactics tried out by Mangin at Verdun. They had been taken up by von Hutier on the Russian front, tried out successfully at Riga and repeated equally successfully in Italy at Caporetto. Now the proof was there; so long as the enemy had reserves he could repeat this process at his leisure and force the Allies to pant along behind him in more or less open country attempting to plug the holes.

But Foch was in no way overawed. After all he had wrestled with similar situations in 1914, in Champagne and on the Yser for instance. He knew that an improvised defence could be very effective. He acted as he had in 1914, issuing orders for formations to hold on everywhere, moving his reserves where they were required and reconstituting a reserve, in particular by bringing the Americans into line in certain quiet sectors of the front; he even made preparations for a counter-offensive from the forest of Villers-Cotteret. This defensive manoeuvre was a complete success: however irresistible each German advance might appear initially, after a few days the exhaustion of the troops and logistic difficulties confined its results to the creation of some salient. The decisive factor however, to which Foch attached due weight and which he exploited to the full, was that the defence could move its reserves by rail and road *more quickly than the attacker could advance on foot*. After the initial surprise when the attack was in a position of superiority, the local balance of forces could be restored comparatively quickly; the Germans knew how to break through but they did not know how to exploit conclusively. Moreover comparison between the speed of advance of the attack and that of the movement of reserves showed that any exploitation in depth was impossible. Such was Foch's tentative conclusion.

So when Ludendorff's final offensive, which took place in Champagne in July, failed against the defences of Gouraud's army, fortunately organised in depth, Foch let loose the counter-offensive that he was holding ready. It was conducted by Mangin and had been planned as a pre-emptive attack, but owing to the delay turned into a large-scale counter-offensive against the German flank. Coming just at the moment when Ludendorff was beginning to run out of reserves, it was completely successful. The tables were turned spectacularly; Foch now hammered away with a series of powerful offensives, but carefully avoiding too prolonged or too deep an advance so as not to expend resources in an exploitation he knew to be impossible. Successive attacks were co-ordinated so that one reacted upon another; Ludendorff was forced to switch his reserves from one point to another and, the attack being initially superior in fire power, these reserves were gradually worn down. Foch had in fact found a better recipe than that which Ludendorff had served up between March and July. Between July and November the enemy front was rolled back everywhere; French territory was recaptured almost in its entirety and Belgium was partially liberated. Foch was preparing a decisive offensive due to be launched on 15 November and visualising an advance through Germany to cut the enemy's communications. On 11 November however the German General Staff acknowledged defeat and accepted the armistice. The Battle of France had been won.

Foch's victory was undoubtedly a victory won by will-power, tenacity and energy – what Napoleon called 'the strength of the spirit'. But it was also a victory won by the mind, a contemplative mind, as his books showed, but also a pragmatic mind capable of drawing lessons from experience and firmly rooted in the realities of life.

In his book *Reputations* Liddell Hart pictures Foch as a visionary wedded to the offensive and basing his views on the pre-eminence of the moral factor. This is a gross over-simplification of a complex character. He was indeed a protagonist of a lofty concept of the 'strength of the spirit', as was essential for anyone destined to carry the terrifying responsibility of conducting a battle. But he was more than that; he could manoeuvre skilfully in the field; he was a commander with a sure eye; he was a general capable of reflecting on tactical lessons and adjusting his methods to suit the possibilities.

Foch's operational experience during the war has been described in some detail in order to show how, stage by stage, he learnt to play the game necessitated by novel conditions of warfare, the experience he gained from the fighting of 1915 and 1916 and the lessons he drew from the defensive phase of the Battle of France. Gradually the outline of the concept that was to bring victory becomes clear. It is of interest to compare it with that of his opponent Ludendorff. He possessed the recipe for the breakthrough attack, but he thought that victory was to be won by exploitation of the break-through in depth – as in Russia. Consequently he wore himself out in offensives that were doomed to be contained by the Allied reserves. When Foch regained the initiative, he was careful not to make the same mistake; he hammered away with limited offensives, thus exploiting to the full the initial superiority in fire power possessed by the offensive. The defender was therefore always in a position of inferiority and subjected to a greater degree of attrition than the attacker. This was the only practicable concept in 1918 because of the slow rate of advance of the attack compared to that of the movement of reserves. Used with artistry it led to the quick collapse of Germany, already undermined internally by four years of war and blockade. The victory of 1918 was therefore primarily a *victory of the mind*, the result of a more accurate grasp of the conditions of the time.

By an irony of fate this concept, which suited one particular situation perfectly, was accepted into French doctrine as an abiding truth. By 1940 fresh conditions obtained; in particular an offensive based on armour with air support could advance quickly, a development foreshadowed in several of the 1918 offensives. So Ludendorff's concept became practicable at last and the French defence collapsed, once again due to an error *of thinking*.

But if, by some miracle, Foch had been able to come back and take a hand before 1940, he would not have made this mistake. He had meditated too profoundly on the subject of battle, on the interplay between tactical and technical factors, not to realise that his recipe would have to be adjusted to the new conditions. The great lesson left to us by Foch, a teacher of un-paralleled vitality, is the value of concentrated and prolonged reflection upon the subject of war.

General Sir John Monash

Malcolm Falkus

At the opening of the present century Australia was a youthful, sparsely populated country. Yet in the space of a few years it created a fine military tradition and her troops won fame throughout the world. This tradition was born in the battlefields of the First World War, and here the Anzac legend, still commemorated each year on 25 April both in Australia and New Zealand, was born.

Like the other Dominions, Australia was quick to give wholehearted and enthusiastic support to the British when hostilities began in August 1914, and in the battles that followed two particular characteristics of the Australian contingent emerged. There was, first, the outstanding courage and resourcefulness of the Australian soldiers. All were volunteers, all matched up to exacting standards of physical fitness, and many had the toughness and adaptability bred in the harsh conditions of the Australian frontier. Time and time again Australian brigades were chosen by British generals to spearhead important offensives, and there is no question that the Australians played a role out of all proportion to their numbers. A captured German officer remarked, 'I have heard much about the fighting qualities of the Australian soldiers. They are not soldiers at all. They are madmen.' If the successes of the Australians were not sufficiently recognised outside that country, this is in part due to the tardy acknowledgement given by Haig and other British commanders at the time, endeavouring, as they did, to bolster home morale by subserving all Allied victories under a general 'British Army' label.

The second outstanding characteristic of the Australian forces in the First World War was the quality of their leadership at all levels. Sadly, again, many of these commanders have received scant recognition. General Sir Harry Chauvel was one of the finest cavalry commanders in the war, and his leadership in the campaigns in Sinai in 1916 and in Palestine and Syria in 1918 was a decisive factor in the brilliant victories there. Brudenell White was another outstanding leader and strategist, who masterminded the Gallipoli withdrawal, and was called by Monash 'far and away the ablest soldier Australia has ever produced'. And there was General Sir John Monash himself, Australia's most renowned soldier, who served with distinction in many of the Australian army's most important and arduous campaigns during the Great War, and who rose to command the entire Australian forces on the western front.

Monash, like Chauvel and others of his great compatriots, was a part-time 'citizen soldier' before 1914. He was born in Melbourne in 1865, son of a German–Jewish immigrant, and retained his Jewish faith. He combined to a remarkable degree a talent for scholarship and a taste for action. At only fourteen he matriculated from school, though he had to wait two further years until he was old enough to enter Melbourne University. Ultimately he graduated in no less than three separate faculties, Arts, Law and Engineering, obtaining his BCE in 1891, MCE in 1893, BA in 1895, and LLB also in 1895. Monash impressed all those with whom he came into contact as a widely read, learned man; a man with an uncanny grasp of detail and an ability to express himself both lucidly and simply. A civil engineer by profession, he could discourse expertly on medicine, on history and on music. The historian Sir Ernest Scott wrote of him that not only was he

> a great soldier and a masterly engineer, but also a tireless student in many branches of knowledge. Only those who knew him well, for instance, realised that the general who had planned the successful operations which gained the Australian victory of 8 August 1918 could have sustained an argument with any musical expert on the interpretation of the symphonies of Beethoven, but he knew those great works as well as he knew the strategic doctrines of Gneisenau or the tactical methods of Moltke.

While at university Monash found time to interest himself in military matters. He subsequently became an officer in the citizen forces of Australia and was promoted to major in 1897, lieutenant-colonel in 1908, and to colonel, in command of the 13th Infantry Brigade, in 1913. Following the outbreak of war in 1914 Monash was at first appointed censor in the department of the Chief of the General Staff, but within a month he was given command of the 4th Infantry Brigade of the Australian Imperial Force. His brigade landed in Egypt in February 1915, where they formed part of the Australian and New Zealand Division under Major-General Sir Alexander Godley. This division, together with the Australian 1st Division and 1st Light Horse Brigade, formed the Australian-New Zealand Army Corps (under overall command of General Sir William Birdwood) from the initials of which comes the famous name of Anzac.

The Anzacs were chosen to play a crucial role in the Gallipoli campaign of 1915, and Monash's brigade was part of the spearhead that landed on what came to be known as Anzac Cove on the morning of 25 April. With only a brief respite for recuperation, Monash and his brigade saw through the whole ordeal from the initial landings and struggle up the cliffs in the face of murderous fire from the Turks above, to the final withdrawal in December. The Gallipoli campaign, conceived by Winston Churchill as a means of capturing the Dardanelles, opening a direct sea link with the Russian allies, and diverting German troops from the hard-pressed western and Russian fronts, was one of the great tragic-heroic episodes of the war. Outnumbered and faced with an unexpectedly well-prepared Turkish army, the Allied troops fought courageously to maintain their precarious foothold for month after month.

Monash led his men with distinction, and showed himself a master of organisation and detailed planning. His brigade was responsible for the defence of the sector known as Monash Valley, and despite crippling losses the superb training and spirit of the Anzac troops enabled them to defy the numerically superior enemy. Monash himself was mentioned three times in despatches, and he was awarded the CB for his inspired leadership. His letters to his wife show something of the appalling conditions the Anzacs endured, and show also the intense pride Monash took in the achievements of his men. 'The thing above all others which stands out uppermost in the terrible fighting which has been incessant since our landing on 25 April is the magnificence of our Australian troops,' he wrote on 14 May. 'I have had plenty of opportunity of comparing them with the troops of British regular units and Territorials, and the British officers are the first to admit that for physique, dash, enterprise and sublime courage, the Australians are head and shoulders above any others.'

When finally the Allied troops were withdrawn from the peninsula on 18 and 19 December, the Australians alone had suffered 8587 killed and 19,367 wounded. The closing months of the campaign, fought in atrocious conditions with thousands of decaying bodies providing a fertile breeding-ground for plagues of disease-carrying flies, rank as one of the great feats of endurance in modern warfare.

After Gallipoli the Anzac forces returned to Egypt for rest, reinforcement and regrouping. Together with new troops, the Anzacs were formed into four divisions, veterans of the Gallipoli campaigns forming the backbone of each, and combined into two Anzac corps. Meanwhile a new fifth division (called the 3rd) was being raised in Australia, and in July 1916 Monash was given command of the new contingent and promoted to the rank of major-general. Thus Monash did not participate in the early Australian involvements on the western front between March and November 1916 – he was at work training his new troops with the tireless energy and attention to detail, tempered by humanity and even gentleness, for which he was by now well known. In these months the four Australian divisions in the field wrote new chapters in Australian war history for their enterprise and endurance during the great First Battle of the Somme, especially in the action to capture Pozières. As the Australian official history of the war notes, 'the Pozières windmill site is more densely sown with Australian sacrifice than any other place on earth'.

General Monash arrived in France on 26 November and for some months his 3rd Division, attached to II Anzac Corps, stayed on the comparatively quiet sector of the front near Armentières. It was at this stage in operations that plans for a full-scale offensive against key points on the so-called Hindenburg Line, culminating in an attack on Arras, were being worked out by the British high command. On 17 March the 8th Brigade of the 5th Division entered Bapaume, and the seizure of this and other towns brought the Allies hard up against the Hindenburg Line. On 11 April came the famous battle for Bullecourt, where for the first time tanks were used to precede the infantry advance. After considerable slaughter of both armies in two great battles, Bullecourt was captured finally on 12 May.

Meanwhile 11 Anzac Corps was being prepared for the attack on the Messines Ridge (a preliminary to the great offensive planned by Haig on the whole Ypres-Armentières front). This corps was part of General Sir Herbert Plumer's Second Army, and for Monash and his division this was their first great engagement. Monash planned his part in the battle with almost German-like thoroughness and his instructions were issued in thirty-six successive circulars. When the attack came Messines was captured brilliantly, with the 3rd Division carrying out to the full its appointed role.

Haig, fatefully, now decided to press on towards Passchendaele, with the Second Army allotted a key role. This attack, the Third Battle of Ypres, was the last of the great British setpiece offensives. It began on 31 July, and on September 1 Anzac Corps formed the spearhead of the thrust against the main ridge of Ypres. In the battles of Polygon Wood, Zonnebeke and Broodseinde, the Anzac troops achieved magnificent successes, though at the cost of fearful losses. Of the latter victory, achieved on 4 October, Monash wrote: 'Our success was complete and unqualified. Over 1050 prisoners and much material and guns. Well over 1000 enemy dead counted, and many hundreds buried and out of reach. We got absolutely astride of the main ridge. Both Corps and Army declare there has been no finer feat in the war.'

The very success of these battles and others elsewhere on the western front induced Haig to attempt the capture of Passchendaele. The attack began on 12 October, and is now a legend for the unsurpassed torments of the cold driving rain, the thick mud, and the demoralising conditions of prolonged trench warfare. Monash's division played as heroic a part as any in the struggle. His men even reached the outskirts of Passchendaele, but were driven back by overwhelming German strength. Not until 6 November did Passchendaele fall to the Canadians.

Monash himself recorded his account of events shortly after the 12 October battle and this shows vividly the difficulties facing his troops:

Considerable rain began to set in on 6 October. The ground was in a deplorable condition by the night of 8 October, and, in consequence, the 66th and 45th Divisions who had taken up the role of the 3rd Australian and the New Zealand Divisions, failed to accomplish more than a quarter of a mile of their projected advance. Even in the face of this the Higher Command insisted on going on, and insisted, further, that the uncompleted objectives of this fourth phase should be added to the objectives of our fifth phase; so that it amounted to this, that Russell and I were asked to make a total advance of $1\frac{3}{4}$ miles. The weather grew steadily worse on 10 and 11 October. There was no flying and no photographing, no definite information on the German redispositions, no effective bombardment, no opportunity of replenishing our ammunition dumps; and the whole of the country from Zonnebeke forward to the limits of our previous captures was literally a sea of mud, in most places waist deep.

In the carnage of Passchendaele the total losses by the British army may have totalled a quarter of a million men, while the Australians alone lost thirty-eight thousand.

After Passchendaele the Australian troops were 'rested' on a comparatively quiet sector of the front, and during this period all five divisions were brought into one corps, under the command of General Birdwood. The next heavy Australian involvement came with the onset of the great Ludendorff offensive, which began at St Quentin on 21 March 1918 and for a time looked like breaking through the entire British line. The Australian divisions were immediately rushed to the front, and passing through retreating British troops headed towards the enemy. Monash wrote of his arrival at British headquarters:

As I stepped into the room General Congreve said, 'Thank heaven, the Australians at last.' Our conversation was of the briefest. He said, 'General, the position is very simple. My corps at four o'clock today was holding the line from Bray to Albert, when the line broke, and what is left of the three divisions in the line after four days' heavy fighting without food or sleep are falling back rapidly. German cavalry have been seen approaching Morlancourt and Buire. They are making straight for Amiens. What I want you to do is to get into the angle between the Anore and the Somme as far east as possible and stop him.' This constituted the whole of my orders. I got them to place a small room at my disposal and give me the use of a telephone and from there worked all night to make the necessary arrangements.

Thanks to these careful preparations the expected German attack, launched the following day, 28 March, was a catastrophic failure. Suffering enormous casualties, the Germans withdrew and so checked what had appeared an unstoppable drive towards the important centre of Amiens. In the aftermath of the fighting Monash showed another of his characteristics, his speedy reorganisation of shattered battle areas. He wrote:

Most of the villages in the neighbourhood had, of course, been hurriedly evacuated by the inhabitants, and I have been at great pains to try and have gathered up all the fowls, pigs, cattle, and sheep and have had them driven back to concentration camps. I quickly had all the villages policed with good stout Australians and we rapidly restored order.

The Ludendorff offensive lost momentum, but major battles continued. Particularly important was the action around Villers-Bretonneux, where the 9th Brigade of the 3rd Division took part in a magnificent defensive stand against the Germans on 4–5 April. But on 24 April, after the Australians had been replaced by exhausted British troops of the 8th Division, the Germans launched another fierce series of attacks, which succeeded in taking a number of key points, including Villers-Bretonneux. Once more Australian troops were brought in to counter-attack, and in the early hours of Anzac Day stormed into the ruined town. 'In my opinion,' wrote Monash, 'this counter-attack at night, without artillery support, is the finest thing yet done in the war by the Australians or any other troops.'

During the lull that followed the saving of Amiens, the Australian divisions continued to show their prowess in what was termed 'peaceful penetration' – quick, covert forays to capture enemy trenches and take prisoners without the preliminaries of artillery bombardment, which served only to alert the enemy. Monash's 3rd Division was particularly prominent in this, and on 9 May Haig noted that this division 'during the last three days advanced their front about a mile, and gained observation over the slopes to the east. The ground gained was twice as much as they had taken at Messines last June and they had done it with very small losses.'

It was at this juncture that Monash received his historic appointment, for at the end of May he was chosen to command the entire Australian Army Corps in succession to General Sir William Birdwood. He was promoted to lieutenant-general and, at the same time, was knighted by King George V at the Australian headquarters at Bertangles – the first time for some two hundred years a British army commander had been so honoured in the field. Monash's rising reputation was noted by Haig, who said of him: 'He is a very capable man. He has made a great success of everything he has touched; a very solid man.' And Lieutenant-General Congreve, who had given Monash his laconic battle orders in the Amiens campaign, described him as the finest divisional commander on the western front.

Describing his command, Monash wrote:

The Australian Corps is much the largest of any of the twenty army corps in France, for it contains all the five Australian divisions, and a very large number of corps troops, comprising a regiment of cavalry, a cyclist battalion, many brigades of heavy and super-heavy artillery, several battalions of tanks, corps, signal troops, ammunition parks, supply columns, mobile workshops, labour battalions, squadrons of flying corps, and many other units . . . it is much the finest corps command in the British Army.

By the close of the war the Australian Corps became even larger, totalling some two hundred thousand, and including two British divisions.

Monash's conception of command and generalship was fundamentally different from that of many British commanders, who continued to regard battles with the 'cavalry charge' romanticism of their predecessors. Monash's approach was on the contrary businesslike and functional. He described his last victory against the Hindenburg Line as 'simply a problem of engineering' and wrote also that the duty of the commander was 'to try and deal with every task and situation on the basis of simple business propositions, differing in no way from the problems of a civil life, except that they are governed by a special technique'. On another occasion he wrote,

I have formed the theory that the true role of the infantry was not to expend itself upon heroic physical effort, not to wither away under merciless machine-gun fire, nor to impale itself upon hostile bayonets, not to tear itself to pieces in hostile entanglements, but on the contrary to advance under the maximum possible protection of the maximum possible array of mechanical resources, in the form of guns, machine-guns, tanks, mortars, and aeroplanes; to advance with as little impediment as possible, to be relieved as far as possible of the obligation to fight their way forward, to march resolutely, regardless of the din and tumult of battle, to the appointed goal, and there to defend and hold the territory gained; and to gather, in the form of prisoners, guns and stores, the fruits of victory.

Monash's first big test came at the important battle of Hamel on 4 July 1918. His careful battle plans included a new role for tanks, Monash insisting that they should advance with the infantry instead of ahead. The plans showed fully his characteristic attention to detail and incorporated the procedure (subsequently widely adopted by the British army for the rest of the war) of ensuring that each participant knew exactly what role and objectives were expected of him. As Monash wrote:

Although complete written orders were invariably prepared and issued, very great importance was attached to holding conferences, at which there assembled every one of the senior commanders and heads of departments concerned with the impending operation. At these conferences I personally explained every detail of the plan, and assured myself that all present applied an identical interpretation. This fixity of plan engendered a confidence throughout the whole command which facilitated the work of every commander and staff officer.

He wrote further:

A perfected battle plan is like nothing so much as a score for a musical composition, where the various arms and units are the instruments, and the tasks they perform are their respective musical phrases. Every individual unit must make its entry precisely at the proper moment, and play its phrase in the general harmony.

The battle of Hamel was an outstanding and complete success, won with very small losses in only ninety-three minutes of combat. 'No battle within my previous experience', wrote Monash, 'passed off so smoothly, so exactly to timetable or was so free from any kind of hitch.'

The victory at Hamel made a big impression on the British high command, and Monash's procedures were soon adopted by the British for nearly every remaining tank-infantry battle.

On 8 August came the next major British offensive on the Hindenburg Line, and this offensive established Monash as one of the greatest generals in the British army. A massive attack was spearheaded by a drive against the central positions in the Somme valley, a drive entrusted principally to the Australians and Canadians. This was one of the vital battles of the entire campaign, and 8 August was described by Ludendorff as 'the black day of the German Army in the history of the War'. Successful beyond expectation, the Germans were pushed back on a wide front with enormous losses. The Australian forces advanced some 12 to 14 miles, and then, in a series of quick blows, reached the Somme near Péronne, while the 3rd Division captured Bray and other towns on the north bank of the Somme.

At this juncture the Germans had fallen back to strongly fortified positions, and, on the Australian sector, came to a stand near Péronne and on the high ground around Mont St Quentin. Mont St Quentin, described as 'a Gibraltar commanding the passages of the Somme and access to Péronne', was a critical position, and Monash decided to capture it as a prelude to Péronne, an action that has been described as the finest single achievement of the war. When Monash put his plan to General Rawlinson, the army commander – a plan that involved transferring his principal forces to the north bank of the Somme and then storming Mont St Quentin with three battalions – Rawlinson replied: 'And so you think you're going to take Mont St. Quentin with three battalions? What presumption! However I don't think I ought to stop you, so go ahead and try, and I wish you luck.' Monash set about preparing his plans, erecting bridges across the Somme and using the 3rd Division to clear the Germans from forward positions.

On 31 August the men of the 17th, 18th and 19th battalions of the 5th Brigade took up their positions. An Australian historian, Peter Firkins, has described the attack:

> While the shell-fragments of their artillery barrage were still falling on the Germans, the Australians rose out of their trenches in the cold pre-dawn darkness, yelling like fiends and keeping up a rapid fire in order to make the Germans think that they were being attacked by a larger force . . . The Australians burst through the enemy defences and charged Fenilla-court and the main height, making up for the lack of numbers by the sheer speed and savagery of their attack.

By 7 am the brigades had reached their main objectives and clung to a precarious foothold in Mont St Quentin. A furious counter-attack by the Germans drove the Australians from their positions on the crest, but they held on grimly. By midnight, when the Australian battalions were relieved by their colleagues of the 6th Brigade, the losses had been staggering: of the 17th Battalion, for example, only eight officers and seventy-five men remained. The day following, 1 September, further savage fighting resulted in the final capture of Mont St Quentin by the 6th Brigade, so allowing the 5th Division to seize the critical German position at Péronne.

These operations, fought over three days, without either artillery or tanks, were carried out with brilliant skill and superb courage. The capture of the German defences on the Mont St Quentin-Péronne ridge was one of the vital blows pushing the Germans from the Somme. Rawlinson wrote: 'The capture of Mont St. Quentin is a feat of arms worthy of the highest praise . . . I am filled with admiration for the gallantry and surpassing daring of the 2nd Division in winning this important fortress.' In all, the Australians suffered some three thousand casualties in the battle, and six men won the Victoria Cross.

With these Allied victories, coupled with Canadian successes at Cambrai, the Germans fell back beyond the Hindenburg Line. As a preliminary to the great offensive against this line, the Australian 1st and 4th divisions formed the spearhead of a Fourth Army drive against forward enemy trench positions. Brilliantly successful, the German positions were overrun and by dawn on 19 September the Australians were poised along the St Quentin canal, looking across it to the main Hindenburg Line.

For the 1st and 4th Divisions this was to be the last operation of the war. There remained the final assault on the German fortifications, judged by the enemy to be impregnable. Haig planned to use the Australian Corps (reinforced by two American divisions to compensate for the withdrawal of the 1st and 4th Divisions) for what he called 'the main attack': an offensive near Bellicourt on the St Quentin canal. The principal onslaught was launched on 29 September, and proved once more a story of tactical triumph for Monash and heroic courage on the part of his troops. Bellicourt was taken after fierce and costly fighting, much of it in hand-to-hand bayonet battles, and after several hours' bitter encounter both Australian divisions cracked the Hindenburg Line. In the succeeding days the Australians pushed farther ahead capturing other key posts at Bony, Joncourt and Le Catelet. On 3 October the 2nd Australian Division broke through the German lines over the whole of the front assigned to the Australian Corps, and on 5 October the 6th Brigade captured Montbrehain in a masterly and decisive stroke.

With these victories the Hindenburg Line collapsed. This marked the end of the war for Australian troops on the western front, for on the night of 5 October American troops relieved the exhausted Australian divisions; and before the Australians were once more called to action, the enemy had sued for peace.

After the armistice Monash was given one more exacting task – the repatriation of the 180,000 Australian troops who were serving abroad. This he and his staff accomplished smoothly in the face of great difficulties, such as the chronic shortage of sea transport. In December 1919 Monash himself returned home to his family and to civilian occupation, and the year following organised the first Anzac Day parade in Australia through Melbourne. After 1920 Monash became first general manager and then chairman of the Victoria State Electricity Commission, serving in this capacity with distinction. He remained interested in military matters, becoming a member of Australia's Council of Defence, and in 1929 both he and Sir Harry Chauvel became the first Australians to attain the rank of full general. When Monash died in October 1931, aged sixty-six, he was given a state funeral. Hundreds of thousands – including many Anzac veterans – lined the Melbourne streets to pay their last respects to Australia's most famous soldier.

Monash's reputation lies principally in his flexible approach to tactics, and to the thoroughness with which he planned his operations. There can be no question that his victories in the closing stages of the war were boldly conceived and brilliantly executed. His businesslike approach to warfare was often at odds with the mentality of many contemporary commanders in the British army, and Monash privately made little attempt to conceal his contempt for some of the British generals under whom the Australians were obliged to serve. Because of his novel approach to battle plans it has been said that Monash was the only general of the First World War who would have been equally at home in the Second. Lloyd George recorded that Monash was 'according to the testimony of those who knew well his genius for war and what he accomplished by it, the most resourceful general in the whole British Army'; and he suggested further that had the war lasted longer, Monash might have risen to become Commander-in-Chief.

As well as his tactical skill, Monash also showed intense humanity and pride in the achievements of his troops, as traced vividly in his letters to his wife, written from the front and published two years after his death. And Monash summed up his attitude to the ordeal he had witnessed for so long when he wrote in his book *The Australian Victories in France, 1918*:

From the far off days of 1914, when the call first came, until the last shot was fired, every day was filled with loathing, horror, and distress. I deplored all the time, the loss of precious life and the waste of human effort. Nothing could have been more repugnant to me than the realization of the dreadful inefficiency and the misspent energy of war. Yet it had to be, and the thought always uppermost was the earnest prayer that Australia might forever be spared such a horror on her own soil.

Field-Marshal The Viscount Allenby

Major General Anthony Farrar-Hockley

The Battle of Arras opened on Easter Monday, 9 April 1917, with the aim of diverting attention from the French offensive impending on the Aisne. At the centre of the battle line was the Third Army under Lieutenant-General Sir Edmund Henry Hynman Allenby, a cavalry officer, aged fifty-six. He was known widely, if discreetly, in British military circles as 'the Bull' because of his great size and uncertain temper. A common cause of his displeasure was failure to comply with one or another regulation, such as neglecting to wear a steel helmet in the trenches.

Allenby believed that discipline and loyalty were inseparable, a precept taught him by his mother in childhood. He was thus an exemplar of loyalty to his Commander-in-Chief, Sir Douglas Haig; but Haig did not reciprocate. Neither man cared for the other. Haig believed that Allenby was lacking in aptitude for high command. At conferences of army commanders he became impatient with Allenby's deliberate, sometimes halting expositions and would ask for another general's opinion while Allenby was still speaking. When a number of army commanders gathered at a tank demonstration, Allenby was the only one whom Haig failed to greet personally.

These examples of their general's attitude were not lost upon his staff. Any request or proposition made to General headquarters by the Third Army was accepted with reservation, examined with suspicion. Thus when Allenby adopted a novel bombardment plan conceived by Major-General Arthur Holland, his artillery adviser, to surprise the enemy just prior to the opening of the offensive, it was repudiated by GHQ.

If Allenby was loyal to those above him, he was no less loyal to those in his charge. Enjoying independent responsibility himself, he assumed – not always justifiably – that the commanders and staff officers who served him also desired the greatest possible degree of independence. It was therefore his practice to delegate powers widely to those he trusted, bringing them together from time to time only to ensure that their activities were co-ordinated. Any individual officer working constructively within the broad parameters of his policy would be assured of his support and, if he made an honest mistake, his protection.

In this spirit Allenby had told Holland that he wished the bombardment prior to the initial assault to aim as much at deceiving the enemy as at damaging his defences. Holland devised a scheme that not only seemed likely to achieve this but also to enhance the bombardment planned to precede the second phase of attack. Allenby thus declined to accept GHQ's objections to it. When an impasse was reached, Haig promoted Holland and sent him elsewhere, providing by way of replacement an officer of orthodox views, heedful of GHQ opinions.

As it happened the Germans withdrew voluntarily to the Hindenburg Line along much of the British front during the weeks immediately preceding the spring offensive so that major adjustments were necessarily made to the Third Army plan. Allenby threw all his energy, of which he had plenty, and imagination, of which he had enough when his capabilities were challenged, into ensuring that his other ideas to surprise the enemy at the outset were implemented to the full. On the Easter Sunday, with less than twenty-four hours to the first assault, Haig sent a message that he still considered the plan to be defective; Allenby must therefore assume full responsibility if it failed. Of course no one, however senior, dared to criticise the Commander-in-Chief in Allenby's presence but, in contradistinction to the practice in Second, Fourth and Fifth Army headquarters, he forbade also any word of criticism of the GHQ staff.

Quite apart from distractions of this sort the army commander had a personal anxiety of his own: his only child, Michael, was a subaltern in a Royal Horse Artillery battery involved in the offensive. He showed no sign of stress or anxiety, however, except to walk slowly up to the casualty office each evening to enquire, in a casual tone, if his son's name was among the lists of killed or wounded.

The opening of the offensive on 9 April 1917 was a success. The front system of German trenches was overwhelmed by the leading divisions of his army; prisoners and enemy field guns taken were numerous. The next phase was not so successful. Third Army had attacked on a broad front, a feature approved by GHQ. In order to exploit the enemy's confusion, arising from the surprise achieved, it was essential that three corps and ten divisional commanders should act energetically to maintain the offensive momentum. Partly due to the appalling conditions of weather and ground, partly to a failure by some of the formation commanders to act decisively and in time, the operation began to falter on 10 April. Attempting too late to influence personally the course of the action, Allenby committed cavalry on 11 April. '. . . It did not quite come off,' he wrote to his wife next day. 'Wire and machine-guns stopped them . . .' So did the surface of the battlefield. It was a precipitate action. Allenby urged his army on so vehemently that three of the divisional commanders signed a formal resolution, protesting ostensibly against the piecemeal thrusts to which they were being committed. If words mean anything, they were protesting against continuance: certainly the scope for offensive action was extremely limited. The resolution was put to Allenby in modified form, rather as a suggestion, with the essence of which he agreed. But it did not persuade him to desist. Wisely Haig intervened, ordering all three armies to suspend operations.

Unfortunately Haig's commitments to the French obliged him to wind up the offensive mechanism twice more in April and May. Attack followed attack to little purpose. Allenby made no demur. A fourth divisional commander, John Shea, became so exasperated with repeated demands to break into an enemy line now fully aroused and freshly reinforced, that he spoke and then wrote so critically of the army policy that Allenby removed him by disciplinary process, though recommending that after a period at home he should be found another appointment.

Within a short time Allenby was himself advised that he was to be moved 'to another appointment'. Although he was informed on the following day, 6 June, that this was not simply a euphemism of the military secretary seeking to convey dismissal from active service, he was none the less downcast and embittered. On leaving France he was convinced that Haig had got rid of him by a stratagem.

Reaching London on 7 June he was at once told to report to the Chief of the Imperial General Staff, Sir William Robertson, and then to the Prime Minister, Lloyd George. At the first of these interviews it became clear that he was not being relegated to some backwater as a result of Haig's animosity; indeed Haig had had nothing to do with his withdrawal from the western front. He had been selected by the Prime Minister for the command-in-chief in Egypt with a view to reopening the offensive against Turkey. Lloyd George's hopes of a Franco-British victory on the Scarpe and the Aisne in the spring of 1917 had come to nothing. His apprehensions were all of further costly reverses in France and Flanders. Sensitive to public opinion, he wondered whether the nation would support another winter at war without any success at all in the field and, long since disenchanted with prospects on the western front, he returned to earlier schemes of operations in the east. Understandably he did not then tell Allenby that he was his second choice for the Egyptian command,* but spoke only of confidence in his ability. What he wanted urgently was an advance into Palestine to capture 'Jerusalem as a Christmas present for the British nation'.

It was arranged that Allenby should embark at Brindisi in a fast warship for Egypt. Characteristically he did not question his orders – what was to be done after the capture of Jerusalem – what was to be the co-ordinated strategy of his own advance and that of the British force moving up the Tigris from the Persian Gulf. What he had received seemed adequate. He understood that he was to ask for the reinforcements he needed, though a look from Robertson suggested that the War Office might not have any to send. When he left Charing Cross station on 21 June his staff carried a number of

* The first choice was the South African General J.C. Smuts, who refused the offer.

briefs prepared for him in Whitehall. A chest of books with his baggage included the Bible and Sir George Adam Smith's *Historical Geography of the Holy Land*. From this range of sources he studied the background to his new command as he journed east.

At the beginning of the twentieth century Palestine was a part of the Ottoman Empire, like Syria to the north and the great deserts to the east and south-east, Nejd and the Hejaz. In the south the Sinai desert separated Palestine from the heartland of Egypt, the Turco-Egyptian frontier running from Rafa, just inland from the Mediterranean coast, to Aila on the Gulf of Akaba, an inlet from the Red Sea. In the Sinai wilderness the mountains were unoccupied; the desert was roamed by Bedouin.

Early in 1915 a Turkish-German force under Colonel Count Kress von Kressenstein crossed the desert to attack the Suez Canal. It was driven back from the eastern bank. During the summer intelligence sources reported preparation of a second Turkish sortie, and so when the British imperial army withdrew from the Dardanelles at the end of the year a number of its divisions were sent to reinforce the canal zone with a view to pushing its defences eastward across the Sinai.

The officer sent to command these operations and, in time, the forces in Egypt, was Sir Archibald Murray. By reputation a good peacetime staff officer, his talents had proved less suited to war. As chief-of-staff of the British Expeditionary Force in 1914 he was a failure. As Deputy Chief of the Imperial General Staff he acted effectively as a personal assistant to Lord Kitchener in the raising and equipping of the new armies, but when he was promoted to be Chief he became a cipher. The War Cabinet insisted on his removal and the Egyptian command was conveniently made vacant.

Despite many difficulties, not least the transfer of the greater number of his field formations to France for the Somme battles in the summer of 1916, Murray had ample forces to push across the Sinai if he had possessed also the necessary determination and audacity – such as Kress von Kressenstein demonstrated in a daring raid on the British lines that summer. Fear that Kress might return with a stronger force to cut the canal stimulated Murray to action. Firm plans were made at last to push eastward to the southern boundary of Palestine. Not surprisingly Murray felt that he might better entrust the conduct of operations to other hands. Delegating his powers in the field to Sir Charles Dobell in mid-October 1916, he removed his headquarters from the canal to the Savoy Hotel in Cairo. Three hundred miles to the east his Australian and New Zealand mounted riflemen, Indian cavalry, British yeomanry and infantry pushed the Turks and their Austro-German supporters from their outpost line in a series of spirited actions which, it may be noted, were almost brought to nothing on two occasions by irresolute generalship. In January 1917 Dobell's Eastern Force reached the Palestine border at Rafa.

At this time Allenby was preparing for the Battle of Arras. Because the projected offensive on the western front had first claim on all British resources, Murray was warned on 11 January to defer any major operations until the autumn. Another of his divisions was transferred from Egypt to France. It was fortunate that dissident activity in other parts of Egypt had recently come to an end, freeing two divisions to compensate the Eastern Force for this loss. The steady if deliberate advance against Kress von Kressenstein's forces was thus maintained. It is much to General Murray's credit that when Kress withdrew again in March to the general line Gaza-Beersheba, he approved Dobell's plans to seize these towns in succession. With the water supplies each contained in the possession of Eastern Force, he reckoned that he would be in an excellent position to mount a general offensive before the winter rains began.

Unfortunately for Murray his professional capability did not match his new spirit of bold enterprise. The construction of a railway and water pipeline from the Suez Canal across the Sinai desert, the growth of forward supply dumps, disclosed to Kress von Kressenstein the intentions of his opponent. To counter them, he began to develop defences from Gaza to Beersheba. The British intelligence staff noted the growth of enemy trenches and bunkers, estimating with fair accuracy the strength of the various positions – though the strength of Kress's immediate reserves was over-estimated. A setpiece attack was planned to capture Gaza, potentially the greater prize of the two original objectives. When the plan was put to Murray for his approval, the organisation of the mounted and infantry divisions remained unchanged from the earlier phase of pursuit. It did not strike him that a deliberate attack might require a somewhat different balance. He accepted also the assumption that if Gaza and its water supplies were not captured by midnight on the first day of attack, the operation must be cancelled. Indeed, as a visitor from Cairo, his knowledge of local resources and conditions was insufficient to challenge it.

It might be said on the British Commander-in-Chief's behalf that these decisions were surely matters for the Eastern Force commander; but Murray had come forward deliberately to oversee the battle. It opened on the morning of 26 March 1917, and despite a slow start progressed steadily to the point of breaking the enemy defences. However midnight struck before success was assured and Sir Charles Dobell broke off the action.

With additional intelligence in his hands Murray came quickly to realise how close they had been to victory. From whatever motives, he signalled to London an exaggerated picture of the outcome: '. . . The operation was most successful and owing to the fog and waterless nature of the country round Gaza just fell short of a complete disaster to the enemy.' The War Cabinet in London was only too anxious to encourage him to try again; Lloyd George was much taken with the idea of a grand drive against Turkey from Russia and the British forces on the Tigris and in Palestine. On 30 March Murray received a telegram suggesting that he should make Jerusalem his immediate objective. Murray's confidence began to ooze away. Not without reason: Kress had plainly reinforced his defence line; Gaza was being made into a fortress. The only additions to the British force were a dozen tanks of an early model, a batch of poison gas shells and a naval bombardment force. None of these sufficed when the assault was launched a second time on 19 April. This failure led to Murray's replacement by Allenby.

The new Commander-in-Chief assumed office on 28 June 1917. Almost at once he left for the Palestine front – now under command of Lieutenant-General Sir Philip Chetwode – returning for a second visit in July. 'I have been motoring and riding round, looking at defence works and water supplies,' he wrote home on 27 July. When he got back to Cairo a telegram from his wife was waiting for him: their son had just been killed in France. The reply he sent and subsequent letters reflect how deeply he was affected by this news. To those about him he showed nothing of his reactions, and he was very much on show just at this time as, in accordance with his practice of knowing all members of his staff, however junior, he was touring the headquarters office by office.

Among those he met was Major Richard Meinertzhagen, recently arrived from the War Office to take charge of intelligence matters in Palestine. Meinertzhagen wrote in his diary.

> Was introduced to Allenby, to whom I talked on intelligence matters for a while. My word, he is a different man to Murray. His face is strong and almost boyish. His manner is brusque almost to the point of rudeness, but I prefer it to the oil and butter of the society soldier. Allenby breathes success and the greatest pessimist cannot fail to have confidence in him . . . The Egyptian Expeditionary Force is already awaking from its lethargic sleep under Murray, and I am happy to say the GHQ will shortly move into Palestine and be near troops instead of wallowing in the fleshpots of Cairo. This move will stamp out the so-called East Force with its iniquitous in-dependent attitude, and the Chetwode policy of much bluster and no action. Chetwode is an excellent soldier but must be driven. If he acts by himself his every action is bluff and he is a very nervous officer, attributing to the Turk all sorts of wondrous strategy and tactics. Apart from this, he is a soldier with sound ideas; what he lacks is the initiative and courage to carry them out as planned. That is just where Allenby will find a very useful and talented servant.

Some at least of these penetrating, if disrespectful, observations might have been confirmed by Allenby if circumstances had permitted. He had known Chetwode for many years and had had him under command as a brigadier in Flanders. At any rate he listened attentively to his views and read carefully Chetwode's appreciation of the operational problem of forcing the enemy line.

That line extended now for 35 miles, beginning in the west round Gaza and extending south-east along more or less continuous trenches for several miles to Khirbet Sihan. From this point to Abu Hureira, 7 miles south-east again, the Turks looked from an eminence across a flat, bare plain towards the British lines. Their defences took the form of a series of redoubts from which they could pour fire into a British assault. Onwards towards Beersheba along ridges and across spurs there were more redoubts, self-contained and lightly wired, passing behind the railway station at Abu Irqaiq to a point where, 4 miles from Beersheba, the ground falls away. Here any defenders would have been at a serious disadvantage to observation and plunging fire. Kress had accordingly accepted a gap between the end of the line and Beersheba, which was patrolled by his 3rd Cavalry Division. To protect it in its isolation the town had been fortified, good use being made of the cactus gardens as at Gaza, among which many of the sandbagged firing bays were set. Barbed wire covered most of the defences but here, as all along the Turkish line, shortage of stocks limited obstacles to double, sometimes single, fences.

Behind this line a further coastal defence position had been sited at Deir Sineid, 5 miles in rear of Gaza. About the same distance behind the Gaza-Beersheba road and at a point roughly equidistant from each town, Tel es Sheria had been made into a stronghold.

The Turkish Eighth Army holding this area under Kress von Kressenstein was believed to comprise five infantry divisions and one of cavalry – say, fifty thousand men. It was in fact only about twenty-thousand strong due to wastage – with fifty battalions in the line supported by 120 guns, 130 machine guns, some manned by Austrians or Germans. An attack very strongly pressed against Gaza would simply drive the garrison back on the switch line Deir Sineid-Hureira. An attack against Hureira must come across the open plain and, all else apart, would have to be made without benefit of observing the effect of artillery fired before or during the assault. The third option appeared to be an attack through the gap between Beersheba and the nearest redoubts 4 miles to the north-west with the aim of attacking Hureira and Tel es Sheria from flank and rear.

Besides the tactical considerations, there was in each of these options a water limitation. The operation would mean the movement forward of a mass of men and horses. There would be water in Gaza for all if they captured the town. The water round Hureira and Tel es Sheria was brackish and fit only for animals. On the right Beersheba had many good wells. Chetwode had no doubt that this was the area of opportunity.

'Once established on the high ground between Hureira and Beersheba, and with Beersheba in our possession, we can attack north and north-westward, always from higher ground, always with observation . . .'

It was Chetwode's idea, but the decision was Allenby's. He decided to adopt it. On 12 July he telegraphed the scheme to London, asking for two infantry divisions and five thousand individual reinforcements to bring his remaining force up to strength. He needed, besides, artillery to complete his fire support to accepted scales and sufficient aircraft of a pattern superior to the German and Turkish complement currently raiding and observing his forward zone. To lay all this out more fully he sent a staff officer to London. There was a sympathetic response from Robertson, but it was not entirely open-handed. Haig was in course of preparing the Third Battle of Ypres. Men, guns and aircraft were not to be found easily. Allenby was persuaded to accept the 75th Division, a skeleton formation in Egypt, for which he was promised additional men and equipment, and the 10th Division from Salonika. As many guns, howitzers and aircraft as could be found would also be despatched.

With the assent to his plans, he received on 10 August further political instructions, though these were still of a general character. He was to 'strike the Turks as hard as possible', to follow up successes vigorously and to the limit of his resources. Allenby accepted without protest the deductions from his minimum bill of requirements. His only other request was that General Bols, who had served him in France, should be sent out as Chief of Staff. From the disbanding Eastern Force headquarters he took Brigadier-General Guy Dawnay as deputy chief. The army was formed into three corps: the Desert Mounted Corps under Lieutenant-General Sir Harry Chauvel, XX Corps under Chetwode and XXI Corps under Lieutenant-General E. S. Bulfin. It was an army now animated by an extraordinary sense of purpose, pervaded by exceptional confidence, due almost alone to the personality of its new chief.

Allenby took his commanders and staff step by step through his ideas for the battle he intended to open: a feint attack on Gaza by XXI Corps, the capture of Beersheba by a combination of infantry and mounted troops from XX Corps and the Desert Mounted Corps, while a light mobile screen held the open centre between Gaza and Beersheba. Subsequently, XX Corps and the Desert Mounted Corps, moving close to the Judean foothills, would attack behind the enemy's eastern flanks, striking both at Hureira and the reserve position at Tel es Sheria. XXI Corps would throw its full weight into Gaza and the Desert Mounted Corps would ride to the coast to cut off the garrison as it attempted to make its way northward.

Like many good plans this one was simple in concept. It required, however, a complex substructure of organisation to mount.

A huge amount of ammunition would be needed adjacent to the line, particularly for the bombardment of Gaza. Rations and forage apart, men and horses would depend on artificial reservoirs for their drinking water from the moment of assembly forward until they could capture sufficient local sources in and north of Beersheba and Gaza. Supply forward to and the collection of casualties from remote and trackless areas during the critical phases of the flank attacks and thrusts by XX and the Desert Mounted Corps called for intelligent guesswork as well as professional expertise. As in France, Allenby gave the widest responsibility to his subordinate commanders and staff, directing only that no administrative device was to be based on optimism; he intended to push men and animals to the limit of their capability from the opening of the battle. Equally, they were not to insure for too many unforeseen contingencies.

'If you want a guide in making your calculations,' he advised his staff at the second of his conferences, held to review progress, 'remember to think your problems through without skipping any intermediate steps.'

At this conference Allenby gave directions concerning the training and recreation of the army before battle. The forward defences were to be thinned out. On a rotating basis one-third of the officers and men in the infantry and mounted divisions would hold the line, one-third train behind the line, one-third assist in administrative support, but spend half each day in sport and recreation. Subject to the capacity of the railway, as many as possible were to be sent to the base on leave.

When the 10th (Irish) Division arrived from Salonika in September, the director of medical services advised that it would be unfit for active service for at least three months; many of its members were recovering from malaria contracted in Greece and others were still succumbing. Allenby toured the reception camps.

'Well, they look all right to me,' he remarked. 'Send them up into Palestine. I'd rather take the risk of having them up there fighting the Turks than fighting each other at the base.'

It was not simply that he wanted to keep the Irish contingent occupied. He needed every soldier capable of manning a weapon in the coming offensive. Time was pressing. Originally he had planned to attack Beersheba in September. Delays in the arrival of troops, aircraft, artillery and plant had necessitated postponement to the end of October. Notwithstanding the problem of water, he did not want to have it supplied by the onset of heavy winter rains.

As preparations advanced anxieties rose also in London. The offensive towards Passchendaele was dragging. Prime Minister and Cabinet were desperate for a victory in the Middle East, perhaps the more fearful of failing also because there was news that two German divisions were being sent there. On 5 October Allenby was asked to state what forces he would need to make certain of reaching Jaffa and Jerusalem; in effect to state a price for a guarantee. He estimated that he would need another thirteen divisions; a reinforcement Whitehall could not hope to supply, though this was not at once admitted. Meantime Allenby toured his units, vented his wrath on those who broke regulations, spent his leisure studying the history of the Holy Land, seeking wild flowers and, sometimes in company with Meinertzhagen, bird watching. With Meinertzhagen also, he watched the progress of the army deception scheme.

It was assumed at GHQ that Kress knew an offensive was being prepared against him – indeed German and Turkish reconnaissance aircraft were permitted into the otherwise tightly controlled EEF air space at random times to obtain the information. But the aim was to convince him that the prime blow would be struck at Gaza. Troop deployment suggested it, wireless messages hinted at it, even Allenby's reconnaissances towards Beersheba were conducted manifestly to accustom the enemy to the sight of mounted movement. Misleading documents were passed to Turkish commanders by various means. The programme was maintained until 31 October.

On 26 October the first elements of the great mass of men began to move into their places by night, slipping from camps and bivouacs left lighted, some filled with dummy figures of men and horses. That night a screen was pushed forward to seek what cover it could find on the flat plain in the centre, seeking to hold off enemy patrols while engineers and pioneers hastened to extend the railhead from Rafa to Karm. They were attacked and all but destroyed at two points yet succeeded in preserving security.

On 27 October XXI Corps began the bombardment of Gaza. British and French warships stood in to the coast, ostensibly embarking troops for a landing behind the enemy lines but actually making ready to take up firing stations abreast of Gaza. Hour by hour, day by day the bombardment continued while XX and the Desert Mounted Corps made ready and began at last their approach marches by night towards Beersheba. The errors in traffic control were negligible. There were none in navigation. A late, adventitious migration southward of Bedouin choked some of the wells on one route, obliging a column of mounted troops to retire 10 miles to take its last drink before battle. Otherwise, one by one, formations, units, guns, engineer plant, motor and horse transport, camel and mule trains moved into position. It was a cold, windless night broken only in the east by intermittent bursts of speculative enemy fire.

At 5.55 am on 31 October the XX Corps artillery began to bombard the Turkish trenches west and south-west of Beersheba. The leading battalions of the 60th Division – commanded by Major-General John Shea whose criticism at Arras Allenby had forgiven – advanced at 8.30 am on the right of the 74th Division. In position east and south-east of the town, the Desert Mounted Corps began its advance under enemy shrapnel at 9.10 am.

For some hours after the battle began Allenby remained in his headquarters near Rafa. Wireless telegraph stations connected him with his corps headquarters and the Royal Navy; multiple telegraph and telephone cables ran to Bulfin's XXI Corps opposite Gaza, to the new railhead at Karm, from which further lines were being run out on temporary poles to the headquarters of XX and the Desert Mounted Corps. Each corps had a liaison officer from Allenby's staff. Reconnaissance aircraft under fighter cover were watching the battle and reporting their observations directly to GHQ. It was from this latter source that the news was first received of the infantry's success on the western side of Beersheba and, early in the afternoon, that the Desert Mounted Corps had failed to break in to the east.

There was little doubt that Beersheba would be captured; forty thousand troops were committed against a defence of five thousand. Allenby was not prepared to delay the outcome: insistent instructions were sent to the corps commander that the town was to be captured before nightfall and advised that he was coming up to see matters for himself. Chauvel then hastened his own orders and shortly afterwards Brigadier-General Grant led the 4th Australian Light Horse Brigade in a dashing charge through the Turkish defences. While some of his squadrons dismounted to overcome the surviving Turkish infantry, Grant galloped on with the remainder into the close, rank streets of Beersheba, surprising the remnant of the garrison and capturing intact almost all the wells and much of the pumping gear.

Despite these and other successes, problems mounted for the Commander-in-Chief. Once he had confirmation that Beersheba and its water was taken, he issued orders to Bulfin to attack Gaza on the night 1–2 November; for it was now more than ever important that Kress should keep the bulk of his forces on the coast while the remainder of the EEF carried out their flank operations under the shadow of the Judean hills. Then came news that it would be 'some days' before the pumps in Beersheba could raise sufficient water for more than a couple of divisions. It was put to Allenby that the flanking movement and concomitant Gaza attack should be delayed. 'We will go forward exactly as planned,' Allenby said, 'to the limit of our resources.' That ended debate.

Slowly XXI Corps advanced in heavy fighting on the western side of Gaza; the Yeomanry Mounted Division watching the flat, open centre reported all quiet, while to the east the leading infantry and mounted formations of Chetwode's and Chauvel's corps were marching across the rock and gravel outcrops of the Judean hills. On the spine of the hills a little band of raiders under Lieutenant-Colonel S. F. Newcombe had cut the Beersheba–Jerusalem road south of Hebron.

Unknown to Allenby however command in Syria had passed to General Erich von Falkenhayn, formerly Chief of the German General Staff. He had available to him those Turkish and German reinforcements – glimpsed earlier by British intelligence – which, under the code name 'Yilderim' [Lightning], were to have counter-attacked the British force on the Tigris. Recognising a greater threat in southern Palestine, Falkenhayn preferred to commit his strength there. As information reached him of the loss of Beersheba and Newcombe's road block, it seemed that Allenby was moving directly through the hills on Jerusalem. Every soldier that Kress could spare from Gaza was therefore sent eastwards towards the Judean hills.

Thus XX Corps and the Desert Mounted Corps marched northwards against increasing resistance, short of water in the stifling heat, short of ammunition due to the difficulties of getting transport across the steep, broken ground. Recovery of the wounded was painful. Expected to attack Hureira and Tel es Sheria on 4 November, Chetwode and Chauvel had to tell Allenby that they could not do so until the sixth. He accepted this on the understanding that the mounted force would break out on the seventh, and ordered Bulfin to make a final effort at Gaza. There were doubts among staffs and some senior commanders that this timetable was practicable, but none dared to gainsay the army commander. His troops did not fail him. Though Hureira and Tel es Sheria were not finally taken until the morning of the seventh, sufficient of a gap was made for six mounted brigades to pass through, Shea's 60th Division following.

The opportunity to cut off the enemy at Gaza had passed however; Kress had withdrawn during the night 6–7 November and was attempting to form a new defence line. At once Allenby told xx Corps to pass back to xxi all the transport it had borrowed and to add some of its own. He did not intend to cling to a defunct plan. As the coast road offered the best line of communication, xxi Corps was to advance as quickly and as strongly as possible. Driving from one corps headquarters to another and often into the forward areas, Allenby pressed his army against the disordered Turks. Falkenhayn's countermeasures destroyed Newcombe's force but could achieve nothing else: the Turkish command chain lacked the ability to react as swiftly as the German staff expected. The spirit of the offensive carried Allenby's infantry and mounted regiments forward to Jaffa on the coast, to possession of the railway junction for Jerusalem and almost up to Jerusalem itself. But in his haste Allenby committed mounted units to the western gorges and steep hill slopes. By the time he had brought up infantry the rains had begun, the Turks had settled into their defences. Controlling his impatience Allenby ordered a halt, brought down the soaked and depleted units to be rested and issued warm clothing, rebuffed a number of brave counter-attacks – of which he had some warning from the German wireless – and put Chetwode's corps to the capture of the Holy City on 8 December. After a day of intense fighting among the boulder-strewn heights on the western approaches, often over the decaying bodies of men fallen in the earlier attempt, the defence withdrew during the night. Next morning the mayor of Jerusalem formally handed his keys to Major-General John Shea. Allenby's army had secured its Christmas present for the British nation.

It had not been cheaply accomplished. The cost was 18,000 battle casualties including 3,802 killed. Against this, half the enemy force in Palestine had been destroyed.* The success was due to Allenby's singlemindedness and the wholehearted response of his troops.

The advance of 60 miles to Jerusalem brought Allenby warm congratulations from the government and a confusing direction from Lloyd George to continue until Palestine was cleared 'from Dan to Beersheba'. Only a few weeks before the Cabinet had been urging caution, apprehensive of a counter-offensive. Now it disregarded the flood waters that interrupted the supplies of the EEF.

Allenby replied that when the rains passed he intended to isolate the Turks

---

* Thirteen thousand battle casualties and fifteen thousand prisoners, but these figures included the many administrative units overtaken on the line of communication.

in Medina by occupying the Jordan valley and, with Feisal's Arab guerrillas, cut the Damascus–Medina railway by the capture of Amman. When railway and roads were improved, he would advance to the line Haifa–Nazareth, but to reach deep into Syria he would need to double his strength. That meant some withdrawal of troops from France.

In the subsequent Allied councils Haig and Robertson continued to advocate a 'western' strategy, arguing that while a victory on the western front would end the war in the Middle East, the converse was not true. But Robertson was dismissed in February and shortly General Smuts came to Palestine as the government's representative to see how the defeat of Turkey in the field might best be managed. It was a wasted journey. In March the Germans launched a huge offensive on the Somme. Two-thirds of the British units in the EEF were hastened to France. By the summer of 1918 Allenby's fighting strength was reduced to sixty-nine thousand, of whom over half were raw Indian troops.

Fortunately the southern half of the Jordan valley had been occupied before these subtractions. Attempts to advance into Transjordan had failed, due partly to a want of tactical subtlety, partly to the unreliability of the Arabs working under Feisal and Lawrence, but two small bridgeheads had been retained. Three Turco-German 'armies' opposed the EEF west and east of the Jordan with a total fighting strength of thirty thousand. Falkenhayn and Kress had been recalled. Command of the Syrian theatre had passed to Liman von Sanders who had long since earned the respect of his ally.

Liman attacked in July, using a high proportion of German troops in an attempt to pinch out the northernmost EEF bridgehead over the Jordan. The operation failed: the Turkish element was plainly not prepared to press the encounter. This and a number of similar experiences convinced Allenby that the enemy was ripe for defeat. There were schemes in Whitehall again to send him divisions from Europe for the winter, but he disregarded them. He could rely only on what he possessed for an offensive – a circumstance that persuaded him to fight higher authority for once when it was proposed that he should send his last Australian mounted and British infantry division to France. As evidence of his need of them he informed London in August that he had issued orders to advance 10 miles to Tulkarm and Nablus. But as he pondered on this plan he thought of something more enterprising. General Wavell, one of his officers, has recorded that,

One morning . . . he returned from a morning ride, strode into his office, and informed the Operations Staff that he had decided on an extension of his plan which aimed at nothing less than the complete destruction of the Turkish armies. The cavalry, instead of turning inland at the level of Tulkarm, were to continue their ride up the plain of Sharon, cross the spur of hills that ran from the main Judean range to the sea at Mount Carmel near Haifa and break into the great Plain of Esdraelon some 30 or 40 miles in rear of the Turkish armies, of the railway that served all Turkish forces west of Jordan, and of their main lines of retreat.

In after years it has been claimed that Allenby had conceived the grand idea many months before and that his somewhat clumsy operations across the Jordan had simply been designed to attract Liman's attention to the eastern flank. This is much to be doubted. Still, a deception scheme was again employed to suggest strongly an offensive in that direction: dummy camps and headquarters, false signals, air action all played their part. Lawrence's agents went out among the eastern villages advising that fodder would soon be sought for a mass of horses and, later, Feisal's guerrillas cut the Hejaz railway at three points under his direction.

Meantime Allenby sped about in his motor car, visiting his units, carrying on a series of skirmishes with the Australians who defied, when they could, his dress regulations for the Jordan valley. During the first half of September the divisions began to deploy. By 19 September thirty-five thousand infantry, nine thousand cavalry were in partial hiding on the plain of Sharon opposite eight thousand Turks and Germans. The Turkish Eighth Army headquarters at Tulkarm, the Eighth at Nablus, the Fourth at Es Salt in Jordan, Liman's GHQ at Nazareth – none had any expectation of attack. A few days before zero Allenby briefed all commanders down to battalion and regiment as to his intentions. One commanding officer asked where he should expect to dig-in after the assault. 'Aleppo,' Allenby replied. This city was 400 miles away.

It was not quite as easy as that of course: the breaking open of a door in the coastal defences incurred almost three thousand casualties, but happily the proportion of those killed was low. When the door opened on 19 September, the Desert Mounted Corps passed through without a moment lost. Three divisions of cavalry rode almost unopposed into and across the enemy line of communication. By that evening they had penetrated to a depth of 25 miles. Just after dawn on 20 September the 2nd [Indian] Lancers supported by armoured cars cleared the Musmus Pass and swept away at Megiddo the enemy attempting to stem the cavalry tide flooding into the Galilean plains. To the north, that morning, the Gloucester Hussars almost captured Liman von Sanders as they raided his GHQ at Nazareth. To the east a composite force – Australians, British, Indians and French – soon took Es Salt and Amman, then swung north along the Hejaz railway. East and north Feisal's Arab guerrillas cut in on weak Turkish detachments, killing, looting, showing no mercy to prisoners.

Day by day Allenby's army continued its advance. The Bristol fighters of the Australian Flying Corps assured air supremacy. Reconnaissance and bomber aircraft of the Royal Air Force were totally integrated with the land battle. By 29 September cavalry columns were passing over the Golan heights. Damascus was reached on the 30th. Less than a month later, 240 miles to the north, Aleppo fell.

It was a spectacular triumph for Allenby, one that earned him in later years such tributes as 'he is one of the great captains of all ages' and 'he is clearly among the few really great generals of British history'. In military terms the advance in 1917 to Jaffa and Jerusalem was a greater achievement; for it was undertaken without the resources in water, food and cover afforded by the countryside in 1918 and against an enemy stronger and more resolute. However, successful direction of the two campaigns surely bestows some title to generalship of the first rank. What, then, were the rare, high talents that transformed a relative failure in France to outstanding success in Palestine?

In Allenby's case they are not easy to find. His career had been long but was not particularly distinguished in the discharge of any appointment or in the enlightenment of his profession. He served competently as a squadron, regimental and column commander in the second South African War, gaining some useful experience of skirmishing in open warfare, but was not at all interested in analysing the lessons of the campaign. He remained aloof from the reformist activities of his seniors – such as Roberts and Ian Hamilton – and contemporaries – such as Haig, Grierson and the Gough brothers – who sought to reorganise, re-equip and retrain the British army to ensure that it would not repeat the mistakes of the late nineteenth century if it went to war again in the twentieth. Nor was this a passing mood of disenchantment on his part, a reaction to three years of hard campaigning. As a commanding officer, brigade commander, even as inspector of cavalry in the years 1910–14, Allenby showed little interest in training, or the developments in artillery, small-arms, aircraft or mechanical transport. A poor performer as commander of a cavalry division in the annual manoeuvres immediately prior to 1914, he did not distinguish himself in command of the British Expeditionary Force cavalry in France and Flanders when war began. His brigades lacked proper direction in the operations round Mons. As the retreat to the Marne began he threw the entire mounted force into disorder when a small force of Germans approached, issuing orders for their engagement appropriate to the drill square, an occasion afterwards recollected with much hilarity by the participants as 'the cavalry field day'.

During his tour as a corps commander in the Ypres salient in 1915, Allenby's reputation was confirmed as an obedient agent of GHQ, a devotee of attack when all the tactical circumstances militated against it. His promotion in war, as in the latter days of peace, owed much to the influence of the Commander-in-Chief, Field-Marshal Sir John French, and one of French's final preferments before he was himself succeeded by Haig was the promotion of Allenby to command the Third Army.

In that, as in his other commands, he lacked real independence in major operational decisions and resources. He was torn between loyalty to his superiors and what he owed to his subordinates. The man who left France was not embittered but frustrated as a commander. In Palestine his directions were of the most general nature. If they were to be given effect, everything – time, sector, disposal of resources, not least leadership – depended upon Allenby personally. He liked that. Abstract problems, tactical problems that lacked the arbitrament of shell and bullet did not interest him. Well aware that his mind was not quick, he enjoyed the exercise of it on problems amenable to prolonged, painstaking thought. In July 1917 he was able to make a decision speedily on the strategic concept for his offensive because he admired and trusted Chetwode's lively and lucid reasoning. Thereafter he had time to 'think through' – advice he applied as much to himself as he pressed it on his commanders and staff officers – all the options open to him. Given the time, his confidence, energy and commanding presence made success overwhelmingly probable.

Allenby's career did not end with the armistice. Within a few months he was appointed High Commissioner for Egypt, retaining also for a time command and political control of the territories he had captured from the Turks. Resolution of the complex problems of Palestine, Syria and Transjordan as well as those of Egypt were too much for a man altogether lacking experience in international politics – as indeed they were too much for a number who had had such experience. In Egypt however he had time to discover for himself the several facets of the national movement for independence and to think through in his painstaking way the options open to the British government. Eventually he came to the view that Egypt must either become independent, while permitting still the maintenance of British garrisons and bases to safeguard the canal, or the United Kingdom must occupy the country with overwhelming military force, ruling by colonial government. He recommended the former. His direct, open methods impressed the responsible Egyptian politicians with whom he worked or consulted. They were less acceptable to some of his fellow countrymen, who believed that the United Kingdom should, in all matters of substance, retain control of Egypt. At the end of his six years of office Allenby had his way, but in so doing had offended a number of senior ministers and officials at home. When he was ready to resign, believing his work to be done, the arrangements for his replacement were extraordinarily discourteous.

Still, he returned home with a great public reputation. His military victories were remembered and honoured. During his latter years in Egypt he had brought his hot temper and bullying habits, which had grown with military power, under control. The effort was said by his enemies to have killed him, for he died not long after retirement. It was a cruel joke, a manifestation of the antipathy provoked by the dark side of his nature; one quickly stifled by the scores of men from his Palestine command – Australians prominent among them – who mourned the passing of the commander who had roused and led them to victory.

General of the Armies John J. Pershing

Donald Smythe

Born in the remote hamlet of Laclede, Missouri, in 1860, the eldest of nine children, John J. Pershing attended the United States Military Academy at West Point, not for any dreams of martial glory, but simply because it offered a free, government-paid education, better than he was likely to receive at an obscure Missouri teachers' college he was attending. Lying about his age to enter, he attended the academy from 1882 to 1886, graduating thirtieth in a class of seventy-seven, but the recognised class leader and First Captain of Cadets.

From 1886 to 1891 he served on the frontier in New Mexico and South Dakota, participating in the last great Indian uprising in the United States, the so-called Ghost Dance Rebellion. The next four years (1891–5) he served as Professor of Military Science at the University of Nebraska, where he earned a law degree on the side, seriously thinking then and later of resigning from what looked like an unpromising army career to pursue the law.

During 1897–8 he returned to West Point as a tactical officer where the cadets disliked him intensely because he was a martinet. Knowing of his previous service with Negro troops, they called him 'Nigger Jack', a term that was subsequently softened to 'Black Jack', a nickname he bore thereafter.

In the Spanish-American War he performed valiantly under fire, acting as 'cool as a bowl of cracked ice', according to an officer who saw him.

After the war he went to the Philippines for the first of three tours (1899–1903, 1907–8, 1909–13), most of which was spent in Mindanao among the Moros, a fierce, warlike people. Among them he had considerable success in imposing American rule with a minimum of bloodshed.

He returned to the United States in 1903, still only a captain, and promptly fell in love with Helen Frances Warren, a girl some years his junior. Recently graduated from Wellesley College, she was also the daughter of Senator Francis E. Warren, a wealthy rancher, chairman of the Senate Military Affairs Committee. They were married in January 1905 in a lavish ceremony attended by President Theodore Roosevelt and other dignitaries.

Almost two years later, when Pershing was suddenly promoted from captain to brigadier-general, leapfrogging 862 other officers, talk circulated that he had been jumped because of his father-in-law's influence. Actually recommendations for his promotion pre-existed the Warren relationship. Because of outstanding work in Mindanao, his work on the newly formed General Staff in Washington, and his brief sojourn in the first class of the Army War College, every general in the army, with one exception, had recommended him for brigadier-general by 1906. None the less Senator Warren facilitated the promotion, especially in committee work. His influence was important, not in gaining the promotion (which would surely have come anyway in time), but in ensuring that it came when it did.

Hard on his promotion in 1906 came allegations in the Philippine and American press that Pershing had fathered illegitimate children during his first Philippine tour, a charge undoubtedly fostered by officers disgruntled over his startling promotion. Pershing denied the accusation, furnishing numerous affidavits, one from his supposed mistress, all contradicting the charge. Yet stories of the reputed scandal continued to circulate, helping to block his appointment as superintendent of West Point in 1912. Pershing's relations with women, at least in legend, were such that many people, including friends, thought that the charge might be true. During his marriage however he was a devoted and faithful husband.

That marriage came to a tragic end in 1915 when, after returning from the Philippines two years before and assuming command of the 8th Brigade at the Presidio in San Francisco, a fire broke out at his home one night while he was away, killing his wife and three daughters. Only a son, Warren, survived.

Pershing suffered terribly. 'I have been able to get so little consolation out of life since that time,' he wrote over a year later. 'About the only respite I have known is by keeping every minute occupied.'

His occupation during 1916–17 was chasing the Mexican bandit, Francisco (Pancho) Villa, who raided an American town in March 1916, killing eighteen people. The pursuit was frustratingly futile, but did provide a measure of training and war preparation for the American regular army and the National Guard which mobilised on the border. It also provided valuable experience for Pershing in handling a relatively large group of men (eleven thousand), the largest he had ever commanded, and gave worthwhile training to a number of young, future American leaders, among them Courtney H. Hodges and George S. Patton, Jr. The latter admired Pershing tremendously, studied his bearing and command practices, and consciously patterned himself after him.

Promoted to major-general during the Mexican campaign, Pershing was the logical choice for command of the American Expeditionary Forces (AEF) when the United States entered the war in April 1917. His only serious rival, Leonard Wood, although better known than Pershing in Europe, was never seriously considered. His Republican political aspirations were anathema to the Democratic administration and an old skull injury impaired his health.

Pershing sailed for France with a skeleton staff in May 1917 on the Cunard liner *Baltic*, planning on board for an army of one million men. One month after his arrival, when he saw the plight of the Allies (the French army had recently mutinied) and realised how massive must be America's contribution, he requested 'at least' three million men. For a long time they came in bits and dribbles, the war effort at home being unco-ordinated and inefficient, with everything in short supply or totally lacking.

The first troop arrivals at St Nazaire in late June, although theoretically regular army, were a nondescript lot, for the regulars had been kept at home, skeletonised and parcelled out as training cadres for the mass of raw recruits. The British and French must have wondered what such troops, really civilians in uniform, would do when they came up against the Germans. In time the Allies came to respect the bravery and initiative of the Doughboy, but throughout the war continued to have serious reservations about the American officer corps, particularly the higher command and staff.

The American build-up was agonisingly slow. Nine months after declaring war, the United States had only 175,000 troops in France, totalling only four combat divisions in various stages of training, only one of which had been in line, and that only on a battalion level in a quiet sector.

By now Russia was out of the war and many German divisions, released from that front, would soon appear in the west, giving Germany an estimated 60 per cent manpower advantage. Italy was still reeling after Caporetto. England's armies, just finished with the disastrous campaign of Ypres and Passchendaele, numbered two hundred thousand less than the previous year. France, recovering from the Nivelle failure and the spring mutinies, had reached her manpower limit and began breaking up battalions to keep up existing units.

Not surprisingly then the Allies began earnest attempts in December to amalgamate American units into British and French ranks.

There was much to be said for the idea. The Allies had the existing staffs of divisions, corps and field armies; they lacked men to fill them. America had the men, but lacked the higher organisations. By the time she created them the war could well be lost under the impact of the massive German assaults expected for the spring and summer of 1918.

As far as the Allies were concerned, amalgamation – at least temporarily – made sense, even from the viewpoint of America. Raw recruits would train better and faster if associated with veterans; consequently American casualties would be lower. Amalgamation would also eliminate the need to develop AEF higher staffs; hence America's weight could more quickly be brought to bear and the war could be ended sooner, which was to America's interest. Finally, amalgamation would relieve the tonnage problem, since it would not be necessary for America to bring over the support troops and impedimenta to sustain full divisions, corps and armies.

Always, in treating of amalgamation, the Allies spoke of an *eventual*

American army. Only for the moment, only *pro tem*, would smaller units be trained and fought in larger Allied units. Later, after they were 'bloodied' and proficient, American regiments would be gathered into their own divisions, American divisions into their own corps, and American corps into their own army. The advantage of this was that it was organic; it permitted the development of larger American units after they had grown to proficiency as smaller ones. In the meantime they would have the benefit of Allied tutelage and experience. How much better this would be, they contended, than to commit a whole American army, virtually untried and untested, to a separate portion of the front. The Germans would surely tear it apart.

These were good arguments, irrefutable in the eyes of the Allies. Even so staunch a Pershing partisan as James G. Harbord, his Chief of Staff, admitted that were he French or English, 'my views on amalgamation would have been the same as theirs'.

Pershing himself admitted that had massive German offensives occurred during the fall and winter of 1917, instead of during the following spring and summer, he would have had no choice but to accede to amalgamation. But he was always suspicious of Allied talk about a separate and independent American army in the future, while clamouring for immediate amalgamation in the present. Such talk he considered so much 'camouflage', 'a downright piece of impudence'. He observed that with rare exceptions the British had never thought to amalgamate Australians, Canadians or Indians into British units, nor had the French attempted it with their Senegalese, Moroccans or other colonials.

The Allies might point out however that the Canadians and Australians had had time – three years of war – to develop their organisations organically. Furthermore, in their formation and development, they had not been confronted with the crisis that loomed up now on the western front: a projected 60 per cent manpower disadvantage during the coming German offensives.

Accordingly in December the Allies began strong attempts to amalgamate American units, becoming increasingly persistent throughout the ensuing months. British or American ships would bring over surplus American companies or battalions for temporary incorporation into Allied units, with the understanding that when the emergency was over they could be recalled for American divisions. As surplus troops, they contended, their temporary incorporation would not interfere with American plans for forming a separate army. Lloyd George, the British Prime Minister, warned Washington in mid-December that the Germans were planning 'a knock-out blow to the Allies before a fully trained American Army is fit . . .'

Alarmed, President Wilson talked the matter over with Secretary of War Newton D. Baker and instructed him to cable Pershing as follows on 24 December: 'We do not desire loss of identity of our forces *but regard that as secondary* to the meeting of any critical situation by the most helpful use possible of the troops at your command.' This was Pershing's basic position also, although Lloyd George, frustrated in dealing with him, came to believe that the general preferred building a separate American army to winning the war.

The crucial phrase in Baker's cablegram was 'critical situation'. How critical must a situation be, and who was to decide? The answer was: Pershing, to whom Baker's cablegram gave 'full authority to use the forces at your command as you deem wise . . .'.

In effect then the United States placed in the hands of its field commander the ultimate decision as to whether to amalgamate, and if so, under what circumstances. The effect was to focus and bring to bear enormous pressures on Pershing, the Allies knowing that if he could be persuaded, cajoled, intimidated, or in some manner won over, the deed was done. Washington, feeling that Pershing was on the spot and knew the situation firsthand, would concur in his decision.

With the exception of Lord Northcliffe, a newspaper publisher, and Marshal Joffre, a sidelined general, the Europeans presented a united front against Pershing on this question. Prime ministers, chiefs of staff, army commanders, ambassadors – all made their pressure felt during the ensuing months, attempting to wear him down.

Pershing resisted them all. If American troops went into Allied ranks, 'very few of them would ever come out', he predicted. Furthermore 'no people with a grain of national pride would consent to furnish men to build up the army of another nation.' His basic stand, held unswervingly throughout the coming months, was summed up in the declaration: 'We cannot permit our men to serve under another flag except in an extreme emergency and then only temporarily.'

He ran a great risk, for the Allies might well be right. Nobody maintained that the Americans were incapable, given time, of providing skilled leaders and staffs. But time was what was lacking. An inexperienced, untrained American army was a gamble and if the Germans tore it apart, as they were to do experienced Allied armies in the coming months, the result could be disaster. Harbord well said of Pershing: 'He risked the chance of being cursed to the latest generation if, through his failure to co-operate, the War were lost.'

Replying to Baker's message of 24 December, putting authority into his hands, Pershing cabled on 1 January 1918: 'Do not think emergency now exists that would warrant our putting companies or battalions into British or French divisions, and would not do so except in grave crisis.' This was his basic position, maintained steadfastly in the months to come.

His objections were the loss of national identity, the problem of reclaiming contingents without disrupting Allied divisions, language difficulties with the French, hard feelings if American casualties resulted from Allied mistakes, and differences in training methods. Specifically Pershing objected to the Allied emphasis on training for trench rather than open warfare.

Trench warfare was as the name implies: static, subterranean, oriented toward the taking and holding of trenches. In an attack the artillery laid down a tremendous barrage on the enemy's trenches, caving them in, destroying barbed wire, and disrupting communications. At a signal the infantry crossed no-man's-land, captured the enemy's front trenches, then repeated the process for as long as momentum lasted, after which they burrowed into the ground like moles, fortifying the trenches captured. It was frontal assault warfare, of limited objectives, and it had not moved the lines more than about 10 miles in either direction since late 1914. It had also heaped up casualties by the millions.

In contrast open warfare was fluid. Open-ended, flexible, oriented to the earth's surface rather than its bowels, it inclined to go around strongpoints rather than into them. Infantrymen hugged the ground, as they must always do, but only temporarily until, momentum regained, the lines swept forward again, probing, enfilading, encircling, cutting off defenders from the side and rear. It was this type of warfare for which Pershing felt Americans had a special genius and in which he desired them trained, especially in America where vast spaces permitted sweeping movements. With men trained to fight *on* the earth rather than within it, he hoped to break open the front and win the war. Victory could be won, he maintained, only 'by driving the enemy out into the open and engaging him in war of movement'.

To Pershing's dismay French instructors sent to America to aid in training taught not open warfare but trench warfare – probably not surprising, as it was the only warfare they knew. At Waco, Texas, after a month of instruction devoted exclusively to trench warfare, an American asked one of the French instructors, 'How shall we know what to do if we should ever have the Germans on the run?'

'This war will be fought out in the trenches,' was the reply; 'in this respect, it has been different, and will be different, from all previous wars.'

This was typical. An American assigned to translate French training documents said that he 'never once saw any mention of open warfare'.

Pershing felt he was being undercut in the United States by French instructors and by a complacent War Department which deferred to their experience. He asked repeatedly that training in open warfare be the principal instruction given before embarkation.

The dispute over training methods was epitomised in the rifle. In trench warfare it was not that important, since artillery did the preliminary work, while grenades and satchel charges did the mopping up. Pershing actually heard of cases where Allied soldiers were so habituated to using grenades that encountering the enemy in the open they instinctively threw grenades at them, rather than shot.

In open warfare however the rifle would be the weapon *par excellence*, as the infantrymen moved forward, hugged the ground, isolated strongpoints, and killed at a distance. Significantly French target ranges were short, under

100 metres. Pershing insisted that Americans be trained to shoot up to at least 600 metres.

To him the rifle was the essential infantry weapon and he complained repeatedly that it was not sufficiently stressed in training at home. A flow of 'teach them to shoot straight' cables went to the War Department, followed by complaints that they were not being complied with.

For their part the French regarded the Americans as a people who had not fired a shot in anger until October 1917 and who surely were foolish if they did not follow French practice, based as it was on three years of hard-fought combat. 'If the Americans do not permit the French to teach them,' said Clemenceau ruefully, 'the Germans will do so . . .'

When President Wilson's confidant, Colonel Edward M. House, passed through Paris in late November 1917, General Philippe Pétain, the French army commander, let it be known, with a deprecating shrug of the shoulders and nod of the head, that he did not think American training was all it ought to be. Pershing 'was a good man but narrow . . .', he said. 'Most of the help proffered by the French had been curtly refused.' A few months later, when Pétain's headquarters issued a manual on the conduct of large-unit offensives, Pershing ordered it suppressed for AEF use.

The dispute about training would be academic, of course, unless the United States got men shipped in sufficient time to be of some use. On 21 March 1918 the Germans launched a massive attack against the British Fifth Army, all but destroying it. In the emergency Pershing offered the Allies 'all that we have'. It was pitifully little: some four divisions (1st, 2nd, 26th, 42nd), all of which had seen some time in the trenches, but only in quiet sectors and only one of them (the 1st) as a full division. Pétain assigned them to quiet sectors, relieving French troops who were sped to aid the British.

Two events at the end of May and beginning of June were important both for Pershing and the separate American army for which he contended. They were the successful American participation in hard fighting (at Cantigny and Belleau Wood) and the Supreme War Council meeting at Versailles. Because they are important they must be treated in some detail.

By the end of May the United States had been at war almost fourteen months and had some 650,000 officers and men in Europe. While of some use in holding quiet sectors, they had participated in nothing bigger than a mêlée at Seicheprey, in which they had not exactly covered themselves with glory. On 28 May however the AEF scheduled an attack. It was to be a limited one, on the regimental level (some four thousand men), against Cantigny, a little village north-west of Montdidier, selected because it was on a hill that provided good observation posts for German artillery. More importantly however Cantigny was to be a test case, revealing the capacity of the American command and staff to plan and carry out an offensive, albeit a minor one. If they could it would reinforce Pershing's argument for an independent army in the near future. If they could not it would reinforce the Allies' contention that, for the moment, American troops could best be utilised in British and French formations. From the AEF viewpoint it was important that the Cantigny operation succeed.

It did. The Americans captured the town, then held it against repeated counter-attacks, taking heavy casualties in their baptism of fire. Although the German defenders were only third-class troops, Pershing was elated by the success.

> This action illustrates the facility with which our officers and men learn [he told the War Department] and emphasizes the importance of organizing our own divisions and higher units as soon as circumstances permit. It is my firm conviction that our troops are the best in Europe and our staffs are the equals of any.

Dining with Pershing and his staff a short time after the battle, Dorothy Canfield Fisher remembered the group's enthusiasm.

> They all talked at the top of their voices . . . about what they thought had been the magnificent conduct of the American troops under fire for the first time in Europe. I remember particularly Pershing's banging his fist down on the table and shouting out, 'I am certainly going to jump down the throat of the next person who asks me, *"Will the Americans really fight?"'*.

The Cantigny success shortened Pershing's patience with Allied criticism of his organisation, especially its staff work. When André Tardieu, recently French High Commissioner in America, ventured some criticism, Pershing told him that he had 'had quite enough of this sort of thing', suggesting that if the French 'would cease troubling themselves so much about our affairs and attend more strictly to their own we should all get along much better'.

While Cantigny was a morale-raiser, it was little more, involving as it did a single regiment, slightly reinforced. Elsewhere the news was just about as black as it could be. One day before, on 27 May, the Germans had ripped open the French lines along the Chemin des Dames in the most dramatic break-through of the war. Achieving a first-day gain 12 miles deep and almost 30 miles wide, they rapidly took Soissons, reached the Marne, and were heading for Paris. French divisions, thrown piecemeal in their path to stop them, 'evaporated immediately like drops of rain on white-hot iron', said a French staff officer.

In these circumstances the Supreme War Council met at Versailles on 1–2 June, not knowing whether this meeting would be their last or whether, as Clemenceau said, the next would be 'in the Pyrenees'. In Paris, 10 miles away, people were leaving the city by the hundreds; the government was packing up its papers preparatory to doing the same.

With the war about to be lost, people's emotions surfaced. They said what

they thought about each other and about the issues. The main agenda concerned the use of American troops, and this time once and for all the Allies
intended to state the case for amalgamation with such forcefulness that even
the stubborn Missouri general would see it.

Stressing the crisis, Ferdinand Foch, the Allied generalissimo, called for
shipping only infantry and machine-gun units from America for the indefinite
future. To Pershing this was intolerable; it meant postponing indefinitely the
formation of a separate American army, which it seemed to him was always
being postponed, however much the Allies agreed to it in principle.

The month before, at an Allied conference at Abbeville on 1–2 May, he had
reluctantly agreed to allow priority shipment of only infantry and machine-
gun units during May and June, postponing until later the shipment of their
complementary artillery personnel, supply units, corps and army troops.
Now Foch wanted to postpone these indefinitely. Pershing pointed out that
his Abbeville concessions had already put him considerably behind schedule
in forming a balanced and integral American army. His supply problem was
becoming acute, as was his transportation. Railway repair workers, for
instance, were urgently needed to repair French rolling stock, without which
supplies would pile up at the ports, and without supplies his forces would
stagnate. Already, under existing agreements, he was some 205,000 men
short for his Services of Supply (SOS).

Foch was unmoved. The Germans were on the Marne; the Fatherland was
in peril. He kept waving his hands excitedly and repeating, 'The battle, the
battle, nothing else counts.'

At this point Mr Graeme Thomson, a British transportation expert, supported Pershing in remarking that it would be a very serious mistake to
permit American rail transportation to further degenerate, it being already
in bad condition. Thomson's words had no more effect on Foch, said Pershing,
'than if they had not been uttered'. Waving his hands the generalissimo said
everything else could be postponed. *'La bataille, la bataille, il n'y a que ça qui
compte.'*

Pershing then played his ace in the hole, the card given him by the American Chief of Staff in Washington, who had cabled on 11 May that the number
of trained men in the United States was getting quite low and hence there was
a limit to the number America could send, even if the Allies had ships. It was
quite impossible, Pershing declared, to send over only infantry and machine-
gun units to the extent Foch demanded: 250,000 men each for June and July,
a total of 500,000. Apart from three divisions ready to embark, only 263,000
trained men remained in the United States.

Foch promptly trumped Pershing's ace. Send them anyway, he said in
effect, even untrained men. The situation required it. *'La bataille, la bataille!'*

To Pershing the proper course was not to bring over untrained infantrymen, but to bring over the trained infantrymen available and use the shipping
surplus to bring over the auxiliary arms, like artillery and SOS personnel,

corps and army troops. Clemenceau had shrugged his shoulders helplessly when Pershing had revealed the shortage of infantrymen. 'Then we can practically expect nothing from the United States after the present schedules are completed,' he said. 'That is a great disappointment.'

'Not at all, Mr Prime Minister,' replied Pershing. 'Every ton of available shipping will be used to bring over the SOS troops that are absolutely needed, as well as divisional and corps troops that are needed to complete the American combat organizations. In the present crisis I consider this essential.'

Foch waved his arms and called for 'the largest possible number of troops, trained or untrained'. Pershing pointed out that untrained combat troops could not be used for two months anyway, so why not leave them in the United States and use shipping to bring over what was needed to complete existing units and build up his SOS organisation? Foch said that men learned quicker in France. Lord Milner, the British War Minister, jumped in with the remark that 'we form a coalition and must make concessions'; therefore Pershing ought to consider sending untrained infantrymen.

Later, when Pershing suggested calling up earlier the latest class of French youth, Lloyd George interrupted, 'Why, General Pershing, you surely would not put those mere boys into the trenches?'

'Mr. Prime Minister,' Pershing rounded on him, 'you have suggested that we put American boys not as well trained as the French boys you refer to into the trenches. I cannot see the distinction.'

Pershing then complained that the Allies, despite promises, were not meeting existing commitments to supply and maintain American troops. Shortages existed in artillery, transport and other facilities. He did not blame them for conditions over which they had no control, but the deteriorating situation pointed up the need to build up the SOS organisation sufficiently to handle the American army when it came into being.

Foch was adamant. 'He saw no reason,' said Pershing, 'why we should not fill up ships in July with men called to the colors in May.'

Suggesting an adjournment Pershing walked out in the yard with his Chief of Staff. He was willing to do everything reasonable to help the Allies in their plight, he told him, but could not see shipping untrained men who could not be used for at least two months when so many other men (non-combat support troops) were needed immediately. Up until 1 May 1918 the War Department had drafted only about 116,000 men a month because of limited shipping facilities. With shipping suddenly available for 250,000 a month, an infantryman shortage had now developed. This would be remedied in time (in May 373,000 men were drafted), but in the interval it seemed the path of wisdom to bring over trained non-combatant troops rather than untrained combatant troops. The former could build up the structure necessary to receive the latter when they came; without the former the influx of the latter would cause the American organisation, in Pershing's words, to 'go to smash'.

When the meeting resumed everyone was keyed up. Tempers were short, exacerbated by the fact that eighteen people were crowded into a tiny room with no window open, making everyone hot and uncomfortable.

'You are willing to risk our being driven back to the Loire?' Foch queried, repeating the question he had asked at Abbeville the month before.

'Yes,' responded Pershing most positively, 'I am willing to take the risk.'

Later, when Pershing remarked that he considered Foch his superior officer, the conference reporter noted that Foch 'made a short remark which was not intelligible'. It was probably just as well; it probably could not have been printed anyway.

'The whole discussion was very erratic,' remembered Pershing, 'as one of the Allies would take exception to nearly every statement made by the other.' Even among the British themselves disagreement occurred over the number of Allied divisions available, Milner exclaiming with some exasperation that it was useless to talk about their resources to meet the German threat when they could not even agree as to what they had. He entered a formal protest against all figures used in the discussion.

Pershing knew that the British and French leaders had little confidence in him, his AEF organisation, and its ability to function as an equal. Both had kept harping, all the way up to President Wilson, about the untried American higher command and staff, warning that its inexperience invited disaster. The French in particular said the Americans should attempt nothing larger than divisional organisations. Corps, armies or groups of armies were out of the question.

At the conference Lloyd George actually proposed that Pershing relinquish control over American divisions training with the British, so that Sir Douglas Haig, the British commander, rather than himself, would determine when their training was complete and when they should be sent into battle. 'I held my temper,' Pershing wrote in his diary, 'but very firmly objected . . . and stated I could not, should not and would not surrender my prerogatives in this manner.'

Only a few days after the Versailles Conference, General Jan Christian Smuts made the extraordinary suggestion of taking the American army away from any American general and giving it to someone more capable of using to best advantage its first-class material, viz., himself.

> Pershing is very commonplace [he wrote Lloyd George confidentially] without real war experience, and already overwhelmed by the initial difficulties of a job too big for him. It is also doubtful whether he will loyaly co-operate with the Allied Higher Commands. He could not get together a first-class Staff either. I fear very much that with the present Higher Command the American Army will not be used to the best advantage; and victory for us depends on squeezing the last ounce of proper use out of the American Army.

Pershing, he suggested, could be retained behind the lines, to handle bases, supplies, training camps, transport, etc.

That such an extraordinary suggestion could actually be made, one so offensive to American national pride, so farfetched, and so unlikely of ever being accepted by any people with any sense of their military worth, may be taken as a measure of Allied opinion of Pershing.

As the conference deadlocked, Pershing suggested that he, Milner and Foch see if they could work out something privately. When the three closeted themselves Foch remained adamant until Chief of Staff General Maxime Weygand (who some said was the brains behind Foch) remarked that perhaps it might be best to leave untrained combat troops in America a month longer, since in any event they could not be used in Europe for several months anyway. Pershing had been saying the same thing over and over without effect, but once Weygand said it Foch immediately agreed.

An agreement was accordingly signed between Foch, Milner and Pershing, which on the assumption that 250,000 men could be transported in each month gave priority to 170,000 combat troops in June and 140,000 in July, a total of 310,000. The rest for each month would be the support and supply troops Pershing desired, a total of 190,000. Any surplus above 250,000 a month would be combat troops.

The agreement was a victory for Pershing, embodying his contention that untrained combat troops should not be used and that the surplus shipping available during the two months should bring over trained support troops. The agreement had far-reaching effects on an American army, for it is hard to see how it could have functioned without the concession about support troops won from the Allies in the Versailles agreement. Even as it was, the AEF was plagued by personnel shortages in the fall.

None the less all agreements were conditioned by what the Germans did. As S. L. A. Marshall later remarked: 'Not Allied pressure, but the remorseless grind of events' would determine the fate of a separate American army.

If Allied defeat continued, the feeding of U.S. divisions into the line piece-meal as they arrived must perforce continue. There could be no choice in this matter. But if the tide could be stemmed . . . Foch could build up his margins, and as the reserve swelled, the constituting of a separate U.S. Army would be to general advantage. And that is exactly how it happened.

At that very moment the German offensive was grinding to a halt, in part because of an heroic stand made by the US 2nd Division, which planted itself across the Paris Highway, blocking further advance. Looking back on the event, American writers have tended to make much of the 2nd's gallant stand, and rightly so, but its importance must not be overestimated. In its sixth day when the 2nd Division deployed, the German offensive had in many ways 'shot its bolt'. All First World War offensives tended to peter out after a week because of difficulties of getting men and matériel forward across devastated terrain in sufficient quantities and speed to keep the offensive moving. Then too the French, while giving way at the centre, had held firm at the shoulders of the salient, at Rheims on the right and west of Soissons on the left. Holding at the shoulders necessarily limited advance in the centre and would eventually make the salient very vulnerable.

None the less frequently in life it is not what the situation actually is that is important, but what it seems to be. French troops, fleeing the Germans, cried *'La guerre finie'* to advancing Americans as they passed. The fact remains, as Harbord later pointed out, that when the 2nd Division went into line on the afternoon of 1 June on both sides of the Paris-Metz highway, 'the French had been retiring along the whole Rheims-Soissons front from one to ten miles a day for five days. No unit along the whole front had stood against the German masses. The first unit to stand was the Second Division and it not only stood but went forward.'

The advance began on 6 June. 'Come on, you sons of bitches,' yelled Sergeant Dan Daly, 'Do you want to live forever?' Apparently some 1,087 of them did not, for the Marine Brigade of the 2nd Division suffered the most casualties that day in its history, not to be exceeded until bloody Tarawa twenty-five years later.

The next nineteen days around Belleau Wood were pure hell. Long, almost unbroken lines of ambulances headed back along the Paris road, carrying men racked by disease, diarrhoea, thirst, exhaustion, weather, wounds and gas. The gas casualties were particularly pitiable; many were delirious, nearly all were blind, crying, moaning and thrashing about.

The struggle for Belleau Wood was neither strategical nor tactical, but psychological. General Böhm, commanding one of the German divisions opposite the Americans, pinpointed the issue: 'It is not a question of the possession or nonpossession of this or that village or woods, insignificant in itself; it is a question whether the Anglo-American claim that the American Army is equal or even the superior of the German Army is to be made good.'

It was a test of wills. Even Ludendorff recognised the consequences when on 8 June he ordered that any American units encountered 'should be hit particularly hard in order to render difficult the formation of an American Army'.

The Germans did their best, but on 25 June, after an all-day artillery barrage, the Americans drove into Belleau Wood and came out the other side. 'Woods now U.S. Marine Corps entirely', read the message to headquarters. The cost was some 5200 casualties, over 50 per cent of the Marine Brigade of the 2nd Division.

Meanwhile American troops began pouring into Europe, more than 300,000 in July, helping to convert a 324,000 Allied rifleman deficiency in March to a 627,000 superiority in November. On 18 July the US 1st and 2nd divisions, together with the Moroccans, spearheaded the Allied attack on the Château-Thierry salient, while some 300,000 other American troops participated in the difficult follow-up drive there in late July and August. On 12 September the American First Army, operational since 10 August and deploying 550,000 men, overwhelmed the vulnerable St Mihiel salient just as the Germans were getting ready to withdraw from it. Two weeks later, on 26 September, it launched a difficult assault on the Meuse-Argonne front, commencing a bitter forty-seven-day battle involving 1,200,000 men, which was only intermittently successful. Finally, on 1 November, it achieved a breakthrough. Ten days later hostilities ceased.

Pershing felt the armistice was a mistake.

> We shouldn't have done it [he commented shortly afterwards]. If they had given us another ten days we would have rounded up the entire German army, captured it, humiliated it . . . The German troops today are marching back into Germany announcing that they have never been defeated . . . What I dread is that Germany doesn't know that she was licked. Had they given us another week, we'd have *taught* them.

He was correct about the German attitude. On Armistice Day General von Einem, commander of the German Third Army, told his troops, 'Firing has ceased. Undefeated . . . you are terminating the war in enemy country.' A decade later Adolf Hitler was preaching the same error.

A few days after the armistice Pershing encountered Clemenceau, with whom he had contended furiously over the amalgamation issue. 'We fell into each other's arms, choked up and had to wipe our eyes,' he wrote in the very last sentence of his memoirs. 'We had no differences to discuss that day.'

Commented Harbord: 'The armistice thus ended two wars for us – the one with our friends, the other with our enemies.'

After the war Pershing served as Chief of Staff from 1921 to 1924, when he retired. His later years were devoted to work as chairman of the American Battle Monuments Commission, which supervised American memorials and cemeteries in Europe, and to his memoirs, *My Experiences in the World War*, which were published in 1931 and won a Pulitzer prize. He died in Walter Reed Hospital in Washington on 15 July 1948.

How to evaluate Pershing?

A careful rather than brilliant or great commander, he worked hard in planning an army on a scale sufficient to tip the balance. Captain B. H. Liddell Hart, an Englishman whom Pershing thought prejudiced against him, wrote in *Reputations Ten Years After*: 'There was perhaps no other man who would or could have built the structure of the American army on the scale he planned. And without that army the war could hardly have been saved and could not have been won.'

In the amalgamation controversy he took great risks. A man who throughout life had stressed preparedness and the fact that in modern war one could not improvise overnight, he none the less seemed impervious to Allied arguments concerning the need for priority shipments of infantry and machine-gun units in the face of expected German attacks during the spring and summer of 1918. As Pershing admitted he was willing to take the risk of the British being pushed into the sea and the French driven back beyond the Loire. History has been kind to him, in that he ran the risk successfully. But he was like a man playing Russian roulette. He lived through it, but he was lucky he did not blow his head off.

On the other hand, even conceding that he might at times have been unnecessarily obstinate and failed to see the gravity of successive crises, he none the less guessed correctly in estimating that they were not as severe as the Allies represented them and that the Germans would not in fact break through and win the war before an American army could be trained and fielded. He may have been saved by luck from being 'cursed to the latest generation', but the fact is that he guessed correctly. The Allies did not need as many priority shipments of American infantry and machine-gun units as they said they did.

In the controversy about rifle training for open warfare he was on less sure ground. Frederick Palmer, who liked Pershing and wrote his biography, said later:

On Salisbury field and at Aldershot in 1914 I heard the same talk about the value of the rifle that I heard later in our training camps in Lorraine; and I saw it put in practice not only by the Canadians, who are our neighbors in western individualism and frontier marksmanship, and by the Australians, but by the British themselves, without being able to go through the trench line to open warfare.

Harvey A. DeWeerd, an American military writer, felt that the secret of advancing against multiple defensive lines lay not in rifle markmanship, but in a combination of artillery, tanks and innovative infiltration methods, such as the Germans had used at Riga and at Caporetto.

For all Pershing's talk about the advantage of open warfare training and his indictment of the Allies for their defensive mentality and stress on trench warfare, the fact remains that during the last five months of the war, when the Germans were gradually pushed back all along the front, the British advanced farther and faster than the Americans. In addition they captured three times as many prisoners.

Confronted with this fact the AEF staff would later argue that the Americans were pushing against the most sensitive part of the German line, the pivot that the enemy had to hold lest we cut vital rail communications to his armies in the north-west, compelling him to withdraw all along the line. There is something to be said for this, which is why the argument still goes on.

None the less Liddell Hart was probably right when he said of Pershing's stress on the rifle, open warfare and the offensive: 'He thought that he was spreading a new gospel of faith when actually it was an old faith exploded . . . He omitted but one factor from his calculations – German machine guns – and was right in all his calculations but one – their effect.'

The key weapon in the First World War was not the rifle, but the machine gun, which killed many, and artillery, which killed more. Against them the American infantryman pitted raw courage, enthusiasm, inexperience, guts, some support from his own auxiliary arms, and his own blood. 'The A.E.F. learned to fight through bitter experience,' said DeWeerd, 'not through any legerdemain with the rifle.'

In America's greatest battle, the Meuse-Argonne, it is questionable how much the AEF engaged in open warfare. Day after day the First Army butted its head against stubborn German resistance, inching its way ahead from 26 September to 1 November until, under Hunter Liggett, who had replaced Pershing as First Army commander, it finally achieved a break-through. In truth it might be argued that the war was eventually won, not by the introduction of any tactic like open warfare, but simply by attrition, by the fact that one side became exhausted before the other. At the armistice the Germans had not one division left in reserve; every one was in line. They had simply run out of men and matériel. Had they not, the war might still have gone on, with Pershing, like Nivelle, removed from command for ordering foolhardy assaults entirely incommensurate with the ground gained.

Marshal of the Royal Air Force The Viscount Trenchard

Gavin Lyall

Perhaps nobody should be called 'the father of the Royal Air Force,' but the fact remains that only one man has been so called. Marshal of the Royal Air Force Lord Trenchard loathed the phrase, though he learnt to live with it, but it took an odd combination of circumstances and a lot of help from others to bring him to that consummation.

Hugh Trenchard was born in 1873, the third of six children in the family of an apparently prosperous Devon solicitor. He managed to spend a happy early childhood by learning as little as possible, first from a private tutor, briefly at a preparatory school, then a crammer for a naval cadetship, his parents having decided on a military career for him at the age of eleven.

Unsurprisingly he flopped and was moved to an army crammer where he excelled at Rugby football and failed twice to get into either Sandhurst or Woolwich. Even the shock of learning that his father was being made bankrupt – the sale of the family house and his mother's jewellery – does not seem to have jolted the young Trenchard into any burst of intellectual effort. Or perhaps the shock was delayed; it might have something to do with the restless energy and touchy pride that run like main arteries through his later career.

Financed by relatives, he finally scraped into the army by the only door left: the militia, which provided a pool of young officers by setting a fairly low-level exam, and then transferring the successful candidates to whatever line regiments wanted them. The 2nd Battalion Royal Scots Fusiliers took Trenchard, and took him out to the Punjab.

In 1893 the British army in India was still that of Kipling's Barrack Room Ballads: the grimy canteens, the dragging hot afternoons, and the main task of inventing ways to stay busy so as to be sane, sober and efficient enough for the rare calls to action on the frontier. Yet Trenchard fitted in well enough. He was neither happy in, nor yearned for, the company of women, which was an advantage to a subaltern living on his pay, but his country upbringing had taught him to shoot and ride, and these were the most respectable pursuits for any young officer. He won the Viceroy's gold medal for rifle shooting and created a battalion polo team – helped by a local bank manager who valued his new-found talent as a horse trader. His brother subalterns called him 'the Camel', partly because of his abstemiousness, partly his lack of small talk, but respected his talent for organising things: polo matches, gymkhanas, rifle competitions. And he was happy with it all – except the lack of real action; he missed the only chance at frontier warfare while home on sick leave for a hernia operation.

The action finally came with the Boer War of 1899. Trenchard had already transferred to the 1st Battalion in order to stay in India; now he switched back, with the help of a friendly general, to the 2nd Battalion, which was posted to South Africa. Once there, he combined his abilities for horsemanship and organisation to raise a mounted company within the battalion. Soon afterwards he led them into a Boer ambush and was carried out, shot through one lung and partly paralysed in the legs by some undefined spinal damage.

At this point Trenchard's career takes on the flavour of a second-rate Hollywood scenario. Sent to St Moritz to help strengthen his remaining lung, he took up bob-sledding and – by crashing on the Cresta Run – somehow readjusted his spine so that he could walk unaided again. He then went on to win the Novice's Cup for 1901, discharged himself from medical care a few months later, and headed back to South Africa

Under the new regime of Lord Kitchener he was set to organising various regiments of mounted infantry – the only effective spearhead force against the Boers – and finally leading one in the last weeks of the war – though the action was meagre. So, faced with the prospect of depot service, Trenchard accepted a job to revitalise – in the odd situation as second-in-command – the South Nigerian Regiment. He did this by supplanting the colonel on active missions (by the local governor's order) and firing the medical officer who in an alcoholic stupor had tried to certify Trenchard as insane.

For seven years thereafter Trenchard tramped his men up and down the Nigerian hinterland, mapping 10,000 square miles of new empire, punishing rebellious tribesmen by making them build roads so as to make their defeat permanent, and finally winning the DSO – an award that seems to have been for cumulative work rather than a single act, and maybe the more worthy for it. And then illness struck again: with an abscess on his liver, he was shipped home. This time his attempts to cure himself by ignoring medical advice slowed things down a bit, but by late 1910 he was back with his original battalion, now in Londonderry, as an acting major.

Time to look at the man himself, now at the end of his thirties. The photographs show a solid figure with a chunky yet austere face, thick moustache and usually the uneasy grin of the 'smile, please' variety. The record shows a near-middle-aged acting major with organisational talent, an aggressive and independent spirit, a good – but not for those days exceptional – experience of active service, a frightening medical charge-sheet and the advantage of being unmarried. Less clearly recorded were the tendencies to keep his thoughts to himself and to give loyalty by choice rather than in the line of duty.

Trenchard's future seemed none too bright. He lacked the conformity and sociability that could have lifted him the next step to battalion commander of a line regiment, and he had neither the training, taste for diplomatic paperwork (his spelling and grammar never recovered from his dilatory schoolwork) nor temperament for a staff posting. He recognised the problem: on indifferent terms with his CO – largely for trying to reorganise parts of the battalion that did not feel the need for it – he fired off applications to join half a dozen Commonwealth or Empire armies. None were accepted. Then an old friend from Nigeria, who had joined the just-formed Royal Flying Corps, wrote to him: 'Come and see men like ants crawling.'

Trenchard went, with his CO's blessing. For £75 he learned to fly – if one hour and four minutes in the air covers that concept – was awarded Royal Aero Club certificate number 270 and accepted by an RFC that was more interested in getting experienced organisers than counting their lungs.

The next step was inevitable. The new Central Flying School made him adjutant to organise the flying course and set the exams which he was also taking himself. He passed himself, although he probably had no illusions about his flying ability, described by an instructor as 'at best . . . indifferent'. At least once he graduated to non-flying jobs, he made little effort to keep up his piloting skill, for which the Royal Air Force may be truly thankful. The same could be said about another, more occasional but equally indifferent pupil at the school: Winston Churchill, First Lord of the Admiralty.

The two years just before the war were probably Trenchard's happiest time. Without greater responsibility, he was not just organising but helping *create* a new service in the company of enthusiasts who believed that aeroplanes could change warfare. Trenchard's ability to become devoted to something new but self-contained was of enormous value to the Corps. He was tough and gruff with subordinates – this was the time when he got the nickname 'Boom' – but it was his job to stop young hot-heads killing themselves. The RFC needed them and not bad publicity.

The outbreak of war and the departure of the RFC's only three squadrons to France brought disappointment: Trenchard was to stay home and train up new squadrons. For three months he did it with a motley collection of aircraft borrowed from flying schools – though the RFC's own aeroplanes were hardly less motley – and mechanics recruited at rates of pay that Trenchard invented himself, to keep them from enlisting elsewhere. But in the November he got his reward: command of 1st wing in France, under a reorganisation that allotted one wing to each British army as the war settled down into its trenches.

Oddly almost the first thing Trenchard did in France was threaten to resign, not for the first or last time. He objected to Frederick Sykes (later Major-General Sir Frederick) being his superior, since he was junior in both age and seniority to Trenchard. The row was resolved by Sir David Henderson staying on as commander of the RFC in France instead of taking over a division, which he wanted to do. Trenchard was saved by another's generosity – a pattern that would repeat itself. Resignation from the RFC would most likely have dropped him into a forgotten pit of elderly, sub-healthy majors at home training establishments.

As it was, Trenchard went to work happy. The first, mobile, months of the war had done more to prove the value of air reconnaissance than its reliability. Now the stagnant armies were calling for more flights and more accuracy: anybody can spot a moving column on a road, but it needs constant photographic coverage to detect the changes in a trench system that may signify a coming attack or strengthened defence. Thanks to Henderson 1st wing got the first photographic unit in the RFC, in time to prepare the Neuve Chappelle attack, and augmented this by the first tentative systems for air-to-ground signalling for artillery observation.

Neuve Chappelle was a failure, and Aubers Ridge little better; one artillery commander told Trenchard that he was too busy, in battle, to pay attention to 'your toys' above. But at least Trenchard had found a loyalty that lasted his own lifetime: General Haig, commander of the new First Army. Their partnership was to be one of the most important of the war.

After a year of command Henderson reluctantly posted himself home to sort out aircraft production problems and, overriding Sykes once more, handed on field command of the RFC to Trenchard. A few months later Haig succeeded Sir John French as C-in-C and the partnership was resumed on a new and higher level.

But meantime Trenchard was having a rather frustrated time. Reconnaissance was now a built-in part of any battle plan, and artillery co-operation was improving – but this was not really the stuff of *aggressive* aerial warfare that he knew must come. A few aircraft dropped a few bombs that were no larger than medium shells, a few others spattered the sky with Lewis guns, carbines and even pistols in an attempt to 'force down' their enemies. And when the real thing began to happen, in that autumn of 1915, it happened because of the 'Fokker Scourge'.

As an aeroplane the Fokker Eindecker earned its place in history solely by establishing, for all time, the value of a fixed gun aimed by pointing the aircraft itself. It was the hired killer of the air with no secondary purpose, and the RFC had nothing to match it, several ideas for firing machine guns through the propeller disc having rusted on the War Office shelves a while before. Rather abruptly the world of the RFC changed to that we know from legend: tired and shaken men sitting down to dinner among empty chairs.

But at least Trenchard could avoid empty chairs at breakfast: he made it a flat rule that every loss was to be replaced overnight from a pool of aircrew held at St Omer. He toured his squadrons incessantly, bullying a commander here, listening to a technical problem there (which he often did not understand but always passed on) and delivering gruff pep-talks almost everywhere. Not all this morale-building was welcome: some squadrons regarded him as an unnecessary and upsetting influence, and one old friend reported him as seeming 'a man who has mislaid affection somewhere down the line'. But on the whole it seems to have worked.

A lot of the credit for this must go to that strange man Maurice Baring, whom Trenchard inherited as an aide – after mutual misgivings – from Henderson. A distinguished writer and something of an aesthete, Baring gave his totally dissimilar commander help that was both loyal and imaginative. He acted as Trenchard's memory, rewrote his prose, and occasionally gave him 'field punishment', staring wordlessly at the sky as they drove away from a squadron he thought his boss had treated tactlessly. It was certainly due to Baring's fluid French that Trenchard was on excellent terms with the French Air Service – which was to be of some importance later on.

In 1916 Trenchard was able to go, gradually, on to the offensive. The first effective British fighters – FE 2bs and DH 2s, both 'pusher' designs with the propeller behind the pilot – were grouped into proper squadrons and, fighting *en masse*, cut the Fokker down to its proper size as an underpowered and flimsy machine. Throughout the Somme battles of that summer the RFC's twenty-seven squadrons dominated the air and, in the words of German General von Below: 'Inspired our troops with a feeling of defencelessness.'

Trenchard's policy was simple enough: 'The aeroplane is not a defence against the aeroplane,' he wrote that year. 'But the opinion of those most competent to judge is that the aeroplane, as a weapon of attack, cannot be too highly estimated.' In practice this meant swarming over the enemy lines and forcing him on the defensive – which often worked, since when troops find the sky full of hostile machines, a squawk goes up to keep friendly aircraft back there (however ineffectively) instead of out of sight on the attack. It was as much a test of senior commanders' nerves as of the aircrews', and Trenchard's nerve was unshakeable.

But was it really within the resources of the RFC? In the five months of the Somme campaign Trenchard lost five hundred aircrew casualties – well over 100 per cent of his starting figure – and this was a heavy mortgage on the Corps' future. New and better aeroplanes could be made, but the RFC was not building up the stock of battlewise veterans that was vital to the success of *any* policy. Even when, as Trenchard had feared, the German air force came back on the offensive, he went on throwing his squadrons forward against the superior new Albatros and Halberstadt fighters – if they could get across into enemy territory before being 'jumped'. The climax came in 'Bloody April' of 1917, over Arras and Vimy Ridge. The Red Baron, von Richthofen, averaged a victory a day throughout the month and in all the Corps lost 316 aircrew, or a third of its strength – and for very little result.

Nobody can say this was an imaginative use of air power, but in fact it was not a use of air power at all: it was the use of an army that happened to include aircraft just as it included machine guns and artillery, and nobody has accused Haig of too much imagination. So Trenchard went on driving his squadrons to the point of exhaustion, and some pilots called him 'Butcher' as often as they called him 'Boom', but the spirit of the offensive remained. And that summer, with the arrival of the first really competitive British fighters – Camels, SE 5s and Bristol Fighters – the air war began to swing in favour of the RFC.

But in London others were having other ideas about the use of aeroplanes. Churchill, now back in the government after a spell in the trenches, had come to the conclusion, or at least the phrase, that there were only two war-winning factors left, both beginning with A: America and the aeroplane. His superiors tended to agree, but the problem was how to get direct political control of the aeroplane; the solution was to form a separate force under an air minister.

In itself the idea was nothing new and had a lot of other advantages. It would stop the bickering between the Royal Naval Air Service and RFC over production facilities, and perhaps even straighten out production itself, which had long been a broth stirred by a succession of cack-handed boards, committees and councils. But a lot of the motivation came from a desire to take the RFC from Haig's control. By then, Prime Minister Lloyd George was looking for any opportunity to cut Haig's power, while Haig was concealing from London the fact that part of the French army had mutinied – which was wise on security grounds, but still shows an appalling gulf of mistrust.

Lloyd George's opportunity came in that June, when a neat formation of Gotha bombers drifted over London in broad daylight, caused six hundred casualties (the worst raid of the war so far) and went home without loss. Night-time Zeppelin raids had been one thing, and they had been mostly defeated, but this brazen slap was something else. It forced the public's rather than the Prime Minister's, hand: there would now be no popular outcry if the government took control of a unified air service and redirected parts of it to strengthen the defence of the United Kingdom and to retaliatory raids on German towns.

Two quick reports by General Smuts – an ex-enemy from South Africa and thus respected as being impartial – produced just the recommendations Lloyd George had hoped for, plus a bonus: it seemed there would be a surplus over requirement of three thousand aircraft during 1918. This was finding caviar in the fishpaste: Haig need be deprived of no squadrons, since the 'surplus' could be used for home defence and strategic bombing. Almost certainly the Royal Air Force would have been created then anyway, but it is still true to say that it was born to handle three thousand aircraft that never came to pass. And in that December Trenchard was summoned home and asked to lead it as the first Chief of Air Staff.

He was the obvious choice, being the most experienced air commander, but politically he was naïvely inexperienced (this may of course have been one of his qualifications in government eyes). His family background had given him no contact with political or even London life, and of his twenty-four years' military service, he had spent perhaps three or four in Britain – and no time at all in Whitehall. His relationship with the London end of the Corps had been largely a one-way traffic of brusque demands for more and better aircraft; he had actually avoided giving evidence to enquiries on the running of the air service.

Trenchard came home in a mood of deep suspicion. He did not believe in a single one of those three thousand 'surplus' aircraft, or in much else about the embryo RAF. He did want the service unified, though mostly to get the RNAS away from the navy, but thought it would be disruptive and wasteful to do it in the middle of a war. He did not believe in the cost-effectiveness of standing fighter patrols – the only way fighters could defend London, there being no early-warning system – and while he wanted to bomb German towns, he thought it should be done only by a very large force; otherwise the morale effect would be on the squadrons that took heavy losses for small results. But most of all, perhaps, he did not believe what he met at the new Air Ministry.

Lloyd George had originally offered the post as minister to Lord Northcliffe, whose sense of propriety allowed him to reply – a contemptuous refusal – in the columns of *The Times*, which he owned. Thick-skinned when it suited him, the Prime Minister then offered the job to Northcliffe's younger brother, Lord Rothermere, knowing full well that Northcliffe would keep a finger in the pie. These noble brothers interviewed Trenchard, Rothermere saying that if he refused the job they would start a press campaign against Haig 'and use you as a lever. We are going to say that Haig has an absolutely wrong conception of air power.'

It was probably to help Haig, as much as anything else, that Trenchard took on the post. 'I knew,' he wrote later, 'that I should have to fight Rothermere and Northcliffe from the day I took the job.' Certainly, to his mind, somebody who knew the real situation in France had to fight the brothers. But he was still a babe in the jungle. When he paid a brief visit to France soon after, Haig observed that his old colleague could 'think and talk nothing else but the rascally ways of politicians and newspaper men'.

And in being at most lukewarm about the new tasks for which the RAF had been created, Trenchard was deliberately pulling a favoured horse. He knew the point of decision was on the western front, and ultimately he was right, but he failed to realise the overwhelming political need for a democracy to appear to try and defend its civilian voters – even if it meant withdrawing crack fighter squadrons from France (which it did). Meanwhile Rothermere complained: '. . . he was insisting on the ordering of large numbers of machines for out-of-date purposes'; (i.e., use over the trenches), and was himself offering to provide four thousand aircraft for anti-submarine patrols.

Most of these four thousand were as mythical as the original three thousand surplus machines turned out to be, and it was one of the last straws on the Camel's back. After less than three months in his post as Chief of the Air Staff, and still two weeks before the RAF came officially into being, he offered his resignation. But the brothers had not won outright; by then a major-general and a knight, Trenchard was too much of a public figure to fall unheard. Knowing that this resignation would force his own, Rothermere handed the decision on up to the Cabinet, which sat on it for over three weeks. In that time the Ludendorff offensive ripped through the Allied lines and started regaining most of the ground won since 1914; when Trenchard's resignation was announced in April it looked all too much as if he had quit when the *military* going got rough.

Two weeks later Rothermere was replaced by Sir William, later Lord, Weir, while Trenchard's old enemy Sir Frederick Sykes came from an army post to take over as Chief of Air Staff. And Trenchard himself sat daily on a bench in Green Park, unemployed.

Possibly he was no luckier than he deserved, but it took some weeks of Weir's persistence and an overheard conversation in which two naval officers agreed that Trenchard was a 'traitor' to bring him back into uniform. With some reluctance he took over command of the Independent Force, the strategic bombing unit of which he had been so dubious.

The force, originally a wing that had grown now to just five squadrons, had been operating off airfields in south-east France for some months. It was Trenchard's task to stabilise and expand the operations, and there was the usual promise of many new squadrons – particularly of heavy Handley-Page and Vickers night bombers – to come. Typically Trenchard adjusted quickly to his new situation, and was soon announcing optimistically: '. . . cloud flying must be practised . . . we must be able to *bomb* in clouds very, very shortly . . .' But the force's most immediate problem was summed up by Duval, the French air commander, in his famous question: 'Independent of whom? Of God?'

Based in a part of France that was not even 'occupied' by the British army, the force was entirely dependent on French charity for its communications – and the French had little belief in strategic bombing. It could expect little help from the established RAF in France, now headed by John Salmond, who resented the force as a squadron-snatcher. But at least Trenchard knew how Salmond felt (and made a point of turning down the offer of fighter squadrons which he thought Salmond needed more), while the old ties and Baring's fluid tongue helped mollify the French. Operations began to build up.

By the end of August Trenchard had only nine squadrons, and never got more before the armistice: 'A tiny part of my own original command,' he later recalled. 'I was not anybody much.' Accepting that he could not achieve concentration he deliberately chose dispersion of his attacks, giving as many German towns as possible a taste of 'total war'. He had no doubt that he was at least partly engaged in what we would now call 'area bombing'. When Weir wrote to him in September saying: 'The German is susceptible to bloodiness, and I would not mind a few accidents due to inaccuracy,' Trenchard reassured his minister that he need have no concern about 'our degree of accuracy when bombing stations in the middle of towns. The accuracy is not great at present.'

This was really the crux of the matter if anybody, Trenchard included, was to believe the force was achieving anything except tie down German fighter squadrons. The value of destroying German war industries and communications was obvious enough, but Trenchard had no great illusions about the force's effects in this direction. In six months its aircraft dropped about 600 tons of high explosives and a good many incendiaries, the vast majority in bombs of 230 pounds and less. A third of this fell on German airfields; the remainder, if totalled together into a single raid on a single target, would not have counted as 'heavy' in Second World War terms. Again the balance was made up by the unmeasurable morale effect: the broken sleep of the worker, the fear for his home and family. And there was certainly a subconscious pressure to believe in such a profit: the loss rate among the force's aircrew ran to over 100 per cent in the period, and one squadron was twice effectively destroyed.

But the idea that a nation's 'will to resist' might be wrecked by new and indirect means, as effective as and quicker than a naval blockade, had taken a deep root in the minds of Trenchard and others.

The armistice brought an abrupt end to an unproven experiment, and Trenchard responded equally abruptly. He handed over the force to Salmond and went home, not even visiting Germany to check, on the ground, the result of his squadrons' work. For the next few months he stayed unemployed, bar a brief visit to quell a mutiny among troops in Southampton docks, where he issued live ammunition to loyal soldiers. Perhaps something in this Gordian Knot approach appealed to Churchill, who was then wearing the two hats of the War Office and Air Ministry, and he offered Trenchard the one post he could hardly have expected: to come back as Chief of the Air Staff. The relationship of the 'Father of the RAF' and his child always seemed to need some help from outsiders.

However, almost the first thing Trenchard did on taking up the job was to fall ill with the influenza that was scything through Europe. As usual he tried to ignore it, but his age – he was then forty-six – medical record and war strain hit back with pneumonia. On what others, at least, feared was his deathbed, he did a totally untypical thing: wrote pleading letters to a certain lady to visit him.

Katharine Boyle had been the wife of a brother officer at Londonderry; now she was his widow. Trenchard had only met her once, briefly, since the war began, but the only conclusion can be the romantic cliché that he had secretly worshipped her from afar all the time. She took over the nursing (Trenchard had retained enough strength to fire three nurses in succession) and Trenchard, once he found he had life as well as love to offer, proposed marriage. Mrs Boyle did not immediately take this seriously, but she accepted him six months later, a period when the RAF was flooded with rumours about misogynist Boom being seen getting out of a taxi with a bunch of red roses.

Reinstalled at the Air Ministry, Trenchard found things less rosy: a new war had begun with the navy and army. It would be literally impossible to list the committees, councils, reports and discussions through which the senior services tried to execute King Solomon's judgement on their baby brother, but it can be said that the admirals had the better case, with the need for specialised squadrons to operate off the new carriers. But their blatant unconcern for the rest of the RAF convinced Trenchard, who had come to believe that the 1917 decision for independence had been a then-or-never one, that giving part to the navy would mean handing everything else to the army. It was to prove a disaster for the Fleet Air Arm later on, but it was an admiral who should have been flown at half-mast for it.

Marriage – which came in 1920, with Baring balancing a wineglass on his head and Churchill insisting on making a speech – helped Trenchard through the long slog ahead. At last he had a private life to give perspective to his professional one; his temper seems to have cooled, his diplomacy improved. At least he stopped resigning: his last attempt had been soon after he became Chief of Air Staff again, though before his wedding. He was dissuaded by his private secretary, but he had been prepared to go that close.

So with one hand he fought off the army and navy; with the other he built the world's first independent air force, complete with its own institutions, ranks, uniforms, flag and tasks. Just how differently Trenchard might have shaped the RAF if it had not been under constant threat of dismemberment we cannot know. We only know what he did.

He accepted calmly the run-down of the RAF to little more than a tenth of its wartime peak, and the 'ten-year rule', which decreed that no service need prepare for a major war until ten years hence. But since aeroplanes dated quickly yet could also be built quickly, Trenchard realised that he could create a force that was really just a nucleus of what would be needed in wartime. If the public wanted something to see for their money, they could have the annual Hendon Air Pageant (which neither the army nor navy could match); for the rest, he chose to spend less on short-lived wood and canvas, more on concrete and morale.

Halton became a training school for ground crews, Cranwell a college for permanent officers, Andover a staff college for future leaders, The five-year short-service flying commission both built a reserve of experienced pilots and kept the promotion ladder clear for Cranwell graduates (Trenchard remembered well that he had spent twenty years as a substantive captain). Later on he added the Royal Auxiliary Air Force: squadrons of weekend fliers recruited mostly from those who drove fast cars or aeroplanes at weekends anyway, and who improved the 'tone' of the RAF – not least in the corridors of power, where their fathers and uncles dwelt.

Operationally he wisely offered the government policies of thrift – notably in the 'air policing' of Iraq, run so successfully by John Salmond, where a handful of old aeroplanes replaced whole divisions of British troops. The RAF was acquiring an identity and a peacetime task. But what about wartime?

Even in peace the spook of strategic bombing continued its long haunting. It had always had more political than military substance: influencing public morale is something politicians believe they know about, and the concept of a single war-winning stroke belongs more to election-night fervour than to staff planning committees. But by now Trenchard was a true believer, and the belief offered the RAF a task that must justify its independence.

In 1921 Trenchard was conjuring, to yet another committee, the prospect of London bombed flat, and the army made the error of admitting its possibility by saying it would hardly matter. The resulting report of the chairman, A. J. (soon to be Lord) Balfour, has a distinct curry flavour: '. . . the position of the General Staffs of the army and navy heroically carrying on their functions at the bottom of a coal pit might in some respects be less disastrous than it seems, seeing that in the contingency supposed they would have very little to do . . .'

By small victories like this, Trenchard was gradually winning the big battle – and tying the RAF closer to the strategic offensive. In 1923 another committee heard him say: 'It is on the destruction of enemy industries and, above all, on the lowering of morale of enemy nationals caused by bombing that the ultimate victory lies.' The fact that the RAF neither had nor was getting anything that could remotely be described as a strategic force was no political paradox: it is one thing to accept the policy, but quite another to announce it to the world, even tacitly, by building the aeroplanes needed. But during this period the actual strength of the RAF was almost the least of Trenchard's worries.

Such Whitehall battles never end in clear victory or even armistice; perhaps they never really end. But from 1926 Trenchard was able to spend far more of his time constructing, rather than defending, the air force. By then his position as Chief of Air Staff had been accepted as equal to that of the First Sea Lord and Chief of the Imperial General Staff (though possibly not by the two holders of those posts, one of whom was Lord Beatty), and an RAF expansion scheme had been approved. This would give 'Home Defence' a total of fifty-two squadrons in a pure Trenchard force: three-quarters were to be bombers, albeit less than half of them 'strategic'. When his ultimate resignation took effect in December 1929, the future of the RAF was virtually assured.

Barely a year after his retirement he returned to public life as Commissioner of the Metropolitan Police. The good he did there in cutting down corruption, reorganising the records and soothing feelings about pay cuts, was quickly interred in the public memory. What most people remember was his attempt to bring a 'well-educated class into the police force' by founding a military-type college at Hendon. It produced some outstanding policemen, but also too much bitterness at the idea of an 'officer class' in a civilian force, and was closed down at the beginning of the war.

After four years on the beat Trenchard went back to semi-retirement. He accepted a few directorships and worked for his meagre pay, and perhaps he offered the Air Staff more advice than it wanted – which he could now do from the floor of the House of Lords, having become the RAF's first peer. When the new war came, he was still only sixty-six (roughly Churchill's age) and hoped for some official appointment in the emergencies of 1940. But although Churchill dickered with the idea, he was unwilling to unleash such an independent spirit in a job of appropriate size. Reluctantly Trenchard came to realise that he had made his last resignation.

Looking back on his work few could call him a man of vision or even much imagination. He could originally accept new ideas, but few of them came after the First World War (to his death he held that Haig's tactics had been unavoidable, and therefore right). He liked to say that the principles of air power had been obvious from the moment the Wright brothers first flew, which nicely discouraged argument about any new uses. He was still opposing the use of parachutes in the mid-1920s, and he never foresaw the rise of a real air defence that came a decade later.

But his great strength was that he could take an idea, turn it into a reality of men and machines, and then make that reality do its job – often far more than its job. Men who can make others do miracles are usually hard taskmasters, and Trenchard certainly was. But while some individuals got trampled, in the end he had done the monumental task of not just creating an air force – and the first in the world – but giving it pride.

Trenchard died in 1956 aged eighty-three (and so much for medical categories). But long before this he had become a legend. To the aircrews he visited in the Second World War he seemed more grandfather than father of the service – although his late marriage had given him two sons just the right age to die in that war – and this time he could just chat about the old days; it was no longer his job to boost their morale for the morrow. And well after the war the local know-all in an RAF training barracks would be called down by some version of: 'So what's your number? – number two?' Your service number showed roughly when you had joined and hence your experience. Everybody knew who must hold number one.

Field-Marshal Gerd von Rundstedt

Andreas Hillgruber

It must surely be exceptional in the history of warfare that a prominent general should be accorded greater appreciation, respect and sympathy, even posthumously, by his enemies than by his own country. But such was the fate of Field-Marshal von Rundstedt under the Third Reich, during the Second World War and in the postwar period. His military abilities were of a high order; his career was marked by great expectations and great disappointments, but severe blame attaches to him. In Germany he has been the target of serious criticism from the most varied quarters; in Great Britain on the other hand he was regarded during the Second World War as Germany's most capable operational commander, as the German army's Grand Old Man, as the 'last Prussian'; even after 1945, when his involvement in the moral ruin of the German *Wehrmacht* through adulteration of the military tradition by Nazi ideological doctrine was plain for all to see, Liddell Hart still described him as 'a gentleman to the core'.

In his early days there was nothing to indicate that he would rise to the highest rank in the German army. Admittedly on his father's side he came from the Altmark aristocracy, from a Halberstadt family with a military tradition dating back several generations. His mother, Adelheid *née* Fischer, on the other hand, came from the well-to-do bourgeoisie. He was born in Aschersleben on 12 December 1875, eldest son (of four) of Gerd von Rundstedt, first lieutenant in the 10th Royal Hussar Regiment. Christened Karl Rudolf Gerd, he went to school in Frankfurt am Main and in 1888 entered the Cadet College in Oranienstein; in 1890 he transferred to the Central Cadet College in Lichterfelde and in 1892 entered the Military College in Hanover. He started his regular officer's career in 1893 as second lieutenant in the Kassel Infantry Regiment. During the peacetime years before the First World War and the war itself there was nothing outstanding or extraordinary about his career; he was stationed in various garrison towns, of which his favourite was Kassel, where he wanted to settle in his old age; promotion followed its slow routine course. The outbreak of the First World War found him as captain, Operations Officer to the 22nd Reserve Division on the western front; after many postings he ended the war as major, Chief of Staff to xv Corps, again on the western front. In 1902 he married Louise von Goetz, known as Bila; their only son (he later became a historian) was born in 1903.

Paradoxical though it may sound, the reason for both his slow 'start' in the Prussian army and his subsequent relatively rapid rise in the *Reichswehr* and then even more so in the *Wehrmacht* under Hitler lies in his enigmatic character. Günther Blumentritt, who was his operations officer during the Polish and French campaigns, then his chief of staff when he was Commander-in-Chief West in 1942–4 and so was one of the few who really knew him, gives this perceptive description: not a typical officer; von Rundstedt was a comparatively complex character, not easy to understand. He was sometimes totally taciturn and sometimes apparently communicative; at times he was excitable and then again apparently imperturbable; he strove in vain for poise and harmony of mind. He was a restless being without enormous self-confidence, a sceptic without capability for enthusiasm or sense of his own superiority. This showed in his marked modesty and in his tendency to prefer his own company where possible – even as a prisoner in Britain in 1945–8 he preferred to be in solitary confinement. Blumentritt says that von Rundstedt's main characteristic is best described as 'self-sufficiency' rather than sheer egoism. He required, and was adept at mobilising, support for his decisions whether official or private; he tended increasingly to avoid clear-cut positions and to vacillate.

On 1 October 1920, only a few months after leaving the old army, he joined the *Reichswehr* as a lieutenant-colonel; by 1923 he had become colonel, by 1927 major-general, by 1929 lieutenant-general and by 1932 full general; from October 1928 he commanded the 2nd Cavalry Division, from February 1932 the 3rd Infantry Division and *Wehrkreis* (Military District) *III*; finally from October 1932 he was Commander-in-Chief Group Headquarters 1. From both the personal and professional points of view these years in the *Reichswehr* were his happiest and most satisfying. He supported Seeckt's concept of the restricted elite army and also the principle of the strategic defensive – a logical conclusion from his experiences of the First World War and Germany's situation under the terms of the Versailles Treaty.

His basic outlook did not change when, like most senior *Reichswehr* officers, he threw himself wholeheartedly into the formation of a conscript army after 1935. On the question, fundamental to future strategy, of the inclusion of armoured forces in the army he took a middle line; in contrast to, for instance, Guderian he opposed concentration of armour into independent formations, making them the major factor in offensive warfare on technical modern lines; his opposition stemmed from his basic concept and his sceptical view of the Reich's unalterably difficult geo-strategical situation, leading to his conviction that the strategic defensive was the correct policy under the changed conditions. He did not however side with the 'pure' traditionalists, who wished to restrict motorisation and technological progress in the army in general and development of armoured forces in particular. Instead his view was that the fire power of the infantry, still in his eyes the primary arm, should be increased by means of new weapons and the inclusion in formations of small and medium-sized armoured units. During these years when the new *Wehrmacht* was forming, he paid special attention to removal of the infantry's 'machine-gun paralysis', which remained his strongest psychological impression from the Great War.

Having been brought up under the Empire, politics, especially the party politics of the Weimar Republic, remained 'a book with seven seals' to him; later, under the Third Reich, Rundstedt the aristocrat looked down on the political goings-on in the Nazi organisations with even greater contempt than the majority of his fellow officers who had imbibed the 'non-political *Reichswehr*' ideology. On 20 July 1932 occurred an episode that was indicative both from the political and sociological points of view: von Papen deposed the Prussian government headed by Braun and took over himself as Reich Commissar for Prussia; von Rundstedt, as Commander *Wehrkreis III* (Berlin), became 'Holder of plenipotentiary powers for the region of Greater Berlin and Brandenburg Province' for a period of six days. For him this was a vexatious interlude, bringing him into a field totally foreign to him and of which he knew nothing (he often used to grumble later that he 'of all people should have been stuck with that'). His attitude during the so-called Röhm putsch of 30 June 1934 was equally 'naïve'. Hitler had ordered the murder of the SA leaders headed by Röhm, whom von Rundstedt like most officers regarded as the army's mortal enemy. Von Rundstedt simply armed his driver and batman in order 'not to be murdered by these people' and went to Hitler with General von Witzleben (his successor as Commander *Wehrkreis III*) to ask that von Schleicher be spared, although he could not conceive that Hitler would have planned to include the general on the murder list. In retrospect von Rundstedt's acceptance of the oath of allegiance to Hitler at the hands of Freiherr von Fritsch, Commander-in-Chief of the Army, on 2 August 1934 is truly symbolic of the self-incriminating thoughtlessness with which the army allowed itself to be ensnared by the Third Reich. On 28 January 1936 the *grand seigneur*, now aged nearly sixty, represented the German *Wehrmacht* at the funeral of King George V in London, attracting the attention of the British public for the first time. Despite the accelerating changes around him he invariably attended service in the Potsdam Garrison Church every Sunday; his son was inclined towards the 'confessional' church, but he himself had no use for Niemöller.

Von Rundstedt was taken completely by surprise by the Blomberg-Fritsch crisis. At an interview with Hitler on 21 January 1938 he did plead that the charges against von Fritsch be cleared up judicially and that his Commander-in-Chief be reinstated – in his eyes a matter of course. His proposal, however, that after the inevitable resignation of von Blomberg Hitler himself should assume overall command of the *Wehrmacht*, as in fact he intended to do in any case, dealt the dictator a trump card; against commanders who opposed the idea he could now use the argument that one of the *Wehrmacht*'s most senior commanders had urged this solution upon him. There can be no doubt that the genesis of Hitler's high regard for von Rundstedt in contrast to other generals, a regard that persisted until 1945 despite occasional conflicts of opinion, lies in this crisis of January 1938. On von Rundstedt's side, from this time onwards his attitude to Hitler was curiously ambivalent, alternating between contempt and admiration; at moments of decision however he invariably opted for further service to 'Führer and Reich'.

In the planned offensive operations against Czechoslovakia during the so-called Sudeten crisis of summer 1938 Second Army under von Rundstedt was assigned to the main front and was to advance from Silesia to capture the fortresses of Troppau and Jägerndorf (Krnov). After the crisis had ended peacefully following the Munich Agreement Colonel-General von Rundstedt (he had been promoted on 1 March) retired at his own request on 31 October 1938. He is said to have remarked: 'It's good that I'm out of that pig-sty Berlin.'

When mobilisation was ordered on 22 August 1939 von Rundstedt was recalled and appointed Commander-in-Chief Army Group South, which was concentrating against Poland in Silesia and Slovakia and was to make the main effort. Although actually present in the Berghof on the same day, 22 August, when Hitler announced his determination to attack Poland, von Rundstedt remained convinced that this would be another 'walk-over war' as in 1938. His association with von Manstein, the most able operational brain in the German army, who was allotted to him as Chief of Staff, offered von Rundstedt his first opportunity to display to the full his great capabilities as a high-level commander in the field. During the war against Poland which opened on 1 September 1939, OKH, the army high command, was in full control without interference from Hitler; following general practice in the Prusso-German army therefore army groups were largely allowed a free hand in carrying out their mission. Von Rundstedt accordingly despatched his Tenth Army under General von Reichenau directly north on Warsaw in order to prevent any retreat eastwards by the main body of the Polish army, which was located farther west, whereas the OKH plan had provided for Army Group South to move south-east across the Vistula. Although the advanced elements of Tenth Army had to be withdrawn from Warsaw temporarily, von Rundstedt's decision proved correct; the most important result of his diversion of the main effort was that large parts of the Polish army were surrounded and destroyed near Radom and on the Bzura, thus considerably shortening the Polish campaign.

For outstanding leadership von Rundstedt was awarded the Knights Cross to the Iron Cross by Hitler, and on 1 October 1939 was appointed Commander-in-Chief East, in other words commander of the relatively small German forces remaining in Poland. His functions as military commander in the occupied Polish areas were considerably reduced with the nomination of Hans Frank as head of the civil administration. The looming clash with Frank and the SS however was left to General Blaskowitz, von Rundstedt's successor, von Rundstedt himself being relieved on 20 October and appointed Commander-in-Chief Army Group B in the west with effect from 25 October; the army group, earmarked to take over the central sector of the front, had its head-quarters in Koblenz and once more Manstein was Chief of Staff. The army high command's plan, still somewhat vague, for the western offensive pro-jected by Hitler for mid-November allotted the decisive role to the northern army group. Von Rundstedt shared von Manstein's doubts about the plan, but he remained loyal to the army high command and left it to Manstein to bypass OKH and submit a counter-proposal direct to Hitler. This was the 'sweep of the scythe'; it turned his own army group into the centrepiece of the revised operational plan, visualising an advance by Army Group A through the Ardennes to the Channel coast to cut off the northern Allied army g oup from the main body of the French army.

After numerous postponements the great German offensive in the west opened on 10 May 1940 in accordance with von Manstein's plan (though Manstein himself had been relieved as Chief of Staff Army Group A on 1 February). It was an overwhelming success, Army Group A's armoured formations driving through to the mouth of the Somme. Then however von Rundstedt gave way to the scepticism born of his First World War experiences concerning the use of armoured formations; he accordingly agreed without demur to Hitler's argument that armour could not operate in the Flanders terrain with its numerous canals and on 24 May halted the German forces on the La Bassée canal, although they were then advancing towards the Channel ports. As a result the British Expeditionary Force, then in an almost hopeless position, was enabled to withdraw via Dunkirk. In the later stages of the French campaign formations of von Rundstedt's army group advanced in rear of the Maginot Line from Champagne to the Swiss frontier and finally, moving through Lyons, took the French army of the Alps in rear. There, as a result of the Franco-German armistice, the advance was halted on 25 June 1940; subsequently German forces were withdrawn to the demarcation line between occupied and unoccupied France, which ran farther north.

Outwardly von Rundstedt reached the zenith of his career when Hitler nominated him field-marshal at a sitting of the Reichstag on 19 June 1940 – though admittedly he was only one among twelve newly appointed field-marshals. On this occasion however confirmation became apparent of the special confidential relationship between the Führer and the German army's oldest soldier; three days earlier Hitler had provisionally ordered preparations for a landing operation against the British Isles (Operation Sealion) and the plan allotted the key role to von Rundstedt's Army Group A. Privately however Hitler now told von Rundstedt that he regarded this merely as a psychological warfare gambit to persuade Great Britain to abandon the struggle, not as a major operation that would actually take place. During the various stages of the subsequent preparations Hitler himself seemed to vacillate regarding the actual execution of Sealion, but von Rundstedt proceeded on the assumption that it was all bluff and was never present at any of the landing exercises on the French coast. On 1 October 1940, after Sealion had been officially cancelled and Army Group B, which had been earmarked for it, had been transferred from west to east (into the Government General of Poland), von Rundstedt became Commander-in-Chief West, assuming overall responsibility for the defence of the occupied French, Belgian and Dutch coasts.

On 14 March 1941, when preparations for the invasion of the Soviet Union were under way, Hitler recalled Rundstedt from the west (his successor was Field-Marshal von Witzleben) and appointed him Commander-in-Chief Army Group South with effect from 1 April 1941. The army group's headquarters was in Breslau and it was planned that it should advance from the southern sector of the Government General and from Rumania into the Ukraine and later as far as the Volga. In Hitler's view the main weight of the invasion should be concentrated on the southern flank, since he gave higher priority to rapid conquest of the economically important areas of southern Russia than to capture of the capital, Moscow. Von Rundstedt however, who only became involved in planning and preparation for the Eastern campaign very late in the day, pleaded in vain for the main effort to be made in the north; he visualised a rapid advance through the Baltic states on Leningrad, thereby gaining touch with the Finns, followed by a move towards Moscow and into the centre of European Russia. His general scepticism about Operation Barbarossa as planned was illustrated by his pessimistic comment on 4 May 1941 to Field-Marshal Ritter von Leeb, Commander-in-Chief Army Group North: 'So see you again in Siberia.'

Meanwhile von Rundstedt adopted an attitude of resignation, not only towards the operational plan but also to orders issued by Hitler for the forthcoming war against the Soviet Union which were in contravention of the rules of international law and the provisions of the Hague Convention; from the outset Hitler was determined that this should be a racial and ideological war of annihilation with no regard for the military ethos. After Hitler had announced this intention with unwonted candour in a speech to over two hundred senior officers on 30 March 1941, von Rundstedt together with the two other army group commanders (von Bock and Ritter von Leeb) did make representations on the subject to Colonel-General Halder, Chief of Staff of the Army.

After the 'criminal orders' (a 'Führer Decree' of 12 May 1941 on 'the exercise of military justice in the "Barbarossa" area and special measures by the troops' and 'Guidelines for the treatment of political commissars' of 6 June 1941) had actually been issued, like most other commanders von Rundstedt confined himself to 'looking the other way' when the troops sometimes failed to carry out the orders. He did not actually set out in his own orders the racial and ideological purposes of the eastern war as did von Reichenau, one of his subordinates commanding Sixth Army; he or his head-quarters however did forward von Reichenau's notorious order of 10 October 1941 to the other army commanders in the army group 'as a model'. Later and until the end of the war he signed a whole series of orders not confined to traditional military matters but including an element of Nazi ideology. Some of these orders, which were drafted by other people, he had undoubtedly not even read; as the *grand seigneur* it was his habit to delegate as many un-important matters as possible. This ability to detach himself from trifles was of value to him as Commander-in-Chief Army Group South in 1941 since the group included Rumanian, Hungarian, Italian and Slovakian formations and the delicate problems of coalition strategy demanded careful handling. Von Rundstedt was cut out by nature for this difficult task and he did it brilliantly.

On another important operational question von Rundstedt found himself in agreement with Hitler. In mid-August 1941, after the victorious frontier battles and Army Group Centre's advance to Smolensk, the army high com-mand and the majority of commanders in Army Group Centre's area urged that the advance on Moscow be resumed as soon as possible with all forces concentrated in order – as they hoped – to capture the Soviet capital and bring the entire campaign to a victorious conclusion. Hitler on the other hand insisted that the powerful grouping of Soviet forces in the area east of Kiev be first surrounded so as to eliminate the threat of a flank attack against German forces advancing on Moscow. Von Rundstedt supported Hitler's decision, saying on 1 September: 'Anyone who wants Moscow must first defeat Budyenny' (the commander of the Soviet group in the Kiev area). The identity of views between the two on this as on other earlier occasions was based on differing premises; Hitler's ideas rested on a mixture of political and psychological considerations, 'economic' wishful thinking and – sometimes accurate – strategic intuition; Rundstedt's views were invariably based upon searching analysis of the strategic situation, other matters being outside his purview. Nevertheless the result of every 'coincidence' between the views of the two increased their mutual respect.

Early in November 1941 von Rundstedt, who had overexerted himself for months, collapsed in his headquarters at Poltava with a heart attack; he insisted however on remaining in command of his army group. The blow was therefore all the greater when Hitler relieved him of his post as Commander-in-Chief on 1 December 1941. His troops had captured Rostov on Don on 21 November but had had to relinquish it again on the 29th following a Soviet counter-attack; von Rundstedt considered withdrawal of the German forces to the line Taganrog-Mius to be inevitable. Hitler however prescribed a halt on an operationally sound intermediate position, but Rundstedt thought this impracticable; referring to his heart attack he requested release from his command in the expectation that this would cause Hitler to change his mind. Instead Hitler granted von Rundstedt's request and appointed von Reichenau as his successor, who then, with covering approval from Hitler, ordered the identical withdrawal planned by von Rundstedt. Although von Rundstedt regarded his removal from command as an insult, this did not lead to estrangement between him and Hitler, as shown by the fact that he was commissioned to 'represent the Führer' at the funeral of von Reichenau, who died suddenly on 17 January 1942.

With the entry into the war of the United States in December 1941 Germany's overall situation changed fundamentally; since the Anglo-American motto was 'Germany first', an invasion of the German-held continent was to be expected in the west sooner or later. As a result, on 15 March 1942, Hitler appointed von Rundstedt Commander-in-Chief West and so he relieved his former successor in the west, von Witzleben. Führer Directive No. 40 of 23 March 1942 prescribed, among other things, unified command of the entire coastline from Biscay to the Netherlands under Commander-in-Chief West. Helped by the agile-minded Zeitzler as Chief of Staff (he was appointed Chief of Staff of the Army on 24 September 1942 and succeeded by Günther Blumentritt) von Rundstedt organised the coastal defences from his headquarters in Paris, then in St Germain and finally back in Paris in the Hotel George V; by reinforcing from other theatres he made every effort to increase the striking power of the German army in the west, hitherto confined primarily to occupation duties. Despite difficulties with the naval and *Luftwaffe* commanders C-in-C West's measures proved their worth, as was shown by the repulse of the Anglo-Canadian landing attempt at Dieppe on 19 August 1942. Hitler's 'answer' to this was the construction of the Atlantic Wall, ordered on 25 August 1942; von Rundstedt and his staff were involved only as advisers and von Rundstedt considered it a 'propaganda exercise'.

He next found himself faced with a task half-operational and half-political. Following the Anglo-American landing in French North Africa on 7–8 November 1942 Hitler decided on 11 November to occupy southern France and disarm the French armistice army and air force. The occupation operation went according to plan but von Rundstedt's main task was to keep in contact with Marshal Pétain, the French head of state with whom relations were strained as a result of the occupation, and prevent him resigning, a step that would have created almost insuperable difficulties for the Germans in France. He met Pétain personally on several occasions and sent General Freiherr von Neubrunn to Vichy as liaison officer. In fact, with his 'non-political' approach von Rundstedt did succeed by 'soldier to soldier' discussions – if such a term can be used – in gaining Pétain's confidence. Delineation of the German and Italian occupation zones in south-eastern France was also complicated by mutual animosities, but von Rundstedt, who was highly respected by Italian senior officers, reached agreement without serious incident. A year later moreover, following Italy's 'defection' on 8 September when the Italian Fourth Army had to be disarmed and its defence zone between the Rhône and the Alps taken over by the Germans, intelligent orders issued by von Rundstedt solved the problem without major difficulty and without leaving hard feelings behind.

During the winter 1942–3 the tide of war turned visibly against Germany both in the east (Stalingrad) and in the Mediterranean; there is much to show that von Rundstedt too was forced to realise that Germany had lost the war militarily. To his intimates he would say in his typical way – as did other German senior officers at the time – that 'the politicals' must now find a formula for a compromise peace. When on leave in Bad Tölz he was invited to the Berghof by Hitler who, he expected, wanted to analyse the military situation in depth with him and then discuss the political consequences. Hitler however launched into a monologue about the fighting on the eastern front without allowing von Rundstedt to say a word. Von Rundstedt thereupon despatched to the Führer's Headquarters a detailed appreciation of the military situation, to which Hitler never replied directly; he did however include certain of its basic ideas in his Directive No. 51 of 3 November 1943, drawing the conclusion however that the anticipated major Allied assault in the west must be met 'with all the forces at our disposal regardless of losses' and that additional defences must be constructed.

Owing to the pessimistic tone of his memorandum and also his age Hitler did not consider that von Rundstedt now had sufficient initiative for this task and so, two days later, Field-Marshal Rommel was commissioned to examine 'defence preparedness of the occupied coastline', initially in Denmark and then in France as well. There was no clear division of responsibility between Rommel and Commander-in-Chief West and they held differing views on the method of dealing with the Allied invasion; von Rundstedt considered that the last remaining chance lay in a mobile defence, defeating the enemy in the heart of France by superior strategy and inflicting such losses upon him that he too would be ready for a compromise peace; Rommel, on the other hand, influenced by his experience of Allied air superiority in North Africa, looked for a decision on the coast itself, in the landing zone, on the first day of invasion. As a result in the second half of December 1943 a clash took place between the two field-marshals, though both were at one in thinking the Reich's overall situation serious in the extreme.

The problem was largely solved by Hitler's decision of 1 January 1944 that Army Group B under Rommel should be responsible for coastal defence from the Netherlands to the Loire, but that the group as a whole should be under C-in-C West, Rommel's direct subordination to the OKW operations staff lapsing. Differences remained however – in temperament, in their views of their strategic task and in their military interests and methods; von Rundstedt disliked Rommel's predilection for technical problems and tactical details, also his desire to be 'up front' with the troops as much as possible; he himself commanded by directives issued through his staff, and in the following months, as the situation at the front became increasingly difficult, he never left his headquarters.

Von Rundstedt was surprised by the strength of the Allied landing in Normandy on 6 June 1944 and especially by the massive use of air power, which made any daytime operational move by the Germans practically impossible. This made nonsense of his concept of a mobile defence as it did of Rommel's objective – to throw the enemy back into the sea on the first day. Over the telephone to Keitel, Chief of OKW, whom he treated with scant respect, von Rundstedt gave forcible expression to his conviction that the war was lost. His appreciations of the military situation given to Hitler on 17 June in *Wolfsschanze II* near Soissons and in the Berghof on 29 June left no doubt of his (and also Rommel's) pessimistic view of the position. Accordingly on 2 July Hitler decided to replace von Rundstedt by Field-Marshal von Kluge, giving him the Oakleaves to the Knights Cross to the Iron Cross as a parting present. Handing over command on the evening of 3 July, von Rundstedt, departed to Bad Tölz to recuperate. As far as anyone could foresee his military career was at an end.

The next few months were to show how deeply he was involved in the Nazi system and Germany's 'final struggle'. He had been embarrassed to receive from Hitler a 'gratuity' in the form of a cheque for 250,000 marks, but to salve his conscience on 12 December 1943 he had placed the money in a special account with the Deutsche Bank – which remained untouched. Though he despised the Nazi Party, was ironical over OKW and its operations staff, who had been his masters in the west, and occasionally made fun even of Hitler himself, he was generally held to be loyal to the Führer and so the German opposition made no attempt to win him over to the resistance. It was significant that in connection with the assassination attempt against Hitler on 20 July 1944 and subsequent events, only the foreign press raised the question whether von Rundstedt might not be cast in the role of a modern Yorck and lead a second 'Tauroggen'. In the witness box of the Military War Crimes Tribunal at Nuremberg on 12 August 1946 von Rundstedt stated emphatically that the idea of initiating or participating in a coup had never entered his head; as a soldier, bound by his oath to Hitler, he would have considered anything on those lines as treason, particularly in the Reich's increasingly catastrophic situation – 'and for all time I should have been held up as a traitor to my country'.

In the light of his career and his character this rigid and narrow viewpoint is understandable and it explains why he complied with Hitler's order on 4 August 1944 to preside over the Court of Honour of the German Reich, which was charged with dismissing from the *Wehrmacht* officers involved in the rising of 20 July so that they might be removed from the competence of the military courts and handed over to the People's Court under Freisler (a fate that overtook Field-Marshal von Witzleben whom von Rundstedt knew so well). Admittedly in the following months von Rundstedt frequently lamented privately that this had been a most painful duty for him. His insensitivity to the role he was playing however was illustrated even more vividly on 18 October 1944 when he represented Hitler at the state funeral for Field-Marshal Rommel in Ulm and lauded his services to Führer and Reich. He never suspected that because of complicity in the 20 July conspiracy Rommel had been faced by Hitler with the alternative of taking poison or arraignment before the People's Court together with persecution for his family; Rommel had chosen 'voluntary' death. There was tragic irony in von Rundstedt's sentence: 'His heart belonged to the Führer.'

By this time von Rundstedt had once more become Commander-in-Chief West. Von Kluge had committed suicide, the Allies had broken through the German front in Normandy and with tremendous effort an improvised front had been formed in the Netherlands, along the German frontier and west of the Vosges. Hitler's purpose was to relieve Field-Marshal Model, who as both C-in-C West and C-in-C Army Group B was overloaded, and to give the reeling western armies a psychological tonic by recalling von Rundstedt, now aged nearly seventy. He was summoned from Bad Tölz to Hitler's headquarters near Rastenburg on 1 September 1944 and, feeling that he must 'answer the call of the troops' and could not leave Führer and Reich in the lurch at this highly critical moment, he accepted. So on 5 September he resumed his old functions in a new headquarters at Arenberg near Koblenz, Model reverting to command of Army Group B; his Chief of Staff was no longer the trusted Blumentritt but General von Westphal, who had been transferred from the Italian front. Though suffering from rheumatism, von Rundstedt now drove out to the front once a week to encourage his men; he did not however abandon his basic method of commanding through his staff, problematical though that was to prove in the kaleidoscopic situation of the next few months.

Only very late in the day, in October 1944 when everything had already been fixed, was von Rundstedt initiated into Hitler's idea of a major German counter-offensive in the west; the operation was planned in complete detail by the OKW operations staff and, according to Hitler, was to 'change the fate of the Reich'. Von Rundstedt, together with Model and other commanders, was opposed to the 'major solution', a German thrust from the Eifel through the Ardennes and across the Meuse to cut off Montgomery's army group in southern Holland and northern Belgium, repeating the 1940 'sweep of the scythe'; in their view the essential conditions for success simply did not exist. Instead they advocated a 'limited solution' – formation of a 'cauldron' round the Allied salient near Aachen and then, if successful, a reappraisal. But their efforts were in vain. The offensive was launched on 16 December 1944 and its failure had to be admitted only four days later. Von Rundstedt protested against the term 'Rundstedt offensive', used both by Goebbels's propaganda and the Allies, since it gave the impression that C-in-C West had been responsible for planning and direction. He himself contributed to this impression however by issuing an order of the day on 16 December to 'Soldiers of the Western Front' which ran: 'Strong offensive forces are moving against the Anglo-Americans today. I need say no more to you. All of you will realise that we are staking our all.'

The proximity of the two headquarters, von Rundstedt's near Koblenz and Hitler's near Ziegenberg in Hesse (until moved to the Reich Chancellery in Berlin on 16 January 1945 owing to threatened catastrophe in the east) enabled the two men to meet more frequently than previously. The curious relationship between them became even closer – Blumentritt's description, not comprehensive but in certain respects apt, is that it was the respect of the usurper paid to the holder of legitimate military authority. It remained unchanged even when, on 9 March 1945, von Rundstedt was once more and for the last time relieved as C-in-C West – after the Americans had succeeded in gaining a foothold on the right bank of the Rhine via the Ludendorff bridge at Remagen, which had not been destroyed.

On 13 February, in view of the imminence of a major assault by the Allies, von Rundstedt had issued yet another inspiring call to the 'Soldiers of the Western Front': 'Guard your German Fatherland, as you have done before, from ignominy and foreign rule' – 'With unshakable confidence we gather round the Führer, our people and our country to guard against a terrible fate.' Now the final decision in the west had been taken. Hitler expressly summoned von Rundstedt to Berlin to take his leave and be presented with the Swords to the Oakleaves of the Knights Cross. His final words were: 'I thank you for your loyalty.'

On the return journey von Rundstedt paid one more visit to the command post, now in the Bayreuth area, of his successor as C-in-C West, Field-Marshal Kesselring.

Von Rundstedt retired to Bad Tölz for medical attention and there, on 1 May 1945, he became an American prisoner of war. During interrogation he suffered a heart attack. He was ultimately taken from Wiesbaden to imprisonment in Great Britain, was held in various camps, spent time in hospital and was taken back to Germany temporarily to testify before the International Military Tribunal in Nuremberg; finally in the spring of 1946 he reached the penultimate stage of his imprisonment in Bridgend Camp. Strained relations with other German generals in the camp, who, he considered, should treat him as the *Wehrmacht*'s most senior officer, increased his unsociability. Some relief from the monotony of prison life, however was provided by work on war histories and even more by talks with Liddell Hart, the British military writer, who considered von Rundstedt a better representative than all other German generals of 'the old Germany', was impressed by his dignified attitude in face of the hardships of prison and presented a favourable picture of him to the British public in his book *The Other Side of the Hill*. Von Rundstedt was not formally released until July 1948, was then placed in solitary confinement in Munsterlager, was moved from there to the British Military Hospital in Hamburg and thence was finally set free.

Von Rundstedt and his wife first occupied two small rooms in the Oppershausen old people's home near Celle and then a three-room flat in the Lerchenstrasse, Hanover. He lived to see the appearance in 1952 of the English edition of his biography written by Günther Blumentritt, his former Chief of Staff and entitled *Von Rundstedt – The Soldier and the Man*. He wrote a short foreword including this: 'I wish to say that I was correctly treated during British and American imprisonment, and many Englishmen, Americans and members of other nations showed me appreciation and regard, for which I can only thank them . . . We must learn by experience that destiny is mightier than man.' No German edition of this book has ever been published.

Von Rundstedt died on 24 February 1953 (his wife had died in the previous October) and was buried in Stöcken cemetery, Hanover. At the funeral, attended by a few relatives (four grandchildren, his son being already dead) and friends, Provost Strasser from Uelzen laid stress on only a *single* side to his nature – his exemplary simplicity and nobility of character; he had been a 'truly religious man', he said.

Against this view of von Rundstedt as a man the historian must set a critical appreciation of his role as senior military commander and the political responsibility he thereby took upon himself – involuntarily. As regards his considerable operational ability and his performance as a commander in the field and C-in-C of army groups, it must be said that under the conditions of the Hitler Reich he was unable to develop his capacity for military leadership to the full, as he would probably have done under the Empire during the First World War. During the Polish and French campaigns he was able to take major decisions of his own within the broad framework of directives from the army high command and so laid the foundations of his reputation; the same applies in lesser degree to the summer and autumn campaigns in Russia in 1941; as C-in-C West in 1942–4 he was still relatively independent, since Hitler's increasing tendency to immerse himself in operational detail, including even tactical moves, and to insist on compliance with his *ad hoc* 'Führer orders' even from senior and very senior commanders, was concentrated primarily on the eastern theatre. For some time it did not seem that the same was in store for the west, but this became obvious at latest during the defence against the Allied invasion and reached its height during the so-called Rundstedt offensive. Hitler treated field-marshals like highly paid NCOs, and in spite of their special 'confidential relationship' von Runstedt was no exception in this respect. He realised how undignified were the small-time military functions allotted to him, but he thought that he must play the part prescribed for him by Hitler because 'Germany's all', the fate of the Reich and its role as a major European power were at stake and all his life this had been his sole 'political' sheet-anchor.

From the time of the so-called Röhm putsch he undoubtedly knew, despite all his illusions, that this Reich of Hitler's was something different from the old Prussia and even from Wilhelmine Germany. His upbringing, however, which had not instilled into him *all* the old Prussian traditions, did not lead him to visualise the possibility of revolt against the criminal orders and political leadership that was visibly carrying the Reich to catastrophe. By 'playing along' without grasping the broader picture, as a field-marshal necessarily should, by assiduously doing his duty and above all by making himself available for activities contrary to the ethos of a soldier, he stands guilty before his soldiers who trusted him and his people whom he served. To the extent that history has so far been able to 'comprehend', this remains as a shadow over von Rundstedt's military leadership; at moments of decision it did not attain the greatness that so many hoped that he, and he in particular, would display.

AIR CHIEF MARSHAL LORD DOWDING

Gavin Lyall

Air Chief Marshal Lord Dowding's place in history was secured by what, in his own eyes, was a failure. He wanted, and hoped, to become Chief of the Air Staff – i.e., military head of the RAF. For good reasons he never made it. Instead he had to become the man who fought the Battle of Britain.

The son of a Dumfriesshire preparatory school headmaster, Hugh Dowding was born in 1882 and spent an unremarkable childhood first in his father's school and then at Winchester. He opted for the army class largely, on his own admission, to avoid learning Greek; on such small pivots can careers, and possibly world events, turn.

At seventeen he passed into Woolwich for a one-year course (it had been shortened from two by the need to churn out officers for the South African War). There Dowding's concentration wandered a bit and his exam position slipped; traditionally, the top examinees all joined the Royal Engineers, the rest the Artillery. It was laziness, according to Dowding, that made him a Gunner and bad advice that put him into garrison, as opposed to the more active field, artillery.

Gibraltar, Ceylon and Hong Kong: three postings in four years, nothing to shoot at with the big guns, but plenty of targets for shotguns, together with the usual round of horse riding and trading. The picture is the normal one of a young subaltern learning the ways of the army – and ways to dodge some of those ways – and making the most of the outdoor life that a warm-weather Empire offered in those days. It took a war to shake many officers out of this comfortable pattern, but Dowding managed it on his own. At the age of twenty-two he transferred to a Mountain Battery in India.

'You can go where you please, you can skid up the trees, but you don't get away from the guns!' These were the 'Screw-Guns' immortalised by Kipling: short-range weapons that could be dismantled and carried by mules and carts that took the Gunners' motto 'Ubique' (everywhere) to absurd lengths – 'The monkey can say what our road was, the wild goat 'e knows where we passed.' For six years Dowding commanded units of such guns, though never in action. But the practice was well up to Kipling's standards, and the main

© Gavin Lyall, 1976.

joy of it was that he was so often out on his own with a troop of two guns, exercising with just a company or so of infantry. It was – for the day and age – an early taste of responsibility, since Mountain Gunners were expected to find or carve their own trails.

It was on such an exercise that Dowding managed to ambush a Gurkha unit that was supposed to be ambushing him, under the command of Cyril Newall. In later life he seems to have enjoyed retelling this story; certainly it was the first time he met the man who would be chosen to command the RAF instead of himself.

But already his interest in warfare was turning more to the administrative and organisational problems of high command – which, for a junior officer, meant staff work. He had applied for a Staff College course, and in 1910 was given a year's half-pay leave to swot up for the entrance exam. He passed in for one of just seven places allocated to Gunners on the two-year course, and enjoyed and profited from his time there. But he came to feel that too much weight was being given to (a) cavalry doctrine and (b) just doctrine. He never rebelled; he was too wise, and too junior, for that. He kept his head down, his mind open, acquired the nickname of 'Stuffy', and went on believing that things in the wide military world were changing a little faster than they were at Camberley.

One day, in a theoretical exercise, he was given command of six theoretical aeroplanes and sent them off to reconnoitre the enemy before he committed himself to any other plans. When senior officers criticised this decision as likely to be ineffective (although this was the only reason why aircraft could have been included in an exercise at this date) Dowding decided to find out for himself.

So, by getting up early and motoring to Brooklands in a borrowed car, he was able to amass a total of one hour and forty minutes in the air and earn his Royal Aero Club certificate (most primary training was done in the early mornings, before the sun caused too much bumpiness in the air). From there, when the Staff College course was successfully passed, he went on to more air training at the Central Flying School to get his RFC wings. It was a vintage time, early in 1914; John Salmond, a future Chief of Air Staff, was Dowding's flying instructor, while Trenchard was Assistant Commandant. But Dowding himself had no particular commitment to the air; he considered a transfer to the RFC but was easily dissuaded by his father, who wanted him in a less risky job. 'My original idea in learning to fly was to increase my value as a staff officer.' Having done just this he went contentedly back to garrison artillery in the Isle of Wight.

This lasted only a few months until the outbreak of war, when he found that the RFC had a first option on his services. His new posting was as commandant of the Dover 'transit camp' through which squadrons for France then flew, but he was soon moved to a new squadron just forming, and rather too slowly for his taste. Dowding felt the same pressure to get into action as any professional officer; all other reasons apart, to write psc (passed staff college) after one's name would mean nothing if he missed a major war that was due to end by Christmas. After badgering Trenchard for a posting, he accepted an offer to go over as an observer rather than as a pilot: 'A fearful insult . . . but I was well enough content.'

He arrived in time for the finale of the 'dash for the sea' that formalised the trench line for the next few years. Six weeks of reconnaissance, hasty changes of airfield as the Germans overwhelmed Antwerp, and firing at enemy aircraft with a broomhandle Mauser automatic – and he was reinstated as a pilot. But almost immediately he was transferred, first to RFC headquarters, then to No. 9 squadron – which was actually called 'the Wireless Squadron' for a while – to help develop the first air-to-ground radio for artillery observation.

He had been with the squadron less than a month before he was given acting command of it – the original CO being transferred for insisting that his squadron's aircraft did not need new wings merely because they flapped a little – but again Dowding was moved soon after; back home to run an experimental aerial wireless school.

In retrospect this may have been a crucial point in Dowding's career. In every way he was ideal for the post: he was interested in technical problems and had experience of air-to-ground radio; he was a Gunner by career, who presumably knew how to communicate to other Gunners; he was now a major aged over thirty, and not to be lightly risked over enemy lines when there were younger men with more flying talent available. He did a good job at the Brooklands school, improving existing radios and guiding work on the first R/T – or voice radio – used in aircraft. But he was being typecast, and not into the attacking mould that Trenchard was trying to establish in France.

After about four months Dowding went out again, this time in full command of a general purpose squadron (effectively, there were no other purposes just yet) in 1st Wing, which was still, although not for long, run by Trenchard himself. By the standards of the time it was not a very eventful six months; the squadron did not run into the Fokkers that scourged other parts of the front, and itself shot down only one German aircraft. Dowding worked hard to improve living conditions – the officers' mess was in a canal barge – and develop new bombsights and camera gear: such things were still being made in squadron workshops. And he had his first run-in with Trenchard.

This was entirely Trenchard's fault: he had sent Dowding a collection of wrong-sized propellers and gruffly ordered him to use them. Dowding did a single test flight before Trenchard recognised his error. Dowding went on fuming that his chief had taken the word of 'some half-baked motor-salesman in Paris' rather than trust an RFC pilot.

The new year in 1916 brought Dowding home, once more to administrative and technical problems – mainly in organising and 'debugging' the first squadron of Sopwith One-and-a-Half Strutters fitted with the new interruptor gear. However he was already designated for higher command: now a lieutenant-colonel, he was to take over 9th Wing, attached directly to HQ in France. Or, in fact, attached directly to Trenchard, who roosted there now as RFC commander.

This situation took much of the direction of the wing out of Dowding's hands; moreover he was soon at odds with Trenchard again over the tactics to be used. In the build-up to the Somme offensive, Trenchard was reaching – particularly now that he had some 'real' fighter aircraft – for air superiority. This involved constant aggressive patrols by small formations – which too often ran into the much larger formations the German fighters were then using. Dowding himself tasted the problem: given special permission to fly over the lines (his new rank would have forbidden it), he was piloting a slow BE2c when it was jumped by Fokkers. The sole armament, the observer's Lewis gun, was jammed by a hit, and Dowding's instrument panel shot to pieces. He spiralled out of the fight and hedge-hopped home with a new perspective on his aircrews' chances in the coming months.

The matter did not come to a head, however, until towards the end of the Somme fighting. Casualties all round had been heavy, but particularly in the squadron of French-built Moranes with Dowding's wing. At the best of times the Morane was accident-prone because of its poor controls, and the Fokkers made up the difference. Dowding suggested that this unit – and others in time – should be 'periodically relieved, as was done in other branches of the Service'. This was a new idea, since Trenchard planned to keep squadrons constantly in action, resting individual aircrew and filling up with replacements – as on the whole he did. But he acceded to Dowding's request for the Morane squadron – though with a not-quite-private note that Dowding was a 'dismal Jimmy' who could hardly be expected to restore squadrons' morale. Not long after, Dowding was promoted to colonel and sent home.

'That finished me with Trenchard till the end of the war and for eight years afterwards,' Dowding recalled. This may not be quite true, but the next fighting command he was to hold would be in the Battle of Britain, twenty-four years later.

'Dismal' is not the right word, but certainly Dowding was, even then in his early thirties, serious and austere to the point of appearing pessimistic. Obviously commanders should be able to fear the worst: one who does not will be unprepared for setbacks. But it is a mistake to show it, and this Dowding did. He recognised the weakness in himself, and never tried to 'do a Trenchard' by visiting squadrons to deliver pep-talks; he knew he had not the touch to create an optimism he did not himself feel among junior officers and NCOs. Indeed he was uneasy in most personal relationships; he was admired or disliked – very few got close enough to *like* him.

Yet behind all this was an immense but unvocalised respect for the sanctity of life, a regret for its loss. As a squadron commander he had ordered the personal effects of two dead German aircrew to be dropped behind their lines (this 'sportsmanship' was less common than legend has it); later in life he supported societies for the humane treatment of animals. But more immediately his concern was for those he commanded: Lord (Sholto) Douglas wrote that casualties were 'with him a concern more heartfelt than it was in the case of any other commander in the Service'.

The next major events in Dowding's life can have done little to conquer his pessimism: early in 1918 he married – and two years later his wife died, leaving him with a son and stepdaughter. And in the first list of officers to be permanently transferred to the new-found Royal Air Force, Dowding's name was missing: he was expected to return to the Gunners. Probably Trenchard had nothing to do with this, though those who drew up the list may have believed they were reflecting his feelings, but it still took the intercession of others to get Dowding restored. Economically, he did not buy the new RAF uniform until the new position was confirmed.

In the 1920s he was at an awkward rank, if not age: too senior to command a squadron or even wing in the active theatres of Iraq or the North-West Frontier, and too junior to command either of those areas – even if Trenchard had been prepared to give him such posts. Most of his work was on the staff, though as such he was sent to Baghdad for a while. It was he who introduced the humane policy of warning native villages by leaflet before they were bombed for real. By 1926 Dowding was back in Whitehall as Director of Training, once more under Trenchard's eye. But this time things went smoothly, Trenchard saying (doubtless gruffly): 'I don't often make mistakes about people, but I made one about you.' Dowding remembered the remark rather than treasured it. Neither man had, or was to, change his own ideas about air warfare.

Dowding's two children lived at the Wimbledon house of his retired father – now handling his schoolmaster's savings adroitly on the stock market – and Dowding himself made his home there whenever he could, commuting to central London, Kenley or Uxbridge. The old sports of riding and shooting were limited, but every winter he treated himself to a skiing holiday in Switzerland, and served as president of the Ski Club of Great Britain. But the life was still a rather solitary one, outside the RAF's social round.

It was a sign of Trenchard's new trust that, in 1929, Dowding was sent out to Palestine to review the sticky Arab-Jewish problem and, tacitly, see if 'air policing' would be needed. In fact such policing really worked only in sparsely populated areas, and Dowding was able to report that changes rather than reinforcements were needed. Back in Britain he spent a few months commanding the Fighting Area (i.e. the embryo Fighter Command) then took a seat on the Air Council as member for Supply and Research. The road to the Battle of Britain began there.

It is impossible to disentangle Dowding's influence from the work of his department generally, or from industries that were already due for a bumper harvest. During the 1920s the aircraft designers had made big advances in the use of metals, monocoque construction, the cantilever (no bracing wires) monoplane and, particularly, aero-engines – culminating dramatically in the Schneider Trophy wins. In parallel the growth of public broadcasting had fed money back into the radio industry to support equivalent developments.

Part of Dowding's job was to sift the wheat and chaff from this harvest. For an example: he did not truly 'pioneer' the monoplane fighter – which was being researched simultaneously in four other countries – but he egged on Sydney Camm and R. J. Mitchell to turn the Schneider Trophy experience into experimental landplane designs – ultimately the Hurricane and Spitfire. Most likely such aircraft would have happened anyway – only a bit later. Similarly, once radar had been proven technically feasible, Dowding urged its development into a practical tool.

There is no coincidence to the fact that much of the work was biased towards the defensive. Trenchard's belief that the only defence was attack had dominated RAF thinking in the 1920s – and to be fair, in the days when fighters had but a small margin of speed over bombers, no margin of armament and no radio either, an effective air defence was impossible. Now the fast eight-gun fighters with voice radio *and* the prospect of early warning changed the whole situation – although not everybody saw it at the time. Political leaders still believed that 'the bomber will always get through' and were encouraged in this by most senior RAF commanders (who had shown no interest in escort fighters for their own bombers). It is slightly ironic that if the ultimate effectiveness of Fighter Command had been widely recognised, more money would have been spent to make it more effective still.

In 1936 the RAF was radically reorganised into specialised commands: Fighter, Bomber, Coastal, etc. It was a big step away from Trenchard's idea that a commander should control all types of aircraft in his area, and indeed most changes in air force organisation since then have been steps back towards mixed forces. The point is worth noting, because it meant that when Dowding became the first C-in-C Fighter Command, he took on, or rather built, a force that had only a single task and no capability for any other. It was a job that demanded rather narrow single-mindedness.

Dowding's true monument is the Fighter Command he created in the next four years rather than his handling of it in battle. Others might have handled it as well or better – the Air Staff certainly believed so – but that is a tribute to what he built; nobody has suggested who else might have built so well.

The keystone of the whole command was not radar but fast and accurate communications. Information from radar and the Royal Observer Corps (radar was then 'blind' inland and in many places at low levels even over the sea) was collected and 'filtered' at group level to avoid duplications. The same information went to Fighter Command HQ at Bentley Priory, where the identical process was gone through except that it covered the whole country rather than just a group area. Each group was subdivided into sector stations – major airfields that controlled other airfields – and group sent down to sector both information on incoming raids and generalised orders to intercept them: i.e., to send up a flight, a squadron or whatever. The sector then controlled the pilots in the air by the final communications link – radio.

But perhaps the oddest thing about Fighter Command was that it was as purely defensive as the Maginot Line. Like that notorious structure, it was designed for the impossible: to fight a preplanned defensive battle without any question of counter-attacking – since Dowding had only interceptor fighters, and short-ranged ones at that. But though the system itself was rigid and the various HQs and radars effectively immovable, the fighting squadrons could be shifted from one end of the country to the other almost as fast as they could fly – and know they would be controlled in the same familiar way wherever they went

Fighter Command HQ itself was planned to stand rather outside the day-to-day fighting: handling that was the work of group and sector. Command itself would be the liaison point between groups, and concern itself with finding reinforcements and replacements. There was to be no question of keeping squadrons in the line when they had been shot to pieces. Not in this war.

The system did not come into being overnight; it came by trial and error, building block on building block. And it is easy to forget how little time Dowding had for rehearsal with his full cast. At the time of Munich there were only five radar stations and three newly formed squadrons of Hurricanes in a mainly biplane force. When the war started the radar stations had doubled, but in a strength of thirty-five squadrons, still only twenty-four had Hurricanes and Spitfires. The annual air exercise of 1939 was only a pale imitation of the reality, and after that everybody was too busy to exercise *en masse*.

As things turned out the greatest unrecognised weakness of the command was at the sharp end: the squadrons themselves. There were too many young pilots making the difficult transition to a new and complicated type of aircraft. There were too many fat-cat commanders who had been posted to fighters to help their careers rather than the RAF. And there was a basic, widespread ignorance about what air fighting was going to be like.

Dowding himself had never been a 'fighter boy', either personally or as a First World War commander, but he did – almost – his best to rectify this. In the minutes of the Air Fighting Committee, which initiated research and made recommendations, Dowding's practical 'show me' approach shines through a lot of fairy-tale mist. He fought for bullet-proof windscreens and armour plate for his pilots' cockpits; he insisted on trials and demonstrations (he even tried to get Bomber Command to provide an armour-plated bomber that his pilots could shoot at with live ammunition). But he ended with a very inadequate idea of what the reality would be.

Because of this, fighters were encouraged to fly in too tight formations, open fire from too great a distance and for too long, and came to believe they would be taking on only unescorted bombers. It was admitted that the squadrons sent to France might meet enemy fighters, but it was assumed that every fighter-to-fighter combat would be a tight 'winding-match'. The threat of the 'Hun in the sun', a phrase dated from 1917 or earlier, had been forgotten. And although Dowding himself brought up the first mention of the Spanish Civil War, where the *Luftwaffe* had been learning its trade, this was not until May 1939, and there was no pressure to find what the Luftwaffe had learnt. As the first independent air force the RAF traditionally thought it could learn little from foreigners, but this attitude fitted young pilots better than it did their top commanders.

This was the house that Dowding built, with its strengths and weakness. Yet he had gone to Fighter Command with no expectation that he would stay there long, least of all to lead it in war: he had every hope of becoming the next Chief of Air Staff in 1937 or 1938. But seniority and a questioning mind were not the only qualifications. He had missed too much of the action in 1916–18 and thereafter to have a reputation as a fighting commander, and his withdrawn life-style (he had not even owned a house since his wife died) made him suspect for the top job, which involved socialising with politicians who held the service's purse-strings. And perhaps hints of his growing interest in spiritualism did nothing to help; the British appreciate eccentricity in their military leaders, but they prefer it to be something tangible, like womanising or model railways.

Even when he knew – in early 1937 – that he had been passed over in favour of his old Gurkha 'enemy', Sir Cyril Newall, he could not really rest secure in his job. The next year he was told he would be retired in July 1939. When his proposed successor smashed a knee in an air crash, he was reprieved until March 1940, then to July, then to the autumn. The last confirmation of this came only in August, when the Battle of Britain was reaching its peak: Dowding's comment, 'I never quite knew exactly where I stood,' has the restraint of an Old Wykehamist. Clearly there was a strong pressure in the Air Ministry to dump him before the real action began.

Inevitably the mistrust worked both ways. He had been promised fifty-two squadrons of modern fighters, and was short of seventeen squadrons, let alone the modern fighters themselves, when the war began. Thereafter the re-equipment went well enough, but the squadron total barely increased because of those diverted to support the army in France. Certainly the army needed all the squadrons it got (and more) but most of all it needed a system to control them. But this was not Dowding's business; he could only see his own task being undermined.

When the German invasion broke in May, the problem got worse. Since the RAF had largely ignored army needs in the 1930s – when other tasks became commands, Army Co-operation was still a mere group – the only pool of useful aircraft was Fighter Command. Without a control system behind them or radar ahead of them, some 250 Hurricanes were lost in France in two weeks, and more were being demanded.

On 16 May Dowding wrote a now-famous letter to the Air Ministry pointing out the situation and subtly asking to be told what *they* thought he should have to defend the country. He also recalled, to two biographers, that on the preceding day he had met the War Cabinet and persuaded them to send no more Hurricanes to France. At that date the British Expeditionary Force was still in position near Brussels and was soon to be ordered to attack *inland* across the German lines of communication, so it would be an odd decision to deny it any air reinforcements even if this attack went well. However, recently opened Cabinet documents suggest that Dowding's memory slipped the dates and that the meeting and decision took place on 3 June, when the Dunkirk evacuation was nearly complete. This makes more sense of his letter to the Air Ministry, and also his own despatch on the Battle of Britain, written in 1941: '. . . it was decided to send no more Fighter Reinforcements to France except to cover the final evacuation.' Final evacuations were not being agreed to on 15 May.

Dowding's memory for dates does not matter; the important thing is that he obviously remembered meeting great opposition about sending no more fighters to France (which he would have met on 15 May) rather than reluctant agreement (as on 3 June). In short, he felt alone in foreseeing the holocaust to come. But he was not alone; since no more fighters *were* sent to France after 15 May (except on a temporary basis) others in the Air Staff and Cabinet agreed with him even before he made his point. Yet the lonely feeling was clearly there, partly in his character, partly in his relations with the Air Ministry, and a lot in his narrow task – retrospectively expanded to saving the Free World – of defending Britain in the air. Dowding was quite right to fear the worst, since that was just what Fighter Command had been created for. Others had wider concerns to worry about.

The system won the Battle of Britain. Despite starting with too few squadrons and facing an enemy based far closer than expected – and thus able to use single-seat escort fighters – the sheer economy Dowding had built into the operation multiplied the efficiency of every RAF fighter. There was no wasteful patrolling: squadrons scrambled only when a raid was plotted, and were usually guided accurately to an interception. But the steady erosion of pilot losses forced Dowding to abandon one of his dearest schemes: the rotation of squadrons to quiet areas in the north. Towards the end of the battle he had to revert to Trenchard's system of 1916, leaving units in the front line and stripping squadrons elsewhere to keep the most battlewise – albeit desperately tired – pilots in those first line units. It was a sad business to abandon a humane principle that had once got him called 'dismal Jimmy'.

This was not the only problem. Nothing could speed the flow of new-trained pilots (men were going into action with less than twenty hours' experience on Hurricanes and Spitfires, and maybe having fired the guns once before) but Dowding did what he could to press-gang experienced pilots from other commands. Meanwhile night raiding had also begun, and interceptions were few and chancy: the command was short of the right aircraft (the Beau-fighter), inland-looking radar, airborne radar – and consequently the men trained to operate such equipment. Frequently Dowding spent most of the night with a night-fighter squadron, snatched a few hours' sleep and arrived at his desk to meet the problems of the day: should he abandon certain bomb-pocked day-fighter fields? (three were evacuated); create duplicate sector operations rooms *off* the vulnerable airfields? (he tried to), rearrange the anti-aircraft guns for which he was nominally responsible? (he set up a committee to handle this).

All these were the sort of problem he had decided were headquarters' concern, but he misjudged how many they would be. A while before, his proposed successor, Christopher Courtney, had arrived to act as deputy – then found there was not enough to do and gone away again. Perhaps Dowding should have delegated more then; now he had no one to delegate to. And so he first missed and then mishandled the biggest operational problem that came up during the Battle of Britain.

It was a disagreement between his two senior commanders: Air Vice-Marshals Leigh-Mallory, commanding No. 12 Group to the north and east of London, and Keith Park, running No. 11 Group in the most vulnerable and active area south of the Thames. Park – whose airfields were the first target during the August phase of the Battle of Britain – played for disruptive tactics, scrambling squadrons as fast as he could and intercepting as far forward as he could, at the risk of being heavily outnumbered. Leigh-Mallory preferred to build his intercepting force into a wing of four or five squadrons – which took time to assemble in the air – and then try for a knock-out blow on a raid that might, by then, have dropped its bombs unhindered. Although a lot of these bombs were falling on Park's No. 11 Group airfields, which could have been protected by a faster deployment from No. 12 Group, in this con-text it hardly matters whether Park or Leigh-Mallory was right. What was certainly wrong was such men using contrary tactics in the middle of a battle and their superior not even noticing, and when he had noticed, being unwilling to take a decision.

Long after the war Dowding said: 'I did not want to have to say you mustn't do this and you mustn't do that. I expected more of my Group Commanders than that. And that was why, by mid-October, I had come to realise I would have to do something about what was going on and get rid of Leigh-Mallory.' But the disagreement had been there from late August; by mid-October the Battle of Britain had petered out.

A straightforward defensive battle can never end in an instantly recognised victory; the Battle of Britain came to be seen as a triumph only later. For the moment, invasion had been merely postponed, while night bombers were ranging unhindered over Britain. Fighter Command's reputation tarnished somewhat and Dowding – who had never been publicised as the commander – was finally and quietly relieved of command. He had had a good long run in the job, but it was hard luck on Keith Park to be shifted to a training command and replaced at No. 11 Group by Leigh-Mallory himself, whom Dowding had not got around to sacking. A hesitancy in command can cause casualties other than those in battle.

Dowding was an awkward person to employ thereafter. Churchill sent him to sweet-talk American manufacturers into producing a certain aero-engine, but this was hardly Dowding's forte. Back home again he wrote a despatch on the Battle of Britain – a good summary that reveals his concern for his pilots' lives along with some vagueness about their practical problems (by – wisely – not trying to copy Trenchard's morale-raising visits, Dowding missed some of the feedback of immediate experience from his pilots). He submitted – at request – some suggestions for RAF economies and made so many new enemies thereby that he turned down a chance to give the RAF in Egypt the same treatment and asked to be finally retired.

In popular circles his reputation grew as the Battle of Britain came to be seen as more and more decisive. In 1943 the government gave him the second peerage earned in the RAF (Trenchard, of course, had been the first), but the RAF never awarded him their top rank. Certainly he had never held their top post, but perhaps there were other reasons as well. Much as he would have liked a professional award, Dowding left it to others to make a fuss about this. He never cashed in on his growing fame, writing neither his autobiography nor even a book about the Battle of Britain – which, properly timed, could have been a best-seller.

Instead he wrote two books on spiritualistic matters. In 1951 he married a widowed lady who shared his interest in the beyond and lived thereafter a fairly private country life. One could say that communication had always been his strong point – he was prepared to talk out his ideas to others – but contact his weak one. Perhaps, well before his death in 1970, in communication with the hereafter, he found also a contact that had been so difficult with spirits that were still partly clay.

Field-Marshal The Earl Wavell

Bernard Fergusson

Archibald Percival Wavell was born at Colchester on 5 May 1883, the son and grandson of generals. His father was then a major in the Norfolk Regiment, but transferred to The Black Watch eight years later to command its 2nd Battalion. In 1896 he won a scholarship to Winchester; in 1900 he passed fourth into Sandhurst; in 1901, despite his youth, he passed out top, and was commissioned into The Black Watch three days after his eighteenth birthday. Four months later he sailed to join his father's old battalion in South Africa, arriving in time to win four clasps to his medal before the war ended. After some years' service in India, including a short campaign on the North-West Frontier, he passed top into the Staff College six months short of his twenty-sixth birthday, ten years below the average age of his successful competitors, and at the end of the course was one of only two officers graded 'A'.

On leaving Camberley he was sent to Russia for two years as a language student, attached at frequent intervals to military units; and on his return, to his irritation, was posted to the Russian section in the War Office. From this he contrived to escape early in the war to France, and in November of 1914 became a brigade major in the 3rd Division. Here he made his mark, but at Ypres in June of 1915 he was wounded in the head and lost his left eye. He was awarded an immediate Military Cross in the first list ever gazetted of that newly created decoration.

For ten months in 1916 he was on the staff at GHQ under the future General Sir John Burnett-Stuart; and from October 1916 until May 1917 was liaison officer in the Caucasus with the Russian Grand Duke Nicholas. In July 1917 he was sent to Palestine as liaison officer between Allenby and the CIGS, Sir William Robertson, who had been his commandant at the Staff College. For the rest of his life Allenby (whose biography he was later to write) and Burnett-Stuart (who survived him, and wrote a moving tribute in *The Times* after his death) were to remain his military heroes. Many found Allenby difficult to serve; he could be something of a bully; but Wavell stood up to him, and despite the twenty-two years of difference in their ages the two of them got on admirably. For most of 1918 Wavell was Brigadier General Staff to Chetwode in xx Corps in Palestine; and after the war ended returned for a year as Brigadier General Staff to Allenby himself, who had become High Commissioner in Egypt as well as Commander-in-Chief.

With the postwar contraction of the army there set in for Wavell, as for Alexander and many others, a long period of marking time in the matter of advancement. After a spell of regimental soldiering in Silesia, in occupied Germany, during which he commanded a company as a brevet colonel, and a period in the War Office, he once again joined Burnett-Stuart as a member of his staff on Salisbury Plain. Here in the late twenties the first fumbling experiments with armour were being carried out. For various reasons these were not as fruitful as they might have been. The authorities were operating on a shoestring; they were trying out too many different types of vehicle; and the officer commanding the Experimental Mechanised Force had a rather pedestrian mind. Fuller, then the principal exponent of armoured warfare, was the obvious choice; but he refused the appointment because he considered that he was not being offered a free enough hand.

In 1930 Wavell was given command of the 6th Infantry Brigade in the Aldershot Command, which had been selected for further experiment in the use of new infantry weapons and vehicles. It was in this appointment that he broke through into widespread notice, partly because of his stimulating and imaginative methods of training, and partly through his lectures: within the command, at the Staff College, at the Royal United Service Institution and elsewhere. His voice and delivery were lacking in fire, but his thinking was original and his language arresting. When in 1934 his tenure was up, he was promoted major-general but went on half-pay for fourteen months before assuming command of the 2nd Division. The financial hardship was alleviated by two paid assignments for which he was highly qualified: the rewriting of *Field Service Regulations*, of which his racy and readable draft was sadly mangled during its passage through the War Office, and the leadership of a military reconnaissance of Palestine and Iraq.

During his two and a half years in command of the 2nd Division he came to wield an enormous, though unsought, influence in the higher reaches of the army. He never had to tout for attention, but increasingly he attracted it. At the very top there was much dead wood; senior officers who had been adequate in their day, but who – to mix the metaphor – had run out of steam. To Wavell's modest quarter in Aldershot flowed a stream of impatient officers of roughly his own vintage, such as Dill, Brooke, Gort, Alexander and Freyberg, worried about the prevailing inertia in high places, both military and political. Among his subordinates there was much talent. His brigade commanders were Victor Fortune, the future Field-Marshal Lord Wilson of Libya, and Arthur Smith, his devoted and highly successful Chief of Staff in the Middle East in after years. Successive brigade majors included Horrocks, Dempsey and Cameron Nicholson: the first two destined to be outstanding wartime corps commanders, and the last to command that same 2nd Division in Burma. There followed a spell as General Officer Commanding

Palestine at the height of the Arab troubles, and at Southern Command at Salisbury: then, in July 1939, five weeks before the outbreak of war with Germany, he sailed for Egypt, to be Army Commander in Chief in the Middle East.

Wavell was now fifty-six. He was physically tough, spending at least an hour a day on a horse and most weekends on a golf-course. His whole career hitherto might be regarded as a spring compressed for the ordeal that he was about to face; and he knew both the geographical and strategic problems of the Middle East, and the limitations and potential of the British armed forces, as well as, and perhaps better than, any of his contemporaries. His resources then, as indeed later even after reinforcement, were woefully small; they would have been smaller still if the troubles in Palestine during the years immediately before the war had not considerably swollen the normal garrison. He opened up the new headquarters with only six officers, with Arthur Smith as his Chief of Staff and Maitland Wilson in command of the British troops in Egypt. During the prolonged inactivity before Italy declared war on 10 June 1940, his appreciations were shrewd and borne out by events; his preparations, within the limits of his resources, thorough; his team trained; and his relations with his naval and air force opposite numbers perfect. In all military history there is no record of a better attuned triumvirate in a long period of crisis than that of Wavell, Andrew Cunningham of the Royal Navy and Arthur Longmore (whose son was later to marry Wavell's second daughter) of the Royal Air Force. With Tedder, who replaced Longmore in May 1941 for reasons still not clear, relations were less happy.

Throughout the Phoney War Wavell had plenty of time to contemplate the situation in which he would be if Italy were to throw in her lot with Germany. She had a quarter of a million troops in North Africa, and three hundred thousand in Ethiopia and Somaliland, though of these last only one-third were European. Nobody at that time contemplated the fall of France, but even so the Mediterranean would obviously be a risky sea route for the British; on the other hand the Red Sea would be closed to the Italians. The eyes of London were focused chiefly on the western front; and throughout May and even into early June of 1940 Churchill was urging the Chiefs of Staff to strip Wavell of eight of his few regular battalions for the benefit of the European theatre. With the connivance of Dill, now CIGS, Wavell procrastinated successfully, and still had these vital battalions when Italy declared war at midnight on 10–11 June. In this argument lay the seeds of the historic clash of character between Churchill and Wavell, which was to continue until Wavell's death ten turbulent years later.

On that fateful date Wavell had eighty-six thousand troops scattered throughout his wide command. To Churchill this sounded a respectable, even a formidable, figure; and many of the signals that poured forth from him during the coming months to add to Wavell's burdens were reproaches concerning what seemed to him the disproportion between 'teeth and tail'. In terms of 'teeth' Wavell was low indeed: nominal divisions and brigades were all several units short, and these below strength, under-equipped, short of ammunition, and in many cases under-trained. To add to his difficulties there were 'strings' attached to the Australian and New Zealand contingents. Their respective governments would not allow them to be split up into any component smaller than a division. He was thus debarred by irrelevant political rules from deploying such troops as he had as recurrent crises flared up – north, south, east and west – during the hectic year that followed.

If nobody else was psychologically ready for the Italian declaration of war, Wavell was. He hit the Italians hard on the very first day with lightning raids. Then came the defection of the French in Syria, and shortly afterwards in Somaliland: in both these countries the carefully co-ordinated plans for mutual defence were no longer secret, and in Somaliland they actually passed into Italian hands. Wavell had been summoned to London for consultations. He calculated that the garrison of Somaliland was more valuable than the retention of that arid, and strategically not very important, country; and for the period of his absence gave Maitland Wilson a free hand for the campaign. Wilson's subordinate, Godwin-Austen, took the decision to evacuate. Churchill was furious to the point of demanding unsuccessfully that Godwin-Austen should be court-martialled. Wavell, having returned, reported the enormous discrepancy between British and Italian casualties, and ended his signal: 'Heavy butcher's bill not necessarily indication of good tactics.' This happy but far from tactless phrase was another nail in the coffin of the Churchill-Wavell relationship.

That relationship brightened towards the end of the year. Marshal Graziani, the Italian general of high repute commanding in North Africa, had been advancing cautiously towards and beyond the Egyptian frontier. As Wavell subsequently put it, he detected some 'unsoundness' in the Italian dispositions: a phrase reminiscent of a Staff College instructor. Belaboured by incessant and gratuitous exhortations from Churchill, worried lest his intentions should be revealed through being confided to too many people, he kept his own counsel to within a tiny circle, virtually restricted to Arthur Smith, Maitland Wilson and Richard O'Connor. To these three alone, old friends of long standing who shared in all his views, he confided his conception of encirclement and a hefty knock-out blow from an unexpected direction; to the last two he delegated the detailed planning.

The culmination of this was the startling victory of Sidi Barrani. Early in the morning of 9 December two squadrons of heavy tanks, with infantry of the 4th Indian Division close behind them, broke into Nibeiwa from the north-west. By the evening of 11 December, for a total loss of 624 killed, wounded and missing, General O'Connor had captured close on 40,000 prisoners, 237 guns and 73 tanks, and the Italian commander General Maletti had been killed. The westward sweep continued. By the middle of February, despite all difficulties of weather, terrain, maintenance of vehicles and lengthening lines of communication, the whole of Cyrenaica was in British hands, as well as 125,000 prisoners and over 1,000 guns.

Wavell had played brilliantly a hand that held no court card other than the quality of his subordinate commanders and the excellence of his troops. He was insistent in his signals home that most of the credit should go to O'Connor. His victory owed nothing to luck; it was due to careful planning, penetrating imagination, the keeping of secrets (no easy matter in Cairo), and refusing to be ruffled by imperious interference from Downing Street. But things were soon to turn against him; and when they did his ration of luck was quickly exhausted: only a few grains of it remained, to help him in Iraq in May and in Syria in June.

On 28 October 1940 Mussolini had presented the Greeks with an ultimatum. It had been contemptuously rejected. The Italians had thereupon invaded the Epirus through Albania, but had been contained, and even thrust back beyond their start line. There were obvious indications that the Germans planned to come to the help of their allies. On 9 January 1941 Wavell was told that support for Greece must now take precedence of all operations in the Middle East. He had already been obliged in the previous November to send a brigade of infantry and two anti-aircraft regiments for the defence of Crete: now he was required to do much more. At first he protested; but on 12 February he received firm orders that no operations were to be undertaken beyond Benghazi, which was to be held as a flank position with minimum forces. Eden (Secretary for War) and Dill (CIGS) were leaving that day for consultations in Cairo. 'It is hoped that at least four divisions, including one armoured division, and . . . air forces may be offered in the shortest time.'

Wavell steeled himself to obey these instructions. Both he and Churchill, when they were committing their thoughts to paper in after years, defended the decision of those difficult days. It remains the most tantalising of all the military-academic arguments arising from the Second World War. What would have happened if Wavell had been allowed to continue forward into or through Tripolitania? Could he in fact have done it with the resources he then had? What would have happened if we had not intervened in Greece? Would the Germans have pushed on into Turkey, Lebanon, Syria, Iraq? Did the intervention in Greece delay the German attack on Russia by six weeks, and were those weeks, having regard to the onset of winter in Russia, in fact crucial?

This is speculation. The hard facts are as follows. Against the advice of two of his senior staff (on a paper submitted by one of them in an effort to dissuade him, Wavell scribbled the dictum of General Wolfe: 'War is an option of difficulties'), he agreed to go in. In making his decision, in so far as it was his decision, he was misled in two respects. He was advised that the Germans could not effectively reinforce the Italians in North Africa until well into April: this deduction was wrong, and they were making their presence felt well before the end of March. Secondly, at a conference in Athens on 22 February, attended by Eden, Dill, Wavell and Longmore for the British – Cunningham sent a representative – and the King, Prime Minister and Papagos the Commander-in-Chief for the Greeks, it was agreed that the line to be held against the Germans would be that along the Aliakmon river. This was reasonably short, inherently strong, and should take the Germans three weeks to reach, allowing just enough time for the British to complete deployment along it. The Greeks agreed to withdraw their troops from the north and from Macedonia to man that shortened line; it was agreed also that General Maitland Wilson should have the overall command.

The strong pressure originally brought on Wavell had suddenly diminished. As Wavell's biographer, John Connell, put it: 'Churchill had had second thoughts. Hesitation and equivocation replaced fierce resolution, and the responsibility for final decision was shifted subtly from London to Cairo.' Eden, Dill, and the three Commanders-in-Chief all shared in it; the die was cast, and the troops sailed. And then, both on his northern and western fronts, the heavens fell in on Wavell.

Although the first contact with the Germans was made in the desert, the whole complicated story will be easier to follow if we pursue the Greek tragedy to its close. Wilson quickly found that the Greeks had failed in their undertaking to withdraw to the Aliakmon Line, a failure that did more credit to their martial spirit than to their military judgement. Elated by the sudden defiance and armed resistance of the Yugoslavs to the German demand for rights of passage through their country, failing to realise how ineffective such resistance would be, reluctant to yield Greek territory without disputing it, the Greeks took fresh and unjustified heart and essayed to hold far more than had been agreed with the British.

On 6 April the Germans under von Brauchitsch attacked both Yugoslavia and Greece with twenty divisions, some of them 'mountain' and six of them armoured. The Yugoslavs were swiftly overrun; the Greeks were caught off balance, too late to scramble back in time to man the formidable position that it had been hoped – probably vainly – that the Aliakmon Line might prove to be. That line was therefore manned by only two Greek divisions and Freyberg's New Zealand Division, which had never before been in action, but in fact fought like veterans; 1st British Armoured Brigade was 20 miles in front as a screen; 6th Australian Division was moving up. On the same day as von Brauchitsch attacked, a British ship discharging high explosives in the Piraeus, the only port capable of supplying Wilson's force, was bombed from the air and blew up. Eleven other ships went down with her, and the Piraeus as a harbour was put out of action for what little remained of the campaign.

There was virtually no air support, the Germans came on fast, vital flanks were turned, and Wilson had no option but to fall back in as good order as he could manage; fifty thousand troops were evacuated from tiny ports and obscure beaches, chiefly from the Peloponnese, in men-of-war, coasters and caiques, but thousands had to be left behind; every gun, tank, armoured car and vehicle abandoned; and quantities of stores and ammunition, of which the Middle East was so short, destroyed. The final organised evacuation was on 30 April. Half of those embarked were ferried only as far as Crete, a mere quarter of the way to Egypt, and their escape was no more than a temporary reprieve.

Crete remained within all too easy reach of the captured airfields of Greece and beyond the effective reach of those in Egypt. Of the thirty thousand British, Australian and New Zealand troops many were little better than refugees from the mainland, and they were short of everything. On 20 May, after six days of heavy bombing of the three airfields, the Germans under Student launched a heavy airborne attack, using both gliders and parachutes; their losses were devastating, but on the 21st they concentrated on reinforcing the precarious foothold they had won at Maleme. Within three days they were landing troop-carrying aircraft there at the rate of twenty every hour, and the defenders despite repeated attacks could not dislodge them. By the end of the month all was over. Superhuman efforts by the Royal Navy on two consecutive and costly nights brought off about half the garrison.

In order to make the Greek intervention possible, and on the faulty assumption that it would be a month or six weeks before the Germans could launch an attack, the defence of the Western Desert had been left to a skeleton force: an under-equipped and unblooded Australian division, and the so-called 2nd Armoured Division, which consisted in fact of a weak support group and one brigade of worn-out tanks, of which not more than half were 'runners' at any given time. When among all his other preoccupations Wavell at last got a chance to revisit the desert, he was alarmed both by the dispositions that General Neame had made and by the state of the tanks. He could and did remedy the former; there was nothing he could do about the latter.

On the last day of March Rommel nosed cautiously forward towards Agedabia. Things went right for him and wrong for the British armour; five tanks were knocked out, two broke down, and only twelve were left in action. Rommel suddenly became aware that he had an opportunity. Brushing aside the cautious objections of his nominal Italian superior, improvising brilliantly, exploiting every stroke of luck, within four days he had reduced the British situation to one of chaos. 3 April was a disastrous day, culminating in the destruction of the main dump of supplies and petrol when friendly forces falling back on it were mistaken for an enemy armoured column, and the dump blown up by those in charge of it. During the night of 6 April, both Neame and O'Connor, whom Wavell had sent up to help in view of his experience, ran into an enemy patrol and were captured; the commander of the armoured division and most of his force were made prisoner thirty-six hours later.

Wavell himself was fortunate not to be captured on the 8th. Flying back from Tobruk his aircraft had to make a forced landing at dusk, in which it lost one wing and the tail. Wavell decided to wait where they were until dawn. They lit a fire and had begun to brew up tea, when a motor patrol arrived in the dark. It was so likely to be hostile that Wavell destroyed an especially secret document that he had on him. The patrol mercifully proved to be a party of Sudanese troops withdrawing to Sollum. Wavell's party climbed on board, and were able by midnight to communicate the news of their survival to a much worried GHQ.

By 13 April Tobruk had been invested and was held by the 9th Australian Division under Morshead. Rommel had done wonders, but having had no time to put them on a proper footing, his lines of communication were long and tenuous, and his fierce jabs against the Tobruk defences brought him nothing but losses. Bardia had fallen to him on the 12th, but the British had succeeded in stabilising the front just west of Sollum. It is some indication of the burden on Wavell of having simultaneous crises on both Greek and Western Desert fronts that he felt obliged to fly to Athens at 7 am on 12 April, returning to Cairo at noon on the 14th.

There was one shaft of light to pierce the gloom just before Student mounted his assault on Crete: the successful conclusion of the campaign against the Italians in Ethiopia. It was nine months since the withdrawal from Somali-land, which had so much angered Churchill. In Kenya, Alan Cunningham, the admiral's younger brother, had a considerable force of seventy-five thousand men: two native African divisions, and the 1st (a European) South African Division. The problem confronting him was appalling terrain, inclement weather and non-existent roads; but at least he had nothing to fear in the way of being attacked. This was not true of the northern front, where General Platt had had to withdraw from the fringes of the Sudan under pressure from the Duke of Aosta, the chivalrous Italian commander, who seemed at one time to be poised to threaten Khartoum. Time was against Aosta, whom no supplies or reinforcements could reach; but in the early days there was much in his favour, particularly so long as Graziani constituted a threat from the desert. Platt had the 5th Indian Division, the Sudan Defence Force and a single mixed squadron of tanks, twenty-eight thousand men in all; but for much of the time he depended on bluff to stem the Italian advance. He had also two guerrilla movements within the Ethiopian frontiers, under Sandford and Wingate respectively, both created by Wavell. Wavell was always aware of the value to be had from detachments operating behind enemy lines. Throughout the North African campaign the Long Range Desert Group, which he also created, had far-reaching effects deriving from its reconnais-sances as much as from its raids.

Immediately after Sidi Barrani, Wavell switched the 4th Indian Division from the desert front to reinforce Platt, replacing it with a newly arrived Australian division. Thus strengthened, Platt was enabled to mount his offensive from the north, while Cunningham advanced from the south at a speed which, in the circumstances, was remarkably fast, capturing in turn the ports of Kismayu and Mogadishu, and using them to simplify his supply problems. Cunningham then turned inland to capture Jijiga and Harar, while Platt tackled the almost impregnable cliff face of Keren, which took two months of hard fighting to reduce. On 5 May the Emperor entered Addis Ababa triumphantly on horseback, and on the 16th Aosta, who was to die as a prisoner, asked for an armistice: there was nothing else he could do.

There was every sign that the Germans would exploit their success in the Balkans eastward and south-eastward. Both they and the British had wooed the Turks for years, but their advances had been coyly rejected: the Turks made it plain that they were ready to fight anybody who violated their frontiers. The Germans now had in Crete a potential stepping-stone to Cyprus, which was practically undefended; to Syria, where the French were in no mood to resist; and to Iraq, though the trouble there had ostensibly ended on the day that Crete fell. This had been a cruel aggravation to Wavell's anxieties in April and May.

Rashid Ali, a former Prime Minister of Iraq, was in German pay. He had seized power on 3 April, and on the 25th, while still openly professing loyalty to the British-Iraqi Treaty, had signed a secret agreement with the German and Italian ambassadors in Baghdad. Under the treaty the British were entitled to move troops through Iraq, and this right was exercised as a trial both of strength and good faith at the end of April and beginning of May, with the passage through Basra of troops from India. Rashid reacted immediately by surrounding the RAF aerodrome at Habbaniya with troops, and attacking it on 2 May. The RAF riposted, and some young pilots under training there actually made their first solo flights 'bombed up', dropping bombs amateurishly but with zest from their training aircraft. Despite the fact that the troops in Iraq had been despatched from India, regardless of all else that was on his shoulders, the authorities in London insisted on Wavell assuming the responsibility for this new campaign, and required him to send military support across from Palestine to help deal with it.

There enters into his recorded signals at this moment a degree of petulance that was never in them before, and it is hard to blame him. 'Your 88 takes little account of realities. You must face facts.' But he managed to drum up some sort of a column out of his odds and ends in Palestine and Jordan. On 29 May Rashid Ali, thirty of his henchmen, the German and Italian ambassadors, and Haj Amin el Husseini, the former Mufti of Jerusalem, who was to survive in obscurity until 1974, stole across the Persian frontier into oblivion.

Another major worry was the situation in Syria and the Lebanon. Until the fall of France in 1940 relations between Wavell and Weygand, C-in-C there until recalled to relieve Gamelin in the closing stages of the French débâcle, had been close, each having a mission at the other's headquarters. Weygand's successor, Dentz, was scrupulously loyal to Vichy and in step with Vichy's growing subservience to Germany. During the last three weeks of May, 120 Axis aircraft were granted transit facilities through Syria, chiefly in the support of subversion in Iraq and Iran. De Gaulle's own private intelligence – which proved wholly erroneous – insisted that the French troops in Syria would switch their allegiance from Vichy to de Gaulle if Syria were invaded by Free French forces. This was accepted in London though rejected in Cairo. Cairo was the better informed.

Nevertheless Wavell was obliged to obey peremptory orders from London; and on 8 June Syria was invaded from Palestine by three columns. Two were Australian: one advancing up the coast, the other by Merjayoun; the third comprised two Free French brigades and an Indian one, under command of the Free French General Legentilhomme. On all three fronts the Vichy resistance was bitter: the more bitter probably because for a year past the French troops in the Levant had had nothing to do but contrast the continuing British defiance of the Germans with the humiliating compliance of Pétain and Laval. Far from welcoming the Free French as liberators, they fought them fiercely as the traitors they deemed them to be. They had the best of the battle, and it came as a surprise when, their honour maintained to their satisfaction, they requested an armistice on 11 July, four days after Wavell had left the Middle East.

Despite all these distractions, too major to be dismissed as mere sideshows, Wavell had still to cope with the desert front. This was urged on him from London as his major commitment, in the same breath as that in which he was ordered to topple Rashid Ali and support de Gaulle in the invasion of Syria. Such urging was gratuitous: he knew as well as anybody that this was his prime task. But it was with a heavy heart, and without the optimism that had hitherto characterised even the most hopeless of his campaigns, that he engaged in Battleaxe, as his new offensive was called. He simply had not the strength for it; his newly equipped armour was not ready for battle in terms either of training or mechanical fitness; and this attack, in which so much optimism had been invested, petered out. It would be difficult for Wavell's worst detractor to arraign him on any charge of culpability. The inadequate machine entrusted to him had been overburdened, and had ground to a halt. Few other men with such inadequate resources, and with so many political spanners thrown into the works, could have kept it grinding on for so long as he did.

News of his supercession arrived before breakfast in his house in Cairo. His old friend and devoted Chief of Staff, Arthur Smith, brought him a telegram announcing that he was to exchange appointments with Auchinleck, Commander-in-Chief India. All he said was: 'The Prime Minister is quite right: this job wants a new eye and a new hand'; and with that he went on shaving, following this process with his usual pre-breakfast ride and swim. Wavell asked for a short leave home, but this was refused him; and on 7 July, having handed over to Auchinleck, he set off for India, visiting Iraq on the way.

It was thirty-three years since Wavell had last been in India, and he had never been east of it; Burma, Malaysia and beyond were a sealed book to him. The slow wartime tempo of India, with the government and GHQ still migrating to Simla for the hot weather, came as a shock. So did India's military weakness. His first signal was to Tedder in Cairo: 'Have just seen India's most up-to-date fighter squadron armed with Audaxes. Does not this make your heart bleed?' There were no modern tanks or armoured cars, and only thirty anti-aircraft guns in the whole country, whereas he estimated his requirements as being over five hundred. Persia seemed to him vulnerable to German penetration. He sought and obtained permission to occupy it with troops from Iraq, and this was achieved in a matter of days with only a token show of resistance; it gave no further trouble, and rendered secure the direct link with Russia.

On 8 September he arrived in London for ten days of consultations. He pointed out the extreme weakness of India, and urged in vain that Burma should come under India rather than Singapore for defence purposes. (Three of his predecessors as C-in-C India, including Auchinleck, had made the same request.) In October he met at Tiflis the Russian commander in the Caucasus, and at the end of the month set off on a quick survey of Burma, Malaya and Singapore. He found Singapore 'very far from being keyed up to war pitch'; and 'as regards Burma, I was horrified by the complete lack of organisation, of military intelligence, and of planning generally to meet any Japanese attack'. On his return to Delhi he renewed both his appeal for tanks and anti-aircraft guns, and for Burma to be put under his command; he was given a halfhearted promise of tanks, with the warning that Russia must have priority, but his question about Burma was not even acknowledged.

Responsibility for Burma was at last belatedly given him in a signal from Churchill dated 12 December – a signal that began with the infuriating phrase: 'You must now look east.' Considering that the Japanese had invaded Malaya four days before and sunk the two great battleships two days before, he was unlikely to be looking elsewhere. He flew to Rangoon as soon as he could to assess what could be done with his scanty resources. The so-called 1st Burma Division was spread all over the country from Mandalay to the southernmost tip of Tenasserim. It comprised ten battalions of Burma Rifles, not all of them regular and all recently expanded with raw recruits; two British, one Gurkha and four Indian battalions, to whom the same remarks applied. Although nominally organised in brigades, they had never trained as such, and the 'division' was short of artillery (one locally manned field battery and four Indian mountain batteries), engineers, signals, transport and medical units. The only RAF unit was a single fighter squadron with sixteen obsolete Buffalo aircraft. There was also a squadron of the American

Volunteer Group, armed with Tomahawks. For a few days he had been able to rejoice in the knowledge that 17th Indian Division, hitherto earmarked for Iraq, and 18th British Division, then rounding the Cape, would be allotted to him; but by the time he got to Rangoon on 21 December, one brigade had been diverted from each to reinforce Singapore, and he was warned that the rest of 18th Division might go there too. (In the event it did, by his own decision after he became Supreme Commander.)

Having despatched to London a forceful appreciation urging the importance of Burma to both India and China, and setting forth his most urgent needs, he flew to Chungking to confer with Chiang Kai-shek. His return to Rangoon airport on Christmas Day coincided with an air raid by eighty aircraft; he counted seventeen bombs within 50 yards of his slit trench, one a mere dozen yards away.

On 30 December he heard from Churchill in Washington that it had been decided to form a supreme command embracing all land, sea and air forces in the South-West Pacific, to be called ABDACOM (American-British-Dutch-Australian Command), and that at the pressing suggestion of the Americans he was to be its commander. He cabled ruefully to Dill: 'I have heard of being handed the baby, but this is quadruplets.' He was to be answerable to 'an appropriate joint body', which would in turn be responsible jointly to Roosevelt and Churchill. Neat, tidy, even logical though this arrangement might seem, the difficulties of setting up such a Colossus, complete with command and staff structures and communications system, would have been bad enough in times of peace; in the middle of a war that had caught everybody unprepared, and in which every front was crumbling so fast that each day brought news of fresh disaster, to have set it up at all was a triumph. His sphere excluded India, which was to be independent, but included Burma, Malaya, Singapore, the Dutch East Indies and the Philippines; his headquarters were initially to be at Surabaya; his second-in-command was to be the American Air Force General Brett, who had been with him on his visit to Chiang Kai-shek, and his Chief of Staff the British General Pownall, an old friend and a proven staff officer, who had taken over command in Singapore only a few days before: he was to hand over to Percival, who was already on the spot. Hutton, who had been Chief of Staff in India, had just taken over in Burma.

The life of ABDACOM was 'nasty, brutish and short'. It lasted only for six nightmare weeks. Headquarters were set up, not at Surabaya, but at Lembang, just outside Batavia (now Jakarta), which was only half the distance from Singapore that Surabaya was. On the way there Wavell visited Singapore, and flew north to visit, at considerable personal risk, the headquarters of two front-line brigades 35 miles north of Kuala Lumpur. He was appalled by what he found, not least by the total ignorance of the higher commanders concerning what was happening in front of them. The troops were bewildered, exhausted and dispirited; the two 'brigades' he saw were down to about four hundred men apiece, and twenty-three guns had been lost the previous day. It was already evident that the best that could be hoped for, other than withstanding siege in Singapore itself, was for a stand to be made in Johore, the last chunk of mainland before the island; but even this was not to be. What remained of the defenders of Malaya proper was slithering down the peninsula, defeated, unco-ordinated, and, with the notable exception of one or two units, totally demoralised.

Singapore was just as depressing. As everybody knows, its defences had always been designed solely against attack from the sea. It had been considered that jungle was almost, and mangrove wholly, impenetrable; but the Japanese had proved themselves masters of both. Nothing had been done, even during the last few weeks, to put the island into a posture of defence; and every suggestion made to the military command that at least trenches should be dug drew the reply that such action would be bad for morale.

The whole story of the loss of Singapore is unutterably painful. It is also familiar and need not be told again. Wavell did his best to inspire in person by his presence the closing days of the defence. He was there four days before it fell, when he tumbled over a jetty in the dark while waiting to embark in a flying boat and broke several bones. Both verbally and in subsequent signals he urged Percival to fight on. On 14 February he telegraphed: 'Your gallant stand is serving purpose and must be continued to limit of endurance.' On the 15th: 'When you are fully satisfied that this is no longer possible I give you discretion to cease resistance.' At 3 pm that day he received Percival's final signal: 'Owing to losses from enemy action water petrol food and ammunition practically finished. Unable therefore continue the fight any longer. All ranks have done their best and grateful for your help.'

It was all over. Nobody could have done more than Wavell to avert the catastrophe, which was probably inevitable anyway. On one point alone has his judgement been seriously questioned. Was he justified in landing, so late as 29 January, the British 18th Division, the last of whose units actually landed on 4 February? With hindsight it is obvious that far more value would have been got from it had it been diverted to Burma. The reason is plain. The most Wavell could hope to do was to win time: time enough especially to build up sufficient air forces particularly in the Dutch East Indies, from America by way of Australia, to dominate the seas and to put an end to the enemy's freedom to move about in them and to effect landings wherever he would. Once Singapore was lost the enemy's fleet would be able to range and dominate the Bay of Bengal. So long as there was a chance of holding the island every effort must be made. The final disaster was due to the disintegration of the garrison and the enemy's capture of the reservoirs, on which the vast population depended for water. Nobody had foreseen the ease with which the Japanese scrambled on to the island. Wavell calculated afterwards that he had lost the race by a month.

The Japanese were ashore on Sumatra before they took Singapore, and within the next few days on Bali, Timor and Java as well. On 21 February Wavell received orders to move his headquarters out of Java to anywhere he liked; he replied with a recommendation, which was at once accepted, that ABDACOM be dissolved. He reached Delhi by way of Colombo on 27 February and at once resumed the reins of Burma. On 1 March he was in Rangoon, which the Governor had already left, and drove out with Hutton to visit HQ 17th Division at Pegu. This formation, which had arrived in Burma early in January, was entirely without training; its units had been made up to strength at the last moment: indeed one battalion received three hundred recruits only three hours before it set off for the front. In normal circumstances the division would not have been regarded as fit to fight for another six months; but these were not normal circumstances.

It has been said that Wavell expected too much of the under-trained troops that were all he had in Burma. It is certain that the reluctance to fight and die that he had witnessed in Malaya had made a heavy impact on him; and he thought he detected a lack of fire in the leadership at all levels, and a lack of resolution at many. Already in the dying days of ABDACOM he had welcomed the offer of General Alexander's services to command in Burma, and Alexander was on the way. Meanwhile he replaced certain commanders, and ordered that Rangoon should be held as long as was possible without the force being cut off and destroyed. The 7th Armoured Brigade, who were to cover themselves with glory during the coming weeks, and a regiment of field artillery, were already disembarking there.

At noon on 4 March Wavell met and conferred with Alexander at Calcutta, and impressed on him the importance of holding Rangoon for as long as he could without risking the loss of his army; but as early as the 6th Alexander decided that to hold it any longer would indeed result in his whole force being cut off. He got out, in fact, in the very nick of time. If the Japanese had continued to hold a roadblock that they had established across his route, things would have been serious indeed; but they withdrew it so that the troops manning it could join in the attack on Rangoon: they had no notion that they were about to find Rangoon an abandoned and undefended city.

It is a measure of Wavell's robust optimism that even while Alexander's success in extricating his army was still in doubt, he directed his Joint Planning Staff in Delhi to address themselves to the problem of the recapture of Burma. This was his constant preoccupation throughout the next year. Fighting in Arakan, where the grain of the country favoured the Japanese, was constant; fighting on the eastern front, where the Chindwin river divided the rival armies, was spasmodic and limited to aggressive patrolling by both sides. Burma could not be recaptured from Arakan: the thrust must be made across the Chindwin in concert with the American General Stilwell's Chinese advancing from the north, and neither of these operations could be undertaken until roads were built through the mountainous, jungle-covered country behind them.

There was at last breathing-space to build up and train new formations. The Japanese had given ample demonstration of their tactical methods: counter-tactics were devised and imparted; morale was improving. Wavell's heart was set on mounting an offensive from Imphal in January 1943; he took much persuading before being reluctantly convinced that this was not feasible. Mindful of Wingate's achievements in Ethiopia, he had sent for him from Britain and caused him to raise a brigade for long-range penetration. The idea was for Wingate's force to insert itself well behind the Japanese lines and to play hell with their communications at the moment when the offensive against them was beginning to bite. Wingate's brigade, organised in seven columns, was already concentrating secretly at Imphal when the decision was forced on Wavell to postpone the offensive until after the next monsoon.

On the face of it there was a strong case for Wingate's operation to be postponed too; but Wingate and his men were keyed up and eager to go, and Wavell was not averse from letting them off the leash. They suffered great hardships, mostly from hunger, and lost about a third of their number; the air supply on which they chiefly depended failed them in that most of the wireless sets on which they depended were lost in action. Nobody decried their achievement in getting so far – Wingate himself and several columns crossed the Irrawaddy and back again; but there was a good deal of speculation as to whether the achievement was worth the casualties. Apart from a certain boost to morale and some minor demolitions, which were quickly made good, there were no startling immediate results; but there were two long-term ones. First they had demonstrated the potential of properly organised air supply, which was to prove the winning card in that theatre. Secondly it became clear after the war that this incursion across what they had thought impassable country was what had encouraged the Japanese to do the same thing in a full-scale offensive; and this was the genesis of the disaster that they brought upon themselves in March and April of 1944.

Slowly and painfully Wavell's resources were building up. Alexander had gone back to make history in the Middle East and Italy; but a new generation of subordinates was coming into being: men of stamina who combined experience with fresh ideas, of whom Slim was the outstanding example. On the Imphal front nothing could be done, apart from making preparations, until after the monsoon that was about to set in. In Arakan he had continued ill luck. Had he had shipping he could have seized Akyab from the sea. At one time a plan for such an attack was well advanced, and troops from 2nd British Division in training for it; but the promised landing craft were reft away for operations in the Mediterranean. He continued with the only alternative, constant probing down the coast; but every time the Japanese, exploiting the manner in which the grain of the country favoured them, had little difficulty in cutting the communications. There were not yet enough aircraft in the theatre to substitute supply by air.

In April he was summoned to consultations in London. In May he accompanied Churchill and the Chiefs of Staff to the Trident Conference in Washington in the *Queen Mary*. During the voyage he saw a document, emanating from the Prime Minister and with a wide circulation, in which the phrases 'complete failure' and 'deep disgrace' were applied to the operations in Arakan. To use his own word, he 'tackled' Churchill about it and the offending paragraph was amended. In June he was called to Downing Street and told of his supercession by Mountbatten. He was offered the appointment of Viceroy of India and accepted it, taking over from Linlithgow in October.

Wavell's most pressing and immediate task as Viceroy was to deal with the famine in Bengal. Within a week of being sworn in he went to Calcutta for three days, seeing the destitutes in the streets by night and dealing with officials by day. He took immediate steps to combat the famine on military lines instead of through an exhausted civil administration that had failed to cope. Order gradually grew out of chaos, but more than a million people are thought to have died.

His political problems were of greater long-term importance; and here he found Churchill no easier to serve as Viceroy than as Commander-in-Chief. His journal, published in 1973, thirty years after his assumption of the office, reveals the earnestness and honesty with which he strove to achieve an honourable solution to mutual antagonism between Hindu and Muslim: an approach that was not so discernible on the part of his successive political masters. It is evident that Churchill intended him merely to concentrate on keeping India quiet for the duration of the war. Wavell saw it as his duty to plan for a lasting, peaceful and prosperous future for the four hundred million people entrusted to him. When Attlee's government replaced Churchill's, Wavell fared no better. The three Cabinet ministers, including Cripps, whom Attlee sent to India in March 1946 to negotiate with the leaders of Congress and the Muslim League, arrived already with a strong bias in favour of the former. One ugly and fully established story is of the stenographer in the office of the Viceroy's private secretary, who passed copies of letters and top secret documents to Nehru, the Congress leader. Nehru showed them to Cripps, who did not scruple to discuss them with him. This was known to ministers in Britain, but not revealed to Wavell, to whose knowledge it came from another source.

Still he pressed on, with limitless patience, striving despite every rebuff from every quarter, including Whitehall, to reconcile the irreconcilable, until on 4 February 1947 he received by hand a note from Attlee to say that he was being replaced. The note did not reveal the identity of his successor; but when Mountbatten was in process of taking over towards the end of March, he told Wavell that he had been offered, and had accepted, the appointment more than three months before, when Wavell had actually been engaged in talks with Attlee in London.

This departure from the strictly military side of Wavell's career is justified by the light that it throws upon his character. He left India with the warm esteem of many with whom he had sometimes had vituperative dealings; Rajagopalachari signed his farewell letter 'Yours affectionately', and Nehru said to him: 'Some failures are greater than successes.'

The last three years of his life were not as happy as they deserved to be. He hated living in London, and after so many years lived at a high pitch he felt at a loose end. He rejoiced in the colonelcy of his old Regiment, with which he spent a week every year; in his golf; in renewing old contacts and picking up new ones in the world of letters; and above all in his family. He was too great a man to repine; although in his final despatch after being relieved of his command in India he had written the following, after paying tribute to the support he had enjoyed from home during four years of war:

> I regret to have one exception to make. During the operations recorded in this despatch [the Arakan and Chindit operations] I received neither encouragement nor help nor understanding of the difficulties, only criticism for the failure of a bold attempt to engage the enemy with inadequate resources, in hazardous circumstances.

In physical stature Wavell was broad and stocky, with a strong chin and a deep furrow running vertically each side of his mouth. Bodily he was as tough as nails, but a bad investment for any insurance company: he was for ever breaking bones in a fall from a horse, and was a positive Jonah when travelling by air. He loved golf, and horses, and swimming. He had no airs or graces. He enjoyed congenial company, and found it hard to conceal his boredom in any other. His long silences were proverbial, and yet he could scintillate. His abiding love was for literature; his anthology of poetry, *Other Men's Flowers*, compiled from the depths of his memory during his arduous time in India, reached, to his own modest astonishment, thousands of people to whom poetry had had no previous appeal.

His subordinates and staff officers adored him, and he 'got through' to the troops serving under him, no matter what language they spoke, to a degree that was the more astonishing because he was so tongue-tied. Except in Malaya, where he arrived on the scene too late to make a proper impact, the troops continued to have confidence in him even in moments of grave adversity. None of those who were made prisoner in Greece, or Crete, or the various reverses in the Western Desert, ever uttered a word of criticism against him. Never throughout his years in command did he have adequate resources for what he was called upon to do. His situation from March to June 1941, with simultaneous crises on his western, northern and eastern fronts and with no reserves in hand, was perhaps the most complicated that has ever faced a higher commander. ABDACOM was hopeless from the outset, and perhaps not even worth setting up.

It is difficult to account for the antipathy between him and Churchill (who incidentally did not trouble to attend his funeral). Those closest to Churchill –

Dill, Brooke and the superb Ismay – never wavered in their sympathy or admiration for Wavell. Perhaps I may quote, in summing up, a sentence I wrote about him elsewhere: 'No blow, fair or foul, military or political, ever got past the shield of his integrity.'

In April 1950 he postponed a projected visit to his Regiment in Berlin to undergo an operation for gallstones. The malady proved to be cancer, and he died in hospital on 24 May. At the funeral service in Westminster Abbey Arthur Smith accompanied the coffin, and the pall-bearers included Mountbatten, Brooke, Montgomery, Wilson and the brothers Cunningham. Then a detachment of The Black Watch took him to Winchester and buried him there in the grounds of his old school.

FIELD-MARSHAL ERICH VON MANSTEIN

Albert Seaton

Erich von Manstein was born on 24 November 1887, the tenth child of Eduard von Lewinski, a general of artillery, and his second wife Helene, *née* von Sperling. Shortly after his birth he was given to his adoptive parents, Georg von Manstein, a general of infantry, and Hedwig, *née* von Sperling, who was the infant's aunt. The Lewinskis, Mansteins and Sperlings were distinguished military families of the Prussian nobility well connected by birth and by marriage, the youngest of the von Sperling daughters being the wife of Field-Marshal von Hindenburg, later the *Reichspräsident*. The von Mansteins lived in style for although they had no landed property, a *Dotation*, voted by the Reichstag to the Mansteins and the Sperlings for their services in the Franco-Prussian War made them independent of their army salaries.

The young von Manstein went to school for five years at the *lycée* in Strasbourg, where his father was stationed, before being sent in 1900 to the *Kadetenkorps*, firstly in Plön and then in Gross-Lichterfelde in Berlin. There, as a member of the nobility, he was enrolled in the Corps of Pages, performing *Leibpagen* and *Hofpagen Dienst* at the Kaiser's Berlin court. In 1906 he entered the 3rd Regiment of Foot Guards as an ensign, a regiment that included among its officers some who were to rise to prominence, among them von Hindenburg, von Schleicher and von Hammerstein-Equord. In 1913 he was at the War Academy.

On mobilisation in 1914 von Manstein became the regimental adjutant of the 2nd Guard Reserve Regiment, forming part of the Guard Reserve Corps, which first saw action at Namur against the French. After being transferred to Masuria to help stem the invasion of East Prussia, it was committed against the Russians in northern Poland. In November 1914 von Manstein was severely wounded. When he returned to duty in 1915 it was as an assistant in the General Staff branch in von Gallwitz's headquarters, firstly in northern Poland and Serbia and then, in 1916, in France for the great Verdun offensive. At the beginning of the Somme battle von Manstein filled a General Staff appointment, although he was not of the General Staff, in von Below's newly formed First Army, where von Lossberg was the Chief of Staff. In 1917 he was transferred from France to Courland as the senior General Staff officer operations with the 4th Cavalry Division, which was campaigning against the Bolsheviks. In May 1918 he was back on the western front in the same type of appointment, but this time with an infantry division, taking part in the May and July offensives and then in the defensive battle in the area of Rheims and Sedan. His experiences during this time, and in particular the heavy casualties suffered by infantry attacking through artillery and machine-gun fire, impressed on him the need for a new concept for the tactical assault.

Defeat and revolution brought about the end of the old imperial army, but von Manstein suffered no break in his military service. At first he was employed in raising a volunteer regiment in Magdeburg before rejoining von Lossberg, who was Chief of Staff of the frontier defence *Oberkommando Süd* in Breslau. In the summer of 1919 von Lossberg was appointed as the chairman of the commission to draw up the plans for the 100,000 army, and von Manstein followed him to Berlin as a staff aide. The Great General Staff had been dissolved by the provision of Versailles, but the German General Staff lived on under the guise of a *Führerstab*. Von Manstein had not completed the War Academy course and his only qualification for admission to the general staff was his long experience of staff duties. First however it was obligatory that he should have completed two years' regimental duty commanding an infantry company, and he did this with the 5th Infantry Regiment at Angermünde. At the end of 1923 he returned to the staff at *Wehrkreiskommando II* in Stettin.

The revolution and inflation had ended the privileged life von Manstein had enjoyed before the war. Unable to get married quarters in Stettin and since the military authorities refused to pay him a travelling allowance, he was obliged to travel daily from Angermünde on a fourth-class monthly railway season ticket, with black-marketeers and carpet-baggers for company. Eventually he made a formal complaint, thus incurring the displeasure of von Seeckt, who struck his name from the list of staff brevets. In this way von Manstein lost two years' seniority, which was not restored to him until thirteen years later when he was already *Oberquartiermeister I*.

Then followed an unbroken sequence of district operational staff appointments in Dresden and Magdeburg until 1929, when von Manstein entered the Ministry of Defence operations department of the General Staff (*Truppenamt TI*). He already spoke good French and had since learned Spanish, and he took advantage of the small monetary grants designed to encourage German officers to travel abroad. In 1931 and again in 1932 he visited the Soviet Union on an official liaison visit, as part of Adam's staff, meeting the leading Red Army commanders and attending manoeuvres in the Ukraine and the Caucasus. Then he returned once more to regimental duty in command of the *Jäger* battalion of the 4th Infantry Regiment at Kolberg, the only time in his service, except in the Guard, when he was allowed to choose his posting. He did not however complete the normal two-year period for in February 1934 he was appointed Chief of Staff to von Witzleben at *Wehrkreiskommando*

III in Berlin. In July 1935 he became the head of the operations department (*Op Abt I*) of the General Staff of the army, roughly the equivalent of the Director of Military Operations, and then, in October 1936, *Oberquartiermeister I*, controlling in addition the other General Staff operational departments (organisation, fortresses, cartography and technical). As *O Qu I* von Manstein acted as the deputy to the two successive Chiefs of General Staff, von Fritsch and Beck.

Von Manstein held this illustrious post until February 1938, an important period during the life of the Third Reich. Hitler had denounced the Versailles Treaty, and by reintroducing conscripted military service had begun to enlarge the armed forces. The German army then reoccupied the Rhineland. Many of these plans were put into execution by von Manstein. Hitler himself, as von Manstein has described, had particular interest in weapon development, except for rocketry which he held to be of little account, and he gave great impetus to the improvement and production of the tank arm and anti-tank weapons. The groundwork for rearmament had however already been prepared by the General Staff; the exception was the concept of assault artillery, the *Sturmgeschütz*, and for this von Manstein alone was responsible.

Von Manstein accorded to Guderian the credit for founding and developing the panzer arm, but he denied Guderian's charge that the General Staff merely hindered it. Guderian advocated the use of tanks in mass as a main arm, supported by motorised grenadiers and artillery moving at tank speed, capable of operative, even strategic, tasks. The General Staff, on the other hand, mindful of the bloody battles on the western front, were determined that the infantry divisions that made up the bulk of the German army, should have their mobility restored by close armoured support, possibly in the form of tank brigades, to overcome enemy field-works and artillery and machine-gun defensive fire. Von Manstein's solution was to form a new arm of assault artillery, equipped with turretless and open-topped armoured tracked vehicles, each mounting a limited traverse 75mm gun, capable of engaging targets with direct fire using high-explosive shell or solid shot. These fighting vehicles were to move on to the objectives together with the assaulting infantry, quickly engaging pinpoint targets, infantry, gun crews or tanks; they could thus provide immediate covering and defensive fire and anti-tank protection, and, if need be, increase the density of the field artillery's indirect fire in depth.

Von Manstein's first paper on this subject, in the autumn of 1935, had a hostile reception, for the Commander-in-Chief, the Chief of General Staff, the Chiefs of the *Heeresamt* and the *Heereswaffenamt* were all artillerymen. Moreover the panzer arm and anti-tank artillery saw the *Sturmgeschütz* as a competitor for materials and funds; the infantry were generally in favour of the new arm, but they themselves wanted to man it. Eventually von Fritsch was won over, because, as a former horse artilleryman, he tended to regard these self-propelled guns as mechanised horse artillery, which of course they were not. In this way the new *Sturmgeschütz* became a branch of the German artillery. So successful was the *Sturmartillerie* that by early 1944 it claimed to have destroyed twenty thousand enemy tanks. These armoured fighting vehicles were eventually taken into use as well by the panzer arm and, after 1943, were copied and introduced into the Red Army in large numbers.

Among the war plans drawn up when von Manstein was *O Qu I* were *Aufmarsch-Rot*, the plan to repel a French invasion, and *Aufmarsch-Grün*, the defence against a joint invasion by France and Czechoslovakia. The concept of *Grün* was used by Hitler in 1938.

Von Manstein first saw Hitler at close quarters on 7 March 1938, after he had lost his *O Qu I* appointment in consequence of the removal of von Fritsch. At Beck's request however he had remained temporarily with the *Oberkommando des Heeres* (OKH). On that morning Beck and von Manstein were called to Hitler who told them of his intention to intervene in Austria. Von Manstein said that he found Hitler's talk logical and convincing and his prognosis essentially correct. The two generals then set to work preparing *Fall Osterreich*, a contingency not previously provided for by the OKH. After the occupation of Austria, von Manstein handed over his duties to Halder, and in April 1938 left for Liegnitz to take over the command of the 18th Infantry Division. He subsequently said that he knew nothing of Halder's plan that autumn to arrest Hitler and put him on trial, although he was informed of the conflict between Hitler and Beck over the question of Czechoslovakia and of the reasons that led to Beck's resignation.

Von Manstein was recalled to the staff for a short period during the occupation of the Sudetenland, when he was von Leeb's Army Chief of Staff, and then again during the August 1939 mobilisation when he was appointed Chief of Staff to von Rundstedt's Army Group South, preparatory to the war against Poland. Von Manstein's talents suited von Rundstedt to perfection, for whereas von Manstein had an inquiring mind and interested himself in detail, von Rundstedt would concern himself with nothing but essentials, reading detective novels so that he might keep his head clear for the great design. In October, after the Polish campaign, von Rundstedt's headquarters was moved to Koblenz on the western front, where it became known as Army Group A.

Hitler had intended to attack France in the winter of 1939, but the start of the offensive was repeatedly postponed. The strategic plan for the opening of the campaign, approved in detail and partly initiated by Hitler, envisaged the heavier blow being made by von Bock's Army Group B in the north into the southern Netherlands and Belgium, while von Rundstedt's Army Group A, on von Bock's left, advanced due westwards towards the Meuse between Namur and Sedan. Von Manstein disagreed with the OKH orders, not because von Rundstedt's role was subordinate to von Bock's, but primarily because the orders, so he believed, conjured up the ghost of von Schlieffen. For von Manstein was attracted towards any grand strategic design which had its origin in boldness and in the unexpected. He and von Rundstedt pressed that Army Group A should be given the decisive role, together with the necessary armour to envelop the Anglo-French and Belgian forces from the South, even though this should mean moving panzer and motorised formations through the heavily wooded Ardennes. Von Manstein was not however an armoured leader by training or experience, and he said that it was a relief to him when Guderian studied his proposals and judged them to be feasible.

Von Manstein's plan for the opening of the campaign was eventually adopted because Hitler, too, favoured the novel and the unexpected. He interviewed von Manstein on 17 February, the occasion of his promotion to command XXXVIII Corps, and heard his plan. Von Manstein was much impressed by Hitler's quick grasp of the essentials and was amazed at his knowledge of technical innovations. Three days later von Manstein's concept had been adopted in the new OKH orders issued on 20 February. Von Manstein believed that his promotion and removal from Army Group A was connected with the unpopularity of his views with von Brauchitsch, the Commander-in-Chief of the German army. Von Manstein's part in the campaign was little different from that of any other infantry corps commander.

Von Manstein thought himself fortunate when he was given the command of LVI Panzer Corps in February 1941. He knew little about the staff planning for the Russo-German War, for he did not receive his own orders until May. But it is perhaps indicative of von Manstein's cast of mind that he criticised the Chief of General Staff Halder's painstaking method of building up the OKH central plan, based on the views and war games of the subordinate army groups, rather than imposing on the army groups a grand design. The criticism of Halder is ill-informed and in some respects unjust, but it illustrates both the strength and weakness of von Manstein's outlook, characteristics that he shared with Hitler.

Von Manstein's corps, part of Hoepner's 4th Panzer Group, itself directly under the command of von Leeb's Army Group North, had only a panzer, a motorised and an infantry division. It made rapid progress however towards Leningrad, on 26 June seizing the Dvina bridge intact by sending forward captured Red Army lorries loaded with German and Lithuanian troops disguised as wounded Red Army men. This elated Hitler, who began to take a hand in the tactics of the battle. The advance soon ran into difficulties, however, due to the stiffening enemy resistance, the widening fronts and the wooded and marshy terrain. Von Manstein was overshadowed by the vigorous Hoepner and the many disagreements between Hoepner, von Leeb, Halder, von Brauchitsch and Hitler. Von Leeb ordered a bad compromise between his own view and the plan advocated by Hoepner, and he sent Hoepner's two panzer corps on divergent axes, one in the direction of Leningrad and the other, von Manstein's towards Lake Ilmen. Both corps were eventually to become bogged down in the forested swamps, and at one time von Manstein was cut off by the infiltrating enemy. On 26 July when Paulus, the *O Qu I*, visited LVI Panzer Corps, a disgruntled von Manstein told him that all armour should be withdrawn from Army Group North, for any rapid advance was out of the question. The same view had been expressed by Hoepner and Reinhardt, the other panzer corps commander.

In the middle of September von Manstein was ordered to Nikolaev on the Black Sea coast to take over Eleventh Army, the former commander of which von Schobert, had been killed. For some time after his arrival von Manstein was severely scrutinised by his subordinates and compared, to his disadvantage with his predecessor. Von Manstein could be charming, but some of his immediate staff disliked him, at least on first encounter, on account of his arrogance and his sharp tongue. Although, as an army commander, he professed to hate paperwork since this kept him away from his divisions, at this period in his career he kept a close control over his headquarters. His routine was like that of many other commanders, reading or hearing the evening and morning reports, and visiting and inspecting during the day; at times he toured forward areas and talked with the other ranks, although it is difficult to say how much he really understood or identified himself with them. But there seems little doubt that, as his success and fame grew, so did his visits act as a tonic to the overtired troops.

Von Manstein's operations in the Crimea during 1941 and 1942 were probably the zenith of his career. His first task was to push the enemy South Front on the Black Sea littoral farther to the east, so isolating the Crimean peninsula, and rescue his subordinate Rumanian Third Army which was in danger of disintegrating under Russian attack. In this he was aided by von Kleist's 1st Panzer Group which enveloped the enemy from the north, so that in the first week of October von Manstein and von Kleist jointly took over a hundred thousand prisoners at Osipenko. Von Manstein then turned back westwards to mount an offensive across the 7-mile wide Perekop isthmus into the Crimea. The Red Air Force dominated the air space and, as Eleventh Army had no tanks, it relied on the armoured assault guns to support its infantry. The fighting was of the bitterest and von Manstein drove his subordinates on to renew their attacks when the divisions were already at the end of their tether. After a ten-day battle, success came suddenly on 28 October with another hundred thousand prisoners and seven hundred guns captured. But when Eleventh Army overran the Crimea it was to become bogged down on a two-sided front, before Sevastopol in the west and the Kerch peninsula in the east. Since the Soviet forces had command of the sea and the air, it appeared that the Red Army might hold out indefinitely.

Von Manstein determined to reduce Sevastopol first. Leaving von Sponeck's XLII Corps with only one German division against the Kerch peninsula, he concentrated the remainder of his force to attack the naval base on 17 December. Again the fighting was desperate and the German casualties were heavy. Von Manstein's daring was challenged and the immediate fate of Sevastopol was decided by the intervention of the Soviet Transcaucasus

Front in the faraway Kuban, which began to land troops in Kerch and behind von Sponeck's defensive line. Von Sponeck asked permission to withdraw westwards behind the Ak Monai narrows where the line could be shortened. Von Manstein refused. The straits of Kerch began to freeze over and when the enemy disembarked more troops at Theodosia in the rear of XLII Corps von Sponeck withdrew against orders and abandoned his guns and heavy mortars. Von Manstein's assistance to XLII Corps had been limited to the despatch of a German infantry regimental group and some Rumanian troops, on whose offensive capabilities he himself did not set great store. The attack on Sevastopol was abandoned, although its defences were by then crumbling fast, and XXX Corps with two German infantry divisions was sent to support XLII Corps and restore the position in front of Kersch. Von Sponeck was removed from his appointment and returned to Germany where he was court-martialled and sentenced to death. Although this sentence was later commuted to one of imprisonment, he was shot by the SS in 1944.

On 15 January 1942 von Manstein's three and a half German divisions recaptured Theodosia, taking 10,000 prisoners and 170 guns. The Red Army troops in Kerch replied by mounting a series of unsuccessful counter-offensives from February until April. On 20 March Eleventh Army itself went over to the offensive using a newly arrived panzer division; the operation was a failure, for the Axis forces at Kerch were far outnumbered by the opposing Crimean Front.

In mid-April von Manstein visited Hitler to discuss his plans for the coming offensive; for he had reversed his priorities and decided to destroy the Kerch bridgehead, which could be reinforced easily by the enemy, before crushing Sevastopol. His plans were accepted without demur, and the Führer told him that after Sevastopol had been taken Eleventh Army was to cross the Kerch straits into the Kuban to intercept the enemy forces recoiling in front of von Bock's summer offensive.

Von Manstein's plan for the reduction of Kerch was again a bold one, for he thinned out the German troops of LIV Corps in the west, replacing them by Rumanians, so collecting a force of six German and three Rumanian divisions for the offensive in the east. A more important factor contributing to his success was the allocation of von Richthofen's VIII Air Corps to his support. The Soviet enemy disposed of three well-equipped armies, but their defences lacked depth and the command was defective; for within seven days of von Manstein's initial attacks, made on 8 May, Eleventh Army was in the town of Kerch. Against 7500 German casualties, the enemy lost 170,000 in prisoners, and over 1000 guns, 250 tanks and 300 aircraft. The Sevastopol garrison had meanwhile remained passive.

The Sevastopol perimeter had been reduced by the first German attack to two-thirds of its former size and measured about 16 miles across. Numerically the attacker and defenders were evenly matched, but von Manstein still set great store on German superiority at arms in that he attacked so strong an enemy in well prepared positions, over difficult and broken country, much of it covered by thick scrub and defended by machine-gun nests built into the rock. The overwhelming superiority of VIII Air Corps decided the issue, however, The attack began on 7 June and the fighting lasted until 4 July, 90,000 prisoners and 460 guns being taken. This time the German casualties were not light – in all about 24,000 men.

In recognition of these victories von Manstein was promoted from colonel-general to field-marshal. But outstanding though these victories were there was nothing in them to suggest that von Manstein had a particular forte as a strategist, nor, except that he had to weigh up the relative priorities between Kerch and Sevastopol, that he was a distinguished exponent of the art of operational command. Von Manstein's success had been due to his boldness and energy, and to his readiness to drive his troops to their limit. The distinction between tactics and operational command is sometimes fine, but von Manstein's achievement would appear to have been little above the major tactical, an ability to reduce thickly defended bridgeheads and fortresses only a few miles across. Indeed this was how Hitler summed him up. The Sevastopol success, remarkable in view of the terrain and the strength and determination of the defenders, fired the Führer's imagination, and he abandoned his earlier intention of putting Eleventh Army into the Kuban and decided to rail it northwards, together with its siege and heavy artillery, to reduce fortress Leningrad. In fact only four divisions went north with the army headquarters, the remainder of the formations being dispersed as far afield as Smolensk and Crete.

The staff of Eighteenth Army in front of Leningrad was none too pleased at von Manstein's arrival. The new field-marshal was soon taken away from his planning task however, for on 4 September Hitler telephoned to say that a serious breakthrough had occurred south of Lake Ladoga near Mga (in the Eighteenth Army sector) and that von Manstein and his staff were to take command there using his own two corps headquarters. The breakthrough reached a depth of only 10 miles. As an operational command the assignment was a minor one, involving six infantry divisions over a space of three weeks. At the end of October Hitler moved Eleventh Army southwards to the area of Vitebsk to meet a big Soviet counter-offensive about to fall, it was wrongly thought, on Army Group Centre. This was in effect the offensive that was to mark the change in the course of the war on the Russo-German front by enveloping and destroying Paulus's German Sixth Army in Stalingrad.

By 24 November twenty German and two Rumanian divisions were entrapped on the Volga. It is probable that Paulus could have broken out in the early stages of the encirclement but Hitler forbade him to do so, being confident that the situation could be restored. Hitler still had the highest opinion of von Manstein's capabilities, and used his Eleventh Army headquarters as a fire brigade, rushing it from one trouble spot to another. He intended that von Manstein should storm his way into Stalingrad. On 21

November von Manstein moved south to the old Don capital of Novocher-kassk, and a week later the headquarters of Eleventh Army was redesignated as Army Group Don, von Manstein being ordered to assume most of von Weichs's Army Group B responsibilities just as he had usurped, on Hitler's orders, von Küchler's functions near Leningrad. Von Manstein's new command consisted of the encircled Sixth Army, Groups Hoth and Hollidt, and Rumanian Third Army; but notwithstanding its grandiloquent designation it was not an army group since its only offensive element, outside the Stalingrad enclave, was the understrength LVII and XLVIII Panzer Corps. In fighting power it could not be compared with a 1941 German army. Repeated delays in assembling the relief force resulted in the counter-offensive being put off from 3 to 12 December.

Hitler continued to forbid the withdrawal of German Sixth Army from the Volga, nor was it permitted to give up any of the Stalingrad positions. He thus robbed it of any offensive capability towards the south-west. Paulus was subordinate to Hitler rather than to von Manstein. Army Group Don's task therefore was to drive, unaided by Paulus, a supply corridor through to the beleaguered Sixth Army. Von Manstein's generalship can only be judged by the way in which he used his two panzer corps, noting this against the day-by-day reactions and developments within the Soviet high command.

Von Manstein decided to use Hoth's main force, LVII Panzer Corps, on the 70–mile-long south-west approach from Kotelnikovo, rather than attack eastwards from the Chir where the Rumanians and XLVIII Panzer Corps stood only 38 miles from Paulus's forward defended localities. In this he did the unexpected. He subsequently said that the choice of the long south-west approach avoided the necessity of having to cross the Don; yet he already had one bridge and a bridgehead across the river. In spite of the paucity of his forces he sketched out his plan according to the grand design used by Hitler for the Kiev encirclement in 1941, two widely separated panzer forces attacking on concentric axes. Von Manstein planned that XLVIII Panzer Corps should not begin its attack until LVII Panzer Corps was halfway to Stalingrad, when it would strike due east into the rear of the enemy resisting the LVII Corps advance. This plan, although it might have had the advantage of surprise, was not without weaknesses, for it split the German armour, and the main force was to move across 70 miles of open steppe in mid-winter, the going conditions, as it proved, being impossible for wheels and difficult for tracks. Nor did von Manstein in fact enjoy the benefit of surprise, for although Stalin and Vasilevsky were convinced that he would select the close approach from the Chir, they were aware from the beginning of December that German armour was being unloaded in the Kotelnikovo sidings. Nor did the nine days' delay add to von Manstein's chance of success.

In the event, distance, terrain and weather played a greater part in the defeat of Army Group Don than the determined Red Army resistance. The main relief thrust hardly got within 30 miles of the enclave, not much closer to Stalingrad than the Rumanians on the Chir. It might have been preferable to have concentrated the two panzer corps and attacked from that sector, the shortest way into Stalingrad, in spite of the Red Army strength there. As it was, both panzer corps were defeated in isolation. Von Manstein's command, resources and activity were however barely adequate for the task; even if he had succeeded in driving a corridor into Stalingrad the outcome would probably have been little different, except that part of Army Group Don might have been lost in addition to Sixth Army. For the Soviet high command already held, and was never again to lose, the strategic initiative. Strategic offensives, already mounted farther to the west, would have re-enveloped Paulus.

The routed Axis forces began to withdraw from the Caucasus into the Ukraine, and von Weichs's Army Group B was withdrawn from the chain of command, its troops being shared out between Army Groups Centre and Don, the latter being redesignated as Army Group South. Hitler was thoroughly dissatisfied with von Manstein's performance, particularly over the subsequent loss of Kharkov, and when the Führer arrived in Zaporozhe on 17 February 1943, he intended to dismiss him. Hitler was somewhat mollified, however, when presented with von Manstein's plan for a counter-offensive, aimed primarily at destroying the forward elements of the enemy South-West Front which was trying to envelop Army Group South from the north. Once again the plan rested on converging offensives of panzer and motorised forces, moving together on near concentric axes, on this occasion from start lines up to 140 miles apart. The troops taking part included two panzer corps of Hoth's Fourth Panzer Army, Hausser's 11 SS Panzer Corps and two panzer corps of von Mackensen's First Panzer Army, which had come up from the Caucasus. The air situation was in the German favour since von Richthofen's Fourth Air Fleet had inflicted a sharp tactical defeat on the Red Air Force. The opposing Soviet ground forces were known to be over-confident, overextended, tired and short of fuel.

The counter-offensive, starting on 19 February, successfully cut off enemy advance elements, and although only nine thousand prisoners were taken, Army Group South claimed twenty-three thousand Soviet dead on the battlefield. Hoth then moved rapidly north-eastwards, enveloping the enveloper by outflanking the enemy South-West Front from the north and driving a wedge between it and the neighbouring Voronezh Front, retaking Kharkov and Belgorod by 18 March. Only the arrival of three reinforcing Soviet armies from the interior, and the mud following the spring thaw, stabilised the Soviet line. Von Manstein's daring strategic blow has since been regarded by his admirers as a masterpiece. It was said to have cost the Red Army forty thousand casualties and the loss of six hundred tanks and five hundred guns, and it left the Germans in undisputed control of the area bounded by the Donets and Mius, much the same line as held in the winter of 1941. Army Group South had been saved from further withdrawal and had earned a respite until the mid-summer. Yet the defeats imposed on the Red Army were limited, being a temporary check and in no way decisive. Vasilevsky, the Red Army Chief of General Staff, whose memoirs are by Soviet standards moderate, said that von Manstein's blow inflicted a reverse because it was totally unexpected. In the long term however it did not dislocate Soviet plans or order of battle.

Hitler's decision, that spring, to destroy the enemy bulge at Kursk, using von Kluge's Army Group Centre to envelop it from the north while von Manstein's Army Group South attacked from the south, was the last German offensive in the east, and the final effort to wrest the strategic initiative from the enemy. Because the German preparations were repeatedly delayed, the Soviet high command had many months' notice of the intention, and heavily fortified and reinforced the area, for according to recently published Soviet figures about 3300 tanks were concentrated there. Von Manstein had advocated earlier that the enemy should be allowed to attack, and, since the Red Army would presumably thrust in a south-westerly direction, he believed that its advance could be enveloped by an armoured force concentrated to the west of Kharkov. Hitler however had wanted to strike first, and von Manstein seems to have fallen in with his plans, for Guderian, who was adamantly opposed to the Citadel offensive, subsequently complained that the commander of Army Group South voiced no real objections at the time, although he certainly was opposed to the repeated postponements. Hitler well realised what was at stake and said, during the preparation, that the mere thought of the battle 'turned his stomach over'.

In the Kremlin similar scenes were being enacted, and discussion and argument as to whether to attack or await the German offensive went on unabated for three months. Stalin, like Hitler, wanted to strike the first blow, and he was over-inclined to listen to Vatutin who advocated this course. Vasilevsky and Zhukov expended effort and mental energy in repeatedly dissuading him. The strain of waiting was trying on Stalin's nerves, and he did not conceal his anxiety and irritability.

During the Kursk battle von Manstein carried out the part assigned to him with some success, but Model's failure in the north and Hitler's decision, on 13 July, to call off the offensive after the heavy losses of only eight days' fighting, spelt the end of the German occupation of the Ukraine. Von Manstein's field leadership was henceforth entirely subordinate to close Führer control.

The German withdrawal in the south was long drawn out, a succession of failures and losses. Hitler was determined to overcome adversity by will-power, *his* will-power, and his generals were forbidden to withdraw or exercise any discretion that involved giving ground. This meant that any mobile defence was out of the question. Von Manstein sought in vain for freedom to make his own decisions. He and von Kluge were agreed that Hitler ought to be replaced by a professional army officer as Defence Minister and

Commander-in-Chief, and in September 1943, according to von Manstein, they tried to urge this course on him. Hitler had come to dislike von Manstein, whom he regarded as inordinately ambitious. In January 1944 von Manstein raised the question yet again and advised the evacuation of the Crimea and the withdrawal from the Dnieper bend. His proposals were flatly and angrily rejected.

As early as 1939 von Tresckow had tried to sound out von Manstein and von Rundstedt on the question of military opposition to Hitler. Neither wanted to be involved. Bodo Scheurig has recounted how, in February 1943, von Manstein told von Tresckow that the Stalingrad catastrophe 'was exceptional' and that he believed that Hitler had 'learned something from it'. Von Manstein still seemed to think armed victory possible. When approached again that summer by the conspirators of *die Berliner Fronde* he told Gersdorff that he (von Manstein) was *persona non grata* with Hitler and suggested that von Rundstedt or von Kluge might try to persuade him to give up the military command. Von Manstein would not agree to a deputation, 'for Prussian field-marshals do not mutiny', and he would have nothing to do with assassination. But when asked if he would accept office as chief of the *Wehrmachtgeneralstag* in the event of a coup, he is said to have replied that he would 'always be loyally at the disposal of the legal government'. By this the conspirators understood that they could not count on von Manstein and believed that all he wanted was firstly security, and then orders. They marvelled that a man should place reliance on his own strategic genius which Hitler would not allow him to use.

Von Manstein's course was nearly run. The Führer maintained the semblance of polite relations with him, but in reality was hostile, even contemptuous. Von Manstein's proposals to withdraw, and in particular the move of his own headquarters from Vinnitsa to Lvov, were discussed openly by Hitler in the presence of Zeitzler, Jodl and others, and were subjected to mockery and sarcasm.

When however Hitler summoned von Manstein to Berchtesgaden on 30 March in order to dismiss him, the dictator was polite, almost cordial. After handing the field-marshal the Swords to his Knights Cross, he announced that he had decided to place the army group in other hands, for Model would be the man 'to dash around the divisions'. The time for grand-style operations in the east, for which von Manstein, thought Hitler, was particularly qualified, was past, and all that counted now was to hang on to what Germany already held. Hitler told von Manstein that there had been no crisis of confidence between them and that he intended to give him another post 'before long'. Von Manstein was then posted to the Führer's reserve, but was not re-employed.

Von Manstein's last claim to fame over the fifteen months of defensive battles and forced withdrawals from December 1942 to March 1944, which took Army Group South from the Don steppe to Galicia, was that he had kept the army group in being as a coherent fighting formation. He was in fact one of the last senior field commanders to do so, for that summer Army Groups Centre, North Ukraine and South Ukraine were to be enveloped and largely destroyed during the great Red Army offensives.

Von Manstein had started his military career with every advantage. In the First World War his experience of command had been limited, but he remained an infantryman at heart. He was an educated and able staff officer with outstanding command ability in the field of tactics, operational command and strategy; this itself is unusual. Yet, except for *Sturmartillerie*, he appears to have contributed little to military thought that was both original and lasting and there was little to set him apart from many other talented German generals of the period. Today, in Germany, he rightly enjoys a great reputation as a strategist, although it is debatable whether his achievements were superior to those of von Rundstedt and von Bock; in the operational sphere he was equalled by Guderian, Hoth and von Kleist. He was determined and bold, and like his fellows and his political master his military audacity bordered on the rash and the insolent, what is known in Soviet military terminology as 'adventurism'. In the first half of the war, against outdated high commands, inexperienced field generals and poorly trained troops, the victories were remarkable. But these successes could not be repeated indefinitely, for such audacity took too little account of the feasible, factors such as climate, distance and terrain, and the steadily improving quality of the enemy troops and high command.

Marshal Georgii Zhukov

———◆———

John Erickson

On 7 August 1915, just a few months short of his nineteenth birthday, Georgii Konstantinovich Zhukov began his military career in the bedraggled style of an obscure wartime conscript in the Imperial Russian Army, which was even then beginning to bleed to death from its grievous battle casualties. For the young Zhukov however the pains of the first days of army life, followed by the overcrowding, stench and brute discipline of the Kaluga training depot, were more than offset by his having been selected for the cavalry, much to the envy of those shunted into the infantry. Cavalry service corresponded immediately with Zhukov's own 'romantic illusions', though that initial decision by the recruit board at Maloyaroslavets, even as it delighted Zhukov, gave his subsequent career a strangely durable cast. Later in life Zhukov came to be identified with the archetypal tough Russian soldier – the traditional infantryman – but for more than a quarter of a century he was bound up with the cavalry and mobile-mechanised forces, progressing from chargers to the novel Soviet 'motor-mechanised' and tank units of the 1930s, culminating in his handling armoured and mobile forces on an unprecedented scale in the closing stages of the 'Great Patriotic War'.

For all the 'hard lying' of the Imperial Army, Zhukov like millions of other Russian conscripts was no stranger to grinding poverty, to labour under cruel conditions and to the malice or indifference of superiors. Born in November 1896 into a desperately poor family in the village of Strelkovka, Georgii Konstantinovich suffered all the deprivations common to rural Russia, but in spite of family misfortune and communal suffering he managed to attend the nearby parish school for three years, passing his first examination with top marks (and acquiring in the process a voracious and enduring appetite for reading and for self-education). At the age of seven Zhukov began working in the fields to help his family and at ten was bundled off to Moscow as an apprentice furrier with his uncle, Pilikhin – not the printer's devil he had hoped to become. Beaten and exploited by the avaricious Pilikhin, Zhukov none the less learned his trade and pursued his studies as best he might, hoping to enrol in one of Moscow's night schools. As he approached sixteen he was a fully fledged craftsman, now lodged out in Moscow and planning to marry his landlady's daughter, Maria, only to have these hopes shattered by his call-up: he could only return home, lend a final hand with the harvesting and bid his family farewell.

With his basic training behind him, Zhukov moved with his reserve cavalry regiment to join the crack 10th Cavalry Division: by the spring of 1916 his was a well-trained cavalry unit and together with thirty other men Zhukov was selected for NCO training, from which he returned in August (1916) to the 10th Division and thence to front-line service. Fighting on the south-western front, he was blown up by a mine in October 1916 and found himself in hospital, followed by a posting to a reserve unit – something of a triumphant return to his fellow cavalrymen now that he sported active service stripes and wore two St George crosses for capturing a German officer and for sustaining heavy wounds.

The new year, 1917, brought revolution, the dramatic crumbling of the dispirited Imperial Army, the Bolshevik seizure of power and finally civil war. In all the flurry of 'democratisation' Zhukov was elected chairman of the 'soldiers' committee' of his squadron; though soon demobilised he became a hunted man and made his way only with difficulty to his home village, where he was stricken with typhus in February 1918. Prevented by illness from joining the Red Guard, he was fit enough in August to volunteer for the new Red Army, enlisting in the 4th Cavalry Regiment of the 1st Moscow Cavalry Division.

Once again force of circumstance and bonds of comradeship came to exercise a singular influence on Zhukov's fortunes. During the civil war he served with Timoshenko's cavalry brigade, one of two brigades in a cavalry division commanded by yet another ex-Imperial Army NCO, Budenny – and here was the nucleus of the famous First Cavalry Army with which Stalin became identified and whose command (Timoshenko, Budenny and Voroshilov plus their protégés) eventually formed part of Stalin's own inner circle. In March 1919 Zhukov joined the Communist Party; later that year he was wounded in the leg during heavy fighting in the Tsaritsyn (later Stalingrad) area, moving on to the 1st Ryazan cavalry course (a commander's* course), joining the fight against Wrangel and ending the civil war amidst the savage, brawling encounter with Antonov's guerrilla armies in Tambov province.

Now a squadron commander, Zhukov after 1921 elected to remain in the Red Army, truncated steadily as its strength shrank to some five hundred thousand (from over five million) by the mid-1920s, subject to fierce economic retrenchment and affording only diminished chances of promotion. Zhukov's fortunes as a regular soldier however prospered, all under the eyes of quizzical but interested superiors: until March 1923 he was a squadron commander in the 38th Cavalry Regiment, becoming in turn deputy commander of the 40th

* The term 'officer' was rigorously eschewed by the Red Army until 1942: *Komandir* and *komsostav* nevertheless denote 'officer(s)' and the officer corps.

Cavalry Regiment (7th Samara Cavalry Division), and in April 1923 commander of the 39th Buzuluk Cavalry Regiment. These promotions came on
the eve of major changes and reorganisation in the Red Army, ushered in by
the 'Frunze reforms' and the transition to a more orthodox military system.
The implications of this critical phase did not escape Zhukov, who realised
that no one could rest on their wartime laurels – those who thought themselves 'past masters, with nothing to learn' must inevitably go to the wall. He
therefore set about learning.

In 1924–5 he attended the advanced cavalry commanders' course in Leningrad in the company of Rokossovskii, Bagramyan and Yeremenko (all future
marshals); in 1929 he went on to the higher command course in Moscow, this
at a time when Soviet military theory was entering a period of exciting and
original development, augmented by the secret Soviet-German military
collaboration involving the elite of the *Reichswehr* (though Zhukov never
attended any course in Germany itself). He seemingly devoured every book,
paper and study he could lay his hands on during these hectic days. In the
spring of 1930 he returned to take command of the 2nd Cavalry Brigade (7th
Samara Division) but was very soon being considered for the post of assistant
cavalry inspector within Budenny's fold. With some reluctance he took up
this post and was soon involved in the demanding work of drafting Red
Army manuals, bringing the bonus of close contact with the leading brains of
the Red Army, in particular, with M. N. Tukhachevskii who was the driving
force behind the modernisation and mechanisation of the Red Army in the
1930s.

In March 1933 Zhukov took command of the crack 4th Cavalry Division,
an elite formation that had fought with Budenny's First Cavalry Army and
which now included one of the new 'mechanised regiments' (the 4th). Once
in this key command in the key Belorussian Military District Zhukov relentlessly set about learning from the ground up how to train, handle and operate
the new mobile strike forces (cavalry currently combined with 'motor-
mechanised units'). He had to accomplish nothing short of producing a
brand-new type of Soviet soldier, the 'tankist'. And so a singleminded Zhukov
set about inspecting, teaching, taking instruction himself, instilling strict
discipline and promoting effective, realistic training. In his view everything
in modern war depended on how the command staff organised its attack and
he placed the greatest emphasis on accurate intelligence, especially when
facing a 'shrewd and subtle adversary'. At this stage Zhukov did not have a
reputation as a martinet with a lashing tongue and ungovernable temper: he
was regarded as a fair commander, asking no more of his subordinates than
he could and would do himself, but also as an officer who would unhesitatingly
hand over any man for court-martial if the good of the Red Army demanded
it.

It is worth dwelling for a moment on these aspects of Zhukov's behaviour
and work methods. In effect his conduct during the Second World War was

nothing but these earlier characteristics writ large: he savaged many a Soviet field commander, but only because of poorly organised attacks, woefully defective intelligence against a 'shrewd and subtle adversary' – in this case, the *Wehrmacht* – and slovenly organisation. Furthermore through these experiments in the 1930s he had learned about the difficulty of co-ordinating various arms, particularly fast-moving tank forces with the slower infantry, but he understood from the outset that the tank must play an independent role on the battlefield and could not be tied exclusively to the pace and performance of the infantry.

Zhukov enjoyed great good fortune in serving at this time with I. P. Uborevich (Belorussian Military District Commander) and in associating with A. I. Yegorov, Chief of the Red Army Staff, both of whom contributed to broadening his operational outlook. But as the grim days of Stalin's military purge drew on, he was even more fortunate in 1936–7 in having the patronage and the protection of Stalin's own military cronies, the First Cavalry Army commanders who survived largely unscathed. Zhukov was not cut down in the murderous military purge that decimated the Red Army's high command and eliminated thousands of officers. Against this bloody background he took command of the 3rd Cavalry Corps and continued to experiment with 'the combat application of cavalry within a mechanised army', followed within seven months by command of the 6th Cossack Corps and ultimately, at the close of 1938 (as the military purge died away), an appointment as deputy commander of the Belorussian Military District with responsibility in peacetime for combat training and in war as commander of a 'cavalry-mechanised group' consisting of four to five cavalry divisions and three to four independent tank brigades.

An operational command came sooner than perhaps Zhukov might have imagined on assuming this appointment. On 1 June 1939 he was hurriedly summoned to Moscow and within hours was despatched to the battlefield of Outer Mongolia, where in the Khalkhin-Gol area Japanese troops of the Kwantung Army were engaging Soviet-Mongolian forces in operations growing in both scale and intensity. On his arrival Zhukov discovered the Soviet corps commander in an HQ located 75 miles from the fighting, 'a bit too far' from the battlefield as Corps Commander Feklenko duly admitted, but even worse in Zhukov's catalogue of sins was the lack of 'thorough reconnaissance'. *Komkor* (Corps Commander) Zhukov at once took this Soviet-Mongolian 1st Army Group by the scruff of its neck and proceeded to prepare a battle of annihilation against the Japanese: two full Japanese infantry divisions, heavy artillery and aviation units moved up, but Zhukov hauled reinforcements from the deep rear, built up an adequate logistics base (across 400 miles of dirt road) and – while preparing a powerful offensive – ostentatiously advertised his defensive dispositions, even to strewing the front line with booklets on defensive tactics. To conceal the noise of his own tanks on the move – including experimental models of what became the T–34 – he stripped silencers and exhaust mufflers from lorries: night movement was masked under the din of Soviet bombing attacks against the Japanese rear.

Anticipating the planned Japanese offensive by four days, Zhukov launched his own enveloping attack on 20 August 1939, splitting his forces into three groups – northern, central and southern. Three days were needed to complete his double envelopment, which utilised tanks, ground-attack aircraft, motorised infantry, artillery and even a parachute brigade, providing the first instance of parachute troops committed as ground infantry. The result was a deadly and decisive Soviet victory, eliminating some fifty thousand Japanese troops in a lesson never wholly forgotten by the Japanese in contemplating any future assault on the Soviet Union: Zhukov's triumph at Khalkhin-Gol therefore assumed political and strategic dimensions going far beyond the confines of a Mongolian river valley. Having brought about a tactically superior concentration of force, prepared effective co-ordination of combined arms and organised centralised command without inhibiting tactical flexibility, Zhukov attacked with a 4:1 superiority in armour, 2:1 in aircraft and $1\frac{1}{2}$:1 in infantry – superiority norms from which he rarely deviated in the future, save in a dire emergency.

All that he had learned he now showed off in a large-scale operation: armour must strike out independently, operations must be conducted 'in depth' (the theory elaborated by Tukhachevskii and others), implemented by thorough planning, adequate reconnaissance and effective operational control, not to mention deception and pre-emption. Here was the essence of the Zhukov 'method', a formidable combination of old professional virtues with the possibilities afforded by modern technology and the vista opened up by high-speed movement, later to be enlarged into the 'non-stop offensive'.

After his victory on the Khalkhin-Gol, Zhukov, in no way tarnished by the military martyrdom suffered by the Red Army in its 'winter war' with Finland, took command of the strategically important Kiev Special Military District: this interlude between victory and catastrophe, which swept over the Soviet Union in June 1941, provides an interesting and certainly illuminating phase in his career. Zhukov brought Bagramyan to his Kiev command: Bagramyan, that successful and eminently clear-headed soldier, sums up Zhukov's characteristics with typical crispness, emphasising his 'iron-hard persistence', his *particular originality of thought*, the 'rare logic' with which he defended his decisions, his directness and 'stern character', which boded ill for military 'good-for-nothings'.

Promoted now to full general of the Red Army, in 1940 Zhukov demonstrated 'complete confidence in himself', exhibiting in his Kiev command not only his military professionalism but also administrative skill and political instinct. His overriding concern was reform of the Red Army, all too urgent in view of the débâcle in Finland. With singular audacity (and possibly Stalin's connivance) he spoke out directly against the inefficiency of 'dual command' (which allowed the military commissar a veto over the commander) and argued for the restitution of unitary command with the commander in sole control of military matters. He also excoriated the senior command, where 'good-for-nothings' had failed to train junior officers properly – 'we stand now in great need of troop commanders who are well trained not only in combined-arms, but also in operational matters': even when unitary command was restored in August 1940 he continued to press the commander's prerogatives, the need for good discipline and the greater study of Russian military leadership and tradition.

This was Zhukov's concept of the Red Army – a well-trained, well-disciplined force, properly organised and equipped, the commander master in his own house, in other words, a highly professional force subject to the minimum of political interference. It was all the more ironical therefore that he should have presided over the crucifixion of the Red Army when on 22 June 1941 the *Wehrmacht* swept upon the Soviet Union with a surprise attack that opened the largest land campaign in the history of the world. At that time General Zhukov was Chief of the General Staff, a post into which he had been catapulted in January 1941 by Stalin, who showed much displeasure at the performance of senior officers in the war games held that month, in which Zhukov, as commander of the 'invading force', had shown just what the panzer divisions might do to shatter Soviet defences on the western frontier. The twenty weeks available to him did not permit either the elaboration or the implementation of sound defence plans, nor could he alone reverse Soviet policy *in toto* or repair all of Stalin's damage to the military system: though aware of the need for full combat readiness, Zhukov could not prevail upon Stalin to follow this course. His irritability in this post must surely have stemmed from his awareness of the appalling constriction imposed on the Red Army by Stalin's straitjacket.

Within five weeks, at the end of July and when the Red Army had been savagely mauled in the frontier battles, Zhukov, who had been sent to the South-western Front on 23 June, was summarily relieved of his post as Chief of the General Staff after a bitter clash with Stalin. Resorting to 'directness', Zhukov had proposed withdrawal from Kiev to avert a military catastrophe, a submission that ignited Stalin's anger. He was dismissed on the spot although that did not save the half million Soviet troops trapped finally in encirclement: well before this débâcle, Zhukov, almost alone in his percipience, had grasped the significance of German armour peeling off the right wing of Army Group Centre to stab an encircling hook deep into the rear of the Soviet forces defending Kiev.

But if he could not save the South-western Front from disaster, at least he could save Leningrad from the threat of immolation. Sent north by Stalin in September, Zhukov took over from Voroshilov, whose crass incompetence had disorganised Soviet defences and imperilled Leningrad itself. Zhukov fastened an iron grip on both demoralised defenders and a disordered defence, throwing out involved and unworkable plans (literally sweeping an array of impressive but irrelevant maps off the table at his HQ). He demanded 'uninterrupted counter-attacks' and concentrated all available forces on the key southern and south-western sectors, rather than spattering them in Voroshilov's fashion: he ordered a final defence position to be manned by Forty-Second Army in the Pulkovo sector, where the heights were feverishly fortified.

While preparing the city for demolition, he divided it into defensive sectors, organised anti-tank and anti-paratroop defences, producing a huge urban fortress. Though German armour did penetrate the main defensive system, incessant counter-attacks had slowed the German advance, which was virtually halted when Hitler decided on envelopment rather than outright storming of the city: on 18 September 1941 Colonel-General Halder observed that the noose round Leningrad's neck could be drawn no tighter. In less than a month Zhukov had mastered the gravest crisis, organised an effective defence and repaired morale, as well as restoring discipline which had crumpled disastrously before his arrival.

The German divisions drawn off from Leningrad regrouped to take part in the huge operation aimed at Moscow. Zhukov also followed them from Leningrad, in response to Stalin's orders to take over the shattered defences of the Western Front, where early in October the giant German encirclement at Vyazma and Bryansk had engulfed yet another half million Soviet soldiers. Koniev, the Western Front commander, excused the disaster on the grounds of German superiority, greater mobility and the effect of surprise, though Zhukov had scant patience with this: in his view there had been time, men and machines enough. Now in late October he had to stitch up a defence line out of the ninety thousand men and limited armour left to him out of six hundred thousand men and numerous tanks deployed at the beginning of the month. Stalin and the *Stavka*, the Soviet GHQ, installed Zhukov as Western Front commander, with orders to hold the Germans off at any cost, which in the event proved to be fearsome even though it saved the Soviet capital.

The defensive battle for Moscow lasted from mid-October to 6 December 1941. It was conducted by Zhukov after his own singular style and in strange, almost astounding, liaison with Stalin. To ensure firm and unbroken operational control Zhukov established his usual tight rein over commanders and maintained his front command post well (indeed, dangerously) forward, at the same time keeping in continuous touch with Stalin, the *Stavka*, the General Staff, adjoining fronts and formation commanders (who received many a flick of the Zhukov whip). He did not like Stalin's demand for repeated small counter-strokes, but was obliged to acquiesce, as he had to acquiesce in Stalin's military parsimony in doling out mere detachments from reserves during the defensive fighting. Yet the *Wehrmacht* never breached Zhukov's defensive front, nor was any Soviet division encircled and obliterated as in previous days: Zhukov's own assessment of the German failure to reach Moscow emphasises mistakes made in assembling the assault forces, the weakness of the flank units and their lack of 'combined-arms units' and the dangerous over-reliance on armour, while the failure to hammer in the Soviet centre allowed Zhukov to switch available reserves to his own flanks.

It was from these flank attacks that the Soviet counter-offensive took shape. On 29 November Zhukov persuaded Stalin of German exhaustion, receiving in turn two armies Stalin had hoarded so carefully and orders to prepare an appropriate plan to use them: Zhukov ruled out an offensive along the whole length of his front, proposing rather to develop the flank attacks – striking to the left and right, while pinning German forces at the centre. On the eve of his counter-blow Zhukov, consulted by Stalin, asked again for tanks – only to be told that there were none available, but that he would receive air reinforcement. Attacking north and south of Moscow on 5–6 December, Zhukov's armies began forcing a German retreat, and with the Soviet advance gaining ground and pace the transition to a general counter-offensive was assured. Zhukov demanded swift pursuit, he 'categorically forbade' frontal attacks and commanded lead units to push on: he used his aircraft skilfully, but the lack of tanks made itself felt at once, whereupon he turned to cavalry formations, ski battalions and airborne units to break into the enemy rear at speed.

Early in January 1942 Stalin proposed a mighty counter-offensive involving every Soviet front, envisaging the eventual destruction of the three German army groups in Russia: it was a wildly ambitious plan, far outstripping the resources then available to the Red Army. Zhukov argued for the main effort to be committed along the 'western axis', where results could be decisive, but to no avail. As the Western theatre commander Zhukov pressed his own offensive, hurling in cavalry corps and an entire airborne corps, making deep penetrations into Army Group Centre's rear but failing – inevitably – to deliver the *coup de grâce*, as Stalin drained strength away to other embattled fronts. Worse, however, was to come.

In formulating plans for the summer campaign, Stalin insisted that the main German thrust would again be directed against Moscow, ignoring growing evidence that the primary attack was being prepared in the south: though paying lip service to defensive preparations, Stalin approved (and encouraged) 'limited' or 'partial' offensives by the Red Army, which grew in scale on the northern and southern wings, thereby placing the Red Army in the dangerous posture of simultaneously attacking and defending. The result was a horrendous catastrophe in the south, which in the summer of 1942 swept entire armies aside and opened up the route to Stalingrad, as well as uncovering the Caucasus (and the oilfields). On 27 August 1942 Stalin brought Zhukov back from the western front, disclosed the calamitous state of affairs in the south and intimated that Zhukov would be appointed deputy to himself as Supreme Commander. Thus at a stroke Zhukov was transformed from 'visiting fireman' to threatened fronts into the chief engineer of the Soviet military machine. In this desperate quest for improved efficiency in the field, Stalin was also persuaded to restore unitary command, thereby revoking the 'anti-panic' measure of commissar control of August 1941 and unshackling the commander – a move close to Zhukov's heart.

In a matter of hours Zhukov was on his way to Stalingrad, now hemmed in by German divisions and even sliced in two by an armoured penetration to the bank of the Volga. His first inspection centred on checking the local commanders' knowledge of their own forces and those of the enemy: thereafter he set about organising attacks north and north-west of Stalingrad to ease the pressure on the beleaguered 'northern group' in Stalingrad, severed from other Soviet units by that German penetration: the directive of 3 September left no doubt about the dire emergency facing the defenders. By 10 September Zhukov had concluded that a breakthrough from the north was not possible; he returned to Moscow in the company of Colonel-General Vasilevskii (Chief of the General Staff) to report to Stalin on the 12th. Here Zhukov referred to the 'other solution' to the Stalingrad problem. Piecemeal attacks with insufficient artillery and tank support, conducted on unfavourable terrain, would never save the situation, only the 'other solution' of a major strategic counter-offensive designed to alter the entire balance in the southern theatre would suffice. A preliminary estimate showed that forty-five days of preparation would be needed before such an offensive could be launched.

This counter-offensive plan 'Uranus' envisaged a three-front operation, committed to an inner encirclement of the German 'Stalingrad group' itself and an outer encirclement to isolate this concentration from outside forces: the first stage involved establishing the two encirclement lines, the second eliminating the trapped armies and preventing any break-out. The additional front, the South-western, added to the present two-front deployment, would strike west of the Don with a blow aimed at the 'operational rear of the enemy in the Stalingrad area': the entire counter-offensive would unroll across a 250-mile front with the pincer movement stretching over a radius of some 60 miles.

Zhukov himself observed that at Stalingrad he acquired 'significantly greater experience in the organisation of a counter-offensive than in 1941 at Moscow', where lack of men and machines did not allow for an attempt at outright encirclement. Yet he did not witness the final triumph at Stalingrad as von Paulus's Sixth Army was reduced to capitulation. He was again at the opposite end of the Soviet-German front, co-ordinating the operation designed to break the German blockade of Leningrad: on 18 January 1943 the ring was broken and the ghastly plight of Leningrad on the point of alleviation. The *Izvestiya* announcement of 19 January of the lifting of the blockade also confirmed Zhukov's promotion to Marshal of the Soviet Union: the Red Army received its reward in the form of the restoration of shoulder-boards –

the *pogon* banished in 1917 – and the restitution of the term *'ofitser'*. It was with this new, battle-tested and increasingly proficient officer corps that Zhukov became identified and they with him, to the increasing discomfiture of the 'political deputies' who were not slow to complain about Zhukov the martinet.

It was therefore as a Marshal that Zhukov embarked upon one of the greatest encounters (and possibly the most decisive) of the Soviet-German war, the battle of Kursk in the summer of 1943. As a result of the frenzied fighting in the south, in which the Red Army failed in its bid to recover the eastern Ukraine, at the end of March 1943 a massive Soviet salient at Kursk jutted between a German salient at Orel in the north and Belgorod in the south.

At Zhukov's prompting the *Stavka* built up a truly massive defensive force, deeply echeloned defences and concentrated formidable reserves: the armoured and mechanised formations, amounting to five tank armies, could be employed not only to seal off penetrations but also to mount a massed counter-offensive. The Reserve Front constituted the greatest strategic reserve ever assembled by the Soviet command, while in the salient artillery regiments for the first time in any operation outnumbered rifle regiments. Fitted out with huge minefields, artillery and anti-tank batteries and defensive works in great depth, the Central and Voronezh Fronts would hold the northern and southern faces of the salient respectively: on Stalin's orders Zhukov would co-ordinate the operations of the Central, Bryansk and Western Fronts, Vasilevskii those of the Voronezh Front. Early in May, when Zhukov had returned to Moscow from a brief inspection of the North Caucasus Front, Soviet intelligence confirmed German movements on the flanks of the salient – data that in turn supported Zhukov's April appreciations and estimates. Now dissuaded from a pre-emptive strike, Stalin and his command sweated out the remainder of May, June and the onset of July before Operation *Zitadelle* (Citadel) opened finally on the afternoon of 4 July.

After five days of this immense battle the German thrust in the north against the Central Front had ground to a halt, snagged in impenetrable Soviet defences; on the southern face however the issue had yet to be decided and on 11 July a giant tank battle was shaping up at Prokhorovka, where Fourth Panzer Army threatened a breakthrough. Both Zhukov and Vasilev-skii authorised Rotmistrov's Fifth Tank Army and Zhadov's Fifth Guards Rifle Army from Koniev's redesignated Steppe Front to intervene in support. By nightfall on 12 July Fourth Panzer withdrew from the scene of this immense armoured joust, leaving three hundred shattered tanks and ten thousand dead: the 'death ride' was over and with it German hopes of finally breaking through the Soviet defences in the southern sector. On 16 July German troops were falling back on Belgorod.

The mighty *Materialschlacht* at Kursk now recoiled fearfully upon the *Wehrmacht*: Zhukov records it as the 'capital encounter' of the Soviet-German war and his part in it was outstandingly important, in planning, preparation and execution. Kursk destroyed any hope of Germany achieving a stalemate in the east: it banished for ever any hope of victory: the strategic initiative had passed irreversibly to the Red Army and henceforth the German army was compelled only to retreat. Zhukov had demonstrated the Red Army's capacity to fight on the strategic defensive against a superbly equipped adversary and to mount a deliberately timed strategic counter-offensive once the defensive battle had been won. Von Manstein's earlier forebodings about Kursk had been realised all too disastrously. Now Zhukov prepared for the kill against Army Group South in its entirety.

Whatever hopes the German command entertained of making a stand on the Dnieper line were shattered at the end of October 1943, when substantial Soviet forces drew up to or were already astride the river line: the Red Army duly entered Kiev on 21 November 1943.

Zhukov's handling of 1st Ukrainian Front has not escaped criticism, particularly his failure in late March to reinforce his outer front and the inner front: in addition, reconnaissance was defective and command posts too often isolated from their subordinate units, allowing First Panzer Army to fight its way out of final encirclement. None the less the German southern wing was effectively shattered and Manstein's head rolled as a consequence. Now the Soviet command turned its attention to destroying an even more powerful concentration – Army Group Centre holding Belorussia. In an attempt to conceal an obvious blow the *Stavka* ordered huge deception measures to persuade the German command that Soviet offensives were being prepared in the Baltic states and once more in the south: meanwhile by mid-May the outlines of Operation Bagration were worked out.

Extending over a 620-mile front, with a depth of 370 miles, Operation Bagration was deliberately timed to open on the third anniversary of the Soviet-German war: with 166 rifle divisions supported by thirty-one thousand guns and mortars, over five thousand tanks and six thousand aircraft, the Red Army outnumbered the Germans by 3:1 in numbers of divisions, 3:1 in guns, 4:1 in armour and just under 5:1 in aircraft, though German defences were well prepared, deep and formidable and the terrain difficult. Zhukov however was now fighting over his old Belorussian Military District command, a fact he exploited by planning thrusts across marshy land and through heavily wooded areas. Early in June he also attended to what had become a familiar routine, dovetailing the general *Stavka* plan with Front operational plans, checking reconnaissance, briefing formation commanders in all arms, making a 'meticulous study of the terrain' and registering enemy defences, with special attention being paid to logistics, both to maintain secrecy and to support the scale of the proposed operations.

The full fury of this Soviet offensive broke over Army Group Centre on 23–24 June: by 29 June 1st Belorussian front with Rokossovskii in command but Zhukov in overall charge took Bobruisk, having encircled the elements of two panzer corps and thus far penetrating German positions to a depth of 70 miles across a 120-mile front.

On 8 July Zhukov flew to Moscow to confer with Stalin, who on this occasion expressed some satisfaction at the Second Front in western Europe but emphasised that the Soviet Union now had the strength to finish off Germany single-handed: he therefore required to know of Zhukov if Soviet armies could reach the Vistula without a pause in their present offensive. Zhukov readily confirmed this and added that Soviet troops must simultaneously seize good bridgeheads, which 'are essential for further offensive operations along the strategic axis of Berlin', whereupon Stalin ordered Zhukov to 'co-ordinate' such an offensive with 1st Ukrainian Front and the left flank armies of 1st Belorussian. The following day Stalin reviewed the operational plan, which envisaged the destruction of enemy forces in the Kovel-Lublin area, the capture of Brest-Litovsk with right flank forces of 1st Belorussian Front and an advance to the Vistula on a broad front, with the seizure of a bridgehead on the western bank.

Soviet operations in the latter half of July completed the ruin of Army Group Centre: the gap torn in the German front was some 250 miles wide and 300 miles deep. Early in August Rokossovskii's forces reached and crossed the Vistula, while Koniev's 1st Ukrainian Front, meeting stiffer resistance, made slower progress. Stalin also demanded that 1st Ukrainian Front capture Lvov before racing for the Vistula: 'You [Zhukov] and Koniev are in a rush to get to the Vistula. It won't run away from you.' Lvov was taken on 27 July and Koniev ordered his armies to sprint for the Vistula, where Soviet troops seized a vital bridgehead at Sandomierz on the western bank. That same day, 29 July, Zhukov was awarded a second 'Hero of the Soviet Union' gold star in recognition of his role in liberating Belorussia and the western Ukraine.

'The Berlin zone of operations' was already on the lips of Stalin, GHQ and Zhukov in October 1944: though Warsaw had burned before the eyes of Soviet troops, Stalin did not want Soviet offensive operations held up too long and required Zhukov to set his armies rolling once more. Zhukov demurred, stressing the need to regroup and reinforce: on the morrow Stalin informed Zhukov that in future the *Stavka* itself would take control of all fronts (thus eliminating the *Stavka* 'co-ordinators' and placing Stalin in immediate overall command) – but Zhukov was to take command of the 1st Belorussian Front now operating in 'the Berlin strategic zone' and would remain as Stalin's one and only deputy. For the remainder of October Zhukov worked on the operation plan for the final campaign directed primarily along the Berlin axis.

Stalin disclosed his decision about the command of the Berlin strategic zone to Soviet commanders assembled in Moscow on 7 November 1944: while this confounded the General Staff planners, it seemed to exclude Marshal Koniev from any significant part in the conquest of Berlin, the great, glittering prize that bedazzled the Red Army. Thus two races were set in motion – one born of the rivalry within the Soviet command and the other projected as Anglo-American and Soviet forces closed in on Germany from opposite directions. The Soviet plan envisaged the main thrust – mounted by tank and mechanised forces – being made along the Warsaw–Berlin axis in one of the most grandiose strategic operations of the Second World War: two enormous armoured thrusts would take Koniev's 1st Ukrainian front from the Vistula bridgeheads into Silesia and Zhukov's 1st Belorussian from its bridge-heads to Poznań, with the axes of the advance of both fronts converging on Berlin. What disturbed Zhukov however was his failure to persuade Stalin of the need to reinforce 2nd Belorussian Front to fend off the danger to the Soviet right flank from East Prussia: the lack of that single army as reinforcement proved to be ultimately a serious embarrassment.

On 8–10 December Zhukov carried out his own front war game with all army commanders and chiefs of arms and services: reinforcement poured in on a gigantic scale to both fronts, which filled out with over two million men, 6500 tanks, 32,000 guns and mortars and almost 5000 combat aircraft, a torrent released on 12–14 January 1945 when Stalin responded to Churchill's request for Soviet action in the east in view of the crisis brought on by the German offensive in the Ardennes. Koniev moved first on the 12th, Zhukov on the 14th.

By now however severe dissensions had broken out within the Soviet high command. Zhukov at the end of January submitted his plan to strike for the Oder and beyond, but Koniev also proposed to advance to the Elbe by 25–28 February and *co-operate* with Zhukov's front in capturing Berlin. The Soviet General Staff agreed with Koniev's proposal, allowing him to fight his way into Berlin, but Stalin had already 'assigned' Berlin to Zhukov: the uneasy compromise allotted Koniev's front to operations to the south of Berlin, while Zhukov took the centre stage and aimed directly at Berlin. But could Marshal Zhukov have taken Berlin even in February, striking on with a 'non-stop offensive' straight from the Oder? This accusation against Zhukov's competence was made (in 1964) by Marshal Chuikov, who castigated 1st Belorussian Front command for lack of skill and true initiative: Zhukov responded with some heat, pointing out that certainly two tank armies and several rifle armies could have been despatched to seize Berlin in a *coup de main*, but there was grave danger that a German offensive from the north could have severed 1st Belorussian Front. The 'tough nut' of eastern Pomerania had to be cracked first and it took Rokossovskii with 2nd Belorussian Front until the end of March to complete the cracking.

At the beginning of April, with the flank threat removed, the way to Berlin was clear: Zhukov had repaired the severed losses his front had suffered and improved the supply situation. Now, in the company of Stalin, Zhukov and Koniev deliberated on the Berlin operation. Zhukov opted for a single frontal assault, Koniev proposed a co-ordinated assault: Stalin resolved this bitter impasse by drawing a line on the map delineating 1st Belorussian and 1st

Ukrainian Front boundaries – but the line ended at Lübben on the Spree, just under 40 miles from Berlin. The implication was that he who drew up to that line first should seize Berlin. That was the conclusion Koniev came to, while Zhukov understood that the original directive and instruction remained: namely, that 1st Belorussian Front was charged with the main attack and the capture of the German capital. Only if Zhukov were held up should Koniev then attack the city from the south.

At 4 o'clock on the morning of 16 April 1945 Zhukov launched his mightiest offensive, using 140 searchlights to illuminate the battlefield and to stun the enemy, and also subjecting him to the greatest artillery barrage ever seen on the eastern front. Yet his assault was stopped dead on the Seelöw Heights. Stalin reprimanded him, Koniev primly argued against shifting Zhukov's mobile forces through the gap he had torn in the south after sliding with smokescreens over the Neisse and on 17 April Stalin gave Koniev permission to turn his own tank armies on Berlin. In a transport of fury and disappointment at the delay, Zhukov, flaying all about him, decided to commit his armour at once and literally hurled Katukov and his First Guards Tank Army into the attack.

By sheer weight of men and metal Zhukov broke through, using armour and infantry in concentric attacks to force his men forward and into Berlin. Koniev pressed his own offensive but was held on the Teltow canal. On 23 April Stalin delivered his verdict and put Berlin in Zhukov's hands: his order to Zhukov and Koniev set up a boundary line in Berlin, setting Koniev's final advance line 150 yards to the *west* of the Reichstag, thus according the ultimate honour of taking that building – the symbol and the substance of total Soviet victory, with the 'Victory Banner' planted atop – to Marshal Zhukov. In the afternoon of 2 May the Berlin garrison finally surrendered and Zhukov's work was done, the bloody frenzy of the Berlin assault over and his reputation as the conqueror of Hitler's capital city secured for all to see.

For little more than a year after the defeat of Germany Marshal Zhukov enjoyed the fruits of victory, second only in popular esteem to Stalin himself as the architect of Soviet triumph. In April 1946 he left Berlin, vacating his post as commander of Soviet occupation forces in Germany for the prestigious position of C-in-C Soviet Ground Forces – or so it seemed. Within three months he had been 'transferred' to the singularly lowly job of commander of the Odessa Military District: within eighteen months he had been virtually banished to the obscurity of the Urals Military District, where he languished officially for more than five years (from February 1948 until May 1953). Like thousands of others Zhukov had fallen victim to Stalin's 'purge of the heroes', the postwar decimation of the Soviet armed forces, which some argue was planned as early as 1944 and its execution entrusted to Bulganin.

In 1946 Zhukov was also expelled from the Communist Party's Central

Committee, possibly for refusing to make proper obeisance to Stalin's 'military genius': his banishment to the Urals may also have been connected with the settling of wartime scores. The real effect of Zhukov's disgrace however was to cow the entire military establishment and thus to implement that unquestioning obedience that Stalin demanded, not to mention the fawning and the sycophancy. Apart from very rare appearances in Moscow, Zhukov had to content himself with running his humble bailiwick in the Urals – it was even rumoured that he proposed to retire from military service –though in 1950–1 he was restored to the status of a candidate member of the Central Committee. But not even Stalin's 'military genius' could solve every Soviet military problem and inevitably Zhukov had to be brought back into the system, already experiencing the direct and indirect strains of the Korean War. A more immediate problem however was the patent inability of General Shtemenko to cope with the duties of Chief of the General Staff: he had bungled what may have been a contingency plan for operations against Yugoslavia and Zhukov was called in to repair the damage. Zhukov was also restored to the position of Deputy Defence Minister and Inspector-General by the summer of 1952 and in August he attended the military co-ordination committee of the Eastern Bloc states.

Stalin's last days are obscured in the blood-red mist of the 'Doctors' Plot', rumours of war and the possibility of yet another murderous purge – hence the elaborate panoply of the great medical conspiracy to kill off soldiers and civilian leaders alike. On 5 March 1953 Stalin died and an entire era passed away with him: on the following day Zhukov was officially named Deputy Defence Minister and bounded back into the Soviet military fold. Almost immediately the post-Stalin leadership had to deal with Beria's attempt to take power for himself: Bulganin, Zhukov and Vasilevskii discussed the situation with Malenkov and now Zhukov used his service with the Urals Military District to move up two Guards divisions from the Urals as reinforcement – for troops in the Moscow Military District could well have rallied to Beria. The marshals, including Zhukov, then settled accounts with Beria: according to Khrushchev's 'memoirs', it was Zhukov who put his pistol to Beria and arrested him. Henceforth, as Dr Garthoff puts it, the Soviet armed forces 'knew sin', with the Party having accorded the armed forces a unique position in supporting (or preventing) a bid for supreme power, even if the melodramatic details of Beria's arrest are not entirely true.

This military weight was also lent to Khrushchev in his struggle with Malenkov, and with Khrushchev's victory Zhukov was rewarded with the post of Defence Minister. Under this new regime headed by Marshal Zhukov the Soviet forces now came to grips with modernisation and above all with the impact of new weapons – principally nuclear weapons – on strategy and tactics.

As Marshal Zhukov became increasingly a soldier-politician, speaking out at home and abroad on a wide variety of issues, the last act of his career was about to open. He had already made enormous inroads upon the old Stalinist style in the armed forces and had adjusted strategic doctrine to the realities of the technology of the nuclear era. This thrust professionalism once more upon Soviet officers and it was only a matter of time before Zhukov turned to placing real curbs on the Party's political lackeys in the armed forces – shades of 1940, when he argued for the autonomy and professionalism of the Soviet officer. He also turned on the political officers themselves, urging them to put their military duties first and relating propaganda to the 'practical tasks of the troops'. In 1956, amidst the turbulence of the de-Stalinisation campaign in the Soviet Union and Eastern Europe, Zhukov was instrumental in menacing the Poles and putting down the Hungarian rising with direct and brutal military intervention. Meanwhile Khrushchev, who had displaced his rivals for supreme power, spared no honour for Zhukov and in the summer of 1957 relied on Zhukov's weight with the military to rout the 'anti-Party group', which menaced his supremacy. In October 1957 Zhukov visited Yugoslavia and was asked by Khrushchev to journey on a little, to Albania, to look into Yugoslav-Albanian relations: on his return Zhukov found himself at the centre of a mighty political storm that ended in his abrupt dismissal, a last and enduring banishment from the seats of power. Marshal Malinovskii took over as Defence Minister: Zhukov was removed from the Praesidium and from the Central Committee, retaining only his actual Party membership and the inescapable prospect of his retirement on his soldier's pension.

Inevitably the charge of 'Bonapartism' was levelled against Zhukov, in addition to a host of other crimes. It is true that Zhukov was heavy-handed and arrogant in this later stage, dealing harshly with the 'good-for-nothings' and betraying his impatience with political interference with military affairs – and his dislike of political officers. Moreover Khrushchev was also nurturing military schemes of his own, being on the verge of discovering the missile; Zhukov would scarcely have been a willing partner in the kind of re-organisation Khrushchev had in mind. Above all, however, Zhukov (as perhaps no other senior officer before or since) controlled the armed forces, through his administrative control of the Defence Ministry, through the weight of his prestige and achievement and through his erosion of Party influence and even Party presence in the armed forces.

It is an express tribute to Marshal Zhukov that there was no one like him in the Soviet military establishment: he exemplified professionalism, soldierly skill, linking Soviet achievements with the heavy tread of a longstanding Russian military tradition. Whatever the wartime catastrophes, he fashioned victories and that *imprimatur* persisted far into the piping days of peace. For this reason, in that he too has become part of tradition, Zhukov's name must be joined to those of Suvorov, Rumyantsev, Kutuzov, Bagration and Brusilov, archetypes of Russian military experience and leadership.

FIELD-MARSHAL SIR CLAUDE AUCHINLECK

Correlli Barnett

In his nineties Claude Auchinleck remains surprisingly little changed from his wartime photographs – still big and straight-backed, quick and decisive of movement; blue eyes still keen; still with a full complement of grizzled hair, though now grey instead of fair; a visage expressing strength and resolution. Upon first meeting him Auchinleck's personality is imposing, even daunting; the embodiment of soldierly authority. Then the reserve melts; there is a joke and a deep chuckle; and friendliness and bluff humour break through. In the words of Sir Alexander Galloway, who served with him in the Middle East, 'He sometimes appeared severe and formidable, but he had great charm and innate kindness.' And in his nineties he still remains restless and energetic, immensely interested in all that is happening in a fast-changing world; he enjoyed life with gusto; a man mellow of spirit and devoid of rancour, even though his career was partially blighted by injustice and calumny.

It was Auchinleck's misfortune, like Wavell's, to bear both in the Middle East and in India high responsibility in the first half of a British war, when commanders have to resist a well-prepared enemy with forces either numerically weaker or, as the result of hasty wartime expansion, professionally and materially inferior. Moreover it is when the general tide of war is running strongly against a country, as it was against Britain in 1941–2, that the pressure from the political leadership on generals to conjure instant victory out of the hat is at its most relentless.

At the very outset of his term as Commander-in-Chief Middle East, in July 1941, Auchinleck found his field forces spread between the Western Desert and the still continuing operations against the Vichy-French in Syria and the Italians in East Africa; his veteran formations tired and disorganised after the disasters in Greece and Crete. Yet the War Premier immediately urged him to attack in the Western Desert without delay; urging which Auchinleck firmly and successfully resisted. In the Crusader offensive in November 1941 the new Eighth Army enjoyed only slight superiority of numbers over Rommel's German-Italian *Panzergruppe Afrika*, while its formations were very uneven in training and battle experience. In particular the corps containing the armour could not compare with the enemy in tactical doctrine and skill or in staff-work and command of a tank battle. The British-built cruiser tank was mechanically unreliable; its 2-pounder gun (like the similar British anti-tank gun) inadequate in killing power. Nor did the Desert Air Force enjoy the overwhelming air superiority of twelve months later.

By the time of the Gazala battles, in May and June 1942, the balance between the Eighth Army and the enemy in terms of training, experience and equipment was beginning to even up. Nevertheless only the new American Grant tanks, forming less than a quarter of the army's tank strength, came near to matching the German Mark IIIs and Mark III Specials in overall fighting power. Since only 112 of the new 6-pounder anti-tank guns had so far been delivered, many units still had to make do with the feeble 2-pounder. It was not until after Auchinleck had left the Middle East that the arrival of fresh divisions, three hundred Sherman tanks, abundant 6-pounder anti-tank guns and the new Priest self-propelled guns finally gave the Eighth Army decisive superiority both in numbers and material.

The British lag in professionalism however was never generally made up, either under Auchinleck or his successor. In Auchinleck's own words in a letter to Churchill in July 1942, Eighth Army was still 'an amateur army fighting professionals'. This was to be Montgomery's judgement too. The problem that confronted Auchinleck in seeking to remedy British inferiority of performance lay in that, as he expressed it in the same letter, they were 'trying to train an army and use it on the battlefield at the same time'. Haig would have understood.

Like Wavell again, and unlike Alexander, Auchinleck was not free to concentrate all his resources and attention on defeating Rommel in the Western Desert, but had to guard against other dangers round the long periphery of the theatre. In the summer of 1941 there was the possibility that Germany would follow her conquest of the Balkans by invading Turkey; in October-November of the same year and from July 1942 onwards it appeared all too likely that the Russian defence of the Caucasus might collapse, so exposing the Middle East theatre, and in particular the vital Persian Gulf oilfields, to a German offensive from the north. While this danger was not finally to pass until the Russian counter-stroke at Stalingrad in November 1942, the Commander-in-Chief Middle East was however relieved of responsibility for defence of the so-called Northern Flank when Alexander succeeded Auchinleck in mid-August.

Then there were also the effects of the Japanese conquest of the British Empire in the Far East between December 1941 and March 1942, which wrecked Auchinleck's hopes of carrying the successful Crusader offensive on to Tripoli in a second bound, so bringing the war in North Africa to a victorious conclusion and paving the way for an invasion of Italy. For two fresh divisions and a consignment of anti-tank guns intended for the Middle East were diverted to the Far East, while Auchinleck himself had to yield two Australian divisions and a hundred tanks to the same destination.

It is against the background of all these dangers and difficulties that Auchinleck has to be judged as a commander.

Perhaps his most outstanding mental characteristic lay in a brisk disrespect for the traditional and orthodox, well expressed in a private letter to the Vice-Chief of the Imperial General Staff in the invasion summer of 1940, when he was commanding a corps in southern England: 'We shall not win this war so long as we cling to worn-out shibboleths and snobberies. I am sure of this. Cobwebs want removing at once.' Auchinleck derived much of his lifelong impatience with stuffiness and convention from his mother, Mary Eleanor Eyre, an Irishwoman from County Galway, whose southern Irish wit and informality reacted against the rigidities of English behaviour and etiquette, and who, since his father died when he was only eight, provided the dominant influence in his upbringing. Furthermore Auchinleck, as a career soldier of small means and an Indian army officer, stood doubly outside the British army 'establishment', in which the often professionally conservative products of 'crack' (i.e., socially fashionable) regiments held such sway.

Auchinleck's impatience with the conventional carried with it an open-minded willingness to consider new ideas, to try novel expedients. As commanding officer of his regiment, the 62nd Punjabis, in 1928–9 and afterwards as senior instructor at the Indian Army Staff College at Quetta, he introduced what were then new and imaginative training methods: the sand table for lessons in tactics and strategy; the combination of the various hitherto unconnected 'schemes' at the Staff College into episodes and aspects of a single 'war'.

It was another mark of his liberal outlook that he was completely free of the common British prejudice against Indians as an 'inferior' race. When plans were being evolved in the 1930s gradually to Indianise the leadership of the army as part of Britain's steady transfer of her rule in India, Auchinleck energetically though vainly argued against the proposal to post Indian officers to all-Indian formations. In his own words later, 'I wanted them spread among British officers, otherwise there was the appearance of segregation. I failed. But when the war came, of course, Indian officers were posted to every kind of unit.' He no less regretted the prewar policy by which the Indian army was not considered fit to be fielded against German troops. Here too his lack of prejudice was vindicated by the experience of war; and in 1941 Indian divisions were among the first British Commonwealth forces to defeat a German army in the Second World War.

Given Auchinleck's cast of mind it is not perhaps surprising that of all his wide reading in military history it was Stonewall Jackson and his Shenandoah campaign in the American Civil War, with (in Auchinleck's own words) 'its deception and manoeuvre', that made the deepest impression on him. This preference for mobile warfare was confirmed by personal experience in Mesopotamia during the Great War, when his battalion took part in an unsuccessful attempt to relieve the besieged fortress of Kut-el-Amara. 'The whole conception was wrong,' he was to recall. 'The Turks should have been manoeuvred out of their positions – not frontally attacked.' As a student at Quetta after the Great War he therefore reacted against the prevailing teaching, which was based on the administration and tactics of the setpiece western-front offensive. And nearly twenty years later the German blitzkrieg victory in France and the Low Countries in May–June 1940 offered him, as he acknowledged, further confirmation of his belief in mobile war.

Auchinleck's temperamental leaning towards the fresh approach and his penchant for mobility, deception and manoeuvre were alike manifested by his plan for the newly formed Eighth Army's first offensive (code-named Crusader and eventually launched on 18 November 1941). Originally he ordered Sir Alan Cunningham, the Eighth Army commander, to study two options: the 'conventional' one of a deliberate advance against the static enemy defences that blocked the coast road and extended inland along the Egyptian-Libyan frontier; and a highly ambitious alternative of a flank march deep through the desert via Gialo and Jarabub aimed at cutting Rommel's communications south of Benghazi. After detailed examination Cunningham and his staff found this latter option logistically almost impossible and strategically very risky because of the very long and exposed line of communication. Instead Cunningham proposed a more modest version, with a tighter wheel by the British armour round the enemy frontier defences and north-westwards on the British-held fortress of Tobruk, then isolated and under siege. Rommel, it was believed, would be forced to give battle in order to defend his communications and preserve his siege of Tobruk, whereupon the superior numbers of the British armour would prevail in the ensuing encounter battle. As Auchinleck put it in his despatch, 'The idea was that by moving wide we should force the enemy to come out and fight on ground not of his own choosing . . .'

Despite one major crisis during the battle and many vicissitudes, this conception was broadly fulfilled in the event, and was crowned with a hard-won success. Nevertheless, even in the 'mini' version evolved by Cunningham and his staff, it was an ambitious plan for an army so hastily assembled. With the benefit of hindsight it seems possible that a more pedestrian conception, following the example of the campaigns of Ulysses S. Grant rather than Stonewall Jackson, might have presented the raw Eighth Army with fewer risks and a task more in keeping with its military temperament.

Auchinleck's predilection for mobility and deception was fully vindicated however during the desperately critical First Battle of Alamein in July 1942, when he gradually wrested the initiative from a Rommel then riding the crest of victory. Instead of posting 1st South African Division in the perimeter around El Alamein, for example, he deployed it in mobile brigade groups in the open desert to the south. Rommel's attempts on 1 and 2 July at penetration and envelopment stuck fast under ferocious flanking fire from these and other mobile groups. Moreover after the first day's fighting Auchinleck evacuated two other infantry 'boxes' (static 'defended localities') in the centre and south of the Alamein neck in order to have his entire force mobile and concentrated.

Mindful of the merely passive defence often offered by Eighth Army units in the past, he ordered immediate counter-strokes, giving ambitious aims or thrust-lines, in the German style, rather than the limited objectives customary in British planning. But the discrepancy between these ambitious aims and the exhaustion and disorganisation of many Eighth Army formations and the rawness of others, exposed Auchinleck to the criticisms of being unrealistic. These criticisms were the more readily made because of the controversial personality of his Chief of Staff during First Alamein, Major-General Eric Dorman-Smith, an Irishman of caustic wit and lively (his critics believed far too lively) military imagination. Yet the choice of Dorman-Smith was another manifestation of Auchinleck's mistrust of the 'establishment' mind. 'I took Dorman-Smith', he wrote after the war, 'because I knew he had a most fertile, active and very good brain. I wanted him because I knew he was a man I could talk to – a fresh mind.' It was Dorman-Smith who suggested to him that British counter-strokes should be aimed at Italian formations, so compelling Rommel to run to-and-fro to their aid with his Germans. The plan succeeded brilliantly: by 16 July Rommel had been completely robbed of the initiative and forced on to the defensive'. In Rommel's own words in a letter to his wife, 'The enemy is using his superiority, especially in infantry, to destroy the Italian formations one by one and the German formations are too weak to stand alone. It's enough to make one weep.'

Although Auchinleck's final attempts to cap his defensive victory by bringing about the collapse of Rommel's front failed in execution, the First Battle of Alamein marks the only occasion in the North African campaign when Rommel was outwitted as well as outfought by a commander of the Eighth Army.

Auchinleck's favourite principles of deception and manoeuvre were no less evident in the plan he and Dorman-Smith evolved at the end of July 1942 for the defence of the Alamein neck against a possible future German gamble at breaking through into the Nile Delta. The key to the plan was a refused left flank running along the Ruweisat and Alam Halfa ridges at right angles to the front of the Alamein position, and intended to block Rommel's expected swing north towards the sea. Auchinleck's defensive layout of minefields and field fortifications was well in hand by the time Montgomery arrived on the scene in mid-August, and therefore determined the basic anatomy of the

Battle of Alam Halfa at the end of the month. However, whereas Montgomery fought a tightly controlled and largely static 'no-risks' battle, Auchinleck had intended the defences along the Ruweisat and Alam Halfa ridges to serve as pivots of manoeuvre for a mobile battle.

Auchinleck's German opponents – Rommel himself, Bayerlein his Chief of Staff and others – admired him more than any other British commander in the Western Desert. As Bayerlein put it, 'It is a pity that no one in Britain recognised the marvellous, though smaller, battles Auchinleck won.' Themselves the products of a long military tradition of mobility and manoeuvre, of flexibility in organisation and command, they correctly felt Auchinleck to be a kindred spirit. Yet at the same time he lies open to the criticism that it was fundamentally unrealistic and mistaken to seek to evolve 'German' plans and 'German' styles of fighting for an army that was the product of a very different military tradition, doctrine and training, and which furthermore lacked as a whole the experience and professionalism of *Panzerarmee Afrika*.

Not that he was unaware of these differences in the characters of the opposing armies. On the contrary he was so keenly aware of them that during his time as C-in-C Middle East he devoted himself, with characteristic energy and willingness to innovate, to trying to carry out thoroughgoing reforms in the organisation of British field formations and their tactical doctrine. The experience of the Crusader battle in 1941 convinced him of the urgent need for reform. The standard British Commonwealth infantry division, essentially an updated version of a 1918 western-front division, was cumbersome and unwieldy, its rifle-and-bayonet infantry only foot-mobile unless an outside transport lift could be provided. To give it greater flexibility Auchinleck therefore reorganised it into three self-sufficient brigade groups, each with its own integral complement of guns, engineers and other services.

The British armour presented an especial problem. Whereas the German panzer divisions, after the experience of the campaigns in Poland and the west, was a balanced force of tanks, trucked infantry and guns, the standard British armoured divisions in 1941 consisted of two tank brigades and a 'support group' of only two battalions of trucked infantry and guns. This tank-heavy structure reflected both the insistence of prewar British espousers of armoured warfare that battles would be decided by the clash of tank versus tank, and the proud cavalry traditions of the charge and of distaste for co-operation with other, more lowly, arms. In Crusader the British armour suffered heavily in the face of the German system of tanks, anti-tank guns and trucked infantry working closely together. Auchinleck therefore decided to create a better balance between tanks and other arms by introducing a new divisional structure nearer the German pattern: one armoured brigade group (itself with a trucked infantry battalion to its three tank regiments) and one 'motor' (or trucked infantry) brigade group, each group to have its own complement of field, anti-tank and anti-aircraft artillery.

Auchinleck's divisional reorganisations of early 1942 served as models for similar reforms in the United Kingdom. Unfortunately in the Western Desert itself the process of reconstruction was still incomplete when Rommel attacked in May.

Far more controversial however was Auchinleck's adoption of the 'battle group' during the crisis that followed Eighth Army's defeat in the Gazala battles, the retreat to Alamein, and the temporary extinction of the British armour as a major factor on the battlefield. He was by now convinced that the conventional infantry division was more of a liability than an asset in mobile desert warfare. What was required, as he explained in a letter to the Prime Minister in July 1942, was 'guns and armour and just enough infantry to give them and their supply organisations protection . . .'. He therefore extemporised 'battle groups' composed of divisional artillery escorted by such infantry as could be permanently motorised, sending to the rear all the remaining foot-mobile, rifle-and-bayonet infantry.

His critics accused him – and still do – of fragmenting the infantry division and dissipating its fighting power. Auchinleck remains unrepentant: 'The "battle-group controversy" is rubbish. In the circumstances existing there was no other way. Infantry and artillery in solid divisional lumps were not and could not be any match for armour until and unless they were dug in with unturnable flanks.'

And this was not to be the case until later in the Alamein fighting. In any event Rommel fought all his battles with extemporised 'groups' of all arms, and with conspicuous success. One may perhaps detect in Auchinleck's critics that tendency towards formalism which was also manifest in the rigid British respect for the hierarchy of command.

Nevertheless the battle group was never intended to be more than a temporary expedient to meet the emergency of July 1942. After the First Battle of Alamein had been won Auchinleck worked out plans for a permanent and truly radical transformation of the British armoured and infantry divisions. From Crusader through the Gazala fighting to the recent battle the decisive weakness of Eighth Army had lain in the inability of armour and infantry to co-operate intimately on the battlefield; a weakness hardly surprising since they lacked common doctrines and common training and, what was more, suffered from that mutually exclusive outlook that is characteristic of different branches of the British army. In *Panzerarmee Afrika*, by contrast, all arms trained closely together according to the same doctrine, and fought likewise. Auchinleck now proposed to solve this chronic British problem by totally abolishing distinct armoured and infantry divisions, and creating instead 'mobile' (or, as the Germans would say, 'panzer-grenadier') divisions, each a permanent and balanced combination of armour and infantry. The two arms – and the artillery – would henceforth train together and fight together under the same divisional commanders; co-operation would be built in to the divisional structure itself.

But these proposals were bitterly resisted by military conservatives and vested interests; in particular by Auchinleck's own Major-General Armoured Fighting Vehicles, Richard McCreery, who had been sent out to Cairo by the CIGS as an 'expert' in armoured warfare, but who was in fact a cavalryman without experience of commanding an armoured division in action, and whom Auchinleck relieved of his post. After Auchinleck's own dismissal in mid-August and McCreery's appointment as Chief of Staff to his successor, General Alexander, his proposals were dropped. At the Second Battle of Alamein in October armour and infantry fought not merely in separate divisions, but in separate and almost completely self-contained corps. As a consequence there was yet another major failure of co-operation between the two arms, causing the breakdown of Montgomery's original 'Master Plan' for the offensive. Only in the case of the New Zealand Division, which retained an armoured brigade group under command for the remainder of the North African campaign, did Auchinleck's scheme survive – and with conspicuous success.

Today all NATO and Warsaw-Pact armies have the kind of combined armour-infantry formations which Auchinleck vainly proposed in 1942; vindication of his originality and forward-looking vision. As a military reformer and innovator Auchinleck has not received his due, for except for Slim he stands pre-eminent in this regard among British generals of the Second World War.

Auchinleck's questing mind was united to a character of massive strength: resolution in adversity; austere professional integrity; reserve; simplicity. Yet although these qualities lend him his greatness as a man, they did not always serve him well as a theatre Commander-in-Chief, as is illustrated by his relationship with Churchill.

From the beginning of this relationship, when Auchinleck was appointed to command the Allied troops in northern Norway in the spring of 1940, to the very end, in mid-August 1942, the pattern was constant – Churchill, sanguine, impatient, in political need of victories, urging offensive action without delay; Auchinleck, realistic, mindful of the lives of his soldiers, resisting this pressure and pointing out in sober detail the forces, equipment and time of preparation needed for success. As he wrote to the Vice-Chief of the Imperial General Staff during the Norwegian campaign:

I have done my best to reduce my estimate to the greatest extent compatible with security, but it would be criminal to pretend that one can make bricks without straw. If HMG think that the commitment involved in the preservation of northern Norway is worth adding to their other commitments, I trust they will set aside *definitely* the forces required for the purpose. I feel very strongly that if they are not prepared to do this it would be better to come away now rather than risk throwing good money after bad by failing to provide the necessary forces.

... I do not wish to appear pessimistic, and I am not pessimistic, but I feel that I must say what I think without fear or favour ...

On taking up the post of C-in-C Middle East on 5 July 1941 he faced almost immediate prime-ministerial pressure to launch a desert offensive within a month or at the most two. After a brisk exchange of signals he bluntly told Churchill: 'I must repeat that to launch an offensive with the inadequate means at our disposal is not in my opinion a justifiable operation of war.' Churchill, perceiving a 'certain stiffness' in his manner, summoned him home for consultation. But to all Churchill's relentless argument and cajolery Auchinleck nevertheless returned a bleak factual analysis of the desert army's unreadiness for battle, and an unbudging refusal to commit his soldiers to a premature offensive. He carried the day, thereby preventing, as can be seen with the benefit of hindsight, a far greater disaster than the Battleaxe offensive, that earlier Churchillian exercise in the premature with which Auchinleck's predecessor, Wavell, had unfortunately complied.

In February 1942, following Rommel's riposte to the Gazala line after Crusader, the struggle of will between Auchinleck and Churchill over the question of an early offensive was resumed. Again Auchinleck refused to yield to Churchill's urging, on the grounds that to attack before 1 June would be to risk defeat in detail and possibly to endanger Egypt. He wanted time fully to complete the Eighth Army's reorganisation, reequipment and retraining. Moreover Crusader had shown that because of the qualitative inferiority of the British armour 'the Army would require a numerical superiority of at least three to two in tanks'; a statement that moved the Prime Minister to scorn. Finally, in May, the War Cabinet gave Auchinleck what was virtually an order to attack before 1 June, in order to recapture airfields needed to cover relief convoys to Malta, which was otherwise expected to fall. In the event Rommel attacked first, on 26 May. The course of the Gazala battles demonstrates that to have attacked when Churchill urged would have exposed the Eighth Army to almost certain catastrophe.

And at the beginning of August 1942, when the First Battle of Alamein had hardly died down, Churchill, this time during a personal visit to Cairo, yet once more applied relentless pressure on Auchinleck to launch a major offensive at short delay. When Auchinleck stubbornly refused to promise a date earlier than mid-September, he sealed his own fate. In the event Churchill's choice as his successor, Sir Harold Alexander, successfully held out for the October full-moon period.

But although Auchinleck's strength of character enabled him to resist Churchill's pressure, with its potentially disastrous consequences, his integrity and reserve, his simplicity, prevented him from employing those arts of diplomacy, flattery even, which were as essential to soldiers handling Churchill as to their predecessors handling Lloyd George, and which may indeed have always been essential qualifications for anyone rising high enough in command to have to work with politicians. He lacked too that glamour, sometimes meretricious, which appealed to Churchill. Instead his austere manner, his uncompromising military realism, contributed largely towards the steady waning of his credit in London.

Twice however this same strength of character saved battles in the balance. Five days after the launching of the Crusader offensive on 18 November 1941, it appeared to the Eighth Army commander, Sir Alan Cunningham, that he had decisively lost, not won, the armoured encounter south of Tobruk on which the whole plan turned, for the British tank strength seemed to be down to forty-four runners, while Rommel was estimated still to have some 120. Cunningham believed that if the remainder of the British armour were not to be destroyed and Egypt placed in danger, Eighth Army should break off the battle and fall back. Auchinleck, flying up from Cairo, found that Cunningham's commanders and staff were in favour of going on with the battle. With the professional intuition that is the mark of a great general Auchinleck saw – or felt – beyond the confusion of the battle into Rommel's own situation. 'My opinion was different from Cunningham's,' he wrote later. 'I thought Rommel was probably in as bad a shape as we were, especially with Tobruk unvanquished behind him, and I ordered the offensive to continue.' Three days later he replaced Cunningham with Lieutenant-General Neil Ritchie, hitherto his Deputy Chief of the General Staff in Cairo. As a consequence of Auchinleck's decisive intervention Tobruk was eventually relieved. Rommel was forced into retreat with losses almost as heavy as he was to sustain at Second Alamein a year later, and the British Empire won its first victory over a German army in the Second World War. Churchill himself wrote that 'By his personal action Auchinleck thus saved the battle and proved his outstanding qualities as a commander in the field.'

The First Battle of Alamein in July 1942 has already been cited as a successful example of Auchinleck's bent for deception and manoeuvre. It turned no less, however, on his qualities of character. For to rally a beaten army after a long retreat is a supreme test of leadership, and Auchinleck took over personal command at a moment when there was a real risk in his own words, of 'complete catastrophe'. Air Marshal Tedder, the Air C-in-C Middle East, wrote of his demeanour at this moment: 'I was deeply impressed by the quick and clear grasp he had secured of an extremely confused and indeed dangerous situation and by the clear-cut and decisive orders he was issuing.'

Auchinleck's sheer dogged will to win was well expressed by his order of the day on the eve of the battle: 'The enemy is stretching to his limit and thinks we are a broken army . . . He hopes to take Egypt by bluff. Show him where he gets off.'

From the very beginning of the battle Rommel himself sensed the strength of will in his new opponent, writing to his wife that Auchinleck 'seemed to view the situation with decided coolness, for he was not allowing himself to be rushed into accepting a "second best" solution by any moves we made'.

Less than three weeks later Rommel, with his great summer offensive now a failure, was writing home that 'it can't go on like it for long, otherwise the front will crack. Militarily, this is the most difficult period I've ever been through.'

The First Battle of Alamein, one of the decisive victories of the war, saving the Middle East at the moment of its gravest danger and paving the way for the offensive victories of Auchinleck's successor, therefore constitutes in all respects Auchinleck's outstanding single achievement as a commander.

Yet it was only because of the defeat of his chosen Eighth Army commander, Neil Ritchie, that Auchinleck had had to fight the desperate battle at Alamein. And Ritchie was the second such chosen army commander he had been compelled to relieve in the middle of a battle crisis, the first being Cunningham during Crusader. Was then Auchinleck, as his critics argue, a poor picker of men?

As an Indian army officer he was certainly handicapped in judging 'form' in regard to the British army's rising men; and, partly because of his pride in his own service, he brought forward Indian army officers he knew well, liked and trusted. In one case, that of Major-General T. S. Corbett, whom he appointed Chief of the General Staff in Cairo early in 1942, personal liking and trust certainly outweighed objective assessment of calibre. Since Auchinleck insisted on Corbett in preference to London's choice of Pownall, a staff officer of high reputation, the appointment did nothing to enhance his already waning credit at home.

The case of Eric Dorman-Smith, a name much on the lips of Auchinleck's critics, and whom Auchinleck appointed Deputy Chief of the General Staff in Cairo, and later took with him as Chief of Staff when he assumed direct command of Eighth Army on 25 June, is quite different. Dorman-Smith possessed a brilliant and original mind, even though he was the kind of maverick, both intellectually and personally, which the 'establishment men' of large organisations like armies often intensely dislike. A whispering campaign was to make him a scapegoat for the shortcomings of others during the Gazala battle, and to blame him for the fragmentation of the army at that time. In point of fact, having been appointed Deputy Chief of the General Staff in Cairo only on 16 June, he bore no responsibility, even indirectly, for the mishandling of that battle, while it was by his advice that Auchinleck sought to repair the fragmentation of the army, in particular by restoring the power of massed artillery fire, first under corps control and on one occasion later under army control.

Moreover, as Auchinleck himself has acknowledged, the successful outcome of First Alamein owed much to Dorman-Smith's ideas. So too did the defensive layout which formed the basis of Montgomery's Alam Halfa battle, while the timing, nature and course of the German offensive move that led to the battle were accurately predicted by Dorman-Smith in an appreciation of 27 July 1942. For all these reasons and although Dorman-Smith was by no means without personal and professional faults (a tendency to lack bread-and-butter practicality being one), he cannot fairly be adduced as proof of poor picking on Auchinleck's part.

Nor presumably can Sir Francis de Guingand, who was Auchinleck's own personal choice firstly as Director of Military Intelligence and then as Brigadier General Staff Eighth Army, and who later became Montgomery's *alter ego*.

There remain the cases of Cunningham and Ritchie.

When Auchinleck chose Cunningham as the first commander of the new Eighth Army in August 1941, Cunningham had just become famous because of his astonishingly swift and distant advances during the conquest of Italian East Africa. In Auchinleck's own words later, 'I asked for Cunningham as I was impressed by his rapid and vigorous command in Abyssinia, and his obvious leaning towards swift mobile action.' At the time Cunningham seemed an imaginative choice; certainly his personality made a favourable first impression on his new subordinates. But in fact there was little in common between the small improvised operations against feeble opposition in East Africa and the forthcoming Crusader offensive, and, as his closest colleagues came to perceive, Cunningham was never as happy and confident in the desert. Furthermore his professional anxieties were sharpened by private health problems. Auchinleck relieved him during Crusader as much because he was clearly suffering from overstrain as because of their differing judgements about the state of the battle. While it is clear enough in retrospect that Cunningham's appointment was a mistake, it is less clear that it showed misjudgement at the time it was made, given the information then available to Auchinleck.

The appointment of Neil Ritchie to replace Cunningham was on the other hand at first intended only as a temporary expedient which would avoid the disruption consequent upon promoting either of the corps commanders engaged in the battle. Later however, when the Eighth Army was back in the Gazala line after Rommel's counter-stroke, it was time to reconsider Ritchie's position. In March 1942 Auchinleck was privately warned that Ritchie lacked the calibre and experience to match Rommel, and that he did not enjoy the confidence of his two corps commanders, Gott and Norrie, both of whom were more senior and much more experienced in field command than he. Auchinleck was in a quandary: could he, without more circumstantial evidence of incapacity than this, sack a second nominee as Eighth Army commander only a few months after sacking his first, and do so when Ritchie had apparently conducted Crusader to a successful conclusion? In any case he had already turned down a suggestion from London that Ritchie should return to Cairo as Chief of the General Staff, on the grounds that Ritchie 'has gripped situation, knows what to do and has the drive to do it'.

So Ritchie stayed on. Yet both before and during the Gazala battle Auchinleck belied his apparent trust in him by trying to 'hold his hand' at long distance by feeding him detailed advice. This served further to sap Ritchie's personal authority over his corps commanders, who felt with justice that he was an independent army commander only in name. Churchill himself felt misgivings, and just before the opening of the Gazala battle urged Auchinleck to take personal command of the army. But Auchinleck refused, arguing that as theatre C-in-C it would not do for him to become immersed in the tactical details of one front. None the less he would have done well to comply with the Prime Minister's wish. For the combination of an army commander of inadequate calibre and ambiguous position, a disputatious committee of formation commanders and an 'uncle' in Cairo proved the worst of all possible worlds when it came to fighting a commander like Erwin Rommel. After an early but fleeting opportunity of inflicting a crushing defeat on the enemy had been lost, the Gazala battles gradually slipped out of the Eighth Army's hands – as indeed the Eighth Army slipped out of Ritchie's. That Auchinleck did not even then take personal command of the army until its defeat had been consummated by the headlong retreat into Egypt must be accounted a further serious error of judgment on his part.

In regard to the whole question of Ritchie and the command of the Eighth Army Auchinleck showed himself less than shrewdly realistic. In delaying so long in relieving Ritchie he also displayed a want of that unattractive but sometimes essential quality in a commander, ruthlessness. The consequences of these shortcomings were disastrous, indeed nearly catastrophic, for the Middle East campaign; and for Auchinleck himself, tragic.

On 3 August Churchill arrived in Cairo already more than half resolved that Auchinleck must go. For First Alamein had failed to expunge from the Prime Minister's mind the shattering defeats at Gazala and the humilating surrender of Tobruk. He felt – as with Wavell a year earlier – that fresh impetus was needed at the top. He had a strong political motive too for a 'purge' in Cairo, in the need to divert public unrest at home over Britain's war leadership by a bold exercise of authority; an exercise which at the same time would serve to identify convenient scapegoats. Since Britain was soon to become a junior partner in joint Anglo-American war-making, Churchill also wanted a brilliant all-British victory first in order to bolster his prestige *vis-à-vis* Roosevelt. Auchinleck, having refused to promise such a victory soon enough, was therefore dismissed on 5 August. For the sake of the desired effect of a clean sweep Corbett and Dorman-Smith were dismissed as well. This was an unquestionable injustice, especially in the case of Dorman-Smith, who, as Churchill himself acknowledged after the war, had had no share in the Gazala defeat, but only in the victory at First Alamein.

Unfortunately the circumstances of 'the Cairo Purge', especially as related in the memoirs of Churchill and others, gave rise to a persistent legend best summarised in Churchill's own words when he wrote: 'It may almost be said, "Before Alamein [Second Alamein in October 1942; Montgomery's battle] we never had a victory. After Alamein we never had a defeat".' Even more injurious to Auchinleck's reputation than this cavalier dismissal of Eighth

Army's hard-won victories under his leadership in Crusader and at First Alamein was the allegation that in August 1942 he planned to retreat into the Nile delta if Rommel attacked again. This allegation, which is wholly without historical foundation, was first made publicly in Churchill's memoirs, and later repeated in even more categorical form by Montgomery, who at the same time made no mention in his memoirs of the defences that were laid out by Auchinleck and formed the basis of his own Alam Halfa battle. Challenged by Auchinleck, Montgomery's publishers formally disavowed the allegation, while Montgomery himself in a radio interview acknowledged that Auchinleck had indeed laid the essential foundations for his own victories.

After refusing the sop of an inferior Persia-Iraq Command, Auchinleck returned to India, there to remain without employment for almost a year, until on the anniversary of Rommel's attack on Tobruk, the eve of his fifty-ninth birthday, he succeeded Wavell as Commander-in-Chief India when the latter became Viceroy. He was the first and only officer to be appointed twice to the post and the last to hold it.

For four months, until the setting-up of South-East Asia Command, he was responsible for the Burma front; once again finding himself in the old, familiar dilemma, caught between the impatience of London and the realities on the ground – in this case the limitations imposed by the long and exiguous line of communication from Bengal up into the Assam hills. Thenceforward he developed India as SEAC's base and training area. In 1947, during the run-up to the partition of British India into the dominions of India and Pakistan, there fell to him the tragic task of splitting into two, regiment by regiment, the Indian army that he had served with such devotion all his professional life. As the Supreme Commander of the new armies of India and Pakistan he was given no operational authority by jealous politicians, and hence was powerless to prevent the communal massacres that followed independence. It was a melancholy close to the career of a soldier who had always sympathised so deeply with Indian aspirations to nationhood.

FIELD-MARSHAL ERWIN ROMMEL

Charles Douglas-Home

When Rommel died at the age of fifty-two he had served in the German army for thirty-four years. Only six of those thirty-four years were actually spent on the battlefield. Most of the others were spent in peacetime or garrison soldiering. The first three of those six years saw Rommel as a young infantry subaltern, rising to the rank of captain, between 1914 and 1917. The last three occurred between May 1940 and March 1943, when as a field-marshal he left North Africa at the end of his desert campaigns.

So, however much one is dazzled by the actual spectacle of Rommel the war lord – or 'the fighting animal' as he was called by his first, and perhaps most distinguished biographer, Brigadier Desmond Young – any assessment both of Rommel the man and Rommel the complete soldier must recognise the fact that for a very large part of his life he was conditioned by the peacetime environment of provincial Germany.

The importance of Rommel in military history springs entirely from his exploits on the battlefield; from his tactical genius rather than his strategic vision. Whereas the history of German arms normally coincides with the history of the development of the German General Staff, in its reaction to the changing strategic environment of first Prussia, then the Second Reich of the Kaiser, and finally the Third Reich of Hitler, with Rommel the national strategic context is less important. He made no great strategic contribution to German military history. The other great figures of German military history – Gneisenau, Clausewitz, von Moltke, Schlieffen and so on – stand in the great central tradition of Prussian grand strategy. Rommel is there too, but entirely because of his tactical engagements, so that his historical position is as it were on the wing rather than in the centre. He was always more at home in the execution – often brilliant execution – of policy than in its formulation.

The fact that Rommel had such electrifying fighting qualities is all the more remarkable when one considers his rather dim, or at least uninspiring, family background. He was born in 1891 near Ulm, the capital of the state of Wurtemburg in the newly created Prussian empire. His father was a schoolteacher, as had been his grandfather before him. His mother was the daughter of a high state official. The family was in the mainstream of middle-class officialdom in provincial Germany. Rommel did not grow up to be a typical young Prussian militarist – his sensible Swabian background saw to that – and his first thoughts of a career before he joined the army had been to become an engineer. But the conditioning of his youth in a society stuffed with ceremonial and over-reverence for the imperial army probably helped to insulate him from the dreadful convulsions that overcame German society in the twentieth century. They actually had no bearing on Rommel's career on the battlefield – except perhaps to show, by his entire ignorance of and lack of interest in his native society, what a dedicated and singleminded soldier he was: a fighting animal, yes; a social animal, no.

Rommel joined the army in 1910 and became an officer cadet in his local infantry regiment. He went to war school for nine months and was then commissioned. While at war school he met and fell in love with a young language student called Lucie Mollin, whom he eventually married in 1916. They went through twelve years of marriage before they had their only child, Manfred. But Rommel's personal life provides an entirely unemotional backdrop to his military career. He was affectionate, punctilious, correct and emotionally always on an even keel. He reserved his emotional energies and outbursts entirely for his military life. Although he once said that the happiest period of his life was spent as director of the War Academy in the 1930s, the evidence of his own war diaries, and his letters home, suggests the opposite – that nothing excited his senses quite like the adrenalin of battle.

However had there been no period of warfare in Rommel's life, or not again after 1917, he would probably have ended his days quietly after a lifetime of dutiful regimental soldiering. He would have had the sort of unimaginative, respected, but hardly admired reputation that would probably have taken him no higher than the rank of Colonel before he reached retirement.

But all this was to change when Rommel went to war. Moreover it was not to be a youthful enthusiasm of Rommel's, which then mellowed with age and responsibility. At any age, and at any rank between subaltern and field-marshal, his passion for the battle tended to get the better of him the moment cordite filled his nostrils.

Rommel was lucky during the First World War to spend so little time in the trenches and so much time in more free-ranging infantry engagements. The historian is lucky too, since Rommel's exploits as a young infantry officer on the eastern front against the Rumanians and Italians are strikingly similar in their basic characteristics to all his actions between 1940 and 1943 as a panzer commander of ever-increasing seniority. Almost every time Rommel came under fire his instinct was to counter-attack immediately, regardless of the odds against him. His first-ever action was with three other men from his platoon against fifteen or twenty Frenchmen whom he found barring their way. He rushed at them shouting, and, though repulsed, was to repeat these tactics throughout his military career on every opportunity and at every scale of operations. 'I've found again and again in encounter actions that the day goes to the side first to plaster the opponent with fire,' he wrote as a divisional commander, who instructed his motor cyclists to drive on with their machine guns firing at anything that moved.

After going into the trenches in 1914 he was posted out of them a year later for training in mountain warfare. This took him first, in 1916, to the eastern front against Rumanian troops, then in 1917 back to France on Hilsen Ridge briefly for operations against the French, before finally returning to the Carpathians for his own personal climax at Caporetto in 1917. There, according to Desmond Young, 'he had been continuously on the move for fifty hours, had covered twelve miles as the crow flies in mountainous country, had climbed up to 7,000 feet and had captured 150 officers, 9,000 men and 81 guns' – and all this after he had received orders not to attack!

These few campaigns were all the battlefield experience Rommel was to get until he returned to warfare twenty-three years later as a major-general in charge of a panzer division. One might have expected the gulf between a twenty-six-year-old infantry captain and a forty-eight-year-old armoured general to be almost unbridgeable in one step – and it is obviously fair to say that Rommel underwent training periods during the intervening years – but it is remarkable how little Rommel's style changed in spite of the ascending scale of his commands, the enlargement of his field of operations, and the great increase in responsibilities which he acquired as he climbed the military ladder.

His tactics remained much the same, only in a continuously changing environment. His basic approach to warfare, to the battle at least if not to the grand strategy of the thing, was to see the battle as some wild dance, an adventure, in which he had to pit his imagination against unpredictable and often improbable odds.

In 1917 his tactics with an infantry company showed themselves to be based on the same inspiration as those which were later unveiled in England by Captain B. H. Liddell Hart, and adopted from his writings by the German tank specialists during the 1930s. Ironically Rommel had pioneered the way on a much lower level in the infantry, but he played no part in the eventual adoption of the principles of 'blitzkrieg,' though once he was given command of an armoured division he showed how quickly and naturally he could adapt to such a new medium.

Basically his tactics relied on deep penetration behind enemy lines accompanied by repeated and unhesitating decisions to attack the enemy's rear areas wherever and whenever possible. He always assumed that the rear areas would capitulate to a surprise offensive. When he assaulted a position he immediately set about securing the flanks of his narrow bridgehead and then pushed as many forces as possible through the gap he had created and secured, so that they broke out and expanded on each side in a form that Liddell Hart was years later to describe as the 'expanding torrent'.

After the excitement of 1917 Rommel's life between the wars was one of singular placidity and military obscurity in contrast to the raging storms which were buffeting Germany outside the cosy official life of regimental soldiering. Germany was grappling with hyperinflation, rebellion, plots, counter-plots, the rise of the stormtroopers, and then of Hitler, while Rommel quietly served out his time as a captain for twelve years, surely long enough to drive any ambitious soldier to despair.

He was, in the way he managed to insulate himself from Germany's turbulent politics, the perfect specimen to play his part in the grand plan of von Seeckt, the founder of Germany's peacetime army. The army was limited to four thousand officers and a hundred thousand men, and it was formed, not so much as a combat force, but as a standing cadre for expansion, with every officer and NCO conscious of the fact that when at some future unspecified but inevitable moment Germany needed a large army again, they would be the basis on which that large army would be built. Rommel emerged from these dim years only when he was chosen to command Hitler's bodyguard in the drive into Sudetenland. He performed the same duties during the Polish invasion of 1939.

On 15 February 1940 Rommel assumed command of the 7th Panzer Division, at the head of which he was to perform arguably the finest military exploits of his career during the swift German invasion of France in May and June 1940. Germany invaded France, Belgium and Holland on 10 May, and France capitulated on 25 June, a second victim (like Poland) of the apparently invincible new blitzkrieg tactics employed by the German panzer forces.

In fact all Germany's panzer divisions – not just Rommel's – took part in the spectacular advance through France, but his division stands out for being one to travel the farthest and for having all its battles brilliantly chronicled by Rommel himself, in his war diaries, which were eventually published in 1950. Rommel's division was also more distinctive than most in the manner of the leadership the panzers received from their commander. This was the age of modern mechanised war, with mass conscript armies, dominated by daunting logistical problems replacing the old cut and thrust of the battle; yet Rommel's leadership was in one sense a refreshing and invigorating step back into an earlier style of command.

Not for him the heavily guarded command vehicle at divisional headquarters, miles to the rear. Not for him decision-making by sticking pins in the map, or some other form of divisional tactics by remote control. He led his division from the front, regardless of personal risk: he was often in great physical danger, but led a kind of charmed life until the nearly fatal accident at the end of his career – but also, let it be said, at great tactical risk too. He jumped from one tank to another, laid his infantry guns, shouted orders live rather than through the wireless, and generally behaved much more like a junior company commander in the infantry than the leader of a formation of 12,500 men and hundreds of vehicles.

This could be mostly explained by his temperament, but perhaps also by the fact that even in May 1940 his experience of modern warfare was minimal, as was his training in leading an armoured division. Indeed when after the Polish campaign he was asked by Hitler what command he would like he made, in his own words, the 'immoderate' request for a panzer division though 'many others were more qualified' and though, as he later confided, 'it did not suit the gentlemen at the army headquarters'.

The speed and distance covered by the 7th Panzer Division across France from Luxembourg to Cherbourg earned it the title of the 'Ghost Division'. In fact the crucial moment came after only two days of the campaign at the crossing of the Meuse. After that the quality of the opposition deteriorated as the French forces disintegrated. It was only for a moment near Arras, when Rommel encountered two British tank regiments and was held up for a few hours, that his lightning advance was even temporarily stilled.

For all that, he was on the face of it encountering enormous odds. And it is much easier for the historian looking back to see how threadbare was the actual opposition to the Germans than it was for Rommel at the time, leading his division as he was from the front.

In fact the crossing of the Meuse so unbalanced the French defences – and Rommel's division was the first German division really to exploit this crossing – that they never properly regrouped. For Rommel this was just as well, because he subsequently took very little account of the danger of the French regrouping and putting in any kind of serious counter-attack. He repeatedly outdistanced his own division and had to go back down the line looking for it. Often he found himself out in front with a dozen or so tanks and some lorried infantry, while only a thin strip, and sometimes even just a disputed road, separated him from the main part of the division miles behind. There is little impression from his war diaries of any feeling of mass movement. Indeed the diaries are more reminiscent of his pamphlet *Infantry Attacks*, which describes his first war exploits, than they are of a senior commander's log.

When Rommel's division finally drove into Cherbourg the brief campaign was over after less than six weeks. In those weeks it had advanced 350 miles – in the last four days 220 miles – sustained 682 of its own men killed, 1646 wounded and 296 missing with only 42 tanks lost. It had captured 97,000 prisoners, 485 tanks and armoured cars, 4000 lorries and several hundred guns. Nowadays, particularly after some of the Middle East wars between Israel and the Arabs, and the war for Bangladesh, we have become more used to the idea of the lightning campaign based on fast-moving armour or air forces, used in the blitzkrieg role. In 1940 nobody was prepared for that kind of speed, and Rommel's daring as a divisional commander – in the risks he took, the imaginative grasp of hitherto inconceivable distances over which to operate – must be seen for the impressive achievement it was in the light of contemporary attitudes to mobile warfare.

His campaign in France was the only one he fought – six weeks – as a divisional commander. Looking back on his life it is probably the summit of his military achievement or the one of which one could say that his capacity for it was most complete, his military qualities most appropriate. Yet it was Rommel's African campaigns, rather than the French one, which are best remembered now.

The exploits of the Ghost Division may have captured the imagination of the Germans through the skilful use of the official information services and probably ensured that when Hitler was casting around for a German commander to take over the crumbling Italian position in North Africa, he was quite ready to accept Rommel. But it was not until he arrived in Africa and led his German/Italian army up and down the desert almost incessantly for twenty-five months – always against British troops – that his reputation spread outside the confines of Nazi domestic propaganda to win for him a permanent place in the history of war.

During his two years in Africa Rommel twice marched 1500 miles eastward up the desert and twice retreated 1500 miles westward down the desert with the British army performing the same movements in reverse. The key to the strategy of the desert war – but not its tactics – was logistics. The reason each army was compelled to beat such a hasty retreat each time it had completed a speedy advance was because it had overstretched its supply lines farther than the 300 or 400 miles that was the farthest from base that a desert army could operate. Rommel tried to defy these logistic imperatives in 1942 by pushing his advance to the absolute limit of his troops' physical endurance and beyond the limits of supply. He failed. The British only succeeded in 1943 when they had first made their supplies absolutely secure for each stage of their advance. They were criticised then, and still are, for the dull, incredibly painstaking way they advanced. But Montgomery was then strategically right. Rommel on the other hand wins all the bouquets for the dazzling brilliance of his tactical footwork in the desert battle, but deserves little praise for his determination to overlook these undeniable supply problems. Unlike Montgomery, he was strategically wrong. The underlying truth of the desert war, which perhaps also explains why Rommel's strategic understanding of it was so faulty, was that both sides were fundamentally reliant on sea supplies to keep them going at all. These sea communications were basically outside their control. The British eventually complied with them, and accepted the shortcomings they imposed on British strategy. Rommel did not.

Along with the fundamental issues of supply there were other factors in the desert war: the personality of Rommel and of the British commanders who opposed him; the harassment, or lack of support, which all commanders received at one time or another from London or Berlin; the morale of their troops; exhaustion, disease, pressure from allies, even the weather played an important part now and then; disparities in equipment, weapons, tanks; anti-tank guns. Yet above all the basic element of the desert was a bonus for a commander of Rommel's calibre. He has often been likened to a naval commander, which is not so surprising since he himself saw desert tactics much more as naval tactics than as land ones. This enabled him to exploit the element to the full, and to free his imagination from all the inhibitions and conventions that seemed to afflict the British generalship. Whatever success or failure attended Rommel's adventures, they always bore the hall-mark of a free-thinking and imaginative tactical genius at work.

If Rommel achieved many tactical triumphs in the desert, however, he was in the end overwhelmed by strategic tragedy. It is true he was nearly at the gates of Cairo before he was brought to a halt in July 1942; it is true that he was thinking in terms of pushing on across the Nile into Asia Minor eventually to link up with the southward thrust of the German armies, which by then had penetrated deep into the Caucasus; and that the British were themselves apprehensive of these possibilities. But the underlying strategic tragedy of Rommel's war was that neither Hitler nor the German General Staff ever entertained the same kind of strategic objectives as Rommel did, neither initially when he was sent to Africa, nor subsequently when his own exploits had created conditions where it was possible, and conceivable, to make deci-sive changes in the strategic emphasis (or lack of it) with which the Germans looked at the whole African operation.

When Rommel was summoned to Berlin to be appointed to the African command he was told that on account of the Italians' critical situation in Africa a German Africa corps was to be formed with two German divisions. But by then all the German energies and interest were almost totally caught up in the immense plan to invade Russia – Operation Barbarossa as it was called. Even before Rommel was called to Berlin, Halder, the Army Chief of Staff, was noting in his diary: 'The war in Africa need not bother us very much. Even now the military situation is better than a year ago, but we must not risk the internal collapse of Italy. Italy must be saved from that. It will be necessary to send some help.' This note really provides the key to the view of the African campaign held in Berlin. Rommel and his two German divisions were sent out to Africa entirely as a defensive operation to save the Italian African empire from collapsing and bringing down Mussolini's regime within Italy itself. All the rest of the German energies were then concentrated on the plan to send a force nearly two hundred times larger than Rommel's to achieve the invasion and defeat of Russia.

As it turned out Rommel's genius on the battlefield, and his distance from Berlin – in the almost unique position of having an independent command – enabled him so to transform the situation he found in Africa and to create there a whole new range of possibilities for German strategy, that he assumed that his leaders in Berlin would also revise their original evaluation of the relative unimportance of his mission. They never did.

The essence of Rommel's approach to desert warfare can find its origins in an earlier tradition of the German army. The army of his youth had been reared in the belief that the Prussian victories of 1866 and 1870 had been won by initiatives of the commanders on the spot, not those at supreme head-quarters. Although there were attempts to restore a tighter strategic control – such as in 1914 – there remained a high degree of independence among divisional commanders. Rommel probably always retained the battlefield mentality of a divisional commander, even when he achieved higher rank. So his command in the desert, being an independent one and relative to the other German operations being so very small scale, probably made it easier for him to behave as though he really was still just in charge of a division. Tactically, from the very start of his fighting experience, he had come naturally to the idea of manoeuvring to exploit every fleeting opportunity that presented itself on the battlefield – the strategy of expedients as it was called at the German war schools.

There was no better place or way to exercise his often extravagant tactical imagination than with a small independent command, fighting in a desert, in a campaign that appeared not to have any central strategical relevance to Germany's main war effort.

If one looks at those twenty-six months of desert campaigning two things stand out, apart from the enormous distances covered by both sides. The first is how Rommel initiated operations at each and every moment that he could. The second is how entirely self-contained the war was in the sense that no feature that was captured, destroyed, attacked or defended had any real wider significance for the war as a whole – though the extremities of the theatre obviously held the key to possession of North Africa as a whole – and how therefore the battle, wherever it was, with whatever British commanders, and whatever strategic background such as the Greek or Russian campaigns, or the bombing of Malta, was much more akin to a boxing match than a classic struggle between nations at war. It was self-contained, almost antiseptic in its insulation from the real world, from civilian populations, from cities, from politics, from guerrillas or local resistance, from refugees, even prisoners of war were somehow often taken and untaken in the same twenty-four hours.

For a field commander such as Rommel this was the perfect element. The moment he arrived he launched an attack, which started more as a reconnaissance, pushed it as far as his resources would go, and until the British weaknesses had been fully exploited, then waited for reinforcements to go on. When, after six months' stalemate in the middle of this 'sand-table', he was routed by Auchinleck and had to retreat right back to where he started, he lost absolutely no time in setting off on the offensive again, within days of his last beleaguered garrison surrendering to the British in a position by then 500 miles behind the British front line. In the words of Auchinleck's despatch, 'The improbable occurred and Rommel attacked.' In a lightning offensive lasting only two weeks he drove greatly superior British forces back out of the bulge of Cyrenaica to the Gazala line west of Tobruk. After a pause of three and a half months he struck again. Once more he totally defeated greatly superior forces in the fierce battles round Tobruk which lasted without a pause for four weeks and then, with ever dwindling resources but never dwindling will and ingenuity, tumbled them back in ten days to within 60 miles of the Nile.

There is a certain grace about his tactics in those desert battles. He is like a cross between a dancer and a welterweight boxer. For instance in the battle that the British code-named Battleaxe (May 1941), which ended in a strategic stalemate but in a tactical victory for Rommel, he achieved that victory – possession of the field – by, as he put it, 'shifting his weight' at the crucial moment, when he lifted his armoured reserve and brought it down on one side of the battle to change the whole centre of gravity of the encounter.

Again in the thick of the battle for the Gazala boxes in June 1942, when he defeated Ritchie and which led straight on to his capture of Tobruk, he dominated the battle in spite of being equipped with fewer forces and inferior tanks. Moreover he did this entirely positionally, by personally taking his main attack round the screen of British defences and staying there until he willed the battle to conform to the shape he wanted it to be.

Perhaps the most spectacular *coup de théâtre* of all his desert exploits is that which has come to be known as the 'dash to the wire', during the Crusader battle of November 1941. This battle he lost to Auchinleck, but not before he had attempted to snatch a striking victory out of a tactical situation that was basically against him.

A position was reached after some days' fighting, which is best described by Auchinleck in his official despatch,

> It looked as if the enemy was hard pressed and stretched to the limit, and this was borne out by his behaviour at this period of the battle; he was thrusting here and there and everywhere in what seemed to be a desperate effort to throw us off our balance, create chaos in our ranks, and so pave the way for regaining the initiative. The enemy it is true had temporarily succeeded in seizing the local tactical initiative, but the strategical initiative remained with us: we were attacking, he was defending. This general initiative it was at all costs essential to retain.

But how nearly Rommel, in his next manoeuvre, created just that chaos and loss of balance which Auchinleck was at such pains to prevent. He put himself at the head of the *Afrika Korps*, set himself a journey of nearly 100 miles to get round behind the main British positions and drove off into the desert as though in command of a battle fleet. In fact the whole plan went wrong at his end: the Germans did not follow in strength behind him, he got lost entirely on his own behind the British lines, and eventually his own staff, well to the rear, had to intervene and give their own orders to the panzer divisions without waiting for Rommel to reappear from his wild-goose chase.

On the other side of the line however his behaviour had a momentous effect – though not for very long. Near panic reigned in the rear echelons of the British divisions, and General Cunningham, the British Commander in Chief, was himself caught up in it, so much so that his already wavering confidence received a fatal blow and he was relieved of his command by Auchinleck within the next two days. Rommel's dash to the wire has remained the subject of keen but unresolved military controversy. Liddell Hart maintained that he was right to try the deep counter-thrust as the one move that offered a good chance of tilting the scales decisively in his favour – Rommel the gambler. Since the operation failed it is easier to conclude that he should not have tried it, that it was doomed anyway, or, though it amply demonstrated Rommel's superb capacity for imaginative and unusual tactical improvisation, that it revealed his deplorable strategic sense as well.

The two saddest aspects of Rommel's later career as a field-marshal at war were the deplorable relations he maintained with his fellow senior officers, and the overwhelming pessimism that afflicted him, and must have affected his judgement, after he was brought to a halt at the El Alamein line in July 1942.

Once he acquired an independent command he appeared to find it impossible to carry on amicable business with any other senior officer, either Italian or German. He had continuous, and acrimonious, disputes with the General Staff in Berlin, with Kesselring, the *Luftwaffe* commander in North Africa and his official German superior, with the Italian General Staff – indeed with everybody except Hitler, and in the end he even fell out with Hitler. This difficulty was naturally aggravated by the strategic cross-purposes between Rommel and Berlin, which I have already mentioned, but there were other factors too. One was the fact that Rommel had risen up through the German army without joining the General Staff, so that he had remained an outsider to this closed, self-perpetuating, most elite world. The other was the dogmatism and virulence with which he came to hold his strategic views, and the apparently impregnable determination to refuse to see the other point of view where German grand strategy was concerned.

Rommel's pessimism also found its origins in this basic dogmatism, coupled with his superb but perhaps too precise powers of analysis. When he was attacking, his superior analytical powers, plus his possession of the tactical initiative, ensured that most of his actions fitted in well with his own analysis of the situation. Things were not so easy when he was defending. His analysis of the situation remained as good, but since he no longer possessed the initiative, or therefore the capacity to impose his own framework on the situation, he tended to accept too easily the logical outcome of this loss of initiative. All the time during his long retreat across North Africa between November 1942 and March 1943 he performed some brilliant withdrawals, but he had lost that zest for real improvisation from the moment in about August 1942 when he realised he was not going to be able to rely on the kind of supplies he believed to be necessary to maintain his position. Only once thereafter – at the Kasserine Pass in February 1943 – when he turned on the Anglo-American armies which were about to squeeze his line of retreat to the west – with

Montgomery's Eighth Army pursuing him from the east – did he show anything like the energy and initiative that characterised his earlier desert battles in a more hopeful and offensive period.

Likewise, when he assumed command of German forces to meet the Allied invasion of Normandy in June 1944 the same pessimism overcame him, this time coloured by his conviction that with such inferiority in the air, defeat was only a matter of time. Again his analytical powers based on his experience in the desert had outstripped the reality of the situation in Normandy.

As he progressed up the military ladder one gets the impression that each accession of greater responsibility, the control of more men, the wider theatre of command, was at the expense of the brilliant but uncomplicated improviser of 1940 – the lost leader of the Ghost Division. His disagreements with other field-marshals, and his own strategic arguments, gradually seemed to preoccupy him more and more, with less and less success. The war diaries become replete with recriminations, less exhilarating, more self-pitying. If the actual high point of his career was to be promoted field-marshal at the age of fifty, as a reward for the capture of Tobruk, by then already he was probably beyond his true level. His death in October 1944 was at the hands of Hitler for a supposed, but hardly active, association with the plot, which misfired on 20 July 1944, to assassinate the Führer. In fact by then his active military career was probably already at an end, for in July, after a lifetime of lucky escapes, he was eventually seriously wounded when a British fighter dive-bombed his staff car on a small road in Normandy. He survived, but only just, ironically to die a few months later by order of the Führer.

He died on 14 October 1944, forced by Hitler to take a suicide pill, or face a trial for treason. He chose the former, in exchange for his family's safety.

Rommel's main impact on the war arose perhaps not so much from the results of his generalship, as from the manner of it. More than any previous war the Second World War epitomised the idea of total war between nations and societies that had mobilised all their resources, not just the military ones; a war played out by decision-makers crouched in the war councils and cabinet rooms of opposing capitals. Rommel did not conform to this pattern. With him the centre of decision was wherever *he* was. He restored to generalship the idea of leadership in battle from the front, regardless of the increased mechanisation or scale of operations. He may thus have epitomised the triumph of the tactician over the strategist, but he none the less brought to the art of the battle a luminous clarity and a tactical imagination that had the quality of genius, even without the strategic judgement to go with it. The desert actually brought out this genius to its best and enabled Rommel to command from the front a force that was, in theory, already too much bigger than a division to make this feasible. However the additional inhibitions of higher command, heavier responsibility, diplomacy and politics seemed eventually to dull his genius. Perhaps it was at the genuine divisional level that Rommel was really at his best.

MARSHAL IVAN KONIEV

John Erickson

Throughout the revolutionary upheavals of 1917–18 in a new-found Soviet Russia, with the old Imperial Army crumbling fast and the new Workers-Peasants Red Army neither fully formed nor manned, thousands of men turned soldier-politician in the guise of the 'military commissars' who functioned first under the Provisional Government and continued to exist under the Bolshevik regime. Some were more soldier than political agent, many were merely flung forward in the welter of soldiers' committees and in the 'democratisation' of the old army, not a few were indeed steeped in the politics and practices of radical activity and could be counted soldiers only by enforced conscription, but all owed their origin to the *commissaires* of the French revolutionary armies of 1792–3, the agents of a revolutionary government who supervised the arming of the *sans-culottes*, instilled revolutionary will, guarded revolutionary probity and whipped up that fervour to fight and to win.

Much of this was now enacted anew in the first perilous days of the Soviet Republic as the 'toiling masses' were summoned to defend the gains of the revolution as their new classless army formed up and in which the military commissar exhorted, encouraged and even educated, at the same time not merely executing but personifying the will of the Party (even if at the outset not all were Bolsheviks, being simply 'tried and tested revolutionaries'). It was left to Trotsky to weld the *voenkom*, the military commissar, into the Red Army and the Soviet military machine: the commissar, who eventually proved to be no mere transitory feature of the military scene, was used to control and to coerce, to guard 'revolutionary vigilance', to show a shining example of revolutionary will (often by heroic self-sacrifice) and to supervise the Red Army's officer corps. Thus at an early stage operational command and political control came into collision, putting the commissar at times beyond the military pale or involving him in an uneasy 'commander-commissar' relationship. It was in this capacity, as a *voenkom* and therefore not wholly on the right side of the military blanket, that Ivan Stepanovich Koniev began his service with the Soviet Republic: yet it was also Koniev – alone of all the former political functionaries transferred to the 'command line' – who attained high military rank as a fighting soldier. Here lies the initial interest, the gathering importance and striking singularity of Koniev's career.

Koniev's 'official biography' begins effectively only in 1918, the year in which he joined the Communist Party: his 'military biography' is rather more fulsome, but several puzzles (not to say mysteries) attend his early political loyalties and affiliations.* He was born into a poor peasant family on 28 December 1897 in the village of Lodeino (in north-east Russia, in the region between Vologda and Vyatka in what is now Kirov *oblast*); finishing the local school at the age of twelve, the young Koniev worked as a woodcutter in the Archangel and Vologda province until the spring of 1916 when he was conscripted into the Imperial Army. Passing his training course, he went to the 2nd Independent Artillery Division as an NCO (*unter-ofitser*) on the south-western front: almost at the same time the man destined to become his great rival – G. K. Zhukov – was mustering with the Imperial cavalry on this same front.

Demobilised in 1917 Koniev returned home in November and with other ex-soldiers worked to set up local soviets in the Nikolsk district of Vologda province. According to his personal military file Koniev joined the Communist Party at the beginning of 1918 and at the first district Congress of Soviets was elected to the district executive committee (*ispolkom*), the local governing body that shortly named him military commissar to a 'fighting detachment' of workers and peasants mobilised to put down the 'counter-revolutionary' revolt of the richer peasantry, the *kulaks*. Fighting in this miniature but savage civil war deep in the rear did not satisfy Koniev and he requested to be sent to the main battlefront, even appealing directly to M. V. Frunze, the military commissar of the Yaroslavl Military District. Eventually in 1919 he was sent together with his 'fighting detachment' to the eastern front, taking up a posting as military commissar to Armoured Train No. 102, used for raiding the enemy rear in the Siberian and Trans-Baikal operations. Here *voenkom* Koniev found himself in the thick of the fighting and was directly responsible for maintaining 'revolutionary discipline', largely by personal example.

His energy and ability took him quickly from brigade to divisional commissar: in February 1921 he returned to European Russia as a delegate to the Tenth Party Congress, only to have a rifle thrust into his hands and like many other delegates storm over the ice of the Neva to suppress the rebellion of his fellow Bolsheviks at Kronstadt. With this bloody affair behind him he moved back to the Soviet Far East as commissar to the staff of the 'National-Revolutionary Army' of the Far Eastern Republic, then in the throes of

---

* In his essay on Koniev, Boris Nikolaevsky (*Power and the Soviet Elite*, London 1966, p. 243) suggests that Koniev was originally associated with the SRs (Social-Revolutionary Party) and even the 'Left-SRs', only joining the Bolsheviks in August 1918. Though the 'official biography' is silent on this point, Koniev's 'military file' flatly contradicts this. There are also other errors in Nikolaevsky's data on Koniev's *military* career.

ejecting the Japanese 'intervention'. Koniev stayed on in the east from 1922 to 1924 as military commissar to the 17th Coastal Provinces Rifle Corps.

At this juncture Koniev's career changed decisively as he transferred to the command staff. To the postwar strain in the Red Army was added political upheaval as Trotsky struggled against Stalin's machinations to retain control of the Soviet military machine, all inevitably dragging the political workers into this deadly feud. For motives that are not quite explained – whether out of a genuine hankering for command and the military life or from sheer calculation over the unhappy lot of the military commissar – Koniev seized on the opportunity provided by War Commissar Frunze's call for political personnel to transfer to the *komsostav*, the regular officer corps. In 1926–7 as an apprentice *komandir* Koniev attended the 'professional improvement courses' for senior command staff, qualifying in July 1927 and thereafter being given command of a rifle regiment (the 50th attached to 17th Rifle Corps); his service record in 1928 described him as 'resourceful, energetic and decisive . . .' After five years in command of a regiment Koniev applied for admission to the Frunze Academy and duly embarked on further studies in 1932. Two years later, having made a considerable impression as a student whom his superiors recommended as being fit for a corps command, he graduated and took over a division, rising to corps commander in September 1937.

Komkor (Corps Commander) Koniev escaped Stalin's military purge, possibly because he was far away from Moscow, fighting in Outer Mongolia as commander of a special Soviet task force covering the Mongolian frontiers against Japanese incursion; the hardships of the Gobi desert were evidently considerable but infinitely preferable to the Lyubanka prison or an NKVD bullet in the back of the head. None the less the purge did reach into the Soviet Far East, pulling down Marshal Blyukher and smashing into the 'Special Red Banner Far Eastern Army' (*ODVA*) which was split into several smaller commands. In September 1938, amidst this military mayhem, Koniev was given command of the Second Independent Red Banner Far Eastern Army and it was from this position that he found himself involved in operations to fend off the Japanese incursion into Outer Mongolia in the spring of 1939.

The first Soviet operations were not markedly successful and in June 1939 another corps commander, Georgii Zhukov, was brought in to remedy this deteriorating situation. (See the chapter on Marshal Zhukov.) Neither Koniev nor Shtern (also a replacement commander in the Far East) emerged with reputations much enhanced and Zhukov's stunning victory over the Japanese scarcely assuaged Koniev's chagrin: henceforth the rivalry between Zhukov and Koniev became an established fact, one singularly useful to Stalin in the kind of manipulation of foibles and weaknesses in which he specialised. In June 1940 Koniev was promoted to lieutenant-general (this on the occasion of the re-introduction of formal military rank for senior officers) and was ensconced as GOC Trans-Baikal Military District, an appointment he exchanged suddenly in January 1941 for command of the North-Caucasus Military District, a sign that war was encroaching inexorably upon the Soviet Union and that the threat now emanated from Germany in the west rather than Japan in the east. As senior commanders were shifted into the European theatre, so the armies and armour of the eastern regions were steadily shunted to the west, among them formations from Koniev's former command in the Trans-Baikal.

So far Koniev had shown himself to be a good and competent commander, well versed in training his men and organising his command, tough (if hot-tempered) and responsible, all of which qualities he needed in his first major operational assignment, one far eclipsing the skirmishes of the civil war – fighting with the Soviet Nineteenth Army in the savage attrition of the 'Smolensk cauldron' in July 1941. Even now the *Wehrmacht* had inflicted dreadful injury on the Red Army in the westerly frontier battles and the entire Soviet western front sagged dangerously. Koniev took over Nineteenth Army on the left flank, one of the reserve armies desperately forming up to fend off Army Group Centre. Already on 9 July a critical situation had developed in the Vitebsk area as panzer units crashed into the Soviet lines, threatening the flank and rear of the main body of Soviet forces on the western front. Koniev at once issued orders to Nineteenth Army (still concentrating east of Vitebsk) to hold the town and to dig in; and without waiting for all his divisions to assemble, he took two of them plus elements of Twentieth Army (on his right flank) and attacked on 10 July, momentarily breaking up the German groups which had penetrated deep into the Soviet defences. Lacking artillery support, Koniev's men went into the assault in scattered groups, often without sufficient ammunition to fight for very long and quite unable to exploit any success. Nevertheless these combat groups 'didn't do badly' (as Koniev put it) and Nineteenth Army's counter-thrust held the Germans at Rudnya and Surazh, checking Third Panzer on the Vitebsk axis. In those grim days, when so many faltered and failed, that was an undoubted achievement.

None of this went unnoticed. At a time when senior Soviet officers, including the Western Front commander Pavlov and his staff officers, were dragged before field courts-martial or shot out of hand for incompetence, Koniev's fortunes prospered. On 11 September 1941 he was promoted to colonel-general and on the following day the *Stavka* (GHQ) appointed him to his first wartime front command, the Western, which had borne the brunt of the initial German attack and which now had to bar the way to the German drive on Moscow as Operation Typhoon developed with thunderbolt speed.

Within little more than a month Koniev's Western Front command, disposing of six rifle armies and some 480 tanks (but only 45 of them modern KVs or T-34s), had been ripped apart by the German thrust along the Moscow axis. Towards the end of September the *Stavka* did begin to react to signs of a major German offensive, but all too sluggishly. Koniev ordered a transition from a 'mobile defence' to a 'stubborn defence', simultaneously deploying his reserves to the north of the Smolensk–Moscow highway. Army Group Centre however swept on and over these Soviet defences and by 2 October no less than twelve German divisions had smashed the junction of Thirtieth and Nineteenth Armies, opening a 20-mile gap which led to Vyazma, while Fourth Panzer Group smashed Budenny's Reserve Front securing the junction between the Western and Bryansk Fronts.

Budenny's collapse left Koniev's flank exposed and by 4 October five of his armies were in dire straits. Belatedly Stalin and the *Stavka* subordinated two armies of the Reserve Front to Koniev and authorised him to fall back on the Rzhev–Vyazma line, but time had already run out. German units effected a massive encirclement at Bryansk-Vyazma, the Western Front was severely mauled and the *Stavka* now had to rush men to fill out the Mozhaisk line in a desperate attempt to cover the approaches to Moscow. On 10 October General Zhukov arrived at Western Front HQ, only to find one of Stalin's special investigation commissions already at work: when he telephoned Stalin that same morning (10 October), Zhukov learned that he had been appointed the new commander of the Western Front, thus displacing Koniev.

If Koniev hoped to placate Stalin in his own report, also dated 10 October, he failed at this time. Stalin at first proposed to replace the entire Western Front command, though Zhukov suggested the retention of Koniev as deputy front commander. Not that Zhukov took a charitable view of the performance of the Western, Bryansk and Reserve Front commands: he found them guilty of 'serious miscalculation', of squandering the time available to prepare for a German attack, of failing to use air and artillery strikes to break up German preparations and of failing to pull out five armies in time, once encirclement threatened. As Western Front commander, Koniev denied these charges vigorously: since the Germans held the strategic initiative along the entire length of the front then, the Soviet command was at a serious disadvantage, German superiority in the air meant only 'withering bombing of our own troops', superior German mobility could not be countered by Soviet troops who were bereft of adequate anti-tank and anti-aircraft defences, and the Western Front scarcely disposed of enough weapons and ammunition. In the last resort, while the German breakthrough to the north could have been checked by some Soviet regrouping, once German units reached Spas-Demyansk the rear of the Soviet armies was gravely threatened and Budenny's Reserve Front could do nothing to shore up this critical situation.

Koniev did continue as Zhukov's deputy, but only for a week. He moved to the right flank, where German forces took Kalinin on 14 October; three days later the *Stavka* set up an independent Kalinin Front with three armies (Twenty-Second, Twenty-Ninth and Thirty-First) plus Vatutin's 'operational group' and put Koniev in command. Clearly Stalin had not lost all confidence in him, nor was there any real reason that he should: and in his own eccentric way, on occasions when Stalin thought that the *Stavka* was to blame (and it was certainly derelict in its slow-witted, bumbling appraisal of and response to this German offensive), then he was inclined to be lenient with the commander in the field. Nor did Zhukov recommend outright dismissal. In fact Koniev's wartime career as a front commander really begins with his appointment to the Kalinin Front and it was here, first in the desperate stages of the defensive battle for Moscow, that he was able to show his paces and develop his own special style of operations.

For the following twenty months, from October 1941 to June 1943, Koniev fought in this theatre to the north and west of Moscow, in the great triangulation of the Kalinin, Western and North-Western Fronts. In late October 1941 the German Ninth Army had succeeded in capturing Kalinin itself, but in the later stages of the defensive battle north-west of Moscow Koniev managed to hold off this German assault on a line running from Selizharovo to the Volga reservoir: the effect was to pinion Ninth Army and prevent it joining with its full strength in the close-range battle to shatter the defences of the Soviet capital.

Koniev played a very effective part in the defensive battle – the consequences of his taking over firm control of the Kalinin Front had been to reduce Zhukov's frontage considerably, thus relieving the nearly impossible strain on the Western Front – and at the beginning of December 1941 it was inevitable that he found himself heavily involved in the coming Soviet counter-offensive. At the very beginning of the month Lieutenant-General Vasilevskii (Deputy Chief of the General Staff) pointed out to Koniev that his front occupied a 'favourable operational situation', adding, 'collect literally everything you can lay your hands on to strike at the enemy'. Vasilevskii's advice was followed in a matter of hours by a *Stavka* directive stipulating that Koniev assemble a 'shock group' of five to six divisions to assist in an operation to break into the rear of German forces at Klin. Having shown himself to be staunch in defence, Koniev presently proved that he could ram his armies forward in attack: there was always a certain neatness, a noticeable precision in his methods and this was already showing at the end of 1941. Klin fell on 15 December after Zhukov's assault was assisted by Koniev: the recapture of Kalinin the next day meant that Koniev could now think of striking to the south-west and accordingly Thirtieth Army (handed over to him from Zhukov's Western Front) was earmarked for a deep thrust into the rear of Ninth Army.

In late December Stalin's decision to activate the flanks fully brought the Kalinin Front an independent strategic role: the destruction of Ninth Army had been planned originally as a joint Western–Kalinin Front operation, but with Thirtieth Army assigned to him Koniev found that this task devolved on his front alone. Koniev's plan called for the main attack to be launched against Rzhev from the north and north-east, thereby encircling Ninth Army and cutting its escape routes to the west and south-west. He also had a brand-new army, Maslennikov's Thirty-Ninth, to assist in these plans:

in all Koniev disposed of thirty rifle divisions, five cavalry divisions and two tank brigades (one-third of all Soviet forces operating on the western axis).

Rzhev however proved to be a formidable breakwater against which the Soviet offensive dashed in vain. Though assigned two 'shock armies' to swell his front, Koniev also found his objectives vastly inflated by Stalin, who wanted the capture of both Rzhev and Smolensk. Like other front commanders, Koniev was the victim of Stalin's policy in the first Soviet strategic counter-offensive of pumping out diminishing manpower across ever expanding circles (and switching armies from one front to another scarcely compensated for losses, fatigue and steadily growing German resistance and recovery).

Late in January Panzer General Model with Ninth Army succeeded in turning the Rzhev 'dagger' against Koniev and split the Kalinin Front in two: disturbed yet determined to finish off Army Group Centre, Stalin on 1 February 1942 put Zhukov in command of the western theatre and instructed him to 'co-ordinate' the Western and Kalinin Fronts. Koniev received seven fresh rifle divisions and one Guards rifle corps, with orders to eliminate the Rzhev 'pocket', though already the would-be Soviet encirclers were themselves in semi-encirclement: between Sychevka and the Volga bend Model's Ninth Army and Koniev's Twenty-Ninth and Thirty-Ninth armies grappled desperately, but this northerly German bastion could not be reduced. In the event Zhukov did not reach Vyazma and Koniev could not take Rzhev: both suffered from Stalin's policy of 'spattering' armies across a vast front and Zhukov's plea in the late spring for one more properly concentrated effort against Rzhev failed to meet with 'the boss's' approval.

For the remainder of 1942 the Rzhev bone remained stuck in Koniev's throat. In August 1942 when Zhukov was made deputy to the Supreme Commander (Stalin) and sent to Stalingrad, Koniev took over the Western Front, conducting the hard, slogging operations to pin down Army Group Centre, assaulting Rzhev and, most important, preventing any German reinforcement of Stalingrad from the centre. These thankless, rain-drenched operations had an undoubted effect: in September 1942 Colonel-General Halder recorded in his *Kriegstagebuch*, 'Sehr gespannte Lage bei Rshev' ('very strained situation near Rshev'), with Ninth Army severely tested. Late in November the *Stavka* discussed further operations against the Rzhev salient and Stalin sent Zhukov northwards from Stalingrad to look into the situation on the Western–Kalinin Fronts at first hand: on 8 December a formal *Stavka* directive instructed Koniev to eliminate the salient not later than the third week of that month (December). But again the Soviet attack faltered, whereupon Zhukov was rushed back to Koniev's HQ to determine the reasons for this failure. Zhukov concluded that there was no point in repeating the operation as the Germans had already reinforced the salient. As for the Soviet mechanised corps from the Kalinin Front trapped by the Germans, Zhukov set about rescuing it by calling up a rifle corps from the *Stavka* reserve. One compensation however was that substantial German forces had been pinned on this sector, plus reinforcements rushed up to hold off Koniev, so that these divisions could not be used in any attempt to relieve their fellows encircled at Stalingrad.

None the less Koniev had been forced to suffer Zhukov's intervention once again: he continued to direct the Western Front, but suddenly in March 1943 he was moved (at Zhukov's suggestion) to command of the North-Western Front. On 16 March Stalin had evidently decided to replace Koniev by Sokolovskii: Zhukov pointed out that in view of the gravity of the situation in the Kharkov area Marshal Timoshenko (then commanding the North-Western Front) should go south and Koniev could take over from him. (Twenty-four years later Koniev returned this favour – if it was a favour – with a bitter attack on Zhukov's failure to eliminate German forces at Demyansk when he was 'co-ordinating' North-Western Front operations early in 1943).

Koniev did not stay long in the north-west: in fact he was on the verge of leaving it forever and beginning a whole new phase in his career. So far he had commanded infantry armies and fronts made up largely of infantry formations, with only limited mobile forces. In the early summer of 1943, when he was appointed to command the Steppe Front – deployed as strategic reserve for the Kursk salient and as such the greatest reserve ever gathered by the Red Army – Koniev at last found powerful armoured forces to hand. His new front disposed of four rifle armies, one tank army – Rotmistrov's Fifth – plus six mobile corps (two tank and one mechanised) as its own reserve; Fifth Air Army also supported the front. With this appointment Koniev had also thrust his way into the front rank of Soviet commanders – Zhukov, Vasilevskii, Rokossovskii and Vatutin, an impressive concentration of talent and experience mobilised for this massive battle. All the senior Soviet commanders at Kursk were thoroughly tested men and it was thus that Stalin must have approved Koniev for this key command.

For a week in early July, from the fourth to the eleventh, the Soviet Central and Voronezh Fronts (holding the northern and southern faces of the salient) fought grinding defensive battles: the Central Front smashed down the German attack, but to the south a critical situation developed towards 11 July, when Zhukov and Vasilevskii ordered the Steppe Front into action, bringing Fifth Tank Army and Fifth Guards Army up to the Prokhorovka area. Rotmistrov's tanks dealt Fourth Panzer a pulverising blow and, as on the northern face of the salient, the German attack was finally deflected. Now it was time for the Soviet fronts to roll forward in a massive counter-offensive, which opened soon afterwards on 23 July, but in order to mount a more powerful blow across a broader front the main blow was delayed to facilitate regrouping.

On 3 August the Steppe and Voronezh Fronts operating in conjunction struck out for Belgorod, taking the German defence completely by surprise: Koniev overran Belgorod in two days and drove on to Kharkov, surrounding the city by 17 August. On the evening of 22 August Koniev, aware that the encircled German garrison was attempting to make its escape, decided on a final night assault and by 11 am on the morning of 23 August this all-important Soviet city was cleared. Five days later Koniev received his reward in the shape of promotion to full general of the army.

Towards the close of 1943 Koniev with his 2nd Ukrainian Front (the revised designation for the Steppe Front) scored a notable success in the southern theatre by opening up an important new passage of the river Dnieper. Having steadily extended his bridgehead opposite Kremenchug, he launched a series of well-organised, short but powerful blows that cut into the deep German defences covering Zhamenka and also loosed Rotmistrov's tanks (Fifth Guards Tank Army) along the Kirovograd axis. Zhamenka fell on 10 December and a month later, on 5 January 1944 – without warning, in that style which was increasingly becoming Koniev's operational trademark – his tanks and infantry attacked Kirovograd itself under cover of a fifty-minute barrage and with the infantry clearing the way for Rotmistrov's tanks, which smashed their way into the town from three directions. Koniev ordered a final night assault on 7 January and then completed the destruction of five German divisions, two of them armoured.

The whole strategic situation in the southern operational zone now began to tilt even more speedily in the Red Army's favour, but it remained to eliminate the German salient reaching from Zvenigorodka in the north to the Dnieper at Kanev, which threatened the flanks of Vatutin's 1st Ukrainian and Koniev's 2nd Ukrainian Front and was presently held by twelve German divisions of First Panzer and Eighth Army. On 26 January Koniev attacked from the east, breaking through the German defences to a depth of 17 miles that same day: two days later Vatutin attacked from the north-west and the two Soviet fronts linked up at Zvenigorodka, trapping ten German divisions in the area of Korsun-Shevchenkovskii. This 'miniature Stalingrad' ended after the sixteen-day battle to liquidate the encircled Germans: the German capitulation brought Koniev Stalin's personal thanks* and his marshal's star on 20 February 1944.

On 5 March 1944 Koniev launched his famous 'mud offensive' on a front running from Zvenigorodka-Uman and aimed at General Hube's First Panzer Army. Amidst the glutinous, all-encompassing seas of mud that accompanied the spring thaw, Koniev attacked south-west of Zvenigorodka, but suddenly swung Rotmistrov's T-34 tanks, which alone could sail these inland oceans of

* I talked at length with Marshal Koniev about his relationship with Stalin: the Marshal recounted details of the nightly reporting to Stalin by radio telephone, with its formality and informality, pointing out that he, as a front commander, could introduce proposals and suggestions useful for him. Marshal Koniev was particularly (and rightly) proud of his meticulous planning, his briefings with his arms commanders and this exactitude enabled him to respond precisely to Stalin. This stood him in good stead in the Berlin operation in April 1945 and he went into great detail over the planning of his armoured thrusts.

Ukrainian mud, northwards to Uman. This huge and vital German base fell on 10 March, with only little resistance being offered, leaving the remnants of Hube's army with its six panzer divisions and elements of Eighth Army completely powerless in the face of Koniev's drive to the southern Bug. Brushing aside German rearguards, Koniev's units reached the river on 12 March, crossed in strength two days later and with Rotmistrov's tanks took the key rail junction of Vapniarka on 15 March, putting them only 30 miles from the Dniester; other mobile columns drove on Vinnitsa and Zhmerinka.

Koniev's successful thrust to the Dniester at once affected Zhukov's plans for 1st Ukrainian Front: Zhukov also set his sights on the Dniester and Chernovtsy, aiming to split the German forces in the south and isolate them from Poland. In some two weeks, as a result of these imaginative and highly effective attacks, Koniev had bounded with his front all the way from the western bank of the Dnieper to the western bank of the Dniester: between them Zhukov and Koniev had encircled Hube's First Panzer Army, but Koniev also raced on past Hube's right flank towards Rumania, reaching the Pruth on a broad front and driving into Rumania as far as Pascani, thereby threatening Eighth Army and Army Group A by this deep encircling move.

On 15 May 1944 Marshal Koniev assumed command of the 1st Ukrainian Front (vacated by Zhukov, though at Stalin's insistence he was still to act as *Stavka* 'co-ordinator' with 1st Ukrainian). Koniev's forthcoming offensive with this front was aimed at Model's Army Group 'North Ukraine' with the object of seizing Galicia and southern Poland, while Rokossovskii attacked Model's left flank and drove into central Poland. Since the German command had anticipated a major Soviet offensive in the south (though in fact the Red Army struck first in Belorussia) Koniev faced formidable defences and considerable German strength. After two days of reconnaissance in battalion strength, on 14 July he plunged into what became known as the 'Lvov-Sandomierz operation', committing Thirteenth Army on his right against Rava Russka and Thirty-Eighth Army to the east of Lvov. This latter thrust encountered heavy German resistance, which even the presence of two Soviet tank armies could not flatten, whereupon Koniev loosed Grechko's 1st Guards in an attack farther to the south.

When the German defences finally caved in, forty thousand men were trapped in the Brody area; Thirteenth Army struck out for the Vistula, but Lvov resisted stubbornly and fell only on 27 July. Reaching the Vistula in the neighbourhood of Sandomierz, Pukhov's Thirteenth Army seized a small bridgehead but was subject to heavy German counter-attacks. There were two distinctive features of this entire operation. In the battle to break through the German defences Koniev committed two entire tank armies – Third and Fourth Guards – through a corridor only 4 miles wide and even as the Soviet flanks were under heavy German attacks designed to seal off the Soviet penetration; and though pressed to commit his main front reserve (Zhadovs'

Fifth Guards Army) in the first phase of the offensive, Koniev resolutely refused to unleash Fifth Guards until the Vistula had been reached. Thus he was able to use a fresh army to counter the growing counter-attacks against the Vistula bridgehead, which finally involved more than a dozen German divisions.

Koniev held the Sandomierz bridgehead tight in his grasp and it was from this vantage point on the Vistula that he hurled his front forward in January 1945 in the final advance into Germany itself. With immensely powerful forces at his disposal – twelve rifle and two tank armies (averaging 1–1,200,000 men, 15–17,000 guns and heavy mortars, 2–3500 aircraft and 2–3300 tanks) – his task was to advance to the Oder, nearly 310 miles away, first destroying German forces in the Kielce–Radomsko area, driving on to the Oder and also capturing the Silesian industrial region (without, Stalin strictly adjured Koniev, damaging the factories and plants).

In a major deception effort Koniev fostered the impression that his main attack would come from his left flank, but on 12 January 1945, preceded by a huge 'artillery attack', one rifle and two tank armies struck out from the bridgehead for Kielce, which fell after three days: while the left flank armies duly developed their attack on Upper Silesia, Sixtieth Army took Cracow and 1st Ukrainian Front was closing on the German frontier across a 170-mile front, crushing Fourth Panzer and Seventeenth Army in its path. By the evening of 23 January Koniev's units had reached both the Oder and the Silesian industrial region: at this point he ordered Rybalko's Third Guards Tank Army to strike from Oppeln into the rear of the German forces holding Silesia, thus threatening an encirclement that precipitated German with-drawal – without ruinous demolition of the industrial installations. On 25 Jan-uary 1st Ukrainian Front was drawn up on the eastern bank of the Oder all the way from Göben to Oppeln and aligned now – like Zhukov's 1st Belo-russian Front – for the assault on Berlin.

Towards the close of 1944 Stalin had intimated that 1st Belorussian Front would undertake the direct assault on Berlin and that the favoured front commander would be Marshal Zhukov, designated for this singular laurel. Marshal Koniev's front would assist in the encirclement operation, a decision that seemed to exclude him from direct participation in the conquest of Berlin. Koniev however had other ideas and in early April, after consultation with Stalin, he managed to broaden this concept of 'assistance' to include the contingency of actually moving on Berlin.

On 16 April 1945 both fronts – 1st Belorussian and 1st Ukrainian – sprang into action, preceded by gigantic air and artillery bombardment. On the first day Koniev was across the Neisse and deep into the German defences, which opportunity Stalin offered to Zhukov who was snared on the Seelow Heights. Koniev acted swiftly: he redeployed his two tank armies under Rybalko and Lelyushenko and received Stalin's permission to send them northwards – on to Berlin. On this occasion there were compelling reasons for Koniev to show

what he could really do with tank armies, which he now exploited ruthlessly:
by 20 April his armoured twins reached Luckenwalde and sliced the two
defending German army groups away from each other, followed by a junction
with 1st Belorussian Front south-east of Berlin and the consequent encirclement of thirteen divisions of the German Ninth Army. In little more than
twenty-four hours, on 25 April, Lelyushenko's Fourth Guards Tank Army
linked up with 2nd Guards Tank Army (from Zhukov's front), thereby sealing
up the Berlin garrison: Koniev had meanwhile committed Zhadov's Fifth
Guards to a westerly drive towards the Elbe, where Soviet troops joined up
with American units at Torgau (also on 25 April).

Not only was Berlin hermetically sealed off, but Germany had been cut
clean in half. But the final prize was denied to Koniev. Though his front took
part in the destruction of the Berlin garrison, it was Zhukov's men who
carried out the last symbolic act of storming the Reichstag. Koniev's 1st
Ukrainian proceeded to eliminate German divisions trapped south-east of
Berlin, while other forces captured Dresden and established another link
with the Americans at Chemnitz, but a sudden new crisis now faced Koniev.
The last of the German army groups, Group Schörner, still remained in
Bohemia and might surrender to the Western Powers: this Stalin refused to
countenance and ordered Koniev to peel off his tank armies and send them
racing south to capture Prague, where General Vlasov, the ex-Soviet general,
had ordered his men to reduce the German garrison. Koniev's tanks driving
from the north linked up with 2nd and 4th Ukrainian fronts already investing
Prague, making a German surrender inevitable. Marshal Koniev thus ended
the war with a part share in the conquest of Berlin and the subjugation of
Prague, no mean achievement, but conferring a subordinate status which
disappointed him and which he was not inclined to forget.

Immediately after the war Marshal Koniev remained as C-in-C Central Group
of Forces and Supreme Commissar for Austria. In 1946, as Zhukov disappeared from the scene, Koniev took over as C-in-C Ground Forces, remaining in this post until 1950 when he became Chief Inspector of the Soviet
Armed Forces: that two-year tour was followed by three years as GOC
Trans-Carpathian Military District (1952–5), one year once more in the post
of C-in-C Ground Forces (1955–6) and a four-year spell (1956–60) as Commander-in-Chief of the newly created Warsaw Pact with its Soviet and East
European forces. At the height of Khruschev's campaign for a German 'peace
treaty' and a settlement of the German question on his terms, Marshal
Koniev was ostentatiously moved back (in 1961–2) as C-in-C Soviet Forces in
Germany, but it was also in 1962 that Koniev – by now an outright opponent
of Khrushchev's plans to cut Soviet conventional forces, reduce military
manpower and rely increasingly on missiles – was shunted out of any operational command and placed in that military rest home for marshals, the
Inspectorate.

Most, if not all, of Koniev's postwar appointments demonstrated his political usefulness to and influence upon the political leadership, rather than emphasising any unique military utility. His rivalry with Zhukov was an important factor in the life of the Soviet military and the Party, but neither Stalin nor Khrushchev could find in him the absolute replacement for Marshal Zhukov: for Stalin, Koniev represented a useful counter-weight to Zhukov; for Khrushchev, Koniev could facilitate a revision of military myths in his own favour, support a fresh 'Army-Party' compact and exercise a benign influence within the armed forces – until Koniev too decided to speak out. The situation was not so simple as saying that Koniev was Russia's 'second soldier' after Zhukov: that position was (and still is) held by Marshal A. M. Vasilevskii, whereas Koniev carved out his own career by combining his military achievement with political manoeuvre. In November 1957 he rather overplayed his hand in the speech which supported Khrushchev's dismissal of Zhukov but which also venomously catalogued Zhukov's military short-comings.

Not all of this however can be ascribed only to Koniev's personal vanity, pique or sheer self-seeking: he represented an outlook, or a disposition, markedly different from that of Marshal Zhukov in his view of the Party's place in military affairs, and though both pressed for high levels of Soviet military strength and preparedness, Koniev never seemed to forget entirely that he had started out as a military commissar, the *voenkom* bound by the principles and enveloped in the presence of the Party. More than that, he was the former military commissar who had alone made the greatest contribution to the Red Army's greatest victories in the field.

GENERAL HEINZ GUDERIAN

John Strawson

General Heinz Guderian was not strictly a war lord at all. He was simply a professional soldier who held high rank in war both as a commander and as a staff officer. But he served one of the most implacable war lords in history. Without Hitler it is doubtful whether the name of Guderian would ever have been widely known outside German military circles. And without Guderian Hitler might not have made quite such a stir in the world. The fortunes and misfortunes of these two men went hand in hand. Blitzkrieg – its theory and practice – held them in thrall.

It was not Guderian who invented blitzkrieg. He simply took hold of other people's ideas, moulded them into precise tactical formulae and trained the men and machines to put these tactical ideas to devastating effect. Indeed no one man was responsible for the ideas. They sprang from the combined deliberations of vanquished military leaders, armchair strategists and political parvenus. It may be argued that one political parvenu was the most far-sighted of all. When Hitler indulged in his endless rantings to Rauschning in the early 1930s, even before he had come to power, his strategic intuition was already uncommonly acute.

'The next war', he had declared in 1932, 'will be quite different from the last world war. Infantry attacks and mass formations are obsolete. Inter-locked frontal struggle lasting for years on petrified fronts will not return. I guarantee that . . . We shall regain the superiority of free operations.' What was more these operations would not need to last long for he would hurl himself upon the enemy like a flash of lightning. Surprise, speed and concentration together would ensure that an enemy already demoralised by threats and lack of will would succumb 'to the first stroke of a single gigantic attack'. Hobbes's great recipe for success in war – the coalition of force and fraud – appealed exactly to Hitler's idea of *Realpolitik*. He had achieved much – the Rhineland, the *Anschluss* and Czechoslovakia – by ruthless manipulation of these two without recourse to war, but if and when it came to war, force would be on such an unprecedented scale and would be delivered with such speed and violence that everything would quickly be over bar the shouting. As for the technique of delivering this single overwhelming attack and the means to do so, all that had been thought of too and this is where Guderian came in.

When the great Hans von Seeckt was Commander-in-Chief of the *Reichswehr* in the 1920s, he set himself three principal tasks. First was to ensure the army's self-identification with the state. In the sense that the army was the first protector of the Reich, that it would do whatever was necessary for the Reich, and in seeing to it that the army was non-political yet at the same time supremely independent – a state within a state – Seeckt succeeded absolutely. Secondly he created an army of leaders – colonels trained to command divisions, lieutenants ready to lead battalions, NCOs ready to become officers, and soldiers to become NCOs. Thirdly, and most apt to our theme here, he laid down training principles which, while not new, had been forgotten and neglected in the mud and blood of Flanders. They were that all the main fighting arms must be properly integrated. In other words Seeckt insisted that mechanised cavalry, infantry and artillery should work as one. Moreover he required them to enjoy the close support of new weapons, such as anti-tank guns and aircraft as well. Herein lay the birth of the mixed panzer groups which gave mobile warfare a new dimension and swept aside army after army opposed to them. Seeckt had always believed in mobility, in the superiority of the attack, in fast-moving grandiose advances which would engulf, stupify and destroy defending forces. What mattered, he maintained, was not the size of armies, but their speed and skill in conjunction with aircraft.

Such notions did not fall on barren soil. Guderian* took them up, and in doing so studied and adapted too the ideas of three British writers, Liddell Hart, Fuller and Martel, who in the 1920s–30s saw that the tank plus its associated weapons was the battle winner of the future, the thing to be supported by other agents of violence rather than be in support of them. In his writings† Guderian paid particular tribute to Liddell Hart, 'who emphasised the use of armoured forces for long range strikes, operations against the opposing armies' communications, and also a type of division containing panzer and panzer-infantry units'. It was exactly this sort of formation that coincided with Guderian's own ideas of close tactical co-operation between

* Born in 1888 in East Prussia, son of a regular army officer, Heinz Guderian was educated at Cadet Schools and the War School at Metz, and was commissioned in the 10th Hanoverian Jaeger Battalion in 1908. He married Magarete Goerne in 1913 and they had two sons. He served throughout the 1914–18 war both as a regimental soldier and on the General Staff. After the war he held various appointments, including in 1922 one in the Army Transport Department of the Defence Ministry. This led to his being on the instructional staff of the Motor Transport School and later to command of a Motor Transport Battalion. In 1931 he became Chief of Staff to the Inspectorate of Motorised Troops and three years later Hitler made him Chief of Staff to the new Armoured Troops Command. The rest of his career is dealt with above.

† During 1936 and 1937 Guderian wrote and published *Achtung – Panzer!* in which the tactics later to be used in the war were clearly explained. But the book was not even translated into French or English.

arms and of what it would do to paralyse and annihilate enemy defences. And it was exactly this sort of formation that Guderian subsequently formed and trained.

When we examine Guderian's contribution to the new revolutionary *Wehrmacht* which the National Socialists created after Hitler's assumption of power, we are at once struck with his astonishing vision of what future battles, that is battles to be initiated and won by the Germans, would be like. Not against him could the age-old accusation about soldiers always waging the last war or the last war but one be levelled. He really was foreseeing what the next war would be like – because its tactics would be of his own making – and therefore preparing for it. His adoption and development of Liddell Hart's doctrine ran something like this. First came the breakthrough on a narrow front, the so-called *Schwerpunkt*. In order to get decisive results with tanks you had to use them in mass and then to move them so quickly that they would get to the enemy's main defensive zone before the guns there could have any effect on the battle. If the enemy's tanks tried to intercept and counter the penetration made, they would instantly be removed from the scene either by overwhelming them with superior numbers of tanks or by destroying them with tactical aircraft. The close co-operation of tanks and aircraft would be a matter of routine throughout the operation. Once the breakthrough had been achieved, closely knit teams of tanks and infantry would mop up the gun areas and fixed defences. In short the key to the whole operation was to expand initial depth on a relatively narrow front to a *combination of depth and width* and by this means to disrupt and destroy the entire enemy defensive zone. The essentials of conducting panzer offensives, Guderian concluded, were 'suitable terrain, surprise and mass deployment in the necessary width and depth'. We shall see later what successes waited on the Wehrmacht as they put these blitzkrieg theories into practice between 1939 and 1942.

It was small wonder that Guderian's tactical theories and tank prototypes made so immediate and profound an appeal to Hitler, for everything that Guderian said and demonstrated about speed, mass, violence and absolute annihilation was simply an echo of Hitler's own concept of warfare. 'I shall never start a war without the certainty that a demoralized enemy will succumb to the first stroke of a single gigantic attack.' It worked in Poland, it worked in France, it might even have worked in Russia if Hitler had paid more attention to what Guderian and others advised. The fact that Guderian's tactics were revolutionary and aimed at destructive domination was itself enough to make them appeal to the Führer and his Nazi revolution, whose theme, as Alan Bullock put it, 'was domination, dressed up as the doctrine of race, and failing that a vindictive destructiveness, Rauschning's *Revolution des Nihilismus*'.

When Hitler as Chancellor first saw the manoeuvres laid on by Guderian to illustrate his ideas about equipment, tactics and the close teamwork of tanks, artillery, infantry and aircraft, he was almost beside himself with enthusiasm. 'That's what I need,' he exclaimed as he watched the panzer units being put through their paces, 'that's what I want to have.' What is more he was in an undeniably strong position to get it, and within a year of coming to power he ordered that the trebling of the army's strength should be completed by October 1934. By that time the promised expansion was well on the way to being accomplished. Twenty-one infantry divisions had been formed and one panzer brigade. Within a year this one brigade had grown into three panzer divisions and command of one of them was given not surprisingly to Guderian. Each division had in it a panzer brigade containing no fewer than 561 tanks and was supported by a panzer grenadier brigade (i.e., motorised infantry) plus motorised artillery, engineers, signal and anti-tank units. A reconnaissance battalion completed the pack. The mixed groups foreseen and planned by von Seeckt had been born, and the division was, as he had also envisaged, designed essentially for bold, thrusting, offensive operations.

What is more the indispensable partner of the panzer, the Stuka (*Sturzkampfflugzeug* or dive attack aircraft) and its associated fellows in Goering's new *Luftwaffe* were making comparably astonishing and ominous strides both in numbers and performance. The Stuka complemented the panzer perfectly. In the first place its diving, screeching howl together with the accuracy of its machine gun or bombs produced exactly the right combination of shock and violence that blitzkrieg demanded. Secondly, until self-propelled artillery came along, it enabled rapid and precise fire power to support panzers over long distances. It was in short fundamental to Guderian's doctrine of self-contained, all-arms teams. Together that peerless pair, Panzer and Stuka, were to carve out for themselves some famous victories.

In 1938 Hitler created a new army post, Commander of Mobile Troops, and appointed Guderian to it. One of the great advantages of this post was that Guderian had direct access to the Führer on all matters concerning the training and organisation of the new panzer formations. With all his dedication and energy, plus an absolute conviction that his blitzkrieg tactics would be battle winners of the future, there was no danger of these new ideas being pushed back to the second row. The year 1938 was remarkable too for the appearance of two new tanks, which caused a good deal of discomfort for all those obliged to argue the toss with them – the Pzkw (*Panzerkampfwagen* or armoured fighting vehicle) III and IV, the famous Mark IIIs and IVs, which were still in service with the *Wehrmacht* when the war ended, and which the great panzer leaders, Rommel, von Manstein and Guderian himself, manipulated with such notable and daring success.

Before either of these events however this same year – 1938 – had seen the first naked use of aggression by Hitler – the *Anschluss*, the annexation of Austria to the Third Reich. Yet when Hitler spoke in Vienna of 'giving thanks to Him who let me return to my homeland in order that I might now lead it into my German Reich', he was hardly in the best of tempers. For Guderian's xvi Army Corps, which had led the way to the Austrian capital with 2nd Panzer Division and the *Waffen-SS* division, *SS Leibstandarte* Adolf Hitler, in spite of meeting no opposition, had made an irritatingly poor showing. General Jodl, Chief of Operations at Hitler's headquarters, held that as many as 70 per cent of the tanks and other armoured vehicles had broken down on the roads from Salzburg and Passau to Vienna. Guderian challenged this percentage, but the point was that the renowned military might of the Third Reich had not performed with that iron efficiency which the Führer expected of it.

None the less valuable lessons were learned, to be applied later in graver military situations. The most telling, Guderian recorded, were those of tank maintenance, road discipline and fuel supply. But all this notwithstanding, the facts were that two divisions had advanced some 500 miles or more in two days, a remarkable achievement for the panzer troops who did it and the General Staff officers who planned it. Nothing like it had ever happened before. Yet it was but a foretaste of things to come. It would not be long before another triumphant march of the panzer troops smashed another people's independence. About a year after the occupation of Vienna, the Führer was able to review his military machine in Prague with no doubts this time as to its efficiency. It was ready for blitzkrieg and within six months would enjoy its first fruits.

Guderian's war service may conveniently be divided into two parts – as a commander in Poland, France and Russia from 1939 to 1941, and as Chief of the General Staff from 1944 to 1945. The first part is mostly a story of success, the second one of shoring up the Third Reich's eastern defences against the Red Army and the fatal strategy of his own Führer. Yet it could be said that Guderian's performance during this time of defeat and disaster encompassed both his finest and his least fine hours.

As might have been expected Guderian's xix Corps, which contained one panzer and two motorised infantry divisions, played an important role in the crushing of Poland. His master, as in all other campaigns, played the leading role. In his various directions concerning operations against Poland, Hitler had made it clear that the whole thing must be done quickly. Hitler had always maintained that the first few days of a military action were politically decisive. To present *faits accomplis* to potential enemies was often to remove their enmity altogether once it was clear that military intervention was hopeless. Moreover the attack on Poland was characterised by another of Hitler's enduring strategic principles – a holding operation on one front, blitzkrieg on another. The pact with Russia had ensured that there would be no intervention against him in the east. Of course he ran the risk of war in the west, but the speed of smashing resistance in the east would neutralise hostility in the west. The whole thing would be over in a fortnight.

That it was over so quickly owed much to the hopelessness of Poland's strategic position and the startling success of all the blitzkrieg theories that

Guderian had so long been advocating. The essence of blitzkrieg was, as we have noted, surprise, speed and concentration. The three things were of course self-sustaining. They fed upon each other. Surprise facilitated speed; speed fostered surprise; concentration enhanced both. The application of these principles was peculiarly suited to the Polish campaign – the first actual manifestation of blitzkrieg. To start with the Polish defensive deployment was such that it invited defeat. Most of their army was strung out along the frontier, which could thus be penetrated anywhere. Moreover, as Germany had virtually outflanked these defences even before hostilities began, because of being able to mount massive *Schwerpunkte* from East Prussia and Pomerania to the north of their victim and from Silesia and Slovakia to the south, the *Wehrmacht*'s two great pincer movements – one to surround and destroy the Polish forces west of the Vistula, the second driving east of Warsaw to cut off everything west of the line Bialystok–Brest–Litovsk–river Bug – swept all before them.

The whole campaign was a classic example of what Hitler had always advocated. About concentration of force there was no doubt; surprise was achieved by negotiating until the last moment and then attacking without warning and in overwhelming strength; the deep thrusting panzer *Schwerpunkte*, together with the *Luftwaffe*'s elimination of the Polish air force and its disruption of Polish communications and command, made speed almost a matter of motoring and replenishment. The panzer divisions did exactly what Guderian had always foreseen for them – they tore open the enemy's defences and penetrated deep into the rear areas. It was the very battle of paralysis and annihilation that Clausewitz had so often recommended. Guderian's own XIX Corps (whose mission was to advance from Pomerania as fast as possible to the Vistula and cut off enemy forces in the Polish corridor) helped to tear open the enemy's front. Guderian, like Rommel never one to lead from behind, put himself in an armoured command vehicle and accompanied the leading panzer formations, in touch both with his own corps HQ and his subordinate divisional commanders. The start of the operation was not quite as successful as the end of the affair. Guderian himself has recorded:

On 1 September at 0445 hrs the whole corps moved simultaneously over the frontier. There was a thick ground mist at first which prevented the air force from giving us any support. I accompanied the 3rd Panzer Brigade, in the first wave, as far as the area north of Zempelburg where the preliminary fighting took place. Unfortunately the heavy artillery of the 3rd Panzer Division felt itself compelled to fire into the mist, despite having received precise orders not to do so. The first shell landed 50 yards ahead of my command vehicle, the second 50 yards behind it. I reckoned that the next one was bound to be a direct hit and ordered my driver to turn about and drive off. The unaccustomed noise had made him nervous, however, and he drove straight into a ditch at full speed.

So inauspicious was Guderian's first taste of blitzkrieg. Yet the whole campaign was over in about two weeks as Hitler had predicted. On 17 September Guderian's corps in its great pincer movement to the east and south had met the spearhead of General List's Fourteenth Army 50 miles south of Brest–Litovsk. Ten days *before* this General Halder, Chief of the General Staff, had already begun planning to move divisions to the West Wall. For it was here that Hitler intended to have his second shot at blitzkrieg and 'one last decisive battle with France'.

The astonishing success of the German armies in the battle for France is well known and has been often described, notably in Alastair Horne's *To Lose a Battle*. Operation *Sichelschnitt* (Cut of the Sickle) was Hitler's greatest triumph, when, as Alan Bullock put it, he achieved in four weeks what the Kaiser had failed to achieve in four years. Guderian's part in it is almost equally well known, for it was a decisive part both in planning and execution. The principal credit for making the plan of campaign must of course go to von Manstein. But it was Hitler who took up the plan with such enthusiasm and it was he who insisted on its execution. Equally indispensable were von Rundstedt, whose army group was responsible for the operation, Halder whose organisation for it was so thorough and sound, and Guderian who showed what his panzers could do when employed with real boldness and skill. On 17 February 1940 von Manstein had outlined his theory to Hitler. Simply expressed it was that instead of making a main thrust in the north where powerful Allied defences would prevent a decisive victory, the weight should be shifted farther south to penetrate *behind* the Allied strength in Belgium, and so cut it off at the roots as a sickle cuts corn. The Führer instantly initiated a new directive which read:

> The objective is to deny Holland and Belgium to the English by swiftly occupying them; to defeat, by an attack through Belgium and Luxembourg territory, the largest possible forces of the Anglo-French Army; and thereby to pave the way for the destruction of the military strength of the enemy. The main weight of the attack across Belgium and Luxembourg will be south of the line Liège–Charleroi.

It was one thing to issue a directive, another to turn it into a proper plan. When the plan had been made it looked something like this. In the north von Bock's Army Group B with some twenty-nine divisions would be the bait and tempt Anglo-French forces into Holland and Belgium, while in the south von Leeb's Army Group C would threaten the Maginot Line. It was in the Allied centre, a centre weakened by distractions elsewhere, that decision would be sought and here von Rundstedt's Army Group A with no fewer than forty-five (including seven panzer) divisions, would smash its way through the Ardennes and race across the Meuse between Dinant and Sedan. Guderian's

Admiral of the Fleet Earl
Jellicoe (*Keystone Press*)

Above right : General Pershing
(*left*) talking to Marshal Joffre
(*Keystone Press*)

Right : Field-Marshal Haig
(*Imperial War Museum*)

Field-Marshal Hindenburg (*left*) and General Ludendorff (*Ullstein Bilderdienst*)

Marshal Pétain (*centre*) with General Wittelhauser (*Photo Harlingue, Collection Viollet*)

General Hamilton (*Imperial War Museum*)

General Mustapha Kemal (*Collection Viollet*)

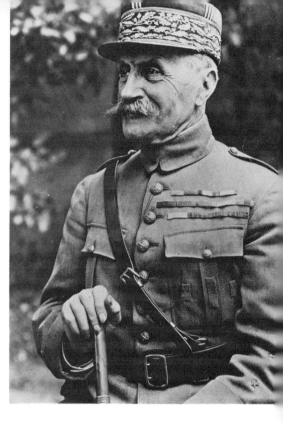

Above: Field-Marshal Falkenhayn (*Ullstein Bilderdienst*)

Above right: Marshal Foch (*Photo Harlingue, Collection Viollet*)

General Monash (*centre*) (*Imperial War Museum*)

Field-Marshal Allenby
(*Camera Press*)

Marshal of the Royal Air
Force Viscount Trenchard
(*Keystone Press*)

Field-Marshal Rundstedt
(*Keystone Press*)

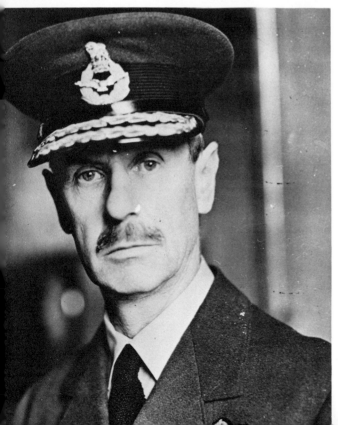

Air Chief Marshal Dowding
(*Imperial War Museum*)

Field-Marshal Wavell
(*Imperial War Museum*)

Above right : Field-Marshal
Manstein (*Imperial War
Museum*)

Right : Marshal Zhukov
(*Novosti Press*)

Field-Marshal Auchinleck
(*left*) and Lieutenant-General
Freyberg (*Imperial War
Museum*)

Field-Marshal Rommel
(*Imperial War Museum*)

Marshal Koniev (*Novosti Press*)

General Guderian (*Ullstein Bilderdienst*)

Above left: Marshal of the Royal Air Force Sir Arthur Harris (*Keystone Press*)

Above right: Field-Marshal Alexander (*Keystone Press*)

General Stilwell (*Keystone Press*)

Admiral of the Fleet Earl
Mountbatten (*centre*) with
Field-Marshal Slim (*right*)
and A. V. M. Vincent (*SEAC
Photo Unit*)

Admiral Yamamoto

Fleet Admiral Nimitz
(*Keystone Press*)

General MacArthur

Fleet Admiral Halsey
(*Keystone Press*)

Admiral Spruance (*Camera Press*)

Above left: Admiral of the
Fleet Viscount Cunningham
(*Imperial War Museum*)

Above right: Grand Admiral
Doenitz (*Ullstein Bilderdienst*)

Marshal of the Royal Air
Force Lord Tedder (*Imperial
War Museum*)

General Eisenhower and
Field-Marshal Montgomery
(*Keystone Press*)

General Bradley (*left*)and
General Patton (*Imperial War
Museum*)

General Spaatz with General Eisenhower (*Keystone Press*)

Marshal Juin (*Keystone Press*)

xix Corps would be the principal *Schwerpunkt* at Sedan – dread name in Franco–Prussian encounters of the past.

In March 1940 in the Berlin Chancellery, Guderian presented his plans to Hitler and the senior generals of Army Group A. Having explained the initial break-in operation and how he would make his way through Luxembourg and the Ardennes, he went on:

> On the fourth day I would arrive at the Meuse; on the fifth day I would cross it. By the evening of the fifth day I hoped to have established a bridgehead on the far bank. Hitler asked: 'And then what are you going to do?' He was the first person who had thought to ask me this vital question. I replied: 'Unless I receive orders to the contrary, I intend on the next day to continue my advance westwards. The Supreme leadership must decide whether my objective is to be Amiens or Paris. In my opinion the correct course is to drive past Amiens to the English Channel.' Hitler nodded and said nothing more.

Thereby hung a tale, for when it came to the reality there were times, in spite of all the glittering success, when the lesson that Guderian had been reiterating almost to the point of tedium – that the panzers must never be allowed to halt – was forgotten or ignored, with in the one case negligible and the other incalculable consequences. On 10 May 1940 the sickle began to cut the Allies down. Guderian's corps poured through the hole made in the French line and had crossed the Meuse on 13 May. The bridgehead was opened into a huge 50-mile gap and panzers flooded through it reaching the Channel a week later. The Allied armies were cut in half. All that Guderian had ever claimed for the conclusive results of blitzkrieg was vindicated. But the advance was not without its ups and downs.

On 16 May to his infinite satisfaction he was in the van of his irresistible panzer troops and all was going well:

> The fog of war that had confounded us soon lifted, we were in the open now . . . I passed an advancing column of the 1st Panzer Division. The men were wide awake and aware that we had achieved a complete victory, a breakthrough. They cheered and shouted remarks: 'Well done, old boy!' and 'There's our old man' and 'Did you see him? That was hurrying Heinz' and so on . . . Now roads had to be allotted among the three panzer divisions – the 6th, 2nd and the 1st – which were pouring through the town [Montcornet] in their headlong drive towards the west.

At this time it must have seemed to Guderian that the only thing that could stop him was lack of fuel or the English Channel. He was poised to accomplish all that he had explained to Hitler at that Chancellery conference two months earlier. Yet to his chagrin and dismay he received a direct order from his superior officer, von Kleist, who commanded the entire *Panzergruppe*, to halt. It seemed that Hitler had forgotten all about his previous agreement. Halder noted that the Führer appeared frightened by his own success, was worried about the southern flank and would not allow any further westward movement. Everything that Guderian had so long been hammering home – that once a panzer thrust had got going, it must above all keep going night and day so that the enemy was continuously subjected to unexpected, always deeper and wider thrusts, disrupting their entire conglomeration of reserves, headquarters and supplies, in short that the integrated panzer, infantry and artillery groups, supported and supplied by Stuka and transport aircraft, must flood relentlessly on, never pausing to be located, checked and counterattacked – all this was apparently forgotten. The Führer, not displaying that calmness so necessary to supreme command, screamed and raved and ordered the panzers to halt. Had the order been obeyed he would have cut off the very source of his success. But Guderian, after threatening to resign and kicking up as much fuss as he could, was permitted to continue with a further 'reconnaissance in force'. And with the broad interpretation he put on it this was sufficient for him to 'press on regardless with the whips out'. By 18 May he had reached St Quentin, next day he forced the Somme. On 20 May he was watching 1st Panzer Division attack Amiens, and the day after that 2nd Panzer Division reached the Atlantic coast.

The game was in the bag. The French army, as Jean Bruller put it in his *Battle of Silence*, 'was smashed to pieces, cut to shreds by the tanks, nailed to the ground by the enemy's Stukas'. The British army on the other hand – largely because Hitler did not insist on the panzers continuing their drive on 24 May – was allowed to slip away to fight another day. None the less *Sichelschnitt* had been, and still is, a campaign of breathtaking success. Not until the first days of galloping through the eastern plains of Poland and Russia a year later would the panzers move quite so fast or so far. Yet it was here that blunders were made from which they never recovered.

Hitler's broad directive for the Russian campaign, Operation Barbarossa, contained some good blitzkrieg stuff. 'The bulk of the Russian Army stationed in Western Russia', it declared, 'will be destroyed by daring operations led by deeply penetrating armoured spearheads. Russian forces still capable of giving battle will be prevented from withdrawing into the depths of Russia.' One of the daring operations was to be led by Guderian, who commanded 2nd Panzer Group, later 2nd Panzer Army. His command lasted roughly six months, was characterised by fierce controversy with his superior officers, took him almost to the gates of Moscow and combined triumphant success with the blackest despair. Guderian gives a full account of it in his book, *Erinnerungen eines Soldaten*, and here we need only highlight certain aspects of it. Apart from the supreme blunder of attacking Russia at all, Hitler's conduct of the campaign had fatal flaws. There was no absolutely clear objective, no master plan, as Montgomery would have put it. At the start of the battle on 22 June 1941 three army groups, respectively under von Leeb, von Bock and von Rundstedt, were directed roughly at Leningrad, Smolensk and Kiev. Guderian's panzer group was in von Bock's Army Group Centre aimed at Smolensk.

In spite of extraordinary advances and fantastic hauls of prisoners, the Red Army was not destroyed nor prevented from withdrawing. In the centre von Bock executed a gigantic pincer movement that converged on Minsk and by 10 July the Germans claimed over three hundred thousand prisoners. A further three hundred thousand were captured in the battle for Smolensk which lasted until August – but by then it was necessary to refit and regroup. Next came the great encirclement of Kiev, a further seven hundred thousand prisoners by the joining up of Guderian's and Kleist's armies. But the trouble was that Hitler had been so encouraged by his successes that instead of choosing one attainable objective like Moscow, he decided to go for Leningrad *and* the Ukraine. On 2 October von Bock's army group resumed its advance on Moscow with Guderian's and Hoth's armoured columns in the lead. They made further astonishing advances and took hordes of prisoners. By 20 October Moscow was only 80 miles away. Now was the moment to concentrate on one objective, but Hitler chose three, von Leeb for Leningrad, von Bock for Moscow and von Rundstedt for the Caucasus. And at about this time Russia's great ally, General Winter, came to her aid.

The Moscow offensive, pressed home right up to early December, failed. Guderian's comments on the whole affair speak eloquently of the actualities of war – bad information, a reckless underestimate of the enemy, ill-preparedness for a winter campaign. Throughout the battle Guderian was subordinate to Field-Marshal von Kluge, commanding Fourth Army, and their relations were constantly strained because of disagreement as to how operations should be conducted.* On 23 August Guderian had had a talk with Hitler at Army Group Centre headquarters at Lötzen and had explained his reasons why Moscow and not Kiev should be the objective. The arguments he used were powerful ones: it was necessary to defeat the enemy's main forces; Moscow, as a key road and rail communication centre, an industrial complex and a psychological prize, could not be ignored; his soldiers with so clear and expected an objective would be capable of one more great effort; and if Moscow were taken the Ukraine would be all the easier to capture later. Hitler would have none of it: 'My generals know nothing about the economic aspects of war.' When eventually the objective did become Moscow, it was too late.

---

* The friction between von Kluge and Guderian had several causes. In the first place during the Polish and French campaigns Guderian had commanded a corps and von Kluge an army. Now, although von Kluge still had an army, Guderian with his panzer group (the equivalent of an army) was commanding the spearhead troops of von Bock's army group yet in deference to von Kluge's feelings Guderian was made subordinate to him for the Russian campaign. Apart from this difficulty, whereas Guderian still believed essentially in rushing forward with his panzers, the more cautious von Kluge preferred to restrain them. Thus was animosity aggravated. Von Bock tried to steer a compromise course between the two.

Guderian's letters home were eloquent about the miseries of the campaign in November and December. On 6 November he bewailed the fact that the enemy was being allowed to gain time while their own plans were being postponed. The winter was more and more advanced and 'with the best will in the world there is nothing you can do about the elements'. The chance of striking a single decisive blow was going and would never recur. Ten days later he recalled that they were approaching their objective 'step by step in this icy cold with all the troops suffering from the appalling supply situation'. Yet the soldiers themselves were fighting 'with wonderful endurance'. A few days later he was near despair. 'The icy cold, the lack of shelter, the shortage of clothing, the heavy losses of men and equipment, the wretched state of our fuel supplies, all this makes the duties of a commander a misery and the longer it goes on the more I am crushed by the enormous responsibility which I have to bear, a responsibility which no one can share.'

By 8 December he had concluded that Moscow could not be taken, the supreme command had overreached itself by ignoring their reports, by making impossible demands, by actually being surprised that the Russian cold could reach $-32°C$. Apart from casualties to troops by sickness and frostbite, the vehicles and guns were being lost too. The tanks were being kept in running order, but 'the gods alone can tell how much longer we shall be able to use them in this cold'. Rostov was the writing on the wall. In short: 'I would never have believed that a really brilliant military position could be so buggered up in two months . . . for months now it has all been one great question mark . . . I am not thinking about myself but rather about our Germany, and that is why I am frightened.' On 16 December he writes that he frequently cannot sleep, his brain going round and round trying to think of what he can do to help his poor soldiers – 'out there without shelter in this abominable cold. It is frightful, unimaginable. The people at OKH and OKW* who have never seen the front, have no idea what the conditions here are like. They keep on sending us orders which we cannot possibly carry out, and they ignore all our requests and suggestions.'

He did not have to endure it all much longer. A row with Hitler on 20 December at Führer HQ in East Prussia was followed by further disagreements with von Kluge, and on 26 December Guderian was relieved of his command. He was in good company in being dismissed. So also were von Rundstedt, von Bock and Hoeppner. Now came a period of what Guderian in his book calls 'On Inactive Service' because of heart trouble which lasted for the whole of 1942. In February 1943 however he was appointed Inspector General of Armoured Troops. Hitler's appeal – 'I need you' – proved irresistible. His duties were precisely defined by Hitler. Guderian was responsible for

---

* OKH: *Oberkommando des Heeres*, high command of the army, which under Hitler's general supervision waged the war on the eastern front. OKW: *Oberkommando der Wehrmacht*, high command of the armed forces, Hitler's headquarters, which directed *all* operations on orders of the Führer himself.

the development, organisation and training of all armoured units. This involved working with Speer, Minister for Armaments and Ammunitions, who noted in his memoirs how often and how outspokenly Guderian would stand up to Hitler, and of course involved also numerous conferences with Hitler himself. During Guderian's time as inspector, the famous Tigers and Panthers were produced and first saw action.

In spite of the terrible losses at Stalingrad, Hitler was determined to mount an offensive on the eastern front in 1943. When Guderian spoke against it in May of that year and asked Hitler why he wanted to attack at all, Hitler replied: 'You're quite right. Whenever I think of this attack my stomach turns over.' None the less the great tank battle of Kursk, Operation Citadel, sometimes referred to as the death ride of Fourth Panzer Army, took place and failed. At that point Guderian retired to his sick bed. Later that year he tried to persuade Goebbels and Jodl to reorganise the supreme command so that a new Commander-in-Chief of the Army – in other words a manager of military operations at OKW – would lessen Hitler's direct influence on the actual conduct of operations and leave him to get on with strategic and political matters. But Jodl produced a question to which there was really no answer: 'Do you know of a better supreme commander than Adolf Hitler?'

The year 1944 was the beginning of the end for the German armies in Europe. In January there was a series of fierce Russian attacks. The so-called Atlantic Wall began to cry out for reinforcements as the Allied threat to it grew, and by June not only had the Anglo-American armies gained a firm hold of the Normandy bridgehead but the Russian summer offensive using over 180 divisions had smashed open the front of Army Group Centre. Although this crisis was overcome in that Field-Marshal Model managed to save something from the wreck, an even greater crisis burst over the Führer, the 20 July plot against his life.

Guderian's part in the events that followed was to say the least of it ambivalent. Many attempts had been made by the conspirators to persuade Guderian to join them. All had failed. And while Guderian admits hearing on 18 July that von Kluge, at this time Commander-in-Chief West, intended to arrange an armistice with the Western powers (this matter is itself one of endless controversy although it is clear that von Kluge did toy with the idea and was certainly party to the conspiracy), he denied absolutely any knowledge of the assassination attempt itself. This made it easier for him to obey the Führer's order to take over from Zeitzler as Chief of the General Staff on 21 July. He justified his acceptance like this:

> The Eastern front was tottering on the edge of an abyss from which it was necessary to save millions of German soldiers and civilians. I should have regarded myself as a shabby coward if I had refused to attempt to save the eastern armies and my homeland, Eastern Germany.

Thus far we may go along with Guderian. His subsequent deal with Bormann and the Führer in order to discover some means of saving 'the Honour of the German officer' is less easy to condone. On the one hand Bormann's directive reads:

> It is the Führer's wish that in the treatment of the events of 20 July 1944, no one should allow himself to attack the Officer Corps, the Generals, the nobility or the Armed Forces as a body or to offer them insults. On the contrary, it must always be emphasised that those who took part in the *Putsch* were a definite and relatively small officer clique.

So far, so good. But Guderian's order of the day issued on 23 July pledged to the Führer the unity of the generals of the officer corps and of the men of the army, and followed it with a general order six days later that required every General Staff officer to be a National Socialist officer leader 'by his attitude to political questions and by actively co-operating in the political instruction of younger commanders in accordance with the tenets of the Führer.' Anyone indisposed to do so would be removed from the General Staff. Moreover the army had to acknowledge Himmler as Commander-in-Chief of the Home Army, and were compelled to introduce the Nazi salute in place of the normal army salute 'as a sign of their unshakeable allegiance to the Führer and of the closest unity between the Army and the Party'.

John Wheeler-Bennett in his great study of the German army in politics had this to say about it: 'There was no longer a man to withstand National Socialism. Their resistance was broken, their first concern was to save their "honour" and at the price of their honour they achieved it. Submissively they accepted the status of a puppet and the mission to preach National Socialism. None refused, none resisted.' And all this was done at a time when Colonel-General Heinz Guderian was Chief of the Army General Staff. It is hardly surprising that he does not have much to say about it in his book, although he does acknowledge that he was a member of the so-called Court of Honour which contained also Field-Marshals von Rundstedt and Keitel and some fellow generals who were collectively required to expel the military conspirators from the army and hand them over to the untender mercies of a People's Court.

Here then was revealed Guderian the Trimmer. Yet this unworthy beginning as Chief of the General Staff is redeemed by the subsequent execution of his duties until final dismissal by Hitler in March 1945. It is a story of slow but sure defeat on the eastern front while making the best of a bad job, standing up to Hitler time and time again, and trying to persuade the Führer's cronies that the war was irretrievably lost and must be ended. A few examples will serve to illustrate the point. On 9 January 1945 we find him arguing the toss with Hitler at Eagle's Nest, the Führer's HQ for the Ardennes offensive, about the need to reinforce the eastern front to meet the Red Army's imminent attack. That he had little influence over the strategic policy of the Third Reich as Chief of the General Staff is made plain by the very fact that the Ardennes battle took place at all, for Guderian would never have allowed Germany's last reserves – particularly the precious seven panzer divisions that had been scraped together – to be chucked away in such a desperate gamble.

In any event on 9 January he was arguing with Hitler for reinforcements needed by the eastern front in view of the massive Russian offensive which he and his intelligence expert, General Gehlen, had long been predicting and which in fact started three days later. Guderian tried first to persuade Hitler to allow him to adjust the fronts of both General Harpe's Army Group A and General Reinhardt's Army Group Centre by relatively modest moves backwards which would shorten their lines and enable them to reconstitute more reserves. But – much more significant – Guderian wanted to concentrate the main defensive strength of the whole *Wehrmacht* on the eastern front in order to counter the gigantic Russian blow that he knew was coming. Hitler in a characteristic explosion of anger and refusal to face facts condemned the intelligence estimate as completely idiotic and a colossal piece of bluff, had some hard things to say about generals' views of operational necessity being no more than excuses for further retreat and absolutely refused to agree either to reinforce the east from the west or to adjust present deployments. Guderian recorded that 'Hitler and Jodl knew perfectly well that if the expected attack should materialize, the Eastern front was quite incapable of holding it with the resources available'. None the less Hitler's decision was that the eastern front must make do with what it had. He even went so far as to thank and congratulate Guderian for creating such a strong reserve there. Guderian's reply was cold comfort: 'The Eastern front is like a house of cards. If the front is broken through at one point all the rest will collapse, for twelve and a half divisions are far too small a reserve for so extended a front.'

When the time came and the massive Russian offensive began on 12 January, the eastern front, as Guderian had predicted, did go down like a house of cards, and within a few weeks the Russians had swept on to the Oder and come within striking distance of Berlin. During these battles Guderian struggled to convince Hitler of the urgency of reinforcements and of the need to create reserves. To start with it was all in vain. Hitler, still at Eagle's Nest, simply repeated his previous answer that the eastern front must make do with what it had, and then when he did start to pay attention dithered about with a panzer corps in so indecisive a way that it wasted its time in railway sidings and was unable to influence battles anywhere. But on 16 January Hitler returned to Berlin. He had decided at last that the western front must go over to the defensive so that the east might be strengthened. Even then his decision to send Sixth Panzer Army, not to the critically threatened central area but to Hungary, made Guderian explode with frustration and anger. It made no difference.

One thing however Guderian did manage to get Hitler to agree to – the creation of the new Army Group Vistula to take command between Army Group Centre and Army Group North. By his suggestion to appoint Field-Marshal von Weichs to the command, it was clear that Guderian himself intended to retain control of the operations to counter-attack Russian troops preparing to advance along the Vistula's west bank. Yet Hitler appointed – Himmler! 'This preposterous suggestion appalled me,' wrote Guderian, 'and I used such argumentative powers as I possessed in an attempt to stop such idiocy.' His argumentative powers did not prevail. On the same day, 25 January, Guderian tried to persuade Ribbentrop of the need to go to Hitler and make him face the fact of imminent collapse in order to make a separate armistice in the west and so allow a transfer of such weight to the east that the Russians could be halted. He was asked by Ribbentrop if the General Staff was losing its nerve and Guderian noted in his memoirs that it would have required nerves of cast-iron both to indulge in such discussions *and* to keep cool and think clearly. Needless to say Ribbentrop blurted it all out to Hitler, who thereupon vented his rage on Guderian and accused him of treason.

So the ludicrous and tragic game went on, Guderian desperately trying to make a few bricks with no straw and so ease an almost hopeless military position, Hitler recklessly dissipating what reserves there were to irrelevant sideshows; Guderian trying to draw in his horns for the final conclusive battle for Berlin, Hitler insisting that they hold on everywhere. When the Russian armies finally reached Küstrin and Frankfurt on the Oder in the first week of February, Guderian made one more effort to persuade the Führer to evacuate Courland in order to muster sufficient strength to counter-attack the Russian flanks in their thrust towards Berlin. He went so far as to tell Hitler he was thinking only of Germany's interests. 'How dare you speak to me like that,' was the Führer's furious and bellowed reply. 'Don't you think I'm fighting for Germany. My whole life has been one long struggle for Germany.' General Thomale was so alarmed by it all that he gripped Guderian's jacket and pulled him back clear of Hitler's fists. Worse was to come. At a further conference on 13 February to discuss an attack from the Arnswalde area on Russian forces north of the Warthe, Guderian engaged in a detailed argument about the attack's timing and insisted that it be done soon and that it could not wait for every round of ammunition and can of fuel to be supplied. Hitler then forbade Guderian to accuse him of wanting to wait. Guderian went further and stated that if General Wenck were not attached to Himmler's HQ, the attack would certainly fail because of Himmler's influence. Whereupon the Führer yelled that he would not permit Guderian to belittle Himmler. Guderian insisted and the disagreeable scene went on for two hours:

His fists raised, his cheeks flushed with rage, his whole body trembling, the man stood there in front of me, beside himself with fury and having lost all self-control. After each outburst of rage Hitler would stride up and down the carpet edge, then suddenly stop immediately before me and hurl his next accusation in my face. He was almost screaming, his eyes seemed about to pop out of his head and the veins stood out on his temples.

Yet extraordinarily enough after Guderian had quietly repeated his demands over and over again, the Führer suddenly stopped raving, told Himmler and Wenck that the latter would take charge of the assault, sat down, called Guderian to his side, requested the conference to continue and with his most charming smile announced that the General Staff had won a battle. 'This was the last battle that I was to win,' observed Guderian, 'and it came too late. I had never before taken part in such a scene. I had never seen Hitler rave so violently.'*

Slowly but surely the German military situation went on deteriorating. On 20 March General Heinrici, now commanding Army Group Vistula, discussed the situation with Guderian at OKH headquarters at Zossen, and complained that the attack Hitler had designed to eliminate the Russian bridgehead at Küstrin would be disastrous and simply result in the German troops being destroyed by Soviet artillery and air power. Guderian's response was uncharacteristic in that he burst out violently that he could not even stay to talk about the matter as he had to leave then and there for another conference with Hitler. He could get nothing done. 'I spend all my time either on the road or listening to drivel.' He was not required to listen to Hitler's nonsense much longer.

The following day at Führer HQ Guderian tried to convince Himmler that as the war could not be won, they must go together to Hitler and urge him to arrange an armistice. When Himmler said it was still too early for that, Guderian pointed out that it was already five minutes past twelve and that if they did not negotiate then, they would never be able to do so. That same evening Hitler tried to relieve Guderian of his post, but since there was no one available to replace him, it could not be done. A week later on 28 March, however, when Guderian stood up for General Busse, Hitler sent him on six weeks' convalescent leave and Krebs took over as Chief of the General Staff. Even then Hitler had a final word for Guderian, urging him to get his health back, since he would be badly needed in six weeks when the situation could be critical. But before six weeks had passed there would be no Führer and no Third Reich either. Guderian went to the Ebenhausen Sanatorium near Munich and became a prisoner of the Americans on 10 May.

How should he be judged? Liddell Hart thought he possessed most of the qualities that distinguish the great captains of history: '. . . *coup d'oeil*, a blend of acute observation with swift sure intuition; ability to create surprise

---

* However much the great Churchill might bully, cajole and outmanoeuvre them, the British Chiefs of Staff had much to be grateful for.

and throw an opponent off balance; speed of thought and action that allows an opponent no chance of recovery; a combination of strategic and tactical sense; the power to win the devotion of troops, and to get the utmost out of them.' It is a fair judgement and is confirmed by historians writing today.* Guderian was thus one of the great commanders of the Second World War. He was uniquely the man who developed the notion of blitzkrieg and then practised it with imagination, flair, boldness and remarkable results. In a conversation with Churchill about the Ardennes offensive, Stalin made a curious reference to Guderian. The best German generals were gone, he observed, and only Guderian was left and he was an adventurer. It was odd to call him an adventurer at a time when he was no longer indulging in his adventurous strokes of blitzkrieg but was striving desperately to pull together whatever he could for a defensive effort to stem the Russian tide. At this point it was Hitler who was the adventurer, not Guderian.

All in all we may conclude that without once being in major and independent command of a campaign (but then with Hitler no German general ever had such autonomy, except perhaps Rommel with his relatively tiny *Panzerarmee*), Guderian was the great architect of victory for a war lord who did not know what to do with victory. One of Guderian's comments on this war lord was that Hitler knew more about active service than the majority of his military advisers. Indeed there was real justice in Hitler's bellowing at Guderian in December 1944: 'There's no need for you to try to teach me. I've been commanding the German Army in the field for five years and during that time I've had more practical experience than any "gentleman" of the General Staff could ever hope to have.' Guderian judged Hitler's will-power to be his most outstanding quality. By it 'he compelled men to follow him'. But Guderian's judgement of Hitler's principal failing was particularly interesting coming from so brilliant a practitioner of blitzkrieg. It was that Hitler's strategic vision, which was bold in the extreme, was not matched by a comparable boldness in carrying it out. Russia was his undoing where his strategy was ruined by 'inconsistency and vacillation'. The Führer, concluded Guderian, was

> a man lacking wisdom and moderation . . . going in solitary haste from success to success and then pressing on from failure to failure, his head full of stupendous plans, clinging ever more frantically to the last vanishing prospects of victory . . . with a fanatic's intensity he grasped at every straw which he imagined might save himself and his work from destruction. His

---

* Richard Humble in his recent study, *Hitler's Generals*, gives Guderian comparably high marks. He calls him the star performer of the Polish campaign, shows what a profound influence he had in creating and exploiting the 1940 breakthrough and reminds us of the incredible speed with which his panzer divisions advanced in the final battles for France. What is more he was 'bluff, outspoken, never afraid to shout Hitler down' and one (the others were von Manstein, von Rundstedt and Kesselring) 'of the élite, the men whom Hitler could never really afford to do without'.

entire and very great will-power was devoted to this one idea which was now all that preoccupied him – never to give in, never to surrender.

At least Guderian, unlike some of the General Staff, who after the war laid *all* the blame on Hitler, was able to acknowledge his master's strength while not failing to note his weaknesses. As for Guderian himself, perhaps the last word we might say is this. His own valedictory despatch he called *Erinnerungen eines Soldaten* (Memoirs of a Soldier). The English version of it is *Panzer Leader*, and it is essentially as a panzer leader *par excellence* that Guderian will be remembered. He died in 1954, aged sixty-six. His portrait still hangs in places of honour at the panzer barracks of the present German army, the *Bundeswehr*. It is a fitting memorial to his place in the history of war.

Marshal of the Royal Air Force Sir Arthur Harris

Martin Middlebrook

'There are a lot of people who say that bombing cannot win the war. My reply to that is that it has never been tried yet. We shall see.'

Between the years 1940 and 1945 a serious and determined attempt was made to secure victory in a war using aerial bombardment as the major means of defeating the enemy. This was a novel and completely untried method of waging war. The enemy was Germany; the bombers were those of the Britain's Royal Air Force Bomber Command joined later by those of the United States Army Air Force. The attempt ended inconclusively but it provided a fascinating subject for later discussion and study. One man came to be more closely associated by the general public with this 'victory through the bomber' concept than any other. He was Air Chief Marshal Sir Arthur Harris, Air Officer Commanding-in-Chief of Bomber Command from February 1942 until the end of the war. It was he who spoke the words quoted above in a filmed interview soon after he took command of Bomber Command.

Arthur Travers Harris was born at Cheltenham on 13 April 1892, son of a member of the Indian Civil Service. After an education at a preparatory school at Sittingbourne and at Allhallows School in Devon, his father wanted him to become a soldier but young Harris refused. There was no family opening in England and after some difficulty with his parents over a choice of career he finished up in Rhodesia with £5 and was left to his own resources. He was sixteen years old.

For the next six years Harris made his own way in Rhodesia – gold-mining, farming, and driving horse coaches and the first motor cars to appear there. He loved his adopted country and would always consider himself a Rhodesian. When war came in August 1914 Harris was twenty-two. He joined the 1st Rhodesia Regiment as a bugler, and at service dinners in later years was often to say of himself that he had been blowing his own trumpet ever since. The Rhodesia Regiment took part in a gruelling campaign in German West Africa with many long marches, hardship and poor rations, but the brigade the Rhodesians were with succeeded in defeating the Germans in this remote theatre of war. By July 1915 the campaign was over, the regiment was disbanded and Harris made his way to England in order to find another way of continuing his war service,

The war in France had by now settled down into the dull stalemate of trench warfare. Arthur Harris had seen enough of infantry work in Africa and looked round for something different. He nearly joined the Royal Artillery but there were no vacancies so he tried the Royal Flying Corps. An uncle at the War Office obligingly helped him to dodge the long waiting list, and in November 1915 he was appointed a second lieutenant and commenced his training as a pilot at Brooklands. In this somewhat haphazard manner the future chief of Bomber Command commenced his aviation career. If he had been in England in 1914 and not Rhodesia, Harris would almost certainly have been one of the enthusiastic volunteers for Kitchener's New Army and might well have been one of the many thousands of infantry casualties on the Western Front.

After less than four months Harris was posted to the Western Front, to No. 11 Squadron at Bertangles, just north of Amiens. The squadron was operating over the Somme front with the Vickers FB5 – the 'Gunbus' – an obsolete two-seater 'pusher' aircraft. Harris's first spell at the front lasted a mere seventeen days; it is not known why he returned to England but he was soon flying again with a Home Defence squadron. He was back on the Western Front again in September 1916, with No. 70 Squadron, again on the Somme, but within three days he was in hospital, probably wounded, and was out of action for the next five months. He went out yet again in June, as a reinforcement to No. 45 Squadron flying Nieuport 1½-Strutters and Sopwith Camels from Ste Marie Cappel behind the Ypres front.

For nearly five months Harris lived the life of a front-line RFC pilot on the Western Front. He was by now a flight commander and regularly led formations of aircraft on patrol over the lines. Below him was being fought the terrible Battle of Passchendaele. The squadron's work was mainly reconnaissance and the protection of the vulnerable observations planes that were spotting for the artillery. Harris was often in action with German fighters, and although there is no record of his achieving any victories he must have been a competent pilot to survive for so long. In November 1917 he returned to England and for several months commanded No. 44 Squadron, one of the Home Defence squadrons which were defending London from Zeppelin and bomber attack, but his Camels had little success against the Germans.

The war finished with Harris as a major in the newly formed Royal Air Force. He had seen a great deal of flying as a fighter pilot but had scored no confirmed victories. He had experienced command of detached flights and of squadrons and had been awarded the Air Force Cross in the last month of the war. Certain aspects of the four-year war had made a great impression upon him – the seeming futility and the slaughter of prolonged land battles under appalling war conditions and the apparent inability of the army to gain a decisive victory at reasonable cost.

The coming of peace found Major Harris as a twenty-six-year-old married man with the responsibility of the first of three children by a wartime marriage (he would marry again in 1938 after a divorce) and facing demobilisation without any secure prospect of employment. The problem was solved in 1919 when, to his own surprise, he was offered a permanent commission in the peacetime RAF. He was sorely tempted to refuse the offer and return to Rhodesia but, in the end, he accepted. Once again Harris's road to Bomber Command had been decided by a somewhat chance decision.

The next twenty years would see many more steps taken along this road. He was soon posted to India to command No. 31 Squadron which was engaged on operations under army command on the North-West Frontier. The niggardly attitude of the Indian army to expenditure on vital stores and spare parts disgusted him and he caused much trouble. This posting was followed in November 1922 by command of No. 45 Squadron in Iraq, where the RAF had just taken over from the army the main responsibility for policing the troublesome tribes. The squadron was equipped with the huge, by the standards of that time, Vickers Vernon and was officially a troop-carrying squadron. But Harris sawed a hole in the floor of the Vernon, put a man on his stomach to look through this hole and converted the aircraft into a highly efficient bomber. The main influence of this period on his future thinking was the lesson that the RAF need not necessarily always operate under army control.

Harris's next appointment was another squadron command, that of No. 58 Squadron at Worthy Down. Again, this was a significant time for him with the Vickers Virginia heavy bombers being pressed by him to develop the difficult skills of night bombing and navigation. In the summer of 1927 he was awarded the OBE and promoted to wing commander, having been a major, or the RAF's equivalent of squadron leader, for nearly ten years. One person who had the opportunity of watching Harris closely during his two years with No. 58 Squadron was Wing Commander Charles Portal, commander of a neighbouring squadron and later to be Chief of the Air Staff and the man who would appoint Harris to command of Bomber Command and control his activities during the years of the bomber offensive.

By November 1927 Harris had been in command of squadrons for most of the past ten years. He had amassed a considerable flying experience in these years, had faced the problems of caring for men and machines in challenging circumstances of peace and war and had made significant contributions to the development of both day and night bombing. For most of the next twelve years he was to serve in various staff positions. Two years were spent on the Army Staff Course at Camberley and a further three and a half years in the Middle East. On both occasions he was to see much of the army and he developed a strong distrust of what he considered to be its completely outdated thinking. These two postings were followed by a pleasant interlude of a few months during 1933 when he commanded a flying-boat squadron.

Harris was next to be involved with bombers again, but this time in the planning and development of the bombers of the future. From August 1933 until May 1937 he served in a series of senior staff appointments at the Air Ministry, firstly in the Operations and Intelligence Branch and then for three vital years as Deputy Director of Plans. During this time he was actively engaged in the development of the new breed of heavy bombers being planned for the 1940s – the Stirling, the Halifax and the Manchester (the famous Lancaster would be a development of this last type) – and also of the role these bombers would play in the war with Germany that looked increasingly more likely.

Harris had plenty of opportunity during this period to exercise his wits in the paper war being carried on with the other major services. One officer who served with him at this time remembers:

> There is no doubt that he did tend to overstate his case but always with good humour which enabled him to keep on friendly terms with his colleagues, no matter how much they disagreed with him. It was a most unpleasant period and I don't think that he can have enjoyed it but it was also a time when Air Power was becoming a reality and not just a dream and this meant bringing about a profound change in the outlook of the other two services. In order to move them at all it was undoubtedly necessary to appear to exaggerate, or rather to assume that the new generation of aircraft then on the drawing board would do what the designers said they would. The rate of technical advance was such that there were many who found this hard to believe.

Harris left the Air Ministry in June 1937, for the next twelve months serving as commander of No. 4 Group in the recently formed Bomber Command. This was a frustrating time with obsolete aircraft and much official hindrance to what Harris thought were essential training facilities – bombing ranges in particular. Then followed a brief trip to the United States in 1938 as head of an RAF mission negotiating the purchase of American-built aircraft; Britain was now rearming as quickly as possible. Harris made some useful contacts with US Army Air Force officers and arranged purchase of the Harvard and Hudson aircraft that would later serve with the RAF.

On his return from the USA he was told that a previously arranged posting as Air Officer Commanding, Palestine and Transjordan, had been cancelled and that he was to go instead to Headquarters Fighter Command to be Senior Air Staff Officer to Sir Hugh Dowding. There is no doubt that if this move had taken place, Harris's wartime career would have been entirely different. He would have spent at least until the summer of 1940 at Fighter Command and, although it is fascinating to speculate on what influence he might have had on the outcome of the Battle of Britain, I know of no senior officer who moved from Fighter to Bomber Command once the war had started. But he talked his way out of the posting and spent the last year of peace in the Middle East. Fate took a hand once more when he was invalided home sick only halfway through the normal tour of duty. The outbreak of war thus found Air Vice-Marshal Harris in England and available for whatever duty his superiors thought him best suited.

Within a week of the outbreak of war Harris was posted to command a front-line bomber group. This was No. 5 Group with headquarters at Grantham and ten squadrons of twin-engined Handley Page Hampdens based on five airfields in or near Lincolnshire. In 1939 Bomber Command was not yet ready for the type of operations that prewar planning, much of which Harris himself had worked on, envisaged for the bombers, and during the eight months of the Phoney War political decisions prevented any real bombing of the German mainland.

During those first frustrating months one important supposition about the modern bomber was proved false. It had been thought that bombers flying in formation by daylight could defend themselves from fighter attack, but when Wellingtons and Blenheims tried this out in a series of bombing raids on German naval targets the theory was proved sadly wrong. Harris's Hampdens were not involved in this unfortunate experiment, but they were ordered to take part in the night flights dropping propaganda leaflets on German cities that went on for several months in the first winter of the war.

Harris was completely opposed to what he considered a futile use of bomber aircraft. He did however find another role for the bomber. His Hampdens were the only aircraft that could carry sea mines, and under his direction the first aerial mining of German coastal waters took place. Later in the war all the groups of Bomber Command devoted part of their effort to this highly successful type of operation and it is claimed that 759 German ships from battleships down to small pilot vessels were sunk or disabled by RAF mines and that eventually 40 per cent of the personnel of the German navy were engaged on minesweeping. The credit for pioneering this mining campaign should go to Harris.

When the Phoney War came to an end abruptly in the spring of 1940 the bombers could at last be used offensively. The Hampdens of No. 5 Group took part in the first raids on German industrial centres, and they also did a particularly good job in bombing the French and Belgian ports in which the Germans were concentrating barges for their proposed invasion of England.

Harris left No. 5 Group in November 1940. During the fourteen months of his active involvement in the bombing war he had done a sound job in developing several tactical aspects of bomber operations and No. 5 Group was certainly in good shape when he left. But there is evidence that like almost everyone else in Bomber Command he was having to learn the hard facts of life about what the modern bomber could and could not do and that he had no specially gifted insight into the secrets of the game. As late as January 1940 he told the C-in-C that he considered that as long as three bombers could keep together in daylight 'the pilots considered themselves capable of taking on anything'. And later in 1940, when Bomber Command HQ was assessing the results of the first night raids on German industry, he joined with others in the optimistic assumption that the bomber crews were finding their targets and hitting them hard. He wrote to the C-in-C complaining that not enough publicity was being given to the bombers' achievements:

> What a riot of publicity would attend such results had they been secured by the Army, and what a catastrophic spate of words if the Navy succeeded in doing a thousandth as much! Yet when the bombers begin to win the war – and we are the only people that can win it, and we are winning it – what happens? Nix!*

Harris was by no means alone in assuming that the bombers were finding and bombing their targets although an intensive review a year later would find that both navigation and bombing accuracy had been appalling during this period. His outburst about publicity clearly illustrates his views on several points: the intense pride in his own service and his hopes and expectations for the heavy bomber, his resentment that the other services still saw the RAF as playing a subsidiary role in modern war and, once again, his tendency to overstate his arguments.

At the end of 1940 Harris was moved again. His old colleague, Portal, had been appointed to the position of Chief of the Air Staff and he asked for Harris to be his deputy chief. These were important moves with bomber men coming to the top positions in the RAF, although Harris was only the number three; there was a vice-chief between Portal and himself.

Harris was to be at the Air Ministry only for the next six months. He was not happy there and only minor aspects of this short period are of interest. He was in London during the worst of the German air raids on the city and was much affected by the sight from the roof of the Air Ministry of London in flames. He naturally hoped that one day the RAF could exact retribution for this, little realising that he would be the chief means of delivering that retribution. He also saw from the German raids that it was easier to destroy a city by fire than it was to blow it to pieces. He never forgot this demonstration and later saw to it that Bomber Command's tactics in attacks on industrial cities in Germany would be based largely on this 'fire-raising' principle.

In May 1941 Harris was offered the job of head of an RAF delegation to the still-neutral United States to hurry along the delivery of the aircraft and equipment being manufactured there for Britain. He was not keen on the idea but it would, at least, get him out of his staff job at the Air Ministry and he agreed to go. He was away until February 1942; it was a period that had little significance in the development of his career.

---

* The two quotations in this paragraph are from *The Strategic Air Offensive Against Germany 1939–1945* by Charles Webster and Noble Frankland, published by Her Majesty's Stationery Office 1961, 1, pp. 200 and 220. The quotations are by kind permission of the Controller of HM Stationery Office.

While Harris was away in America, Bomber Command had been having a rough time. By the end of 1941 the bombers had been operating in their strategic role of bombing German industry for twenty months and towards the end of this period some effort had been made to measure the effectiveness of the bombing. A careful examination was made of over four thousand photographs taken by aircraft at the moment of bombing in a hundred raids. It was found that only one aircraft in five had bombed within 5 miles of its target! Furthermore during the same period the German defences had been hardening and Bomber Command's losses had increased steadily. Bomber Command was ordered to give up long-distance raids for the time being and conserve its strength. A few weeks later the Commander-in-Chief, Sir Richard Peirse, was removed and sent to a command in India. His replacement was Arthur Harris who took over in February 1942; Harris's promotion to Air Chief Marshal and his knighthood soon followed.

Before describing Harris's activities during what was to be the climax of his career, it would be useful if a quick look were taken at the role that had been planned before the war for Bomber Command, at the way this role had to be amended by wartime realities and at the new Commander-in-Chief's own views on how his bombers should be used.

In the years following the First World War much thought was given by the leaders of many nations to the role of the bomber aircraft in any future war. Two factors influenced British thinking on the subject – the frightful casualties incurred during the land battles on the Western Front and the damage and casualties caused in London and other places in England by German Zeppelins and Gotha bombers. To summarise briefly the development of British thinking, it was decided that if war with Germany came again the Royal Air Force would have two roles. The first would be to defend Britain from German air attack, but the effort devoted to this defence was to be no more than necessary to achieve that aim. The majority of the RAF effort was to go into the heavy bomber, which would be used offensively, by daylight if possible, in attacks on German industry. If this could be done on a large enough scale, the defeat of the enemy in land battle would be assured when his supply of war material ran out. This policy was supported with intense fervour by RAF bomber men like Portal and Harris. It was not of course accepted completely by the other services, who saw their own eminence in military affairs thus reduced.

These theories had taken some bad knocks since 1939. The daylight bomber had not survived and Bomber Command had been forced to carry out its offensive by night. The targets it had been allocated had been individual factories, shipyards or other acceptably warlike objectives, although there was no international law limiting the use of the bomber. But the experiences of 1940 and 1941 had proved that bomber crews could not with certainty find and hit these small targets. Something else would have to be tried.

Harris arrived at Bomber Command HQ at High Wycombe as this crossroads was reached. There were several options open to the Air Staff. Bomber Command could be virtually disbanded and the dream of crippling or even defeating the enemy completely by strategic bombing abandoned; the remaining bombers would then be limited to providing direct support to the army and navy. Or Bomber Command could somehow solve its target-finding problems and resume the bombing of the vital German industrial targets – what might be called 'precision bombing'. Or again there might be a compromise, with Bomber Command adopting a different kind of bombing that was within the limits of its capabilities. There had been a prewar line of thought that instead of the specific attack on German industrial premises a more general attack on large cities should be tried; this would so demoralise the civilian population that the enemy would collapse, not through a shortage of war material but by the refusal of the civilians to carry on the war.

This last was the Air Staff's solution to the problem in early 1942. The bombers could not find the factories so they would be sent to the more easily findable large cities and bomb these instead. A famous directive, issued on 14 February 1942, ordered Bomber Command to resume full-scale operations and stated 'that the primary object of your operations should now be focused on the morale of the enemy civil population and, in particular, of the industrial workers'. Eighteen German industrial cities and towns were listed for the first phase.* But this new type of attack – 'area bombing' – was only intended to be a temporary expedient. If the new navigational aids being developed could bring about an improvement in target-finding ability and bombing accuracy then precision bombing was to be resumed; the directive listed twelve individual targets for this eventuality.

When Harris arrived at High Wycombe eight days later this directive was waiting for him. He set about his task with enthusiasm.

Harris undoubtedly saw his first task as being the re-establishment both of Bomber Command as a major force and of the policy that strategic bombing would be the major means of causing the defeat of Germany. He was perfectly happy with the new directive; he felt that the morale of the German civilian was a valid target and that the destruction of industrial cities would gradually cripple Germany. Area bombing would work if sufficient determination was applied to the direction of the bomber offensive and sufficient aircraft and crews made available for its execution. Harris would show all the determination in the world; the War Cabinet must be persuaded to supply the aircraft despite the insistent demands from many other theatres of war.

He was eager for an early success so he sent his bombers to two comparatively small cities, Lübeck and Rostock. These targets on the Baltic coast were easy to find and only lightly defended. Harris used them as guinea pigs for his tactic of destroying cities by fire. The bomber crews found their targets; the old buildings in Lübeck and Rostock burned well.

* *Ibid.*, IV, p. 144.

Next he set out with what at that time was a plan of outstanding boldness –
to collect together a thousand bombers and destroy a major defended city.
Bomber Command's strength of front-line aircraft at that time was only just
over four hundred, but Harris was prepared to risk these and his entire training organisation; he also appealed to Coastal and Flying Training Commands
for help and this was promised. However a not surprising Admiralty decision
prevented the Coastal Command contribution; the navy had no wish to assist
in what they correctly guessed was a mammoth public relations exercise that
might rebound upon them. The story of how Harris still put a thousand
bombers into the air and caused severe damage to Cologne is well known and
will not be repeated here, but there were a number of political and operational
results that should be mentioned.

The war-weary people of Britain were tremendously heartened by the news
that a thousand bombers were raiding Germany, although they did not know
that most had to return to their training units soon afterwards. The War
Cabinet was also suitably impressed and decided that Bomber Command
should be backed with further supplies of aircraft. Operationally, valuable
lessons had been learnt by the introduction of a 'bomber stream', in which all
aircraft flew the same route to the target, and by the concentration of the
attack over the target to only ninety minutes, which saturated the defences.
Harris had taken great risks in sending out all his training aircraft, in using
the bomber stream, and in packing so many aircraft over Cologne at the same
time with the attendant risk of collision. But the experiment worked and
only forty aircraft, an acceptable proportion, were lost. With this one bold
and quite brilliant stroke Harris had restored the standing of Bomber Command, and at the same time proven a new set of bomber tactics.

The story of 1943 can be told more quickly. The year saw two series of
raids on particular areas of Germany, which later became known as 'Battles',
and the start of a third. By the spring of the year Bomber Command had a
more powerful force of bombers than ever before, the majority of which were
for the first time the four-engined types planned before the war. It also had
the specialist Pathfinder Force, which found and marked the targets for the
less experienced crews of the Main Force. All of the Pathfinders and a proportion of the Main Force also had a new navigational device, an airborne ground-
scanning radar set called H2S.

The first battle was that of the Ruhr, waged between March and July.
Nine of the Ruhr cities were raided, some of them several times. Raids on
cities in other parts of Germany were interspersed with the Ruhr raids in
order to keep the German defences at full stretch. The Ruhr raids were very
successful: the Pathfinders, using a blind-bombing device called Oboe, were
at last able to penetrate the Ruhr haze and at the end of the battle much of this
important industrial area was in ruins.

In July and August followed the short, sharp Battle of Hamburg. This was
beyond the range of Oboe, but being situated on a distinctive river was easily

identified by H2S. Four heavy raids by Bomber Command assisted by two smaller American daylight raids destroyed the city. The main feature of these raids was the huge 'firestorm' that developed when numerous small fires joined together and formed one huge conflagration.

By autumn of 1943 Harris was ready for the third of that year's great bomber campaigns – the Battle of Berlin. This was a major turning-point in the bombing war and it would be as well to pause here and review Harris's achievements to date and the relationships he had established both with his superiors and with the men he led.

There is not the slightest doubt that in his first year and a half at Bomber Command Harris had been brilliantly successful. Under his direction the bombers had for the first time in the war started to cause serious damage to Germany. The press and public loved him – he would be known popularly as 'Bomber' Harris for the rest of his life.

One of his greatest achievements had been the raising of morale in the dispirited force he had taken over early in 1942. He saw to it that Bomber Command was soundly administered, that aircrew received sound training, that aircrew and aircraft losses were replaced promptly and that the best available equipment was pushed through to the squadrons as quickly as possible. On top of this sound basis for good morale, Harris showed that he possessed great powers of leadership. He rapidly became known as a commander who was completely dedicated to the job of winning the war, who did as much as he could for his men, but at the same time also expected them to give their best. The amazing thing is that he achieved all this without moving from his headquarters. The majority of his men never saw him. Their name for him was 'Butch' – short for 'the Butcher'; it was a title, not of resentment, but of wry admiration for his hard-driving methods.

Harris was well served and much admired by those who worked closely with him. His Deputy C-in-C was Sir Robert Saundby, his former flight commander in the Vernon squadron in Iraq; the two were very close, Saundby occupying the same house as his chief. As for the remainder of his staff, any-one attempting to research a book will still find an impenetrable wall of loyalty. There was rarely any trouble with the group commanders; Harris visited their headquarters only occasionally, but they were often at High Wycombe and spoke daily with their chief by telephone. Ideas from within the command were given full consideration, unlike ideas from outside, and numerous tactical improvements were the result of initiatives taken at group level. A good example of this was the precision bombing and later the low-level marking pioneered by No. 617 Squadron, the Dambusters.

Harris devoted some time to day-to-day operations; for instance, at the morning conferences he personally decided whether a raid should take place during the coming night and selected the target. But much of his time was devoted to what he saw as the continuing battle to keep Bomber Command in the forefront of the British war effort. In his home he prepared a 'conversion room' with an impressive display of photographs showing the destruction caused by his bombers in Germany. Five thousand people were entertained by Harris and his wife at their home during the war, mostly so that they could see the conversion room. He was very disappointed when the Chiefs of Staff of the army and navy declined to visit him and be 'converted'.

Another task for Harris was his constant fight to retain and build up his aircraft strength. He bitterly resented the decisions that forced him to give up squadrons to Coastal Command and to the Middle East, feeling this was a betrayal by the RAF of its true purpose. He had a great ally in the Prime Minister who – at least in this period – fully backed the bomber offensive; with Churchill's help he was able to resist many of the demands made on him.

This leads on to one of the most important aspects of Harris's leadership of Bomber Command. This was his relationship with the Air Ministry and the way he interpreted its directives as the bombing war progressed. In June 1943 another famous directive had been issued, the Pointblank Directive. This reflected the overall strategy agreed by the British and American Chiefs of Staff for the use of both countries' bomber forces in Europe in the year leading up to D-Day. The main aim was still the general attack on German industry and on civilian morale, but priority was given to selected industries – for precision daylight bombing of the factories by the Americans, and for night attacks by Bomber Command on the cities and towns containing those factories. Some of the towns on the priority list were not large ones and a higher degree of target finding than before would be required, but it was hoped that the Pathfinder Force could now cope with this.

Soon after receiving this directive, however, Harris began planning his own offensive for the winter of 1943–4. In his dealings with the Air Ministry he made no attempt to conceal that he intended to concentrate on Berlin and raids on the city started in November. Although Berlin as a target was within the overall aims of the Pointblank Directive and Harris's plans were, initially at least, approved both by Sir Charles Portal and by Churchill, the concentration on this one target, which was not on the Pointblank priority list, did not reflect the spirit of the joint Anglo-American plans although the directive contained ambiguous passages and was capable of different interpretations.

Oft-quoted statements by Harris at this time show both his old methods of pitching his claims as high as possible and his belief that the bomber could still win the war on its own: 'We can wreck Berlin from end to end if the U.S.A.A.F. will come in on it. It will cost us between 400 and 500 aircraft. It will cost Germany the war'* (3 November 1943, letter to Churchill). And, in a letter on 7 December to the Air Ministry pleading that priority be given to his best bomber, the Lancaster: 'It appears that the Lancaster force alone should be sufficient but only just sufficient to produce in Germany by April 1st 1944, a state of devastation in which surrender is inevitable.'*

* *Ibid.*, 11: p. 9 (Churchill letter); p. 56 (Air Ministry letter).

Thus was reached the major turning-point in the bomber war with an all-out effort being made on the German capital. Here was the last chance to fulfil the bomber dream of defeating the enemy before the land campaign that would follow the invasion of Normandy. Many others no longer saw the bomber as capable of pulling this off and thought that Bomber Command should instead be attacking the selected Pointblank targets. But Sir Charles Portal and Churchill backed Harris.

It is only possible here to describe briefly the outcome of the Battle of Berlin. Thirty-five major raids were launched on Germany between November 1943 and the end of March 1944, but roughly half of these were again on targets other than Berlin to prevent the Germans from concentrating their defences. But Berlin was not an easy target to find and hit in winter conditions, even with the latest navigational aids, and, being of modern construction, did not burn easily when it was hit. At the same time the German night-fighter organisation was steadily mastering the bombers' tactics and caused casualties that became unacceptable. The climax came in a raid on Nuremberg on 31 March when ninety-six bombers were lost. In his memoirs Harris does not mention this raid and the maps showing the cities bombed by Bomber Command throughout the war do not include Nuremberg although many smaller places are shown. When 1 April 1944 came, with heavy damage caused in Berlin and the other winter targets, there was still no sign of the hoped-for collapse of German industry. The morale of the tough and disciplined German people was still intact.

One more aspect of the Battle of Berlin should be noted. From January 1944 onwards the Air Ministry cooled in its enthusiasm for Harris's attacks on Berlin and started putting pressure on Bomber Command to adhere more closely to the Pointblank Directive. An issue was made over the comparatively small town of Schweinfurt, the home of most of the German ball-bearing industry. The Americans had raided Schweinfurt by day, at heavy cost, and Harris was urged to attack it by night. He made no secret of his dislike for this selective type of bombing, calling targets such as Schweinfurt 'panaceas'. He believed that the only way to success was to keep hammering away at the larger targets – the 'city targets' – and would not be diverted from his current campaign against Berlin. It was only after a specific instruction was issued by the Air Ministry to Harris that Schweinfurt was attacked in February.

This period marks the time when Harris and the Air Ministry started going their separate ways. An example of this can be seen in the targets selected by Harris for attack in March 1944, the last stage of the Battle of Berlin. A directive from the Air Ministry at the start of the month updated Pointblank and listed six targets as now being top priority for attack by Bomber Command: Schweinfurt, Leipzig, Brunswick, Regensburg, Gotha and Augsburg. Harris could always claim that on any one night he could ignore this priority list for weather or tactical reasons, but the lists of targets his bombers actually raided in that month reads: Stuttgart (twice), Frankfurt (twice), Berlin, Essen and Nuremberg. In other words he was taking advantage of the freedom he was allowed for weather considerations to pursue the general offensive against large German cities at a time when the Air Ministry was calling on him to put more effort on smaller, more selectively important, targets. This difference of approach will be seen again in the last winter of the war, but the bomber offensive on Germany was about to be suspended and the bombers turned on to what was the very antithesis of all Harris's hopes. Bomber Command was required to give direct support to the coming invasion of Normandy.

For exactly six months, from April to September 1944, Bomber Command was ordered to give top priority, firstly to preparing the way for the invasion and then to supporting the Allied ground forces after they had landed. This was tactical rather than strategic bombing and it was masterminded by Air Chief Marshal Sir Arthur Tedder, the RAF officer who had been selected Deputy Supreme Commander of the Allied invasion forces. Harris was not unduly keen to take his bombers away from the offensive on Germany and he had some misgivings over the ability of his force to bomb accurately the targets allocated – gun positions, railway yards and junctions, army camps, airfields, flying-bomb sites, ammunition factories and many more, all in German-occupied France, Holland and Belgium. Failure to bomb accurately would result in the deaths of thousands of friendly civilians.

Nevertheless throughout the summer of 1944 most of Bomber Command's effort was devoted to these targets. They were hit with far greater accuracy than anyone had dared hope. A valuable contribution was made to the success of the invasion and, at the same time, great strides were taken in developing the tactics of more accurate bombing.

The autumn of 1944 brought another turning-point in the bomber war and a potential crisis in Harris's career. Bomber Command had now grown to be a massive force of well over a thousand four-engined bombers and had shown during the summer that certain types of precision bombing were possible. It would continue to receive requests from the army for help with tactical targets and Harris usually met these promptly, but a great debate now took place over how the main effort of Bomber Command should be employed.

There were three views. Sir Arthur Tedder urged that the bombers should concentrate on forcing the collapse of the German army by severing the communications between Germany and the battlefield. Sir Charles Portal, although originally a supporter of Harris's general offensive on Germany, now believed that a sustained attack on the German oil industry was the best way to bring about the collapse of the German army. But Harris had never changed his view that the continued general bombing of German industrial cities would cause the collapse. In November he wrote to Portal: 'Are we now to abandon this vast task, which the Germans themselves have long admitted to be their worst headache, just as it nears completion?'*

So there were three claimants for the use of the bombers. There is no doubt in retrospect that either Tedder's or Portal's plans were within Bomber Command's skills and, if either one had been pursued singlemindedly, would have shortened the war. But it was Harris's determination that prevailed. He stated bluntly that he should be left to pursue his own policy or else he was prepared to resign. Portal was in a quandary. 'Bomber' Harris had been built up as the great hero of the RAF in the dark years of the war; it would be embarrassing to replace him now. Furthermore there was a possibility that, if Harris went, the Americans would try to bring Bomber Command into a unified Allied air command under an American commander, with the result that the last independent force under British control would go. Harris was allowed to stay.

That last winter of the war was in many ways a sad time. Directives continued to arrive at Bomber Command ordering attacks on selected industries. Harris never completely ignored these, but neither did he ever give full compliance. Portal, who had earlier allowed and even encouraged Harris to pursue the old RAF policy of the general attack on industry and civilian morale, could not now tighten the restraints on Harris. Oil was bombed, transportation was bombed, but Bomber Command's main weight continued to fall on the city target. A whole series of devastating raids struck the German cities and it is probable that more destruction was caused by Bomber Command in that last winter than in all its raids of the previous war years. Dresden, destroyed by Bomber Command with huge loss of civilian life in February 1945, later became the symbol of this period; but it should be stated that although Dresden was on Harris's list of cities still requiring attention, it was also one of several targets behind the German eastern front that Bomber Command was ordered to attack in order to help the Russians, and that the Americans also joined in the attack on Dresden.

The end of the war in Europe duly came in May 1945. Germany's cities lay in ruins but the morale of her people never did crack, and although Germany's industry was largely destroyed only in the very last stages of the land battles did the German army fail to get supplies of war material. This is not to say that the bomber had not failed to make a most valuable contribution to the victory, but it had not been able to bring about that victory on its own. Probably the last man to have held on to that theory had been Sir Arthur Harris.

Harris and Bomber Command were not included in the great rush of honours and adulation after the war. Harris's request for a special campaign medal for Bomber Command aircrew was refused; his own share in the post-war honours were a GCB in 1945 and a baronetcy when Churchill returned to

* *Ibid*, III, 82.

office in 1953. Neither could be considered adequate reward for his wartime achievements, but he was probably being made to pay for his obstinacy in the last winter of the war and for the view, which became fashionable when the war was safely won, that the bombing of cities was immoral.

Harris was never offered another position in the RAF nor any other official occupation and he retired to spend his time between South Africa and England. He nurses a healthy dislike for institutions like the BBC and for postwar historians who criticise him, but he rarely enters into undignified argument.

No individual comes out of such a review of his life without less praiseworthy aspects of his character and lifestyle being revealed, but let it be stated quite clearly that Sir Arthur Harris was a man of the highest principles and patriotism who served the British Empire well in two world wars. That service did not become outstanding until February 1942 when he took over Bomber Command, but the resurgence of spirit in the command that he brought about, the courage shown in sending out the Thousand Bomber Raid, the development of new tactics in 1942 and 1943, the undoubted successes of the Battles of the Ruhr and Hamburg – all these were quite brilliant achievements attained in the face of fierce opposition over Germany and, sometimes, at home. But then it all started to go wrong with the Battle of Berlin. Harris had become the leading apostle of the strategic bomber theory: it was his bad luck that he never received the aircraft strength required to crush the German will to resist; that the strength he did have was constantly being diverted from his main aim – although by the justifiable exigencies of war; and that the remorseless progress of conventional war required the invasion of Europe in 1944. On the other hand he was the victim of his own repeated overestimation of what could be achieved in this untried field of war.

It is surely not without significance that after Germany fell the Americans intended to bomb Japan out of the war with massed bomber fleets making incendiary attacks on the main Japanese cities and that Japan collapsed suddenly after two atom bombs, the ultimate weapon of aerial attack. Since 1945 major war has been kept at bay mainly by the universal fear of atomic attack from the air. The scale of explosive power and the means of delivery have changed with the years, but the principle is exactly the same as the one Harris was attempting to prove in the Battle of Berlin.

The pros and cons of the last year balance neatly. Under Harris's direction Bomber Command was a major factor in the success of the invasion, but he undoubtedly went astray in the last winter. Perhaps he was tired: the strain of deciding every morning for two and a half years whether his bombers should be risked that night must have been appalling. Those who shrank from controlling him at this time should bear the ultimate blame.

Whatever the final verdict of history on this bluff, forceful, determined man, several points are clear. There can be no doubt that Harris will go down as one of the great leaders of men. He should be honoured by the RAF, alongside Trenchard, as one who put air power 'on the map'. He will be remembered as the man who tried so hard to bring about the end of the Second World War without recourse to the terrible carnage of the first.

FIELD-MARSHAL THE EARL ALEXANDER

———◆———

Nigel Nicolson

Men followed Alexander because they found in him all the qualities which they most admired. He projected the army's idealised image of itself. He was brave, gallant, charming, modest and professional. He won all his battles except two, Dunkirk and Burma, which he salvaged. If he cannot be ranked among the greatest of British military commanders, it is because he lacked Napoleonic qualities. His temperament was calm more than brilliant, his methods persuasive more than forceful, and his contribution to the art of command (particularly of allies) greater than his contribution to the art of war. A study of his campaigns reveals no major movements that astonish by their originality or daring. Even now that everything is known, it is still slightly puzzling that Alexander could have achieved so much by his grace of manner and professional reliability, and it can only be explained by adding to his other qualities a steely determination, which he was at pains to conceal but managed nevertheless to convey to his subordinates. Lacking Marlborough's genius, he matched his gift for diplomacy. He was able to sway men gently and almost imperceptibly.

He exercised his will by assuming that everyone would wish to do it. If they had other ideas, Alexander would either accept them or evolve a compromise. This is one of the most difficult methods of command. Traditionally generals are expected to lay down a plan of action and enforce it, not present a series of alternatives for discussion. In the heat of action and in the lower ranks of command, such moderate methods are almost impossible, and in tight corners Alexander often showed himself capable of firm and rapid decision. But when campaigns were being planned, he did not retire to the solitude of his caravan and emerge with clear-cut operation orders. He fashioned his plan by seeking advice, listening to argument, thinking aloud, and planting the seeds of his intentions in other men's minds, so that when they germinated they became as much their intentions as his own. He would never force a course of action upon an unwilling commander. He knew that if he did so, it would be executed with misgivings; and that if it failed, he would have lost his subordinate's confidence for the next round.

The method worked. There were moments in the Second World War when

Alexander's gentle touch aroused the suspicion that in the end he would always concede to a stronger will like Montgomery's or Patton's, but his tact and sympathy made him not only acceptable, but indispensable. He was the only Allied general with whom nobody could quarrel, the only one except Eisenhower of whom it could be said that trust and respect survived his mistakes. Calm under stress and courtesy under provocation are among the rarest of human qualities, to which people will always respond, in war as in politics, if they are combined with dedication, competence and success. It is not a sign of weakness. If you can twice save a British army from annihilation, and twice force the capitulation of a German army group in the open field, as Alexander did, you cannot be accused of insipid leadership. He gave the impression, and proved it when crisis came, that he always had something in reserve, that no situation was so desperate that it did not allow of some remedy. He had the resilience of an explorer or mountaineer. He was at his best when he had to make the most of elements that broke in his hands, and he could produce a high gloss on the poorest of human material.

His character was formed by his aristocratic upbringing, his youthful love of painting and mechanics, and his experiences in the First World War. Alexander was both a romantic and an intensely practical man. He enjoyed adventure, wild places, strange peoples and the hazards of unpredictable odds. As a boy he had the run of his family's great estate at Caledon, in County Tyrone, the third of four brothers, heirs to a semi-feudal tradition. His father, the Earl of Caledon, died when Alexander was six, and his mother allowed her sons the freedom of Ulster's countryside, where they shot, fished, climbed and painted. These pleasures never left him. He was at heart a countryman and an artist. He was never an intellectual: he seldom read or thought or talked profoundly. He was able more than clever. He was popular at Harrow because he instinctively liked people and assumed that they would like him, and he enjoyed sports, particularly athletics and cricket, at which he excelled more than at his work. When he passed out of Sandhurst he was placed 85th out of the 172 cadets of his year, and joined the Irish Guards as a Second Lieutenant in 1911 without intending to make soldiering his permanent career. He wanted to paint, and to become President of the Royal Academy was his highest ambition.

The First World War changed all that. When it broke out he was exactly the right age, twenty-two, and had had three years of peacetime soldiering, which gave him a style of leadership that rapidly matured under fire. First as a platoon commander, then as company commander and commanding officer of his battalion, he displayed a gift for leading men that left all his contemporaries behind. What was expected of an officer under the crippling conditions of trench warfare was courage under fire, a combination of cheerfulness, forethought and firmness, and an ability to make friends of the soldiers without loss of authority. All junior commanders aspired to these things: Alexander managed them superbly. He was fortunate to have

Irishmen under his command, men of the breed he had grown to know so well at Caledon, 'who love their leaders', he once said, 'and who have natural good manners'. What a characteristic phrase!

His attitude had its roots deep in chivalry. To him war was not a grotesque massacre by young men of other young men with whom they had no personal quarrel; nor even a crusade to defend liberty against tyranny, for Alexander gave little thought to the ultimate causes of his wars. For him it was an opportunity to test a man's merit and mettle, to strengthen his stamina and courage, and to show that he could retain and refine the decencies of civilised conduct in conditions which proclaimed their very opposite.

He rose during those four years in Flanders from lieutenant to the temporary command of a brigade. He became one of the youngest majors in the British Army, and then its youngest lieutenant-colonel. He was twice wounded: once, severely, on the river Aisne, and again at Passchendaele. He won the MC at Loos, the DSO on the Somme, and the Legion of Honour, and was unlucky not to be recommended for the VC. He fought his battles as if he did not expect to survive them, but with a coolness and a magnificent disdain that caused one of his Guardsmen to say in recollection, 'He was the most perfect man, morally, physically and mentally, that I have ever met.' He emerged from the war as the most respected officer in his regiment, perhaps in the whole Brigade of Guards.

The experience left indelible marks upon him. He had become a professional, in small-arms, minor tactics, map-reading, the care of men. He had learnt that he was capable of anything demanded of him. He knew what a battlefield was like, and was determined that if he were ever called upon to lead an army, he would not forget what orders actually meant in execution. He had acquired a respect for the Germans, and had learnt not only their language but their way of thinking. He had come to enjoy war. 'I shall be almost sorry when it is all over,' he wrote to the colonel of his regiment in 1917, and if this seems a paradox in the character of man so gentle, it was because Alexander had come to love what he knew he could do best, and he relished risks. As soon as the Great War was over, he looked, in high spirits, for a new one.

He found it in the most unexpected place and circumstances, in Latvia, where he was appointed by the Allied Commission to command a brigade of German Balts, the *Landeswehr*, and led them in a campaign to expel the invading Bolsheviks. Alexander, still only twenty-seven, was simultaneously confronted by three totally unfamiliar challenges: he was in command of foreign troops, many of them his ex-enemies, whose loyalty to him was doubtful; their supplies of food, clothing and other essentials were pitifully inadequate for winter warfare in the Baltic; and he was engaging in a mobile battle across forests and frozen lakes. But he managed to weld his brigade into the most effective fighting force operating on any front against the Bolsheviks. He was wounded for the third time in his career, but led the

Landeswehr in a general offensive, flanked by the Lettish army and the Poles, to free the whole of Latvia from Bolshevik control. They advanced 100 miles in twenty days in the mid-winter of 1920 to reach the Russian frontier, and then Alexander resigned his command to return to regimental duties in England. It had been his first taste of an independent command in the most adverse conditions of war.

During the next twenty years Alexander had a more active career than peacetime soldiering normally allows. He took the 1st Battalion of the Irish Guards to Constantinople in 1922, when the Turkish capital was simultaneously threatened by the Greeks and the insurgents under Mustafa Kemal, and although no fighting resulted, he showed once again his imperturbable confidence under threat and his gaiety in relaxation. After an interval with his battalion at Gibraltar and again at home, he went to the Staff College in 1926, the War Office for a short period, and then to Northern Command at York as GSO1. At the age of nearly forty he married Lady Margaret Bingham, daughter of the Earl of Lucan.

In 1934 he was given command of the brigade at Nowshera on the North-West Frontier of India, an exceptional appointment for an officer who had had no connection with the Indian army. With habitual energy he set himself to master the intricacies of mountain fighting and the language of his Indian troops, and led them in two brief campaigns against the tribes. His four years in India added to his reputation and self-confidence. All his characteristics had emerged: leadership by persuasion and example; his understanding of men; his delight ('joy' would not be too strong a word) in facing dangerous odds; his habit of delegation, which some mistook for laziness, but which relieved him of detailed administration to concentrate upon the operational plan; his physical courage and his mental calm. By this time he was one of the most experienced officers in the army. He had fought over most types of terrain, from mountains to ice-bound plains, handled tanks, artillery and aircraft in action, commanded everything from a platoon to a brigade and soldiers of several nationalities. He gave a zest to soldiering, a nobility to war. Field-Marshal Templer, who had been with him in York, and was to serve under him again as a divisional commander in Italy, summed up his qualities like this:

> He had great panache. He was a *beau sabreur*. He had chic, but he never showed off. He had the aristocratic gift. He could be fun. He was always prepared to be kind and amusing, and had excellent manners. His supreme quality was that he was so transparently honest. All his foibles, frailties and strength of character combined into a man for whom anybody who met him would willingly die.

The Second World War came at the right moment to make full use of his character and talents. His greatest opportunity coincided with his prime. In 1939 he was commanding the 1st Division at Aldershot, and he took it to

France as one of the four divisions in the original British Expeditionary Force. For the first seven months there was little action. The BEF constructed field-works on the Franco–Belgian frontier, but when the Germans attacked in the west in May 1940, the BEF moved forward from their prepared positions to the river Dyle in Belgium, guarding the approaches to Brussels. During the next few weeks the army retreated from river to river, to maintain their unity after the collapse of the French on their right, and the Dutch and Belgians on their left. They were still intact when they gathered at Dunkirk to retreat still farther by the only route now available to them, the sea.

Hitherto Alexander's main role had been to sustain the morale and cohesion of his division more than manoeuvre it in combat, for his men were never intensively engaged during the long retreat to the coast. But at Dunkirk he was given a task which demanded all his skill and legendary calm, and for the first time made his name nationally known. He was appointed commander of the rearguard, about twenty thousand men, when Lord Gort was ordered home. He was to save what he could of the BEF, and if and when the Germans threatened to overwhelm him, he was given authority, at his own discretion, to surrender.

The recent publication of the contemporary documents has revealed the dreadful dilemma by which Alexander was confronted. He had been told by Lord Gort that his prime duty was to save his three divisions by evacuating them to Britain. But without informing Alexander, Gort had simultaneously told the French that Alexander would assist them in holding the Dunkirk perimeter so that the French too could embark. If there was to be a sacrifice, it would be shared between the Allies. Churchill in Paris had made equivalent promises to the French government. So when Alexander was faced by the French demand that they and the British should man the perimeter shoulder to shoulder until the last, he was torn between the orders he had received directly and those repeated to him at second-hand. He chose the former. By doing so he saved from annihilation or imprisonment three of the best divisions in the British army, but left ashore eighty thousand French soldiers who covered the last stages of his withdrawal, thirty thousand of whom were captured.

It is the fate of these thirty thousand which has created in France a legend of Dunkirk that differs widely from the British, but the French have overlooked the fact that while Alexander was in command, five times as many French soldiers were evacuated as British. That the final rearguard was all French cannot be quoted to Alexander's discredit: he had more than fulfilled his undertaking that the evacuation would be carried out *pari passu*. He had been the coolest of all those exhausted and harassed men, insisting that the greatest danger in time of stress is panic. He had been constantly on the move between the beaches and the front line, organising and encouraging his men, and in the final few hours he had stood on the shell-torn mole at Dunkirk while the last of them embarked. When all were gone, he took a motorboat parallel to the beaches and close inshore to make certain that none were left stranded, shouting through a megaphone, 'Is anyone there? Is anyone there?', and when he received no answer, he himself embarked on a destroyer and reached Dover safely in the early hours of 3 June. His achievement was immediately recognised and acclaimed, above all by Winston Churchill, who wrote in his memoirs:

> Nothing ever disturbed or rattled him and duty was a full satisfaction in itself, especially if it seemed perilous and hard. But all this was combined with so gay and easy a manner that the pleasure and honour of his friend-ship were prized by all who enjoyed it, among whom I could count myself.

It was this friendship that brought Alexander to the highest rank of field command, a friendship that was deepened during the next eighteen months while Britain awaited a German invasion. Alexander first commanded 1 Corps on the Lincolnshire and Yorkshire coasts, and in December 1940 he was promoted GOC Southern Command. In both areas Churchill was his frequent visitor, and their mutual trust and liking grew. He was designated for the command of the first expeditionary force which could mount a major counter-attack on the periphery of occupied Europe, but when the Japanese war broke out and the pitifully small British force in Burma seemed about to succumb, Churchill called upon his favourite general to retrieve a desperate situation.

Alexander landed in Burma on 5 March 1942 to find that the key battle had already been lost. The army was not only in retreat but in despair. It seemed impossible that Rangoon could be saved, but mindful of his orders from Wavell he attempted it. The result was to place his force in even greater jeopardy, and it was only by a combination of luck and sang-froid that he was able to extricate it in time to form a new line across the centre of the country. Here he held out for a few weeks, but it became clear to him that the ultimate solution could only be a retreat to India. He had under his command not only British and Burmese, but several unreliable Chinese divisions, who looked for their orders more to their Generalissimo Chiang Kai-shek and their American field commander Stilwell than to Alexander himself. He was dealing with gritty characters in circumstances of extreme peril. His troops were facing the masters of jungle warfare, with exposed flanks, no air support, and a complete severance of supply and reinforcement. The Burmese were beginning to desert, the Chinese to waver, and the British were decimated by tropical disease. Alexander's strongest asset was the determination of his corps commander, General Slim. So they retreated, first to Mandalay, and then for 300 further miles across roadless and bridgeless jungle to the relative security of Assam. The monsoon descended just in time to prevent a Japanese pursuit.

He had again saved a beaten army by a combination of forethought, perseverance, example and good luck. Two defeats in succession (for it was difficult to regard Dunkirk and Burma in any other light) would have ended the effective careers of most generals, but Alexander emerged from them with heightened prestige. Even before the Burma campaign was over, Churchill designated him for yet higher command, and it can only be because the character of the man had once again proved equal to extreme adversity, and Churchill loved him for it, tacitly acknowledging that he had imposed on the army in Burma a task far beyond its powers.

Returning to England in July 1942 emaciated but still buoyant, he found himself appointed to command the British First Army in the coming invasion of French North Africa. Within a week or two he was removed from this post to one yet higher. He was made Commander-in-Chief Middle East. A few days later Montgomery was promoted to command Eighth Army, and the two men found themselves respectively the producer and director of the biggest desert drama the world had ever seen.

Alexander, the most admired soldier in the British army, and in supreme command of its most important theatre, decided that his subordinate, Montgomery, must take first place not only in planning and fighting the coming battle, but in public esteem. He deliberately effaced himself. Montgomery had a flair for arousing adulation, and enjoyed it: Alexander was embarrassed by it, and was incapable of jealousy. Eighth Army, he felt, must identify itself with a single commander, and Montgomery's self-confidence and authority would grow with his success and fame. So Alexander gave him his chance, never countermanding his orders, rarely suggesting an element in his plan, and supporting him by every possible means, political, administrative and psychological, to achieve their common object, the defeat of Rommel. It was a remarkable demonstration of his self-control. By remaining remote from the battlefield, Alexander was risking his own authority and the confidence of the troops: he was waiving his right to dictate tactics or correct errors in them, or to use the reserves as he thought best; and he was risking the loss of Churchill's confidence, for the Prime Minister continued to believe that a Commander-in-Chief who did not conduct the actual battle was not worthy of his salt.

The gamble, based on Alexander's careful assessment of a particularly gifted and difficult subordinate, paid off. Montgomery won Alam Halfa with brilliant cool-headedness. He then won Alamein. But there was a price to pay for Alexander's modest demeanour. Alamein was won at a greater cost than Alexander would have allowed had he been in direct command. The battle lacked his style and rhythm, and there was no follow-up after the breakthrough which could have pinned Rommel against the coast. Furthermore Montgomery took advantage of Alexander's permissiveness to ignore his advice, and increasingly to write his own orders. In Sicily and Italy this had damaging consequences to the Alliance. It was not that Alexander had lost his killer-instinct somewhere between brigadier and lieutenant-general (as John Keegan has suggested), nor that he lacked the mental energy to frame a strategically lethal plan. It was simply that he weighed up the advantages of controlling Montgomery more tightly, against the certainty that Montgomery would resent it and be less effective in consequence.

In Egypt Alexander had seen himself as the organiser of another man's victory, and it must have come as a relief to him when Eisenhower appointed him Commander-in-Chief of all the Allied ground forces when they united in Tunisia. Now he had two and a half armies which he could manoeuvre instead of one – the Eighth, First and the American Corps. At first he failed to combine their movements in the most efficient way. If he had had more time and a Napoleonic vision he could have trapped Rommel at Mareth, and then at the Wadi Akarit; and when the Axis armies were united within a tight perimeter round Bizerta and Tunis, his first attempt to crush them was fumbling. He then conceived the plan of piercing their centre by a concentrated attack on the German model, and rolling up their flanks right and left. He did, it is true, have many advantages. He was attacking in overwhelming strength a weakened and beleaguered enemy. But the *coup de grâce* needed careful organisation, and a simplicity intelligible to every man under his command, while puzzling to the enemy. This he achieved. It was a great victory: 250,000 men surrendered to him in the open field.

Then came the invasion of Sicily. The campaign illustrates both Alexander's strength and his weakness. Montgomery took control of the planning to the annoyance of the air and naval commanders (Tedder and Cunningham), and once on shore was allowed by Alexander to shoulder aside Patton's Seventh Army in an attempt to break through west of Etna having failed to do so on the east. All Alexander's tact was needed to soothe hurt American feelings, and allow them a full share in a campaign that lasted only thirty-eight days. As it progressed, order and goodwill succeeded initial confusion and recrimination. But it was not an unalloyed triumph. The Germans escaped across the Messina strait, and neither Eisenhower, who alone had the necessary authority over army, navy and air, nor Alexander, his deputy, did much to stop them.

From Sicily, in September 1943, the Allies invaded the mainland of Italy, with Alexander still in overall command of the land forces. When the landing at Salerno ran into serious trouble, it was Alexander who gave heart to the Allied divisions by his personal intervention on the beaches, who arranged their rapid reinforcement, and cancelled provisional plans for re-embarkation. He was once more in his element, commanding troops in a tight corner, and he was able to retrieve a desperate situation caused by hasty and over-optimistic planning. Once the battle was won, the Allies held securely a third of the Italian mainland. They fought their way up the peninsula, using its entire breadth but making their main effort on the two coastal flanks. It was a slow and brutal business. The battles on the rivers Volturno, Sangro,

Garigliano and Rapido, the three attempts to capture Cassino and its famous abbey, ended in stalemate and high casualties. The army in Italy was fulfilling its allotted function by keeping twenty of the best German divisions away from Russia and north-west Europe, but the campaign was stagnating.

In an attempt to loosen it, Alexander suggested to Churchill in December 1943 the idea of landing a major force at Anzio, 60 miles behind the enemy's right flank. The plan was a good one, but it was conceived on too small a scale. A force of three divisions was not strong enough to open the road to Rome, and the Anzio Corps found itself hemmed in for four months a few miles from the beaches where they had landed in January, and was at one moment in danger of being thrown into the sea by the greater forces which Kesselring was able to bring against it. Although the operation failed in its original object, it forced the Germans to disperse their effort and threatened their main communications from a flank. In May 1944 this threat proved decisive. Alexander launched his main attack from the Cassino front, broke the line at Cassino itself and south of it, and timed the attack from Anzio to cut off the German retreat, a plan which owed much to his Chief of Staff, John Harding. It was not wholly successful, because the American army commander, Mark Clark, preferred to take the direct route to Rome ('The great prize', as he called it) rather than advance north-east to cut the main roads from Rome to Cassino, as Alexander had ordered. The victory was not as complete as it might have been. Still, Rome was captured on 4 June, two days before the landings in Normandy.

The Italian campaign was now reduced to a major diversion. Alexander was convinced that if his armies were left intact, he could conquer the whole of Italy before the end of 1944 and advance through northern Yugoslavia to capture Vienna ahead of the Russians. Whether he could in fact have accomplished this grand design during winter and through mountainous country must remain a matter for debate. It was the only occasion when Alexander seriously questioned his orders. Churchill supported him, but the Americans insisted that Alexander must give up seven of his divisions to stage a landing in southern France in direct support of Operation Overlord. With what he had left he must do his best to keep as many German divisions as possible engaged in Italy. The war would not be won there, nor from there. It would be won by the convergence in central Europe of the Russian armies from the east and the Allied armies from France. The Italian campaign had fulfilled its function. Now it must be allowed to simmer.

At this low ebb of his campaign Alexander was promoted Supreme Allied Commander in the Mediterranean with the rank of field-marshal. He was now responsible not only for Italy, but for Greece, the Balkans, and liaison with the Russian armies advancing into Rumania and Bulgaria. He played an important role in stabilising the British political and military position in Athens at Christmas 1944, and arranged with Marshal Tito the co-ordination of his own forces in Italy with the Yugoslav partisans. But it was in Italy itself that he made the boldest and final stroke of his military career. He was discouraged from attempting a major offensive by Alanbrooke, who advised him to contain the German forces by limited attacks. Instead Alexander proposed to force the capitulation of all the enemy forces facing him, and by his energetic advocacy of the plan he won the Chiefs of Staff's consent.

Although Mark Clark was now in command of the army group, it was Alexander who drew up the master plan. It succeeded brilliantly. Attacking first with Eighth Army on the Adriatic flank, and then with the Fifth in the centre, he captured Bologna, and broke the German army into pieces against the Po. His armoured columns ranged the north Italian plain at will, reaching the French and Austrian frontiers less than three weeks after the offensive began. It was a total victory. On 29 April 1945 the German plenipotentiaries signed at Alexander's headquarters an instrument of unconditional surrender. A million men marched into captivity.

Confronted by his achievement it is impossible to deny Alexander's claim to greatness. But it was greatness of his own special kind. Liddell Hart wrote of him: 'He was a born leader . . . but he might have been a greater commander if he had not been so nice a man, and so deeply a gentleman.' One finds in his later career recurrent examples of his 'niceness' acting as a brake upon his determination. He won his battles, but he could have won some of them more economically if he had been as tough in mind as he was in spirit. His reluctance to create friction at the top sometimes resulted in wasted or muddled effort lower down. When he was a young officer it seemed that he could do no wrong. But when his seniority required of him forethought extending over weeks and months, instead of hours and days, he did not always display an imagination equal to his courage. Against the Tunis victory one must put the uncertainty of his touch before and after Mareth; against the battles of Salerno and Anzio, which he ultimately won, one must place the planning, which was confused or over-optimistic. The last round in Italy was, in my opinion, his finest achievement, and the one least recognised. When all is said Alexander's accomplishment was that men of all ranks and nations *wanted* to be commanded by him; and after six years of war that can be said of few others.

He was Governor-General of Canada from 1946 to 1952, and then for two years served his old friend Churchill as Minister of Defence. He was not happy in politics, which his generous soul found too competitive and his uncomplicated mind too intricate. He spent fifteen years in semi-retirement, occupying his time with a diversity of interests, including painting, and died in 1969, when he was aged seventy-seven, loaded with honours and sustained by the affection and gratitude of the entire nation.

General Joseph W. Stilwell

Riley Sunderland

American General Joseph W. Stilwell (1883–1946) prepared, planned and commanded the first successful Chinese offensive of modern times against a great power, in northern Burma 1944. He reorganised, trained and supervised the arming from British and American stores of the five Chinese divisions involved. In another role, that of Chief of Staff to Generalissimo Chiang Kai-shek and also in compliance with the orders of the US War Department (now the Department of the Army), he strove from April 1942 to October 1944 to provide Chiang and his government with a battleworthy army of from sixty to ninety divisions. Had he succeeded with this project he might have changed the history of Asia and the Pacific. The originality of his achievements, the pioneering nature of his tactics, the continuing existence of the political and cultural factors in and the political consequences of his failures make his experiences in the Second World War important and instructive. And, much of the American experience in China was to be repeated in Vietnam.

A critical essay on Stilwell as soldier and commander must be based on his military life. Graduating from West Point in 1904 he had (as his associate Major-General Haydon L. Boatner reminds us) only some five years with troops between 1904 and 1940. These were three years as a lieutenant in the Philippines and at Monterey, California, and two years as a battalion commander with the 15th Infantry Regiment in China. His gift for languages led him to spend several years learning and teaching French and Spanish. This in turn led to his making a survey of Guatemala and to his later being a corps staff officer in France during the First World War.

After the war, over a period of twenty years, Stilwell was a language officer in China, student at the Infantry School ('Benning' to the American army) and at the Command and General Staff College ('Leavenworth'), back to Benning on its faculty, and finally American military attaché to China 1935–9. The last experience was most fruitful for it led him to study the Chinese army in large-scale combat with Japan in 1937–9. An interval teaching reserve officers, 1933–5, introduced him to the types of civilians who would fill the American armies of the Second World War. Though in these several posts he learned a great deal about the conduct of operations and about the

German, Chinese and Japanese armies, this in the 1930s was not the way to general officer's rank in the American army and Stilwell did not expect such rank.

What saved Stilwell from retiring as colonel in 1939 was that in China and at Benning he had become well acquainted with General (as he later became) George C. Marshall, in 1939 appointed US Army Chief of Staff. Marshall thought Stilwell might be capable of high command, and quickly nominated him for brigadier-general. Commanding the 7th Infantry Division he impressed Marshall as a troop trainer and as a tactician. Moving up to III Corps he did so well that one observer called him Marshall's 'best corps commander'.

Japan attacked Pearl Harbor on 7 December 1941 and the United States was openly at war. Stilwell was soon called to Washington as potential commander of the American army contingent in a projected Anglo-American amphibious move into what was then French North Africa. He was thus on hand when the Chinese and American governments agreed to have a high-ranking officer head the current US Military Mission to China and also be Chief of Staff to Chiang in the Generalissimo's role as Supreme Commander of a newly formed Allied China theatre. Stilwell's directive from the War Department (not, one must note, from the Joint Chiefs of Staff) told him to improve the effectiveness of American assistance to China and 'to assist in improving the combat efficiency of the Chinese Army'. So that the current programme of sending American military equipment ('lend-lease') to China would support and complement Stilwell's anticipated training projects he was authorised to 'supervise and control' lend-lease. (He did not administer it. This was the task of his logistician, Major General Raymond A. Wheeler). Stilwell was also designated military representative of President Franklin D. Roosevelt. Finally, as senior officer present, Stilwell would command the American air and ground forces sent to China, Burma and the Indian base area. Marshall summarised Stilwell's task in two words: 'Support China'.

Stilwell's attempts to support China were handicapped throughout by the decision of the American government to make its main effort in Europe, and by the impossibility of one man's serving two masters if the two did not agree. Stilwell could not serve both the American War Department and Chiang. Until early 1944 Roosevelt was ambivalent, rejecting Marshall's (and Stilwell's) approach yet shrinking from provoking a confrontation by recalling Stilwell. Then, as will be seen below, early in 1944 he adopted the Marshall–Stilwell view and crisis followed.

While Stilwell's posts were being created the Japanese were making steady and unexpected progress in an invasion of Burma. Stilwell was therefore directed by the War Department to go to Burma immediately after reporting to Chiang in his wartime capital of Chungking. In Burma Stilwell would command the Chinese troops sent to reinforce Burma's Indian, British and Burman defenders. The War Department expected this arrangement to improve Sino–British co-operation. Perhaps, but the assignment had its interesting side in that Stilwell was a resolute Anglophobe.

By June 1942 four Japanese divisions with adequate air support had driven Burma's Allied defenders back into India and China. The defenders had been road-bound and afraid of the Burmese jungles. Again and again the Japanese hooked behind them, cut their lines of communication, and forced them to abandon weapons and transport to retreat past the Japanese roadblocks. Chiang Kai-shek had added to Stilwell's difficulties. He had interfered with Stilwell's attempts at counter-attacks by sending orders that bypassed Stilwell. No professional enjoys such treatment, particularly when defeat follows on it, and Stilwell's resentment was both lasting and poorly concealed.

The only Allied success had been that of the American Volunteer Group of fighter aircraft. Commanded and trained by a retired American fighter pilot, Claire L. Chennault, and using the tactical system Chennault had tailored to counter Japanese aircraft and doctrine, these 101 volunteers and their Curtiss-Wright P-40s had destroyed more Japanese aircraft than they had lost. They were the only Allied air unit to do this in the period December 1941 to June 1942.

Japan's occupation of Burma completed its blockade of China and created the local situation Stilwell faced until his recall. Within China, the Generalissimo's three hundred odd divisions were far under-strength, badly fed, inadequately armed and immobile through lack of transport and supply. About thirty were loyal to Chiang, the rest followed other Nationalist politicians. Lend-lease for these men, supplies for the tiny American air force Chennault had organised from the AVG, now had to be flown from India over Japanese-held Burma to Kunming in China. From Kunming to Chennault's fields was another haul over a line of communication whose worst stretch was a dirt road (Kutsing-Tushan) longer even than the entire Ledo Road from India to China. Indian airfields from which supplies would be flown to China had to be built. The railway to their projected sites and to British and Indian army bases needed much work. Indian ports were either too far (Karachi, Bombay) or congested (Calcutta).

Differing national policies made for more complications. Probably surmising that the Pacific war would be won or lost by what the Japanese and Americans did in the Pacific's waters and islands, Chiang thought his and China's ends best served by his accumulating arms to use in a postwar settlement of accounts with the Chinese Communists. Nothing in his wartime actions suggests that he thought the physical condition, training, organisation and morale of the Nationalist divisions relevant to that end. The government of India, already supporting the war against Germany and Italy in North Africa and the Mediterranean, was reluctant to use India's men and wealth to rescue a China whose ambitions in Burma and Tibet they knew and feared. The British government thought the United States unduly concerned with a China that demanded much and would contribute little. Most of the officials concerned in these several governments believed that the Allies had not mastered the problems of jungle war. A few, such as British Major-General Orde Wingate and Stilwell, saw the solutions, but in the then climate of opinion they were inevitably thought to be eccentric.

In this situation the attitude of President Franklin D. Roosevelt, that the United States should ask nothing from China in exchange for American assistance given to China (as against Marshall's and Stilwell's contrary views), determined American policy. Not until 3 April 1944 did Roosevelt send Chiang a message that completely reversed his previous course and adopt the Marshall–Stilwell *quid pro quo* approach.

Against this background of logistic problems and diplomatic conflict Stilwell planned and sought support for a number of projects to improve the combat efficiency of the Chinese army. To bring enough weapons into China to complete the armament of the first thirty American-sponsored Chinese divisions (and to train a second thirty), Stilwell with the enthusiastic support of the US Army Service Forces undertook completion of a road from India to China across northern Burma, to be paralleled by fuel pipelines. The Japanese had to be cleared from Burma to reopen ground communications with China (by Rangoon had been Stilwell's first idea) and so Stilwell sought Chinese, British and American support for an attack on Burma from Indian and Chinese bases. To prepare a Chinese contingent he set up schools and unit training centres, and despatched teams of American instructors and liaison officers to selected Chinese divisions. Inevitably the number of American servicemen in India and China grew as these several logistic and training projects slowly matured.

Complications were introduced by Brigadier-General Claire L. Chennault's (as he had now become) telling Roosevelt and Chiang that if he were given 147 bombers and fighters, with replacements, and a very small supply tonnage flown in to China, he could defeat Japan. Chiang in January 1943 made clear his support for the Chennault Plan. These views also meshed perfectly with Roosevelt's thinking, for they permitted him to give Chiang what Chiang wanted without asking anything of Chiang in return, e.g., rebuilding his army. Therefore at the Trident Conference (Washington, May 1943) Roosevelt announced his support for the Chennault Plan, though Marshall and Stilwell warned that if the air effort provoked the Japanese the latter would take Chennault's air bases – for whose defence the Chinese army was now not to be prepared. To preserve an option, however, Trident also directed planning a Burma campaign.

Chennault did not defeat Japan with a small air force. For this he blamed Stilwell, charging that Stilwell had failed to support him. Chennault's estimate of what the aircraft and ordnance of the 1940s could do is an interesting example of the mystique of the aeroplane. He was not however alone among his contemporaries in his enthusiasm. But it is odd that he should have held it so long, long after experience in Britain and in Germany in 1940–2 should have shown the view mistaken. Thus in May 1940 the Air Ministry had advised the British Cabinet that dropping 28 tons of bombs per night on the Ruhr offered the possibility of halting industry there in a couple of days. Two years later, in May 1942, the RAF made the famous thousand-bomber raid on Cologne without ending the war yet four months later in October 1942 Chennault was making his promises to Roosevelt. Perhaps word of the thousand-plane raid and similar developments did not reach Chennault in the remoter parts of Asia, but Roosevelt should have known better.

The Burma offensive, whose planning was directed by Trident, became more probable during the Quadrant Conference of August 1943 in Quebec. Quadrant directed a major engineering effort in India and Burma to support operations in Burma and China, and also created a tri-service, Anglo–Sino–American command to conduct operations in South-East Asia. This was South-East Asia Command, Admiral Lord Louis Mountbatten, Supreme Allied Commander. Stilwell was made Deputy Commander, but the administrative slip that failed to give him orders confirming him in the post (after twenty-five years nothing more seems to have been involved) left him *acting* only and introduced one more irritant, and a major one.

In October 1943 Stilwell surveyed his situation in a memo to himself, as was his practice, and decided there was nothing more he personally could do to affect the course of events in China. Thereafter he gave most of his time and attention to South-East Asia Command and Burma, a course in which he persevered until Chiang called him to China on 26 August 1944.

By coincidence the northern Burma campaign began on 30 October 1943. Chinese trained in India and sent to Burma to protect the progress of the road to China (Ledo Road or, much later, Stilwell Road), met elements of the first-rate Japanese 18th Division of Lieutenant-General Shinichi Tanaka. Both sides were reinforced, and a stalemate developed. Stilwell was not present; Brigadier-General Haydon L. Boatner, USA, deputy commander of the Chinese army in India, commanded. Meanwhile Stilwell was preparing for the next great Allied conference, Sextant, in Cairo in December 1943. In so doing Stilwell suggested that Chiang seek American support for ninety divisions.

Chiang's presence at Cairo did not help his cause. Roosevelt and Winston Churchill, much against the wishes of the US Joint Chiefs, reduced the size of the projected Burma operations below what Chiang had been led to expect. Concurrently American strategic planners had begun to think that America could use bases in the Marianas rather than in China to defeat Japan. Roosevelt moreover seems greatly to have lessened his estimate of Chiang.

Immediately after Sextant Stilwell decided to go to northern Burma and take local command. For one thing, Boatner was seriously ill. Given the scale of operations, Stilwell would function as a corps commander. His later actions show he sought to end the northern Burma campaign by destroying the 18th Division in one decisive battle. He left Roosevelt and Marshall to persuade

Chiang that it would be in Chiang's interest to commit some of the first thirty divisions in Yunnan province to Burma operations. The two American leaders began their effort on 17 March 1944. Chiang demurred and on 3 April Roosevelt adopted the Marshall–Stilwell approach by requesting Chinese action in return for American lend-lease.

While Stilwell campaigned and Roosevelt negotiated, the Japanese invaded India with three divisions and South-East Asia Command sent Wingate and his Chindits (with a rifle strength of two divisions) to cut the lines of communication of both the Japanese attacking India and those facing Stilwell. The resulting battles around Imphal and in central Burma kept major Japanese forces from northern Burma and must be seen as an essential factor in Stilwell's campaign.

On 31 December Stilwell arrived in northern Burma. He enjoyed a critical advantage not present in his first battles with the Japanese – air supply made possible by air superiority. His forces could dispense with a ground line of communication and concentrate on attacking that of the Japanese, thus dramatically reversing 1942. He combined reinforcement and envelopments to break the stalemate and then moved the Chinese 38th and 22nd divisions well into the Hukawng valley on the trace of the Ledo Road. The arrival of Galahad, a brigade-sized force of American infantry trained on Chindit lines to conduct deep jungle penetrations on air supply, led to Stilwell's first attempts at a decision.

Twice he sent Galahad around the Japanese right flank and across their line of communication, while the Chinese made the frontal attack. At Walawbum (4–8 March) the Japanese had had the foresight to cut a bypass through the jungle and used it to escape the trap. At Inkangahtawng (12–23 March), Galahad again enveloped, but the Japanese reacted vigorously while the site of the Galahad block was beyond supporting distance by the Chinese. While Galahad was being withdrawn, Stilwell thought himself free to visit China. In his absence his northern Burma staff radically changed the concept of Galahad's employment by using it as a static flank guard. As a result one of its battalions was besieged at Nhpum Ga (28 March–9 April). The resulting relief operations plus the siege significantly reduced Galahad's combat effectiveness through sickness and physical fatigue.

At this point, though the period of campaigning weather before the monsoon rains was growing short, Stilwell had done two important things: he had steadily driven back the Japanese until he was within striking distance of the strategic key to northern Burma, the airfield and town of Myitkyina; and he had fixed the attention of his opponent, Tanaka, on the Hukawng valley. (The Generalissimo's belated decision to cross the Salween into Burma over 11–12 May would have been another distraction). So Tanaka did not notice that over 28–30 April Stilwell sent all of Galahad, two Chinese regiments, and some three hundred Kachin irregulars east and south out of the Hukawng valley and on to Myitkyina. (Myitkyina's capture would permit a great expansion of air supply to China by permitting the use of a lower route and so the Joint Chiefs of Staff on 3 May reaffirmed that Stilwell was to take the town. They did so in the course of giving him a new and overriding mission which Myitkyina was to facilitate, that is, giving China-based air support to imminent American operations in the western Pacific). No more than the threat to Myitkyina did Tanaka appreciate a renewed threat to his right flank. Stilwell's last and most successful envelopment was forming.

The long-range strike at Myitkyina began with a brilliant overrunning of the airfield on 17 May, a coup which, in large part as a result of Nhpum Ga, Galahad was in no condition to exploit by occupying the town. The envelopment of Tanaka's flank by the Chinese 112th Regiment took place on 25 May. The envelopment was a success in that the 18th Division escaped only by abandoning its artillery and motor transport, but Myitkyina degenerated from coup to siege. The town finally fell on 3 August. As desired, hump tonnage, thanks to the new route, rose from 13,686 in May to 25,454 in August.

Then China claimed Stilwell's attention. Fearing that a new type of American long-range bomber (B-29s) might be based on Chennault's fields, and disturbed by the operations of a reinforced, better-supplied Chennault, the Japanese on 17 April had begun a major drive to take his bases (Ichigo). (After the war they denied having aimed at creating a line of communication from Manchuria to South-East Asia, saying they lacked the necessary resources.) Marshall and Stilwell in early 1943 had warned of exactly this. The weight of the drive fell on the troops of a Chinese Nationalist general, Hsueh Yueh, whom Chiang feared as a possible rival, and so on or about 5 June Chiang embargoed the shipment of arms and supplies to him. Stilwell enforced the embargo, as did his successor Lieutenant-General A. C. Wedemeyer until Chiang lifted it on 22 February 1945. (Neither general reported the embargo to Washington.) So the Japanese moved forward steadily, meeting significant resistance only at Hengyang (28 June–8 August).

As the Japanese advanced the American government concluded that China might be driven to seek a separate peace. Seeking to revive the Chinese armies, and at the 4 July recommendation of the Joint Chiefs, Roosevelt asked Chiang to give Stilwell command, under Chiang, of all Chinese forces. In this event Stilwell planned to arm sixty Nationalist divisions, and but five Communist. He contemplated no political moves or suggestions. Chiang agreed in principle to Stilwell's command, but the long (6 July–18 October) negotiations broke down in October. A Chinese scholar, Dr Liang Chin-tung, with access to Chiang's records, traces the break to Stilwell's refusing the Generalissimo's orders of 8 and 11 September that Stilwell's Burma forces renew their eastward drive in order to support Chiang's Salween divisions and to the language of a demand by Roosevelt on 16 September that Chiang 'at once' give Stilwell command. At Chiang's insistence Roosevelt recalled Stilwell on 18 October. In so doing he told Chiang that he and Churchill, not Stilwell, were responsible for the Allied strategy of which Chiang had bitterly complained to him. By October 1944 the relationship between the President and the General-issimo was not what it had been.

Stilwell's recall should not be confused with a relief. He had, as Roosevelt told Chiang, faithfully executed the orders of his superiors. They in turn awarded the Oak Leaf Cluster to the Distinguished Service Medal together with the highest grade of the Legion of Merit for his services in the China–Burma–India theatre. They later employed him to command the US Army Ground Forces (1945), the Tenth Army (1945), in which post he would have played a major part in the projected invasion of Japan, and, finally, Sixth Army (1946) whose headquarters were in the Presidio of San Francisco. This attractive place, which overlooks the Pacific, was only an afternoon's drive away from his beloved house at Carmel.

Stilwell died in San Francisco of cancer in 1946. At his wish, his ashes were scattered over the ocean off Point Lobos, a place of superlative beauty in an area marked by natural beauty, and very near his house.

Such then was Stilwell's career. The part that concerns us is his work in the Second World War. To analyse it let us now consider relevant cultural and military factors, the personal traits that affected his operations, his military ideas and their probable sources. The principal military factor may be quickly presented. It was that the United States and the British Commonwealth agreed in March 1941 to make their main effort in Europe. This in turn reflected Germany's strength and the logistical difficulty of Asian operations. Japan could not long survive Germany's defeat. Pacific operations had second priority and with one exception, transport aircraft, the China–Burma–India theatre was last. So many American transport aircraft were assigned to hump operations that Marshall thought victory in Europe was significantly delayed.

The cultural factor was that into the twentieth century Westerners without previous, substantial experience in Asia tend to see Asian governments and societies as mirror images of their own. This results in unreal expectations and in placing unreal demands upon Asians and Asian organisations. No Western power has been free of this, though in recent years the British record has been the best. Once Great Britain had won the eighteenth century contest with France in India, the British could lay a foundation that withstood the blunders that caused the Mutiny and the several Afghan disasters. Britain in Asia then had a century to digest the lessons of these experiences and prepare for the return of power to Asian hands. Relative latecomers, the other Western powers, did not have time to adapt their preconceptions to Asian reality.

And so most influential Americans saw the Chinese Nationalist government as the image of their own. They did not see Chiang and his associates as presiding over an uneasy coalition of regional military forces, or as having very limited authority, or as not sharing the American goal of quick, simple military victory. Nor could they perceive the implications of the pervasive Chinese practice of bargaining, or adopt the concept of *quid pro quo* as Stilwell and Marshall urged. Rather, they thought the Americans need only show their wonderful new ways and machines to the Chinese and the Chinese would cheerfully and gratefully adopt them

A specifically American trait that affected Stilwell and the American effort in China was American identification with and reliance on technologically intensive projects. Chennault's air force in China and the immense and costly air transport route to China were, as Lieutenant-Colonel Gordon K. Pickler of the US Air University maintains, quintessentially American. Stilwell's programme, that is, placing American commanders and staff officers in a group of Chinese divisions, the creation of service schools, retraining and rearming the divisions, was not the programme the United States preferred. Not until the winter of 1944-5 did part of it, retraining and rearming, get priority and then it was too late. Some numbers will illustrate; American troop strengths in China on 15 August 1945, at the war's end, were:

Air   34,726
Ground 22,151
Other   5,492

In India in November 1944 there were:

Air   102,467
Ground 81,353

These then were the public factors with which Stilwell dealt.

Next we may consider Stilwell's personal qualities as they affected his work. His career will have suggested some: initiative, openness to innovation, great energy, resilience, or, as Marshall wrote at the time: '. . . tremendous energy, courage, and unlimited ingenuity and imagination . . . alert . . . his training and understanding are on an unusually high level . . .' Other traits were less helpful, and in the China–Burma–India theatre he was handicapped by his Anglophobia, obsessive nursing of grudges, verbal indiscretions and excessive reserve.

One possible source of his Anglophobia, and which also illustrates his nursing of grudges, was suggested by a member of his family who ascribed it to the rudeness of two Englishmen in China. Many years before, they had taunted him while he was playing badminton. That might well be, for the man who later drew up a seventeen-page handwritten list of the difficulties he had met in dealing with South-East Asia Command would have let such an episode fester, and grow. Then there was Stilwell's dislike of pomp and ceremony, which he seems to have associated with Britain, and which may reflect his rejection of the grand style kept by his maternal grandparents. A last influence may have been family history. Old families have long memories and attitudes survive the events that bred them. One of the court that condemned Charles I and who suffered for this the ghastly penalty for regicide was brother of the Nicholas Cooke, alias Stilwell, who founded the family in New Amsterdam.

The Anglophobia was not free of ironies and inconsistencies however. Stilwell and Field-Marshal Earl Wavell were related by marriage, while General (later Field-Marshal the Viscount) Slim and Stilwell became personal friends.

Another trait that affected operations because it too angered men whose support Stilwell needed was his flair for words. Nicknamed 'Vinegar Joe' by a student at Benning, he had a talent, not always wisely used, for acid turns of phrase, e.g., dubbing the Generalissimo 'Peanut'. These indiscretions were so widely known that Marshall warned Stilwell he was offending not only Chiang but Roosevelt. It was the deplorable part of a gift that filled his private papers with humour and satire. Much of it, such as the diary of a family visit to Japan purportedly kept by his infant son Ben, is charming.

His reserve and secretiveness were excessive. He would not tell his staff of his plans, let alone try to win support for his projects from either Roosevelt or Chennault. He left it to Marshall and Secretary of War Henry L. Stimson to win Roosevelt's support for him while Lieutenant Joseph W. Alsop of Chennault's staff regularly corresponded with the President's right-hand man, Mr Harry L. Hopkins. (This in turn led Hopkins and Marshall to differ so violently about American policy towards China that to preserve their relationship they agreed not to discuss it.) As regards Chennault, who was after all Stilwell's air commander in China, Stilwell made no attempt to win his support or even to keep him informed. A superior should not have to win the support of his subordinate, but given the fact of the Chennault–Roosevelt and Chennault–Chiang relationships, Chennault was a most atypical subordinate.

Staff planning in the China–Burma–India theatre began only in April 1944, on the initiative of Major-General Daniel I. Sultan, Stilwell's new deputy. Sent to Stilwell in northern Burma, the plan drew no response. To get some reaction, Sultan and his chief planner, Colonel William M. Creasy, in accordance with the plan transferred a Military Police platoon from Stilwell's combat headquarters to China. That brought an angry blast, and telling Creasy, somewhat needlessly, that this would make or break his career, Sultan in June sent Creasy to explain. The interview ran something like this:

Creasy saluted and said: 'Sir, I sent your MPs to China.'

Long silence, then: 'Who the hell gave you authority?'

'Sir, I was trained that the silence of a superior means approval.'

More silence.

'OK, Colonel, you've got your approval. Carry out the plan!'

Creasy had his approval and in a few years he had his general's stars, but it was an odd way to run a headquarters.

The man who had these traits, traits that often warred with one another to his great handicap, had equal conflict between public image and private reality. His house, Llanfair, was set in a uniquely beautiful geographic enclave. For a few miles along the California coast above Big Sur there grew the Monterey cypress with its extraordinary flat top as though trimmed, there was the eucalyptus, Easter lilies grew wild, little flocks of quail ran about, people had flowerbeds instead of lawns, and there was Llanfair just off the Pacific beaches. The western sun flooded the upstairs sitting-room and set aglow the amethyst glass plate from the Forbidden City. The redwood beams of the ceiling, the adobe walls, the austere northern Chinese furniture, the books that covered one wall, but yet were only a part of his library – all were marks of the centuries of gentility that Stilwell shed when he affected the plain, rough old soldier. One wonders what the press would have made of his collection of silk brocades in a magnificent camphorwood chest. The press knew nothing of them and so Stilwell could perfect the image that was his trademark. But it was image, not reality.

The famous diaries were to Stilwell what a psychiatric session might be to another man, as well as aids to memory. Into them he poured the rages, frustrations, and bitterness of an intensely reserved, sensitive man who had been given as he wrote 'a mission and no means'. The diaries were neither the outer nor the whole man and their content surprised many service associates. No man is a hero to his valet and still less can a public figure be unaffected by the appearance of the uninhibited fantasies he had suppressed in his lifetime.

From the man and his traits we pass to his operational methods, which reflected Stilwell's willingness to innovate and adapt. The heart of his tactical system was repeated envelopment by troops on air supply, to destroy the enemy in place. In using air supply to give jungle mobility superior to the Japanese, and in using that mobility to attack Japanese flanks and rear installations, he and Wingate thought alike, and were ahead of their contemporaries in India and Burma. To execute his envelopments, Stilwell developed an air-ground team. His infantry depended on air supply, close air support, and air evacuation by the US Tenth Air Force under Major-General Howard C. Davidson. 'Air parties' (in local usage) with forward air controllers in liaison aircraft (L-5s) foreshadowed today's USAF tactical air control parties and supplied the connecting link between ground and air. The passage of twenty-five years has brought no significant improvement to this system.

Stilwell's use of Galahad demonstrated his tactical thought. Brigadier-General Frank D. Merrill, who with Colonel Charles N. Hunter alternated in command of Galahad, described it as playing the role of strategic cavalry. That is, since it was far more mobile than its Japanese opponents it could march around their flanks to strike their lines of communication. This is not a novel manoeuvre in war. It is the way Allenby used the Desert Mounted Corps against the Turks and Germans in Palestine in November 1917. The novelty lay in Stilwell's recognising that in northern Burma in 1944 infantry on air supply could play a classic cavalry role. As will be seen Stilwell was well acquainted with the Palestine campaigns.

His familiarity with these campaigns of the First World War suggests inquiry into the origins of his approach to the problems he met in the Far East. Two sources can be readily identified. Stilwell's books included *Five Years in Turkey* by Liman von Sanders. Victor of Gallipoli as commander of the Turkish Fifth Army, Chief of the German Military Mission to Turkey from 1913 to 1918, Liman von Sanders changed the course of world history by his command of Asian troops. His German Mission, moreover, supplied commanders and staff officers to Turkish divisions, corps, armies and army groups; directors and instructors for service schools; staffs, troops, specialists and equipment for the Turkish transport, supply, medical and signal services; air support, and elite infantry organisations. In concepts, roles, missions and experiences the German effort in Turkey in 1913–18 foreshadowed that of the United States in China in 1941–5. Stilwell's copy of the grand old Prussian's account of this was well read. Its example of Western officers holding key command and staff positions in Asian Nationalist forces was not lost on him, nor did he forget the increased combat efficiency that might be obtained through a relatively few logisticians and trainers.

A second source was the German Military Mission to China. When in 1938 at Japanese insistence Adolf Hitler recalled them, a considerable number of their papers were given to Stilwell (then military attaché) through his assistant, Major Frank Dorn. Some of the papers went to Washington, others (copies?) were still at Carmel in 1965. The fact of the transfer argues for good relations between the two groups of professionals, German and American. Stilwell therefore knew that the German Military Mission to China had organised a group of training divisions in which German officers held certain command and staff assignments – just as they had in Turkey. Chinese held other posts and filled the ranks. In so doing they had on-the-job training and valuable experience in a unit trained and organised to high professional standards.

When the Sino–Japanese War began in 1937 these Germans continued to hold command and staff roles behind a veil of diplomatic discretion. One may assume they wanted combat experience while the Chinese wanted their help. So, some years later, a former member of the mission recalled that a Lieutenant von Schmeling was killed in action commanding a Chinese battalion during the Shanghai fighting. Here then was the precedent for Stilwell's belief that Chinese Nationalists would accept Western commanders and here too is the probable origin of his suggestion of 27 April 1942 to the Generalissimo that a Chinese corps of 100,000 be formed with Americans as '. . . higher commanders and principal staff officers . . . until such time as Chinese officers can be substituted'. A possible American origin of the command arrangement is that from 1916 to 1930, by Act of Congress, US Marine Corps officers were seconded to the Haitian gendârmerie. The Haitian episode, and the success of the marines, was well known in the States, but unlike the German experience I do not recall any of its records as having been in Stilwell's hands. A final interesting link between Turkey and China is that General Hans von Seeckt, who established the German Mission in China, served in Turkey under Liman von Sanders. Seeckt earlier created the famous 100,000-man *Reichswehr* after the First World War. The number suggests Stilwell's proposed 100,000-man elite force.

Stilwell's handling of British and American infantry has been most controversial, oddly so for a man who wrote with such sympathy of the infantryman and so prided himself on being one. From first to last, eight American battalions fought as infantry at Myitkyina. American Second World War infantry divisions had nine such but the impact of the eight was far less than that of a division. To begin, two were engineer battalions. Showing an absence of contingency planning, they had not been prepared for the role. The troop equivalent of three more battalions were organised by the War Department as an infantry regiment less headquarters and headquarters company, which the department expected the China–Burma–India theatre to provide from Galahad veterans, but the theatre was not told of this concept and made no preparation to ready these fine, experienced volunteers to be combat units. Training and organisation had to be provided on the battlefield. The balance of the eight were the three Galahad battalions. The War Department had decided not to provide replacements. Stilwell did not try to improvise a replacement system and limited himself to returning medical evacuees. Of these latter, 250 were not returned to their units but were sent off as the American contingent of a little Sino–American task force, Purple. Its American commander lost his way, Purple contributed nothing but a further drain. As is well known, at Myitkyina the remnants of Galahad finally had a morale breakdown.

Stilwell was so anxious to have American infantry that one may wonder why these difficulties arose. The answer begins with the intricacies of command structure within India and Burma. SEAC, not CBI Theatre, had operational control of infantry. India Command, not CBI, controlled training facilities so that Stilwell could not simply order his staff to get ready for a specific number of battalions. And so weeks were lost in sorting out Galahad's status and facilities, even though they were present and Marshall personally interested. Later, as regarded the New Galahad with its three battalions the US War Department contributed more complexities by failing to make sure CBI knew its intent. It does seem that CBI could have done something in the line of field expedients to prepare the two engineer battalions. Finally Galahad like the Chindits believed they would have one very hazardous mission of ninety days followed by relief. Both organisations took a corresponding view of medicine and field sanitation. Neither was given replacements.

Stilwell's Chinese units faced the same hazards and combat environment as Galahad and the Chindits, but stayed combat effective and were not withdrawn. Significantly they had replacements and practised excellent field sanitation. Stilwell believed he could not let northern Burma become a fight from which Westerners were excused and so told Marshall that he had to keep an American flavour in the fight (for which his superiors had not made adequate provision for they did not believe they could explain to the American public why American soldiers had to be sent to an area squarely between two of the world's greatest sources of manpower, India and China).

There may have been still a third factor, Stilwell's limited experience with troops, none of it in combat. This might have led him to misread the situation.

In retrospect the intricate command structure in India, the War Department's failure to make clear its intent with the New Galahad, the original concept of the Chindits and Galahad as high-intensity, short-lived forces interacted to produce a series of failures to meet the realities of combat in northern Burma. The situation was exacerbated by Wingate's death soon after his men were committed. Given this situation there was not a great deal that Stilwell could have done. Sending the 250 Galahad evacuees to Purple Force was ill advised. At the time both Stilwell and Merrill were uneasy over the step. Something could have been done to prepare the engineers. Stilwell certainly had authority to withdraw Galahad and the Chindits sooner than he did. Whether he was justified in fearing an adverse Chinese reaction is unknowable at this time. Later the Chinese were to comment sardonically on their having replaced Galahad at Walawbum and Inkangahtawng.

Appraising Stilwell as a soldier and commander must be distinguished from appraising the American effort over which he presided and much of which he did not command. He was not the first nor will he be the last soldier to find himself 'given a mission and no means'. The question rather is how Stilwell played the hand he was dealt. He may be faulted for his inability or unwillingness to win the friendship or at least the neutrality of Chennault, of Roosevelt, of Chiang. Perhaps he could not have done it, but that is not the point. He did not try. His Anglophobia hurt him when he was discussing future operations with the British, many of whom came from GHQ (India). When men doubt postwar Chinese ambitions it is not helpful to tell them they compare unfavourably with Clive. Clive had other worries. It was in these fields of personal and inter-command relations that Stilwell had his serious failures.

In spite of these failures and against assorted cultural, diplomatic, logistical and military obstacles Stilwell did organise and command the first Chinese offensive of modern times against a great power. In so doing he showed technical virtuosity of a high order in his pioneering use of air-supplied infantry in South-East Asian jungle. His repeated demonstrations that properly led, fed, trained and equipped the Chinese soldier could defeat one of the most formidable infantries presaged China's again becoming a great power. It has been suggested that Stilwell's views were out of step with global strategy. In telling Marshall as late as 24 May 1944 that Japan would have to be defeated on the mainland of Asia he was certainly out of step with the main thrust of Anglo-American strategy of mid-1944 but his continuing effort to strengthen China was consistent with an enduring theme in American policy and in accord with Marshall's order: 'Support China.' It is worth pointing out that some 10 per cent of the messages in Stilwell's personal file were to and from Marshall. Marshall always knew what Stilwell was doing and when he disapproved corrected him.

In all, only a most versatile soldier of high martial skill could have done what Stilwell did.

Admiral of the Fleet The Earl Mountbatten

Vice Admiral Sir Ronald Brockman

That a Prince from a German Principality should join the Royal Navy at the age of fourteen and forty-four years later become First Sea Lord; and that his younger son, after a further forty years should be the first son to succeed a father as First Sea Lord must surely constitute events which, when taken together would have involved almost astronomical odds.

Mountbatten's father, Prince Louis of Battenberg, encouraged by Queen Victoria's son Alfred, and her daughter Alice, became a naturalised British subject in 1868, at the age of fourteen, and entered the Royal Navy with an intense enthusiasm and devotion to his new country and service. He rose by outstanding merit to the highest commands in the Royal Navy and from 1912 to the end of October 1914 was the First Sea Lord. It was he who alone took the responsibility, in the absence of ministers away for the week-end, to cancel the demobilisation of the Fleet on Sunday, 26 July 1914, thus preventing the dispersal of all the reservists to their holidays and enabling its passage from Portland to its war base at Scapa Flow to be effected on Friday, 1 August 1914, immediately prior to the outbreak of war. Nevertheless, he was hounded out of office by the pathological attitude of the press and public to anyone of German name and origin.

In 1917 when the Royal Family abandoned their German names and titles, Prince Louis took the name Mountbatten, and was created the first Marquess of Milford Haven.

The family were all multilingual, speaking three or four languages, and young Louis was fluent in German and French, a qualification which was to stand him in good stead in the higher ranks of the Royal Navy which he entered as a Naval Cadet on 8 May 1913 at the Royal Naval College, Osborne, where he was at the time of his father's forced resignation from the post of First Sea Lord on 28 October 1914, on account of his German parentage. It had a traumatic effect on him. Lord Louis had been to some extent over-shadowed by his brilliant elder brother, Prince George, whose early retirement from the Royal Navy as a Captain and premature death before the Second World War were sad losses. The future Admiral of the Fleet passed modestly into the Royal Navy at Osborne, forty-second out of a term of eighty-two cadets; he passed out of the Royal Naval College, Dartmouth, eighteenth in the term; and at the end of the additional period at Keyham he was top of the term, a position he was never to lose. The treatment accorded his father had left its mark; sheer hard work and determination to succeed were to be the outstanding traits of Lord Louis in the years ahead.

He would also be the first to admit how much his character was formed by and how much he owed to his parents. His father's outstanding qualities as a naval officer are well known and he was at his best in his relations with his children; but the influence of his mother, Princess Victoria of Hesse (a grand-daughter of Queen Victoria), is unquestioned and it is from her that Lord Louis absorbed the progressive thought and ideas which have always been characteristic of him.

From his earlier days he was accustomed to accompanying his parents in visits to members of the family all over Europe and especially to kings and emperors whom he would maternally address as uncle or cousin. During these visits he became acquainted with the leading statesmen of the day.

As a midshipman in July 1916 he joined the *Lion*, flagship of Vice-Admiral Sir David Beatty commanding the Battle Cruiser Fleet. Early in 1917 he was transferred to Beatty's new flagship, the battleship *Queen Elizabeth*, when the latter became Commander-in-Chief, Grand Fleet. Thus the young Louis had the opportunity of being a shipmate of one of the really outstanding admirals of the First World War, and Beatty's example of leadership cannot fail to have left its imprint on the young midshipman.

Beatty was well known for keeping in close touch with ship's companies. On such occasions as ships' concert parties and sporting occasions, he would take the opportunity of addressing the crews and giving them the inspiration and fighting spirit he possessed in such measure. Mountbatten followed a similar practice throughout his career; and those who served in the South-East Asia Command in the Second World War will long remember the Sup-reme Commander's talks from a soap box during his frequent visits to the front, taking everyone into his confidence about future planned operations and inspiring them to even greater efforts against the Japanese.

Probably the best of Beatty's characteristics midshipman Louis imbibed in the First World War was the instinct for the offensive and for taking the initiative. This is reflected clearly in Mountbatten's actions in HMS *Kelly* and the 5th Destroyer Flotilla; in his preparations as Chief of Combined Operations for the landing in Normandy; in his South-East Asia Campaign; and in his devolution of power in India.

Then in 1917 came the change of name and, as a younger son of a marquess, young Prince Louis of Battenberg became Lord Louis Mountbatten. Although in 1946 he received a peerage and became Viscount and in 1947 Earl Mount-batten of Burma, his many friends and most of the lower deck of the Royal Navy still refer to him affectionately as Lord Louis.

He served briefly in K6 of the 12th Submarine Flotilla and in 1918 was promoted sub-lieutenant and appointed as first lieutenant and second-in-command of HMS P31, in the Portsmouth Escort Flotilla. She had a ship's company of fifty: the captain was a twenty-four-year-old lieutenant and, apart from two warrant officers, Lord Louis was the only officer, a great experience for a young eighteen-year-old in the last months of the war operating in the Channel.

In 1919 the Admiralty decided to send the 'War Babies' (the term used to refer to those youngsters who had been sent to sea at round about fifteen or sixteen years old) to catch up with the general education they had missed. The course consisted of two terms at Cambridge, where Lord Louis went to Christ's College. He attended lectures and tutorials as an undergraduate and as a voluntary subject read ethnology.

He also joined the Cambridge Union and made such a name for himself in the debates that he was elected to the committee at the end of his first term, and was invited to lead Cambridge against Oxford in the inter-varsity debate, a distinction never reached by any other serving officer. Oxford's motion 'that the time was ripe for a labour government' was overwhelmingly defeated under his leadership.

In 1920 he accompanied his cousin, the Prince of Wales, on his Empire tour in the battle cruiser *Renown* to New Zealand, Australia, the Pacific colonies and the West Indies.

It was during this tour, as flag lieutenant, in charge of the signal department of the *Renown*, that he conceived the idea of making use of the ciné cameraman, embarked for the cruise, to make a film to teach fleet manoeuvres. This was the first instructional film ever made in the services, but it was rejected by the Board of Admiralty on the grounds that Their Lordships could see no possible application of film for instructional purposes.

On 4 August 1921, the seventh anniversary of the outbreak of World War I, Lord Louis' father was specially promoted to Admiral of the Fleet in recognition of his services to the Royal Navy, which he joined fifty-three years before, and a partial atonement for the injustice which had forced him to retire as First Sea Lord in October 1914. Five weeks later he died.

At the end of 1921 Lord Louis again accompanied the Prince of Wales on his second Empire tour on board the *Renown*, this time to India, Burma, Ceylon, Malaya and Japan, which gave him an early first hand knowledge of those countries which in later years were to play such a big part in his life.

It was in Delhi in February 1922 that he became engaged to Edwina Ashley, daughter of Lord Mount Temple, who owned the Broadlands estate in Hampshire, and granddaughter of Sir Ernest Cassel, the great financier. She inherited Broadlands from her father and great wealth from her grandfather. This affluence had, however, only one really noticeable effect on Lord Louis – he was more determined than ever to succeed in his naval career on his own merits and worked harder than ever. They were married in July of that year.

In 1923 he joined the battleship *Revenge*, then forming part of the international fleet in the Dardanelles and at Constantinople. The following year he attended the Officers' Long Course at HM Signal School and qualified as a communications specialist, coming out top of his course. For the next nine years he held specialist wireless appointments at sea and at the signal school. When Fleet Wireless Officer of the Mediterranean Fleet during 1931 and 1932 his staff drew up a list of over twenty innovations and improvements which he introduced in the fleet of seventy ships, the effect of many of which is felt to this day.

Lord Louis' progress in the navy between the wars was marked by early promotions on sheer merit; and there was no doubt in the minds of his contemporaries that he was marked for high command in the future. His powers of command and leadership were outstanding; and it is not without interest that former Able Seaman Wincott, one of the leaders of the 1931 mutiny at Invergordon, has said that, if Lord Louis had been in command of the fleet at that time, there would have been no trouble.

To the general public Lord and Lady Louis at Brook House in Park Lane, their millions, their parties, his polo, conveyed a very different picture to that known to the Royal Navy. That Lord Louis lived a full life is accepted; but what was not known, except to his naval contemporaries, were the long hours of work extending well into the night which Lord Louis put into his professional activities such as the Long, and later the Advanced, Communications Course; culminating later in the writing of the navy's wireless telegraphy handbooks.

He was promoted to commander in 1931, and in 1934 achieved one of his declared ambitions, to command his own ship, HMS *Daring*, one of the most modern destroyers in the Mediterranean Fleet. Eight months later her flotilla was sent to Singapore to change ships with the old wartime V and W class destroyers of the China Fleet.

In 1936 he was promoted captain and selected for service in the Naval Air Division, for, although he never qualified as a service pilot, he had a long history of flying experience. His father had taken him up on his sixth birthday in an airship. In 1911 he flew as a passenger in the first naval Short biplane, piloted by Lieutenant Longmore, afterwards Air Chief Marshal Sir Arthur Longmore, who was Air Commander-in-Chief in the Middle East in the Second World War. Then in 1918 he spent some of his leave learning to fly with the newly formed Royal Air Force. He proved an apt pupil but could not be granted 'wings', as his course was unofficial. Lord Louis was still flying solo in light aircraft as late as 1944 in the South-East Asia campaign.

He was in charge of policy in the Naval Air Division and led the Admiralty campaign against the Royal Air Force to have the Fleet Air Arm returned to the Royal Navy, a battle won just in time to be effective before the outbreak of the Second World War. He also got the 20mm Oerlikon gun adopted for close range air defence against the total opposition of the various

Admiralty departments concerned by finally going straight to the First Sea Lord.

In 1938 he was selected for the Higher Commander's course at Aldershot, where he met many of the generals he was to have dealings with later in the war. The following year, in August 1939, he commissioned HMS *Kelly*, the latest destroyer flotilla leader and was appointed Captain (D) commanding the Fifth Destroyer flotilla. As war was imminent he reduced the commissioning procedure from three weeks to three days by working hand-in-hand with his ship's company night and day.

He had an adventurous career in command of the *Kelly*. In December 1939 she was mined in the North Sea but towed back to her builder's yard on the Tyne and repaired. In May 1940 she was torpedoed by an E-Boat off the German minefield in the North Sea. So heavy was the damage that her starboard gunwhale was awash, but Lord Louis succeeded in getting her back to the Tyne under tow after ninety-two hours of frequent air attack. While she was under repair, he commanded the flotilla from other destroyers which carried out bombardments of places as far afield as Cherbourg and Benghazi and fought in day and night actions against enemy destroyers. In the night action of November 1940 his ship, the *Javelin*, had her bow and stern blown off by a salvo of torpedoes, but again he got her under tow, this time to Devonport. He rejoined *Kelly* on completion of her repairs and, during the Battle of Crete, after having sunk the last of the *caique* invasion fleet and bombarded Maleme airfield, the *Kelly* herself was sunk in May 1941 by twenty-four Junkers eighty-seven dive bombers and capsized under full helm at thirty-four knots, with a loss of more than half the officers and men. Lord Louis was among the survivors picked up by the *Kipling* and taken to Alexandria, where they were all cheered by the whole Mediterranean Fleet.

So remarkable was the morale of the *Kelly* that the surviving members of the ship's company formed a reunion association which now meets biennially at a dinner, usually held on board the RNR Training Ship, HMS *President*, in London. It is run by the men and the officers are invited as their guests. Such an association run by the survivors of a destroyer's ship's company is without precedent and is a fitting tribute to Lord Louis' great power of leadership.

After the *Kelly* and the majority of the rest of the flotilla had been sunk, Lord Louis was appointed to command the aircraft carrier *Illustrious*, then being repaired in the USA following damage in action off Malta.

At the invitation of the Chief of US Naval Operations he visited the US Pacific Fleet in Pearl Harbor and gave lectures on the war at sea to their officers. He also went to sea in an American aircraft carrier and destroyer leader and made many valuable contacts with the US Navy.

It was during this visit to Pearl Harbor in October 1941 that he was recalled by the Prime Minister, Winston Churchill, to succeed Admiral of the Fleet Lord Keyes (on whose staff he had served as a young lieutenant in 1927) as adviser on combined operations. After informing him of his new appointment, Churchill said he hoped he appreciated its importance. Mountbatten replied that he would sooner be back at sea with his friends. The Prime Minister turned on him and asked him whether he had no sense of glory. He pointed out that he was offering him a chance to take part in the highest direction of the war and what could he hope to achieve by returning to sea, except to be sunk in a bigger and more expensive ship.

The Prime Minister went on to emphasise that the commando raids were to continue in order to keep up the offensive spirit and to gain essential experience of landing on enemy occupied coasts, and to harass the enemy; but these raids were also to be the cover for the prime task of Combined Operations Headquarters which was to be preparation for the invasion of Europe.

Lord Louis was instructed by Churchill to work out the philosophy of invasion, to land and advance against the enemy. New landing craft, appurtenances and appliances had to be designed and quickly constructed in large numbers: the three services had to be trained to act together as a single force in combined operations. The Prime Minister emphasised that at that time in October 1941 all other headquarters in Britain were engaged on defensive measures and that combined operations headquarters was to think only of offense: the south west of England was to be turned from a bastion against Hitler's invasion into a springboard to launch a cross-Channel attack. Churchill followed these instructions by ensuring that Mountbatten was in a position to get things done by arranging, in March 1942, for him to be advanced to the acting rank of vice-admiral (at the age of forty-one) and with the honorary ranks of Lieutenant General and Air Marshal (unique appointments) – and most important of all, with a seat on the Chiefs of Staff Committee.

He was a generation younger than his colleagues on the COS Committee; indeed the First Sea Lord, Sir Dudley Pound, had been a senior captain commanding the battle cruiser *Repulse* in 1921 when Lord Louis was serving in the ship as a very young lieutenant. Nevertheless, in spite of the difference in age and substantive rank, they all treated him as an equal at the COS meetings. It was appreciated, however, that all this was not necessarily to his advantage; he had, in effect, been lifted out of his generation, and many felt that unless he could revert to the rank of captain and be given a further command at sea, his subsequent naval career might be cut unduly short.

Lord Louis' upbringing and background stood him in good stead when he became a member of the COS Committee and attended Cabinet Defence Committee meetings in 1941. Many other forty-one-year-old naval officers would unquestionably have been overawed, if not positively frightened at such rapid advancement to the rank of acting vice-admiral and at having to deal with cabinet ministers – but not so Lord Louis.

Many ministers and senior officers stood in obvious dread of Winston

Churchill's overpowering attitude. But Mountbatten remembered him as a gay and pleasant colleague of his father's whom he had known well since the age of twelve. This left Lord Louis' opinions unclouded by too much respect and he soon felt that he was talking on equal terms with the Prime Minister and his colleagues.

Ten days after his acting promotion, Combined Operations carried out their biggest and most dramatic raid on St Nazaire, on 28 March 1942. The object of the raid was to put out of action the great dry dock in St Nazaire harbour which was the only one on the Atlantic coasts big enough to take the German battleship *Tirpitz*.

The plan was to ram the gate of the dock with a destroyer, *Campbeltown*, crammed with high explosive. It was a most hazardous voyage, entailing a long run-in under heavy fire, but surprise was complete. Torpedoes were also fired into the harbour installations and commandos landed and carried out more demolitions. The next day, after the raid was over, and the *Campbeltown* was crowded with German officers inspecting her, the ship exploded. This daring and courageous operation, for which no less than five VCs were won, ensured that the *Tirpitz* was never able to come into the Atlantic.

In April 1942 Harry Hopkins, personal adviser to President Roosevelt and General George Marshall, Chief of Staff of the US Army, arrived in London to discuss American plans with the British government and chiefs of staff. During this visit General Marshall asked to come and inspect the Combined Operations Headquarters and, as a result, the US Chiefs of Staff sent officers of their three services to join the staff of Lord Louis. Combined Operations Headquarters thus became the first integrated inter-allied inter-service head-quarters in history and the forerunner of all that followed later in the war. American units were also attached to Combined Operations for amphibious training and the strength of the command rose to 50,000 officers and men of the three services.

On 19 August 1942 a one-day raid (Jubilee) was carried out against the enemy in Dieppe. Although the planning was carried out by the force comman-ders and not by COHQ, this raid had been suggested originally by the Chief of Combined Operations in order to gain experience from carrying out an assault on a port before the detailed planning for the Normandy landings (Overlord) was started. The plan included the capture of the port and then sending in a 'cutting-out' party onboard coastal craft and tank landing craft three hours after the assault. They were to 'cut out' barges suitable for use by the allied invasion forces and tow them back to England.

This raid has been described by many as a catastrophe. The losses were unquestionably high, but, costly as it was, Dieppe taught the planners lessons which had to be learnt. At a briefing meeting prior to the raid the Prime Minister turned to Mountbatten's chief naval planner, Captain Hughes-Hallett and asked whether he could guarantee success? The CIGS, Field Marshal Sir Alan Brooke, broke in and said that if he, or anyone else, could guarantee success there would indeed be no object in carrying out the operation. He pointed out that it was just because no-one had the slightest idea what the outcome would be that the operation was necessary. Churchill said that this was not a moment at which he wanted to be taught by adversity. The CIGS replied that in that case the idea of invading France must be abandoned, because no responsible general would be associated with any planning for invasion until an operation at least the size of the Dieppe raid had been carried out, on which plans could be based. This dramatic confrontation made it quite clear that such a raid was essential.

One of the lessons learnt at Dieppe was the need for overwhelming fire support. It was the inadequacy of the bombardment support which prevented the capture of the port, yet full and overwhelming bombardment would have destroyed the port facilities. This experience led to the conclusion that the only way in an invasion to obtain a port intact was to bring over a prefabricated mobile one. It was this conclusion that led to the famous *Mulberry* artificial harbours, which ultimately played such a vital part in the D-Day operations.

During the following months, as the date of the invasion drew nearer, Combined Operations Headquarters was a hive of activity. Into it flowed a seemingly endless stream of ideas, some of which – like PLUTO, the Pipe-Line Under the Ocean which carried petrol to the Normandy beach-head – were brilliant.

Mountbatten also appointed scientists to his staff at COHQ and ensured that they were fully concerned with all operational planning. The leading part they played in Combined Operations Headquarters' planning for Overlord proved the value of this decision.

While combined operations raids continued on continental coasts, the formation of the Combined Commanders Committee late in 1941 took over the problem of preparations for re-entry into Europe as advocated by the Prime Minister to Lord Louis. General Sir Bernard Paget and Air Chief Marshal Sir Sholto Douglas were in favour of an attack in the Pas de Calais area; Mountbatten alone pressed repeatedly for the Cherbourg or Baie de la Seine areas. He pointed out the formidable coast defences in depth developed by the Germans in the Pas de Calais area, which could dominate the Straits of Dover; while the deep water port of Cherbourg, coupled with the local command of the sea in the western area, demanded an attack in the Baie de la Seine. His counter to the criticism that there were no harbours in that particular area was that such a problem could be solved; and it was indeed by the construction of the *Mulberry* harbours. It must be emphasised that he was the only senior officer who held this opinion; he forced his views through and General Eisenhower, on his appointment as Supreme Allied Commander for the Allied Expeditionary Forces late in 1943, had no hesitation in approving the plans for landing in the Baie de la Seine.

Mountbatten had by this time just left for South East Asia; and all that he accomplished so successfully in his two years as Chief of Combined Operations was vindicated on 12 June 1944 when Churchill, Field Marshals Smuts and Alan Brooke (Chairman of the British Chiefs of Staffs Committee) and the three US Chiefs of Staff, General Marshall (Army), General Arnold (Air Force) and Admiral King (Navy), visited the landing beaches and on return sent the following signal to him in his South East Asia Headquarters:

> Today we visited the British and American Armies on the soil of France. We sailed through vast fleets of ships with landing craft of many types pouring more and more men, vehicles and stores ashore. We saw clearly the manoeuvre in process of rapid development. We have shared our secrets in common and helped each other all we could. We wish to tell you at this moment in your arduous campaign that we realise that much of this remarkable technique and therefore the success of the venture has its origin in developments effected by you and your staff of Combined Operations.

(Signed)	Arnold	King
	Brooke	Marshall
	Churchill	Smuts

Lord Louis' experience afloat and ashore, especially as Chief of Combined Operations and his membership of the Chiefs of Staff Committee, coupled with his outstanding powers of initiative and leadership and his ability to work on terms of close friendship and amity with other nationalities, bore fruit in his next appointment.

In May 1943 at the Washington Conference (Trident) the British and US governments had decided to co-ordinate in South East Asia the British Commonwealth land and air forces, the US land and air forces and the British Eastern Fleet, which were at that time under three separate commands. As a result of this decision Mountbatten was entrusted at the Quebec Conference (Quadrant), held in August 1943, with the formation of the South East Asia Command.

In October he arrived in Delhi to take up his new command. His task – to grip the war against Japan in South East Asia. As Supreme Allied Commander South East Asia he had the three service commanders-in-chief under him and his American deputy, General Stilwell. They were all a generation older than him. It was obvious that for a forty-three-year-old naval officer, still some five years below the top of the captain's list, though wearing the uniform of an acting full admiral (the youngest the Royal Navy had ever had), the situation was fraught with personal risks. His subordinate commanders-in-chief and his deputy would need very careful handling.

Much of his subsequent success in South East Asia Command and in his relations with his three commanders-in-chief, all a generation senior to him in the services, was due to his knowledge of what was going on in London and Washington and, perhaps above all, of what the reactions of the Prime Minister and the President were likely to be in various circumstances.

He arranged that the naval, army and air directors of plans should owe their single service allegiance to their respective commander-in-chief, but that their joint allegiance as a planning committee for inter-service plans should be solely to him; and he met them regularly to ensure his views were well known.

A week after landing in Delhi, with only a small personal staff, he flew to Chungking to call on his neighbouring Supreme Commander, Chiang Kai Chek. After four days of intense talks he flew back via parts of the Burma Front, finally visiting the army/tactical air force headquarters for Burma, which at that time was established at Barrackpore near Calcutta. Here he met General Slim, acting Army Commander, Air Marshal Baldwin and the senior members of their staff. He was invited to address them, without any warning or preparation and not having discussed any policy with his staff or commanders-in-chief. Entirely on his own initiative he made three points:

1. When the Japanese carried out their usual outflanking movements through the jungle his forces were to stand fast and not fall back on their supply lines: they would be supplied by air.

2. He had heard that there were one hundred and twenty men in hospital suffering from tropical disease to every one battle casualty. He was setting up a medical advisory team of tropical disease experts to deal with the problem.

3. He had heard that in the monsoon all active fighting stopped. The war would last twice as long at this rate. In future his forces would march on, fly on and fight on and gain the great advantage when the enemy expected both sides to stop.

It is fair to say that not one of Lord Louis' staff thought that any of the three points was really practicable. In fact 1. was a triumphant success as it stopped all further retreat, though Lord Louis had to divert American transport aircraft from supplying China 'over the hump' against President Roosevelt's orders. The improvement as a result of 2. was dramatic; within one year the rate of tropical disease cases had dropped to ten for every battle casualty, and 3. was the master stroke of the Burma campaign and largely responsible for the ultimate Japanese rout.

Mountbatten's first offensive was to restore the morale of his men which was at a very low ebb. He toured his whole command to meet the men of all services and of all nations. He would start off by gathering them round and saying 'I hear you call this the forgotten front. I hear you call yourselves the forgotten army. Well, let me tell you that this is not the forgotten front, and you are not the forgotten army. In fact, nobody has even heard of you'. He would then go on 'But they will hear of you, because this is what we are going to do . . .' and he would proceed to put them in the picture. As well as the pep talks, he obtained special broadcasts for the forces on All India Radio; and arranged to have a major station built in Ceylon, Radio Seac, to cover the command. He demanded films, gramophones, theatrical shows by ENSA, and also arranged for SEAC news stories to be published in the British press. He also set up the command's own newspaper called SEAC, edited by Frank Owen who had been editor of the Evening Standard before the war; and a picture magazine called *Phoenix*. After a while the men began to feel that people actually cared about them and this boosted their morale.

The problems of establishing the command structure were daunting. Unlike Eisenhower whose inter-service inter-allied staff included US and British soldiers and airmen only, without naval officers (other than one public relations officer), Mountbatten had a well balanced inter-allied inter-service integrated staff of sailors, soldiers and airmen. The formation of the command headquarters was therefore straightforward, but difficulties arose in regard to the control of the naval, land and air forces which it took all his skill, tact and ingenuity to solve.

In regard to the navy, in all matters concerning the security and support of the land campaigns and amphibious operations in the theatre, the naval commander-in-chief was subordinate to the supreme commander. The latter had, however, wider responsibilities in regard to the security of sea communications and with offensive action at sea against the enemy, for which he was responsible to the Admiralty. This unsatisfactory aspect had been discussed by Mountbatten with the First Sea Lord at the Quebec conference, and Dudley Pound (who unfortunately died soon after) had urged him to accept it, promising him his strong personal support. The arrangement was very confusing at first, as it was difficult to be sure when naval forces were under the Supreme Allied Commander and when they were under the Admiralty. However, a generous interpretation of Mountbatten's position by the successive Commanders-in-Chief Eastern Fleet, Admirals Sir Bruce Fraser and Sir Arthur Power, enabled co-ordination to be achieved with the other services in every department where this was necessary.

In regard to the land forces, the position was complicated by the fact that the Deputy Supreme Allied Commander, Lieutenant General Stilwell, US Army, had four differing responsibilities: as Deputy SAC he was responsible to Mountbatten: as Chief of Staff to the Supreme Commander of the China theatre, his allegiance was to Generalissimo Chiang Kai Chek, who was, of course, independent of the Combined Chiefs of Staff: as the Commanding General of the United States China–Burma–India theatre, he was responsible to the US Joint Chiefs of Staff: as Commander of the Northern Combat Area Command, he commanded the 1st and 6th Chinese armies. This final responsibility complicated matters as, at the Cairo conference in November 1943, the Generalissimo had refused to let his large Chinese forces come under any one other than the Supreme Allied Commander. Stilwell offered to take 'operational control' from General Slim, the 14th Army Commander, but from no other general, and then only until his forces advanced as far as Kamaing.

This was awkward for the 11th Army Group Commander-in-Chief, General

Giffard, who now only controlled two out of the three fronts. But worse was to come for on 16 June 1944 the Chinese 22nd Division captured Kamaing and, on behalf of the Generalissimo, Stilwell now insisted on being freed from control by Slim and would only take orders from Mountbatten, thus in effect creating him the sole commander of the allied land forces in addition to being Supreme Allied Commander.

This lasted until 12 November when a new land forces command was agreed to by the Allies and a new Army Group Commander-in-Chief took over. The job had been no sinecure since Mountbatten had had to settle matters such as inter-corps boundaries, the amount of tonnage allocated on the common lines of communication to the Central and Northern Combat Area Commands, and other purely land force matters. He had to pay even more visits than usual to Stilwell's front.

Relations with India Command were also complicated. The US Joint Chiefs of Staff had urged that India Command should be subordinate to the South East Asia Command. The British government, however, decided that it was constitutionally impracticable to place troops in India under a commander not responsible to the government of India. They further considered the two commands were too large for one man to manage effectively. South East Asia Command therefore retained control of operations and India became the base for all three services, both commands remaining equal. It might well have been an unworkable proposition, but with goodwill between Mountbatten, and Auchinleck, together with the wise backing and support of the Viceroy Field Marshal Lord Wavell the arrangement worked well.

As regards the air forces, it is here that it may be unquestionably said that Mountbatten made one of his greatest contributions to the success of the South East Asia campaign. He was so dissatisfied with the separate control of British and US air forces that on 11 December 1943 he issued a directive of great political consequence. He turned the British Air Commander-in-Chief into the Allied Air Commander-in-Chief with all air forces under him. He grouped the RAF and US Army Air Force in Burma into a single integrated force under the US Air General. Great improvement in morale and efficiency resulted.

On 7 March 1944 Mountbatten received a severe injury to his left eye from a piece of bamboo while on a visit to the Chinese front, and was in an American military hospital near the front, with both eyes bandaged, when the Japanese followed their attack in Arakan with a bigger attack by the 15th, 31st and 33rd Divisions, cutting off the 4th Army Corps on the Imphal Plain. He insisted on having the bandages removed from his eyes, thus risking losing the sight of his left eye, and flew on 13 March to the Army/Air Force Burma HQ at Camilla. Then and there he decided to move the 5th and 7th Indian Divisions from the Arakan Front to the Central Front by air, and, as he had no spare transport aircraft, he took thirty off the American 'Over the Hump' route into China for a second time against President Roosevelt's orders and saved the Battle of Imphal. Only three weeks earlier he had persuaded the President to let him take the Hump aircraft to supply the troops cut off in the 'Administrative Box' on the Arakan front, but had been expressly warned not to do it again. This was the first time that the ultimately responsible commander had moved large forces from one front to another by air, and at a critical stage in a battle on both fronts.

In spite of his considerable success in getting additional transport aircraft from British and even more from US sources, there were not enough aircraft to maintain the 14th Army by air in their thrust down the middle of Burma. Yet without this thrust Burma could never be liberated until more landing ships and landing craft arrived to capture Rangoon by sea.

The advancing troops needed nearly double the tonnage which the air forces could deliver at sustained rates. Mountbatten solved the problem by calling on them to work at double these rates. These rates had been carefully computed as a result of long experience in both the British and US air forces and were only authorised to be exceeded for a few days at a time to meet a grave emergency. So he took a very grave risk in asking the air forces, flying and ground crews, to work at this extra rate in the tropical climate and terrain of Burma for month after month.

They responded magnificently. The Royal Air Force flew 196 hours a month instead of 100 and the Americans 204 instead of their 120, and the airlift rose to over 77,000 tons a month. Mountbatten never ceased to pay tribute to their fantastic continuous high pressure effort, which he had called for and on which he had staked his career.

That the recapture of Burma was not followed by the recapture of Malaya and Singapore was the most disappointing feature of the South East Asia campaign and no blame for this failure can be attributed to Mountbatten. After the capture of Rangoon in June 1945, steps were taken at once to launch operation Zipper, the reconquest of Malaya, for which plans had been prepared many months earlier. All forces were at sea at the time the bombs were dropped on Hiroshima and Nagasaki; they had to be diverted to the lee of the Andaman and Nicobar Islands, and no landings were permitted until General MacArthur had accepted the surrender of the Japanese in Tokyo Bay on Sunday, 2 September 1945. That the landings would have been a complete success was confirmed by the fact that the intelligence of the whereabouts of the Japanese forces was proved to be one hundred per cent correct.

With the end of the war in the Far East, Mountbatten was immediately faced with a number of difficult problems. Among them were the recovery of allied prisoners of war and internees, the treatment of Burmese (and Indians) who had assisted the Japanese, and relations with the Burmese generally, in which he successfully followed a liberal line: the control and eventual return of Japanese prisoners of war: the transfer to his command from General MacArthur of responsibility for the Netherlands East Indies and Borneo: the supply of rice from Thailand to the starving populations of much of this vast area; and the return of civil government to the ex-colonial areas of Malaya and Singapore, of French Indo-China and the Netherlands East Indies.

All these responsibilities brought with them daunting political and administrative problems. He faced and tackled them with his characteristic self-confidence, vigour and clarity of mind, suffused by a wise liberal attitude which set a tone for future relations with the population of colonial territories.

To exercise these responsibilities Mountbatten had transferred his headquarters to Singapore, where he remained until he gave up his command in June 1946, when, as Viscount Mountbatten of Burma, he returned to London in time for the victory parade in June 1946. After a short period of leave and the senior officers war course, it had been announced that, now in his proper rank of Rear Admiral, he would take command of the 1st Cruiser Squadron in the Mediterranean Fleet in April 1947. Early in 1947 it was, however, announced that he was to become the last Viceroy of India and he arrived in New Delhi in March of that year to succeed Lord Wavell.

As it is Mountbatten's career as a service officer which is being considered here, this is not the place to give an appreciation of his work in India until June 1948. Suffice it to say that his success there, with the aid of Lady Louis, was accomplished with dignity and style; and that the transfer of power was accomplished to two states, India and Pakistan remaining within the British Commonwealth.

It was, as may be imagined, with some difficulty that he managed to return to naval life; and only his foresight in obtaining a promise in writing to this effect from the Prime Minister in 1947 enabled him to accomplish it. He took up his appointment as Flag Officer Commanding the First Cruiser Squadron in the Mediterranean Fleet in October 1948 and remained in command until his return to the Admiralty as Fourth Sea Lord in April 1950. It is not without interest that the Prime Minister, in spite of his promise, sent a Cabinet Minister on holiday to Malta in 1949 in an attempt to seduce Lord Louis away from the navy to a cabinet appointment: and this approach was to be repeated in later years under a different administration. It is a measure of the esteem in which he was held in the highest political circles.

His appointment as Fourth Sea Lord and Chief of Supplies and Transport was unquestionably an imaginative one in the light of his probable future in the Navy. The two years experience of the civil side of the Admiralty which this appointment gave him was to prove of inestimable value to him ten years later in his proposals for the reorganisation of the Ministry of Defence.

His next three years, from 1952 to 1954, were spent in command of the Mediterranean Fleet, at that time still the major command afloat and with a fleet which, although not of prewar size, was still a powerful force.

The establishment of the NATO headquarters outside Paris had led to prolonged thought about the southern flank, culminating in 1953 in the establishment of the allied naval command in the Mediterranean and Mountbatten as the first Commander-in-Chief, with a new and separate headquarters in Malta. Close working relationships were rapidly effected with the French, the Italian, the Greek and the Turkish navies; these countries and the United States were an integral part of the allied headquarters. Mountbatten's immense wartime experience and prestige ensured not only a happy and efficient allied staff, but also that his voice was heard in high level planning and discussion at Supreme Headquarters, Allied Powers, Europe, outside Paris.

Mountbatten's next appointment in 1955 had been a matter of some consideration in the highest circles during 1954. Apart from him, there was one other outstanding admiral eminently qualified to be First Sea Lord; and there was a possibility that Mountbatten would be appointed Second Sea Lord for three years, before becoming First Sea Lord. Fortunately wiser counsels prevailed: leading politicians were anxious to have Mountbatten in the senior naval appointment in Whitehall, where his knowledge and experience could be used to the full; and even at this early stage consideration was being given to how best to use his talents in the Ministry of Defence.

He was therefore appointed First Sea Lord in 1954 to take over early in 1955. This was the culmination of his naval career and the appointment to which his ambitions had been pointed from an early age. To follow his famous father after forty years and to sit in his father's old office in the west block of the Admiralty was an emotional experience which meant a great deal to him.

His principal aim on joining the Board was the rebuilding of the Navy after ten years of peace and the supercession of the old pre-war and wartime vessels remaining. It was a subject to which the C-in-C had given much thought with his staff in the Mediterranean in 1954 and now was the opportunity to put his ideas into practice. In his four years as First Sea Lord from 1955–9 he was greatly helped by the outstanding Secretary of the Admiralty, Sir John Lang, with whom he had established close and friendly understanding when he was Fourth Sea Lord. With the latter's help the 'way ahead' committee was formed with the First Sea Lord in the chair, and with almost the same membership as the Board of Admiralty. This powerful committee achieved the streamlining of the navy ashore and afloat, at home and abroad; the closing of many support bases, the scrapping of old ships and the reduction of what may be fairly described as the mass of old ironmongery in the reserve fleet. The money and manpower saved were then devoted to better uses, principally the rebuilding of the submarine fleet and the introduction of nuclear propulsion (leading at a later date to the emergence of the Polaris force); the building of the guided missile destroyers with the British *Seaslug* weapon; the reconstitution of the amphibious warfare squadron with the Royal Marines afloat in the commando carriers with helicopter support; and the rebuilding of the frigate force centring around the Leander class of which about forty were finally built and which were generally acknowledged to be the best of their type in the world.

For the *Dreadnought*, the first of the British nuclear submarines, Mountbatten, against advice, insisted on the purchase from the United States of their power reactor and machinery. He was determined that there should be no mistakes in this unknown field and that it would be sensible to build on American experience; the success of this policy and the full backing in the early days of Admiral Rickover, US Navy, has ensured no accidents or failure in the Royal Navy's nuclear submarine force.

He was also determined that the navy should not be left behind in guided missilery. In the ten years since the end of the war British scientists had produced *Seaslug*, a beam rider guided missile. Lord Louis was told that the system was obsolescent, to which he replied that every system that worked was obsolescent and that it was essential that the Royal Navy should get into the act. In the event *Seaslug* provided a great success; efficient in action, reliable and not difficult to maintain.

During this period more than one suggestion was made to Mountbatten by Conservative Prime Ministers that he should leave the Admiralty prematurely and go to the Ministry of Defence. He was, however, determined not to finish his time as First Sea Lord until he could see an end to all that he had planned for the navy, and the appointment of the first Chief of Defence Staff in 1957 suited him well, as it was understood that he would succeed at the appropriate time. This came in 1959 after he had been First Sea Lord for four years.

Based on his wartime experience on the Chiefs of Staff Committee, Mountbatten had for many years been considering the future of the Ministry of Defence; and had collected in writing the thoughts of many senior officers. Now was the time to put his ideas into practice; and he was under no illusion about the difficulties he would face with the three Departments of State, the Admiralty, the War Office and the Air Ministry. Lord Louis had throughout, however, the tremendous backing support of Harold Macmillan and, through the Prime Minister, of successive Ministers of Defence.

First to be accomplished was the reorganisation of CDS's staff, a small and specially selected team of officers from the three services; the acceptance of the Vice Chief of Defence Staff as a member and later as Chairman of the Vice Chiefs of Staff Committee; and, most difficult of all, the appointment of CDS's Director of Plans. Here Lord Louis applied the principle with which he had solved a similar problem during the war in South East Asia Command. His Director of Plans would be chairman of the committee of the three service directors of plans; each director of plans would be responsible individually to his own head of service, but as a corporate body the directors of plans would report to the Chief of Defence Staff. Thus in the face of much opposition the first hurdle was surmounted.

Secondly, before any reorganisation of the ministry could be attempted, the commands abroad had to be dealt with. Both in the Far East and the Middle East these were organised on the basis of a commanders-in-chief committee; whereas a unified Ministry of Defence would wish to deal with a unified Commander-in-Chief in the field. Hence Mountbatten's insistence on the appointment of such officers.

Lastly came the question of the Ministry of Defence itself. The reorganisations referred to had taken time and it was not until he had been two years in his appointment that the time was ripe for the final step. The draft of the amalgamated Ministry of Defence was prepared by his personal secretaries, more than one of whom had served with him for several years and knew his mind. This draft was revised and finalised by Mountbatten during his annual summer leave in Ireland and with the blessing of the Minister, Peter Thorneycroft, put into the Whitehall machine. It is of interest that General Lord Ismay and Lieutenant General Sir Ian Jacob, the famous team from the wartime Cabinet Office, both of very independent turn of mind and known to have been critical of Mountbatten in the past, pronounced themselves in favour of the scheme. So a major Whitehall revolution was accomplished. Many people may rightly claim credit for their part in the Ministry's evolution, but there is no question that the initiative came from Mountbatten and that all his experience of command and administration went into its foundation. The long hard hours of work which he put into this scheme was in many ways a relief, because he suffered a tremendous blow early in 1961 when Lady Mountbatten died suddenly and unexpectedly in Borneo during one of her visits overseas as Superintendent-in-Chief, St John Ambulance. Thus ended tragically a wonderful team partnership, for each had an individual career and yet each complemented the other – indeed in many ways Lady Mountbatten's sharpness of mind and intellect surpassed those of her husband and much was the good advice she gave him.

Before retirement only one project remained dear to Mountbatten and this was the integration of the three service intelligence organisations under the Director Generalship of Major General Sir Kenneth Strong, who had been Eisenhower's wartime chief of intelligence. Such an obvious step was long overdue and this was accomplished immediately before Mountbatten's retirement in July 1965 following his sixty-fifth birthday.

Throughout his service life Lord Louis had worked hard but he also played hard. He excelled in two quite different sports, as an oar in service pulling boats and as a polo player. So it can be seen that he applied the same ingenuity, daring and dedication to his play as well as his work, and with the same degree of success.

With a man of such striking individuality and personality as Lord Louis, the question will inevitably be asked whether he contributed anything original or lasting to the military act in its broadest sense, taking military here as referring to all three services? This is not an easy question to answer because no major war is ever the same as the previous one and technological advancement is apt to make earlier contributions out of date. There can, however, be no doubt that Mountbatten will be remembered for two outstanding contributions during the Second World War: the Normandy landing in 1944, and the development of air power in the South East Asia campaign and the air supply of an army advancing south through Burma.

In the case of the former, his major contribution was to fight the combined commanders on where to land in France. They all wanted the Pas de Calais, and the German High Command thought we must go there. For a young and comparatively inexperienced sailor to argue against generals such as Paget, Devers, McNaughton, and airmen like Douglas and Spaatz, did take moral courage as well as firm convictions. That the Combined Chiefs of Staff had no doubt about Mountbatten's contribution to the Normandy landing is shown by the signal sent to him in South East Asia from the beaches.

As far as the campaign in South Asia is concerned, his principal contributions lay in his decision, backed only by Slim, to fight on through the monsoon weather of 1944: his diversion of American transport aircraft from the Indo-China supply route on two occasions, in contravention of Roosevelt's orders, and the unheard of insistence that British and American transport aircraft crews and ground staff should work for months at double sustained rates, which alone made possible the 14th Army's advance from the North of Burma right through to Rangoon before the onset of the monsoon.

Mountbatten's personal relationships during his service career are of much interest. A man of such enthusiasm, initiative, original thought and drive was bound to arouse controversy, especially among those who did not know him well or had not served with him at close quarters. Between the wars in command of destroyers there is no question that Lord Louis was admired and beloved by all of his ship's companies, although he was a strict disciplinarian.

In later years with his own headquarters and personal staff relations were of the happiest. The Admiral was always approachable; although staff meetings might be initiated by a long discourse from the Commander-in-Chief, everyone present was encouraged to take part and Mountbatten would always change his mind if he could be persuaded that his original thoughts were wrong.

It is no secret that friction did arise in a few cases with senior officers of the Royal Navy in the Second World War who were of an earlier generation and who did not relish the young acting admiral, almost twenty years younger. As Supreme Allied Commander, South East Asia, relations with the Commander-in-Chief East Indies Fleet were far from easy until the advent of Admiral Sir Bruce Fraser.

In later years Mountbatten's wartime experience in high command lent great weight to his views on the Chiefs of Staff Committee; but his tactful handling of many difficult problems prevented serious discord arising, and it is fair to say that in his time the Chiefs of Staff presented a united front. His contribution to bringing the three services together within the Ministry of Defence and outside it, especially in the commands overseas, was one of his most significant achievements. He was both the architect and the builder of the structure which now exists.

Field-Marshal The Viscount Slim

———◆———

Lieutenant General Sir Geoffrey Evans

August 1914, and among the first in the long queue to join the army was twenty-three year old William Joseph Slim. Thus had it not been for the holocaust of the First World War, Slim would not have made the army his career nor, in the Second World War, would his country have had the services of a commander whose name finds a prominent place in the register of the great captains of history.

Born in the city of Bristol on 6 August 1891, Slim was brought up in a hard school and in a family with no military connections; money was tight and the chances of advancement in life entirely dependent on his own efforts. His father, a man of much charm and to whom his son was devoted, owned a warehouse near the docks and dealt in wholesale ironmongery. His mother, one of three daughters of an upper-middle-class Somerset family, was a woman of very strong character, and, like some great men whose mothers were of that calibre, there can be little doubt that her son inherited from her those traits of integrity and firmness of purpose which he was later to display. On the other hand the valuable characteristics of boundless enthusiasm, modesty, human kindness, broadmindedness and tact were gifts from his father.

In Slim's early boyhood his father suffered a severe financial setback, due to the default of his partner, and the family moved to Edgbaston, a suburb of Birmingham; moreover it was necessary for William Slim to go to work after school hours to augment the family exchequer; but in due course, after an improvement in his father's finances, he was sent to King Edward's Grammar School, Birmingham, to complete his education.

During Slim's adolescence, his father was a great companion and took a deep interest in his two sons' activities (the elder brother took up the medical profession). It was on account of the history books, especially military history, with which he plied his younger son, that the latter was fired with the ambition to become an officer. But the chances of attaining that goal were nil, for in those days parents paid to send their sons to Sandhurst; furthermore, since an officer's pay was a pittance (second lieutenants 5s per diem), it would have been essential for him to receive an allowance to maintain the required standards. Because his parents were unable to find the money, another profession had to be found for him.

While at school, Slim's first inclination had been to become a schoolmaster, but as time passed it was decided to put him into the well-known steel firm of Stewart and Lloyds, and this he joined just prior to the First World War. Nevertheless, if he could not be a regular soldier, Slim was determined to involve himself in military matters and, through friendly influence, obtained permission to join the Birmingham University Officers' Training Corps. By August 1914 he had reached the rank of lance-corporal in this officer-producing unit; three weeks later he realised his life's ambition when he was granted one of the first commissions in Kitchener's New Army and posted to The Royal Warwickshire Regiment. A career that was to take him to the highest post in the British army had begun.

Slim's initiation to active service was a rude one when 9th Service Battalion, The Royal Warwickshire Regiment, the battalion in which he was serving, was sent to Gallipoli in July 1915, for almost exactly one month following its landing on the peninsula it suffered thirteen officer and four hundred other-rank casualties in four days' fighting. Among the seriously wounded was Slim, the bullet just missing his spine and passing through his shoulder.

Until then he had endured the heat, the flies, the unsuitable rations, the scarcity of water and the exhaustion with his men; he also experienced the plight of the wounded as they jolted down the steep, boulder-strewn hillsides to lie on a beach still under fire; of utmost importance he saw the effect on morale of maladministration and the lack of touch between the high command, the staff and the troops. By chance he made his first contact with Gurkhas, some of whom, having lost contact with their unit, joined to fight with his company. Their cheerfulness and courage in unspeakable conditions made a deep impression on him.

Dispirited by what he had seen of active service, he was invalided to England, but with the resilience of youth he rapidly recovered both mentally and physically. It was then that a lucky conversation with a brother officer brought about his application for a regular commission in a regiment in which he understood he could live on his pay – The West India Regiment. Although his application was granted he never in fact served with that regiment.

The early months of 1916 found Slim back with his battalion, now transferred to Mesopotamia, where he was wounded again (on this occasion in the arm) and awarded the Military Cross. During this period he also effected a transfer to 6th Gurkha Rifles, but continued to serve with The Royal Warwickshire Regiment until the end of the war.

Unconsciously no doubt active service had taught him many lessons. He had learnt how to handle men and get the most out of them at all times; he had seen the ghastly waste of life through sending men on valueless raids, ostensibly to maintain morale, and the enormous casualties resulting from fruitless attacks to capture ground of no tactical importance; he had realised, too, that if regimental officers and their men are to give of their best, they must have the fullest information their commanders can give them without prejudicing security. These and his experiences in Gallipoli were in the forefront of his mind when, thirty years later, he rose to a position that made him responsible for the lives of many thousands of soldiers.

In 1925 Slim married, and throughout the years between the wars his career followed that of any officer who took his profession seriously. Following a tour as adjutant of his battalion, he was selected for the Staff College at Quetta, where he made his mark as an outstanding student and – as a result of the junior staff appointments that ensued – became comparatively well known in the Indian Army. But when he was posted to the Camberley Staff College as the Indian Army instructor in 1934, he gained a high reputation in British army circles as well. Both his fellow instructors and his students testify to his qualities of stability, keen intellect, down-to-earth manner, keen sense of humour and his affability at all times. As far as the army was concerned, Slim's training for high command came with his selection to attend the Imperial Defence College.

Aged forty-six, and above the normal age to command a battalion, Slim returned to India in 1938, and it was only after considerable deliberation on the part of the selection board that he was appointed to command a battalion of 7th Gurkha Rifles. But not for long, as within a few months he was promoted to commandant of the Senior Officers' School in India and, on the outbreak of war in 1939, to command 10th Indian Infantry Brigade forming in Jhansi in the United Provinces (or Uttar Pradesh as it is today).

At that time the Indian Army was in a parlous state for active service outside India and against an enemy armed with modern weapons of war. The material in the shape of officers and men was available and of a high order, but they needed intensive training and equipping. Whereas in European armies the age of mechanisation had arrived, the Indian Army still depended on pack mules and carts, and a few lorries, for transport; its automatic weapons were obsolete, wireless sets were non-existent, as were infantry armoured vehicles and anti-tank weapons. Yet it was planned to despatch some formations overseas for the defence of Egypt and the Middle East, with little time and even less means to train them for this new role.

It was in these circumstances that Brigadier Slim took over his new command with a completely new staff and units that neither knew him nor each other. Nevertheless by his personality, his forceful and imaginative training, improvisation and the confidence he inspired, he quickly welded his brigade into a happy and enthusiastic team. Fortunately almost a year was to elapse before 10th Indian Infantry Brigade, as part of 5th Indian Division, sailed from India to take part in operations against the Italians in the Sudan and Eritrea.

·　　·　　·　　·　　·

In August 1940 Italian forces in Abyssinia crossed the frontier with Sudan to capture a few small frontier posts, including Gallabat, some 300 miles southeast of Khartoum. In November of that year Slim's brigade, positioned about 100 miles north of Gallabat to oppose an enemy advance from that direction, was ordered to recapture Gallabat and the adjoining Italian post of Metemma, with the object of opening a caravan route to supply the loyal chieftains in revolt against their Italian masters. Owing to the steps taken to ensure surprise, Gallabat was quickly captured, but the attack was then disorganised by casualties inflicted by the Italian air force, and though Slim was anxious to continue with a fresh plan, his staff advised strongly against it. They did so on the grounds that enemy reinforcements were reported on the way and his primary task of preventing an enemy advance on Khartoum could well be seriously prejudiced. Reluctantly Slim accepted their advice and also the fact that his first battle of the war had been a failure.

Characteristically he took the blame on his shoulders for he wrote long after the war: 'Like so many generals whose plans have gone wrong I could find plenty of excuses but only one reason – myself. When two courses of action were open to me, I had not chosen, as a good commander should, the bolder. I had taken counsel of my fears.'

Wounded for the third time during the operations in Eritrea, in January 1941 he was invalided to India, unruffled, but undoubtedly influenced by his experience at Gallabat. The wound was only a flesh one, and having quickly recovered he was promoted in June 1941 to major-general in command of 10th Indian Division, engaged in quelling the Iraqi revolt of that year and in preparing against a possible Axis threat to the oilfields of Iraq and Persia. The last occasion on which he had fought in this country the enemy had been the Turks; this time it was to be the Vichy French.

Coincidental with his arrival plans were in hand to occupy Syria, a hotbed of Axis influence, and part of the plan involved an advance into Syria by forces from Iraq up the right bank of the river Euphrates towards Aleppo, The formation selected for this operation was Slim's 10th Indian Division. with its first objective the capture of the important bridge over the Euphrates at the strongly defended town of Deir-ez-Zor. It faced a difficult task since Deir-ez-Zor was 200 miles distant across an almost waterless desert, subjected to severe dust storms; furthermore the troops had not been in action before. The essence of Slim's plan was for an infantry brigade to approach the town from the south while a mobile column made a wide westerly turning movement by night to attack from the north, the whole operation to be under the command of the infantry brigadier.

By noon on 1 july the brigade was within 7 miles of Deir-ez-Zor, despite several air attacks, which, though unnerving for the inexperienced Indian and Gurkha soldiers, caused few casualties. Satisfied that all was going well, Slim, not wishing to breathe down his subordinate's neck had returned to his headquarters, only to be woken during the night with the news that the mobile column had insufficient petrol, due to sandstorms and bad going, to reach their objective. In consequence the brigadier had had no alternative but to call it in and modify the extent of the turning movement. Driving through the night Slim arrived at the brigade headquarters at dawn on 2 July, and considering that the assault would not succeed on the revised plan, ordered petrol to be collected from every available source, including immobilising the transport on the lines of communication. That night the motorised column set out again, while Slim anxiously awaited news of its progress since the outcome might well put his force in a worse position, or at best render the operation abortive.

The mobile column passed through successfully, and with the combination of its surprise attack from the north and the brigade's assault from the south, the enemy fled. Not only did they leave behind large quantities of petrol and ammunition, but they did not have time to blow up the bridge. In the circumstances Slim's action was a bold one and no doubt memories of Gallabat influenced his decision on this occasion.

In the meantime stirring events were taking place thousands of miles away in Burma. The Japanese invaded that country on 16 January 1942.

By 6 March Rangoon had fallen. The British, Indian, Burmese and Chinese forces (the last under command of the American General Stilwell) had moved to positions several miles to the north of the city from which General Alexander, who had been flown from England to command the Allied forces in Burma, planned to deny to the enemy the two main routes leading from Rangoon to Mandalay. To this end he gave Stilwell the responsibility for the road and railway on the eastern side and 17th Division and 1st Burma Division the task of defending the road running close to the river Irrawaddy through Prome on the west. Immediately it was clear to Alexander and General Brooke the Chief of the Imperial General Staff in London, that as a matter of the utmost urgency a corps commander be appointed to command the Indian and Burma divisions, and Slim was selected.

Few commanders can have been faced with a more unfavourable situation than was Slim when he arrived on 19 March 1942 to assume command of what was termed Burcorps. In the place of desert and open country to which he had been accustomed until then, the terrain was jungle and rivers; the troops he was to command did not know him; their training, equipment and transport were unfitted for operations in this type of country and their morale had undergone a severe shaking as a result of continuous withdrawals. His 'skeleton' headquarters had been hastily made up from officers drawn from Headquarters Burma Area Army, wireless communication was practically non-existent except through the cavalry regiment; there were no maps and transport was at a premium. Most disturbing was the fact that there was no hope of reinforcements nor of replacing casualties to men and material, so that both had to be carefully preserved. Of Japanese movements little was known, particularly since the small Royal Air Force contingent had been overwhelmed, and often the first intimation of the enemy's presence was a hail of tracer bullets accompanied by the shrieks of their soldiers as they hurled themselves from a flank or from the rear. But above all was the uncertainty as to the future. Was it to be a complete withdrawal from Burma or was there to be an opportunity for a counter-offensive? Somebody, at some time, had to make the decision so that plans could be realistic.

Yet despite the pressing problems, both present and future, Slim quickly inspired confidence among his juniors by his personality alone and his frequent visits to the troops. Crisis followed crisis in quick succession as the corps withdrew northwards. Units were cut off from time to time, Chinese formations, sent to his assistance, came and went according to the whim of Generalissimo Chiang Kai Chek, and Japanese appeared at unexpected places necessitating rapid changes of plan. But throughout Slim displayed robustness and resilience of a very high order, and whatever he may have felt inwardly he always appeared to his subordinates, commanders and staff alike, both imperturbable and in complete charge of the situation.

At last, on 19 April, the decision was taken to withdraw Burcorps to north-eastern India. There was a long way to go, the 600-yard wide river Chindwin had to be crossed while in close contact with the Japanese and time was short before the monsoon broke in May. This last factor was of vital importance, for once the rains came the tracks leading into India would become impassable and Slim's corps would perish from starvation and disease.

Continually harassed by an enemy, whose morale was at its highest due to a succession of victories, with the British and Indian soldiers in rags, starving, racked with malaria and soaked to the skin, the rearguard of Burcorps, still carrying their personal arms, reached India and safety on 19 May.

'The Army in Burma, without once losing cohesion had retreated nearly 1000 miles in some three and a half months – the longest retreat ever carried out by a British Army' (British official history). Of these, Slim had commanded his corps for exactly two months. Evidence that his soldiers realised he had done all that was humanly possible was the rousing farewell they accorded him when he relinquished command shortly after the retreat was completed.

Errors there may have been and not surprisingly in the conditions. Thirteen thousand killed, wounded and missing, plus the loss of the tanks, most of the guns and transport, was a high price to pay and this could well have undermined the confidence of some commanders. But not so Slim, who at once set himself to conduct a self-examination to analyse the causes of defeat and to study the Japanese psychology, so that if called upon again to fight them he would be better prepared. Although he was later to conduct operations on a far greater scale, some may be of the opinion that the retreat from Burma was Slim's greatest test as a commander.

Within a few weeks of returning to India, Slim was appointed to command the newly raised xv Corps with his headquarters in Calcutta. This, with iv Corps facing the Japanese in eastern India, formed Eastern Army.

In the main his responsibility was to defend Bengal from seaborne attack and assist the civil authorities to maintain law and order over many thousands of square miles, tasks made no easier by the fact that one of his three divisions was immobilised in Calcutta through lack of transport. Unrest throughout India came to a head in July, in particular in Bengal, where riots, destruction of communications, murder and arson brought the supply of men and material to the fighting front to a standstill. So bad did the situation become that the army was called in and though stretched for numbers, even to the extent of employing the venereal patients in the hospitals, Slim gradually restored order and was able to concentrate on training his corps.

Although many had realised what steps were necessary to combat Japanese tactics, Slim clarified them by issuing a series of memoranda that were to form the basis for fighting in jungle conditions. In these he laid great emphasis on acclimatising the soldiers to jungle surroundings and the importance of patrolling, which he described as 'the master key to jungle fighting', since it developed the initiative of junior leaders and their men, increased their physical fitness and enabled them to move about in the jungle with confidence.* Of extreme significance was his statement – 'there are no non-combatants in jungle warfare' and every administrative unit and head-quarters was made responsible for its own defence.

Referring to the attack he dwelt on the importance of rarely attacking frontally and the necessity to assault from a flank or rear, while holding the enemy in front. He also made the point that, contrary to the opinion of the time, armour could be employed almost anywhere, except in swamps, but should always be accompanied by infantry for close protection and reconnaissance. Finally he drew attention to Japanese psychology and the fact that when their rigid plans were disrupted they became confused and consequently easier to overcome, and that this disruption could best be brought about by mobility in the jungle, surprise and offensive action.

Not content that only his formations should be more than a match for the Japanese, through his Chief of Staff he concentrated on the efficiency of the personnel of corps headquarters. They too had to be hard and ready to move at short notice in all manner of transport – train, lorry, boat, aircraft, or even on mules or porters. Thus, since the essentials for jungle fighting were at last

---

* Jungle warfare does not allow for the employment of large formations in any one place at any one time. It is a war of battalions, companies and platoons, seldom of divisions and brigades. Hence the importance of highly trained junior leaders.

put on paper, officers and men going into action knew what to expect and how to react to the varying situations.

While Slim was preparing his command for the future, an offensive, under direct control of Headquarters Eastern Army, had opened in July 1942 in the Arakan peninsula, south of Calcutta, on the eastern shores of the Gulf of Bengal. Its object was to capture the Japanese airfields on Akyab Island and so remove the air threat to Bengal and Calcutta in particular. It had begun auspiciously, but by March 1943 not only had it been brought to a halt but a retreat was in progress, and Slim, with only an operational headquarters, was sent to restore the situation, a task that he, with the help of the monsoon which brought all movement to a standstill, carried out successfully. But yet another disastrous campaign had a devastating effect on morale throughout the whole of Eastern Army, and the myth of Japanese invincibility reached alarming proportions. Changes in the higher command and a completely fresh approach were required, and when General Sir George Gifford was appointed to command Eastern Army, a most successful combination that was to last for the ensuing eighteen months came into being. Both generals had a respect and liking for one another and shared similar characteristics of integrity and dislike of flamboyant publicity. Both understood the soldier, his needs and his training. But further changes in the chain of command were envisaged and while planning for another Arakan campaign, Slim was removed from xv Corps in October 1943 and appointed to act for Gifford as Commander-in-Chief Eastern Army.

With the arrival of Admiral Mountbatten as Supreme Commander South-East Asia Command in October 1943 and the formation of a new headquarters – 11th Army Group – with General Gifford at its head, Slim, now fifty-two years old, was confirmed in the command of Eastern Army, the name of which was changed to Fourteenth Army. But complications arose as Stilwell, who commanded the Sino-American forces (a part of 11th Army Group) operating in the far north of eastern India, refused to take orders from Gifford. However the impasse was overcome when Stilwell agreed to come under the orders of Slim, whom he had met during the retreat from Burma and for whom he had a high regard. Stilwell, a physically and mentally tough soldier of sixty, was not an easy man and the fact that the relations between him and Slim remained cordial throughout speaks much for the tactful and clever handling of the former by the latter.

As Slim had experienced when first arriving in Burma, the problems facing him were again numerous and critical, but on a larger scale. To begin with his front was enormous, some 700 miles as the crow flies, and roughly followed the line of the length of the Indo–Burma frontier. Most of it was a tangled mass of jungle, river and mountain, some rising to over 10,000 feet. There were neither roads to carry the modern weapons of war nor airfields; lateral communications were non-existent between Stilwell's forces in the north, iv Corps based on Imphal in the centre and xv Corps in Arakan, 250 miles farther south. The lines of communication both to IV and XV Corps were totally inadequate to support the comparatively few British and Indian troops facing the Japanese; their rations were unsuitable and insufficient and the incidence of malaria was so high as to render some units unfit for battle. Finally, morale generally required a considerable boost.

Since any form of offensive operations was unthinkable until conditions had vastly improved, Slim concentrated his whole energy towards rectifying this appalling situation.

Thus, during this period of 'approach to battle', through his meticulous attention to the logistic situation, the health, welfare and discipline of his soldiers, by his insistence on an aggressive outlook and the confidence he inspired in his staff and subordinate commanders, he laid the foundation for a series of resounding victories, culminating in the complete defeat of the Japanese in Burma.

By December 1943 the situation had improved to the extent that offensive operations, at least on a limited scale, could be contemplated. Stocks of food, ammunition and petrol were increasing, airfields had been built and roads forward to the Burma frontier were nearing completion. Meanwhile the Japanese, who were aware of the preparations to make the Imphal plain a base for the reconquest of Burma and considered their best hope of remaining in Burma was to capture that British base before an offensive could be launched, were planning an all-out assault on Imphal.

In brief their plan envisaged a limited offensive in Arakan in February 1944 to draw Slim's attention and his reserves from the main assault on Imphal scheduled to be launched in early March. In the estimation of General Kawabe, the Japanese overall commander in Burma, victory would be complete before the monsoon broke in May, after which he would turn to the defensive. The threat to Burma would therefore be removed for many months to come and the defeat of the British would no doubt have a most damaging effect on the political and internal situation in India.

On 4 February 1944 the storm broke with a determined attack on XV Corps in Arakan, and Slim was called upon to fight his first battle as army commander. He was also as certain as he could be that a major attack on Imphal could shortly be expected.

Judged by the size of the forces engaged, the Arakan battle, which lasted three weeks, was not of great magnitude, yet since it concluded in the complete defeat of the Japanese it marked the turn of the tide. For the first time British and Indian troops stood their ground while supplied by air. In Slim's own words: 'It was a victory, a victory about which there could be no argument and its effect, not only on the troops engaged, but on the whole of XIV Army, was immense.' He had won the first round, but the Japanese had compelled him to commit such reserves as he had.

About this time too arrangements were well forward for the fly-in of Major-General Wingate's Special Force to central Burma. The object of this operation was to cut and keep cut the enemy's communications to their forces opposing Stilwell, engaged in pushing a road eastwards to join the old Burma Road and so reopen a land supply line to China. In Wingate, Slim had another difficult subordinate but again through his tactful but firm handling he succeeded in keeping this dedicated man under control.

So, by the end of February, Slim had four major and widely separated operations on his hands: Stilwell's advance towards the Burma Road, the Arakan battle still in progress, Wingate's operation due to take place in a week's time and, lastly, the pending assault on IV Corps at Imphal. Since his presence was necessary to discuss plans with the respective commanders from time to time, long flights were entailed calling for considerable mental and physical stamina. Of these he had ample.

For a number of reasons it had been clear to Slim that the reoccupation of Burma would have its beginnings in the northern (Stilwell) and central (IV Corps) fronts. It was equally clear that with the precarious lines of communication, it was unlikely that he would ever be able to concentrate a force across the river Chindwin, the first major obstacle, more than equal to that which the Japanese could bring against him. His first major battle *had* to be a success, and therefore the only alternative was to inflict a crippling blow upon the enemy *before* re-entering Burma. This was likely to be achieved only if the Japanese attacked first and it seemed that this they were about to do.

Throughout the Imphal/Kohima battle – described by one Japanese historian as 'the disaster at Imphal was perhaps the worst of its kind yet chronicled in the annals of war' – Slim followed a policy of allowing the enemy to batter his head against the Imphal defences and to suffer enormous casualties in so doing. Furthermore he reasoned that once the monsoon burst the Japanese lines of communication would become impassable, and without food and ammunition they would lay themselves open to destruction.

For four months, March to June, the battle raged at Imphal and Kohima. Crises were almost daily occurrences in the early stages, but due to Slim's resilience and determination never to admit defeat, together with strong backing given him by Mountbatten and Gifford, they were overcome. That the Japanese sprang many surprises causing extremely anxious moments, there is no doubt.

To reinforce IV Corps a division with its guns and mules was flown at short notice into Imphal from Arakan, a remarkable feat in the circumstances. When the Japanese cut all land communications with Imphal, the greatest air supply operation in the history of war was put into effect by the combined efforts of Fourteenth Army and the Royal Air Force under the command of Air Marshal Baldwin; and by resisting the many demands from above that he hurry with the relief of Imphal, Slim maintained his policy of wearing down the enemy. The final outcome was proof that he was right in his conception of how to conduct the battle. When he saw that the time had come for a counter-offensive, he judged he could call upon his officers and men, although they were reaching the point of exhaustion, for one more effort and he launched a pursuit that drove the enemy back to and beyond the river Chindwin.

Out of some hundred thousand of the enemy who had taken part in the operation, fifty-three thousand were killed, wounded or missing at Imphal and Kohima; most of their tanks, guns and equipment were either captured or destroyed, and of the three Japanese divisions engaged two were no longer fighting entities. In all the Japanese had suffered the greatest land defeat in their history, the back of their Burma army had been broken, the belief in their invincibility had gone forever, and Slim had succeeded in his strategic aim. Apart from solving the problems of terrain, weather, disease, the complicated logistic situation and the number of formations that could be supported, his way into Burma lay open.

The period between the victory at Imphal in June 1944 and the capture of Rangoon provides a picture of the qualities of generalship at their highest level. At the bottom of the scale of priorities for men and material, until the war in Europe was won, Slim had to make do with the barest resources to fight a mobile campaign in the most difficult conditions of terrain and climate and against an enemy who paid no lip service to the term 'the last round and the last man'. What he lacked in resources, he made up with improvisation, cunning, the fullest use of surprise and the maximum exploitation of the capabilities of the Royal Air Force.

Although the political object of the advance into Burma was the capture of Mandalay, the capital and, with Rangoon, possibly the only name known to those outside the campaigning area, Slim rightly believed that the complete destruction of the enemy was his main aim. Once this was accomplished, then all the Mandalays, Rangoons and in fact the whole of Burma, would fall into his hands. When the initiative passed to him after the battle of Imphal and in pursuance of this aim, he exerted continuous pressure on the Japanese, never allowing them to recover from one blow before he delivered the next.

An example of his flexibility in conducting the campaign was his sudden and complete change of plan after the advance into Burma had begun, a change that brought about one of the most brilliant strokes of strategy of the Second World War. Originally all available information had pointed to the fact that the Japanese intended to fight north of the wide Irrawaddy river and Mandalay. Then, when this proved to be incorrect, and it was clear that the enemy intended to make the Irrawaddy his main line of defence, Slim did not hesitate to divert one of his two corps to a different objective. Moving with great secrecy by jungle tracks, and crossing the Irrawaddy several miles to the south, while still giving the Japanese the impression that Mandalay was his objective, he struck at Meiktila, 70 miles south of the capital. This was the nodal point of the enemy's line of communication with their formations around Mandalay and west along the Irrawaddy. Furthermore, by his timing and wide dispersion of the various crossings of the Irrawaddy, he brought confusion to the minds of the Japanese commanders and uncertainty as to which was his main thrust.

For the Japanese the results of the Meiktila battle were cataclysmic. Slim was quick to take advantage. For logistic reasons alone it was essential for him to reach Rangoon before the monsoon broke. By creating a mobile corps of armour and lorried infantry of a size hitherto unseen in the Far East, and supplied by air, he gave his adversaries no chance to reorganise nor to establish a planned defence. During the race to Rangoon, in one month, this mobile force, urged on by the army commander, advanced 370 miles against a series of 'fight to the end' delaying actions by courageous Japanese remnants. By 5 May it joined up with the seaborne landing at Rangoon, just as the rains began.

Except for destroying isolated formations and units, the campaign was over. In nine months of incessant fighting from 6 August 1944 to 5 May 1945, Slim had taken his army, including heavy tanks and monster vehicles, through 1000 miles of largely undeveloped country and crossed two wide rivers – one of which was strongly defended – with inadequate equipment, to inflict a mortal defeat upon the most resolute of opponents.

Although it would be wrong to say that nobody could have accomplished what Slim did in Burma, it would be true to say that nobody could have done it better. Any judgement of his feats should be based on what he did with what he had – or rather with what he had not. The measure of his greatness as a commander lies in the fact that he never had enough to do what he had to do.

But what of the man himself, his physical appearance and his approach to high command? Stockily built and of medium height, 'God and his parents had given him the right physical characteristics – the British bull-dog jaw etc', as one senior Royal Air Force officer, who served constantly with him, summed up. Or as Winston Churchill remarked, 'He has a hell of a face.' Yet the strength of character in that face was ever lightened by the twinkle in his eyes.

During his rise to army commander he had commanded every sub-unit and formation from a platoon to a corps (all, with the exception of a battalion, in battle). He was therefore a highly experienced and balanced soldier and the combination of his physical and mental qualities gave him the necessary robustness to withstand the shocks of modern war. Never was he inflated by success nor depressed by misfortune, and his equable temper was a great asset when dealing with awkward persons and critical situations.

In his relations with his superiors Slim was a model of tact though he never hesitated to make his opinions crystal clear; consequently he invariably had their confidence and full support. Equally his handling of subordinates was such that, difficult as some may have been, he obtained their trust and loyal co-operation.

In the exercise of command he did not believe in the chief of staff system prevalent in other armies, preferring to put over his personality without an intermediary. And he had the knack of creating a happy atmosphere within his own headquarters, which permeated throughout whatever formation he was commanding. None feared to use their own initiative.

Of him it could well be said that he was a soldier's general, for there was no 'brass hat' about him. He knew how to talk to the regimental officers and their men in their own language, be it English, Urdu or Gurkhali. Whether his audience was troops in the forefront of the battle (and he was with them as often as the situation permitted), administrative units, clerks in head-quarters or men in the reinforcement camps, he made a point of putting them in the picture within the bounds of security. In addition he introduced both the humorous and human touch, interpolating his remarks on the war with more personal subjects such as rations, pay, mails, leave and beer.

In the operational field Slim's success in Burma sprang from his meticulous strategic and logistic planning based on an uncanny ability to see into the future. Always one move and sometimes more in advance of his enemy, he was also at times ahead of his superior commanders.

Before the war few, if any, had any experience of jungle warfare and none of fighting the Japanese. Time and again the line of communication was the vulnerable point, for the Japanese were adepts at cutting it and forcing the British to retreat. But Slim was quicker to grasp the potentialities and value of air support in the jungles of Burma than even most air force officers. Both he and Mountbatten realised that air superiority, the movement of troops by air, supply dropping and air landing of supplies, would allow for operations to be staged in country devoid of adequate communica-tions and likewise nullify the normal Japanese tactics of envelopment and penetration.

As a result a revolution in jungle warfare took place, and supply by air became regarded as normal practice by the army and air forces.

In the realm of organisation Slim foresaw that standard formations were unsuitable and that a combination of mule and motor transport was best fitted for the terrain. Yet when the necessity for speed arose and the country permitted, he immediately placed some formations on a completely mechan-ised and motorised basis, as he did for the thrust on Meiktila and the rush to Rangoon.

Tactically the employment of armour also underwent a revolution. The jungle did not permit the use of tanks in large numbers as in Europe and Africa. Instead squadrons and troops were placed in close support of infantry and found themselves climbing steep jungle-clad slopes to operate with great effect on the summits.

Above all, Slim proved beyond doubt that jungle warfare is primarily a matter of logistics in which improvisation must play a major part.

On the conclusion of the war and following a year as Commander-in-Chief Allied Forces South-East Asia, Slim, a general and fifty-five years old, returned to England as commandant of the Imperial Defence College, at which he had been a student ten years before. It seemed that his military career was drawing to a close since he was told that this would be his last appointment, and in 1947 he left the army to become deputy chairman of British Railways. But within twelve months he was recalled to the active list by Prime Minister Attlee to succeed Field-Marshal Montgomery as Chief of the Imperial General Staff. So he became the first Indian Army officer in history to be appointed military head of the British army.

In the war as an army commander he had been protected from the blasts of political pressure by a supreme commander. Now he had to deal direct with prime ministers, for both Attlee and Churchill held that office during Slim's term at the War Office. With the former his relations were always cordial, and in Attlee's own words, 'Bill Slim was first class. He was the best anybody had.' With the latter, largely because they did not know one another well, there was some strain at first. But this was soon dissipated for shortly after they came together, Churchill, when comparing Slim with another service chief, remarked 'When a man cannot distinguish a great from a small event, he is no use. Now Slim is quite different, I can work with him.'

For four strenuous years Slim steered the army through a difficult period. Political pressure was demanding a return to peacetime establishments and the abolition of, or at least a reduction in, National Service, while large numbers of troops were still needed to meet the requirements of Malaya, East Africa, Hong Kong and the Korean War. The revolt in Egypt with all its repercussions was also taking place. It was a testing period, and when in 1952 his term as Chief of the Imperial General Staff came to an end, Slim looked forward to having time to write, an occupation that had always interested him. It was not to be.

In the course of his travels round the world as Chief of the Imperial General Staff, Slim had visited Australia and met Prime Minister Robert Menzies, on whom he had made a deep impression. And it was on the latter's recommendation that the Queen called upon Slim the following year to go to Australia as Governor-General, a post he was to hold for seven years.

His 'straight from the shoulder' approach, his ability to sound the right note in his speeches and broadcasts and his strong sense of humour soon appealed. It is often said by Australians that he was one of the greatest and most popular governor-generals the country has ever known.

Appointed a Knight of the Garter in 1959 and raised to the peerage in 1960, Viscount Slim returned to a semi-public life as Constable and Governor of Windsor Castle in 1963, which position he occupied until 1969. Much in demand to attend service functions, he took a deep interest in the problems of the officers and men who had served with him. But his health began to fail, as did his sight, to an extent that he had to hand over an office that had given him much pleasure. Moving to London he died peacefully in 1970.

The impressive military funeral accorded him in St George's Chapel, Windsor, was attended by representatives of the Queen and other members of the Royal Family, by the Prime Minister, the Diplomatic Corps and by a host of officers and other ranks of all three services, who came to pay their last respects to a man who, to them, will always be affectionately remembered as – Bill Slim.

Admiral Isoroku Yamamoto

Captain Roger Pineau

When the Commander-in-Chief of the Imperial Japanese Navy's combined fleet learned that his striking force had succeeded in surprising Pearl Harbor, he said, 'It does not do to cut a sleeping throat.'

What sort of man was this who had not wanted to war against the United States, yet planned, organised and ordered the attack on Pearl Harbor, and then lamented that the severance of diplomatic relations occurred *after* the outbreak of hostilities?

Unlike the moment and place of his death, which are precisely recorded, his birth is known only to have occurred on 4 April 1884 in the north-west city of Nagaoka in rugged Niigata prefecture, on Japan's main island of Honshu. He was born into the family of Sadayoshi Takano, an impoverished but well-read schoolmaster, who already had five sons and a daughter. When pressed for a name, the father said, 'My age is fifty-six, let's call him that.' Thus the name Isoroku, written with the characters for five, ten and six.

His childhood was rigorous, physically and mentally. There was gardening in summer, clearing deep snows in winter, fishing throughout the year, and a constant struggle with the written complexities of the language.

Stories conflict about Isoroku's early life and where the seeds of adult thought, prejudice and action were sown. It is said that his father risked unpopularity by letting the children visit an American missionary, who first taught the future admiral about Christianity. On the other hand Willard Price, who interviewed Commander Yamamoto in 1915, wrote:

> Young Yamamoto began to hate America when his father told him tales of the hairy barbarians, creatures with an animal odor, owing to their habit of eating flesh, who had come in their black ships, broken down the doors of Japan, threatened the Son of Heaven, trampled upon ancient customs, demanded indemnities, blown their long noses on cloths which they then put in their pockets instead of throwing them away.

This alleged hatred – which first appeared as Second World War propaganda – is not manifest in his peacetime actions or utterances.

As early as middle school in the 1890s young Japanese had military training. Isoroku's greatest adventure each year was the military manoeuvres in which thousands of boys from several prefectures participated. Army officers commanded the exercises; the youngsters carried real weapons, but not live bullets.

As the new century dawned Yamamoto applied for admission to the naval academy at Etajima, on the Inland Sea. His application was accepted and, of three hundred applicants, he scored second highest in the entrance examination. It was only forty-seven years since Commodore Matthew C. Perry had come from the east with his black ships to 'open Japan'. The Meiji Restoration, which exposed Japan to the full influence of the Western world, had been under way for just thirty-two years. In 1894 the Japanese navy had tested its mettle against China and found it good. After a slumber of three centuries this fledgling country was awakening, and it wanted a powerful modern navy.

Naval training was rigid and spartan. All activities of the naval cadets were conducted in military formation during their three academic years at Etajima. Students were forbidden to drink, smoke, eat sweets, or go out with girls. The fourth year was spent on board naval vessels – close to currents, storms and winds – so these future naval officers could learn to live and fight at sea.

Isoroku stood seventh in the class of 1904. The Russo–Japanese War had begun that February, and he was proud to be ordered to cruiser *Nisshin*, part of the protective screen for *Mikasa*, flagship of Admiral Heihachiro Togo. Like him, thirty-five years hence, Isoroku would command the combined fleet.

Isoroku's baptism of fire came on 27 May 1905 in the battle of Tsushima Strait when *Nisshin* was struck by Russian shells. He wrote home:

> . . . I realized no fear when the shells began to fly about me, damaging the ship and killing many men. At 1850 hours a shell hit *Nisshin* and knocked me unconscious. I was wounded in the right leg and two fingers of my left hand were severed. The Russian ships were utterly defeated, however, and their dead littered the sea. When victory was announced at 0200 next day, even the wounded cheered.

Hector C. Bywater called it 'one of the most decisive naval actions in history', the first great Asian naval victory over an occidental country. It was almost decisive for Isoroku, who came within a finger of missing his career (the loss of three fingers constituted a mandatory discharge). He spent two months convalescing in the hospital before his return home to Nagaoka for a hero's welcome and chance to rest.

In the decade after Tsushima his career followed the usual peacetime naval pattern. He was on the whole a serious young man, not given to carousing like so many youthful naval officers. He read extensively, even books in English, including the Bible. To the jibes of more frivolous fellows he replied that the Japanese had much to learn from foreign books. He taught cadets on training cruises to China and Korea. In March 1909 his squadron briefly visited west-coast ports of the United States. Back home by July, this observant lieutenant had got an inkling of the country and people he would oppose three decades later.

In 1913 Isoroku's father died at eighty-five, and his mother followed shortly. This led to his adoption into the Yamamoto clan. (It is common Japanese practice for a prominent family, lacking a male heir of its own, to adopt a promising young man to perpetuate the family name.) At twenty-nine, this lieutenant showed promise, and the adoption was solemnised on 19 May 1915 at Nagaoka. The following three years were devoted to study, mostly to naval aviation and foreign affairs, and in 1918 he married.

On 5 April 1919 Yamamoto was ordered to language study in the United States. Largely at his own instigation he had a corollary assignment to make a study of petroleum at the same time. He was well aware that oil was the life blood of modern navies. The language study was carried out at Boston, where Yamamoto rented accommodation at 157 Naples Road in the suburb of Brookline.

Contrary to some biographers, he was not enrolled for two years at Harvard. His only application, in fact, was made in September 1919 for enrolment as a 'special student in English' for the next spring term, but he withdrew during the first month of that term. He got on well with acquaintances in Boston, readily performing the plate-balancing dance, answering questions about his distant homeland, and teaching *shogi* (Japanese chess) at which he excelled. He learned to play poker and promptly mastered it. Anticipation, bluff and luck appealed to his temperament, and poker became a passion of his life.

Isoroku's life was not all plate-balancing, poker and English, however, as he pursued his interest in oil and its relationship to naval policy. He approached the problem assiduously, reading omnivorously, visiting nearby oil installations and refineries, literally sleeping only three hours a night and devoting every waking moment to his studies. He became proficient at English and learned a lot about oil, but decided he needed to see the oilfields of the south-west, which he did when, after promotion to commander, he received for First World War service the Small Cordon of the Rising Sun with a cash award.

He was ordered home in early May 1921 and reached Yokohama on 19 July. After three weeks of leave he returned to Second Fleet, this time as executive officer of light cruiser *Kitagami*. In December 1921 he went to the Naval Staff College as an instructor.

In June 1923 he embarked on a nine-month trip to Europe and the United States with Admiral Kenji Ide, the naval vice-minister. They studied reactions to the Washington Disarmament Conference of 1922, which had established the 5:5:3 ratio of naval arms for Great Britain, the United States and Japan. He returned from that journey a captain, arriving at Yokohama on 31 March 1924.

His first major post came on 1 December 1924 as executive officer of the naval air station at Lake Kasumigaura. This two-year-old base, about 40 miles north-east of Tokyo, had been built at the suggestion of a British air advisory mission to Japan. It was the training ground for most of Japan's naval aviators.

Yamamoto became one of Japan's leading theorists on the military applications of aviation. Although he never learned to fly, the fliers loved him for his unstinting championship of naval aviation, and with his capacity for bold imaginative decisions he gained the respect and admiration of younger officers for his strong leadership. In this he was an exception. The Japanese navy, from its early days, had stressed gentlemanly qualities in its officers. Unfortunately however there was a tendency to equate gentlemanliness with an easy-going affability. This produced many bright and charming flag officers, but few real fighting leaders.

After a year at Lake Kasumigaura, Yamamoto returned to the United States as naval attaché on 23 February 1926. As Admiral Ellis M. Zacharias, one of the few American naval officers who knew him well said:

> . . . his selection in itself indicated the growing significance attributed to this outpost of Japanese intelligence . . . He was an air enthusiast and a brilliant tactician keenly interested in the operational problems of naval strategy. His arrival in Washington represented a significant change in Japanese intelligence methods and also in the subject which most interested our Japanese friends. His predecessors had concentrated on information of a tactical nature: problems and techniques of gunnery, technological details of our vessels, battle order, and detailed data on technical progress in our fleet. Now, it seemed, the naval attaché office in Washington was no longer interested in these tactical and technical data. Suddenly operational problems within the framework of highest strategy shifted to the forefront of the subjects on the Japanese shopping list . . .

> I always felt, after Yamamoto was appointed commander in chief of combined fleet and wartime leader of Japan's navy, that the first plans for the Pearl Harbor attack originated in his restless brain right here in Washington . . . great naval strategist that he was, he recognized even at that early stage of sea-air-power development the significance of carriers.

Yamamoto's biography, compiled by the Office of Naval Intelligence, described him as 'exceptionally able, forceful, and a man of quick thinking'.

He returned to Japan on 5 March 1928 with a low opinion of his future enemies, telling a correspondent, 'The United States Navy is a social organization of golfers and bridge players.' He returned to sea in August 1928 as captain of the light cruiser *Isuzu*, and moved to the aircraft carrier *Akagi* in December, before returning once more to shore duty on the Navy General Staff in October 1929, with concurrent duty in the Bureau of Naval Affairs. He was responsible for many innovations while in these posts, and remained in the last until assigned as a naval aide to the next London naval conference in 1930.

He was made rear-admiral before departing from Yokohama in November 1929 for a stormy Pacific crossing. From Seattle he went overland to New York City, and thence to London. There he was influential in obtaining equality for Japan in submarines and light cruisers, and it became clear to the naval world that Yamamoto was the voice of the Imperial Japanese Navy. He returned home in mid-June 1930.

In September he was assigned to Naval Air Corps headquarters, and was shortly named Chief of the Technical Division. The Manchurian Incident of 1931, which precipitated war with China, gave him occasion to improve naval aircraft. He insisted on torpedo bombers and long-range bombers, and most of all he demanded a fast carrier-borne fighter plane. Mitsubishi finally produced the Zero.*

In October 1933 Yamamoto took command of Carrier Division 1, and at sea worked out practical problems of air warfare. Training continued at a furious pace. When numerous accidents and casualties evoked grumbling among the fliers, Yamamoto railed, 'Our fleet suffers in comparison with the air strength of other navies. Time is short for Japan to catch up. We must accept the cost of intensive training. I regard death in training as a hero's death.' This odd mixture of fanaticism and patriotism inspired the pilots. Yamamoto posted the names of pilots killed in training, and the list was venerated by salutes from the living.

With the increase of militarist control in Japan, naval limitations came under increased criticism, and at the same time Britain requested a 1935 naval conference. Yamamoto was recalled from sea duty for briefing as delegate to preparatory talks in 1934.

With Great Britain and the United States sending high-ranking officers, the Japanese navy's sending a rear-admiral displayed Japan's contempt for the talks. He was however a safe Japanese choice, just fifty years old, eager to please his superiors, but not politically obligated. At a send-off party he promised to achieve Japan's basic aims of establishing a 'common upper limit' on overall naval tonnage, agreement to abolish all offensive weapons such as battleships and aircraft carriers, and abrogate the 5:5:3 treaty by the end of the year. He said, 'I am carrying the unanimous support of the Japanese nation in my suitcase. If I retain that, there is nothing the empire need fear.'

On arrival in Seattle on 1 October he refused all newspaper interviews, except to say that 'substantial reductions in armament are quite possible'. He travelled to New York City locked in his train compartment, refusing even to read American newspapers, which nevertheless gave him considerable publicity.

American headlines were also publicising General William 'Billy' Mitchell,

* Named from the fuselage markings 'oo', the last two digits of the Japanese year 2600 (AD 1940) when the plane went into production.

who was campaigning for increased air power for the United States. He prophesied war with Japan, and said the United States should be building military planes against that eventuality. This evoked Yamamoto's only public remark *en route* to New York: 'I do not look upon relations between the United States and Japan from the same angle as General Mitchell. I have never looked upon the United States as a potential enemy. Japan's naval plans have never included the possibility of an American–Japanese war.'

In New York his associates turned reporters away saying, 'The admiral speaks no English.' The falsehood went unquestioned. On 9 October, however, in interviews at the Hotel Astor he declared that Japan would advocate drastic reductions in naval armament. In a press conference upon arrival at Southampton he announced in fluent English, 'Japan can no longer submit to the ration system. There is no possibility of compromise by my government on that point.' That dockside statement doomed the conference to failure, even before it opened on 23 October. When Japan formally denounced the Washington naval treaty on 29 December, the American delegates went home

Yamamoto stayed on in an effort to win over the British, at least, to Japan's claim for naval parity. Conversations dragged on into 1935 and Yamamoto remained obdurate. He confided to colleagues, 'If we are patient, the day will come when we can make England and the United States bow to us.'

Press and public had been stunned when Yamamoto – himself so obsessed with aircraft carriers – proposed to abolish all capital ships. He went further and said that, given a free hand in Asia, Japan might agree to a world programme of disarmament. When asked how the United States and Great Britain could defend their Far East interests without capital ships, he said, 'The only defense they need is justice and international friendship.'

To a suggestion that the three powers exchange information on their naval building programmes, Yamamoto countered bluntly, 'Such an arrangement would be of no advantage to Japan. We can always find out what other powers are building, but you cannot know what we are doing.' This candour was not fully appreciated until the Second World War finally revealed Japan's warship programme of the 1930s.

While in London, Yamamoto was promoted to vice-admiral, and in Tokyo on 2 December 1935 he was named Chief of Naval Aviation. A year later he was concurrently appointed Vice Minister of the Navy. In these prestigious posts he was able to push his favourite weapon – air power. However he still had to contend with the conservatives of the Navy General Staff. In October 1934 studies were begun on new battleship designs. In 1937 Navy Minister Mitsumasa Yonai told the Diet that the Japanese navy had no force to match the combined strength of Britain and the United States, and 'no intentions of building to such a level', still construction continued on 73,700-ton battleships *Yamato* and *Musashi*.

The 'mighty battleship' concept was popular in the Japanese navy, but

Vice-Minister Yamamoto did not go along with it. While it died hard with the admirals, field grade officers, especially naval aviators, supported Yamamoto. He spoke movingly about battleships: 'They are like elaborate religious scrolls which old people hang in their homes – a matter of faith, not reality.' And, 'In modern warfare battleships will be as useful to Japan as a samurai sword.'

While Japanese doctrine held that carriers provide an 'air umbrella' for the striking force of battleships, Yamamoto preached that carriers should project fire power deep into enemy territory. That became doctrine in 1938, and Japan began building 30,000-ton, 30-knot carriers *Shokaku* and *Zuikaku*. Thus Japanese warship construction reflected both points of view. When fellow admirals argued that only a battleship could sink a battleship, Yamamoto replied that torpedo planes could also, and cited the oriental aphorism, 'The fiercest serpent may be overcome by a swarm of ants.'

Japan's expansionist programme was moving ahead in China along with the build-up of its naval strength at home. Yamamoto realised that if the programme was to succeed, war with the United States must be avoided, or at least delayed. He thus opposed army officers who wanted to ally with the European Axis. Navy Minister Yonai shared his view, but they stood largely alone.

The 'government by assassination' wave of the early 1930s flared again toward the end of that decade. Yamamoto's extreme opposition to war netted him so many enemies that he was offered a bodyguard. When he demurred, Yonai insisted. In July 1939 when an ultranationalist plot to kill him was discovered, Yonai sent him to sea as Commander-in-Chief of the combined fleet, promoted to full admiral. Yonai later said, 'It was the only way to save his life.'

He had been commanding the combined fleet only a few weeks when Germany invaded Poland. He knew that time was short, and his duty was clear. The Japanese navy must protect the homeland, and the fleet must be ready for any emergency. Training became even more rigorous. A fleet pamphlet read: 'With tenacious and timeless spirit we are striving to reach a superhuman degree of skill and fighting efficiency.'

Yamamoto's last hope for avoiding war had been that the navy stand firm against the Axis pact. But the new navy minister, after a mild protest, reluctantly went along with the army. The signing of the pact of 27 September 1940 sealed Japan's fate. Her commitment was limited to joining the Axis in war only if the United States joined Great Britain, but cautious Japanese regretted even that. Yamamoto, calling the pact 'impulsive' and 'irrational', knew that it made war with the United States inevitable. He told intimates that he was thinking of retiring to tend chestnut trees in his Nagaoka garden.

Prime Minister Konoye asked Yamamoto what chance Japan had in a war against Britain and America. With usual directness, he replied, 'If we are told to fight, regardless of consequences, we can run wild for six months or a year, but after that I have utterly no confidence. I hope you will try to avoid war with America.' Yamamoto also faced a personal dilemma. He had fought strenuously against the pact, and continued to argue vehemently against war with America and Britain. Now he was confronted with the need to prepare his navy so that Japan might at least have a fighting chance. Such preparation, as he saw it, included a devastating blow against United States naval forces in the Pacific so that Japan might negotiate a peace before being utterly defeated. His strong feeling about this arose from his keen awareness of the great disparity in basic strength between Japan and the United States.

This awareness is memorably apparent in a statement made at a Tokyo meeting of his old Nagaoka schoolmates on 18 September 1941:

It is a mistake to regard Americans as luxury loving and weak. I can tell you that they are full of spirit, adventure, fight, and justice. Their thinking is scientific and well advanced. Lindbergh's solo flight across the Atlantic was an act characteristic of Americans – adventuresome but scientifically based. Remember that American industry is much more developed than ours, and – unlike us – they have all the oil they want. Japan cannot vanquish the United States. Therefore we should not fight the United States.

Today these words make Yamamoto stand out like an island of sanity in Japan's lunatic rush toward war, but they caused a furore in all quarters of the government. Even Konoye spoke out, saying Yamamoto was irresponsibly pro-United States and pro-British. On learning this, Yamamoto, in his only known display of temper, shouted, 'I am Japanese. As a Japanese I do only what is best for my country. It is Konoye and his friends who are irresponsible.'

Early in 1941 Yamamoto said, 'We have no hope of winning a war against America unless the United States fleet in Hawaiian waters can be destroyed.' By April 1941 a staff study convinced him that an attack on Pearl Harbor was not only necessary but feasible. He ordered Rear-Admiral Ryunosuke Kusaka, of Vice-Admiral Chuichi Nagumo's First Air Fleet, to work out the operational plans. Kusaka, who knew his own boss, replied, 'The idea has appeal, but is risky. Admiral Nagumo will not like it.'

Nagumo and most other senior staff officers believed that the entire Japanese fleet would be needed to support the army's invasion plans for the rich resources areas to the south – the Philippines, Borneo, British Malaya and Sumatra – and, besides, there was no sense in stirring up the United States.

In September 1941 the various plans were war-gamed with Admiral Osami Nagano's Navy General Staff. Everyone approved the strikes in Burma, Malaya, the Central Pacific islands, the Dutch Indies and the Philippines. Hawaii appeared too risky. The war-gamers concluded that even if a Pearl Harbor attack succeeded, Japan would lose two or three carriers, and that was too costly.

But Yamamoto was adamant, and continued training for his plan as if it had unanimous support. He also continued his argument saying that the United States was bound to enter the war anyway. Finally he convinced his opponents that Japan had enough ships and planes to strike Pearl Harbor and simultaneously support the army's southward moves. Had he failed to persuade, he confided during a chess game, 'I'll resign, Watanabe. Either Nagano will approve, or he will fight this war without me.' By the end of October he had convinced all the doubters except Nagano. In a final show-down Yamamoto threatened to take over the carriers and personally direct the attack. His plan was adopted on 3 November.

In early November Yamamoto ordered Nagumo's task force to sail from the Inland Sea. The ships departed separately over several days, but all were gathered by 21 November at Tankan Bay in the bleak Kurile island of Etorofu. Thence the task force moved stealthily out of the fogbanks on its clandestine southward way to launch the fateful attack of 7 December 1941 on American ships and airfields at Oahu. And so the fury of modern war came to the Pacific. Japan rejoiced at news of the attack. The United States, stunned to disbelief at first, reacted promptly.

The next day, on board flagship *Nagato* at Hashirajima, Yamamoto and Watanabe interrupted their chess game to hear a short-wave radio broadcast from America. President Roosevelt was asking Congress to declare war on Japan as a result of the 'day that will live in infamy'. The American people, united as never before, were angry and clamouring for revenge. Yamamoto said, 'That's too bad, Watanabe. If I die before you, tell the Emperor that the navy did not plan it this way from the beginning.' After Pearl Harbor, Japan's naval war in the Pacific depended on Yamamoto. The Navy General Staff remained the official source of decision on Japanese naval action, but Yamamoto and his officers shaped all future fleet plans.

Yamamoto's prestige was unrivalled in Japan, as his ships and planes scored victory after victory. From Pearl Harbor to the Indian Ocean, from the Marianas to the Java Sea, the successes of combined fleet operations were complete. His headquarters exuded a feeling that in postwar years the Japanese called 'victory disease'. But Yamamoto, no victim of this malady, remained unmoved by his successes. He told Admiral Shigeru Fukudome, 'It is easy to open hostilities, but difficult to conclude them.' And he lamented Japan's lack of diplomatic offensive toward peace negotiations.

The first-phase operations of the Japanese war plan called for the surprise invasion of Thailand, destruction of the United States Pacific Fleet, and air strikes on the Malay Peninsula and Luzon, followed by conquest of the Philippines, Borneo, British Malaya (including Singapore) and Sumatra. When these were secure, amphibious forces would seize Java and the rest of the Dutch islands. A defensive perimeter would run from the Kurile Islands through Wake, the Marshalls, and around the southern and western edges of the Malay Barrier to the Burmese–Indian border. These operations were to be completed by late March or early April.

Immediately after the Pearl Harbor attack Yamamoto set his staff to work on studies for second-phase operations. Several plans emerged, but the army opposed them as too risky. Tokyo however offered no plans for second-phase operations. The situation so disgusted Yamamoto that he made his own plans for decisive action. He saw an attack on Midway as the best means of luring the United States fleet into battle, and studies toward that end were begun in late March. Kuroshima and Watanabe were sent to Tokyo to sell this idea, but the Navy General Staff rejected it.

Admiral Yamamoto opposed the traditional Japanese strategy of keeping the fleet in home waters to await the enemy's arrival. He argued that if he could annihilate the American fleet in the Pacific and set up air patrols between Wake, Midway and the Aleutians, then the Imperial Japanese Navy could cruise at will throughout the Pacific and land troops anywhere.

When the Navy General Staff initially rejected the Midway plan, Yamamoto made his position clear in a message to them:

> The success of our strategy in the Pacific depends on our destroying the United States fleet, especially its carrier task forces. The proposed operation against Midway will draw out the enemy's carriers and destroy them in decisive battle. Should the enemy avoid our challenge we shall still gain by the advancing of our defensive perimeter to Midway and the western Aleutians without obstruction.

The Navy General Staff remained intransigent on the subject until 18 April 1942 when General Doolittle's sixteen B-25s launched from carrier *Hornet* bombed Tokyo and other cities of the Japanese homeland. These strikes so depressed Yamamoto that he withdrew to his cabin for an entire day, but their effect on the Navy General Staff was to eliminate all opposition to an early-June attack on Midway.

Even while the Midway operation was being studied and rehearsed, developments that would influence it profoundly were taking place on the north-eastern approaches to Australia. There the long-planned invasion moves towards Tulagi in the Solomons and Port Moresby in south-eastern New Guinea precipitated the Battle of the Coral Sea on 7 May. When Japanese forces finally withdrew from the battle area three days later, it was with a slight numerical advantage over the enemy, but without taking Port Moresby. Worse was Japan's deprivation of carriers *Zuikaku* and *Shokaku* in the approaching Battle of Midway.

Yamamoto was so sure that the American fleet would be lured out of Pearl Harbor by a Japanese attack on Midway that there was no room in his consciousness for consideration that the enemy might know of his plan. But the United States had succeeded in breaking Japanese codes and knew that Midway was scheduled for invasion during the first week of June.

The results are familiar. The Japanese attempt to take Midway was met by a ready and wrathful enemy. The assault was repulsed with the devastating sinking of four Japanese aircraft carriers and loss of the cream of Japan's naval aviators. Midway was thus not only the first defeat in battle that Japan and Yamamoto had ever suffered, it was the battle that doomed Japan to lose the war.

'Midway was a victory of intelligence, bravely and wisely applied,' says naval historian Samuel Eliot Morison. Admiral Chester Nimitz commented, 'Had we lacked early information of the Japanese movements, and had we been caught with carrier forces dispersed . . . the Battle of Midway would have ended differently.'

For Admiral Yamamoto it was an indescribable blow. Too stunned to speak, he could only groan as he read the tragic reports.

Following the repulse at Midway, Yamamoto focused on a southward move. He saw the southernmost end of the Solomons chain as a base for attacks against Allied lines of communications he had not yet been able to disturb. Airfield construction was begun on Guadalcanal. When Admiral Nimitz spotted this activity its reason was apparent, and he quickly chose that island for the first American invasion of the Pacific war.

The struggle for Guadalcanal started on 8 August 1942 when American troops landed there and at nearby Tulagi. In the next six months Yamamoto tried twice for a decisive surface engagement without success. The struggle ended on 8 February 1943, exactly six months after it began, with an amazingly successful Japanese evacuation.

However successful, evacuations win no battle or wars, and Yamamoto could read the handwriting on the wall. He had sortied from Hashirajima in *Yamato* on 17 August to direct Operation 'KA', the effort to dislodge Americans from Guadalcanal. He put in at Truk on the twenty-eighth and soon thereafter wrote to a friend, 'I sense that my life must be completed in the next hundred days.'

To compensate the Emperor for the loss of Guadalcanal, Yamamoto promised a crushing air offensive on some of the Allies' newly acquired advance bases. At Truk, on 11 February 1943, Yamamoto transferred his flag from *Yamato* to sister ship *Mussashi*, Japan's newest battleship.

On 25 March 1943 an operational directive by Imperial General Headquarters spelled out the terms of a revised policy for South-East Area Operations. Operation 'I' called for close co-operation between army and navy air arms to intensify their operations, with main efforts in the New Guinea area.

Admiral Yamamoto reacted to this directive on 3 April by moving with his staff from Truk to Rabaul in two flying boats. Yamamoto and Vice-Admiral Jisaburo Ozawa (Third Fleet) set up their headquarters with the local commander, Vice-Admiral Jinichi Kusaka. Rabaul's land-based planes were augmented by planes from Ozawa's Third Fleet carriers for Operation

'I'. Yamamoto split it into two phases, the first on 7 April against the lower Solomons, the second against New Guinea on 11, 12 and 14 April.

Accepting aviator claims that they had sunk several warships and two dozen transports and shot down 175 enemy planes, Yamamoto halted Operation 'I' on the 16th. Actual Allied losses from these strikes were one destroyer, one tanker, one corvette, two transports and some twenty-five planes. Yamamoto never lived to learn the truth.

He had decided to inspect the bases of the upper Solomons. At 5.55 pm on 13 April 1943 a radio message informed all parties concerned that Commander-in-Chief Combined Fleet would visit Ballale, Shortland and Buin on the 18th. The schedule, worked out by Yasuji Watanabe, was meticulously detailed about Admiral Yamamoto's itinerary for that day:

0600 depart Rabaul in medium attack plane, escorted by six fighters
0800 arrive Ballale, and depart at once for Shortland in Base Force 11 subchaser
0840 arrive Shortland
0945 depart Shortland in subchaser
1030 arrive Ballale
1100 depart Ballale by plane
1110 arrive Buin
1400 depart Buin
1540 arrive Rabaul*

The coded Japanese message reached its addresses, but it was also intercepted by United States listening posts, where intelligence experts were able not only to understand what it said but also to realise what it meant. On 18 April Admiral Yamamoto was entering a combat zone where he might be vulnerable to Allied attack. Should an effort be made to get him? Did Japan have anyone as good or better to take his place? Admiral Chester W. Nimitz, Commander-in-Chief Pacific Fleet, put the question to his top intelligence officers at Pearl Harbor and Washington. 'Would the elimination of Yamamoto help our cause?' The answer was an unqualified 'Yes!' The plan was put in motion to get Yamamoto.

Sixteen P-38 Lightnings at Henderson Field, Guadalcanal, were fitted with extra fuel tanks to provide the necessary range. Pilots were briefed on the mission to intercept the targets 30 miles north of Ballale. The trap was set.

Yamamoto spent 17 April in conference on further war plans. During an evening game of *shogi*, he suddenly said, 'I am not satisfied with the way things went today, Watanabe. You better stay here tomorrow and continue the planning talks to settle all details.'

* Captain Watanabe showed me a notebook in which this itinerary was detailed in his own hand. I mentioned that the twenty-minute difference in time between the Rabaul-Ballale, and Buin-Rabaul flights was understandable, but hadn't he made a five-minute error in the subchaser ride? He explained that the five-minute difference allowed for an adverse set of tide and current on the northward leg.

At 6 am next day Admiral Yamamoto took off from Rabaul in his green-striped bomber with Rear-Admiral Takata, Commander Ishizaki, and Commander Tobana. In a second bomber were Admiral Matomi Ugaki, Rear-Admiral Kitamura and Commander Muroi.

As Captain Watanabe sadly told me, 'My chief was a very punctual man.' Precisely on schedule the two Japanese bombers were starting their landing approach when the Lockheed Lightnings struck, and both were shot down. Ugaki's bomber plunged into the water, within sight of the Buin control tower. Ugaki, Kitamura and the pilot were injured but survived. Yamamoto's aircraft caught fire and crashed in the jungle: there were no survivors.

Rabaul headquarters was in turmoil at news that both bombers had been shot down and the Navy Ministry ordered that Yamamoto's death be kept a strict secret. Mineichi Koga, Yamamoto's own choice as his successor, arrived at Truk on 24 April for conference with Yamamoto's staff, but still the secret was kept.

With the Allied invasion of Attu on 11 May the combined fleet had to come out of its lethargy and return to conduct of the war. On 17 May *Mussashi* departed from Truk with her sorrowful cargo and news, and arrived in Tokyo Bay four days later. On 21 May the public announcement finally came: 'Admiral Yamamoto, while directing general strategy in the front line in April of this year, engaged in combat with the enemy and met gallant death in a war plane.'

After a state funeral on 5 June his ashes were placed in two urns. One was deposited in Tokyo's Tamabuchi Cemetery alongside Togo's ashes. The other urn went to Nagaoka for burial beside the ashes of his father. A modest grave marker was cut as he had requested, an inch shorter than his father's. Yamamoto's military contributions to his country were considerable. His emphasis on aircraft and aircraft carriers in the Japanese building programme showed real foresight regarding the future of naval warfare. His emphasis on the aircraft torpedo proved to be fully justified. His development of carrier task forces – which he used to begin the war and the United States used in ending it – showed remarkable imagination. In naval leadership he had few modern peers. As combined fleet staff officer Goro Takase said, 'His concern for subordinates struck the heart of every sailor, and each was ready to die for him. His leadership pervaded the lowest reaches of the navy and inspired every man. There was never any wavering in his command.'

With all his naval genius he made mistakes in the Second World War; let us review the major ones. He should not have ventured so far into an active war zone, and for doing so he paid with his life. He should have struck at Guadalcanal with all his might, by going after it piecemeal he lost it, the rest of the Solomons and other early gains. He failed to concentrate his forces at Midway; and the dispersals were critical.

Finally what about Pearl Harbor mistakes? Admiral Morison in *The Rising Sun in the Pacific* says:

Thus, the surprise attack on Pearl Harbor, far from being a 'strategic necessity,' as the Japanese claimed even after the war, was a strategic imbecility. One can search military history in vain for an operation more fatal to the aggressor. On the tactical level, [it] was wrongly concentrated on ships rather than permanent installations and oil tanks. On the strategic level it was idiotic. On the high political level it was disastrous.

It is curious that the man who instigated, spearheaded and insisted upon the Pearl Harbor attack was the one person in all Japan who knew more about the oil resources of the United States than any other. Curious that that man – last child of an aged father, the plate-balancing, folk-dancing, Harvard enrollee who became Japan's fleet admiral Commander-in-Chief of the combined fleet – was betrayed by his own expertise into making one of the most colossal military blunders in his own country's, and indeed the world's, history. Whether he was the hero or merely the dupe of a lost cause is a nice discrimination, depending on how far one judges that his hand was forced by the ultranationalist insanity that led Japan to disaster. For after all Isoroku Yamamoto had told his old Nagaoka schoolmates before Pearl Harbor, 'Japan cannot vanquish the United States.'

Fleet Admiral Chester W. Nimitz

Henry H. Adams

'A man he seems of cheerful yesterdays and confident tomorrows.' Fleet Admiral Chester Nimitz commanded men and ships and aircraft amounting to more military power than had been wielded in all previous wars combined. The 'cheerful yesterdays and confident tomorrows' that had been foreseen by the editor of the yearbook on Nimitz's graduation from the Naval Academy had stood him in good stead as he co-operated with Army General Douglas MacArthur to bring Japan to complete and utter defeat.

In contrast with the theatrical MacArthur, Nimitz was modest, quiet, compassionate, humane, courteous. His light blue eyes could on occasion assume a glacial chill, but when he was pleased, their gleam seemed, as one of his officers put it, 'to light up the room'.

When he arrived at Pearl Harbor on New Year's Eve to take command of the Pacific Fleet, just twenty-four days after the Japanese attack, he found pessimism everywhere. He blamed no one; he told his officers to look ahead, not back. It was like magic. Although there were many worries to come, there was no more unreasoning defeatism. Yet Nimitz had no illusions about the difficulty of his new job. 'I will be lucky', he wrote to his wife, 'to last six months. The public may demand action and results faster than I can produce.'

He produced a great deal in those six months. From pinprick raids, including one on Tokyo, his forces went on to stop the Japanese in the Coral Sea and to defeat them in the Battle of Midway, and at the beginning of the seventh month started the offensive at Guadalcanal.

The future fleet admiral was born on 24 February 1885 in Fredericksburg, Texas, a small German–American community, tightly knit, and generally apart from the more prosperous cattle ranchers nearby. Chester's father died before his son was born, and his mother soon married her husband's brother William and moved with him to the nearby small town of Kerrville, Texas. Here Chester grew up, helping in his parents' small hotel and leading the normal life of a small-town boy.

He was eager for an education, but there was no money in the family to provide for more than high school. He decided to apply for admission to the US Military Academy at West Point, New York, and to make the army his career in return for an education. When he called on his congressional representative to ask for an appointment to West Point, he was informed that all were filled.* 'But', continued the congressman, 'I have an opening for the US Naval Academy. Are you interested?'

Nimitz had never heard of the Naval Academy, and he had never thought of a career at sea, but he would grasp at anything to get an education. He never regretted his decision to accept. After much hard studying, Nimitz was sworn in at the Naval Academy on 7 September 1901. He graduated as a passed midshipman on 30 January 1905, nearly six months early because of the need for officers in an expanding fleet. He stood seventh in a class of 114. His first duty station was the battleship *Ohio*, flagship of the Asiatic Fleet. When the *Ohio* arrived in the Far East, the Russo–Japanese War had just been fought. A little later, the *Ohio* paid a courtesy call to Japan, and Nimitz met Admiral Togo, the victor in the Battle of Tsushima. The meeting left a lasting impression, and Nimitz honoured Togo for the rest of his life, although they never met again.

At the end of two years, Nimitz was promoted to ensign and soon was given command of the *Panay*, an old gunboat. This command lasted only a few months before he was moved up to command the destroyer *Decatur*, if he could get her under way, that is. The ship had been laid up for years in Cavite. Nimitz had to scrape together a crew, fuel, and supplies to get his decrepit 420-ton dreadnought to the navy yard. Later the *Decatur* served in Philippine waters, and this led to an event that might have wrecked his career. He ran the ship aground near Manila. He was removed from command and court-martialled, but was convicted only of 'neglect of duty' and the official reprimand had no effect on his career.

Sent home, he was promoted and in January 1909 was assigned to submarine duty. He soon grew disenchanted with the dangerous gasoline engines used in American submarines and campaigned for their replacement with diesels. He set about learning all he could of diesels, and this interest led to several interesting future assignments. He commanded the first diesel submarine in the US Navy, and his growing recognition as a submariner brought him an invitation in 1912 to address the students of the Naval War College.

In April 1913 he married and the next month sailed with his bride to Europe where he was to study diesel engineering in Germany and elsewhere. On his return to the United States he reported to the New York navy yard to supervise the installation of diesel engines in the oiler *Maumee*. During this time he received several tempting offers from industry to leave the navy and become a diesel engineer. He rejected them all, and when the *Maumee* was commissioned, he served aboard in the dual capacity of chief engineer and executive officer.

---

* Appointment to the American service academies are made by members of the US Senate and the US House of Representatives, each of whom annually has a quota. Appointees must pass an entrance examination.

With war drawing closer to America, the *Maumee* was assigned the task of working out underway fuelling techniques. When the United States entered the war she was assigned to a mid-Atlantic station to refuel American destroyers ordered to report for duty with the Royal Navy. Nimitz was thus instrumental in pioneering a technique that later made possible the highly mobile naval war in the Pacific in the Second World War.

In August 1917 Nimitz reported for duty as aide to Rear-Admiral Samuel Robison, Commander Submarine Force Atlantic Fleet. Robison took an interest in the young man, now a lieutenant-commander, and they became lifelong friends. The admiral lost no opportunity to help his protégé's career, and advised him away from the engineering specialty that might limit his career.

After a tour in the office of the Chief of Naval Operations, as senior member of the Board of Submarine Design, Nimitz became executive officer of the battleship *South Carolina*, a key assignment that indicated he was being considered for appointment to the senior ranks.

His most challenging duty was the establishment of the submarine base at Pearl Harbor which came to him in 1920. Using salvaged war materials, he was to erect an entire base, including a machine shop and a foundry on a spot where giant cacti thrived. On completion Nimitz was promoted to commander and ordered to the Naval War College in Newport, Rhode Island. Its president was the brilliant non-conformist Rear-Admiral William S. Sims. In the war-gaming, Sims stressed the carrier as the new capital ship of the navy, and the assumed enemy was always Japan. Here Nimitz experimented with the circular formation for naval ships rather than the traditional line of battle. It was to become the standard carrier formation in the Second World War.

On completion of his War College studies, Nimitz was happy to serve once again with Admiral Robison, now Commander-in-Chief US Battle Fleet. His flagship was the battleship *California*, and Nimitz became his aide, assistant chief of staff and tactical officer. Under Robison, Nimitz had the opportunity to try out the circular formation with the Battle Fleet. He also urged that the navy's lone aircraft carrier, *Langley*, be incorporated into the force rather than being left to her own devices where she would not bother the battleships. Both experiments worked well, but after the departure of Robison and Nimitz, conservatives lost no time in abandoning them.

In the fall of 1926, Nimitz began a series of routine, often mundane, appointments which ended only with command of the cruiser *Augusta*. He was elated, for the *Augusta* was to go to Shanghai to become flagship of the Asiatic Fleet. This was a happy tour, which lasted from mid-summer 1933 until 1935. Under Nimitz the *Augusta* became a crack ship and visited the Philippines, the Netherlands East Indies, Australia and Japan.

Upon leaving the *Augusta*, Nimitz reported to Washington as Assistant Chief of the Bureau of Navigation, later known as the Bureau of Personnel. Here he learned the importance of politics in the military. He was much concerned with manning the new ships that were beginning to come into service under the building programme of President Roosevelt. He held this post until, in 1938, he was promoted to rear-admiral and briefly commanded Cruiser Division 2. Surgery terminated this command, but on his discharge from the hospital he became Commander Battleship Division 1, with his flagship the *Arizona*. During this command his division worked on refinements in underway replenishment and in bombardments in support of amphibious operations.

Owing to the shortage of sea-going billets for flag officers, his command of Battleship Division 1 lasted but a year. Then he went back to Washington as Chief of the Bureau of Navigation in 1939. His reputation as a keen judge of men grew, and he was consulted by many senior government officials, including the Secretary of the Navy and the President. At this time Nimitz was fifty-four years old, and he had had a well-rounded career, with the exception that he was no aviator. His lack of aviation experience brought him into conflict with Rear-Admiral John T. Towers, who was Chief of the Bureau of Aeronautics. Towers believed that he should assign all senior aviation commands. Nimitz had no intention of allowing Towers the authority that belonged to the Bureau of Navigation, but he was always ready to listen.

Nimitz's quiet brilliance was bringing him the reputation he deserved. President Roosevelt summoned him one day and offered to make him Commander-in-Chief US Fleet. Nimitz refused, for he considered himself too junior. The appointment went instead to Admiral Husband E. Kimmel, whose career ended in ruins at Pearl Harbor as the Japanese bombs fell.

On the afternoon of 7 December 1941 Nimitz was spending the day at home. When news of the Japanese attack on Pearl Harbor came over the radio, he rushed to his office. There were preparations to be made for the casualties, reinforcements to be sent, and plans to be made for the huge surge of enlistments that would come. Several congressmen called asking to join the navy. Nimitz's invariable reply was, 'Go back and vote us appropriations, for we're going to need them.'

On 15 December President Roosevelt and Secretary Knox decided to change the high command of the navy. The commander-in-chief post would be brought to Washington and be given to Admiral Ernest J. King, who would work under the Chief of Naval Operations, Admiral Harold Stark. In a few months Stark was sent to London, and King took over as Chief of Naval Operations as well. The President and the Secretary also personally selected Nimitz to relieve Kimmel as Commander-in-Chief Pacific Fleet (Cincpac).

Nimitz had four main objectives when he took over as Cincpac: to safeguard shipping between the United States, Hawaii, Midway and Australia; to divert the Japanese from the East Indies; to hold the line against further Japanese expansion in the Pacific; and to restore morale to the badly shaken Pacific Fleet. His only remaining offensive weapons were his carriers, and he proposed to use them on raids to keep the Japanese off balance.

Rear-Admiral Claude Bloch, Commandant of the Fourteenth Naval District based in Hawaii, had once worn the four stars of Commander-in-Chief US Fleet when Nimitz had been a junior rear-admiral. He had seen Kimmel lose the battle line, and he was not going to let Nimitz throw away the carriers. But Vice-Admiral William F. Halsey, Jr, scorned Bloch's defeatism and offered to lead the carrier raids himself. Thus supported, Nimitz lost no time in letting Bloch know who was in command and sent Halsey on his way. The raids amounted to little, but they did encourage morale, both in the fleet and in the United States, helping to offset the constant flood of bad news from South-East Asia.

In April area commands were established in the Pacific. General Douglas MacArthur became Commander-in-Chief South-West Pacific, commanding all the Allied troops, ships, and aircraft in that area, with headquarters in Australia. Nimitz added to his title of Cincpac that of Cincpoa, Commander-in-Chief Pacific Ocean Area, having under his command all naval forces, army units, and both army and naval aviation. Both commands were international in scope, having been approved by the Combined Chiefs of Staff, and Allied units served under both Nimitz and MacArthur.

While Halsey was taking General James Doolittle's aviators on their Tokyo raid, trouble was building up in the Coral Sea area. It became evident that the Japanese were mounting an amphibious operation against Port Moresby on the south-east coast of New Guinea. Loss of Port Moresby would mean a distinct threat to Australian communications and would deprive MacArthur of the base he was planning to use in his planned New Guinea campaign. Co-operating with MacArthur, Nimitz in early May sent a carrier force into the Coral Sea. In the ensuing action, the first in history where the surface ships never sighted each other, the American forces lost an oiler, a destroyer, and the carrier *Lexington*. The Japanese lost a light carrier and had a large one damaged, but the invasion force turned back, the first time the Japanese had been stopped in the war. Thus, while American losses were heavier, it was a strategic victory for the United States.

Much more important was the Battle of Midway fought on 4–6 June 1942. The action is described in the chapter on Admiral Spruance. From Pearl Harbor, Admiral Nimitz, who technically retained tactical command, could only wait for the reports which would tell him the outcome. He had already done his work. His was the staff that had deciphered the Japanese messages revealing the battle plan. He had made the decision to virtually ignore the thrust against the Aleutians, and he had positioned his carrier forces on the flank of the Japanese carrier force.

To work off his tensions Nimitz liked to shoot on a pistol range he had set up outside his office. He found that he could exclude from his mind everything but squeezing the trigger. On 4 June Admiral Nimitz expended a great deal of pistol ammunition.

When it was evident that the Battle of Midway had been won, Nimitz considered it the high point of his career. His vastly outnumbered forces had turned back the Japanese for the second time, and this time the victory was both tactical and strategic. The Japanese lost four of the six carriers that had raided Pearl Harbor. The Americans lost the *Yorktown*, but the Japanese were never again able to go on the offensive. They would win battles in the future, but never another campaign.

With the victory at Midway, American forces prepared to begin the long roads to Tokyo. General MacArthur, after repulsing Japanese overland attempts to take Port Moresby, began a drive in Papua designed to gain control of New Guinea. Meanwhile Nimitz's Pacific Ocean Area forces were about to react to the Japanese building an airbase on Guadalcanal in the Solomon Islands.

As he prepared to assume the offensive, Nimitz had tacked above his desk a list of three questions he expected his planners to be able to answer:

1. Is the proposed operation likely to succeed?
2. What might be the consequences of failure?
3. Is it in the realm of practicability of material and supplies?

Nimitz and King met about every two months, usually in San Francisco, and many decisions made in these meetings required only formal approval by the Joint Chiefs. Nimitz liked to listen to the debate and then make his decision. Neither he nor Admiral Spruance, who became his chief of staff following Midway, was a 'paper man'. They liked to talk things out, make the decisions, and keep their energies free for the things that only they could do. Nimitz and Spruance were great walkers, and they thrashed out many decisions of the war during the 5–10 mile hikes they were accustomed to take.

Nimitz considered one of his most important duties that of getting to know the officers and as many of the enlisted men in the Pacific Fleet as he could. The commanding officer of every ship or force arriving in Pearl Harbor was expected to make a call, and these calls were not merely social. Each officer was examined closely about the state of his command, and remedial action was taken if appropriate and possible, Nimitz entertained at dinner frequently. After a social hour with two drinks, dinner was served, and the talk was both serious and light. Guests might hear an analysis of the war, talk of music and books, of which he was inordinately fond, or professional topics. There was never any of the character assassination common in gatherings of professionals in almost any activity. Nimitz would never speak ill of a subordinate except to his face.

The overall objective of both MacArthur's New Guinea drive and the one under Nimitz in the Solomons was the recapture of Rabaul on the island of New Britain. For the Solomons operation, a South Pacific command was established, subordinate to Nimitz, working in co-ordination with MacArthur. Vice-Admiral Robert L. Ghormley was named Commander South Pacific Area and South Pacific Forces. Directly in command for the assault on

Guadalcanal was Vice-Admiral Frank Jack Fletcher, who had under him Rear-Admiral Richmond Kelly Turner, in charge of the amphibious force, and Major-General A. Archer Vandegrift, commanding the 1st Marine Division. Fletcher himself commanded the carrier force as well.

The Marines landed on Guadalcanal and the nearby small island of Tulagi on 7 August 1942. Hard fighting ensued on Tulagi, but the airfield on Guadalcanal was easily taken. The surprised Japanese had retired into the jungle.

The seizure of the airstrip, later named Henderson Field, was the only thing in the fifteen-month Solomons campaign that was easy. The Japanese struck back shortly after midnight on 9 August in a naval surface attack that caught Turner's forces by surprise and sank three American and one Australian cruiser at a cost to themselves of one hit on the flagship. It was the greatest uncompensated loss in American naval history. The reasons for the defeat sum up to a mixture of inexperience and over-confidence and at the same time excessive caution on the part of Admiral Fletcher, who had withdrawn his carriers out of range of the battle area.

At first the Japanese underestimated the number of Americans on Guadalcanal and committed most of their efforts to the drive on Port Moresby, trying to throw the Americans out of Guadalcanal by naval power and a few reinforcements. A series of actions followed in which the carrier *Enterprise* was damaged. Then in the next few weeks the carriers *Wasp* and *Saratoga* were hit, and the former had to be sunk. Also damaged was the battleship *North Carolina*. The marines on Guadalcanal meanwhile were fighting for their lives in a series of perimeter battles around Henderson Field. Beset by the Japanese, jungle rot and malaria, the marines felt bitter over their supposed abandonment by the navy. Admiral Turner was cautious in view of his naval losses, and Admiral Ghormley in his headquarters at Noumea seemed unable to end the bickering.

Nimitz eventually reached the unwelcome conclusion that he had no choice but to relieve Admiral Ghormley. Admiral Halsey was making an inspection tour of the South Pacific preparatory to taking over command of the carriers in the South Pacific. As his plane came to a stop in Noumea, Ghormley's flag lieutenant handed Halsey a message from Nimitz: 'Immediately upon your arrival at Noumea, you will relieve Vice-Admiral Robert L. Ghormley of the duties of Commander South Pacific Area and South Pacific Force.'

Although Ghormley was cordial and friendly to Halsey, on his return to Pearl Harbor, he demanded of Nimitz the cause for his relief under such humiliating circumstances. Nimitz was sympathetic. 'Bob,' he said, 'I had to pick from the whole Navy the man best fitted to handle that situation. Were you that man?'

'No,' replied Ghormley. 'If you put it that way, I guess I wasn't.'

The fighting on Guadalcanal reached a climax in November when the Japanese mounted an all-out effort to drive the Americans out, attacking by sea and land in co-ordinated actions. American losses were heavy, but the

Japanese were repulsed and made the decision to evacuate the island. By the end of January Guadalcanal was free of the Japanese.

On a visit to the island Nimitz contracted malaria and had to enter the hospital at Pearl Harbor on his return, but he was not so incapacitated that he could not meet King in San Francisco the following month. This was a period of relative inactivity in the Pacific war, and King was anxious to speed things up. He proposed that South Pacific Forces assault Bougainville at the north-west end of the Solomons chain. Nimitz opposed the move, since Bougainville was beyond range of fighter cover from Guadalcanal. Objectives in the Central Solomons, especially Munda, would have to be taken first. King then proposed that Central Pacific forces seize objectives in the Gilberts that spring. Nimitz, usually the advocate of the bold move, again cautioned patience. He could do it in the fall when the new big carriers began to join the fleet, accompanied by new battleships, cruisers and destroyers.

In March, at a conference in Washington where Nimitz was represented by Spruance, the objectives for 1943 were determined. Halsey's South Pacific Force would move up the Solomons towards Bougainville and Rabaul, while MacArthur's South-West Pacific Force would go only as far as Cape Gloucester on the southern end of New Britain. For lack of ships, planes, and troops, the assault on Rabaul was postponed to 1944. In the end it was bypassed.

These decisions freed a good number of ships for the Central Pacific, and Spruance was able to win approval of Nimitz's desires of recapturing Attu and Kiska in the Aleutians, which had been the only Japanese gains from the Midway operation. Also he won tentative approval of a Central Pacific campaign against the Gilberts and Marshalls. Final approval was given after the British members of the Combined Chiefs of Staff concurred.

During the following months Nimitz reorganised much of his command. He appointed Spruance to command the Central Pacific Force when it came into being and replaced him as Chief of Staff with Rear-Admiral Charles H. McMorris.

The recapture of Attu and Kiska took place without difficulty. In fact, the Japanese had evacuated the latter before the Americans stormed ashore. Meanwhile planning for the Central Pacific drive had begun. As discussed in the chapter on Admiral Spruance, the Joint Chiefs' directive was to bypass the Gilberts and proceed directly to the Marshalls. The more everyone looked at this idea, the less he liked it. All discussions hung on the fact that the Marshalls were out of range of landbased aircraft from any base the Americans had and were within range of several Japanese airbases. If the Gilberts were taken first, then the Americans could be supported by air power based in the Ellice and Phoenix Islands. The Gilberts could then be used to support subsequent landings in the Marshalls. Spruance was the most forceful advocate of the Gilberts, and Nimitz soon accepted the idea. Approval was given by the Joint Chiefs on 20 July, and the planning for the Gilbert operation went ahead.

Nimitz meanwhile had his eye on the progress of the Central Solomons campaign. At his suggestion, after taking Munda, Halsey bypassed the heavily defended island of Kolombangara to take lightly held Vella Lavella Island farther up the chain. Once the strong Japanese island positions were bypassed, they were useless so long as the Allies controlled the sea and sky, for they could neither be reinforced nor evacuated. Halsey was now ready to plan to move on to Bougainville, scheduled for 1 November, nearly simultaneous with the forthcoming assault on the Gilberts.

D-Day for the Gilberts was 20 November 1943. Apprehension at Cincpac headquarters mounted as early reports came in from the Gilbert Islands. Although the going on Makin was as easy as expected, the fighting on Betio was much heavier than anyone had foreseen. Nimitz however remained confident, saying, 'I've sent in there everything we had, and it's plenty. I don't know why we shouldn't succeed.'

By the next morning the news from Betio had improved, but news had come in that the light fast carrier *Independence* had been torpedoed by an enemy plane, and at the morning conference Nimitz and his staff considered the implications of this attack. In the view of the aviators, led by Admiral Towers, Spruance was keeping the carrier groups too close to the beachhead, enabling the Japanese to find them easily. The carriers, the aviators argued, should not be confined to supporting the troops ashore; they should be free to roam widely, giving distant support against ships, planes and bases that might threaten the success of the operation by bringing in additional forces from afar.

Surface officers, thinking of the Japanese reactions to Guadalcanal, wanted the carriers nearby to intercept any Japanese flanking movements and to support the men fighting ashore. These differing viewpoints were never completely settled, but in the case of the Gilbert operation Nimitz did radio instructions to Spruance to give the carrier groups a little more scope.

Shortly after Betio had been declared secure, Nimitz and members of his staff visited Tarawa in order to study the defences that had exacted so heavy a toll. The Marshalls operation was scheduled to begin in just over two months, and ways had to be found to prevent any more bloody Betios. No one in the Cincpac party had ever seen such a scene of devastation. Thousands of Japanese corpses remained still to be buried. 'It's the first time I've smelled death,' said Nimitz softly.

Back in Pearl Harbor Nimitz gave every assistance to Spruance and Turner in studying and applying the lessons of Tarawa to plans for the Marshall Islands operation. On the island of Kahoolawe he had constructed the types of pillboxes and blockhouses the Japanese had built on Betio. Ordnance experts set to work to discover what kind of bombing and gunfire could destroy them. They learned that general area fire was useless; it merely stirred up clouds of dust obscuring targets and disturbing the defenders not at all. It took direct hits with armour-piercing shells and bombs to do any good. Other improvements were for the increased use of tracked amphibians to transport troops across the reefs, better supply of ammunition and better communications.

Before the Marshalls operation began Nimitz attended a meeting in San Francisco with King which set the course of the Pacific war for the next few months. MacArthur would continue his drive west along the northern coast of New Guinea, and Halsey in the South Pacific would complete the encirclement of Rabaul by taking Green and Emirau Islands, as South-West Pacific troops took the Admiralties. This left the Central Pacific forces free to proceed with the conquests of the Marshalls and later that summer the Marianas.

Conquest of the Marshalls began on 31 January 1944, without any of the difficulties that had beset the Gilberts. Fast carriers destroyed all Japanese aircraft in the Marshalls, and the Japanese were helpless to bring in others. So well did things go that Nimitz queried Spruance whether they could proceed with the capture of Eniwetok, using the uncommitted corps reserve. Spruance agreed, and that atoll was taken in mid-February, while Rear-Admiral Marc A. Mitscher's carriers, Task Force 58, covered the assault by raiding Truk, the most publicised Japanese strongpoint in the Pacific.

While the Marshalls operation was proceeding, Nimitz hosted a major conference at Pearl Harbor on future strategy for the Pacific war. MacArthur opposed the whole concept of the Central Pacific drive, arguing that the troops and ships it consumed could more profitably be employed along the New Guinea–Halmahera–Mindanao axis. He had won an ally in Cincpac headquarters in the person of Admiral Towers, who argued that Nimitz's forces could support MacArthur by driving through the Bismarcks, Admiralties, Palaus and on to the Philippines. The Marianas, he argued, were of little use and had the drawback of having no usable harbour to support the vast number of naval ships that would be available by then. MacArthur's representative argued that the use of the Marianas for bombing Japan with B-29 long-range bombers would be 'just a stunt'. The capture of Truk, currently in Central Pacific planning, was overly risky and should be abandoned. Everything should be subordinated to a return to the Philippines, for American air and sea power based there could cut Japan off from her resources region in South-East Asia and the large islands nearby.

Nimitz generally concurred with these arguments. Admiral Sherman and Major-General Richard Sutherland, MacArthur's Chief of Staff, went to Washington to sell the results of the conference to the Joint Chiefs of Staff. They reckoned without Admiral King, who firmly killed the plan and buried it so deep it would never rise again until after the war, when it would be debated anew by historians.

By 11 March everything was settled, and the Joint Chiefs had their directive ready. MacArthur would make a 400-mile leap to Hollandia on the north coast of New Guinea on 15 April, supported by Mitscher's fast carriers. Truk would be bypassed, and Central Pacific forces would invade the Marianas beginning on 15 June and the Palaus on 15 September. Both would join the invasion of Mindanao on 15 November. Whether Luzon or Formosa would follow was left open, but the target date for either was 15 February 1945.

Soon thereafter Nimitz found an invitation from MacArthur inviting him to come to Brisbane for a meeting. Despite MacArthur's repeated refusals to come to any meeting anywhere, Nimitz had no hesitation in accepting the invitation. He and MacArthur would be having to work together even more closely in the future, and despite the general's efforts to take over command of all of the Pacific war, Nimitz felt that personal acquaintance would make things easier. On 25 March Nimitz and some of his staff arrived at Brisbane. Although Nimitz found MacArthur inclined to pontificate and to be jealous of his prerogatives, he was also considerate and persuasive. Nimitz was more amused than bothered by MacArthur's pomposities and genuinely respected his fighting abilities.

Planning had continued for the Marianas operation, and the assault on Saipan took place on schedule. An immediate concern was the movement of the Japanese combined fleet to oppose the landing; Nimitz hoped for an opportunity to destroy the Japanese navy and prepared to watch with confidence Spruance's moves to meet the enemy in the Philippine Sea.

The story of the Battle of the Philippine Sea is told in the chapter on Spruance and need not be repeated here. Spruance's caution in refusing to risk the beachhead met with Nimitz's approval as far as the record was concerned. In any event the great American victory in the Battle of the Philippine Sea stilled most criticism.

Differences in views between MacArthur and the navy continued during the summer, and it was to take the Commander-in-Chief, President Roosevelt, to settle them. MacArthur believed he had given a solemn pledge for the United States that the Philippines would be liberated, and his proposal was that after the landings on Mindanao, the rest of the archipelago be liberated as quickly as possible. Nimitz and other naval officers favoured bypassing Luzon and other northern Philippine islands and seizing Formosa, which would serve as a base for a landing on the coast of China, whence the American naval and air power could be allied with the Chinese land power in the decisive actions of the war.

In view of this impasse President Roosevelt decided to take a personal hand. He determined to meet Nimitz and MacArthur in Pearl Harbor to settle the matter for once and for all. He had just been renominated for an unprecedented fourth term as President, and there was no doubt that his journey to the Pacific would be valuable politically. He did not invite members of the Joint Chiefs of Staff to accompany him, for he was determined to make his decisions personally as he was wont to do in his meetings with Churchill and Stalin. Admiral King, arriving in Pearl Harbor two weeks before the President, was in a sour mood, for he believed Mr Roosevelt's forthcoming conference was only a political stunt. He was further annoyed at Mr Roosevelt's decision to accept a British fleet in the Pacific, for he feared their logistic needs would hinder rather than help the US Navy. In addition he felt that the American forces had brought victory near in the Pacific, and now that it was assured there was no need for someone else to come in and share the glory. He was prepared to accept the Royal Navy units if they contented themselves with operating south of the Philippines against Borneo and Sumatra and kept out of the way of the real fighting.

After an inspection trip of the Marshalls and Marianas with Nimitz, King returned to Washington, on the way back passing in the Pacific the heavy cruiser *Baltimore*, which was carrying President Roosevelt to Hawaii. Mac-Arthur meanwhile, after protesting that he was much too busy to leave his command, had been ordered by General Marshall to proceed to Hawaii to meet Admiral Nimitz and the President. Since he had no choice but to come, he determined to make good use of every opportunity to dominate the meeting.

The *Baltimore* entered Pearl Harbor on 26 July. Following publicity photographs and drives past cheering crowds, the President, Nimitz and MacArthur got down to business. In the living room of Mr Roosevelt's quarters a large map of the Pacific had been set up. At issue was what would happen after the recapture of Mindanao. MacArthur, in line with his promise to return, spoke for Leyte in the central Philippines to be followed by Luzon, where Manila is located. Nimitz, supporting the navy position, argued for Formosa. His heart was not in the argument however for he was coming to the conclusion that MacArthur was right. At length Mr Roosevelt made up his mind. The Philippines would be liberated.

After the Marianas operation Admiral Halsey relieved Admiral Spruance for operations against the Carolines in preparation for the invasion of the Philippines. Under Halsey the Fifth Fleet was renamed the Third Fleet, and Task Force 58 became Task Force 38. There was hard fighting for Peleliu. Yap was bypassed, and the magnificent anchorage of Ulithi Atoll was seized and made available as an advance base from which to mount the Philippine invasion.

During these operations Task Force 38 raided the central Philippines and found the defences there so weak that Halsey recommended the invasion of Mindanao be cancelled and Leyte be substituted for it and that the operation be advanced a month to mid-October. Nimitz and MacArthur concurred, and the matter was put up to the Joint Chiefs who were then meeting the British at Quebec. Called from the dinner table, they conferred briefly and gave their blessing.

The invasion of Leyte took place on 20 October 1944. Nimitz had transferred almost all of his amphibious ships and troops to MacArthur's command, leaving the Third Fleet little more than Task Force 38 and its logistic support ships. Vice-Admiral Thomas C. Kinkaid, under General MacArthur, commanded the Seventh Fleet, which comprised the attack transports, cargo carriers, landing ships and craft, old battleships and cruisers, escort carriers, destroyers, destroyer escorts, and myriad other kinds of vessels needed for an amphibious assault. The Third Fleet and the Seventh Fleet had no common superior short of the Joint Chiefs of Staff in Washington.

Once again the Japanese navy emerged, and the ensuing Battle for Leyte Gulf was the largest ever fought. They planned a pincer movement, one force transiting Surigao Strait to attack Leyte from the south, and a very powerful one converging from the north through San Bernardino Strait. In addition they sent their remaining carriers down from Japan to serve as decoys and pull Halsey's Third Fleet from the area, so that their surface forces could penetrate Leyte Gulf and knock out the beachhead.

Halsey felt he could safely leave the force approaching from the south to Kinkaid and the Seventh Fleet; this left him free to concentrate on anything coming from the north.

All afternoon of 24 October Mitscher's aircraft pummelled the Japanese force in the Sibuyan Sea as it headed for San Bernardino Strait. But Halsey's mind was on another question: where were the carriers? Late that afternoon they were located well to the north, and Halsey, overestimating the damage Mitscher's planes had done in the Sibuyan Sea, took all his force north to attack the empty carriers. The Japanese had not been able to replace the aviators lost in the Battle of the Philippine Sea; they hoped to lure Halsey away from San Bernardino and were prepared to lose the entire northern force to do so.

Kinkaid meanwhile committed his entire combat force to dealing with the southern threat. No one was guarding San Bernardino, although an ambiguous message addressed from Halsey to the Third Fleet and intercepted by Kinkaid led him to believe that Halsey had left a powerful surface force there.

During the night Kinkaid's old battleship force annihilated the Japanese in Surigao Strait as Halsey sped north. Admiral Kurita, commanding the central force in San Bernardino, transited the strait and emerged into the open sea, opposed only by weak escort carrier groups.

At Pearl Harbor Nimitz was keeping a close watch on what was going on, although the messages reaching him were far from telling the full story. But he was coming to the conclusion that Halsey had left San Bernardino unguarded, and he wondered whether he would be forced to break his rule of never interfering with the commander on the scene.

Kinkaid meanwhile was having second thoughts on whether Halsey had left a surface force, designated Task Force 34, at San Bernardino, and as the powerful Japanese force under Kurita began shelling the vulnerable escort carriers and their accompanying destroyers and destroyer escorts, radioed an inquiry. He was dumbfounded to learn that Task Force 34 was 300 miles north with the carriers.

Nimitz at length intervened, asking Halsey the whereabouts of Task Force 34. The message contained end padding for cryptographic security which read like part of the message and seemed insulting to Halsey. In a rage he turned his surface force and a carrier group back and thus spent his time running back and forth between the battles. He got back to San Bernardino at 1030 the next morning, too late to do any good.

The slender American forces off San Bernardino never hesitated. They fought magnificently, losing two destroyers, a destroyer escort and two escort carriers to Kurita and to *kamikaze* aircraft, which made their first appearance at this battle. At length Kurita paused to regroup, and then turned back, abandoning his mission. Goliath had run from David.

Despite the heavy criticism of Halsey for his actions in the battle, Admiral Nimitz refused to censure him then or later. He once remarked that when he arrived at Pearl Harbor soon after the attack, he found himself surrounded by caution, and that Admiral Halsey was the only one who would undertake difficult, dangerous jobs and carry them through to a successful conclusion. 'I will not', concluded Nimitz, 'be a party to anything that detracts from him and his reputation.'

Admiral Nimitz could always forgive errors of commission. He found it difficult to sympathise with those who just wished to play it safe.

Halsey's Third Fleet remained in support of Philippine operations well into January 1945, suffering much damage from the attacks of *kamikaze* aircraft, now that the Japanese fleet had been reduced to impotence. Nimitz meanwhile was deep in the planning for the forthcoming Iwo Jima and Okinawa operations.

It had become clear during the Philippine campaign that losses there would not leave enough men for the planned invasion of Formosa in the spring of 1945, so, as Admiral Spruance recommended, Okinawa was substituted. Okinawa lies closer to Japan than Formosa, which made it a more valuable objective, but its nearness meant that shorebased Japanese air power would be more of a threat. Every available carrier would be needed.

For the invasion of Iwo Jima, Nimitz moved his headquarters to Guam, leaving the administrative staff at Pearl Harbor and taking only his operational staff to the forward area. Although the fighting at Iwo Jima was much more difficult than Nimitz and his staff anticipated, Iwo Jima was worth the cost as a base for fighters accompanying the B-29s to Japan and as an emergency airfield. Thousands of airmen's lives were saved by the American airfield on Iwo Jima.

The landing on Okinawa on 1 April 1945 was unexpectedly easy, because the Japanese had adopted a policy of not resisting an invasion at the beachhead. They were now planning to let the Americans come up against their prepared positions inland.

If the troops ashore were having a comparatively easy time for the moment, the ships of Spruance's Fifth Fleet were not; Japanese-based *kamikazes* were attacking in numbers, and ships were getting hit, especially the carriers and the destroyers that were assigned to picket stations to give early warnings of

Japanese air attack. Then the troops ashore ran into the prepared Japanese defences, and the whole attack seemed to be bogging down.

Noting the situation Nimitz flew to Okinawa, where he was politely received by Lieutenant-General Simon Bolivar Buckner, who pointed out that they were on the ground, with the implication that what was going on there was none of Nimitz's business. Nimitz pointedly reminded him who was in command by remarking, 'Yes, but ground though it may be, I'm losing a ship and a half a day. So if this line isn't moving within five days, we'll get someone here to move it so we can all get out from under these stupid air attacks.' Buckner got the line moving, and Okinawa was declared secure on 21 June.

The naval losses however did not keep American ships from operating off the coast of Japan until the end of the war. Nimitz knew of the decision to drop the atomic bomb, but he had no part in it. He believed that Japan could be beaten without it.

On 2 September, at the Japanese surrender ceremony, MacArthur signed the document for the United Nations; Nimitz signed for the United States.

Soon after the surrender Nimitz returned to the United States, and 5 October was officially designated 'Nimitz Day'. Nimitz disliked such pomp but bore it manfully. On that trip he called upon Secretary of the Navy James Forrestal, with whom he had had many differences. Forrestal suggested that he become head of the General Board, an elder statesman's role, or that he become a kind of unofficial adviser in semi-retirement. Nimitz refused both offers and claimed what he believed was his by right, the office of Chief of Naval Operations. Forrestal tried to dissuade him, but without success.

'All right,' Forrestal yielded, 'but it can only be for two years, no more.'

Nimitz was not bothered by the limitation. 'That suits me exactly,' he said. 'I think that the CNO's term should be limited to two years.'

As Chief of Naval Operations, which post he took over on 15 December 1945, Nimitz was faced with the problems of rapid demobilisation of the navy and of making more efficient what was left. He was also much involved in the proposals to unify the armed forces. He did not object to unification, but he did object to a single chief of staff of the army, the navy and the air force, and he objected to having the army commanding all troops and the air force all aircraft. This would have stripped the navy of its carrier and anti-submarine air elements and would have eliminated the Marine Corps. When unification came these objections were met, and the navy retained its air and its marines.

After his tour as Chief of Naval Operations was over, he devoted himself for a time to acting as 'good will ambassador' for the United Nations, and later served for eight years as a regent for the University of California.

Nimitz died on 20 February 1966, and at his own request was buried in a simple funeral in the Golden Gate National Cemetery alongside the Pacific where his command had brought him the affection, respect and admiration of the men he had commanded and the men he had defeated.

General of the Army Douglas C. MacArthur

Stephen E. Ambrose

Above all else, Douglas MacArthur was a general of extremes. If he planned and directed some of the most brilliant offensives in military history, he was also in command during some of the most disastrous defeats ever suffered by American armed forces. At the beginning of the Second World War his men were caught by surprise at Clark Field and throughout the Philippines and badly mauled by the Japanese. No satisfactory excuse for this blunder has ever been made. But during the course of the war MacArthur executed the island-hopping strategy that made a shambles of the Japanese war plans. In Korea, he almost singlehandedly pushed through the idea of an amphibious assault on Inchon – he was opposed by almost every high-ranking officer in his own command and by nearly all his superiors. The result was a breath-taking success. But then he moved forward towards the Yalu without proper reconnaissance, with a dangerous gap between the two wings of his advancing armies, and as a result suffered a severe defeat at the hands of the Chinese, whom he had badly underestimated.

Nevertheless MacArthur has a solid claim to greatness. He was a general officer in three major wars, which must be something of a record. During the Second World War and the Korean War he established himself as *the* master of amphibious operations. He had been a dashing junior officer and a competent division commander in the First World War. As a theatre commander in the Second World War and again in the Korean War he showed himself to be remarkably flexible and a master at combined (air, sea and ground) operations. Nor were his abilities limited to making war. He was an innovative Superintendent of West Point, bringing much-needed reform to that institution; indeed he is the father of the modern academy. He performed adequately as Chief of Staff of the Army during the depression and was outstanding as head of the military occupation of Japan after the Second World War.

Throughout his career MacArthur, a man of enormous talents with an ego to match, created controversy. In part the mixed and extreme reaction to him was a result of his personality, in part to his methods of leadership, in part to his rigidly right-wing politics. He was actively hated by a large

number of civilians and by his fellow military men, while being simultaneously praised to a remarkable degree by others. Major-General Edward
Almond called him 'the greatest man alive', while Lieutenant-General George
E. Stratemeyer went further: MacArthur was the greatest man since Christ,
the greatest general in world history, 'the greatest man who ever lived'. One
of MacArthur's operations officers declared, 'We look to MacArthur as the
second Jesus Christ.' MacArthur enemies meanwhile were nearly as extreme
in their denunciations.

One of MacArthur's associates put the general in some perspective. 'He's
too enormous. I don't really understand him. No one could.' There can be no
doubt as to the accuracy of the confession. MacArthur was different from
other generals – in all the vast literature about him, pro and con, he is hardly
ever compared to anyone else – and to come to a conclusion about the nature
of his generalship or his character is extraordinarily difficult. One can record
events, sayings, decisions, reactions, but they do not constitute a believable
portrait. He simply refused to fit into any known category, even that of
great man, and the human mind finds it difficult to comprehend the unique.

Douglas MacArthur was born on 26 January 1880 in Little Rock, Arkansas.
His father, a Medal of Honor winner in the Civil War, was a regular army
general. Young Douglas MacArthur was thrilled by his father's stories of the
Civil War and of his activities in the Far East, where he was the hero of the
Philippine Insurrection and the military governor of the islands. In 1899,
thoroughly steeped in the military life, young MacArthur went up the Hudson
River to West Point, where he quickly established himself as an authentic
genius. He eventually graduated with the highest marks ever received there.
He made a dashing figure in his cadet grey – tall, trim and handsome. His
mother, upon learning that Ulysses S. Grant III's mother had gone to the
Point to see to his interests, came up the river too in order to manage her
son's social life. She stayed with him until her death in 1936, dominating his
personal life. Those who knew her agreed that the best descriptive adjective
was 'formidable'.

After graduation MacArthur served briefly in the Philippines, where he
engaged in hand-to-hand combat with brigands. Back in Washington he was
a military aide to President Theodore Roosevelt and worked in the War
Department. In the First World War he proposed the formation of an all-
American division made up of National Guard units from many states, which
became the Rainbow Division. He held various posts in the division, eventually becoming its commander.

A brigadier-general when the war ended, MacArthur was one of the best
front-line general officers in the war. He was always in or near no-man's land,
either leading a charge or reconnoitering. Once, out alone at night on the
southern front, he heard the rumbling of German vehicles on the move. He
immediately realised that the enemy was pulling back and that he could hit
them before they re-established their lines. There was no time to consult

division or corps; he had to move at once. Gathering up his battalions he ordered them to 'advance with audacity', and he had them moving by 3.30 that morning. They struck out quickly, silently. MacArthur's night attack was a huge success and won him his fourth Silver Star.

Even as a young brigadier, MacArthur did not live as other men did. He got into trouble with GHQ because he refused to wear a helmet, did not carry a gas mask, went unarmed, always had a riding crop in his hand, and was usually in the trenches, seldom in his headquarters. In every case he was violating a specific regulation. Someone at GHQ ordered an investigation; the results were so laudatory that it almost became a joke. When Pershing heard of the investigation he bellowed, 'Stop all this nonsense. MacArthur is the greatest leader of troops we have, and I intend to make him a division commander.'

Following the war MacArthur came home to assume the Superintendent's position at West Point. He was the youngest Superintendent in history, and had been out of the Academy for only sixteen years, so many of the faculty had been full professors while he was only a plebe. Teaching methods were antiquated – they had not changed since the Civil War. Congress, returning to normalcy, was cutting back the appropriations, even though equipment was worn out and obsolete.

The assignment was a tough one, but extremely important because the Military Academy required inspired leadership to establish a bridge between the traditional and the modern. Much was necessary to liberalise the academic education and to bring the tactical instruction up to date. The army itself, always conservative in its policies and methods between wars, was slipping into the routine of preparing for past rather than future wars. As MacArthur said, 'How long are we going to go on preparing for the War of 1812?' And as one cavalry officer's wife remarked, 'After World War I the cavalry went right on training to fight the Indians.'

MacArthur felt that the cadets were too much isolated from the rest of the nation. To do away with cadet provincialism he gave the cadets more opportunity to see the rest of the service and the outside world. He improved the curriculum too, placing more emphasis on the humanities and social studies while not neglecting science. In changing the curriculum he offended the old, entrenched professors, and even more the alumni. MacArthur found it difficult to work with the senior members of the faculty, mainly because he was a supreme egotist who could not bring himself to pay proper respect to the professors. He badly hurt their feelings by announcing his intentions without consulting them or asking their advice. He felt a strong sense of mission and considered his programme so obviously necessary and his actions so clearly correct that he never explained himself fully to the Academic Board; the members consequently saw him as a brash young man meddling in areas he did not understand.

MacArthur's majestic bearing and his astonishing record of accomplishment intimidated people. At an Academic Board meeting one afternoon a senior professor kept interrupting MacArthur, until finally the latter exploded. He banged his fist on the table and shouted, 'Sit down, sir. I am the Superintendent!' When he ended his tour in 1922 no one doubted it. He had permanently changed the academy, bringing it into the twentieth century and making it into one of the outstanding military colleges in the world.

The next decade and a half was an unhappy period for MacArthur, as it was for others of the heroic cast like Winston Churchill and Charles de Gaulle. There were no great issues, no great causes. He had a disastrous marriage to Louise Cromwell Brooks, a bright, giddy, rich divorcée who was very much of the jazz age; there was a great gulf between their interests. The divorce was public and loud. His second marriage, in 1937 to Jean Faircloth, was highly successful. She was a Southern belle who had been brought up to be an army wife, and she had the personal qualities that enabled her to live with a genius who cherished himself.

From 1930 to 1935 MacArthur was Chief of Staff of the Army. He spent most of his time warning about the dangers of the coming war and of the scope it would take, fruitlessly pleading with Congress for more money for the army.

When his tour as Chief of Staff ended, MacArthur went to the Philippines, to build there an army for the Commonwealth, one that could provide self-defence for the islands by 1946 when they were to become an independent nation. He took young Major Dwight D. Eisenhower with him. MacArthur had the highest possible opinion of him. In personal reports MacArthur said that he was the best staff officer in the army, a man for whom no position was too high. He expected that Eisenhower would go right to the top in the next war.

MacArthur lived in the Manila Hotel in isolated splendour. In those days a white man still commanded respect in the Far East, and a white general was akin to a god. He had only to utter a wish to have it fulfilled. Convinced that Orientals were most impressed by the flashy display, MacArthur appeared at reviews dressed in a white uniform of his own design made of sharkskin material, with four stars on his shoulder, a red ribbon at the base of his lapels, his General Staff insignia on his left breast, a gaudy, gold-braided cap on his head and an enormous corncob pipe in his mouth. By resigning from the United States Army after two years in the Philippines (he was reactivated in 1941), he fulfilled a boast he had made as a cadet – Quezon made him a field-marshal in the Commonwealth Army.

All was not ritual and regalia. MacArthur did what he could to build up the Philippine army. His target date for readiness was 1946; but since the Japanese attack came five years early, it is impossible to judge the efficiency of his methods. What is certain is that the half-trained, under-armed Filipinos were no match for the Japanese in 1941.

MacArthur did not think that the Japanese would come. Invasion, he predicted, 'would cost the enemy – at least a half million of men as casualties and upwards of five billion of dollars in money'. He thought no enemy, after studying the lesson of Gallipoli, would ever again attempt an attack against a coast defended by modern weapons. In any case the Philippines held no strategic or economic value for the Japanese. He felt that he was the only white man who understood Oriental psychology, and he argued that those who feared a Japanese attack 'fail fully to credit the logic of the Japanese mind'.

There can be no doubt that it was MacArthur who failed in the Philippines. Six hours before the attack on Clark Field destroyed his entire bomber force of four squadrons on the ground, the War Department had informed him of the Pearl Harbor attack and said that the nation was at war. His chief airman, Lewis Brereton, asked permission to attack Formosa, but MacArthur refused. Later MacArthur denied that he had received any hard news about Pearl Harbor, but the messages the War Department sent – along with the acknowledgements from the Philippines – are now in the archives for all to see. He also denied that Brereton made the request, and implied that Clark Field was Brereton's fault (which in part it was, since the B-17s were lined up wingtip to wingtip, an easy target). The documents bear out Brereton's claim to have made the request. In his memoirs MacArthur declared that an attack against Formosa would have been disastrous, since he had no fighter planes to protect the bombers. This was a valid reason, but it did not agree with his earlier assertions that he never heard Brereton's request.

In the ensuing struggle for the Philippines MacArthur was slow to recognise how badly the battle was going, slow to pull back to Bataan, and slow to stockpile supplies on the peninsula. As a result the troops went on half-rations the day they took up their positions on Bataan; in the end hunger and weakness proved to be more dangerous than the Japanese. MacArthur begged the War Department for men and supplies, but Washington had written off the Philippines and started to build up a base in Australia, whence the counter-offensive could some day be launched. All the War Department wanted from the men on Bataan was time.

It was a realistic policy, but that did not help the defenders. Chief of Staff George C. Marshall patiently explained to MacArthur that the navy was doing its best and trying to build its forces for later assaults. As historian Forrest Pogue puts it, telling MacArthur that was like telling 'a man dying of thirst that he must wait for a drink of water until a well could be dug and a water main laid. Thoughts of well-dressed officers sitting in comfortable offices and sleeping in clean beds excited the anger of the battlers of Bataan and deepened their suspicions of a faceless enemy called Washington.'

It was at this point that MacArthur began to build up an active persecution complex. It had always been latent; now it became virulent. In 1943 Robert E. Sherwood visited his headquarters. He reported that MacArthur and his staff seemed to think the War Department, the State Department, the Joint Chiefs of Staff, even the White House itself, were 'under the domination of "Communists and British Imperialists".' In December 1944 MacArthur told Clark Lee, 'Yes, we've come a long way since Melbourne, despite the Navy cabal that hates me, and the New Deal cabal.' He complained that Roosevelt 'acted as if he were the directing head of the Army and Navy'.

There was something much bigger involved than MacArthur's personal feelings. They were merely the surface manifestation of a gigantic struggle over the direction of American foreign policy. Roosevelt, Cordell Hull, Harry Stimson, and most of all George Marshall – in short, official Washington – had decided to defeat Germany first in the Second World War. This was partly a strategic decision forced upon the policy-makers. Germany was the more dangerous enemy, Europe was closer than the Far East, so shipping men and supplies there was easier, and so on. But it was also a foreign policy decision of the highest magnitude, for it meant that in the government's estimation Europe was more important than Asia, at least to Americans living in the middle of the twentieth century.

MacArthur violently disagreed. He believed that Asia was the key to the future, and that it was on that continent and its offshore islands that America should make her major commitment. The split between Marshall and MacArthur could not have been more decisive. Their argument was to dominate American foreign policy discussions for the next two decades. MacArthur had important followers in the United States, led by Senator Robert A. Taft and the Asia-firsters, while Marshall had the backing of Roosevelt and Truman, and thus the power. In many ways the argument continues to this day.

Marshall stuck to his Europe-first policy, no reinforcements arrived in the Philippines, and slowly the forces on Bataan fell back. President Roosevelt ordered MacArthur to leave the islands (he had planned to go inland and organise guerrilla warfare activities) to take command of the South-West Pacific Area, with headquarters in Australia. Along with his wife and four-year-old son, he made a dramatic escape on PT boats.

At a press conference in Australia, held shortly after he arrived, MacArthur announced, 'I came through and I shall return.' The Office of War Information thought the phrase a good one, but asked MacArthur's permission to change it to 'We shall return', since presumably MacArthur would need some help. He refused permission, and 'I shall return' it stayed.

The emphasis on 'I' became more pronounced as the war went on. His headquarters exercised the tightest conceivable censorship on news coming from the area; all communiqués emanating from headquarters gave the impression that MacArthur was personally directing the campaigns. His communiqués became famous. One newsman computed that between the fall of 1942 and October 1944, the MacArthur communiqués reported Japanese losses of from 150,000 to 200,000, while the Allied casualties listed in the communiqués amounted to 122 killed, 2 missing and 529 wounded. The communiqués always began, 'MacArthur's Headquarters', giving the impression that he was in the field leading the men (in fact he was in Australia, where of course he belonged).

Whatever anyone thought about the way MacArthur managed his public relations, few could criticise his fighting methods. In a skilful, bold campaign he made his way back to the Philippines. On New Guinea and at the Admiralty Islands, in some of the toughest campaigns of the war, MacArthur's leadership and strategic policy paid huge dividends. His end-runs in the Dutch East Indies cut off enormous numbers of Japanese troops without any major cost to the Americans. The island-hopping campaign was one of the keys to American victory in the Pacific and MacArthur seems to have been the man who made the strategy. The concept of hitting the enemy where he was weakest, not strongest, was a major strategic contribution drawn from MacArthur's First World War tactical experiences.

On 2 March 1945 MacArthur set foot again on Corregidor. He waded ashore, to say into a handy microphone, 'People of the Philippines, I have returned . . . Rally to me.' Five months later, at Yokohama, he accepted the Japanese surrender. He was sixty-five and had led a life full enough to satisfy any man. But much more was to come; his greatest triumphs and failures, as well as his bitterest controversy, lay ahead.

In Japan, where he was a virtual dictator, MacArthur revealed a side no one had suspected. His politics, at least in regard to Japan, turned out to be liberal and democratic. While running one of the fairest and most honest military occupations in all history, he allowed the Japanese to write their own, new, constitution. The Emperor was no longer deified, but became the symbol of the state and of the unity of the people. Supreme power resided in the Diet, elected by universal franchise. MacArthur gave the Japanese, for the first time in their history, a Bill of Rights. He saw to it that Japanese women got a new status, with equal opportunities in employment, education, marriage, voting and property rights.

On 25 June 1950 the North Korean army launched a surprise attack across the 38th parallel. President Harry S. Truman immediately authorised MacArthur to furnish the South Koreans (ROK) with ammunition and supplies. The war that resulted was, for the military strategist, one of the most fascinating in history. It was in reality two wars. In the first eight months it was a war of movement and manoeuvre, with troops from both sides moving over the rugged, mountainous terrain almost as easily as troops move through the desert. Both sides suffered from over-confidence and as a result came face to face with total disaster. There was brilliant generalship both north and south of the 38th parallel. Then, after April 1951, the war came to resemble the First World War. Both sides dug extensive trench systems. Artillery took over as the major weapon. Two years of stalemate followed.

The first North Korean attack had driven a panicked and helpless ROK force before it. The Korean troops threw away their arms and equipment so that they could run faster. MacArthur rushed in American troops from Japan, but these ordinary GIs, grown soft in the occupation delights of Japan, were hardly ready for combat. Still, they did what they could, and they managed to slow the onrushing wave. At enormous cost, they bought time.

It was still an open question as to whether time was worth buying. In comparison to the world situation the United States had never been more unprepared. It did not have enough troops, enough veterans, enough arms and equipment (and what it did have was in poor condition and badly worn), enough anything. On 13 July Lieutenant-General Walton H. Walker took command of all US Army forces in Korea, calling them the American Eighth Army, which was a pretentious name for a force that consisted of an under-strength 24th Division and elements of an infantry regiment. Within a week parts of two more divisions arrived, and Walker established a perimeter around Pusan, on the south-eastern tip of the peninsula.

During August and September 1950 Walker's men held off determined North Korean attacks. Shifting his limited forces brilliantly, Walker managed to hold on. In Japan, meanwhile, MacArthur was building up a striking force. Walker and his men felt that if MacArthur had given them more of the available force, they could have broken out of the perimeter and dealt the enemy a major, perhaps decisive, blow.

MacArthur was thinking of bigger things. He had made his reputation in the Second World War with amphibious landings, and now he saw a chance to repeat. He planned to go ashore with his x Corps at Inchon, the port of Seoul, and cut the North Korean supply line. Planners in both the army and navy were opposed. The local commanders were opposed. There were not enough landing craft, the port was small and had to be approached along a narrow channel through a maze of mudbanks, and the tides were among the highest in the world.

MacArthur insisted on going ahead. On 13 September 1950 ten United Nations warships entered the harbour and shot up the floating mines. They then went in closer to draw enemy fire; when it came they blasted away at the port's defences. The date was the 191st anniversary of the Battle of Quebec, which MacArthur found gratifying. Wolfe's victory on the Plains of Abraham emboldened him to go ahead with Inchon, and he declared that the more he thought about Quebec the more he thought he was right at Inchon. He put it this way: 'I imagine that Wolfe thought to himself, if his brigadiers and his admiral believed his plan unfeasible, then General Montcalm must have reasoned that Wolfe would not try it. And if able American officers think Inchon impracticable, doubtless the Communists do too.'

Even MacArthur's own staff was opposed, but by this time he was pretty thoroughly out of practice in listening to advice from anyone. In 1951 he said that he had got more and more into the habit of heeding the advice of only two men. The first was George Washington, who built the country, and the second was Abraham Lincoln, who saved it. Their writings, MacArthur said, contained the answer to 'pretty much everything'.

Inchon represents one of the only battles in modern military history in which the commander deliberately rejected the results of careful scientific staff planning and decided to follow his intuition. But it worked – magnificently. The marines got ashore, raced to Seoul, broke the siege at Pusan and drove on to the 38th parallel, the prewar boundary. MacArthur had won a victory unmatched in American history. Still, it had been hard on the nerves, and the shaken navy declared afterwards that even though it was successful never again would they participate in such an attack.

After Inchon, MacArthur was in an expansive mood. But he also had learned something from the Second World War. This time he did not take sole credit (although he might have been justified), nor did he neglect the army's sister services. He wired back to the United States, 'The Navy and Marines have never shone more brightly than this morning,' and when he went ashore he stayed away from personal references. He told Admiral Struble, 'I've lived a long time and played with the Navy a long time. They've never failed me.'

When MacArthur's troops reached the 38th parallel a basic political decision had to be made. Contrary to the usual story MacArthur did not make it. The United Nations, reaffirming its previously stated purpose of unifying Korea and holding free elections, implicitly gave him permission to drive north to the Yalu river and inflict total defeat upon the North Koreans.

The advance went well. On 15 October Truman flew to Wake Island to confer with MacArthur (it was their first meeting) and to set a future course. MacArthur, whose abilities as a prophet were somewhat suspect after his 1941 statements about Japanese intentions in the Philippines and about the efficiency of Filipino army, said the Korean War would be over by Thanksgiving. Truman asked about the prospects for Russian and Chinese intervention.

Very little [the general replied]. Had they interfered in the first or second month it would have been decisive. We are no longer fearful of their intervention. We no longer stand hat in hand. The Chinese have 300,000 men in Manchuria. Of these probably not more than one hundred to one hundred and twenty-five thousand are distributed along the Yalu River. Only fifty to sixty thousand could be gotten across the Yalu River. They have no air force. Now that we have bases for our Air Force in Korea, if the Chinese tried to get down to Pyongyang, there would be the greatest slaughter.

Later, when the Chinese did come and drove MacArthur back past Seoul, he denied ever having made such a statement. On another occasion he hedged by saying that when he made the prediction he assumed he could bomb the Chinese across the Yalu. In a third version he explained that he was dependent upon the CIA for his intelligence, the implication being that he had received the wrong information. The record is clear enough: whatever the reason, he did say the Chinese would not come in, and that if they did he would wipe them out.

The lightly armed Chinese came, hit MacArthur's widely scattered forces, and inflicted a crushing defeat. There was an outcry in the American press, with journals like the *Washington Post* and the *New York Herald Tribune* demanding MacArthur's recall. The *Herald Tribune* roundly declared, 'Unsound deployment of United Nations forces and a momentous blunder by General MacArthur helped insure the success of the enemy's strategy.' Truman stuck with MacArthur, partly because General Matthew Ridgway was conducting the actual operations on the ground and was able to stiffen the resistance, but mainly because he did not want to face the political repercussions. MacArthur spent most of his time in Japan now, issuing public letters and giving exclusive interviews to nearly every correspondent who showed up.

His theme was always the same: he should be allowed to bomb beyond the Yalu, and he should be authorised to use the Chinese forces on Formosa against the Communists on the mainland. He argued that there was no substitute for victory, and he said flatly and honestly that he could not understand Truman's policy (after MacArthur's defeat near the Yalu, Truman changed his policy from one of forced reunification in Korea to one of the *status quo ante bellum*). With deep sincerity and great eloquence MacArthur described the horrors of the war, and declared that in all conscience he could not subscribe to a policy that aimed toward a stalemate. The sacrifices of the United Nations troops and of the people of South Korea had to be made meaningful, and this could only be done by achieving victory in the war (meaning reunification under the South Korean government).

The real issue was not the use of troops in Formosa or the bombing across the Yalu – these were tactical matters. MacArthur was again questioning the fundamentals of American foreign policy, and arguing for the adoption of an Asia-first attitude. Hoyt Vandenberg, Chief of Staff of the Air Force, explained to MacArthur that American power was not unlimited, and that if he committed the air force across the Yalu as MacArthur wanted he would be unable to meet a Soviet threat in Europe. The argument did not impress MacArthur. He contended that if Asia fell to Communism, so would Europe.

Every member of the Joint Chiefs of Staff disagreed. During the Senate hearings that followed his dismissal, MacArthur said they supported him and implied that Truman and the State Department were rejecting the advice of all their professional military advisers. This imposed upon the Joint Chiefs the painful duty of saying publicly that MacArthur was mistaken. Chairman Omar Bradley put their position best. 'So long as we regarded the Soviet Union as the main antagonist and Western Europe as the main prize,' he explained, the strategy advanced by MacArthur 'would involve us in the wrong war at the wrong place at the wrong time and with the wrong enemy.'

In December 1950, and again in early 1951, Truman issued general orders that no one in government service should make a statement on foreign policy without clearing it with the State Department. The orders were obviously aimed at MacArthur. It was to a certain extent a muzzling, but nearly every member of the armed forces thought MacArthur had gone too far in his public disagreements. As a professional soldier he obviously had a duty to disagree with the administration when he thought it was wrong, but his criticism – most people felt – would have been more effective and listened to more closely if he had made it privately.

In April 1951 MacArthur sent a letter to Republican Representative Joseph Martin, who read it in the House of Representatives. In the letter MacArthur raised all the basic points again. As he saw it, he was explaining to a confused and bamboozled public what a ruinous course their civilian leaders had chosen – he was in short doing his duty. As Truman saw it, MacArthur had issued a direct and unavoidable challenge.

Harry Truman was not a man to back down. He also was not the man to handle a situation like this with any subtlety or grace. Like a bludgeon he used his powers and fired MacArthur. 'I could do nothing else', he explained, 'and still be President.'

MacArthur returned for his hero's welcome, while Truman's popularity sank to the lowest point possible. The President was confident however that upon reflection the public would back him, and the indications are that it did. MacArthur toured the country repeating his message, but rather quickly he began to fade from the centre of the public's conscience. By 1952 the people were glad enough to elect Eisenhower and get the war over with on Truman's original terms – the restoration of South Korea. The Europe-first policy remained in force throughout the 1950s.

MacArthur took up residence in the Waldorf Hotel in New York, where he lived a quiet life and wrote his memoirs. He still lived in isolated splendour, still baffled visitors with his astonishing memory and forthright views. On occasion he went out into the public, where he could still move people to deep emotion. Once he visited President John Kennedy and out-quipped one of the best ad-libbers ever to live in the White House. He had not lost the capacity to surprise – no one had expected MacArthur could be a humourist. With all of his many sides he remained true to his central characteristics. Looking over his eighty-odd years as he wrote his memoirs, he could not find a single major mistake to confess. He remained independent, relied on no one, did not allow people to get close to him, and defied understanding.

But he was not immune to all the laws of human nature. As an old man his thoughts more and more returned to earlier, happier days, to baseball games on the West Point Plain, to the battles of the First World War. In

May 1962 he delivered one of his last public addresses. It was to his first and most lasting love, the cadets of West Point. He ended by saying, 'Today marks my final roll call with you. But I want you to know that when I cross the river my last conscious thought will be of the Corps – and the Corps – and the Corps.

'I bid you farewell.'

Fleet Admiral William F. Halsey

James Bassett

When Fleet Admiral William Frederick Halsey, Jr, veteran of forty-four years in the navy at the age of sixty-two, swept beneath San Francisco's Golden Gate Bridge on the gun deck of the battleship *South Dakota* on 15 October 1945, a veteran war correspondent wrote: 'The war's most famous naval formation, Halsey's Third Fleet, came home today.'

These fourteen ships hardly constituted the whole Third Fleet, of course, for Halsey had commanded 105 American men-of-war and twenty-eight British vessels during the Pacific campaign's final weeks.

But they were the first home, as indeed Halsey's minuscule carrier strike team had been first to blast the enemy in the precarious hit-run days of early 1942. And their commander, as the pre-eminent American naval historian Samuel Eliot Morison avowed in 1948, was 'one of the most famous sea fighters of this or any other war'.

The twenty-two thousand men aboard the homebound flotilla comprised a small segment of what Lord Nelson termed his 'band of brothers', whether seamen or task force admirals. They were typical of the fighters Halsey had trained so diligently during four long years of combat after the Pearl Harbor disaster.

In character, in methodology, Halsey was a rare combination of Nelson and John Paul Jones. Britain's greatest admiral said at the outset of the Franco–British imbroglio in the late eighteenth century: 'What the country needs is annihilation of the enemy.' Halsey said on his first visit to Guadalcanal in 1943: 'Kill Japs, kill Japs, and keep on killing Japs!'

Jones told the fledgling American Congress: 'I wish to have no Connection with any Ship that does not sail fast, for I intend to go in harm's way.' Halsey, in October 1944, retorted thus to a false Japanese claim that his presumably decimated force was withdrawing: 'The Third Fleet's sunken and damaged ships have been salvaged and are retiring at high speed toward the enemy.'

Halsey has been compared with General George Patton. That is wrong. They were both warriors; but Halsey was a man of no pretence, no deliberate flair, no lack of compassion. True, had he been a soldier, he doubtless would have been a tank or air commander.

He followed the edict of General Nathan Bedford Forrest, a cavalryman in the Civil War: 'Get there fustest with the mostest.'

From birth, Halsey was predestined to become a navyman. The swash-buckling ancestral Captain John Halsey was commissioned as a privateer by the governor of Massachusetts in 1704, and became the hero of a book entitled, *A History of the Robberies and Murders of the Most Notorious Pirates*. A century later Captain Eliphalet Halsey sailed the first Long Island whaleship around Cape Horn. He was followed in the next fifty years by a dozen more Halsey whaler-men.

Then came William F. Halsey, Sr, Annapolis class of 1873, who rose to captaincy in the doldrum era before President Theodore Roosevelt perceived the need for a potent naval arm as an instrument of national policy.

Halsey, Jr, barely managed to enter the Academy in 1900 after 'Mother camped in [President] McKinley's office' to ensure young Bill one of five extra presidential appointments.

Those four gestative years were an important part in forming Halsey's character. He played gutsy fullback on the football team, despite his relatively small size, and even threatened to 'bilge' (quit Annapolis) for low grades rather than forsake the game. But academically smarter classmates tutored him to a near-perfect 3.98 grade in his plebe year.

As his command career advanced, Halsey surrounded himself with brains. Two of his Second World War staff subordinates attained the heights of CNO (Chief of Naval Operations). His 1945 British liaison officer, Michael LeFanu, was ticketed for the chairmanship of the British Joint Chiefs of Staff until leukaemia struck him down in 1970.

Halsey was fortunate to receive his ensign's commission when he did, in February 1904, four months early because Teddy Roosevelt's naval expansion programme required a sudden influx of new officers. First duty for Ensign Halsey was aboard the coal-burning battleship *Missouri*, precursor to his final flagship, *The Mighty Mo* on which Japan signed the formal surrender papers forty-one years later.

Within three years he was a proud division officer in the new USS *Kansas*, a primary unit in Roosevelt's globe-girdling Great White Fleet. Thus he first cruised the seas that would become part of the Halsey legend, from Australia to Japan itself.

During a boring lull, after a stint as destroyer executive officer in 1910, Halsey almost forsook the navy for a civilian career. Fortunately friends dissuaded him. His next assignment as skipper of the destroyer *Flusser* led to a lasting friendship with Franklin D. Roosevelt, then Assistant Secretary of the Navy and 'almost a professional sailorman'. The future president used *Flusser* to survey Maine's coastal waters.

Halsey had captained the spanking new oil-burning destroyer *Jarvis* for a year when the European war began, but soon was transferred to Annapolis as discipline officer.

Then came the American declaration of war on 6 April 1917. After impatiently 'nursing midshipmen' for eight months, freshly commissioned Lieutenant-Commander Halsey received orders to Queenstown, Ireland, where he took command of the destroyer *Benham*.

By May 1918, after transfer to the destroyer *Shaw*, Halsey had been blooded by attacking his first German U-boat. A month later he was 'as proud as a dog with two tails' at having his initial multi-ship command, another American destroyer and two British sloops.

And soon after that, Halsey learned 'a lesson that [stood by him throughout his] naval career'. Receiving an SOS from a torpedoed American destroyer, he radioed British headquarters at Queenstown that he was *en route* to aid her. Such a message, said Halsey years later, may have sounded 'presumptuous, but it would have been silly to request [orders]. The Admiral himself always pointed out that since the man on the spot had so much better information than the man at headquarters, it was impossible for HQ to give proper instructions.' Halsey never questioned the decisions of the 'man on the spot' in the Second World War, when he had overall charge of the vast South Pacific area. Nor did he take kindly to second-hand guessing from his superiors when he himself was that targeted man.

For his patrol actions, he was awarded the Navy Cross. His terse recollection: 'There was a very wide distribution of the Navy Cross to commanding officers of naval vessels during World War I. It did not have the prestige that attaches to the award in World War II.'

Between war duties for Halsey were much the same as for most of his associates, with some notable exceptions. As military fervour cooled, fleet manpower dwindled, and regulars had to make up for loss of the reservists. Yet 'making bricks without straw', as Halsey described destroyer operations in the early 1920s, was excellent training for his future career as Commander South Pacific, when he directed Operation Shoestring.

Shorthanded during practice exercises, Halsey replied, 'when a squadron of nineteen destroyers maneuvers by whistles – at night, blacked out, at 25 knots – it's no place for ribbon clerks'. In truth, the doughty sailor never suffered 'ribbon clerks' within his domain if he could prevent it.

A stint at naval intelligence in Washington, DC, was followed by two years as naval attaché in Berlin. After sixteen months of leisurely Mediterranean destroyer duty, Halsey came home, won his captain's fourth stripe, and in February 1927 took command of the *Reina Mercedes*, the Naval Academy's disciplinary vessel, which that spring also headquartered Annapolis's first fulltime aviation group. Prophetically, this detail was commanded by Lieutenant Dewitt C. Ramsey, whose No. 2 man was Lieutenant

Clifton A. F. Sprague, both would become renowned air admirals in the next war.

'My whole career changed right there,' said Halsey. 'I became fascinated with [aeronautics],' handling controls whenever possible, 'eating, drinking, and breathing aviation.' But when he was granted permission to take air training at Pensacola, he flunked the eye examination. Back at sea, Halsey doggedly retained his consuming interest in flying, now that 'planes had become an integral part of the fleet'. He spent much of his duty periods as commander of a nineteen-unit destroyer squadron monitoring torpedo drills from the sky.

Following a tour at the Army War College, where his classmates were Omar Bradley and Jonathan (Skinny) Wainright, two others destined for heroic service, Halsey accepted a tantalising offer from Ernest King, Chief of the Bureau of Aeronautics, to take command of the converted cruiser-carrier hulled *Saratoga*. There was a proviso: Captain Halsey at the age of fifty-one must pass the aviation observers' course at Pensacola. 'The world of aviation suddenly reopened to me,' he wrote. 'I was so excited that I regarded the privilege of commanding the *Sara* merely as a pleasant bonus.' He added succinctly: 'That night I took my last drink of liquor for a solid year.'

Fortuitously, as so often happened, Halsey's aerial instructor was a lieutenant who later joined his closeknit Band of Brothers on the USS *Enterprise* staff Bromfield Nichols took the 'old man' in firm hand, but permitted him to be reclassified as a pilot trainee rather than mere observer. One year later, having fitted corrective lenses into his goggles, Halsey won his cherished gold wings.

Saratoga, which Halsey captained for two years and which flew his rear-admiral's two-starred flag for another two years, 'initiated [him] into the marvels of fleet aviation'. He said later:

> To employ this mighty arm of naval warfare and employ it properly, you have to know its limitations as well as its potentialities. I think I know something about them now, after six years of carrier experience; but I knew little enough then, and I had to learn the hard way – from others, while bearing the responsibility for their actions.

By 1938, commanding Carrier Division 2 (*Enterprise* and *Yorktown*), Halsey was learning fast. He was equally astute in making necessary tactical innovations in the fledgling art of air-sea warfare. Some seem deceptively simple today: requiring a single radio wavelength for all the scouting planes of a carrier task unit to ensure that every ship will receive simultaneous word of an enemy sighting. Or ceaselessly drilling into his pilots their need for special instrument expertise in returning to flight decks during foul weather.

This was likewise a period when Halsey's obdurate distrust for the Japanese grew and, when USS *Panay* was bombed in late 1937 while on Yangtze river patrol, Halsey's worst forebodings seemed confirmed. Little wonder then that the Pearl Harbor attack came as scant surprise to Halsey – or that he would emerge as the most outspoken foe of the Emperor's minions from 7 December 1941, through the surrender aboard his flagship *Missouri*. Halsey was implacable. He hated. And that is what made him such a formidable adversary.

In January 1939 Halsey commanded two of the navy's five carriers (some one hundred would be in service by V J-Day) with his flag in *Enterprise*, the 'Big E', to which he would bring worldwide fame within scant years.

By April 1940 Halsey's units had joined the Pacific Battle Fleet in Hawaii. His flag again flew from *Saratoga*, during joint army-navy war games repelling a mythical invasion of the West Coast, in which his single carrier's aircraft had to ward off shore-based army planes. This foreshadowed Halsey's later activities, when he resolved that the best place to hit the enemy's air force was at his airfields.

He won a significant technical battle over usage of voice versus keyed radio transmission from ships to planes. The simpler oral system was chosen after proof that it could not be jammed even at distances of 150 miles, as some old-fashioned critics had claimed. Likewise he was an early convert to radar, a top-secret new invention that 'was said to be almost supernatural'. Like voice radio and instrument flying, radar became a Halsey totem, to be perfected as a vital weapon. He awesomely mentions spotting a destroyer squadron at 78,000 yards under 'freak weather' conditions.

'If I had to give credit to the instruments and machines that won us the war in the Pacific,' he said, 'I would rank them in this order: submarines first, radar second,. planes third, bulldozers fourth.' Not, you will note, the atom bomb.

Halsey's allegiances extended upward to his respected superiors as well as downward to his handpicked aides. When Admiral Husband E. Kimmel, also Annapolis class of 1904, was elevated in February 1941 over many a disappointed senior to lead the Pacific Fleet, Halsey was delighted, though admittedly 'astonished'. To the day of his death, Halsey defended Kimmel, who bore the burden of blame for Pearl Harbor's vulnerability ten months later. Disdaining any political danger to his own career, Halsey stood up steadfastly for his old comrade, whose plight he attributed primarily to a paucity of long-range patrol planes.

Halsey himself admitted to having underestimated the quality of Japanese military prowess 'despite emphatic warnings' from Far Eastern military experts. 'Let me confess here [in his memoirs] that I revised my opinion after December 7. The Jap naval aviators who made that attack were good – very good indeed.'

On 27 November, ten days before the débâcle, Halsey participated in a conference called by Kimmel, concerning defences of the American 'picket-line islands'. These included Midway, Wake, Johnston and Palmyra; all were woefully undersupplied with men and arms. It was Halsey who successfully urged ferrying a dozen marine F4Fs (Grumman Wildcats) to Wake in lieu of army planes, which were restricted to venturing more than 15 miles from dry land. He also drew the job of hauling this small aerial contingent to that distant land speck, at the same moment when the controversial 'war warning' came from Washington, DC, predicting a Japanese strike against the Philippines, Borneo or Malaya. Halsey's task force, which departed from Pearl Harbor at 7 am on 28 November, comprised his flagship *Enterprise*, three heavy cruisers and nine destroyers.

'Before we shoved off,' recalled Halsey, 'I asked Kimmel, "How far do you want me to go?"' He meant, if his force had to cope with Japanese submarines, an event that might 'precipitate war'. Kimmel's reply was, to quote Halsey, 'characteristic'. He snapped: 'Goddammit, use your common sense!'

In short, Halsey was irrevocably 'the man on the spot' again, but now with a nation's fate possibly riding upon his broad shoulders. Yet Kimmel's curt order to him was 'as fine . . . as a subordinate ever received. It was by no means an attempt to pass the buck. He was simply giving me full authority, as the man on the spot, to handle the situation as I saw it, and I knew he would back me to the hilt.' These were the kind of conditions under which Halsey would perform at his peak, from the South Pacific to Tokyo Bay, in the ensuing four years. He never shrank from authority. But he detested being hobbled by vague, dogmatic or plainly irrational mandates.

Battle Order No. 1 promptly sped from the flagship. It informed all hands that they were 'now operating under war conditions', 'instant action' loomed, and 'hostile submarines' might lurk in the area. Moreover Halsey directed that aircraft and destroyer torpedoes carry warheads, bombers live weapons, and that pilots were to sink 'any shipping sighted and shoot down any planes encountered', since his was the only American force in the area. When his operations officer, who was not privy to the exact nature of the mission, protested that 'this means war', Halsey said quietly, 'I'll take [the responsibility]. If anything gets in my way, we'll shoot first and argue afterwards.'

Significantly, a mighty Japanese carrier-battleship fleet had sortied from its homeland base on 26 November, *en route* to Hawaiian waters along a northerly course. Had the enemy proceeded more directly, Halsey's pitiful array might well have been intercepted, and his brilliant career ended before it began.

On 4 December the marine fighters were launched towards Wake. Three mornings later, at 8.12 am, Halsey received the historic dispatch: 'Air raid in Pearl Harbor X This is no drill.' For the first time in Pacific Fleet records battle flags were unfurled.

During a fruitless twenty-four hours his force sought the now-withdrawing foe, always with garbled intelligence from GHQ, until fuel ran so low that *Enterprise* had to return to Pearl Harbor. Halsey's flag secretary notes:

'We watched the entry (past the sunken vessels) from the bridge. The Admiral was silent for a while, then we heard him mutter, "Before we're through with 'em, the Japanese language will be spoken only in hell!"'

Admiral Chester W. Nimitz, having replaced Kimmel as Commander-in-Chief Pacific, sent for Halsey on 9 January. The Japanese, he said, had seized Britain's Gilbert Islands for a probable move against Samoa as a step towards severing American supply lines to the South-West Pacific. The situation was desperate, for the Americans had no operative amphibious teams ready for countermeasures.

'So,' Halsey recounted, 'it was up to the fast carrier task forces.' His initial chore: to head a combined force formed around *Enterprise* and *Yorktown* in a lightning strike against both the Gilberts and the Japanese-held Marshalls.

Halsey accepted the war's first offensive assignment 'with something less than enthusiasm'. Later he frankly acknowledged that he was aware of the enemy's illicit fortification of the Marshalls with airfields and submarine pens. He also knew that a previous game-board exercise had ended with defeat for the American 'team' attempting to assault Kwajalein.

Nevertheless Halsey's group probed deep into hazardous waters on 1 February to bomb the northern Marshall strongholds of Wotje, Maloelap and Kwajalein. The *Yorktown* unit under Rear-Admiral Frank Jack Fletcher hit Makin in the Gilberts, and for good measure Jaluit and Mili in the southern Marshalls. These raids drew an unexpected dividend: the Japanese high command weakened their forward echelon, which was vastly superior to the available American forces, by calling back one-third of their combatant ships for fear that the home islands might be endangered.

'When our task forces sortied for the Marshalls raid,' Halsey wrote, 'you could almost smell the defeatism around Pearl. Now the offensive spirit was reestablished; officers and men were bushytailed again. So, presently, was the American public. At last we had been able to answer their roweling question, "Where is the Navy?"' This was the barest beginning. But like future Halsey actions, it indeed had that salubrious effect, and he thereby won his first of four Distinguished Service Medals.

Another 'morale raid' followed against Marcus Island, less than 1000 miles away from Tokyo, before Halsey was summoned again to Cincpac's office to discuss 'something top-secret' that had originated with the Joint Chiefs in Washington, DC.

Lieutenant-Colonel James H. Doolittle had drilled sixteen army air corps B-25 crews in simulated flightdeck take-offs, and was ready for the supreme surprise – a dagger thrust into the heart of Japan itself. Said an emissary from Navy Commander-in-Chief King: 'They might not inflict much damage, but they would certainly give Hirohito plenty to think about.'

Halsey opined, 'They'll need a lot of luck,' then promptly accepted the delicate job of taking Doolittle's raiders within 400 miles of Tokyo 'if we could sneak in that close'. He had *Enterprise* and *Hornet*, the latter new to the Pacific, plus the usual screen of cruisers and destroyers.

By the time the 18 April 1942 D-Day was set, Halsey had been elevated to Commander Carriers Pacific Fleet. When the two carrier groups conjoined roughly between Pearl Harbor and Kamchatka, Halsey announced on the bullhorn: 'This force is bound for Tokyo!' A great cheer arose. Part of the crew's enthusiasm, recalled Halsey, arose from the grim fact that Bataan had fallen just four days earlier.

Doolittle's take-off was made 650 miles out, because a Japanese picket boat spotted their approach, and relayed the phenomenal news to enemy HQ. As Nimitz wrote afterwards in a co-authored book, *The Great Sea War*: 'The physical effect of the raid on Tokyo was slight. Few of the Japanese public even knew that the city had been bombed, but Japan's rulers knew and were disturbed. The raid was to have an important effect on strategic developments.'

The United States was still on the defence, albeit strategically active. Admiral King ordained: 'Hold what you've got, and hit them when you can.'

Reporting back to Cincpac, Halsey was informed that the South Pacific area was 'warming up', with the Japanese massing for invasions of New Guinea and the Solomons. *Lexington* and *Yorktown* were on the scene; Halsey got orders to join them with his two carriers. To his lasting regret, he was still 1000 miles away when the first carrier battle in history – Coral Sea – was fought. At a heavy cost, including *Lexington*, an oiler and destroyer, the foe's attempt to seize Port Moresby was thwarted.

Halsey, still running south-east at flank speed, was 'mad as the devil' with an admonition that he stay within coverage of American land-based air, and beyond reach of enemy shoreplanes. So the frustrated task force commander abandoned plans to pick off the retreating Japanese ships. In the process however he did discover that his adversary had finally mastered radar technique.

Still embittered, Halsey read a dispatch from Nimitz on 16 May to 'Expedite return'.

'We re-entered (Pearl Harbor) on May 26', Halsey recounted, 'for me to face the most grievous disappointment in my career. The trouble brewing was the Battle of Midway. Instead of being allowed to fight it – and I would have been senior officer present – I was sent to the hospital.' From the heights above GHQ, 'I watched them sortie [under his frequent command relief Vice-Admiral Raymond Spruance] on May 28 to win the crucial carrier duel of the war.'

Not until early September was Halsey deemed sufficiently recovered from shingles to resume active duty. At Pearl Harbor he found that his carrier task force, again formed around *Enterprise*, was still being shaped.

Since 7 August the American invasion of Guadalcanal, under Vice-Admiral Robert L. Ghormley, had been badly mired down by a series of naval defeats, intramural command squabbles, a huge Japanese troop build-up and (as Nimitz's book noted) 'a new plunge' in Allied morale. Nimitz himself had just completed a visit to the South Pacific in late September to study the problem firsthand. He came to the conclusion that the problems were just not being solved, and that time was running out. He therefore decided, on 16 October, that aggressive fresh talent must replace the lagging Ghormley.

Halsey and a small staff had departed from Pearl Harbor a day earlier on a tour of the South Pacific. As his Coronado seaplane settled on to the placid waters of Noumea Harbor, New Caledonia, a whaleboat nuzzled alongside. Ghormley's flag lieutenant was aboard, and when Halsey disembarked he was handed an envelope stamped 'Secret'. It said: 'You take command of the South Pacific Area and South Pacific Forces immediately.' Colonel Julian Brown, the admiral's intelligence officer, clearly remembered Halsey's response: 'Jesus Christ and General Jackson! This is the hottest potato they ever handed me!' Halsey himself wrote: 'My reactions were astonishment, apprehension, and regret, in that order.'

He had no 'inkling of the appointment'. He knew the current situation was at the crisis stage. He had no experience 'campaigning with the Army, much less with Australian, New Zealand and Free French forces'. Finally, Ghormley had been his good friend for forty years, since they played on the same academy football team.

'My war career', Halsey explained, 'was divided into three phases. From the outbreak until May 28, 1942, I commanded a task force at sea. From October 18, 1942, until June 14, 1944, I commanded an area and the forces within it. During the rest of the war I commanded a fleet.' Beyond doubt, that middle phase was the hardest, meanest most difficult of all.

Japan had settled into Rabaul and Bougainville the previous January. They had begun their descent down the obvious ladder towards the New Hebrides and New Caledonia. Goal: thinly defended New Zealand and Australia.

On Guadalcanal they had built an airstrip 555 miles from Allied-held Espiritu Santo in the threatened New Hebrides. Over his Joint Chiefs' objections, Admiral King determined to challenge the enemy at that very point.

Immediately after taking charge, Halsey called his principal commanders to Noumea, including Marine Major-General Alexander A. Vandegrift, Major-General Millard Harmon, and Rear-Admiral Richmond Kelly Turner, who led respectively the island contingent, the army land and air forces, and the amphibious support groups.

'Are you going to evacuate or hold?' he asked.

Vandegrift declared he could 'hold', provided he got more seaborne aid than heretofore.

'All right,' said Halsey. 'Go on back. I'll promise you everything I've got.'

He was better than his word. He scrounged shipping from Pearl Harbor, and whenever that was denied him he cannibalised homebound vessels of their weaponry and electronics for his own depleted squadrons. He visited Guadalcanal, which Ghormley had not done, and threatened to stencil 'South Pacific Fighting Force' on everybody's breeches if total unity were not observed. Thus Comsopac assembled the first real tri-service combined command in American military history.

Navy Secretary Frank Knox was pleased.

'Men of the aggressive fighting type must be preferred over men of more judicial, thoughtful, but less aggressive characteristics.' The secretary likened thrusting Halsey into this tight situation to Lincoln's ultimate replacement of 'the brilliant, polished, socially attractive McClellan [by] the rough, rather uncouth, unsocial Grant'.

Not that Halsey lacked the social amenities. He did not. But now, in this desperate instance, he represented total toughness.

On 23 October the Japanese tossed down the gage with an all-out attempt to recapture Henderson Field. Halsey responded by throwing a two-carrier task force against the strongest enemy fleet since Midway. From his tiny Noumea command post aboard the ancient merchantman *Argonne*, he flashed a simple order: 'Attack repeat attack,' then chafed and fumed and read pulp magazines as the faraway action commenced off Santa Cruz Island. *Hornet* was sunk, *Enterprise* badly mauled. But Nimitz termed it a 'long run . . . strategic advantage', for the foe's momentum was blunted and Henderson Field was held at tremendous loss to the Japanese.

Several skirmishes followed. Finally came the climactic Battle of Guadalcanal, which prevented the landing of 13,500 enemy soldiers on the island, and allowed substantial Allied reinforcements. It lasted four murderous days. Japanese losses were two battleships, a heavy cruiser, three destroyers and ten troop-filled transports. American fleet losses included three light cruisers and seven destroyers. Damage to other vessels was intensive on both sides.

President Roosevelt, Secretary Knox, Admirals King and Nimitz radioed their congratulations, which Halsey promptly relayed 'to the men who had done the fighting', ending with the heartfelt phrase, 'To the glorious dead: Hail heroes, rest with God.'

On 18 November Mr Roosevelt promoted Halsey to full admiral. While custom decreed that the navy could have only four such lofty officers at the same time, Congress immediately stamped its approval on Halsey's fourth star.

With Guadalcanal secured by February 1943, Halsey moved assuredly up The Slot to New Georgia and Bougainville. This brought him into MacArthur's strategic territory, although he still reported to Nimitz. He resolved the tricky protocol issue with aplomb, and visited the haughty general at Brisbane, once the Joint Chiefs had accepted his operational plan in April.

'The respect that I conceived for him that afternoon,' recalled Halsey, 'grew steadily during the war.'

Privately he confided: 'I can work for Doug MacArthur, but he sure as hell could never work for me.'

By December 1943 the South Pacific had become a garrison activity, with the Japanese effectively controlled, their southward advance forever ended. Halsey went to Washington, DC, to accept his second DSM from Knox. 'A forceful and inspiring leader,' read the citation, '[he] indoctrinated his command with his own fighting spirit and invincible determination to destroy the enemy.'

There followed a few more island-hopping expeditions in conjunction with MacArthur until, on 15 June, Halsey could safely turn over the housekeeping duties. He was now ready for the final third phase of his career: command of four quadruple carrier task groups that formed a fleet.

'Almost alone among senior admirals, Chester [Nimitz] and I advocated invading the central Philippines, building a major base, and jumping from there to the home islands of Japan, via Iwo Jima and Okinawa,' Halsey recounted. He did *not*, though, espouse landings in the Western Carolines, which he felt could easily be bypassed.

None the less Halsey departed from Pearl Harbor with the Third Fleet on 24 August 1944, his four-star flag flying over the new 45,000-ton battleship *New Jersey*, bound for a somewhat truncated Carolines invasion (Peleliu and Ulithi). There would follow a few weeks of softening up the Japanese strongholds, along with heavy air strikes against the middle Philippines.

Halsey's overall command now embraced five hundred-plus vessels, combatant and logistical, the greatest naval force ever assembled. Under Spruance, this was the Fifth Fleet.

In mid-September, during three hectic days, almost four thousand aerial sorties knocked down 173 enemy planes, blew up 305 on their fields, sank an estimated hundred ships, and destroyed a vast quantity of shore installations. Halsey's losses totalled a mere nine planes and ten men. More to the point, Halsey had proven his case for moving quickly into the heart of the Philippines, which he 'found . . . a hollow shell with weak defenses and skimpy facilities . . . the vulnerable belly of the Imperial dragon'.

As the Carolines action neared, Halsey's bold estimate came under consideration by the Combined Chiefs of Staff (American and British) at Quebec. They radioed for MacArthur's opinion. The general replied that he could indeed omit the intermediate steps, and land at Leyte on 20 October – two months ahead of the original schedule.

President Roosevelt himself revealed in his January 1945 'State of the Union' address how

Admiral Halsey reported that a direct attack in Leyte appeared feasible . . . Within the space of 24 hours, a major change of plans was accomplished which involved Army and Navy forces from two different theaters of operations – a change which hastened the liberation of the Philippines and the final day of victory – a change which saved lives which would have been expended in the capture of islands which are now neutralized far behind our lines.

Halsey drew the task of 'neutralizing the northern flank', as Nimitz chronicled, with a series of air assaults that roamed from Okinawa to Luzon and even Formosa. Two American cruisers were torpedoed off the latter island, but towed to Ulithi. This prompted over-enthusiastic Japanese pilots to declare they had demolished eleven carriers, two battleships and three cruisers. Believing this erroneous information, an enemy force moved southward to 'mop up remaining [American] elements', and sailed straight into the jaws of Halsey's baited trap.

On 15 October he radioed Cincpac: 'The Third Fleet's sunken and damaged ships have been salvaged and are retiring at high speed toward the enemy.'

When a Japanese scoutplane finally ascertained that Halsey's immense command was essentially intact, the enemy force turned tail, and the Third Fleet resumed its direct support of the Leyte beachhead. Net enemy toll: 140 ships sunk, 248 damaged; 1225 planes destroyed in the air or on the ground.

Since Jutland, no major naval engagement has been more fought-over by armchair analysts than the Battle for Leyte Gulf. Nimitz, having viewed it from his Pearl Harbor eyrie, pronounced it 'for complexity and magnitude without parallel' in naval annals. For his part in the four-day encounter and the ensuing actions, which finished Japan as a sea-threat, Halsey earned his third DSM. Yet some scornful critics dubbed it the 'Battle of Bull's Run', because of what occurred after Halsey's key decision.

Here, in brief, is the scenario.

Having been thwarted in their attempts to stall the Philippines landing, the Japanese evolved a new plan called 'Sho-Go' (Victory Operation), which moved forward in their typically unalterable fashion, once triggered.

They strengthened their Philippines-based air force both to hit Allied vessels in Leyte Gulf, and to cover a triple-pincered drive to defeat the Third and Seventh fleets, thus cutting Allied support for MacArthur's beachhead. Virtually all of the reduced Japanese navy was thrown into this last-ditch try.

One force of battleships, cruisers and destroyers moved south through Surigao Strait. Another, paced by the super-dreadnoughts *Yamato* and *Musashi*, took the middle passage through San Bernardino Strait. The third, which included four carriers, came south from the Inland Sea. What followed, as Nimitz recounted, was a series of engagements 'notable on both sides for remarkable achievements as well as for lost opportunities'.

Yet the outcome was inevitable, for the American forces were vastly superior, the Japanese were perilously dispersed because of the Allied submarine menace, and their communications were poor – fortunately at a moment when the American divided command was having its own information-sharing problems.

Confident that the old Seventh Fleet battleships and escort carriers could hold the line, Halsey first aimed his planes against the foe's centre force on 24 October. Their main target was *Musashi*. Torpedoes and bombs disabled her, and she began dropping far astern of the main body. Discouraged by failure to attain landbased air defence, the Japanese commander signalled .reverse course.

Now began the really controversial phase, when Admiral Thomas Kinkaid of the Seventh Fleet assumed that Halsey provided his back-up against heavy enemy assaults, whereas Halsey deemed his mission offensive rather than defensive.

Nimitz's orders themselves may have caused this confusion. One portion told Halsey to 'cover and support' South-West Pacific forces. Another said: 'In case opportunity for destruction of major portion of the enemy fleet offers or can be created, such destruction becomes the primary task.'

Halsey needed no further directive. This suited his combatant spirit to a T. After receiving exaggerated enemy damage reports from his carrier pilots, he elected to head north for the Japanese carriers, not aware that these were decoys, almost empty of aircraft. As always, he was determined to 'get the carriers'. Besides, he firmly believed that Kinkaid was 'amply strong to handle' any Japanese hit-run surface attacks.

'My decision to strike the Northern Force was a hard one to make,' Halsey wrote later, 'but given the same circumstances and the same information as I had then, I would make it again.'

While he was ploughing north with his fast carrier task fleet, Kinkaid's ancient battlewagons ambushed and thoroughly trounced the enemy's southern contingent in Surigao Strait.

But then the fleeing Japanese centre force, under a tart admonition from Tokyo, returned to the fray through San Bernardino Strait on 25 October. Although Halsey was puzzled why Kinkaid had 'let [his carrier commander] get caught like this . . . I still was not alarmed. I figured that the 18 little carriers had enough to protect themselves until the victorious old battle-wagons arrived.'

For his part, Kinkaid was becoming increasingly alarmed at the absence of Halsey's fast battleships and at least a division of carriers, as his escort carriers came under attack. A series of despatches flashed to the Third Fleet appealing for aid.

Halsey replied that he was 'still engaging enemy carriers', but that five of his own carriers had been ordered south immediately. Suddenly came the ill-starred message from Cincpac which hit Halsey 'as if I had been struck in the face'. It demanded: 'The whole world wants to know where is Task Force 34?' This Nimitz despatch, an 'insult' as Halsey then read it, was worded in such fashion because an inept encoder used the first six words as 'padding' to make the basic question harder for the enemy to decipher.

Half of his four task groups were immediately spun off by the angered Halsey to assist Kinkaid. He personally took these two units south.

Despite 'having turned my back on the opportunity I had dreamed of since my days as a cadet', Halsey counted all four Japanese carriers, a cruiser and two destroyers sunk, plus a pair of battleships, cruisers and four destroyers damaged. Once within range of the enemy's regrouped central force on 26 October, Halsey attacked with considerable success. He scattered his opponents in total disorder after they had inexplicably withdrawn while mauling the American escort carriers.

Following judicious review, Admiral King agreed with Halsey that the Japanese fleet was indeed crushed, with scant likelihood that it would ever again pose a serious threat. So the 'Battle of Bull's Run' achieved its proper due from the highest military echelons. MacArthur's despatch especially delighted the still smouldering Halsey, for it expressed the general's 'feeling of complete confidence and inspiration when you go into action in our support'.

Kinkaid drew his deserved share of praise. Between them the two admirals had sunk 306,000 tons of irreplaceable Japanese combatant shipping. American casualties: 37,000 tons.

For three more months Halsey lent Third Fleet backing to MacArthur. It was an arduous interlude, marked by a destructive typhoon that convinced him that fleet weather data must be improved, and by the appearance of the diabolical *kamikaze* ('divine wind') suicide dive-bombers.

His last action was a daring sweep through the China Sea. On 11 December, a banner day, the Third Fleet sank forty-one ships (127,000 tons). Having 'wrung the China Coast dry of profits [and] proved that its defenses were flimsy', he turned over command to Spruance on 26 January 1945, after eighty-five gruelling days at sea.

Roosevelt pinned the gold star representing Halsey's third DSM at the White House, with a citation that gave him credit for 'painstakingly' preparing for recapture of the Philippines and then executing his support mission through 'daring tactics'.

Halsey rejoined the fray on 18 May, with USS *Missouri* now his flagship, and his dual chore that of cleaning up the Okinawa area and preparing for the ultimate American invasion of the Japanese homeland scheduled for November. Shortly before, a four-carrier British task group under Vice-Admiral Sir Bernard Rawlings augmented the American fleet. Rawlings, who became one of Halsey's most admired friends, flew his flag in the battleship *King George V*.

Thus bolstered, the Third Fleet sortied Leyte Gulf on 1 July to launch the Pacific war's final stage. Halsey carried a broad mandate: 'We would attack the enemy's home islands, destroy the remnants of his navy, merchant marine, and air power and cripple his factories and communications. Our planes would strike inland; our big guns would bombard coastal targets; together they would literally bring the war home to the average Japanese citizen . . . Our next port of call was Tokyo itself.'

Halsey was adamant in polishing off the ragtag Japanese naval units at Kure, although his carrier task force commander demurred. National morale, the impending entry of Russia into the conflict, and exactment of stiffer peace terms framed his rationale. 'My only regret', Halsey told his subordinates, 'is that our ships don't have wheels, so that when we drive the Japs from the coast, we can chase them inland.'

During that month, the Third Fleet bombarded the homeland with impunity. It added insult to grievous injury by broadcasting in plain language Japanese to the hapless targets exactly what would occur.

On 9 August, a week after Nimitz forbade attacks on soon-to-be atomised Hiroshima and Nagasaki, Halsey was blasting at southern Hokkaido. The previous day Russia declared war, and Japan offered to surrender.

Immediately Halsey made plans for the certain occupation as 'the only military unit at hand with sufficient power to take Japan into custody at short notice . . . until occupation troops arrived'. Marine landing forces were quickly patched together, for prisoner-release and security purposes.

The atom bomb had been dropped on Hiroshima three days earlier, on Nagasaki that fateful 9 August.

Pending formal capitulation, Halsey kept up his guard against last-minute enemy surprises. On 14 August his fliers destroyed 422 grounded planes around Tokyo, before the All Pacific Ocean Areas despatch arrived on the 15th, suspending offensive operations.

Halsey's estimate of the role of the A-bomb and Russia's belated war declaration as a face-saving excuse for 'the Nips' was borne out later by a statement from the Japanese Naval Chief of Staff. Submarines and aircraft brought the empire to its knees, and neither the bomb nor Russia was the 'direct cause of the termination of the war', he suggested.

Said Halsey: 'I hope that history will remember this.'

So the formal surrender occurred on the veranda deck of *Missouri*, with MacArthur as master-of-ceremonies. American and British fleet units lay peacefully at anchor in the shadow of Mount Fujiyama, having steamed through the narrow passageway to Tokyo Bay on 29 August at 'the supreme moment' of Halsey's career.

The Second World War was finished, with both a bang and a whimper.

In USS *South Dakota* Halsey proceeded with a small task group to San Francisco, where he arrived on 15 September for the first of a series of triumphal receptions. Five stars denoting his elevation to fleet admiral now emblazoned his flag. He had earned his fourth DSM. And, much to his annoyance, he was sent on a five-week speaking tour of the country, to show the navy's colours at a time when the service finally realised it would soon be locked in a battle for budgetary survival against the exuberant air force.

Halsey remained on active duty until 1 April 1947, despite his wish to retire. Wisely he rejected an appeal from New Jersey Republicans to run for governor. He lived to see his exploits transformed into a motion picture, *The Gallant Hours*, and died on 16 August 1959 at the age of seventy-six.

'He had', as his autobiographical aide wrote, 'jumped from the obscure pages of the "Navy Register" to the front pages of the world's newspapers, and from there into the pages of history.' Certainly he was the best-known, best-loved American admiral of his generation, doubtless the prime combat commander of the war, and the most decorated.

> Admiral Halsey's mind [was] the Navy's mind – well-trained within professional limits. But his spirit [was] the historic spirit of leadership . . . When he commanded the Third Fleet, he did not send men into battle, he led them in. It is morale that wins wars, and what personal leadership does for morale is nowhere better stated than by Sir Thomas Malory (in describing King Arthur): 'All men of worship said it was merry to be under such a chieftain, that would put his person in adventure as other poor knights did.'

Admiral Raymond A. Spruance

———◆———

Henry H. Adams

No major, high-level, wartime commander in the US Navy has received as little public recognition as Admiral Raymond A. Spruance. To say that he did not seek publicity is to understate the matter; he positively shunned it. The role Admiral Spruance played in the victory over the Japanese, however, can hardly be overstated. He commanded in the Battle of Midway, the invasions of the Gilberts, the Marshalls, and the Marianas, the Battle of the Philippine Sea, and the invasions of Iwo Jima and Okinawa. Under his astute leadership the use of carrier air and amphibious forces reached their highest peak, although he was neither an aviator nor an amphibian.

Spruance was born in Baltimore, Maryland, on 3 July 1886, but his family soon moved to Indiana. There was little warmth and affection in the Spruance household, his father being an austere, undemonstrative man, and his mother too busy with her intellectual pursuits to devote much time to her children. When he was six the boy was sent to live with his maternal grandmother in New Jersey. His school career was unspectacular, but he always received high grades. When he was thirteen he returned to the Indiana home. He remained there until he entered the Naval Academy at Annapolis, Maryland, on 2 July 1903.

In the academy Spruance attracted little attention. He remained a shy, quiet young man, who studied hard and graduated twenty-fifth in his class of 209. His first command was the first of the torpedo boat destroyers built for the US Navy, the 420-ton *Bainbridge*, DD-1, then assigned to the Asiatic Fleet.

He exhibited the leadership methods that he was to follow throughout his career. He did his job well and expected his subordinates to do the same. He was never lavish in praise, because he expected superior performance as a matter of course. He became known for his skill in shiphandling and for his interest in the welfare of his men. If anything, he erred on the side of austerity.

In 1914 he returned to the United States and married. He had various assignments in engineering both ashore and afloat, until it became evident to him that he was in danger of being trapped in his speciality. He never again requested an engineering billet. He had risen rapidly in rank and was promoted to commander just before the First World War ended.

Spruance considered resigning from the navy rather than face the lean peacetime budgets that would follow. He was fortunate however in being given command of a brand new 1100-ton destroyer, *Aaron Ward*, which was assigned to the Pacific. *Ward* was one of a six-ship elite division led by Commander William F. Halsey, Jr.

Two more different men can hardly be imagined. Halsey was aggressive, gregarious, an extrovert. Spruance was introspective, calm in emergencies, little given to socialising. Yet despite their differences what they had in common was more important. Both were fearless leaders, utterly dedicated to duty, each with absolute integrity, each able to command the respect of his seniors and juniors and to get the best out of the men who worked for them.

The two men became close friends. At sea the division, led by the aggressive Halsey, became noted for its daring manoeuvres. Spruance was known for his complete calm on the bridge, giving the correct orders at the correct time in a quiet voice, even when collision seemed imminent.

Having known command of a high-speed destroyer, Spruance was distressed to learn in 1921 that once more he would be assigned to work in his speciality, this time in the Bureau of Engineering in Washington, where he became head of the Electrical Division. It seemed that his career was headed for the dead end of specialist officers.

His work in the bureau and possibly Halsey's glowing fitness reports got him back to the main stream in 1924, when he was assigned as commanding officer of the destroyer *Dale*. His command was brief, for Vice-Admiral Philip Andrews, Commander US Naval Forces, Europe, asked for him as Assistant Chief of Staff. Andrews was a hard man to get along with and could easily ruin the career of a naval officer. Spruance however learned how to handle the old man, and their families became friends. On completion of this duty, Spruance received an outstanding fitness report, a rarity from Admiral Andrews.

Spruance relieved Halsey in command of the destroyer *Osborne* in European waters and engaged in many 'show the flag' visits before returning to the United States to become a student at the US Naval War College at Newport, Rhode Island. This was the first of three assignments to the War College that Spruance would have before the Second World War, this one as student, and twice later as instructor. After the war he would return once more, this time as President.

Spruance's performance at the War College and his successful commands of destroyers made him one of those watched for possible high command, and he never had another engineering assignment. While at the college he was promoted to captain and then served a tour as Chief of Staff to Commander Destroyers, Scouting Force, in California. After two routine years he was ordered back to the War College for three years.

In the spring of 1938 Spruance received orders to command the battleship *Mississippi*. No matter that she was an old, tired ship. She was a battleship, and therefore one of the most prestigious commands the navy had to offer. As before, he ran the ship to the satisfaction of his superiors and the crew alike. His tour in command ended only when he was promoted to rear-admiral in early 1940.

Spruance's first assignment as an admiral was as commandant of the newly established Tenth Naval District, with headquarters in San Juan, Puerto Rico, where he reported on 26 February 1940. In view of the war in Europe, the United States was attempting to strengthen its position in the Caribbean, establishing a series of bases in defence of the Panama Canal and shipping moving between North and South America. After the fall of France in June the presence of French ships in Martinique and elsewhere caused much apprehension, and they became partially Spruance's responsibility. The following month his command was elevated to a Sea Frontier, embracing the whole of the Caribbean. It was an area where anything might happen as a result of American efforts to ensure that Germany gained none of the French or Dutch colonies in the area in violation of the Monroe Doctrine.

Like most naval officers Spruance longed for another command at sea, and was gratified when he was ordered to Pearl Harbor as Commander Cruiser Division 5, breaking his flag in the heavy cruiser *Northampton*, on 17 September 1941. This assignment led to a reunion with Halsey, who was commander of the task force to which the division was assigned. Halsey, by this time a vice-admiral and a qualified aviator, was in the carrier *Enterprise*. On 28 November Halsey's Task Force 8 sortied from Pearl Harbor to deliver fighter planes to Wake Island. Delayed by heavy weather, Task Force 8 was still at sea when the Japanese attacked Pearl Harbor on the morning of 7 December 1941.

Until Admiral Chester W. Nimitz took over as Commander-in-Chief Pacific Fleet in late December 1941, Halsey's task force patrolled north of the islands in futile steaming. After Nimitz's arrival Spruance's division supported Halsey during his raids in the Gilberts and Marshalls, pinpricks of no strategic value, but morale-builders for the shaken American public. More raids followed. The most important was on Tokyo, in which General James Doolittle flew army bombers from the carrier *Hornet*. Halsey commanded the force and Spruance's division was part of the escort. Spruance felt the raid was a waste of time, diverting carriers that might better be used elsewhere and needlessly risking valuable ships for the sake of a few headlines.

He was right about the diversion of the carriers, for while Halsey's ships were returning from the Tokyo raid, the Japanese opened a drive on Port Moresby on the southern coast of New Guinea. American efforts to stop this move led to the Battle of the Coral Sea in early May 1942, and each side lost a carrier. Halsey's force rushed to the South Pacific, but before it could arrive the battle had been fought.

When Spruance returned to Pearl Harbor he learned that Halsey was ill and had recommended that Spruance succeed him in command of Task Force 16. He also learned that he was about to have the challenge of his life.

The Japanese were mounting a major sea effort aimed at Midway Island, which lies at the western end of the Hawaiian chain, some 1200 miles north-west of Honolulu. Admiral Yamamoto's real goal was to lure the American fleet into battle so that it could be destroyed. He well knew that American industrial power made a complete Japanese victory impossible. He had estimated that he could 'run wild' for a year, and then the United States would inevitably begin to win. If he could destroy the American fleet, the American government might be inclined to sue for peace and allow Japan to retain her conquests in South-East Asia.

Unknown to Tokyo the Americans were breaking several Japanese naval codes, and Nimitz had a very good idea of Yamamoto's plans. What the Americans learned was enough to shake anyone. Nearly every serviceable ship in the Japanese navy was committed to the Midway operation, including ten carriers, a large number of battleships, and many other ships constituting a force far superior to what the American navy had available to oppose them.

The Japanese had an incredibly complex plan, with major units moving all over the ocean, a thrust against the Aleutians thrown in as a diversion. And in that complexity lay the only American hope.

The main Japanese invasion and covering forces were approaching Midway from the south-west, while a four-carrier striking force would be poised to the north-west. Admiral Nimitz's access to Japanese plans enabled him to place his slender forces where they might do the most good. He largely ignored the threat to the Aleutians and planned to hit with his carrier strength at the flank of the Japanese carrier force while it was engaged in striking at Midway. In addition to Spruance's Task Force 16 with the *Enterprise* and *Hornet*, he had Rear-Admiral Frank Jack Fletcher's Task Force 17 with the damaged *Yorktown*, a victim of the Coral Sea battle. Rushing back from the South Pacific, the *Yorktown* entered the yard at Pearl Harbor and was sufficiently patched up in seventy-two hours to take its place in the battle.

Aboard the *Enterprise*, Spruance retained Halsey's staff. Chief of Staff Captain Miles Browning was an experienced aviator, but Spruance would soon show that, aviator or no, he could grasp the essentials of handling and committing aircraft in battle as well as anyone.

Spruance with Task Force 16 left Pearl Harbor on 28 May 1942. His mission was 'to hold Midway and inflict maximum damage on the enemy by strong attrition tactics'. In a separate letter Nimitz had instructed, 'You will be governed by the principle of calculated risk.' By this he meant that it was more important to save his carriers than it was to hold Midway. Since Yamamoto was more interested in the destruction of the American ships than in the capture of Midway, it is apparent that that unfortunate island was really a stalking horse in the battle to come.

Admiral Fletcher took Task Force 17 to sea on 30 May and joined Spruance the following day in a position about 325 miles north-east of Midway. Then it became a matter of waiting until the enemy should show himself. Fletcher, as senior, was in tactical command, but each force operated independently. Spruance had complete responsibility for his own flight operations and strike schedule.

Early sightings by Midway aircraft of the occupation force ships confirmed Nimitz's intelligence analysis, and Spruance and Fletcher could expect the Japanese carrier force to turn up where predicted. They had one great advantage over Vice-Admiral Chuichi Nagumo, commanding the Japanese carrier force: they knew about where he would be; Nagumo had no knowledge of their whereabouts. In fact he thought they were probably in Pearl Harbor.

Nagumo however was too old a hand to neglect searches for a possible American carrier force, but he was over-confident and the searches were perfunctory. The one search plane assigned to the sector where the Americans were was late in getting off.

On the morning of 4 June a search plane from Midway spotted Nagumo's force. The pilot had seen only two of the four Japanese carriers, and the position reported was 40 miles in error, but both Fletcher and Spruance knew that the time to act was now, before surprise was lost. Since the *Yorktown* was recovering its early morning search, it was up to Spruance to launch the attack, which he did without delay. Owing to the lack of accurate information as to where the Japanese carriers were, as well as the fact that some of the air units were participating in their first action against the enemy, co-ordination of the air units was lost. Some squadrons never found the Japanese at all, and of those that did, many planes were shot down. At the time the American planes reached the Japanese carriers, Nagumo's aircraft were changing their bomb loads to torpedoes, having belatedly discovered the American carriers. He was helpless to launch aircraft. He had to depend on the fighters then in the air.

American torpedo bombers were nearly wiped out and they obtained no hits. But, by providence, dive-bombers arrived while the torpedo planes were sacrificing themselves. The bombers did their deadly work. When the attack was over, carriers *Akagi*, *Kaga* and *Soryu* were ablaze. The fourth, the *Hiryu*, escaped this attack and soon retaliated.

As Spruance was recovering the survivors of his air squadrons, he could only watch as planes from the unscathed *Hiryu* scored three bomb hits on the *Yorktown*. Fletcher had to shift his flag to a cruiser and he later turned tactical command over to Spruance. Attacks that afternoon located the *Hiryu*, and she was soon burning fiercely. All four Japanese carriers were out of action and would soon sink.

Spruance made the decision that during the coming night he would steam eastward, away from the Japanese, for a few hours, before turning back to be in position to strike again the next morning. He had not located the Japanese main body, and he knew it contained battleships and at least one carrier. He had no desire to run into a Japanese surface ambush at night where the enemy would hold all the advantages. Spruance has been criticised for excessive caution in this decision, but postwar analysis has vindicated his judgement. Yamamoto had set that precise trap. Spruance's caution kept him from throwing away the victory that he had won.

The next day was devoted to pursuit and to fruitless attempts to save the *Yorktown*. During the night Yamamoto had recalled ships from the Aleutian sector to support at Midway. Then, realising he had lost the battle, he made the decision to withdraw. Spruance's forces never did catch up. After one late afternoon strike, the planes returned after dark. He made the decision to turn on the lights of the carriers, disregarding the danger of exposing his force to submarine attack. The peril was real, for the next day a Japanese submarine finished off the *Yorktown*. Spruance however preferred to risk his task force rather than condemn his aviators to almost certain death when it lay in his power to save them.

After the battle Spruance was detached and ordered to report as Chief of Staff to Admiral Nimitz. While it was rumoured otherwise, no implication of rebuke was meant. Spruance's command of Task Force 16 was an emergency measure; only Halsey's illness gave him his opportunity to command at Midway. Long before the battle Nimitz had picked him for his Chief of Staff, and Spruance had been so informed.

When Spruance reported for duty, the principal decision to assume a limited offensive in the Solomon Islands had already been made, but he was fully occupied in the day-to-day support of South Pacific forces in their slim hold on Guadalcanal and in planning for future operations in the Solomons. Spruance became deeply involved in plans and estimates for the forthcoming Central Pacific campaign, having no idea that he would later command most of its operation.

On 5 August 1943, after fourteen months as Chief of Staff and, for part of that time, Deputy Commander-in-Chief Pacific Fleet and Pacific Ocean Area, Spruance, who was now a vice-admiral, was named Commander Central Pacific Force. Admiral Ernest J. King, Commander-in-Chief US Fleet and Chief of Naval Operations wrote: 'Spruance . . . was in intellectual ability unsurpassed among the flag officers of the United States Navy.'

Spruance's first task as Commander Central Pacific Force was to seize positions in the Gilbert Islands. Originally the Joint Chiefs of Staff and Admiral Nimitz had favoured a direct assault on the Marshalls, but Spruance was opposed. The Marshalls were known to be heavily defended, and that was about all that was known about them. The Japanese had fortified them while keeping all foreigners out for many years. Furthermore the Marshalls could not be successfully reconnoitered from existing American bases, whereas the Gilberts could. From the Gilberts, landbased air power could scout out the

Marshalls and could support the landings there. Spruance further argued that the Gilberts would be a far easier undertaking and that the lessons learned there could ensure success in the Marshalls. A direct assault on the Marshalls might well fail. Gradually he won his superiors around to his line of reasoning; the invasion of Tarawa Atoll and Nauru Island was approved in July, with the target date of 15 November 1943. Invasion of the Marshalls would be planned for January 1944.

Spruance's most pressing job was to select a staff and the subordinate commanders for the Gilberts. He kept his staff small. He hated paperwork and liked most staff planning to be done in conference. He would listen to all sides, make the decision, and then go for a walk while his staff attended to the detailed planning that had to be done. Chief of Staff Captain Carl Moore complained that Spruance was always off on a long walk when a decision was needed. Although this sounds like the exasperation of a conscientious man who wants to get on with the job, it is so frequent a complaint that one wonders whether Spruance was not yet ready to make certain decisions and would think them out on his walks. Once they were made he seldom had need to change them. In an emergency he could make up his mind quickly and usually reached the right decision.

For his amphibious commander, Spruance selected his old friend Rear-Admiral Richmond Kelly Turner, while command of the troops went to Major-General Holland M. Smith, United States Marine Corps. Looking more like a businessman than a marine, Smith belied his appearance, being one of the most dynamic of commanders.

Early in the planning Spruance expressed dissatisfaction with Nauru as a target. Turner and Smith agreed. Lying 380 miles west of Tarawa, Nauru was too far off for the naval forces assaulting both places to be mutually supporting. It was also too close to the Japanese base at Truk, which could not be watched from any American position. Forces attacking Nauru could be surprised by the Japanese and possibly be wiped out before the Tarawa forces could come to their assistance. Turner and Smith had other objections: Nauru was rugged and would present too difficult an amphibious target. To have sufficient troops for a successful assault would require all the transports assigned to the entire operation.

On 2 September, when Admiral King was visiting Pearl Harbor, Spruance brought up these objections. King asked him what he would take in Nauru's place, and Spruance replied promptly: 'Makin.' Makin Atoll lies 100 miles north of Tarawa, that much closer to the Marshalls, and it has a lagoon for a fleet anchorage and islands that could be developed into airstrips. After consideration King agreed to submit the change to the Joint Chiefs of Staff. Makin was promptly approved.

The Gilbert Islands, British until the Japanese seized them early in the war, are composed of some sixteen coral atolls, each made up of low-lying, narrow islands and reefs surrounding a lagoon. There is very little dry land

and the areas of these islands are generally described in acres rather than square miles. Nevertheless there was plenty of room for the Japanese to dig in. Everyone agreed that the Japanese defences should be obliterated by massive gunfire and bombing on the morning of D-Day before the assault troops landed. There were two principal attack forces, one under Turner for Makin, with elements of the army's 27th Division, and the other under Rear-Admiral Harry W. Hill, with the 2nd Marine Division, for Tarawa. A small force embarked in the submarine *Nautilus* would capture the undefended atoll Abemama, which was done without incident. Makin was expected to be easy, and it should have been. Yet it took four days as a result of the inexperience of the green army troops.

At Tarawa the initial target was Betio Island on the southern part of the atoll. The Japanese were protected in shelters by layers of coconut logs, coral sand, and reinforced concrete, which made them impervious to anything but a direct hit with armour-piercing shells or bombs. The much-heralded preliminary bombardment levelled nearly everything in sight, but the Japanese defenders were largely unhurt. The marines were forced to wade long distances to reach shore as the unpredictable tide failed to give enough water over the reef. To capture the 291-acre island took four days with thousands of casualties.

Although the high casualty rate caused much criticism, Spruance's judgement in taking the Gilberts first was vindicated. Kwajalein Atoll in the Marshalls was much more heavily defended than Tarawa had been. It is problematical whether a direct assault would have succeeded. As it turned out, the valuable lessons of Tarawa were applied, and the assault on the Marshalls was comparatively easy.

The Marshalls lie north-west of the Gilberts and consist of twenty or so atolls, Kwajalein, near the centre, being the largest in the world, some 65 miles long. The final plan for the Marshalls called for the seizure of Kwajalein in the first phase, and Eniwetok, about 300 miles north-west in the second. On Kwajalein the principal objectives were the islands Roi and Namur in the north-east corner and Kwajalein Island in the south. Undefended Majuro Atoll was added because its lagoon would serve as a fleet anchorage and an advance base.

D-Day for the Marshalls was 31 January 1944, but only preliminary landings took place that day. The main assault followed on Roi, Namur and Kwajalein the next morning. The team of Spruance, Turner and Smith remained intact, but the new carrier commander was Rear-Admiral Marc A. Mitscher. This change displeased Spruance, for it was done without consulting him, and he had not been impressed with Mitscher as captain of the carrier *Hornet* at Midway. It took some time for Mitscher to win Spruance's confidence, but when he did it was never shaken.

All the lessons learned in the Gilberts were applied in the Marshalls, particularly in the preliminary bombardment, so that the conquest of the

Marshalls went swiftly, and the floating reserve was not needed. Spruance considered that of all the major operations in the Pacific war, the Marshalls operation gave the most gain for the least cost.

So swift was the capture of Kwajalein that Spruance recommended the Eniwetok operation proceed immediately, using the ten thousand troops of the corps reserve as the assault force. Nimitz approved, and D-Day was set for 17 February. To cover the assault Spruance directed Mitscher's Task Force 58 to raid the Japanese stronghold of Truk on the same date, leaving one carrier group in support at Eniwetok.

Spruance hoped to destroy a major portion of the Japanese combined fleet during the Truk strike, but Task Force 58 was detected on the way in and the Japanese fleet hastily withdrew to Palau. The raid nevertheless cost the Japanese 15 small naval ships, 24 merchantmen, and nearly 275 planes. American losses were minimal. The raid was a worthy complement to the invasion of Eniwetok, which went smoothly and with only minor delays and difficulties.

As a result of the Marshalls operations, Spruance was promoted to admiral. He would retain command of the Central Pacific Forces, now also designated the Fifth Fleet, for the next major operation, the conquest of the Marianas. First however he had to help out in another way. Task Force 58 was being borrowed by MacArthur for the conquest of Hollandia on the northern coast of New Guinea. To protect his right flank, Task Force 58 first raided Palau. Again Spruance hoped to strike at the combined fleet, but again it eluded him.

Planning for the Marianas was on a scale never before seen in the Pacific. Unlike the small atolls of Micronesia, the Marianas are composed of volcanic islands rising high above the sea, the three largest being Saipan, Tinian and Guam. Over 125,000 troops were assigned to the Marianas operation and 535 combatant and auxiliary ships. The nearest base was Eniwetok, which was little more than an anchorage, and 1000 miles distant. Pearl Harbor was 3500 miles away. The operation is the more impressive when it is noted that the landing on Saipan took place just over a week following the Allied landing at Normandy.

The Spruance, Turner, Smith, Mitscher team remained intact for the Marianas, and, like their commander, his subordinates had all been promoted, Turner and Mitscher becoming vice-admirals and Smith a lieutenant-general. Spruance was content to leave the detailed planning in their capable hands. D-Day for Saipan was set for 15 June 1944. Guam was tentatively set for 18 June, and Tinian was left indefinite, depending on the progress on the other two islands. The assault on Saipan took place on schedule with no more than the expected difficulties. Movement ashore however was slow and operations fell well behind schedule.

Spruance meanwhile was concerned with another danger, for submarine scouting reports revealed that the Japanese were at last committing a major fleet to oppose the Americans in the Marianas. These reports caused Spruance to postpone the Guam assault indefinitely and to prepare to meet the Japanese fleet in the Philippine Sea west of the Marianas.

Although the Battle of the Philippine Sea was an overwhelming American victory, it brought Spruance more criticism than anything else in his career.

Spruance was overwhelmingly conscious that his overriding mission was the seizure of the Marianas. Protection of the beachhead took precedence in his mind and coloured all his decisions. Experience in all previous battles had shown that the Japanese had a propensity for complex plans, with diversions and flanking attacks. He feared that while he was opposing a force west of the Marianas, one or more Japanese task groups might slip around his flanks and destroy his beachhead as they had so often attempted to do at Guadalcanal.

Spruance had Mitscher's Task Force 58, consisting of fifteen carriers with fast battleships, cruisers and destroyers. These were divided into four task groups, of which two were off to the north attacking the Bonins to prevent Japanese aerial reinforcement of the Marianas. Turner had a powerful but slower force of old battleships, destroyers, cruisers and escort carriers, whose job was to support the forces ashore. In a pinch they could be used in a fleet engagement.

After a conference with Turner, Spruance borrowed seven cruisers and eleven destroyers from him to strengthen Task Force 58. He recalled the two groups from the Bonins and rendezvoused with them at noon, 18 June, some 180 miles west of Tinian. All ships fuelled, and Spruance created a special task group of battleships, cruisers and destroyers to take station west of the carriers. Spruance then issued his instructions: 'Task Force 58 must cover Saipan and the forces engaged there and this can be done best by proceeding west in daylight and towards Saipan at night.'

It was not easy to proceed westward in the daylight hours, for an easterly wind meant that Task Force 58 would have to turn back toward Saipan every time it conducted flight operations. The Japanese on the other hand could continue to advance as they launched and recovered planes.

Spruance had good reason to believe that the Japanese would run true to form and attack with diversions, for sightings indicated that there were at least two forces. The main body under Vice-Admiral Jisaburo Ozawa, had come up from Tawi Tawi; another was coming from Batjan. Spruance had no way of knowing that the two forces had joined on the afternoon of 16 June.

Ozawa was badly outnumbered in every category of ship and aircraft, but he held the advantage of the wind and of longer-range planes. He intended to stay out of range of the American planes and send his aircraft to attack the American carriers, fly on to Guam for refuelling and rearming, attack again on the way west, and return to their carriers. It was a good plan, but it failed.

Mitscher recommended that Task Force 58 steam westward that night in order to close the enemy and be in a position for a powerful early morning strike. Spruance refused on the rather slender evidence that reported jamming of a submarine transmission indicated two enemy forces in the area. He held fast to the idea that the Japanese would slip behind him and attack the beachhead. Even if they had, his critics have argued, no serious harm would have been done, for Turner's slower ships could have held off any threat until Task Force 58 should come to the rescue. The troops ashore had sufficient food and ammunition to hold out until the battle was decided, and the vulnerable transports and supply ships had already moved to waters east of the Marianas.

When dawn searches on 19 June revealed no trace of the enemy, Spruance instructed Mitscher to keep the airfields on Guam and Tora neutralised. This move effectively spoiled Ozawa's plan of shuttle bombing. The Mariana bases were not available to him.

Shortly before 10 am radars picked up many aircraft approaching from the westward. This was the first of four massive raids Ozawa sent off from his carriers that day. When they were over, the Japanese had lost 219 aircraft. Before the battle was over they would lose 176 more. The cost to the Americans was one bomb hit on a battleship and a few near misses. Pilot losses were less than a tenth of those of the Japanese.

Free now of any apprehension of a flanking move, Spruance was anxious to speed west after his defeated opponent, but the necessity of turning east to recover and launch aircraft meant that little westering was made good. Not until night brought flight operations to an end could Task Force 58 steam west at high speed.

Ozawa was making his way north-west, for his force had fallen victim to American submarines and had lost two carriers including his flagship, the new *Taiho*.

Early morning searches found no trace of the Japanese. All day Spruance waited. It was not until mid-afternoon that a search plane spotted Ozawa's retiring force. The report was garbled and contained a 60-mile error in the Japanese position, but Mitscher and Spruance had no hesitation in launching an attack, even though it was at extreme range. On their way American planes found and sank two oilers. Then they located the main body and sank one and heavily damaged two carriers, a battleship and a cruiser. Ozawa lost forty aircraft in the short action.

Spruance approved Mitscher's decision to turn on the lights to guide the returning airmen home. Although there was much confusion, most planes landed safely. Many downed aviators were picked up by destroyers, and losses were incredibly low.

Nimitz and King both supported Spruance in his decision not to steam west on the evening of 18 June. As it turned out, there was no flanking force, and the task force might well have annihilated Ozawa's ships. On the other hand American ships might have been lost or damaged, slowing future operations. The most important Japanese casualties were their trained carrier pilots. Their loss meant that in the forthcoming Battle for Leyte Gulf in

October, the surviving Japanese carriers would be only decoys manned by a handful of airmen.

A crisis that required Spruance's attention soon developed on Saipan. Two marine and one army divisions were fighting there, and General Smith was infuriated at the slow progress of the army's 27th Division, the same division that had angered him at Makin. He recommended that the commanding general be relieved; and after a review of all the facts and taking counsel with Turner, Spruance agreed. The relief of an army general by a marine caused a bitter inter-service row, but Spruance came in for none of the blame. It was all directed against General Smith of the Marine Corps.

It took twenty-four days to complete the conquest of Saipan, and soon Spruance was able to proceed against Tinian and Guam. The former was invaded on 24 July and the latter on 21 July. There was hard fighting for both islands, but the end was never in doubt. Admiral Spruance was relieved by Halsey on 26 August, and the Fifth Fleet became the Third Fleet. The same ships remained, but they had a new taskmaster.

On his return to Pearl Harbor Admiral Spruance recommended to Admiral Nimitz that the next objectives for the Fifth Fleet be Iwo Jima and Okinawa. Nimitz replied that the Joint Chiefs of Staff had decided on Formosa, once MacArthur and Halsey had completed the conquest of the Philippines. Spruance believed Formosa would be too difficult and that it was too far removed from Japan to be decisive. Iwo Jima would bring Tokyo within range of fighters, as fighters based on Iwo Jima could escort the big B-29 bombers beginning to operate from the Marianas. It would also afford a valuable emergency landing field for damaged bombers. From Okinawa, American forces could control the East China Sea and could reach southern Japan. Formosa would not serve either of these purposes well.

Spruance returned from leave to find his plan accepted. After the Philippine fighting, there were not enough troops to assault Formosa. In a meeting of King, Nimitz and Spruance, Iwo Jima and Okinawa were designated the next targets.

In the Iwo Jima operation, Spruance again had the skill of Turner, Holland Smith and Mitscher available to him. To cover the landing, Spruance sent Mitscher's Task Force 58 on a two-day raid on Tokyo so the Japanese would be more interested in defending their homeland than in reinforcing Iwo Jima.

General Smith demanded a ten-day preliminary bombardment, since it was evident that the Japanese were well dug into the volcanic island. Everyone knew that Iwo Jima would be the most difficult target since Tarawa. Despite Smith's demands, Spruance limited the pre-invasion bombardment to three days. He felt that when the bombardment started, American intentions would be revealed, and each day's delay in landing would increase Japanese reinforcement. He did authorise one additional day if, in the judgement of the commander of the bombardment group, it would be useful.

As the big guns began bombarding Iwo Jima, Task Force 58 achieved complete surprise at Tokyo on 16 February. The weather was bad and the results disappointing, so halfway through the second day Spruance directed Mitscher to return to Iwo Jima to support Turner.

Landings took place on schedule on 19 February, and the fighting ashore was intense. At sea the Japanese struck with *kamikaze* (suicide) planes and succeeded in damaging the carrier *Saratoga* and two escort carriers, one of which sank. A number of other ships were also damaged.

A second raid on Tokyo took place on 25–6 February, but was again hampered by bad weather. On the withdrawal Spruance ordered Okinawa bombed and photographed (the operation to seize that island was only a few weeks off). It soon became evident that although much hard fighting lay ahead, victory was assured at Iwo Jima, and Spruance felt it safe to withdraw his carriers to get ready for Okinawa.

Since the operation there would require two full corps comprising the Tenth Army, and the preponderance of troops would be army rather than marine, Army Lieutenant-General Simon Buckner replaced General Smith. Turner and Mitscher remained.

The Japanese navy no longer offered any serious threat, but the enemy air power did. Experience in the Philippines and at Iwo Jima with the *kamikazes* worried Spruance and his staff a good deal. To weaken Japanese air, Task Force 58 raided Kyushu on 18–19 March. Over seven hundred enemy aircraft were destroyed and much damage was done to ground installations. Several American ships were hit by *kamikazes*, including the carrier *Franklin*, which survived because of Spruance's decision to stay and protect her only a few miles from the Japanese coast.

A portion of the Royal Navy was being assigned to the Fifth Fleet, and Spruance foresaw endless difficulties in logistics, methods of operation, and possible national vanities. He need not have worried. Task Force 57, under Vice-Admiral Sir Bernard Rawlings, performed to his complete satisfaction.

The landings on Okinawa took place on 1 April 1945, following nine days of preliminary carrier strikes and a week of bombardment. Ashore the fighting was stubborn and heavy, the Japanese commander skilfully withdrawing from one prepared position to another. There was no chance that he could win, for he had no hope of reinforcement or evacuation. The main danger to the operation was from the *kamikaze* aircraft of the fanatical Japanese. At one point the Japanese committed their remaining naval strength in a suicide raid. Mitscher's aircraft disposed of this threat quickly, sinking most of the force, including the giant battleship *Yamato*.

While the US Navy was supporting the troops ashore, the Royal Navy Task Force 57 was protecting the southern flanks. British carriers were less susceptible to suicide attacks because of their armoured flight decks: not one had to be withdrawn from service, while several American carriers were knocked out of the war by *kamikazes*.

Spruance's able subordinates were taking care of the present fighting, so he was free to turn his mind to future operations. He advocated a landing on the China coast somewhere north of Formosa to complete the encirclement of Japan. He felt an invasion of Japan was unnecessary and that the cost in American and Allied casualties would be too high. Although he knew nothing of the existence of the atomic bomb, he, along with many naval leaders, believed Japan could be brought to her knees by the combination of sea blockade and air bombardment.

Spruance was relieved by Halsey on 27 May, and the Fifth Fleet once more became the Third. When he returned to Nimitz's headquarters at Guam after leave, he found that he was to command the Fifth Fleet in an amphibious invasion of Kyushu scheduled for 1 November. He was engaged in planning this operation when the war ended.

After the war Spruance commanded all naval forces in Japan and on 24 November relieved Admiral Nimitz as Commander-in-Chief Pacific Fleet and Pacific Ocean Area. He had to deal with all the problems of demobilisation, while trying to maintain some semblance of a fighting navy. His tour was short, for he had always wished to retire as President of the Naval War College, and that post became available sooner than expected. He became its President on 1 March 1946.

As President, Spruance modernised and revitalised the curriculum, emphasising the interdependence of strategy, tactics and logistics. Lessons learned and advances made during the war were incorporated, so that future students could benefit from their seniors' experiences. Most of all, the emphasis was on principles rather than rigid doctrine that might become outdated.

Spruance retired on 1 July 1948 and moved to California. In January 1952, to his surprise, he was appointed Ambassador to the Philippines, arriving in Manila the next month. He proved to be an effective ambassador, although he seems to have attempted to intervene in Philippine affairs more than was strictly according to protocol. He worked for land reform, and he made American desires felt in the election in which Ramon Magsaysay opposed incumbent President Elpidio Quirino. Although he enjoyed strict neutrality on his staff, his influence was subtly felt. Magsaysay was elected in 1953. Spruance's most solid accomplishment was the negotiation for American bases in the now independent Philippines. These negotiations he brought to a successful conclusion before departing for home on 1 April 1955.

Once again in California, and a neighbour of Admirals Nimitz and Turner, Spruance interested himself in civil affairs. He died on 13 December 1969.

A quiet officer, he depended on good men to do the jobs he gave them. He refused to take the credit he believed his subordinates had earned, and so remained little known to the public. A brilliant strategist, a leader of men and a fearless fighter, he earned the respect of all who knew him. He was, as Admiral Nimitz characterised him, 'an Admiral's Admiral'.

Admiral of the Fleet The Viscount Cunningham

Lieutenant-Commander Peter Kemp

Andrew Browne Cunningham was born in 1883, the second son and third child of a Scottish family of considerable eminence in medicine and the church. His selection of a naval career came somewhat fortuitously in 1892 at the suggestion of his father, who had noticed his interest in boats and the sea. After a year's special schooling in the navy class at Edinburgh Academy and three years at Stubbington House, a preparatory school which used to 'cram' for the navy, he passed into HMS *Britannia* in 1896.

His first service at sea after passing out of HMS *Britannia* in 1898 was on the Cape of Good Hope station, and when the Boer War broke out in the following year the young Cunningham managed to get himself attached to the Naval Brigade operating ashore and saw a fair amount of action. If there was not much to be learned in this type of warfare to help him along his naval career, it was nevertheless a useful lesson in responsibility and self-reliance, and brought him one inestimable advantage too. This came from the necessarily close contact in which he lived with the seamen of the Naval Brigade, bringing him an early recognition of the many qualities and the adaptability of the British seaman. It was a knowledge that he never lost throughout the whole of his naval service and that was later to make him so inspiring a leader in battle.

After passing for sub-lieutenant Cunningham was appointed to the battle-ship *Implacable* in the Mediterranean and had the good fortune six months later to be selected to fill a vacancy in the destroyer *Locust*. It was his first introduction to this branch of the navy, and it was in destroyers that almost all his naval service up to the rank of captain was spent.

The ten years that preceded the First World War were years of great change and advance in the navy. The old Victorian navy was still dying hard – Cunningham in fact spent a year in a sail training ship – but under the forceful direction of such men as Sir John Fisher, Sir Percy Scott, and others, the new navy of 1914–18 was being born. For two years after leaving the *Locust* Cunningham served in training ships, mainly organising the instruction of direct-entry boys, and through this duty took an active part in the regeneration of naval gunnery and other fighting specialisations that the new navy was demanding. Later in his life Cunningham always considered these two years in training ships as the most valuable and satisfying of his career, again bringing him into closer contact with lower deck life than would normally fall to the lot of a young lieutenant.

After two years in cruisers in the Mediterranean, Cunningham was appointed to his first command, Torpedo Boat No. 14. She was one of thirty-six vessels originally designed as coastal destroyers but later re-rated as torpedo boats. They were known in the navy as 'oily wads' since they burned oil fuel in their boilers at a time when most destroyers were coal-fired. From TB14 he was appointed in command of the *Scorpion*, a Beagle-class destroyer, and he was still in her, in the Mediterranean, when war was declared in 1914.

Except for a very brief period in command of the destroyer *Rattlesnake* when the *Scorpion* had to return to England for a refit, Cunningham spent almost the whole of the war in command of the same ship. When she was finally paid off in January 1918 he took command of HMS *Termagant* in the Dover Patrol, and was still serving there when the war ended in 1918.

It had been a good war for Cunningham. Three years in the Mediterranean, which had included the Dardanelles campaign and other destroyer operations along the Levant coast, had included his promotion to commander in 1915; the year in the Dover patrol and service in the 1919 campaign in the Baltic under Sir Walter Cowan, in which Cunningham commanded the destroyer *Seafire*, ended in his promotion to captain. But it was not only the two steps in promotion that were important landmarks; it was also his intimate knowledge of the Mediterranean, and especially the eastern Mediterranean, which was to stand him in even greater stead in his later career.

Command of destroyers throughout these wartime years had brought him not only the self-confidence and quick thinking that are almost the inevitable result of command of small, fast ships in wartime; it also brought him a great deal of fighting in both large and small engagements, and a consequent belief in the power of gun and torpedo in close action as the decisive factor in naval warfare. In this belief he differed from many naval officers of his time who saw the big battleship gun fired at long range as the final naval weapon. He had also seen in the Dardanelles the use of naval aircraft in battle and, again differing from many of his contemporaries, was prepared to accord it a far more dominant role in battle than many could yet foresee.

On his promotion to captain at the beginning of 1920, Cunningham was of course at the bottom of the captains' list, and the years between the two world wars were sticky ones for promotion. The rapid run-down of the navy after the armistice of 1918; the notorious 'ten-year rule', which virtually precluded any new naval building; and the Washington and London naval treaties, which laid down maximum naval strengths for Britain, the United States, France, Italy and Japan, had the effect of clogging the captains' list, and Cunningham had to serve nearly thirteen years in that rank before promotion to rear-admiral in 1932. His close connection with destroyers was by no means broken during these years, as in addition to serving as Captain (D) in the 6th and 1st flotillas, he also spent two years as captain-in-charge of the destroyer base at Port Edgar in the Firth of Forth. Other appointments were flag captain to Sir Walter Cowan on the American and West Indies station, a year's course at the Imperial Defence College, command of the battleship *Rodney*, and commodore of the Royal Navy Barracks, Chatham.

As a rear-admiral Cunningham went back to destroyers, commanding the flotillas in the Mediterranean as Rear-Admiral (D) with his flag in the cruiser *Coventry*. This appointment took him through the Italo–Abyssinian war, a period that disgusted him by the pusillanimity of the sanctions against Italy imposed by the League of Nations and by the defeatist attitude adopted by the Chiefs of Staff Committee in London. But it was a period in which extensive planning for a possible war with Italy engaged Sir William Fisher, Commander-in-Chief Mediterranean, who had Cunningham and his staff with him, and it was a period, too, of intensive exercising at sea to make sure that the plans were viable. Some of this planning was used to very good effect three or four years later when war against Italy had become a reality.

Cunningham left the Mediterranean in 1936 to face a bleak future. He was now a vice-admiral but there was no prospect of any worthwhile sea command for him in the foreseeable future. In the normal run of events he might, perhaps, have hoped for a shore command at home as the final step in his naval career. The serious illness of Vice-Admiral Sir Geoffrey Blake in 1937 brought Cunningham a temporary appointment in Blake's place as second-in-command of the Mediterranean fleet, and at the end of 1937 the appointment was made permanent when Blake was invalided. This proved to be the great turning-point in Cunningham's naval career, as he stepped naturally into those future appointments that Blake had been expected to fill.

The second of these appointments came in 1938 when the new First Sea Lord, Sir Roger Backhouse, appointed Cunningham as Deputy Chief of Naval Staff at the Admiralty. It was Cunningham's first staff appointment and one which, in his own words, filled him with horror since he felt unsuited for the job through lack of staff experience. He took over from Admiral Sir William James in October 1938, a few days after the signing of the Munich agreement, and at once fell into the midst of the naval rearmament programme then in full swing. Perhaps not unnaturally, the first and biggest of the problems placed squarely on his plate was the chronic shortage of destroyers needed for escort work in the event of war, and typically he drew upon his own experience of the First World War when he commanded the *Seafire*, one of a class of small destroyers produced in large numbers with a minimum of building time. He recommended a new class based on the lines of the 1917 S-class, small destroyers of about 1000 tons, and forty-eight of them were built. Unhappily they lacked the necessary endurance to be of any value for convoy work in the Atlantic, though they were of considerable use in the narrower waters of the Mediterranean and the North Sea.

Cunningham's first few months at the Admiralty were not entirely happy, for Sir Roger Backhouse was a First Sea Lord who was not prepared to delegate any of his work. All that came Cunningham's way were responsibility for the naval reactions to the civil war in Spain, a fruitless visit to Berlin to protest at Hitler's decision to build U-boats up to 100 per cent parity with Britain, and a few minor decisions on new naval equipment. Somewhat hamstrung by his chief's decision to handle all major, and many of the minor, day-to-day decisions himself, Cunningham was unable to show himself in his best light in the weekly meetings of the Deputy Chiefs of Staff.

These unhappy days came to an end in March 1939 with the serious illness of the First Sea Lord, so serious indeed that he was never able to return to the Admiralty. Cunningham was thrown into the heart of naval affairs in the middle of an international situation that was rapidly degenerating into war. As substitute for Backhouse he represented the navy at the meetings of the Committee of Imperial Defence, and much of the burden of the last intensive months of rearmament and rapid increase of naval personnel fell on his shoulders. There were also discussions with the French navy on areas of collaboration in the event of war, in which Cunningham took a notable part.

With Backhouse's illness showing no signs of allowing him to return to the Admiralty as First Sea Lord (in fact he died on 15 July 1939), it was arranged to bring home Sir Dudley Pound to take over that post and to replace him as Commander-in-Chief, Mediterranean, by Cunningham. By early June he was back in the Mediterranean with the rank of acting admiral, flying his flag in the *Warspite*, and for the next few months the fleet was kept busy in exercises of all descriptions. Cunningham was always a great believer in training for war, and hated to see ships swinging idly round their mooring buoys when they could be at sea exercising. Although the fleet which he now commanded was considerably inferior in numbers to that of Italy, which all knew was certain to be the enemy when war came, in skill and expertise it was vastly superior. And of even more importance was the exceptionally high degree of morale that Cunningham as its leader instilled into every man under his command. He had the priceless quality of inspiring confidence in all who served with him, and not only a memory that could pick out any officer or rating who had served in any ship he had commanded but also the time to stop for a word and a greeting. He looked the complete part of a fighting admiral with his genial countenance and the piercing blue eyes of the born sailor, and his reputation as a distinguished destroyer captain of great dash and daring gave promise that the necessary blend of resolution and courage lay behind the looks. Even in the blackest days of the war in the Mediterranean there was never any whisper of defeat among the men who manned the fleet.

For the first nine months of the war, with Italy remaining a non-belligerent, Cunningham watched his fleet dwindle away as his ships were withdrawn to more active areas of warfare. They came back to him as the war situation in France deteriorated and threatening noises from Italy foretold her eventual involvement. Cunningham, anxious as ever to get to close grips with the enemy, had his plans ready to occupy Crete if the first Italian action, as seemed possible, was directed against Greece, and to make a sweep into the central Mediterranean to test the Italian naval reaction should Greece prove not to be the Italian target. In the event, the sweep into the Mediterranean produced no Italian reaction whatsoever, either from the air or on the sea.

It was the fall of France and the signing of an armistice between her and Germany that brought Cunningham his first big test as Commander-in-Chief. A French squadron under the command of Vice-Admiral Godfroy, consisting of one battleship, four cruisers and three destroyers, formed part of his fleet and with France now out of the war, posed an embarrassing problem. The solution proposed by the authorities in London was to present these ships, together with those at Oran, with an ultimatum to the effect that if they would neither continue the fight against Germany and Italy nor agree to disarm and immobilise themselves, they would regretfully be sunk by British ships. Cunningham, distressed beyond measure at the thought of having, in the last resort, to open fire on his erstwhile allies, did his utmost to settle the business by diplomacy. For some hours it was touch and go, with British and French ships facing each other cleared for action, but in the end Admiral Godfroy was won over to Cunningham's proposals for a peaceful and honourable solution. It was, in its way, a small triumph for Cunningham's common-sense outlook and skill in winning the French crews over, as compared with the result at Oran where the British squadron was forced to open fire on the French ships lying in harbour there after a blank refusal to accept the ultimatum.

The loss of the French fleet to the Allied cause in the Mediterranean raised tremendous problems. There was now nothing to defend the western Mediterranean, which became virtually an Italian sea. The main fleet base at Malta was untenable except for a submarine flotilla, since it was wide open to air attack from Sicily and southern Italy. Cunningham's only base in the eastern Mediterranean was Alexandria, lacking proper dockyard facilities for the adequate maintenance of a fleet and with a supply route from home of 8500 miles around the Cape of Good Hope. He had no long-range reconnaissance aircraft; the Royal Air Force in Egypt was unable to provide fighter cover when the fleet went to sea; and the only Fleet Air Arm element at his disposal was the small and antiquated aircraft carrier *Eagle*, though later she was reinforced by HMS *Illustrious*, a new and larger fleet carrier.

It was against this background that Cunningham had to devise a viable strategy that would in the end knock Italy out of the war. As he saw it, such a strategy involved the continued supply of weapons, ammunition, oil and food to Malta so that the island could continue to defend itself; the perpetual harrying of the Italian supply routes from the mainland to her armies in

North Africa; and the denial of the central and eastern Mediterranean to the Italian battlefleet. Similar tasks in the western Mediterranean, beyond Cunningham's reach, were left to a powerful squadron known as Force H, based on Gibraltar. On paper it appeared a superhuman task, but the Italians played into Cunningham's hands by their reluctance to venture their larger warships in battle. The first sign of this Italian reluctance to engage was at the action off Calabria on 9 July 1940 when a powerful Italian squadron turned away behind smoke rather than face the fire of Cunningham's elderly ships, even though they considerably outnumbered the British force in cruisers and destroyers.

The Fleet Air Arm attack on Taranto followed quickly, a typical example of Cunningham's determination to retain his freedom of naval movement in the central Mediterranean, in which of course the needs of Malta played an important part. As he developed his Mediterranean strategy, Cunningham never took his eyes off Malta, which to him was always the lynch-pin of the war against Italy, and the attack on Taranto was a vital move in his overall strategic concept. Its success in putting out of action half of Italy's battleship strength for a long period made easier the continuing naval burden of keeping Malta in the battle with supplies for all her needs.

As the Mediterranean war spread, so the essential task grew. The Italian ultimatum to Greece on 28 October 1940 involved the fleet in the occupation of Crete, with the development of Suda Bay as a forward base, and the convoying of troops and supplies to Greece. It was in this convoy requirement that Cunningham was able to deal another blow at the Italian fleet off Cape Matapan, a stunning night action in which three 10,000-ton Italian cruisers and two destroyers were sunk. Cunningham's handling of the air element of the fleet was both masterly and extremely effective in the run-up to the action, and though the big prize, the battleship *Vittorio Veneto*, escaped, there could be no denying that Cunningham, with his fleet inferior in numbers and age to the Italian, still held the whip hand in the Eastern Mediterranean. His boldness in attack had paid immense material and moral dividends, and success had followed success in an almost inevitable sequence.

It is perhaps easy for a leader to command success when he has achieved so great a moral ascendancy over his enemy as had Cunningham in the first nine months of the Mediterranean war, but it is perhaps in adversity that the true greatness of a leader emerges. The lack of success of Italian armies in North Africa and Greece brought German armies and air forces into both Greece and North Africa, and Cunningham, already dangerously stretched following the aid to Greece, found his fleet dwindling almost daily. German dive-bombers based in Sicily made the running of supplies to Malta a particularly hazardous affair, the passage of every convoy cost him heavily in merchant ships and escorts sunk or severely damaged. The evacuation of British forces from Greece when that country was overrun by the German army was even more costly in ships, and the subsequent evacuation of Crete after a successful German airborne attack reduced the Mediterranean Fleet to a dangerous imbalance by the great loss of destroyers.

Yet Cunningham was as indomitable in defeat as he had been in victory. When he heard that there were still soldiers in Crete waiting to be taken off after the evacuation had officially ended, he called on his remaining destroyers to make one last effort. Though the crews were tired almost beyond endurance after four days and nights of heavy fighting, they cheerfully responded to his call. He sent a signal to them, 'Stick it out, we must never let the Army down', and it was reported by his staff that he remarked that although it took the navy three years to build a new ship it would take three hundred years to build a new tradition.

The cost of Crete to the Mediterranean Fleet was two thousand officers and seamen killed, with five times that number wounded. Including ships which had to leave the Mediterranean for major repairs, the fleet lost two of its four battleships, its only aircraft carrier, five cruisers and eight destroyers. With what was left Cunningham still had to face the overriding need of keeping Malta supplied, and added to this was the nightly replenishment by sea of the fortress of Tobruk, cut off by the Axis armies from all access by land. Somehow these essential tasks were done; somehow the battered fleet answered all the calls that Cunningham made upon it. It was a triumph of inspired leadership, a result of the affection in which this indomitable admiral was held by all whom he commanded.

In March 1942 Cunningham was told by the First Sea Lord that he was to become his representative on the Combined Chiefs of Staff Committee in Washington. It was ordered that his departure from the Mediterranean was to be kept secret for as long as possible so that the enemy should not know that he had left the station, a compliment to the skill with which he had led the fleet for just short of three years. He arrived in Washington at the end of June.

All staff work irked Cunningham, and he was no more happy in Washington than he had been in London when he was Deputy Chief of Naval Staff. He found Admiral King, the US Chief of Naval Operations, a difficult man to get close to and lacking flexibility when any questions of joint Anglo-American operations were discussed. Cunningham, who throughout his more senior appointments had been admirably served by his staffs, fretted when he himself was tied to a desk. It came as a great relief to him when, three months after arriving in Washington, he was selected as naval Commander-in-Chief for Operation Torch, the landings in North Africa, with General Eisenhower as Supreme Commander.

Three months after the Torch landings, Cunningham added the post of Commander-in-Chief, Mediterranean, to that he already held as naval Commander-in-Chief of the expeditionary force for Torch. By then the British Eighth Army, advancing westward along the North African coast after their victory at El Alamein, and the Anglo-American armies, moving eastward from their Torch landings, had both reached Tunisia. It was time that the naval forces, from the eastern and western Mediterranean, both of which had the same task of destroying all Axis seaborne communications from the European mainland to Tunisia, came under a single naval command. Cunningham was on the spot and was already deeply engaged in the planning of operations that were to follow the clearance of the whole North African coast. There could be no other choice. With his appointment as Commander-in-Chief came promotion to admiral of the fleet.

The greatest dividends accruing to the Mediterranean Fleet from the occupation of the whole length of the North African coast were the complete removal of any threat to the re-supply of Malta and continuous fighter cover for the fleet in all its operations. Malta, denied to Cunningham as his main fleet base since the entry of Italy into the war, once more became available, and its central position in the Mediterranean brought Cunningham the key he needed for the total defeat of Italy's navy.

It was from his headquarters at Malta that most of the detailed planning and control of the amphibious assault on Sicily and, after the conquest of that island, on the Italian mainland across the Straits of Messina and at Salerno, were carried through. Cunningham's close knowledge of the sea conditions likely to be met on the southern Sicilian beaches, and his anxiety to minimise as far as possible the hazards to assault craft and their troops committed to a landing on those beaches, made him protest vigorously against proposed army amendments to the overall plan which, in his view, took too little account of the naval problems of landing across open and defended beaches. A compromise solution was found which removed some of the expected dangers. In the event the assault went in during a short period of rough, north-westerly weather and some of the assault craft broached-to in the choppy seas off the beaches. It was typical of Cunningham that eight hours after the first landings he was off the Sicilian beaches in a destroyer to see for himself how the naval assault craft and the troops they carried had fared.

The assault landings on the coast of Calabria opposite Messina and farther up the mainland at Salerno followed quickly after the capture of Sicily. In the combined, and naval, planning for these operations Cunningham again had to play a major part, and the unqualified success of both assaults was a tribute to the meticulous care with which the plans were evolved. These three operations – Sicily, Calabria and Salerno – represented by far the largest amphibious operations yet carried out by British forces since Gallipoli in 1915, and were the greatest and most detailed in which Cunningham was involved throughout the whole period of his Mediterranean command. Their success set the crown on his strategic concept of his Mediterranean campaign, and his final reward came when it was to Malta that the Italian fleet, when it surrendered, was led by HMS *Warspite*, Cunningham's flagship at the start of the war.

The date was 10 September 1943, and the naval campaign that had resulted in this remarkable victory had lasted just three years and three months. It was almost entirely Cunningham's campaign, carried through and stimulated by his decision to carry the war to the enemy on every possible occasion and by his fortitude and unquenchable optimism during the days of adversity. To the officers and men of his fleet, he was a towering figure throughout.

While Cunningham had been arranging the details of the Italian naval surrender in the Mediterranean, the Combined Chiefs of Staff, with President Roosevelt and Mr Churchill, were in conference at Quebec. It was at that meeting that the First Sea Lord, Sir Dudley Pound, was struck down by the illness to which he was to succumb seven weeks later. Cunningham knew well that he would be personally involved, and as the news of Pound's illness became progressively worse, his appointment as Pound's successor became more certain. It was on 5 October that the appointment was published.

Cunningham's only previous Admiralty service had been for some eight months in 1938–9 when he had been Deputy Chief of Naval Staff. It had not been a happy period, and he had welcomed his subsequent sea appointment with considerable relief. He did not like staff work and mistrusted his ability to hold his own with his fellow Chiefs of Staff and with politicians. But by the time he took over as Chief of Naval Staff the war at sea in the Atlantic had been won, and convoys were regularly crossing the Atlantic virtually without hindrance from German U-boats. Although there were still the inevitable ups and downs of naval actions at sea, the broad base of final victory had been established and Cunningham had little more to do than to keep the well-oiled machinery running smoothly.

Planning for the assault on north-west Europe was already under way when Cunningham took over, and beyond making decisions about the various naval force commanders and putting as much pressure as was possible on the construction of landing craft, there was little for him to do. But the great problem that exercised him was the future role of the Royal Navy after the war in Europe had been won. He was anxious that it should be used to the full in the Pacific, but met some opposition from the Prime Minister and very considerable opposition from the US Navy in the shape of Admiral King. After some months of argument, the Prime Minister was won over to Cunningham's views, but Admiral King refused to be convinced. It took a direct order from President Roosevelt to get him to agree to a British Pacific Fleet operating alongside the US Navy in the Pacific, and to the end he remained unconvinced of its value in those waters. In the event the British Pacific Fleet, built up and maintained at sea with a great amount of effort, did little more than operate on the sidelines of the main Pacific actions.

Cunningham has been criticised since the war for his insistence on this costly gesture. There was still much work for the Royal Navy to do in European waters after the collapse in Germany, both in policing the disarmament of the remaining German naval units and in such areas as port and mine clearance and the reopening of the European seaborne trade routes. Yet the Pacific venture was typical Cunningham. He was never the man, when there was fighting still to be done, to allow any ships that could be used actively against an enemy to remain unused. It is possible that, during the early stages of the campaign for a share in the Pacific war, the Admiralty did not fully appreciate the new conception of naval war that had evolved in that theatre, with fleets operating for weeks at a time some thousand of miles from their main bases. The Americans had solved this problem with a huge and intricate organisation of replenishment at sea and, on purely administrative and supply grounds, had no wish to see a British fleet dependent for its sustenance on the American organisation. As a result a vast British fleet train of tankers, fresh-water carriers, ammunition ships, victualling ships, auxiliary aircraft carriers to carry spare aircraft to replace losses, and supply ships of every description, had to be built up from scratch to support the British fleet at sea for the periods required for meaningful operations in distant waters on the American scale. It was a vast naval investment in a venture that had few dividends to offer.

In the meantime the assault landings in Normandy had been successful and all could now see that the final stages of the war in Europe were being played out. Cunningham's task in this great and victorious campaign was to keep the remnants of the German navy from interfering with the momentum of advance, and of opening the northern European ports for military supplies as they were captured. The German 'small battle units' – midget submarines, explosive motorboats, etc – proved less of a menace than had been feared, but port clearance developed into a formidable naval task. There was still much vicious naval fighting, particularly in the clearance of Antwerp, but Cunningham had too firm a naval hand on these waters for there to be any room for doubt as to the final outcome.

With the ending of the war, Cunningham had to face what was possibly his greatest task. This was to determine the shape and strength of the postwar navy, particularly with reference to the ships still under construction which had been ordered under the war building programmes. Though Cunningham played an active part in the endless discussions in the Chiefs of Staff Committee which centred round this problem, he had little heart in them. He had spent just on fifty years in the navy, and he was seeing his world coming to an end. His relief as First Sea Lord was appointed on 1 March 1946 and at the beginning of June Cunningham left the Admiralty for good. He was glad to go.

Cunningham was an admiral of the 'old' navy, in which, speaking very broadly, the ships were platforms for their guns. He never specialised in any particular branch and never really appreciated the technical developments that the Second World War brought in its train. Right to the end of his career his standard of excellence in a warship was the number of guns or torpedoes she carried on the smallest possible tonnage. This no doubt was a legacy of his long service in, and love of, destroyers. A sentence in his autobiography, *A Sailor's Odyssey*, recording a passage in a destroyer in 1946, is perhaps typical of his outlook.

> I crossed from Liverpool in the new Battle-class destroyer *Solebay*, a fine enough ship which seemed to carry every mortal weapon and gadget except guns. I noted at the time that 'these "Battles" fulfil my worst expectations. An erection like the Castle Rock, Edinburgh, on the bridge. They call it a director, and all to control four guns firing a total broadside of about 200 lbs. We must get back to destroyers of reasonable size and well-gunned.'

Cunningham was blessed with good fortune throughout his career. It started when he obtained command of his own ship as a junior lieutenant. The First World War came at the right time for him and carried him safely over the two selective promotion hurdles to make certain of his reaching flag rank. The successive illnesses of Sir Geoffrey Blake and Sir Roger Backhouse were indeed responsible for his ultimate appointment as Commander-in-Chief, Mediterranean, shortly before the outbreak of the Second World War, and in the conditions of that war there was no one in the navy better qualified to hold that important post. He was extremely well served by an excellent staff, who took much of the burden off him, and he was wise enough to use a staff as it should be used.

In his role as Commander-in-Chief he was the entire fighting admiral, decisive, firm in his tenacity to hold the essential strategical requirements of the situation, generous to all young captains who tried their best even when they failed to achieve success, and utterly loyal to all under his command. He would never tolerate 'yes-men', or excuse failures in courage or seamanship, but to all the rest he brought an inspired leadership which carried the Mediterranean Fleet triumphantly through the months of adversity after the fall of Crete. During these black months he was probably the paramount figure in the Royal Navy, a tower of strength whose influence spread well beyond the limits of his own particular command. His service in destroyers had early brought him into a closer understanding of the men of the lower deck than is possible in larger ships, an understanding that he never lost throughout his long career. It was that, as much as all his other military qualities, that brought him to the top of the tree.

Cunningham retired in 1946, full of honours. He was twice Lord High Commissioner to the General Assembly of the Church of Scotland, in 1950 and 1952. He lived quietly at his house at Bishop's Waltham, close enough to Portsmouth to retain contact with the navy he had always deeply loved. He died in 1963 at the age of eighty.

GRAND ADMIRAL KARL DOENITZ

Lieutenant-Commander Peter Kemp

Karl Doenitz was born in 1891, son of an old-established and worthy Prussian family. There was no family tradition of naval service, and Doenitz himself was attracted to the navy only by reason of the technical education and training that would become available to him by service in its ranks. At the age of nineteen he therefore joined the Imperial German Navy, and at the outbreak of the First World War four years later was serving as a junior lieutenant in the light cruiser *Breslau*. As such he was involved in one of the very first naval episodes of that war, the escape of the *Goeben* and *Breslau* from the clutches of the British Mediterranean Fleet and their subsequent arrival at Constantinople and nominal sale to the Turks. This inglorious demonstration of British sea power, which resulted in the Commander-in-Chief being put on half-pay for the remainder of the war and the court-martial of a cruiser admiral, gave Doenitz a loss of belief in the vaunted invincibility of the Royal Navy and a belief in the German navy's (and incidentally his own) superiority in skill and tactics over the greatest naval power in the world.

For two years, though the ships were nominally Turkish, Doenitz remained in the *Breslau*, engaged in occasional tip-and-run operations in the Black Sea. Fear of the Russian Black Sea Fleet kept the two German ships within easy retiring range of the Bosphorus, and Doenitz learned what it was like to serve in a squadron whose range of operations was limited by the need to preserve an easy and accessible retreat whenever an enemy ship appeared over the horizon.

In 1916 he returned to Germany and was transferred to the submarine service. After his initial training he was appointed to *U 39* as a watchkeeping lieutenant and in 1918 was given command of *UB 68*, one of the German U-boats in the Mediterranean, based in the Adriatic at the Austrian port of Pola. There he came in contact with *Kapitanleutnant* Steinbauer, one of the more adventurous of the U-boat commanders of the First World War, and it was probably from him that he imbibed the theory of the night attack on the surface, relying on the small silhouette of a submarine's conning-tower to slip through screening destroyers unseen under cover of darkness. Certainly he and Steinbauer agreed to rendezvous at sea on one of the Allied convoy routes and try to prove their theory. Steinbauer failed to arrive at the rendez-vous and Doenitz was left on his own to test out the new idea. By good fortune a convoy duly obliged by arriving in the vicinity and Doenitz found no difficulty in penetrating the destroyer screen, reaching the merchant ships unobserved. He sank one ship with a torpedo, but later, when diving, lost control of the submarine and had to blow the main ballast tanks to prevent the boat going too deep and becoming crushed by the pressure. *UB 68* sur-faced in the middle of the convoy and Doenitz abandoned ship. He was picked up by a destroyer and spent the next ten months in a prisoner-of-war camp in Yorkshire.

It was unquestionably this single convoy action that turned Doenitz's thoughts towards new tactics designed to combat the long historical success of the convoy principle in defence of trade at sea. Though himself no naval historian, and probably unaware of the centuries of naval experience in which convoy had always seen seaborne trade safely through against even the greatest of privateering attacks, it was obvious enough to him, and indeed to every German naval officer, that the British adoption of convoy in 1917 had snatched from the U-boats a campaign which they had been winning. The traditional submarine attack, delivered in daylight with the submarine sub-merged, no longer had any validity against ships escorted in convoy. Did the answer, then, lie in *UB 68*'s experience in the Mediterranean?

It was to be sixteen years before Docnitz was able to test out his new theories in submarine tactics. He returned to Germany from his English prisoner-of-war camp in 1919 and was asked, and agreed, to serve on in the German navy. But it was a navy that, under the terms of the Versailles Treaty, was not permitted to include submarines among its ships. During the years of the Weimar Republic orders had indeed been placed for the surrepti-tious building of U-boats in foreign dockyards, particularly those of Spain, Holland and Finland, and to a small extent Doenitz was able to keep in touch with submarine development by reason of these orders. But his service in the navy was mainly with destroyers and cruisers, and by 1934–5 he had reached the rank of captain and commanded the cruiser *Emden*.

When Hitler seized power from the tottering Weimar Republic in 1933, the prospect of a considerable naval rearmament grew appreciably brighter. Erich Raeder, Commander-in-Chief Navy, met Hitler for the first time within days of the *coup d'état* and was won over by promises that the navy would have a fair share of the priorities when it came to rebuilding the armed forces. By a mixture of deference and flattery, Hitler assured himself of Raeder's loyalty, retaining his regard by approving the ambitious 'Z' plan of naval building that would give Germany a powerful and balanced fleet by 1944 and one strong enough to challenge Britain by 1948. Though Raeder's loyalty to Hitler was never in doubt, it was different so far as the Nazi Party was concerned. He was never himself a party member and maintained a strict order that no naval personnel were to take part in politics. He loathed and distrusted Goering and his relationship with other party leaders was aloof and cautious.

Doenitz was quite the reverse. Though not a party member because of Raeder's ban, he was an ardent believer in the Nazi faith and a fanatical supporter of Hitler. He was too young and junior in the early days to cut much ice with the party, but as he rose in rank and importance after the outbreak of war, he cultivated the party leaders and was on terms of friendship with most of them, and even with Goering, always a strong anti-navy man, whom he recognised as the most powerful man in Hitler's immediate entourage. When he succeeded Raeder as Commander-in-Chief at the beginning of 1943, he relaxed the order under which naval personnel were forbidden to take any part in politics. Raeder called him 'Hitler-Youth Doenitz'.

From the moment of seizing power, Hitler's eyes were turned towards the domination of Europe. His basic plan, in outline, was to deal first with continental Europe and then with Britain and her empire, although it was acknowledged throughout the party that Britain was always the principal enemy. From this philosophy arose the negotiations for a naval agreement with Britain, proposing the building of a German navy up to 35 per cent in tonnage of that of Britain, with 45 per cent in the case of U-boats, a figure that in certain circumstances could be, and eventually was, raised to 100 per cent. The underlying idea was that Britain, essentially a rharitime power, would be satisfied with this degree of naval superiority and thus likely to remain quiescent in the case of German adventures in Europe. The Anglo-German naval agreement was signed in London in 1935.

The building of U-boats in Germany had, in fact, begun before the signing of the naval agreement with Britain, and the ink was hardly dry before the first operational flotilla was in existence. In command of it was Captain Doenitz, later appointed Senior Officer Submarines, a post in which responsibility for all aspects of submarine development, policy, and training was placed on his shoulders. This gave him the chance to develop his theories and to plan and carry out exercises in which they were put to the test.

Doenitz's submarine philosophy was based on two precepts. The first of them was that the submarine's prey was the merchant ship pure and simple. It was for him the be-all and end-all of submarine warfare; the sinking of an enemy warship was no more than an added dividend to the profit and loss account of merchant ships sunk per U-boat on patrol. The war against trade was to be prosecuted with complete ruthlessness and disregard for the loss of civilian lives. The doctrine of the Hague Convention, by which merchant ships were to be stopped and searched, and provision made for the safety of the crew before being sunk, was anathema to Doenitz. He spent much time going through the small print of the Convention in search of loopholes through which his U-boats could sink merchant ships without warning. It was typical of him that he could put forward the proposition that a merchant vessel making an SSS signal in wartime, which meant 'Am being attacked by a submarine', was acting as a naval intelligence source and was thus not protected by the rules of the Hague Convention.

His second precept was that a submarine was basically a surface vessel capable of submerging, and thus should fight as a surface vessel. In terms of a war directed against an enemy's trade, as represented by her merchant ships, this was a brilliant conception, completely reversing the generally accepted view that a submarine's role in war was to lie submerged during daylight and sink by submerged torpedo fire such targets as came within her range. Doenitz counted on the surface attack at night to bring him his dividends, realising that the tiny silhouette of a submarine's conning-tower was almost invisible at night and that the surface speed of a submarine almost invariably exceeded that of a merchant ship. These two factors were enough, in a war directed against trade, to load the odds in a submarine's favour, by combining virtual invisibility with the tactical ability to reach the optimum firing position irrespective of the relative positions of submarine and target when the first contact was made.

He lost no time in devising exercises in the Baltic which would show whether or not his theories were correct. A master of detail in the training of submarine crews, he put his men through a rigid and demanding groundwork that gave them, both officers and lower deck, a supreme confidence in the design of their submarines and in their capacity to handle them in all conditions of weather. From that stage he tested out their skills in night surface attacks using the rest of the German fleet to play the part of an escorted convoy. Their ease of penetration through a destroyer screen to within a range of 600 yards of their target without being sighted confirmed that he was on the right lines.

His next development of the night surface attack theory was to use a pack of U-boats against a convoy. His idea was to spread a line of U-boats across the probable path of a convoy, with the U-boat that actually sighted it shadowing it on the surface until the rest of the line could be called in. Once assembled, the whole of the pack was then ordered to make its way ahead of the convoy to be in a position to attack during the following night.

The control of such a tactical manoeuvre created immense problems, principally as to whether the most efficient direction should come from a command submarine at sea or from a shorebased headquarters. Doenitz tried out both methods, discovering that he could exercise a greater degree of planning and control from a headquarters ashore equipped with a sophisticated communications network. He was quick to realise the one obvious drawback of such a system of control – that a large volume of signals from his U-boats at sea would give an enemy's direction-finding system considerable scope for plotting U-boat positions. This was a risk he was prepared to accept, both in the interest of the more efficient control obtained from a shore headquarters and from his belief that no efficient system of high-frequency direction-finding had been evolved in Britain.

For the next three years, 1936–9, he built up the German U-boat arm on lines designed to provide him with a force that would operate in wartime in accordance with his theories. Apart from frequent fleet exercises in which his doctrine of the wolf-pack attack on the surface at night was brought to a remarkably high degree of efficiency, he concentrated his thoughts on the most efficient design of U-boat for this particular purpose. His general requirement for such a type of warfare was the smallest practicable U-boat, because of the 'invisibility' aspect, and the greatest practicable endurance in terms of fuel stowage, because of the requirement that they would need to operate, in any war against Britain, at vast distances from their home ports. His engineers discovered that, by a small increase of 17 tons in displacement of the standard 500-ton U-boat, the endurance could be increased from 6,200 miles to 8,850 miles by the incorporation of additional fuel tanks. This was the Type VIIC boat, built in large numbers. For more distant operations the 740-ton U-boat, with an endurance of 13,450 miles, was designed. This was the Type IX boat, and they were built in the ratio of one Type IX to three Type VIIC. And finally, for the really far-distant operational areas, such as South African waters and the Indian Ocean, large tanker U-boats from which operational boats could refuel at sea, were designed. These were the Type XIV boats, with a surface displacement of 1,688 tons, and known to the U-boat captains as 'milch cows'. These however did not begin to come forward in appreciable numbers until the end of 1940 or the beginning of 1941.

It was during these four years, when he was responsible for the whole development of the U-boat arm, both in *matériel* and doctrine, that the foundation of his future brilliant career was established. So far as the U-boat was concerned, Doenitz was a completely dedicated man, selecting and training his crews himself and instilling in them a firm belief in his revolutionary ideas of submarine warfare. Although not himself a widely 'approachable' man, he took pains to meet his submarine captains on every available occasion, and more often than not when a U-boat returned to harbour after exercises Doenitz would be waiting on the quay as it secured alongside to greet captain and crew. It was in this way that he became revered by his U-boat commanders and crews, who looked upon him almost as a father figure.

During these years he was fortunate in two respects. The first was that he remained in his appointment throughout the whole period of four years and was not, as was the case in most other navies, shifted to a new appointment after two and a half years or so. This worked two ways, giving him a continuity in his command in which he had plenty of time to develop and perfect his tactical theories, and at the same time gave to his commanding officers a feeling of security in the knowledge that the command would not be changed and that they would not have to readapt to the philosophy of a new leader.

In the second case the naval high command in Berlin was only too ready to recognise in Doenitz the expert on submarine warfare and broadly to accept all his requirements without question. Doenitz, it must be remembered, was still a relatively junior officer during these years and it was fortunate for him that in Raeder, Commander-in-Chief Navy, he had a superior who was prepared to give him his head in all aspects of submarine warfare.

Doenitz was not only a dedicated man so far as submarines were concerned, he was also completely singleminded in respect of the enemy against whom he was training his U-boats in his new tactical doctrine. Almost alone in Germany during these years of 1935-9, he believed that Britain would be the enemy when war came, and every aspect of his training methods was directed to this end, even to the extent of asking for training exercises to be carried out in the Atlantic instead of in the Baltic or North Sea. Raeder firmly believed that Hitler could deliver the goods when he promised that there would be no war against Britain before 1945, and in fact laid down his schedules for the rebuilding of a balanced fleet, known as the 'Z' plan, geared to this date. In spite of his fanatical devotion to Hitler this was perhaps the one case where Doenitz differed from his Führer, though he was much too canny to say so. There may well have been some wishful thinking in Doenitz's firm belief, for he was far from being an Anglophile and was only too eager and ready to get something of his own back after the 1914-18 defeat. But be that as it may, at least he was proved correct in the event and was the only important German naval officer to be so.

The showdown, which proved Doenitz right in his assessment, was the abrogation on the part of Germany of the Anglo-German naval agreement on 26 April 1939. This action served notice on Britain that the rapidly growing tension between the two countries, engendered by the German occupation of Czechoslovakia and the consequent British guarantee to Poland, provided not only grounds for war but also realisation that German naval rearmament was now moving into top gear. Under Raeder's 'Z' plan, the strength of the U-boat arm had been fixed at 233 boats by 1948, but the abrogation of the naval agreement was clear enough evidence to Doenitz that Germany would no longer have until 1948 to build up her balanced fleet. He pressed hard for the German shipbuilding industry to be ordered to concentrate its resources on a rapid U-boat building programme to the virtual exclusion of all other types of warship, but the best he could achieve was a decision by Raeder that priority of construction was to be concentrated on battleships and U-boats. In any case it was by now far too late to expect the industry to produce large numbers of U-boats in time for the war that was so obviously only just around the corner.

When Britain declared war on Germany on 3 September 1939, Doenitz had no more than fifty-seven U-boats, of which forty-six were operational. Of these, only twenty-two were Type VII boats suitable for Atlantic operations. Allowing the usual ratios of one-third of a total submarine force on patrol in their war areas, one-third on passage to and from their patrol areas, and one-third in harbour for rest and refit, Doenitz found himself with no more than seven U-boats available for operations in the Atlantic. This was obviously far too few for efficient wolf-pack tactics, though it did not preclude the night surface attack against merchant ships when they were intercepted. It was not until October 1940 that Doenitz at last had sufficient U-boats to put his wolf-pack theories into operation in dead earnest. They proved devastatingly effective, and during this month his U-boats accounted for sixty-three merchant ships of a total tonnage of 352,407 tons.

The mechanics of the pack attack were fairly complicated and required minute and intensive control from Doenitz's headquarters ashore. It was not difficult to learn, with some exactitude, the date and times of departure, and the number of ships involved, in the convoys leaving Canada for Britain. Normal intelligence services gave him this information. The individual boats in a wolf-pack were then spread on a line at right angles to the estimated course of the convoy at about 25 to 30 miles apart, depending on the visibility, in the hope that one of the boats would sight the convoy. When it did so, it sent a sighting report on the high-frequency U-boat wavelength back to Doenitz and continued to shadow the convoy, remaining on the surface but at maximum visibility range where it was unlikely to be sighted by the convoy escorts. While shadowing, the U-boat continued to report to Doenitz any alterations of course or speed made by the convoy, together with the weather conditions and any other relevant information.

As soon as the first sighting report was received at U-boat headquarters, signals were sent on the same U-boat wavelength to the other boats forming the wolf-pack, directing them to close the U-boat that had made the original sighting report. Even their proper closing courses were worked out by headquarters and signalled to each individual boat. As they approached the convoy, the shadowing U-boat would home the approaching boats in on medium wave until all had made contact.

All U-boats in a wolf-pack had strict orders not to attack the convoy until the whole pack had arrived. They then took up a position ahead of the convoy estimated to coincide with the convoy's arrival at that position after dark, and attacked throughout the night. The method of attack was to rely on their virtual invisibility to get within the screening escort vessels and then right among the merchant ships, closing to a range of about 600 yards before firing their torpedoes. At such a range they could hardly miss. As soon as it began to get light in the morning the U-boats broke off their attacks and, at maximum speed, proceeded on the surface on the same course as the convoy, relying on their superior speed to draw ahead. On the approach of darkness they turned and bore down on the convoy again for the next night's attack. And so on, night after night, until all the U-boats had used up all their torpedoes.

Doenitz remained in close control throughout the whole of the operation, a stream of signals from his headquarters directing every movement of every individual U-boat except during the actual night attacks, when each U-boat captain used his own skill and initiative to get within range and to sink as many merchant ships as possible. It was U-boat headquarters who decided when the first attack was to be made and when the pack was finally to be drawn off, the courses to be steered during daylight to overtake the convoy and reach a position for the next night attack, which U-boat was to shadow and report, and so on.

As Doenitz had foreseen, there was no British defence to this form of attack. Between the two wars the Royal Navy had developed the Asdic, a device that could locate a submerged submarine by means of a supersonic beam reflected from the submarine's hull. Great, and as it turned out unjustified, reliance was placed on the Asdic to defeat any U-boat campaign such as had occurred during the 1914–18 war, and it was in a spirit of some complacency (so far as the question of defence of trade was concerned), that the British Admiralty entered the war in 1939. But Asdic was valueless against any vessel on the surface, and so the Atlantic battle, in its early days, developed almost entirely into one of human eyesight as to who could see the other first, the U-boat captain looking for a convoy or a watchkeeper in an escort vessel looking for a U-boat. In a contest such as this the dice were loaded heavily in favour of the U-boat. As yet radar, which was later to play a significant part in the battle, was metaphorically speaking well over the horizon so far as escort vessels were concerned, and air patrol and escort was limited to the range of existing aircraft, a matter of 200 miles or so from the nearest shore airfields.

This was the situation that Doenitz exploited with consummate skill and unrivalled determination. No trouble in its execution was too great for him, and even the smallest details of the campaign were, by his instructions, brought to him for decision. He had his trials and setbacks, as for example the faulty design of the torpedoes, which had a tendency to run too deep and thus pass underneath the ships they were supposed to hit. There was faulty design, too, in the pistols with which the torpedoes were armed, both magnetic and contact, resulting in premature explosions or failure to detonate. He ferreted out the causes of these failures, had them rectified, and brought the designers and the Inspectorate of Torpedoes, the body responsible for testing the designs, before a court-martial.

If he had his setbacks in the campaign, he had his strokes of good fortune also. By far the most important of these was the vulnerability of the British naval codes, in one of which all signals to convoys and their escorts were made. During the Abyssinian crisis of 1935–6, a great volume of signals had been made in the administrative naval code from the Mediterranean and the Red Sea, and as a result it had been partially reconstituted in Germany. This gave a useful insight into the operational code, so that it, too, was partially reconstituted. Although there were occasional changes of codes during the first four years of the war, the German *B-Dienst*, the branch of their naval intelligence department which dealt with cryptography, steadily penetrated them and was able to pass to Doenitz a great deal of accurate information about the movements of convoys at sea. In addition, from early 1942 until June 1943, the *B-Dienst* presented Doenitz with the daily signal from the British Admiralty giving convoy positions and the Admiralty's assessment of all U-boat dispositions. With this information at his command, Doenitz not only knew the convoy movements but was able also to safeguard some of his U-boats by withdrawing them from positions which the British Admiralty had estimated with too dangerous a degree of accuracy.

In his overall direction of the main U-boat assault on British seaborne trade, Doenitz yet found time to plan and direct such other individual actions as promised a worthwhile dividend. The best remembered of these is *U 47*'s penetration of Scapa Flow on the night of 13–14 October 1939 and her successful attack on HMS *Royal Oak*. This was planned entirely by Doenitz, who had studied the chart of Scapa Flow and detected a narrow gap between two of the blockships through which a U-boat might squeeze. Knowing his commanding officers intimately, he selected *Kapitan-Leutnant* Prien for the job, and could not have made a better choice. The success of this operation brought him a personal reward in the shape of promotion from commodore to full admiral and, a year or two later, direct access to Hitler, whom he was able to infect with his own doctrine that it was only through U-boat operations that the defeat of Britain could be achieved.

In November 1942 Admiral Sir Max Horton was appointed to succeed Admiral Sir Percy Noble as Commander-in-Chief, Western Approaches, and as such responsible for the conduct of the war against U-boats. Where Admiral Noble had been hampered in his command by the chronic shortage of escort vessels and the need often to throw them into the battle before they could be fully trained in all the intricacies of anti-submarine warfare, Admiral Horton's arrival in the hot seat at Liverpool corresponded with the gradual delivery of the anti-submarine frigates ordered under the accelerated wartime building programmes. The initial trickle grew gradually into a good-sized stream, which for the first time since the start of the war allowed escort groups to be built up and adequately trained for the great battle of the oceans.

Horton, as of course also Doenitz, realised the overriding importance of morale in the Atlantic battle. Just as did Doenitz, so Horton insisted on a very high degree of skill and devotion in his headquarters organisation so that the captains of escort vessels and of aircraft could have complete confidence in all its operations. Just as Doenitz took pains to be on the quayside when his U-boats came in from their patrols at sea, so Horton went personally to sea in the small escort vessels and flew in the aircraft which kept watch above the convoys. Both had been active submariners during the First World War. It was now to be a battle of wits between the two, and Doenitz was already beginning to see the writing on the wall.

He had had his first inkling of it in February 1942 when U-boat losses began to rise alarmingly. The cause of the losses was the introduction of 1½-metre radar in both surface and air escorts. U-boats on passage across the Bay of Biscay found themselves being attacked from the air by aircraft diving suddenly out of clouds or down sun. U-boats attacking a convoy at night were surprised by an escort vessel approaching at full speed, until then not seen by the U-boat captain. Doenitz and his technical experts were quick to recognise the cause as a new type of radar installation of much longer range and considerably greater accuracy than any used in the Atlantic so far, but it took until August to provide the cure. This took the form of the Fu MB, a search receiver that told the U-boat when it had been located by radar, often in time for it to submerge and escape destruction.

But for Doenitz the net was closing in. What he had feared from the introduction of the 1½-metre radar in February 1942 became a reality in February 1943 when the first 10-centimetre radar sets were used in the Atlantic. The Fu MB was unable to register the pulses of this new radar, and sudden surprise attacks again became the order of the day. And it was at this juncture, perhaps in despair at the failure of the Fu MB, that he made his biggest tactical mistake of the war. He ordered all U-boats crossing the Bay of Biscay, whether inwards or outwards, to stay on the surface and fight it out with the aircraft with their anti-aircraft guns. It was a disastrous order which resulted in many losses. The toll in February was nineteen; in March, fifteen; in April, sixteen; and in May, a staggering thirty-seven. These were losses on a scale that spelled disaster. And it was not only the 10-centimetre radar that was responsible; more powerful depthcharges dropped in a wider pattern, and particularly the ahead-firing mortars, first 'Hedgehog' and then 'Squid', played a significant part in the total.

In May 1942 Hitler asked for Doenitz to be present at the regular Führer conferences held to discuss the overall war situation so that he could report personally on the progress of the U-boat war. Doenitz grasped with both hands this opportunity to push himself forward in Hitler's notice, oozing a confidence in ultimate victory that became music in Hitler's ears after the more realistic assessments of Raeder. It was enough to ensure him preference over the better qualified Admiral Carls as Raeder's successor as Commander-in-Chief Navy when the change came in January 1943.

Raeder had sent in his resignation following a demand from Hitler, which incidentally Goering had stirred up, that all major warships were to be scrapped, their guns mounted as fixed batteries ashore, and their crews used to swell the U-boat fleet or to be drafted into the army. This demand from Hitler arose through the débâcle in the Arctic when the pocket battleship *Lützow* and the heavy cruiser *Hipper* had been prevented from attacking a convoy to Russia by the spirited defence of four British destroyers, aided later by two British cruisers. Doenitz, on his selection as Raeder's successor, had at first agreed with Hitler's order, though a few weeks later, after he had explained the realities of naval warfare, he had to return and plead for the retention of the big ships.

Brilliant as had been his direction of the U-boat campaign, Doenitz was out of his depth as Commander-in-Chief. This became quickly apparent in his handling of the Mediterranean campaign, particularly during the evacuation of Tunisia and the Allied assault on Sicily. He had a personal belief that the solution of these two problems lay in the organisation of supplies to the embattled armies, and he insisted that German and Italian naval ships, from cruisers downwards and including submarines, should be used for ferrying supplies and not for fighting. Such an incredible misuse of sea power was very largely responsible for the huge surrender of German and Italian soldiers in Tunisia and the comparative ease and safety with which the assaulting British and American divisions were landed over the Sicilian beaches. The Italian navy had been eager enough to fight and oppose the landings, but Doenitz's insistence that their ships should be used for supply purposes effectively tore the heart out the still willing Italian naval officers.

The growth of Allied air power in the Atlantic, and particularly the closing of the gap in mid-Atlantic beyond the range of shore-based aircraft by the use of escort carriers, brought to an end the tactical doctrine of the surface U-boat attack. The gap was closed in May 1943 and Doenitz was forced, for the first time in the war except for the short Norwegian campaign in 1940, to withdraw all his U-boats from the north Atlantic. He must have known then that the war at sea was lost, that the whole basis of his strategy to defeat Britain at sea had collapsed. For two more years he beguiled Hitler with fairy stories of new U-boat developments just around the corner which would swing the balance back into Germany's favour. It may well be that he even talked himself into believing them. But one by one they folded in his hands. The Schnorkel, or breathing tube, by which a submarine could run her diesel engines while still submerged and thus achieve a high underwater speed, was the first modification that was going to do the trick. It was effective to a very limited extent when first introduced, but the tight-knit convoy system deve-loped by the British and Canadian navies beat it. The Walther U-boat, in which high test peroxide was used to drive a turbine, was the next step that was going to revolutionise submarine warfare, but too many teething troubles and defects delayed its appearance almost until the war had ended. And as the sea war closed in on Germany, it was by a crash building pro-gramme of midget submarines that the tide of disaster would be turned. Their losses were stupendous; their successes virtually nil.

Of all the top Nazis who surrounded Hitler as the gates of Germany herself were breached by the Allied armies, only Bormann and Doenitz remained truly loyal to the Führer. On 26 April 1945 Goering attempted to take over the leadership of the Reich, and Hitler, mad and screaming with rage, ordered his immediate capture and execution. Himmler, unaware of the detestation in which he was held by the Allies, had already tried to make a separate peace with the British and Americans and a furious Hitler branded him as a traitor. Goebbels, with his family, committed suicide. Feeling himself surrounded by treachery, and immolated in his Berlin bunker with Bormann and Eva Braun, Hitler rewarded Doenitz's faithfulness by nominating him in his will as his successor.

It had long been Doenitz's ambition to oust Goering as second-in-command of the Reich, and all his meetings with Hitler since his appointment as Commander-in-Chief had had this end in view. Now, with Hitler's suicide, his great ambition was more than realised and he found himself the new Führer. On 1 May he assumed office as Chancellor of the German Reich. He realised that Himmler's abortive attempts to make a separate peace had made any chance of a unilateral armistice with the Western Allies quite impossible, but he still hoped to be able to make some sort of a bargain with them. He believed that the Allied powers would recognise him as the German leader, negotiate with him, and leave him in his exalted position to lead the German nation through the difficult years of national reconstruction. His dream lasted no more than three weeks, and on 22 May he was arrested. With the rest of the Nazi leaders he was tried at Nuremberg as a war criminal and sentenced to ten years' imprisonment. He was released from Spandau in 1956 after serving his sentence and now lives in retirement in a small flat at Aumühle, south of Hamburg.

As Admiral Commanding U-boats Doenitz was, without any doubt, the most brilliant commander of the war. As Commander-in-Chief Navy he was a sorry failure. He had neither the grasp of strategy nor the breadth of vision necessary to survive in the rarified atmosphere of top naval command. He was more a man of cunning than of deep naval thought, and it was this cunning, allied to a degree of tactical brilliance in a new conception of sub-marine warfare, that took him inevitably to the top. There was plenty of deep thought in his revolutionary ideas of overcoming the disabilities of the conventional submarine in its lack of speed when submerged, and he had the skill and enthusiasm to train his submarine commanders to a pitch of excel-lence that ensured the outstanding success of his tactical ideas. So long as there remained gaps in the Allied anti-submarine defence, he and the U-boat service he directed were unbeatable, but once those gaps had been closed, he had no answers to the problems. After May 1943, when the Atlantic air gap had been closed and the new technical weapons had become widely available, he squandered his U-boats in a completely ruthless attempt to swamp the defence by weight of numbers, knowing full well that he was sending most of them to inevitable death. Up to the last moment he refused to acknowledge the defeat that had been staring him in the face for the last two years of the war, and at the end his judgement snapped and he indulged in a series of wildcat schemes that not only had no hope of success but were prodigal in the extreme of human life, the lives of the U-boat men he loved.

Doenitz claimed that the first knowledge he ever had of the Nazi atrocities in the concentration camps was when he saw photographs of Buchenwald in the American army newspaper *Stars and Stripes* after the final surrender in Germany. This is probably true, possibly because he was too wrapped up in the sea war to inquire what had happened to the millions of Jews in Germany who had disappeared. Certainly he, and other German naval leaders, protested to Raeder about the notorious 'Crystal-Nacht' before the war, and Raeder conveyed these protests to Hitler. But Doenitz was throughout his career a man of overweening ambition who would allow nothing to stand in the way of his march to top command. Such things as Jews and concentration camps were completely irrelevant in his approach towards the top of the ladder. There is, perhaps, a touch of sadness in the thought that a man so brilliant in the tactical sphere, the complete submariner in every aspect of submarine warfare, should have failed so signally at the very moment when he grasped in his hand the ultimate fruits of his life work.

Marshal of the Royal Air Force Lord Tedder

Air Chief Marshal Sir Christopher Foxley Norris

Broadcasting some time after the Second World War, a well-known war correspondent had this to say about Tedder:

> In no way did he fit, or seek to fit, the accepted picture of the war-time leader of combat forces. His chosen approach was that of the calculating intellectual, not the forceful militarist (which is scarcely surprising considering his outstanding academic achievements). He was happiest and most successful behind his desk, out-thinking the enemy; perhaps least at his ease and effective when in the company of the men he led and who fought and died under his leadership. Nevertheless it was by the quiet charm of his personality and the witty advocacy of sound causes among his colleagues that he scored his greatest triumphs. Himself a sensitive and introspective man, he could always see the other fellow's point of view and tolerate it, even if he did not welcome it. It was because of his tolerance and understanding that he gained the tolerance and understanding of others. His was always the policy of subtle persuasion rather than direct confrontation. Lacking the glamour of others, or indeed the desire for it, he nevertheless became a leader among leaders, a great man amid greatness.

The interesting thing about this appreciation is that, perhaps apart from the last half-sentence, a more thorough study of Tedder shows it to be almost entirely fallacious.

Like many military leaders of his generation, Tedder had no early thought of a career in the armed forces. *Pace* the previous reference to his 'outstanding academic achievements', his record at school and university was not remarkable. His work there showed a steady and thorough approach rather than any eye-catching brilliance. He won a university prize but not a first-class degree; he wrote and published a seventeenth-century naval history (his only published work for the next forty years); and then he disappeared into the Colonial Service.

Only the outbreak of the First World War brought him into the forces, and, again like so many of his contemporaries, his service of choice was the army. It was a minor physical mishap that led him thence to the Royal

Flying Corps in 1915. His subsequent career falls conveniently into three phases: the First World War; the inter-war years; and the Second World War, naturally by far the most significant of the three.

Tedder's record in the First World War was more interesting for the portents it provided for the future than for any outstanding contemporary performance. Having managed to survive the sketchy preliminary training, he joined No. 25 Squadron in France. A small, quiet, somewhat aloof man, gifted with a sense of humour whose acidity sometimes clouded any pleasantry; already married and perhaps more set in his ways than many of his comrades, he made little impact on the latter and provided no more memorable contribution to the practice or theory of air fighting than did most newcomers. It is thus not easy to obtain first-hand evidence of his activities or potential. What is significant however is that though his contemporaries scarcely noticed him, Trenchard did. He is on record at the time as considering Tedder 'a practical thinker and a reliable man, who saw the essentials and was not too detailed'. Perhaps not a very glowing description, but the last phrase certainly proved prophetic. Later, questioned about his initial observation of Tedder and the paternal attention he gave to his career, Trenchard expanded: 'What I liked about him was that he determinedly set about sorting the essentials of his job from the trivia; and then got on with it. He had a great gift for getting his priorities right.'

Not surprisingly, shortly afterwards Tedder was given command of No. 70 Squadron. He took over from a glamorous and dashing leader and to his fellow officers he came as somewhat of a disappointment. He was described as 'unimpressive', 'a wet blanket', 'not much of a leader', and perhaps most illuminating, 'the sort of chap who always wore his hat slap on the middle of his head'. But, as Trenchard had noted, he defined the essentials of the squadron's task and saw to it that they were accomplished as effectively as the tools to hand permitted. He did not do a great deal of flying himself; but he improved the administration, the supply, the serviceability; and the comfort and welfare of his men. His squadron, like others, suffered heavy casualties at various times. To reduce them, he re-examined operational procedures and revised tactics. He showed that he could formulate new ideas and, another pointer to the future, that he could fight them through the opposition of high and remote authority, with determination amounting to obstinacy and with eventual success. He accomplished much but in such an unobtrusive manner that he gained little immediate credit or reputation.

At the end of his tour of command he returned home and effectively filled various training and personnel appointments. When peace came he had seen enough of the RFC/RAF to wish to make a full service career; the authorities had seen enough to welcome him in.

Tedder's career between the wars followed the turgid processes of all such periods, when the winning of any promotion is a notable and laborious achievement. He was fortunate that he was involved in certain events which gave him further useful experience and at the same time confirmed the authorities' good opinion of him.

He successfully commanded a squadron during that Near Eastern panto-mime known as the Chanak Incident – a piece of Turkish delight sufficiently sticky to damage several reputations. He demonstrated again his administra-tive ability, and his care for both the maintenance and supply of his machines and the welfare of his men. For the former he saw the need to organise on an adequate but not an over-elaborate logistic base, comprising a well-stocked air stores park and an efficient repair system. With the latter he demonstrated a new sureness of touch, firm control being blended with quiet good humour and a humane sympathy. He was never to be a traditionally inspirational leader but he somehow encouraged people to want to do things. It is interest-ing that he recognised some deficiencies in himself in this field ('I wanted to be liked, but I wasn't much'); and here and later made various calculated experiments in the art of what would today be called man-management.

In Turkey he had contrived to keep out of politics and avoid entanglement in the web of intrigue that surrounded even the most straightforward activity. But in various Whitehall appointments he learned that such involvement becomes almost inevitable. He learned also to identify the villains of the piece in governmental circles, and acquired a well-founded dislike and distrust of ministry control and its practitioners. He noted that the aims of many of the policies in force were not only misjudged but wholly negative. Reaction to any positive proposal for improvement and development took the form of automatic obstruction at worst or reductions and procrastination at best. Economy in the worst sense was the only ascertainable motive for such reaction. When finally the pressure of world events forced the hands of those in charge, it was nearly too late and the essential expenditure had to be made hastily and therefore wastefully.

Again, as one who had always taken the trouble to master his subject, Tedder suspected a system under which the individuals who held the reins and purse-strings showed no such mastery and apparently saw no requirement for it. He himself held various appointments in the training and armament fields in the 1920s and 1930s. The personal stamp he put on them was that he always maintained one basic aim, to attain or improve operational efficiency. To him elaborate ritualistic training exercises were anathema if the end product were only artificial, unrealistic skills; complicated and ingenious weapons and armaments were equally unacceptable if they had no chance of proving battleworthy. These were his criteria, not those of the economist or the boffin, and it disturbed him that decisions on such matters had to be vetted by and often fought out with people who had little practical qualifica tions to assess them.

In 1936 Tedder once more enjoyed the pleasures and responsibilities of command when he became Air Officer Commanding the Far East Air Force

in Singapore. It is noteworthy that although he took the responsibility seriously, the pleasure was also genuine; there was little sign of the dedicated
backroom boy, more at home behind his desk than in the field. In this, his
first experience of high command, he characteristically laid the emphasis on
the realities of operational performance as against the façade of formalised
exercises and flag-showing. He observed two basic deficiencies in the command
as a whole. One was the lack of a proper professional air staff organisation,
geared to and designed for operational proficiency; this he promptly rectified.
The other was the notable lack of inter-service co-operation and of appreciation of the other services' problems and requirements; this he did what he
could to correct, without much success but with a useful memorandum for
the future. Yet he did not blame his colleagues; indeed the fault was not
theirs; 'I can see little justice in hunting in the Far East for scapegoats. To
my mind there is no need to go further than Whitehall to apportion the
blame.'

He was not to be spared the rigours of Whitehall for long. In 1938 he was
recalled to the Air Ministry as the Director of Research and Development.
Always an important appointment for the long-term efficiency of the Royal
Air Force, it became even more critical under the imminent threat of war
and with its outbreak in 1939. On the recommendations and decisions made
in the Directorate would largely depend, both in the short and long term, the
ability of the RAF to master its enemies and play a telling part in overall
victory. Tedder had to make many of the decisions personally, and here for a
change he found himself opposing and rejecting many apparently promising
proposals. The eternal cry from the Treasury, 'No money', was at last temporarily hushed, but resources and time were still limited and many bright ideas
had to be discarded either because their promise was not sufficiently definite
to justify allocation of our stretched material and intellectual resources; or
because that promise was so remote that it could not influence the present
conflict. Many an ingenious brainchild fell at the latter hurdle, but by no
means all; Tedder for example strongly supported Barnes Wallis's 'bouncing
bomb', which later broke the Ruhr dams and also Whittle's jet engine, though
the latter eventually entered operational service too late to have any major
effect on the war's outcome. As Trenchard had commented, it was a matter
of getting his priorities right; had he got many of them wrong, the balance of
success in the air war would have been gravely threatened.

One of Tedder's difficulties in sorting the jewels from the tinsel was that
the latter often enjoyed support at the highest level. Both Churchill and
Beaverbrook, Minister of Aircraft Production in 1940–1, were fascinated by
gimmicks. Churchill indeed remained so throughout the war; and by no
means all his hobbyhorses were fallers, e.g. the Mulberry harbours, Pluto, the
flail tank and so on. He referred to them himself as his 'toys' and found an
almost childish enjoyment in them; but Tedder had to apply strict standards
of realism to all those that entered his purview (he chaired the Air Arma-

ments Board which brought him into contact and sometimes conflict with the comparable projects of the other services). On occasion this also brought him into dispute not only with Beaverbrook but with Churchill personally. The legend of the polite, suave diplomat found no foundation in these discussions. Tedder never thumped tables, and distrusted people who did ('If they have to make a row, they're probably trying to cover up a weak case'); but he argued forcibly, sometimes acidly and pulled no punches. He stuck to his guns (or bombs as the case might be), and earned a reputation as a strong and convincing debater, but also as an obstinate and sometimes awkward man in argument. If not actually making enemies, he generated hostility and impatience among those he opposed.

Thus when Air Marshal Longmore, C-in-C Middle East Air Force, in late 1940 requested Tedder as his deputy, in making an alternative choice the Chief of Air Staff may have been influenced by outside pressures to choose someone likely to fit more smoothly into an inter-service environment. But fate now decided to play a hand. The officer first selected for the job was shot down *en route* to Cairo. Tedder was sent after all; and horizons of unimagined breadth opened in front of him. He was proceeding to what proved the most vital air commander's role in the Second World War, because in the event it was the campaigns in the Middle East that proved that air power, far from being an adjunct and supporting arm to the land and air battles, was the dominant and pervasive factor in all modern warfare.

When in December 1940 Tedder finally reached Middle East Command, tails were well up. All three services had got off to a good start. The navy had tipped the balance of warship strength by their brilliant air raid on Taranto. The army had blunted and repulsed against heavy odds any Italian threat to the Egyptian bases, and made considerable territorial gains; the Royal Air Force, with equipment often pathetically obsolete, had seen off the Italian air force not only in the Western Desert but in Abyssinia. Nevertheless the commanders did not delude themselves that these victories demonstrated any lasting superiority or offered prospects of sweeping development of local successes. The resources for this were not available and the means to provide them were insecure and geographically over-extended. In spite of Taranto and the currently strong position of Malta, sea passage through the Mediterranean remained hazardous. Most troops and their equipment still had to circumnavigate the Cape to reach Egypt. Most aircraft flew the sketchy and improvised central African route after being unshipped and assembled at Takoradi in Nigeria.

Tedder was delighted to find that his appointment was defined as Deputy to the Commander-in-Chief (Longmore) with particular responsibility for supervising operations in the Western Desert and Egypt. Furthermore, almost at once circumstances led to his temporarily assuming direct command of No. 202 Group in the desert. He welcomed the opportunity for first-hand observations and confirmed that he was never happier than when so occupied.

'The best week I've had from the Service point of view for years. It is difficult to express how exhilarating it was in the Desert. It was partly the air, keen and sparkling, and partly the magnificent feeling among our men.'

Later extracts from his diary endorse the admiration he developed for both air and ground crews and the enjoyment he derived from their company. 'I passed four pleasant, inspiring hours standing in the crowded Mess Tent, talking to British, Australian, many South Africans, New Zealanders and Rhodesians. Towards the end, we had some songs.' And again, 'So far as our fellows are concerned they are quite literally incredible. How they keep going, flung as they have been from one campaign to another and then again to a third, under foul conditions, I cannot imagine; but they do.'

The tributes were well earned; but these are scarcely the words of a cool, calculating, desk-bound intellectual. Nevertheless he did not establish a close bond of comradeship with those whom he commanded. It was not true to say he was a *faux bonhomme*; perhaps however he was a *bonhomme manqué*.

Outside his own operational squadrons Tedder's first impressions of the Middle East were less favourable. Within the Middle East Air Force he was concerned at the paucity and obsolesence of the aircraft and equipment, the tenuousness of its supply line and the cumbrous inadequacy of its mainten-ance and repair organisation. About the inter-service situation he felt even more apprehension. One fundamental defect in the command arrangements was at once obvious. The army and air force headquarters were collocated in Cairo alongside the political authorities (whose influence in the campaign was always considerable). The navy, in the person of Admiral Cunningham, stead-fastly refused to move from their own seaside headquarters at Alexandria, so that throughout the prolonged eastern Mediterranean operations essential inter-service communications depended on the telephone line and wireless telegraphy, and the vital element of personal discussion was often missing. Tedder's relationships with both Cunningham and Wavell were good and he had genuine respect for them; but he found the former disturbingly tradi-tional and singleminded in his approach to what were essentially joint-service operations – and had to be so if they were to have any chance of success. Tedder liked and admired Wavell, as he did Auchinleck later, although pro-fessionally he became impatient of what he saw as their rigidity and hesitance. It was the lower levels of army commanders and the clumsy, top-heavy staff structure within which they had to operate that caused him early and growing unease; an unease that was to prove amply justified by the performance of some of those commanders and staffs in the operations that lay ahead.

There were clouds building on the horizon. The first, considerably bigger than a man's hand, was the arrival of *Luftwaffe Fliegerkorps 10* in Sicily in January 1941. This, apart from its intrinsic threat, was a menacing indication that in the Mediterranean the Germans had weighed their Italian allies in the balance and found them wanting; and were now determined to redress that balance. This development immediately affected not so much air as sea operations in the central Mediterranean. The passage of convoys became ever more hazardous; and Malta became a commitment to our British commanders, although it always remained a thorn in the side of the enemy. As long as the British retained the airfields they had won in Cyrenaica, the Sicilian bases of the *Luftwaffe* could be counterbalanced. But other major developments were brewing which made their retention increasingly improbable.

The arrival of the *Luftwaffe* was only the forerunner of a general drive by the Germans to the south. Yugoslavia was invaded and occupied and Greece threatened. The British government and the Chiefs of Staff were on the horns of a dilemma. To fail to send forces to the aid of Greece would be to betray an ally, and to do so before the eyes of the world (and especially Turkey), which would draw its own conclusions as to our credibility and capability; yet to send even considerable forces would be unlikely to stem the overwhelming tide of the German invasion and would seriously endanger the British position and prospects in Cyrenaica. On strictly military grounds Tedder was against the operation. He appreciated that with the forces available and the geographical situation the British had no chance of maintaining air superiority; without it, defeat was not only inevitable but would be crushing.

The battle for Greece, and more especially for Crete, provided a strange paradox for the protagonists and practitioners of air power. On the one hand the failure of the British air force to hold the ring and provide air cover for the army, which otherwise should have had a good fighting chance of at least temporary success in Crete, was indisputable; the air force also failed to repel the vulnerable German air transports; and it failed disastrously to protect the navy against air attack throughout the operations, resulting in crippling losses to British warships. All this is beyond argument. On the other hand the campaign can be represented as a victory for the apostles of air power, because it demonstrated once and for all that where geographical or other considerations precluded the establishment of air superiority and consequently the provision of air cover, land and sea operations, certainly in daylight, should never be undertaken; and if circumstances, such as military misjudgement or political compulsion, led to their being undertaken they would fail and fail lamentably. Without airfields that the air force could protect and maintain in operational condition in Greece and Crete, air power could not play its part; and the campaign was doomed from the start. Over Crete the vulnerability and paucity of local airfields and the remoteness of Cypriot and Egyptian bases meant that the British aircraft sortie rate was far below that of the *Luftwaffe* on its Greek mainland airfields; nor did the British even have numerical superiority, indeed in effect considerable inferiority since most of their defensive aircraft lay beyond their maximum operating range. They were bound to lose; and it did not help that even when warships might have been given air cover, their location and movement were either not divulged to the RAF or were notified too late for the provision of what help could have been given.

Tedder foresaw all this and said so with foresight not hindsight. His constant theme was that the whole Mediterranean campaign was in essence a battle for airfields. If the army could advance and provide ground for forward airfields, the air force could cover it and help to force the enemy to further withdrawal. It could also cover the passage of naval vessels and supply ships along the flank, and deny the passage of enemy ships. If the airfields could not be provided, then the air force could not establish and maintain air superiority for the land and naval battle; and British operations by land and sea could not succeed without that air superiority. The Cretan débâcle proved his contention to the hilt. Nevertheless he was a big enough man, even at that unhappy time, to write in his diary, 'The Balkan affair was inevitable; we had to support Greece.'

Others were unable to take such a broad view. No one could blame Cunningham for bitterness over his losses but he reacted, as others before him and after him, by demanding a 'private air force', a force exclusively devoted to the needs of the navy. He quoted, inappropriately, the success of Coastal Command (whose main opponent of course was the submarine not the aircraft) and put strong pressure on the Chiefs of Staff to give him what he wanted. Tedder (Longmore had unfairly been made the scapegoat for Crete and Tedder replaced him in May 1941) had sympathy with his feelings but none for his solution. He was convinced that flexibility was a vital element of the successful application of air forces. When the navy's need was paramount, they would be given the maximum air effort available; but a day or a week later the need and the emphasis might, indeed almost certainly would, lie elsewhere; and the whole of the air effort must lie ready under the hand of the air commander to allocate and apply where the immediate need arose. If a part of it were irrevocably sealed up in a naval locker, or an army one for that matter, there would not be enough effort to apply. To his credit, and in spite of the equally unhappy experience of the army in the Cretan campaign, Wavell saw the point and the principle and neither pressed his own bid for a 'private' air force nor supported Cunningham's.

It may be appropriate here to mention a factor, sometimes overlooked, which consequently distracted and handicapped the Middle East commanders. One tends to think of the Middle East campaign as the 'Desert War', the Allies (largely Commonwealth) swaying to and fro in combat with the German and Italian armies in the Western Desert, with the navies fighting a comparable conflict in the Mediterranean, Malta of course playing a unique and critical part. What is not always appreciated is how many side issues and other commitments distracted them and diverted their forces, either actually or potentially.

Passing mention has already been made of the earlier campaign in Abyssinia and the southern flank of the area, a minor masterpiece in itself. The major diversion and catastrophe of Greece and Crete has been dealt with at more length. But the Middle East commanders constantly had to take their eye off the immediate ball to look over their shoulders eastward and north-ward.

In 1940 and again in 1941 forces had had to be diverted from the main battle to Syria and Iraq, to deal first with the Vichy French and later with Rashid Ali. More seriously, or so it appeared at the time, major diversions were envisaged to deal with any southern lunge by the massive German forces advancing through the Caucasus. This threat never materialised but it persisted for two years and the equivocal attitude of the Turks gave continuing cause for concern. More difficult still, after the end of 1941 there was a constant drain, especially of aircraft, to bolster sagging British forces in the Far East; involving diversion of resources, either by redirection of aircraft and troops already *en route* to the Middle East or by actual withdrawal of those already serving there. Tedder, as always seeing the broad picture, complied with the demands made on him, but he could not avoid expressing the view that squadrons so diverted might be too little and too late to serve the purpose planned for them in the vast theatre of the Far East; whereas they would have proved critical in tilting the fine balance between the forces directly confronting each other in the Western Desert.

Malta also, its defence and its maintenance, could be described as a diversion, but it was not so for the desert battle. On the contrary it was an essential element of it. If effective forces could continue to operate from it, the supply line to the Axis forces in Cyrenaica was always at risk and their operational potential could never be fully developed. If Malta could be eliminated, as it so nearly was, the resulting logistic advantage could well have been decisive. Tedder saw this clearly, as did his colleagues, and Malta was never given anything but high priority in all planning, although many of the operations so planned were near or total failures. He turned a blind eye to certain irregularities in the process:

> It would occasionally happen that by an understandable administrative error a new Wellington being sent to the Middle East would stop to refuel at Malta, and an older machine would actually arrive at the intended destination. Then again aircrew would often be so charmed by the scenic beauties and the peaceful way of life they found in Malta that they would decide to stay.

In spite of such external issues, Tedder always saw that the outcome of the Middle East war must lie in victory or defeat in the desert. He was determined that the RAF would play a full, if necessary predominant, part in that outcome. To do so it must establish superiority over the enemy air force; to accomplish this, offensive action was essential, since numbers were evenly balanced and sophisticated air defences could not be provided. Once again this called for flexibility, mobility, forward operation and a high sortie rate. This again called for good serviceability, which demanded an efficient repair and maintenance system. In Air Vice-Marshal Dawson, Tedder found the right man to provide this and gave him a free hand to cut across orthodox practice and staff procedures. Results spoke for themselves. Not only was air superiority established over an enemy numerically comparable and often actually better equipped; it soon developed into air supremacy so that when the army was defeated and had to retreat, it did so scarcely without interference from the enemy air; as General Freyberg put it, 'Thank God you didn't let the Huns Stuka us – we were an appalling target.' When in turn the enemy retreated, British air attacks turned his retreat into a shambles.

Tedder, always enthusiastic about the performance of his own men, was often less so about that of the army. He yielded to nobody in his admiration of British soldiers' fighting qualities; but he thought that they were sometimes poorly officered and often badly led from the top, amateurs fighting the German professionals. 'We cannot in a few weeks remedy the results of over twenty years of [Army] neglect, or hope effectively to educate the Army which generally speaking has not troubled to study or even think about the air aspect seriously since flying began.' These were harsh words, spoken in the aftermath of yet another desert reverse. But Tedder was never just a negative critic. He worked hard to remedy matters; he insisted on co-located tactical headquarters and on improved communications and the improved use of them; he disseminated at all levels the knowledge of what the air could and could not do, what it should and should not be asked to do. When final victory in the Western Desert came at Alamein and after, no one had played a greater part in preparing for and achieving it; and most of his army colleagues were generous in their acknowledgement of this, as indeed was Winston Churchill, who had not always been an admirer of Tedder.

A significant by-product of the steady advance westwards of the Middle East forces was that it brought them into closer contact with their American comrades. In particular it brought together Tedder and Eisenhower. Tedder already had considerable experience of the United States Army Air Force. The Americans had taken a little time to size up the quiet, somewhat acidulous air marshal; he in turn had crossed swords with them over what he saw as undue political pressures or unsound military practices. But he had been quick to appreciate their fighting quality, and his absorption of them into the Middle East Air Force as part of a fully integrated fighting team had been a most successful experiment, promising both professionally and personally for the future.

The initial situation between Middle East commanders and those of Operation Torch had elements of awkwardness. The former were flushed with victory, often delayed, hard-won but now clear-cut. Their expertise was proven and they, especially Montgomery, were perhaps too ready with advice. Command arrangements for the whole theatre had to be urgently arranged and there was considerable potential for friction, since to the existent interservice pressures were now added those between nations. Tedder was determined that the new command system must have two essential attributes.

There must be a single unified air command for the whole Mediterranean theatre, although under it geographical division into North-West African Forces and Middle East Command was dictated by sheer distance. And the subordinate air commands must be functional and flexible, this not being made any easier by the fact that the American air force was still labelled 'Army'. There must be no private exclusively allotted air forces, since rapid switching of full weight to the point of immediate need alone could exploit the essential flexibility of air power.

Such a command, with Tedder at its head, was eventually established. At the same time he readily accepted full subordination of the command and himself to the comparatively unproved direction of Eisenhower. Eisenhower was quick to appreciate this and insisted in turn on total international integration of his forces; his own partnership with Tedder was perhaps the most closely integrated of all.

In June 1943 as a necessary preliminary to the invasion of Sicily it was decided to eliminate any threat from the small Italian-garrisoned island of Pantelleria. The plan was to attack the heavily armed and fortified island with a great weight of bombs, and then to complete the operation with a seaborne landing. In the event the latter proved unnecessary since the bombing so devastated the communications and morale of the garrison that they surrendered without a fight. Two points justify the inclusion of this comparatively minor incident in this narrative.

Firstly it brought Tedder into contact with Professor Zuckerman, a scientist sent out to analyse and report on the results of the bombing. Tedder was much impressed by both analysis and report, and a partnership between the two men developed which had great influence and value in the planning of the air aspects of the invasions of both Italy and Normandy. Secondly, to Tedder's mind, the lesson of Pantelleria far from being one of unalloyed triumph for air power, presaged considerable dangers for the future. It was all too easy. 'If the enemy has strong defences and puts up a stout resistance, just send for the Air Force and bomb them out of the way.' It was a tempting deduction and a pleasant prospect; but Tedder saw that it could mean a wasteful use of an elaborate and expensive force; and that in many circumstances it might prove a lot easier said than done. He was right, and proven so at Cassino, at Caen and at Walcheren. He worried about the army becoming over-dependent on bombing and unready to play its own part in the battle. 'The Army having been drugged with bombs, it is going to be a difficult task to cure the drug addicts.' He, the prophet of air power, was also the first to admit its limitations and liability to misuse.

When planning began for the invasion of Sicily (Operation Husky) it soon became clear that the first essential was to ensure British supremacy in the air. But it was no longer necessary for Tedder to convince his colleagues of this; indeed when Montgomery proposed variations in the plan which might have left certain Sicilian airfields uncaptured, it was Admiral Cunningham who objected most strongly. In the event the all-out air attacks that eliminated the Sicilian airfields from which the army or navy elements of Husky could have been threatened once again exemplified the proper use of air power in joint operations.

Thereafter the major decision for the Allied staffs was where to aim the next blow. Tedder always favoured Italy (as opposed to Sardinia) but an attack as far north up its coast as air cover could be provided; his squadrons were already engaged in crippling the Italian communications systems. As an airman he saw the immense advantage to the Allied strategic offensive against Germany offered by the use of central Italian airfields, attacks from the south bypassing and dispersing the enemy's strongly established northern air defences. As a tactician he opposed the concept of a steady frontal assault up the whole length of Italy, over-dependent on Pantelleria-type air support. He convinced Eisenhower that a landing in the Naples–Salerno area was feasible if communications could first be disrupted; if enemy air could be suppressed at the critical period; and if counter-attack by land could be blunted by Allied air. He was proved right, but only by the narrowest of margins at one stage of the Salerno battle; and that margin was only maintained when, having already been deprived of one-third of his heavy American bombers, Tedder managed to persuade the Chief of Air Staff against great opposition to let him retain all his Wellington night-bomber squadrons until the crisis was past.

At the end of 1943 Eisenhower and Tedder were transferred from the Mediterranean to assume high command and share the planning for the invasion of north-west Europe, Operation Overlord. Here once again an early task was to resolve difficulties over the air command. Firstly of course the overall position of Eisenhower and Tedder (now the Deputy Supreme Commander of all three services) was different, in that in the Mediterranean they had held command over all the Allied forces in the area. Now they held it only over those forces specifically allotted to Overlord; enormous forces indeed, but there were still very large forces in the area outside their command. On the air side Tedder's position was complicated *vis-à-vis* Harris and Spaatz, the respective commanders of the two strategic air forces, and Leigh-Mallory the Air Commander-in-Chief for Overlord. One cannot help having some sympathy for the latter, for Tedder, nominally having responsibility across the board, in the event inevitably concentrated on air matters, and Leigh-Mallory often found his own position confusing and embarrassing. Nor was the Deputy Supreme Commander's position entirely clear in relation to Bedell Smith, the Chief of Staff to the Supremo.

Tedder decided to rely upon argument and persuasion rather than rigid definition of powers and responsibilities. He was confident that if he could establish the correct uses for all the air power available and demonstrate their correctness, he could rely upon all his associates to help him apply it;

and although there were periods of major difficulty and disagreement his confidence proved justified.

The first essential was to produce air superiority over the actual invasion area. This was currently enjoyed, but its maintenance depended on unrelenting offensive effort aimed not only at the Luftwaffe in being but most notably by the strategic air force attacks on aircraft production and the fuel industry. Secondly every effort had to be applied to helping the invading forces to get ashore and established without heavy losses. Thirdly their advance thereafter had to be assisted in every way, including airborne operations and all forms of close support. Tedder's plan was a phased series of operations using both the strategic and tactical air forces; in the final preparatory phase everything would be concentrated on communication targets to seal off the invasion area (the need for continuing diversionary attacks to conceal the location of that area could not be forgotten) and interdict all logistic and reinforcement surface movement, particularly by rail. The target system was so large and diffuse that the strategic air forces would have to make a major contribution to the implementation of this plan.

This plain statement of fact disguises an intense period of argument, dispute and contention. After full consideration of all alternative target systems that could contribute to the invasion's success, and relying heavily but not blindly on his previous experience, Tedder concluded that the communications to the invasion area offered the best prospect. The strategic commanders had to be persuaded of the need for their contribution and to agree to divert effort from their own offensive programmes; it was not easily done, but it was done. Churchill had to be persuaded that his deep apprehension about the threat of heavy French civilian casualties was unfounded; it was finally allayed, but again it was not easily done. The clear merits of the plan and Tedder's advocacy, supported also by now by his unrivalled reputation in this field, finally won the day. As with so many of his victories, some of the hardest fighting had to be done around the conference table.

The success of the plan is now history, well attested by our opponents; throughout the rest of the campaign Tedder continued to play a decisive role in the progressive allocation of Allied air power in both direct and indirect support of the general battle, even though later in 1944 the direction of the strategic air forces reverted from the Supreme Commander to the national Chiefs of Staff.

Tedder, as deputy, was involved in the overall strategy; in the arguments that developed over it; and in the personal disputes that followed the arguments. Although not questioning Montgomery's initial plan to hold and absorb the enemy's strength on the left to allow sweeping advance on the right, Tedder considered that the pressure applied on the left was over-cautious; certainly it resulted in failure to produce the airfields needed and planned for tactical operations. Later the disagreements broadened and deepened.

Montgomery concluded that the only valid follow-up plan must consist of a single overwhelming thrust; and that to ensure its success (under his command) the great proportion of Allied forces and their support, particularly logistic, had to be applied to this thrust. Eisenhower saw the merits of this plan but felt that it had to await the capture of the necessary supply ports, especially Antwerp. He did not give it the full support Montgomery proposed, because he was unwilling to concede the initiative and ease the offensive pressure on the remainder of the front. Politically it also had drawbacks since it would have been unpalatable to the American Chiefs of Staff and public; the American forces and commanders would at least have appeared to be relegated to a secondary and subordinate role. Montgomery felt free to criticise Eisenhower strongly over this, and won the backing of the Chief of the General Staff who followed suit. Tedder supported Eisenhower, and as a result was regarded by his British colleagues almost as his evil genius. They decried Eisenhower's military capability and held that much of his incapacity resulted from bad advice.

The whole issue has been fully aired by the respective protagonists. It is relevant here only to note that Tedder at least analysed the arguments pragmatically and dispassionately. When he reached his conclusions he stuck by them and by his superior. It is a matter of debate, which will never be fully resolved, as to whether those conclusions were correct.

Space does not permit further record of Tedder's career, which undoubtedly reached its peak as the Second World War closed. How can he be summed up as a wartime leader? How prominent a place does he merit in the history of modern warfare?

Paradoxically perhaps, in an inherently modest man, the best summation is to be found in extracts from the final passage of his own *With Prejudice*:

It is our custom and our history to find ourselves involved in war for which we are inadequately equipped, and suffering from that mental inertia which lays us open to the charge of habitually thinking in terms of the last war but one. The war which broke out in 1939 found us running true to form. At that time the very idea of air warfare as such was new . . .

. . . The Mediterranean campaign provided us with a clear step-by-step demonstration of the development of air power and its relationship to land and sea forces, and introduced in rather brutal terms the new factor of air superiority and its effect on the operation of land and sea forces. To attain that position air forces must be adequately equipped, trained for battle and securely based . . .

. . . One of the outstanding characteristics of air power proved to be its flexibility and the terrific concentration made possible by a unified air command – a unity only achieved by a faith born of mutual understanding between all branches and ranks of the air forces.

It was Tedder's contribution both to victory and to military history that he appreciated these fundamental principles; that he insisted on applying them; and by demonstrating their validity, finally convinced others of it also.

This was his professional contribution. As to the man himself, there were always present some contradictions and obscurities that led him to be misunderstood and sometimes disliked; but the fact of greatness is surely beyond dispute. It was perhaps best expressed by Harold Macmillan in *The Blast of War* (writing in February 1943):

Tedder is really a very interesting man. He has that rare quality of greatness (which you can't define but you can sense). It consists partly of humour, immense common sense and a power to concentrate on one or two simple points. But there is something more than any separate quality – you just feel it about some people the moment they come into a room. And Tedder is one of those people about whom you feel it.

FIELD-MARSHAL THE VISCOUNT MONTGOMERY

———◆———

Ronald Lewin

In the eyes of Hitler and the German high command the conflict at Alamein was a sideshow. In the eyes of Churchill and the British people it represented the turning of the hinge of fate, an occasion for the ringing of bells. Montgomery's victory over Rommel among those desert sands rapidly established his reputation, but more than three decades have now passed since October 1942 and an increasing perspective makes it easier to ask how far his *réclame* as a commander was actually founded on reality – how far, that is to say, the first victory with which he is identified owes its fame to his own generalship on the field of battle, and how far the military truth may have been falsified by extraneous factors.

Montgomery's philosophy, oft-repeated, was that if you give your troops, your people and your government a victory they won't be much concerned about anything else, and Alamein was a justification for the Roman triumph which all three of these groups desperately needed in the autumn of 1942: a clean-cut victory, with the enemy on the run. Before it occurred the Eighth Army was 'brave but baffled': unconscious, in the main, that during the first battle of Alamein in July it had already, under Auchinleck, inflicted on Rommel a decisive defeat. The British public, emotionally exhausted by apparently universal disaster, looked for a sign. And Churchill now passionately required some symbol of success – success, above all, in the Middle East. Here was the focus of his personal strategy. 'Rommel, Rommel, Rommel, Rommel! What else matters but beating him?'

It was thus not surprising that the news of Montgomery's victory provided an excuse for Mafficking. The beginning of the end was suddenly in sight. As the war rolled on, and no major disasters followed, it became increasingly evident that for the British Alamein was a genuine turning-point. By an inevitable logic, therefore, it seemed at the time that the man who had won so famous a victory must by definition have been a great general. Was the nature of his battle magnified by the scale of its consequences?

These are important considerations – particularly important in Montgomery's case, since it was not once but twice in his career – in Normandy as at Alamein – that he was committed to a battle which *had* to be won.

Most defeats allow of a second chance, but if Rommel had reached the Suez Canal or Overlord had failed something irretrievable would have occurred. All the same the truth is that Montgomery's reputation, inflated though it may have been by wartime relief at his successes, is firmly rooted, nevertheless, in the military skills with which he tackled these critically significant conflicts. He and Gort were the only soldiers who made it possible for the nation to breathe again: Wavell, Alexander and Slim had their triumphs, but none was as crucial as Montgomery's. Yet public rapture and prime-ministerial approval, which nominated him so immediately as a candidate for Valhalla, are essentially irrelevant. At the core of the conquering hero was the great captain. This is what matters.

Montgomery is one of those commanders whose qualities intensify rather than expand during the course of their lives: the child was the father of the man, and manhood stiffened but did not substantially modify the template of childhood. Under the stress of experience other commanders have sometimes developed entirely new aptitudes and even new personalities. The strong mental gifts, the robust and resilient character, the temperamental contradictions that transported Montgomery from Alamein to the Sangro and from Normandy to the Baltic were fixed, *data*, at a very early stage in his career.

The chaos of his temperament – for the field-marshal who dominated the battlefield could never set his own inner house in order – derived from many sources. There were the contrasting grandfathers – Sir Robert Montgomery, the hero of the Punjab, and the *gemütlich* Dean Farrar. There was the even greater contrast between that gentle saint his father, the Bishop of Tasmania, and his iron-willed idiosyncratic mother, whose overpowering influence on the boy she harried made him an uneasy mixture of rebel and conformist for the the rest of his life. There were the freedoms of a childhood in Ireland and Antipodes, and the constraints of St Paul's School and Sandhurst. By the time Montgomery was commissioned into the Royal Warwickshire Regiment in 1908, at the age of twenty-one, all these influences had coalesced, and he then was what he would always be.

A lucid, decisive mind; a penetrating intelligence which cleared no room for the intellectual or the aesthetic; a self-opinionated assurance; an absolute courage which could deviate into foolhardiness or folly; a desire to please, coupled with an itch to be an Ishmael; a kindliness and intermittent humanity marred by ruthlessness, intolerance, and sheer lack of empathy; a marvellous capacity for ignoring the inessential, combined with a purblind insensitivity about the obvious; a deep but unsophisticated Christianity; a panache, a burning ambition, above all an individuality – such were the gifts which both good and bad fairies brought to Montgomery's cradle, and such was his soldier's stock-in-trade.

What Montgomery did during the First World War is less important than what the war did to him. A DSO earned as a platoon commander during the

First Battle of Ypres in October 1914 was a laudable beginning. After recovering from his wounds, however, he spent the rest of the war as a staff officer. Not for him the distinction of commanding a front-line battalion in his early twenties like, say, his contemporaries Alexander and O'Connor; still less the dramatic individual exploits of his future opponent Rommel at Caporetto. It is what he discovered, rather than what he achieved, that conditioned him as a commander.

In feeling a revulsion from the carnage he had witnessed Montgomery was not of course alone: indeed there were other generals in the Second World War who were so affected by memories of the past that their fear of casualties impaired their generalship. Montgomery drew a different conclusion: casualties are inevitable in war, but *unnecessary* casualties are unforgivable. He could be granite when the occasion demanded: there was no hesitation about his readiness to accept 100 per cent casualties in the 9th Armoured Brigade during the Supercharge operation at Alamein. But he had learned, and never forgot, that the duty and science of the commander is meticulous preparation; that the staff officer should be the servant of the fighting man; and that while defeat of the enemy is the first priority, soldiers must be sent into the attack with every possible material aid to execute plans in which nothing has been slurred or overlooked. It is not surprising that in his *History of Warfare* he selected Monash as 'the best general on the Western front in Europe', nor that he remarked in his *Memoirs* how 'by the time the 1914–18 war was over it had become very clear to me that the profession of arms was a life-study'.

The next twenty years, therefore, were transformed into a learning process. Montgomery applied himself to the science and practice of warfare with the self-abnegation of a monk, not even allowing his happy but tragically brief marriage to distract him from his life's purpose. There was an integrity about his professionalism which is perhaps more familiar in the German than in the British army. Wherever he went, at Camberley, at Quetta, in Egypt, in Palestine, he was a cynosure both because he was a 'loner', a man for whom soldiering *tout pur* seemed more important than social amenities, but also because he manifestly excelled. He was a memorable Staff College instructor, an outstanding brigade commander, and as successful a GOC of a military district in the troubled Palestine of 1938 as he had been a brigade major in the dissident southern Ireland of 1921. Yet there was a shadow. Wavell recalled how, in the spring of 1939, a new commander for the 3rd Division was required. At the selection board he, as GOC Southern Command, said he would accept Montgomery. 'There was something like a sigh of relief from the other Army Commanders . . . everyone always agreed that he ought to be promoted, but every other commander who had a vacancy for a major-general had always excellent reasons for finding someone else more suitable than Monty.'

An able and original mind that makes no attempt to disguise its qualities is bound to arouse hostility, particularly among the conservative – and the

British army commanders of 1939 were no firebrands. But 'too clever by half' was a self-imposed tag which Montgomery would wear throughout his career. The assurance which was his strength in battle became his Achilles' heel in his personal relationships. Over and over again he would wound or offend while remaining impervious to the reactions of others. Sometimes, too, he would treat as 'a great joke' what nobody else found in the least funny: like Bottom, he could play the ass while unaware of his metamorphosis. His military gifts were so great that he was able to survive and succeed in the army in spite of these limitations, but when he became an ally, when he had to deal with Americans as equals and superiors, his incomprehension of their susceptibilities put both him and his country at risk.

Still, Wavell secured for him the 3rd Division, which he took to France in 1939 as part of Alan Brooke's corps. And it is in the *Alanbrooke Diaries* that one can observe most intimately the quality of Montgomery's performance as a fighting divisional commander during the 1940 blitzkrieg. Meticulous training before the battle, which paid dividends during it; cheerful tranquillity amid confusion; foresight, energy, decision, appropriate action – these were the characteristics which impressed Brooke at the time and later, when he was CIGS, caused him to support Montgomery like a father. For it should be observed that however inept he may have been in personal relationships, by the simple evidence of his professional *expertise* Montgomery obtained one of the vital assets for a commander in the field: he secured his home base. Brooke after Dunkirk and Churchill after Alamein, the military and political supremos, became Montgomery's men. These were no easy conquests, but they gave him their confidence in a measure which no other British commander – not even Mountbatten or, in a final analysis, Alexander – was to enjoy for so long and throughout so many crises.

Thus it was natural that Montgomery's should have been the first division to be re-equipped after Dunkirk, and that he should have found himself increasingly responsible for the defence of south-eastern England's threatened counties. Here – for the first time – he was able to demonstrate on a wide scale an aspect of the great captain's genius in which only Slim was his equal – that of persuading large formations of troops to believe in their task, to believe in themselves, and to believe in their leader. This was the gift Liddell Hart attributed to Marlborough – 'the power of commanding affection while communicating energy'. Montgomery was soon to need it in another field, for in August 1942 (twenty-four hours after he had been put in command of the forces for Operation Torch, the invasion of north-west Africa), he was instructed to fly out to Cairo and take over the Eighth Army.

One yardstick by which to assess Montgomery's generalship at Alamein is to ask what would have happened if Gott, whom he succeeded, had not been killed by a German fighter before he even assumed command. 'Strafer' Gott, the old desert hand, was worn out. Even as a corps commander he had lacked distinction. There can be little doubt that had he survived the Eighth Army would not have fought under him as a unified force; it would not have been gripped by a firm central control; the armour would have continued to act like a private army; there would have been few fresh ideas in the battle plan; the artillery would not have been used, for the first time, to produce massed fire as a matter of course, and the Desert Air Force would not have been integrated so closely and so comfortably into the army's operations. In the event all of these possibilities were averted.

There were general and specific reasons. At bottom lay the fact that within an astonishingly short space Montgomery imposed his will on his officer corps and his personality on his troops. This was an achievement of the same order as Slim's restoration of morale in the Far East – and Montgomery went further, since he created the impression that it was *his* army and that only he knew the right way home. It was a feat of generalship that half won his battles before a shot was fired – to inject a new sense of purpose and confidence into a puzzled, uneasy multitude, a critical, jaded, intelligent army of such diverse origins, Australia, New Zealand, South Africa, India and Great Britain. Between Alamein and Tunis the charisma of his personality never waned, and the vice of his will was never relaxed. If his sackings were sometimes effected with ill-considered brutality, if the technique of his personality cult was sometimes in bad taste, this was as nothing compared with the fact that when the Eighth Army linked up with the First in Tunisia they arrived in the spirit of conquerors with a trail of victories in their wake.

Some of the specific reasons may be found in his handling of Alam Halfa (the battle which should really be named Second Alamein), where Rommel's last thrust for Cairo and the Nile delta was halted. Many of Montgomery's hallmarks are visible: the careful preparation and practising; the ensuring that all know their tasks; the co-ordination of artillery and air power; the calm refusal to be bustled into an unprofitable pursuit; the eye fixed unswervingly on the battle to follow. Perhaps Montgomery's greatest gift to the Eighth Army at Alam Halfa was that he made it all seem easy.

The problem in Operation Lightfoot, or Third Alamein, was to destroy or at least hurl into irreversible retreat a still-menacing *Panzerarmee*. Montgomery had advantages denied to his predecessors. From the sinking reports and the secret intelligence he knew of Rommel's critical lack of supplies – especially fuel. (Indeed 'Ultra' the system of intercepting and decoding signals on the Germans' highest command nets, provided a flow of hard information about his enemy's plans and problems, whose full effect on his generalship, though profound cannot yet be fully evaluated.) American convoys were now pouring abundance into the depots of the delta. The Sherman with its high explosive shell at last provided a possible counter to the 88mm and, with the 6-pounder anti-tank gun, finally released the 25-pounder for its proper role as a field gun – just at the time when experiment had made it possible for a single observer to direct swiftly and simultaneously a great volume of gunfire. There were fresh divisions, large stocks, and good new commanders hand-picked by Montgomery himself. Behind him, moreover, lay the shock-absorber of Alexander. But too many British generals in the desert had started with high hopes and a reasonable chance – Operations Battleaxe and Crusader, Gazala – and ended in defeat or stalemate. Montgomery was the lucky general Napoleon preferred – the one who knew how to make use of his luck.

The dust and smoke of the great dogfight at Alamein have not obscured certain basic facts – the remorseless preparations; the essential simplicity which, as in all Montgomery's plans, characterised Lightfoot; the careful marshalling of reserves; the imperious control of his armour; the calm sustained under pressure. This battle which *had* to be won was at no time in danger of being lost. Never before had Rommel so danced to a British commander's tune. At this distance it seems clear that the doubts of some of his subordinates, of Tedder, of Churchill back in London, were unjustified: the only thing they had to fear was fear itself. Montgomery, unlike Wavell or Auchinleck, had dared to resist his Prime Minister until Lightfoot could be fought on his own terms, and thereafter he was always master of the field. Those who worship the Rommels and Pattons of this world find such good housekeeping uninspiring, but his troops, at least, could be grateful to Montgomery for never undertaking an operation *à l'improviste*.

This was what he always did best – the orchestration of a setpiece battle. Here in Egypt, supremely in Overlord, and later on in north-west Europe (in the Reichswald, and at the Rhine crossing) he found the challenges which he was best equipped to answer. Yet between the breakthrough at Alamein and his departure from Italy, by contrast, there were few occasions when he performed as more than a *bon général ordinaire*. One remembers the flawless action at Medenine, and the brilliant left hook and night drive at Mareth. Above all one recollects how, during an inter-Allied planning situation of great fluidity and confusion, it was Montgomery alone who diagnosed and demanded the correct scheme for the Sicilian invasion.

From Alamein to Tunisia, however, it became clear that in a war of movement he lacked the fingertip-feel that he exercised so magisterially in a position battle. Throughout their prewar friendship Liddell Hart had tried to interest him in the importance of exploitation: he never mastered it, and one of the great question marks hanging over his thesis that after Normandy he should have been given forty divisions to drive into the north German plain is precisely the doubt as to whether he could have driven them. At Alamein he was like a political leader who promises one thing ahead of an election and does something else afterwards. There was much talk of a *corps de chasse* before Lightfoot, but where was the chase?

It was strange too that he seemed to mislay his genius when he met a mountain. (A good Staff College question would be: 'Devise a Montgomery plan for Cassino.') His snap victory between the towering flanks of Wadi Akarit was due to Tuker of the 4th Indian Division: over the last days of the

Eighth Army before the Tunisian *massif* at Enfidaville it is better to draw a veil. Neither in Sicily nor in the slow drag up Italy is there any element of distinction or originality in his generalship. In Sicily, too, he laid a depth-charge: his cavalier treatment of Bradley and Patton, and his open distrust of American military skill, were never to be forgotten or forgiven. Yet all these uncertainties were dissipated when he returned to London at the beginning of 1944 and in his old school, St Paul's, set about making ready for Overlord, the greatest assault crossing in history. He had not only come home: he had come into his own.

Command of the land forces in the invasion of Normandy was Montgomery's by right because in 1944 he was the only officer in the Allied armies who was completely equipped for the task. The others who were considered – Marshall, Alan Brooke, Alexander – had manifold and manifest qualities, but none possessed Montgomery's battle skills or his immense capacity for organising the preliminaries to an operation of war. Those gifts so often praised by his comrades-in-arms – clarity of vision and simplicity of conception – were now seen at their quintessential, and they were supported by a will-power that enabled him to keep his objective consistently in sight.

The basis of the Overlord scheme was so elementary as to appear naive: get ashore, hold on the left and break out on the right. Yet all the complexities of the campaign cannot conceal its simple bone structure – though Montgomery triumphantly concealed it from the Germans. He himself has been somewhat vociferous in maintaining that everything went exactly as he had forecast, which is untrue – he would certainly have liked to seize Caen in the earliest stages – but no big battle is 100 per cent perfect, and he would have been wiser to admit the incidental failure while rightly pointing to an overall success. This derived from his favourite doctrine, that the commander must always achieve balance while denying it to his enemy.

Commanders who enter action without confidence in their plan or their strength are already unbalanced. Montgomery was poised from the start, for his successful insistence (with Eisenhower's approval) on an enlargement in scope and force of the initial Cossac plan for the assault was fundamental to all that followed. Once he was ashore on the right width of front and with sufficient troops he was never flurried. The air interdiction programme weakened the panzer divisions, his own tactics pinned them in the east, and the Americans were released for an end-run whose execution was Patton's but whose conception was Montgomery's. His errors were absorbed in his achievements – except in the field of human relations.

Eisenhower never properly comprehended Montgomery's Normandy strategy, and had it not been for Alan Brooke's careful coaching Churchill might well have exploded in a frenzy of frustration over the halt before Caen. The Americans – and the press – were equally misled. All came to believe that he was seeking and failing to break out on the British front, and his apparent failure caused public criticism and private back-biting at SHAEF. (Alan

Brooke fortunately was not distracted from the truth.) This was to the good in so far as the Germans were taken in, but otherwise disastrous. The vein of egocentricity in Montgomery led him to underestimate Eisenhower as a soldier, much though he respected him as a man. Once Montgomery had spoken he felt no need to explain, or to ensure that he had been understood by his superiors. After the crossing of the Seine this attitude became intolerable.

The debate about the single thrust as compared with the broad front will never end, yet the issue is simple. Even if Eisenhower had been ready to make huge transfers of supplies from the American armies to sustain a pre-dominantly British thrust; even if all the waterways between the Seine and north Germany could have been surmounted; even if the Scheldt could have been swiftly opened; even if Montgomery was capable of giving such a thrust the right impulsion; nevertheless, as Eisenhower told him, 'The American people would not stand for it.' Which meant that Roosevelt and therefore Churchill would not stand for it. An alert commander in the field, Montgomery still lacked a vital piece of equipment – political antennae. During and even after the war he never grasped the validity of Eisenhower's judgement: by a pertinacity which at first was laudable but ended by being myopic he reached a point, at the end of 1944, when the Supreme Commander came within an inch of sacking him. This personal tragedy would have been an incalculable blow to the Anglo-American endeavour: the responsibility would have been Montgomery's alone.

It fits the pattern of this man of contradictions that he dallied unpardonably over what should have been obvious and easy – clearance of the approaches to the vital port of Antwerp – and yet could undertake in relative haste the most daring and imaginative enterprise of the campaign. Nobody has a right to accuse Montgomery of being incurably cautious without first analysing Operation Marketgarden, which we typically think of as 'Arnhem' because of its final phase of failure. The reasons for that failure were varied, technical, and partly beyond Montgomery's control: the broad concept, which he and Dempsey devised, still lifts the heart by its panache, and reminds one how, unlike the commanders in 1914–18, Montgomery was unfailingly receptive to new devices – massed artillery used like a single gun, heavy bombers in a tactical role, the 'funnies' of the 79th Armoured Division, airborne troops. When he reached the Rhine there was hardly an instrument in the current military orchestra that was denied a part in his final, grandiose composition. Yet Marketgarden once again had emphasised Montgomery's ineradicable weakness – the inability to supply an effective impulsion in mobile operations. Granted all the difficulties of terrain, the doggedness of the airborne troops at Arnhem was not sufficiently matched by the plan for their relief – or by its execution.

Montgomery's personality stands insistently between the critic and his generalship. It is impossible to evade. If he evoked love and respect, he was also hated and sometimes despised. There are few neutrals in this disputed terrain. Yet the danger has always been that preoccupation with the feet of clay might prevent a clear vision of the towering stature, for the height and scale are there in unrivalled dimensions. The man who cast a magic wand over the Eighth Army and made the return to Europe seem like an exercise in military logic did so because, in a generation of outstanding soldiers, he was the most completely equipped battlefield general his country had ever produced. His creed was that 'operations must develop within a predetermined pattern of action'. For all his flaws of character and his military misjudgements, the record stands that it was his habit to put the whole of that creed victoriously into practice.

General of the Army Dwight D. Eisenhower

Don Cook

Dwight David Eisenhower was not born great, nor did he achieve greatness. But when greatness was thrust upon him, he met the challenge.

Yet in the aftermath of victory his successes were so clouded by the inevitable military and political controversies over his handling of vast and complex responsibilities that it has taken three decades of sifting, sorting and analysing the records and the memoirs and counter-memoirs to gain some solid measure of his stature as a military commander. What emerges is the certainty that in the overall Eisenhower was more sound and correct in his judgements and decisions than those who were opposing him, and that his 'command influence' across the whole kaleidoscope of the Second World War in Europe was a great deal more decisive and precise than his critics accepted at the time or were subsequently prepared to concede. When Eisenhower was wrong, his errors were often generosity in seeking to accommodate conflicting points of view in some wider interest of Alliance harmony always uppermost in his mind and an essential quality of leadership in a Supreme Allied Commander; or failure to impose his judgement and follow his own instincts out of basic respect and sensitivity for men under his command, which can be a grave weakness in a commander. To his critics this simply reinforced the superficial picture of Ike-the-inexperienced or Ike-the-uncertain or Ike-the-committee-chairman. But the record spread full shows Eisenhower as a military man of greater command qualities, more steel, depth and grasp than many of the experienced, ambitious and often egocentric subordinates who served with him were prepared to see in his accommodating personality and his rather modest, self-effacing and seemingly diffident approach to his job.

He was catapulted from the obscurity of the American peacetime army with very little evidence of any special qualifications or preparation for his role. He took his place in what was certainly the most high-powered, experienced, intelligent, volatile, strongminded and colourful cast of military and political characters ever assembled to make history. At the top, Churchill and Roosevelt, George Marshall and Alan Brooke. The sailors Cunningham and King, the airmen Spaatz and Harris, the army commanders Alexander and Montgomery, Bradley and Patton, and then a host of strong supporting

players. If Eisenhower at first moved in this company with a certain diffidence, he was also moving with a confidence of his own. A man with less than
greatness in him would simply not have survived among these men for four
continuous years from May 1942 to May 1945.

His qualifications and preparations for supreme command were in fact a
good deal better than the rather banal record of farmboy-to-president would
indicate. The qualifications were his own, there to be realised and developed
with a little bit of luck in assignments along the way, which placed him in
proximity to superiors from whom he could learn even when the going was
pretty dry and shallow in the army of the inter-war years. As for professional
preparation, he was the product of an American military education and training system that produced out of the slimmest resources (118,000 officers and
men in 1938, including the Army Air Corps) an unprecedented flow of top-
flight divisional, corps and army commanders and staff officers on whom
victory rested in the Second World War. The very hand-to-mouth existence
of the American army in the Depression years tended to force its dedicated
and determined career officers to concentrate on quality and on technical and
theoretical study and innovation about their profession, simply because they
had little else to work with in the way of real resources of men, equipment and
money.

Eisenhower grew up at the turn of the century when the American Civil
War was still a living memory and Texas and Kansas where he spent his
boyhood were still frontier country. He was one of seven sons of parents of
intense and simple piety whose lives were marked by struggle, bankruptcy
and disappointment, and who were sustained by hard work and deep honesty.
Ike, extrovert and athletic, decided to try for an appointment to a service
academy for the simple reasons that have motivated hundreds of other
American boys – a chance for a free education (with pay), which his parents
would otherwise be hard put to afford, and the attraction of adventure and a
career. His mother, a deep pacifist, was clearly against his decision but never
said a word. Like many other midwest farm boys, he would have preferred the
navy, but as it turned out he was a few months too old under navy regulations
for admission to Annapolis, and so when he passed the common entrance
examination for the two academies he took an appointment to West Point.
He entered as a cadet in June 1911 at the age of twenty-one, older than most
of his classmates.

He enjoyed West Point, took to its rigid and sometimes bizarre disciplinary
system laconically and with a sense of humour, collected his full share of
demerits as well as friends, and graduated about the middle of his class in
1915. His cadet years were marred principally by a severe injury to his knee
on the football field, which ended his career as a football player, almost ended
his career in the army, and bothered him all of his life (worst of all when he
again wrenched it badly on a beach in Belgium after a forced landing in a
light aircraft in September 1944). He was commissioned as a second lieutenant

of infantry and reported to San Antonio, Texas, just as the Mexican border troubles were building up before the entry of the United States into the First World War.

Those war years, as his classmates headed for France, were almost a total frustration for Eisenhower, punctuated finally by a sharp reprimand from the War Department for persistently trying to get his orders changed for overseas instead of accepting them as they came, keeping him at home. He was gaining in the army a reputation, which he did not particularly like, as an officer with 'special qualities', as an instructor, a trainer, an organiser – and a football coach. But as a young major of twenty-eight he was given the task of building, organising and commanding literally from the ground up the army's first tank corps training facility at Camp Colt, near Gettysburg, and wound up with some ten thousand men under his training orders when the war ended.

There followed a dreary round of routine postings in the run-down army's peacetime camps, until Brigadier-General Fox Conner requested Eisenhower for his staff in Panama where he was commanding in 1922. Conner, who had been Pershing's Chief of Operations in France, was an officer of exceptional breadth, intelligence, culture and character. He took Eisenhower under his wing, and was a decisive influence in broadening and deepening a somewhat shallow and superficial streak in him in three years of service in the Canal Zone. Conner then manoeuvred the army system to ensure that Eisenhower got the opportunity to move to the top. After his Panama service Eisenhower sought a long-overdue appointment to the Infantry School but was turned down by the Chief of Infantry. Conner, who had then moved up to the General Staff, got Eisenhower transferred first to the adjutant-general's department for duty as a recruiting officer, and then promptly had him assigned to the Fort Leavenworth Command and General Staff College on the adjutant-general's quota! Eisenhower wrote in thanks, and asked for advice as to how he should prepare for the course in view of the fact that he was in effect going to postgraduate school before taking his degree.

> You may not know it [Conner replied], but you are far better trained and ready for Leavenworth than anybody I know. You will recall that during your entire service with me, I required that you write a field order for the operation of the post every day for the three years you were there. You became so well acquainted with the techniques and routine of preparing plans and orders for operations that included their logistics that they will be second nature to you. You will feel no sense of inferiority . . .

Eisenhower graduated at the top of his class in Leavenworth. He followed this with a course at the coveted War College in Washington, which was then more than enough to carry him into the orbit of the two senior professionals of the American military establishment – General John J. Pershing and General Douglas MacArthur. Eisenhower's tour of duty with Pershing – first eighteen months in Europe with the Battle Monuments Commission and then as a staff officer coping with the turgid prose of Pershing's war memoirs – was simply dull and dim.

He then spent six years in the exalted company of MacArthur, first when MacArthur was Army Chief of Staff and then when he went to the Philippines to command and organise the Philippine Defense Force. There is little in Eisenhower's writings or comments to reveal his feelings about MacArthur – certainly nothing to show that he was greatly impressed. The most noteworthy aspect of their association was that Eisenhower came out of it with an entirely opposite approach to military command, to his subordinates and to himself from that of the imperious MacArthur. (Even then MacArthur used to refer to himself in the third person – 'MacArthur then said to the Senator . . .') When the Second World War broke out in Europe in September 1939 Eisenhower requested immediate transfer back to duty in the United States, resisted all advice and appeals from MacArthur and others to stay on in the Philippines, and arrived back in San Francisco at the end of the year.

His first assignment on return was at the Presidio in San Francisco, command headquarters for the western United States, where he was logistics planning officer. Shortly after he took over, General George C. Marshall, the army's already venerated Chief of Staff, arrived to watch an amphibious landing exercise. Marshall and Eisenhower had met only once before, a brief encounter in Pershing's outer office ten years earlier. On this second occasion Marshall's only laconic comment, mindful of his own days of service in the Philippines where the best military batmen are still recruited, was: 'Have you learned to tie your own shoes since coming back, Eisenhower?'

In the next two years in the expanding army of 1940–1, Eisenhower finally got a regimental command, which lasted only eight months, and then was shunted back to staff duties, moving up rapidly first as Chief of Staff of the 3rd Infantry Division, then Chief of Staff of the ix Army Corps, and finally, as a brigadier-general, Chief of Staff of the Third Army headquartered at San Antonio, where his military career had begun twenty-five years before. Five days after Pearl Harbor he got a telephone call from Washington: 'The Chief says for you to hop a plane and get up here right away.'

Eisenhower now began his long and close association with Marshall, who almost certainly made the greatest single contribution of any one American to victory in the Second World War. The wartime American army was Marshall's creation. He was a great soldier and a great gentleman, head and shoulders above every other officer who served under him in a rare combination of character, intelligence, professional and political leadership and ability. The entire army recognised this (with perhaps the exception of MacArthur and his staff). There was no politicking with General Marshall, and to be selected by him for a job or a promotion was the purest measure of an officer's ability and quality that the American army has ever known.

Marshall had summoned Eisenhower to Washington because of his experience of staff work and his familiarity with the Philippines and the military problems of the Pacific – as well as the personality of General MacArthur and how he worked. In those first weeks of 1942 American attention was entirely on the agony of the Bataan retreat, Corregidor and surrender. As deputy chief of the War Plans Division, Eisenhower was in charge of scraping together what meagre resources could be supplied for the fight and giving such co-ordination as could be given to the chaotic events in the South-West Pacific. In the midst of this General Marshall ordered a sweeping reorganisation of War Department machinery and War Plans became a full-fledged Operations Division, a kind of Washington command post for Marshall in directing America's global strategy and tactics. At the same time he moved Eisenhower up to be its director, and a few weeks later promoted him to be major-general. Marshall bent his own rule against promotions for staff officers in Washington on the grounds that Eisenhower was in fact his 'subordinate commander' taking decisions and issuing orders from the operations division.

With all of the focus on the Pacific, Marshall and President Roosevelt never for a moment wavered from the conviction that Europe was the first strategic priority and that the war against Hitler had to be won first. Eisenhower played no part in any of the early conferences on grand alliance strategy, but in March 1942 at Marshall's direction he thrashed out with the operations staff the first basic strategic concept for fighting the war. It recommended a vast concentration of American forces in the United Kingdom, rejected their use in any peripheral attacks at the flanks or fringes, and urged that the military priorities should be to gain air superiority over the Continent and then strike from Britain straight across the Channel into France and western Germany.

Marshall and Harry Hopkins took this staff paper, with some refinements and alternative proposals for a cross-Channel operation, to London in April. They got agreement in principle from the British – but with reservations and differences about timing and circumstances that were to cloud things for many months. Still, the two nations had begun to come to grips with the problems of a joint strategy to defeat Hitler. Returning to Washington, Marshall ordered Eisenhower to Britain to make an inspection and recommendations for the organisation of an American command to handle the vast build-up that was to follow. Just as abruptly, when Eisenhower had finished his task and reported back, Marshall named him commanding general of the European Theatre of Operations in London to carry out the plans he had recommended. At the same time he was to be the senior American representative in joint planning with the British for the cross-Channel attack.

Eisenhower arrived in Britain to take command on 24 June 1942, a few months before his fifty-second birthday. Barely three weeks after he had taken over and made his first acquaintance with the senior British officers with whom he was to work intimately for the next four years, General Marshall and Admiral Ernest J. King again flew to London to resolve the argument about where and when Allied forces were to attack in 1942. In three weeks Eisenhower had seen enough of the practical problems and heard enough from the British to be increasingly impressed with the military and logistic dangers of a weak or premature attack across the Channel. But he was loyally carrying out his directive to get agreement at least on preparations for an emergency strike at France if the Russians suddenly began to collapse in the face of the German drive across the Ukraine.

For five days in London, Marshall and King strained every argument and much temper and nerves on the subject of a cross-Channel attack. The British were adamant that neither the logistic sea-lift, nor the trained divisions, nor the air superiority would be ready to take on the Nazi armies in Europe in 1942 (which was then half over). Finally, on the sixth day with Churchill taking the lead, everybody turned to the possibility of landings in North Africa – an alternative that the strategic planners had always listed, and which the British had favoured but had kept quiet about until they saw the moment to push it forward. Agreement quickly fell into place, and on 24 July, exactly one month after landing in London, Eisenhower found himself selected almost automatically to command an Anglo-American operation against North Africa. For political reasons, because the attack would be against French territory, there was not even any consideration of the supreme command going to the British. Eisenhower was on the scene in London, had Marshall's confidence, the background of war plans in Washington and a growing acquaintance and understanding of the British and how they operated.

Remarkable in Eisenhower from the day he set foot in London was his deep, visceral dedication and determination to make Anglo-American co-operation a living and working reality. He brought with him a simple conviction about this which was as basic and unshakeable as his own patriotism. Moreover he made it work. It was not easy, for he was dealing with Britain at its prideful finest hour, and at the same time American chauvinism was on the increase along with American might and power. But Eisenhower was probably the least chauvinistic American and the least chauvinistic military commander in history. He never lost his American patriotism or pride; he simply added another patriotism to it.

A few months after the North African landings, when the Casablanca Conference had produced another long Anglo-American strategic wrangle with a compromise outcome that left some Americans feeling that they had again been diddled and out-manoeuvred by the British, Eisenhower wrote a revealing and remarkable personal letter to his successor in the operations division at the War Department, Major-General Thomas T. Handy. Worried about bitterness developing at the top, he pleaded with Handy to approach the British 'in a frank and honest way' but to avoid 'dealing with our military problems on an American vs. British basis'. He said he was not so naïve as to hope for complete objectivity, but he wrote:

I am not British and I am not ambidextrous in attitude. But I am not going to let national prejudice or any of its related evils prevent me from getting the best out of the means that you fellows struggle so hard to make available to us. The problem is never out of my mind for a second.

By this time the entire Allied command in North Africa had become aware of Eisenhower's famous dictum: 'I don't mind calling somebody a son-of-a-bitch but I'll be goddamned if I'm going to have anybody calling somebody a British son-of-a-bitch or an American son-of-a-bitch'. There may be something trite about this and it is not all that obvious years later how overwhelmingly important it was in energising and welding Allied harmony. But Eisenhower knew its importance and with the Supreme Allied Commander setting the tone, every other echelon on down had to respond accordingly. Greatness is often a realisation of simple basics, and this alone would have secured Eisenhower's place as a commander – but there was much more to it than simply keeping the show together.

The chief planning argument over North Africa, which was thrashed out between the Chiefs of Staff in what Eisenhower called 'the trans-Atlantic essay contest', involved harmonising the British view that the landings should be pushed as far east towards Tunisia as possible, and the American view that it was dangerous to get everything trapped inside the Mediterranean dependent on the single sea-lane through the Straits of Gibraltar, and that therefore there had to be a landing in Morocco on the open Atlantic. There was sound strategic judgement in both arguments, and after much juggling and balancing of forces and shipping, three landing sites were agreed. The Americans would land at Casablanca on the Atlantic coast and at Oran inside the Mediterranean, and a predominantly British force would hit Algiers and then push for Tunis. Lieutenant-General Sir Kenneth Anderson, in command of what was to be designated the British First Army, would become Eisenhower's ground commander when the landing phase was over.

Eisenhower flew to Gibraltar to establish his command post for Allied Force Headquarters inside the Rock on Wednesday 4 November. On that same day Montgomery's attack at El Alamein, which had begun on 23 October, reached its climax with a breach of Rommel's lines and the start of pursuit of the *Afrika Korps* across Tripolitania. From the United States and Britain the Allied convoys converged on North Africa and achieved far greater strategic and tactical surprise than the planners had thought possible. The armies hit the beaches on the morning of Sunday 8 November. Planning had been generally sound (except, for example, that all the signal equipment for an entire task force had been put in one ship, which was badly shot up, leaving the unit crippled for communications when it got ashore) and the landings generally went off smoothly.

It was just as well. Back at the Rock, while the landing craft approached the beaches, Eisenhower was locked in absurd argument with General Henri

Giraud, who must certainly rank as one of the silliest men ever to wear the stars of a French general. Giraud had been smuggled out of France by submarine in the misplaced belief of the American State Department advisers that the French in North Africa were ready to rally to his call and rid themselves of the Vichy yoke. When he arrived in Gibraltar he made the incredible demand that before continuing on to Algiers he should replace Eisenhower as supreme commander, and that the Allies should immediately invade southern France as well! Hour after hour for nine hours this bizarre discussion went on in the dripping, dank, crowded Gibraltar cave. Finally everybody went to bed, and next day when Giraud learned that the troops were successfully ashore in North Africa, some reality took hold and a fuzzy compromise that satisfied his obtuse personal honour was reached. In any case all this was swept away within hours by Eisenhower's first major decision as supreme commander – and certainly the most politically controversial decision that he took in the entire war: his recognition of Vichy Admiral Jean Darlan, who was unexpectedly in Algiers when the invading forces landed.

Of all that has been written about the Darlan deal, which is plenty, Eisenhower said all that needed to be said from his own standpoint when he made his decision at Gibraltar 'after going off alone for an hour or so' and then assembled his British and American staff officers in the Rock and told them:

> The military advantages of a cease-fire are so overwhelming that I will go promptly to Algiers and if the proposals of the French are as definite as I understand, I shall immediately recognize Darlan as the highest French authority in the region. None of you should be under any misapprehension as to what the consequences of this action may be. In both our nations Darlan is a deep-dyed villain. When public opinion raises its outcry our two governments will be embarrassed. Because of this we'll act so quickly that reports to our governments will be on the basis of action *taken*. I'll do my best to convince our governments that the decision is right. If they find it necessary to take action against this headquarters, I'll make it clear that I alone am responsible.

The Darlan affair was scarcely a test of Eisenhower's military abilities, but it certainly was a test of his readiness to take command decisions. He had not underestimated the political furore, and he was perfectly aware of what he was doing. But he got his ceasefire and the Allied armies headed east for Tunis while the controversy boiled on and on, for weeks and weeks.

For Eisenhower the first phase of the North African campaign had been almost entirely political, but the military test was now beginning. Four days after the landings, British paratroopers were dropped on the Algerian port of Bône, east of Algiers, and a small British task force with practically no reserve to back it up pushed through to the Tunisian town of Tabarka on 15 November. By 28 November the British were through the mountain passes and within sight of Tunis itself – but cold winter rains were turning all of

Algeria into a quagmire and there was nothing moving forward to put any weight behind the advance. Meanwhile Axis reinforcements were being rushed into Tunisia and Rommel's experienced though weakened *Afrika Korps* was retreating intact towards the Mareth Line on the country's southern border. The Allies would soon be facing very strong enemy forces.

This was the low trough of Eisenhower's career as a commander. Everything began going badly and his control of events was the weakest in the history of the war. He was nagged by the political situation, not only in Algiers but from London and Washington as well. His Allied command structure, which had been good enough for planning, did not have a cohesive and effective grip on military operations and battle. He did not yet have a strong team of subordinate commanders with clear-cut tasks and the means of carrying them out. His relations with Anderson were distant and uncertain, compounded by Eisenhower's own uncertainties in action for the first time in his career. His American forces were green and not yet battle-tested. The front lines had overreached logistic reinforcements in the air as well as on the ground. In the dash to Tunisia, which had been largely unopposed, forward units had been pushed ahead to sieze points that were easy to take and looked good on the maps, but were then highly exposed and dangerously dispersed when they had to be defended. Lateral roads were poor (all roads were poor) and command and co-ordination of the widely scattered forward units was weak, to say the least. Partly this was Anderson's fault and partly it was Eisenhower's fault and partly it was simply due to lack of previous experience in joint Anglo-American operations.

As things worsened and morale sagged Eisenhower drove to the front on 22 December, and in appalling weather he saw for himself that off the roads the tanks, half-tracks, trucks and artillery simply sank in the icy and glutinous Tunisian mud. Not even motorcycles could be manhandled free. Military manoeuvre off the roads had become impossible. On Christmas Eve at Anderson's headquarters he called off a planned attack and ordered the armies on to the defensive. On Christmas Day, as he ate dinner in the British mess, he got a telephone flash that Darlan had been assassinated, and left immediately on a thirty-hour drive back to Algiers in sleet, rain and snow.

Darlan's death eased the political problems somewhat, but Giraud was still playing the primadonna in military matters. He refused to place himself or his troops under British orders. Eisenhower would probably have saved a lot of trouble by telling him to go to hell and sit with his troops in the Sahara. But seeking to rally and accommodate the French, whose forces he felt he needed, he split the front-line command by establishing a forward command post of his own. Giraud could thus report to him and take his orders from an American instead of being under Anderson who was supposed to be in command of the entire front. Instead of improving control this only compounded the confusions.

Most serious for Eisenhower personally was the situation that had been allowed to develop at the lone American corps headquarters in the front line under Major-General Lloyd Fredendall, who was holding the south central front in Tunisia under Anderson's command. Fredendall had been perfectly competent getting his forces ashore at Oran against almost no opposition, but when he moved forward to face the Germans, he lost his grip. To Eisenhower's silent anger when he toured the lines and saw what was going on, Fredendall had dug himself into a mountain command post in a valley ravine. Engineers, busy blasting out the corps command post, had not even laid the minimal minefields to protect the forward positions of the troops against the oncoming veterans of the *Afrika Korps*. Fredendall seldom left his dugout, as though he expected to fight a Maginot Line battle instead of pursuing the enemy. Moreover he had split his 1st Armoured Division into separate commands, and the divisional commander did not even know what each was doing since they were taking their orders from corps headquarters direct. This was the mess into which the Germans struck with their attack through the Kasserine Pass.

The battle of Kasserine Pass was the first real 'blooding' of the American troops under Eisenhower – and a serious blooding for Eisenhower himself. The intelligence section had warned of an impending attack but misjudged where the Germans would strike by a good 50 miles. In the early morning hours of 14 February Rommel hit the Americans on the northern flank of II Corps at Faid Pass – which by chance Eisenhower himself had visited in a night inspection of the front only an hour and a half before the attack opened up. (As a Supreme Commander, Eisenhower could never be faulted for not knowing his front lines; he toured constantly and was away from his headquarters visiting subordinate commands about one-third of the time throughout the war.)

He found the local battalion commander at Faid confident about how quiet things were, yet he had to order him to get minefields laid on his front 'first thing in the morning'. By then the Germans were knocking the combat command of the 1st Armoured Division to pieces. Rommel then opened up in a pincer movement from the south through the exposed American position at Gafsa and on to the Kasserine Pass, where he sent the remainder of the 1st Armoured and the 34th Infantry reeling back in retreat. Anderson had insufficient forces to put in any relieving attack from the north. All the Americans could do was shorten lines, fall back, regroup and finally begin to hold in the hope that Rommel would run out of steam. Meanwhile Eisenhower was stripping equipment out of other formations to replace losses, and sent Major-General Ernest Harmon forward to stiffen Fredendall – who promptly told Harmon to take over and went to bed for twenty-four hours. By the time he woke up the attack was spent. On 22 February Eisenhower urged Fredendall to go over to the offensive, but both he and Anderson were afraid that Rommel had not yet shot his bolt. Eisenhower did not himself have enough grip on the battle to order a counter-attack, and the result was that the Desert

Fox slipped back through Kasserine Pass intact and unpursued with only slight losses.

The worst about Kasserine Pass from Eisenhower's standpoint was that it had all been foreseeable and every weakness had been exposed – his intelligence section, dispersal of units, bad organisation of forces, a weak American commander, greenness of American troops and failure to carry out rudimentary battle preparations in face of the *Afrika Korps* veterans. But it was not until 4 March that he finally bit the bullet and acted on endless advice (including General Sir Harold Alexander's tactful comment, 'I'm sure you must have better men than that'), relieved Fredendall and brought the legendary George Patton up from Morocco to take over II Corps. Never again did an American corps headquarters dig itself into a mountain command post far from its front, and never again was Eisenhower so slow to relieve a faltering commander. He wrote to Patton almost as if he were writing a memo to himself:

'You must not retain for one instant any man in a responsible position where you have become doubtful of his ability to do the job. This matter frequently calls for more courage than any other thing you will have to do, but I expect you to be perfectly cold-blooded about it.'

By the time the battle was over, new command arrangements for North Africa, which had been worked out at the Casablanca Conference in January, came into effect. Alexander arrived from Cairo to take over on the ground, and Air Marshal Sir Arthur Tedder came to take hold at last of the sprawling and badly directed air operations. The British Chief of Staff, Field-Marshal Sir Alan Brooke, chortled in his diary:

> We were pushing Eisenhower up into the stratosphere and rarified atmosphere of a Supreme Commander where he would be free to devote his time to the political and inter-allied problems whilst we inserted under him one of our own commanders to deal with the military situations and to restore the necessary drive and coordination which had been so seriously lacking.

Brooke had taken a rather jaundiced view of Eisenhower from the outset of their first London staff conferences – but since he was pretty jaundiced about everybody this probably did not seem all that noteworthy at the start. His diaries (secret until 1957) were loaded with sour reflections on Eisenhower, and more importantly he aired his prejudices constantly to Montgomery in correspondence and conversations, which almost certainly tended to spur Montgomery in his own arguments and feelings about how Eisenhower was doing his job. Brooke was one of the truly brilliant soldiers of the war, but he was an aloof, reserved and somewhat enigmatic personality even for his own countrymen. He had a rapid-fire incisive grasp of both detail and broad strategy, and was incomparable in organising and presenting his views. He was distant and dour as only an Ulsterman can be – probably compounded because much of his time throughout the war had to be spent arguing with and curbing that restless and relentless genius, Winston Churchill. Brooke would probably have been superior in field command to any other British general in the war if Churchill had not picked him to run the army and the Chiefs of Staff. He did not suffer fools gladly, but he seems to have had difficulty in accepting and understanding Americans, and realising that they were not fools simply because they had a different national personality and a somewhat relaxed attitude towards themselves without the particular sophistication of the British.

The narrow view that Brooke took of the new command set-up was not, fortunately, the attitude with which Alexander, Tedder or Admiral Sir Andrew Cunningham, who had become Eisenhower's naval deputy, approached their tasks. There was nothing condescending about them in their dealings with Eisenhower, who had been pleading for 'command reinforcements' and for his part knew in his own mind exactly what his role should be and how he wanted to play it.

This was quickly demonstrated in the smooth and confident working relationship which Eisenhower established with Alexander. When Alexander took over command of the newly formed 18th Army Group, he made no bones about the greenness of American troops and his lack of confidence in their battle readiness compared to the veterans of Montgomery's Eighth Army which he was also commanding in the south at the Mareth Line. Eisenhower for his part told his American commanders to stop bellyaching about criticism and get on with forging forces 'which will enhance the reputation of the American Army with the British'. But when it came to the final phase of the Tunisian campaign, Eisenhower stepped in to insist to Alexander on a change of plans to give the American II Corps a much greater and more decisive role in defeating the Axis forces.

Alexander planned to use the Americans more or less piecemeal in defensive actions in the centre while Montgomery pushed up past them from the south to compress the enemy into the north-eastern corner of the coast, like a piston in a cylinder. At a conference in mid-April to approve the final battle strategy, Eisenhower told Alexander that he wanted the American corps used as a unit with a clear assault objective in the destruction of the Axis forces 'which would give a sense of accomplishment to the American people which they richly deserve'. More important from the military standpoint, he emphasised to Alexander that it was absolutely essential to the future conduct of the war for the American army to gain battle experience 'on a large scale', and that II Corps, which was now under Major-General Omar Bradley, 'had never had a chance to exert its power as a unit'. There was no argument. Alexander promptly organised one of the most remarkable logistic operations of the war. He shifted the full American corps of four divisions from the centre to the north in only two days, across the rear area of the British First Army, and assigned Bradley the objective of striking along the Tunisian coast to capture Bizerta.

Bizerta fell to Bradley on 7 May, and the British entered Tunis the same day to complete the encirclement and capture of approximately 275,000 Axis troops. Eisenhower's insistence on decisive employment of American troops had meshed completely with Alexander's tactical appraisal of where and how to use them. It had been a precise example of effective Allied command relationships under Eisenhower – of which there were endless others before the end of the war, usually not much more than discussions and advice between the Supreme Commander and subordinates which did not even make the war records but were a deft and constant influence on military operations. With a new strong team of commanders (and a new British intelligence chief at his headquarters, Brigadier Kenneth Strong), Eisenhower was showing his instinct and precision about when, where and how to intervene from above to keep his own hand on events. But Tunisia had become so much Alexander's victory in the public eye that back in Washington General Marshall called in his army public relations director and told him: 'You can tell some of these newsmen from me that I think it is a damned outrage that because Eisenhower is self-effacing and not self-advertising they ignore him completely when, as a matter of fact, he is responsible for the coordination of forces and events.'

At the Casablanca Conference, after much discussion and deep argument between the British and American Chiefs of Staff, an invasion of Sicily had been agreed upon as the next strategic move in the war. Eisenhower took no part in these discussions, having spent only one day at the conference to report on the immediate problems of the North African campaign. But he leaned more towards the British view of keeping up the momentum in the Mediterranean than the American view, which was against anything that might seem to divert from or delay the main assault against Festung Europa across the Channel.

Eisenhower's view was a fairly pragmatic one. Logistics dictated that it would in any case take the remainder of 1943 and into 1944 to provide the build-up for the cross-Channel attack. Therefore in the meantime it would be a mistake not to use the resources present in the Mediterranean to keep on the offensive. The real strategic problem was that the Chiefs of Staff at Casablanca had left hanging in the air the question of what to do after Sicily. Another conference was then convened in Algiers in May, with Churchill present and dominating the discussions far into the night every night. It was then agreed to allow Eisenhower to go for the Italian mainland *if* enemy forces collapsed quickly in Sicily. But this did not allow for much real advanced strategic planning.

In mid-June, on the way to Sicily, Eisenhower picked off the Italian island of Pantelleria. It was an operation that was his own if ever there was one during the war. An air base on the island would have been a considerable threat to the Sicily landings, but Alexander was thoroughly opposed to attempting its capture. Tactical or geographical surprise was impossible against the island's rocky coastline with heavy coastal defences. Tedder was also doubtful, but Eisenhower resolutely insisted that air and naval bombardment could reduce Italian resistance on the island to a point where a landing could succeed. He brought Cunningham, the British admiral, around to his support, and then ordered Tedder and the American air commander, Major-General Carl Spaatz, to produce the air assault which went on almost constantly for three weeks. Cunningham's sea armada added its naval guns in the final stages, and then, when a British landing force arrived offshore, the Italian commander hoisted the white surrender flag before a single soldier had to land. It was a marked success for Eisenhower as well as for air power and naval guns.

General Lauris Norstad, who was in North Africa in those days as a colonel in the air force when it was still part of the army, later wrote: 'I may be somewhat prejudiced since I was there at the time, but I think history will support my own feeling that the actions of Eisenhower early in 1943 created the U.S. Air Force in fact if not in name.'

Sicily, however, turned out to be far from a textbook campaign for medals or historians. In retrospect it bore the mark of a command that was still feeling its way. The North African landings had taken place against either no opposition or token resistance from the French, but now the Allies were about to land for the first time against the Germans. Montgomery, full of himself from North Africa, moved in and dominated the planning. Alexander was still not sure of his American forces and Patton and Bradley were relegated to secondary strategic objectives. The invasion force for Sicily was in fact greater than the D-Day landings in Normandy – seven divisions against five. But once ashore Montgomery bogged down in front of markedly inferior German forces which knew how to use good defensive terrain. Patton, after some tough arguments with Alexander, was finally allowed to cut loose; but his dash to the western end of the island was of little strategic importance. The summer heat in July was murderous for troops and equipment. Patton nearly ruined his career when he inexcusably lost his temper and slapped a soldier hospitalised with shock and battle fatigue. A mere sixty thousand Axis troops fought delaying actions for a full month against the Allies with five hundred thousand men – nearly a ten to one superiority. Eisenhower left direct control of the battle to Alexander, and his role was weakened further by the fact that he was in Algiers, Tedder commanding the air was near Tunis, Cunningham in charge of naval forces was in Malta while Alexander, of course, was in Sicily.

But as Supreme Commander, Eisenhower's big mistake was his failure to land simultaneously on the toe of the Italian boot when Allied forces went ashore in Sicily. This would have cut off the Axis retreat route from the island and would have been a relatively safe operation well out of range of any strong enemy counter-attack by either land or air. Eisenhower admitted his regrets about this to his naval aide and diary-keeper of the war, Captain Harry Butcher, halfway through the Sicily operation. It is true that he did not have a clear-cut directive from the Combined Chiefs of Staff to go for Italy, and he was probably also inhibited by Marshall's feelings about getting bogged down in the Mediterranean and the need to bring Marshall along step by step. But if Eisenhower had asserted his own authority he would certainly have had the backing of the British in going for the mainland at the same time as Sicily, and he could almost certainly have carried Marshall with him. As it turned out, with Montgomery's slow progress up the east coast of Sicily, the Germans fell back in good order and then got away from Messina and back across the straits with three good divisions relatively intact. Montgomery captured the town on 17 August, and then crossed to the toe of the Italian boot unopposed on 3 September.

By this time Mussolini had been overthrown and the weakness of the Allied military performance in Sicily was pretty much overtaken by the political success that the campaign was reaping. Secret negotiations for an Italian surrender began in Lisbon on 19 August, and after much complex manoeuvre and argument a surrender document was signed in Sicily the day Montgomery landed on the Italian mainland. Meanwhile preparations for a major Allied landing farther north, at the Bay of Salerno, had been pushed forward rapidly, to coincide with the public announcement of the surrender (which was to be kept secret for six days).

The battle of Salerno was 'a damn close-run thing' as Wellington said of Waterloo – the closest the Allies ever came to a major defeat under Eisenhower's command. The choice of Salerno for the attack was dictated primarily by the fact that it was the point farthest north up the Italian coast where the Allied air forces could still fly fighter cover over the beaches – a fact that the Germans were able to figure out as well as the Allied planners. The Germans were therefore waiting at Salerno with plenty of seasoned reserves only hours away ready to be thrown into action as the landings developed. It was primarily Alexander's responsibility, General Mark Clark, commander of US Fifth Army, being the operational commander.

But above all it was a battle that would not have been won without the rapid and decisive functioning of Supreme Allied Headquarters under Eisenhower. The mistake of divided headquarters during the Sicily operation was not repeated. All the senior deputy commanders were together at Eisenhower's advance headquarters at Amilcar near Tunis when the battle was joined. Throughout there was tight co-ordination and control from the Supreme Commander down through the subordinate command echelons, with the air, naval and ground commanders all working closely in appraising the rapid developments and meeting them with promptness, efficiency and decisiveness to pour in the reinforcements and the fire power that turned the tide. Tedder and Spaatz combed the Mediterranean to put practically every aircraft available over the beaches, while Eisenhower bombarded the Combined Chiefs of Staff to return three groups of B-24 bombers that had been withdrawn from his command over his protests two weeks before the landings.

Cunningham, with the Italian fleet now surrendered and in the bag, came through with a massive Royal Navy concentration off the beaches to plaster the German positions with more than three times the tonnage in shellfire at much greater accuracy than the air forces were able to rain down from the skies.

With insufficient sea-lift to push needed reinforcements to the beaches, Eisenhower released the 82nd Airborne Division to be dropped to Clark's assistance. He got the American Chiefs of Staff to allow him to hold in the Mediterranean eighteen landing craft that were on their way to India and the Pacific (although cargoes of steel rails had to be off-loaded from them before they could be pressed into combat use). At the height of the battle Eisenhower relieved an American corps commander under Clark, Major-General E. J. Dawley. Alexander had been dissatisfied with Dawley's performance when the Germans thrust through in their big counter-attack against the beaches, but as a British commander he was reluctant ,to act drastically against an American senior officer. He told Clark: 'Wayne, you've got a broken reed there.' Clark agreed, but demurred that Dawley had been his senior at West Point, etc, etc, and that he had brought in another general to stiffen things as deputy corps commander. This was not very satisfactory, and Alexander told Eisenhower his opinion of the situation. Eisenhower flew to Salerno and acted on the spot. The Fredendall lesson also had been learned.

By 18 September the combined ground, air and naval efforts that Eisenhower had brought to bear at Salerno under the leadership of Alexander and Clark had turned the tide. Alexander, who was in constant direct communication with Brooke in London, signalled: 'I can say with full confidence that the whole situation has changed in our favor and that the initiative has passed to us.' Like the victory in Tunisia it was a battle in which the drama of the beaches and the headlines for the commanders on the spot greatly overshadowed Eisenhower's own role in ensuring that victory had been possible.

In early December, three months after Salerno, President Roosevelt, *en route* back to Washington from the Teheran Conference with Churchill and Stalin, informed Eisenhower that he had been selected to command the cross-Channel invasion of Europe, the code designation Overlord. The decision was a surprise, certainly to Eisenhower, who had assumed from the first that the command would go to General Marshall. But in the end Roosevelt decided that Marshall's guiding hand was much more vital over the whole global direction of the war from Washington. Eisenhower arrived in London in mid-January of 1944 to begin the intensive six months of final preparations for the greatest Allied combined operation of land, sea and air forces in history – quite probably for all time.

Basic planning for Overlord had been under way in London since the spring of 1943 in a special joint planning group under Lieutenant-General Sir

Frederick Morgan. His recommendation that the invasion take place across the beaches of Normandy was accepted. But Morgan had been told to plan on the basis of an invasion force of only three divisions. Eisenhower and Montgomery, who was to have overall command of the landings, took an immediate decision that this had to be increased to five divisions. With the outlines of the plan set and the beaches fixed, detailed preparations for the D-Day landings then passed to Montgomery and Bradley, who would command the Americans. It was to be their battle. Eisenhower's concerns were now in the wider spheres – above the beaches and the use of air power; behind the beaches and the massive logistic build-up of forces that would pour across after the landings; and beyond the beaches with the European resistance movements, civil affairs and political problems, the French in particular, intelligence operations, cover planning to throw the Germans off in assessing where the invasion would hit – and grand strategy for the armies when they broke out for the final conquest of Germany.

From a command standpoint the air problem for Eisenhower was the most vital and difficult of all. His British Deputy Chief of Staff, Major-General John Whiteley, bitterly summarised the attitude of the airmen as 'hoping that Overlord will meet with every success but sorry they can't give direct assistance because of course they are more fully occupied on the really important war against Germany'. Eisenhower was determined that he had to have both tactical and strategic air forces based in Britain under his control to fight the battle of Normandy. There was no particular problem about assigning the tactical air forces, but the RAF's formidable 'Bomber' Harris balked vigorously at any 'interference' from Eisenhower with his strategic forces and his massive area bombing of German cities every night. For Eisenhower the issue was so vital that on 22 March, at the height of a long and complex inter-service and inter-governmental wrangle, he recorded in a diary memorandum: 'If a satisfactory answer is not reached and the matter settled at once, I will request relief from this command.' It was the first and only time in the war when he even thought of such a drastic act. Later that same day the British Chiefs of Staff met and finally resolved the controversy by agreeing to place Harris's Bomber Command under Eisenhower's 'direction' (rather than his command or his control), with Tedder as Deputy Supreme Commander, acting, in Churchill's phrase, as 'the air lobe of Eisenhower's brain'. The Americans had been more than ready to do the same with Spaatz's strategic forces in Britain, and finally with some semantical flexibility Eisenhower got what he felt would be a workable arrangement if not an ideal solution. He and Tedder then turned to another long wrangle with the air forces over how they wished to employ strategic air power in support of the invasion.

Both had become convinced that a massive air offensive against the French railway network and key bridges should be mounted. But the airmen balked. Harris objected that his forces, trained for night area bombing, would be wasted on such small targets. Spaatz wanted to concentrate his daylight precision bombing with Flying Fortresses against the German oil refineries, arguing that he could cripple the *Wehrmacht* by cutting off its supply of gasoline. The RAF then produced a War Cabinet directive of 1940 forbidding air attacks against targets in occupied Europe which carried any risk of heavy civilian casualties. Eisenhower consulted the commander of de Gaulle's Free French forces in Britain, General Pierre Koenig, who gave a forthright opinion which was relayed to Churchill: 'This is war and it must be expected that people will be killed. We would take the anticipated loss to be rid of the Germans.' Churchill still agonised that the plan 'will smear the good name of the Royal Air Force across the world', but Eisenhower and Tedder were adamant. Finally the War Cabinet ruling was reversed. Tedder drew up a list of seventy marshalling yards as priority targets for a strategic bombing campaign, which then got under way in mid-April. Even Harris's night bombers showed greater effectiveness than their commander had predicted, and civilian casualties were mercifully far fewer than had been feared.

By D-Day in June rail traffic in France had been cut to a mere one-third of its January level. Eisenhower's 'direction' of the bomber forces continued until September, and was utterly essential not only in sealing off the Normandy beaches against strong German counter-attacks, but in then paving the way for the break-out of the Allied armies with massive air support in the battles for Caen, St Lô, Falaise and elsewhere. Not for the first time in the war, Eisenhower had shown himself to be a good deal more realistic and practical about the command and use of air power than some of the airmen themselves.

Then less than a week before the scheduled landing date, Air Marshal Sir Trafford Leigh-Mallory, the air commander for D-Day, came to Eisenhower in frantic alarm over fresh intelligence of German forces in the area where the airborne landings were due to take place behind the American beaches under Bradley. He forecast desperately that 'at the most only 30 per cent of the glider loads' were now likely to get through the defences, and urged Eisenhower to call off what he said would turn out to be a 'futile slaughter' of two American airborne divisions. Eisenhower wrote later than 'it would be difficult to conceive of a more soul-racking problem', but he grimly decided that Bradley *had* to have the airborne drop to support the seaborne landings. He wrote to Leigh-Mallory that 'there is nothing for it' but to go through with the plans, and ordered him to go back over 'every last detail' to minimise the hazards as far as possible and in particular to avoid any word or action leaking out that would needlessly depress the troops involved.

On the eve of D-Day Eisenhower arrived at the US 101st Airborne Division and stayed on the field talking with the troops until they began taking off around midnight. They seem to have cheered him up more than he was able to cheer them up. He then drove two hours back to his headquarters near Portsmouth to await the first flash of the D-Day landings. In the overall,

D-Day went remarkably well, the airborne landings included. Around noon that day a messenger brought a personal note to headquarters from Leigh-Mallory. It was sometimes difficult to admit one was wrong, the air commander wrote to Eisenhower, but never had it been a greater pleasure than in doing so now. He congratulated Eisenhower for the decision to stick to the plans, and apologised for having added to his worries with his dire warnings.

From D-Day on, the leitmotif of the last eleven months of the war for Eisenhower was a long, running series of arguments and conflicts with the British over strategy, tactics and command arrangements, step by step across Europe until the completion of the conquest of Germany. In part these were differences of strongly held convictions, in part it was a matter of personalities, and in part it was a basic problem of national approach, of which Eisenhower later wrote:

> There was a considerable difference in the methods used by the British government and those used by the Americans in communicating with and supporting a theater commander. The American Chiefs of Staff, with the approval of the President, gave a theater commander a mission, provided him with such supplies and troops as they deemed adequate, and let him alone to fail or succeed. If he failed, he was relieved and a new commander assigned. As long as he was succeeding they largely let him make his own decisions. The British government, on the other hand, kept in close touch with almost every tactical move in our theater.

Thus Roosevelt seldom communicated with Eisenhower at all. Marshall expected to be kept thoroughly informed by Eisenhower, and he replied with constant observations, questions or suggestions which rarely impinged directly on operational matters. But Churchill and Brooke were used to keeping up a stream of tactical advice and direct orders to British commanders in the field, and they certainly did not play coy with Eisenhower. Churchill lectured him unceasingly on politico-military concepts. Brooke had strong views about the strategy he wanted to see applied to cleaning up the Germans, and did not deeply conceal his lack of confidence in how Eisenhower was running the war. Montgomery added his own particular brand of exacerbations over tactics, objectives, orders, personalities and command arrangements.

It is a measure of Eisenhower's greatness as a commander and as a person that these differences never got out of hand. He spent endless hours in complex and often emotional arguments with these three British leaders without ever giving offence, without ever allowing any breach in the alliance to develop, and at the same time without ever compromising his own considerable authority or allowing his own concepts to be undermined. He was accommodating in manner and in discussion, but while being understanding he could also be tough and unyielding. The British were ready constantly to criticise him for vagueness or uncertainty or lack of clear, firm leadership, but in fact he was often trying to avoid on their behalf the very kind of showdown decisions that the British could not win. This may not have been ideal leadership, but it is a rather wry commentary on how Eisenhower rode these storms that Brooke openly regarded the British officers at SHAEF, who were indeed strongly loyal to Eisenhower, as being under his domination – while Bradley and the senior American commanders felt just as openly that in decision-making Eisenhower was dominated by the opinions of his senior British staff. An allied commander faces problems and limitations in leadership, as well as opportunities, which never arise in purely national enterprises.

Fundamental to a great deal of the Anglo-American wrangling over the conduct of the European campaign was Eisenhower's concept of a 'broad front strategy' against Brooke's determined preference for a single major thrust to finish off the Germans. The Combined Chiefs of Staff had given Eisenhower a simple, straightforward directive which said: 'You will enter the continent of Europe and, in conjunction with the other United Nations, undertake operations aimed at the heart of Germany and the destruction of her armed forces'. It was then left to Eisenhower and the planning staff of Supreme Allied Headquarters to decide how this directive was to be carried out.

In substance Eisenhower decided to advance on Germany on a broad front following the break-out from Normandy, with the aim of forcing the Germans to stretch their own defences all the way from Switzerland to the mouth of the Rhine. His intention was that the Allies would then probe and push all along this line, prepared to take advantage of weaknesses which were certain to show since the Germans could not be strong everywhere. This long line would then give the greatest advantage of tactical surprise for the final thrust across the Rhine and into the 'heart of Germany' (which was not specifically defined in the directive of the Combined Chiefs of Staff). Brooke on the other hand regarded this as unimaginative, wasteful and time-consuming – as well as dangerous, because neither could the Allies be strong everywhere along a broad front. Brooke's great strategic principle was 'concentration of forces', and once the armies were out of Normandy he and Montgomery pleaded with Eisenhower almost incessantly for a major single thrust into the 'heart of Germany' across the north, with everything concentrated to complete the job in one blow while the rest of the Allied divisions pinned the Germans down on the defensive.

It is quite probable that this difference of strategic approach derived at least in part from the vast difference in British and American military resources. Brooke and the British army simply *had* to think in terms of effective concentration of forces because they did not have the resources to fight any other way. Eisenhower on the other hand could plan the campaign with an enormous tidal wave of American military power building up behind him. When Germany surrendered he had ninety-one Allied divisions on his order of battle – sixty-one of them American. Nor did Eisenhower feel that there was all that much contradiction between advancing towards Germany on a broad front and then concentrating forces for a major thrust, or series of thrusts, when the opportunity came. But Brooke saw a world of difference of approach, timing and execution.

The first major argument that Eisenhower faced after D-Day, which reflected this fundamental difference, was over Anvil – the code designation for the invasion of southern France which finally took place on 15 August. A force of seven divisions was to be withdrawn from Italy, and the British pleaded bitterly for the operation to be called off so that Alexander and Clark could continue a major drive north to the Po valley and on to Trieste. This was of course a reflection of Churchill's 'soft underbelly of Europe' strategy, which he argued would aid Overlord by drawing German forces away from France. The British had already lost the argument several times in the Combined Chiefs of Staff, but this did not deter Churchill – who changed the code designation of the operation to Dragoon 'because I am being dragooned into it.'

Eisenhower had to bear the brunt of two long and personal confrontations with the old warrior on the subject in early August, one of which lasted for six solid hours. He wrote to Marshall afterwards that he had 'said no in every form of the English language at my command.' Eisenhower, for his broad front strategy, wanted to open the big French ports of Marseilles and Toulon, complete the liberation of France and bag the German forces in the south and south-west, get the French army in Italy back on its native soil and move more Allied forces up to the borders of Germany at the southern end of the Rhine. He contended that smaller Allied forces in Italy would continue to pin down just as many Germans. In the end, when Churchill finally accepted that he could not change Eisenhower's mind, he flew off to Italy and went aboard a destroyer to watch the landings near St Tropez. When Eisenhower heard this he again wrote to Marshall that 'with all of the fighting and mental anguish I went through in order to preserve that operation, I don't know whether to sit down and laugh or cry'.

But in the meantime, as the battle of Normandy raged and ebbed, difficulties of a deeper and more intractable kind were building up between Eisenhower and Montgomery. The two men could scarcely have been less alike in personality and temperament – Eisenhower open, convivial, conciliatory, modest and in the habit of working closely with a staff that participated actively in the decisions; Montgomery secretive, abrupt, austere, dogmatic, an egocentric who kept to his own caravan and used his staff simply to provide him with information and carry out his orders. It was probably part of Montgomery's vanity also to have Eisenhower always come and see him – for he never visited Supreme Allied Headquarters once throughout the entire war. In any case the first major conflict that developed between the two in Normandy was not over strategy or even tactics, but simply over fighting.

Montgomery, in his original plans for D-Day and the Normandy battle, intended to take the city of Caen on the first day of the landings and then thrust south-east to Falaise on the most direct route to Paris in good tank country with good airfields. He described all this to the assembled Allied commanders at St Paul's School in London when everybody including King George VI gathered in mid-May for a final briefing on the invasion plans – but he conveniently leaves this out of his memoirs. He did not capture Caen immediately, but this was not particularly held against him since it was probably over-optimistic anyway. The Germans then poured their heaviest concentration of armour into holding that corner of Normandy, and Montgomery turned failure into virtue by deciding that he would now operate to pin down the German armour while the break-out from Normandy would be carried out by the Americans under Bradley on the right, in a vast wheeling operation to entrap the enemy at the opening of the drive across France.

As Basil Liddell Hart comments in his *History of the Second World War*:

> It was the 'Monty way' to talk as if any operation that he had conducted always proceeded exactly as he intended, with the certainty and precision of a machine – or of divine providence. That characteristic has often obscured his adaptability to circumstances and thus, ironically, deprived him of the credit due him for his combination of flexibility with determination in generalship.

Montgomery compounded the controversy over these events by asserting in his postwar memoirs and repeating at every given opportunity that 'Eisenhower never fully understood' his Normandy strategy or how he was fighting the battle. Eisenhower understood perfectly well, and approved the strategy. So did Bradley, who wrote with the fullest generosity about his relations with Montgomery during this period. Eisenhower's argument with Montgomery was about speeding up the fighting. He wrote to Montgomery on 6 July:

> I am familiar with your plan for generally holding firm with your left, attracting thereto all of the enemy armour, while your right pushes down the peninsula and threatens the rear and flank of the forces facing the Second British Army. However, the advance on the right has been slow and laborious. It appears to me that we must use all possible energy in a determined effort to prevent a stalemate . . . We have not yet attempted a major full-dress attack on the left flank supported by everything we could bring to bear . . .

Montgomery dismisses this as 'Eisenhower like a football coach, up and down the line all the time encouraging everyone to get on with the game'. It was not a happy opener for the months ahead. The capture of Caen was not completed until 20 July, six weeks after D-Day. After that, Montgomery and all the other commanders quickly caught up with and outran the planned 'phase lines' and were across the Seine ten days ahead of expectations. As they raced on, Montgomery, with Brooke's blessing, argued with Eisenhower to abandon the broad front strategy in favour of a single thrust.

Meeting Eisenhower on 23 August Montgomery proposed that the advance in central France be halted now that it was beyond Paris, and that logistic support be switched entirely behind his 21st Army Group for a dash straight across the north, crossing the Rhine above the industrial Ruhr and into the heart of Germany to end the war. He asked that the US First Army be taken away from Bradley and placed under his command to give him the force to do the job. Bradley at this same time was proposing to Eisenhower that he be given the logistic backing to continue his thrust across central France towards Metz, with the aim of crossing the Rhine and outflanking the Ruhr to the south.

Eisenhower was neither blind nor deaf to the advantages of a single thrust against the disorganised and retreating Germans. He knew perfectly well that at this point he did not have sufficient logistic support available to go on maintaining a 'broad front' advance everywhere. Nevertheless a division still required something like 600 tons of supplies every day even when it was sitting still, and by that time Eisenhower had thirty-six divisions in action in France. He was also aware therefore that even if he reduced supplies to Bradley, Patton and the rest of his forces to a minimum there still would not be enough for Montgomery to mount and sustain the kind of operation he was proposing. Moreover Montgomery wanted to push across some of the most difficult fighting terrain in Europe, involving endless river crossings, crowded with towns and villages which could be turned into one defensive strongpoint after another. Finally Eisenhower simply did not accept the thesis that the Nazis would collapse and surrender if a single Allied force thrust itself into Germany's vitals. The capacity of the German army to recover, regroup and hit back was probably the most impressive military quality shown by any army on either side in the Second World War, and the Nazis were not the giving-up kind of men.

Nevertheless some concentration of force was called for, and Eisenhower came down on Montgomery's side – but with much more limited objectives in view than the end-of-the-war dash that Montgomery thought was possible. He agreed to switch the main logistic support to Montgomery, and also to direct the First Army to cover Montgomery's southern flank while remaining under Bradley's command. Eisenhower's primary objective was to capture the Channel ports and the big harbour of Antwerp in order to break the logistic bottleneck for the growing Allied forces. But with Montgomery's objectives in view he also turned over the First Airborne Army for the operation against Arnhem in the hope that it might at least be possible to secure a bridgehead across the Rhine. This was the limit of what Eisenhower regarded as possible with the resources he could muster for Montgomery. It also fitted into his 'broad front' strategy for closing to the Rhine from north to south before attempting to move into the heart of Germany.

Relations between Eisenhower and Montgomery were so strained and the arguments so difficult that the tendency seems to have been for both men to seize upon any agreement in sight with relief, and then go away and emphasise what each saw in it while ignoring serious fundamental differences which still remained. Eisenhower was not clear enough nor categorical enough in spelling out to Montgomery exactly what were *his* priorities and limitations for a northern thrust, and Montgomery for his part was more than ready to take what he had been given and read into it a go-ahead for *his* objectives. This was the kind of misunderstanding that would probably never have arisen between Eisenhower and Bradley, or even Eisenhower and Alexander. But to the end of the war and beyond, Montgomery never wavered in his conviction that Eisenhower did not do enough to allow the 21st Army Group to win the war before the winter of 1944.

This however was not at all the view of Montgomery's loyal and highly respected Chief of Staff, Major-General Sir Francis de Guingand, who wrote subsequently that 'throughout the war this was the only major issue over which I did not agree with my chief'. With a much clearer grasp of the logistic problems, and much closer contacts with Supreme Allied Headquarters, which Montgomery never deigned to visit, de Guingand's conclusion quite simply was that it would have been impossible to supply the operation which Montgomery wanted to mount, even if Eisenhower had stripped everything else naked and moved all of the main transport services to support the 21st Army Group. He goes on to add:

> We would have been very lucky to find any Rhine bridges intact and to bring forward bridging material would have been a lengthy affair. In any case we had not yet 'phased in' the bridging material which would be required for the Rhine. Even assuming that such a force or spearhead did cross the river, I cannot see how it would have produced a German capitulation. If we had been able to get a sizeable force across the Rhine into Germany in the autumn, the Germans after a period of crisis would have produced sufficient troops to strangle its effectiveness.

When the airborne operation against Arnhem failed, and Montgomery had to give up his ideas about thrusting into Germany and concentrate on the more mundane problem of finishing off the Scheldt estuary so that the port of Antwerp could be opened to supply the Allied forces, including his own, he opened up on Eisenhower with a fresh attack over the command arrangements. Things were going wrong, he contended, because there was no single ground commander to take hold, and at the very least there should be one commander north of the Ardennes to direct an assault against northern Germany. To this Eisenhower was finally stung to reply: 'The Antwerp operation does not involve the question of command in the slightest degree.' But Montgomery was also relaying his complaints and his proposals and expectations to Brooke in London.

In early December, Churchill and Brooke asked Eisenhower to come to London with Tedder for a major discussion of the military situation. Like the bleak winter in North Africa two years before, this was again a low point for Eisenhower. But this time he had vastly superior forces under his command and a great deal more experience and confidence in his own judgement. The London meeting nevertheless was a pretty grim affair. Brooke recorded in a diary entry of 12 December:

> Ike explained his plan which contemplates a double advance into Germany north of the Ruhr and by Frankfurt. I disagreed flatly with it, accused Ike of violating principles of concentration of force which had resulted in his present failures. I stressed the importance of concentrating on one thrust. Amongst other things, discovered that Ike does not hope to cross the Rhine before May!

But whatever Brooke's ideas about strategy, whatever Eisenhower's plans, whatever Montgomery's agitations about the command arrangements, the Germans were about to change everything.

Four days after the London meeting, on the morning of Saturday 16 December, General Bradley left his 12th Army Group headquarters in Luxembourg around 5 am for a four-hour drive in foggy, icy weather to Versailles for a conference with Eisenhower on future operations and logistics. By the time he arrived at Supreme Headquarters first reports had begun to come through of some attacks on his thinly held Ardennes front to the north of Luxembourg. Bradley, probably influenced by his own army group intelligence, which had been fairly sanguine about possible enemy activity, thought they were probably only small spoiling attacks. Eisenhower, whose intelligence chief, Major-General Strong, had been warning of the possibility of an Ardennes offensive, immediately took the view that it did not make much sense from a German standpoint to try simple spoiling attacks in this area, and that this was something major, He was right. The Battle of the Bulge was on.

When Eisenhower assembled a staff conference with Bradley at 2 o'clock that afternoon, Strong went over the growing intelligence reports and gave his opinion that this was again a classic German General Staff operation to attack out of the Ardennes, and he forecast that the Germans would head for the Meuse and then turn north towards Brussels and Antwerp in an effort to circle Montgomery's forces in the rear and split the Allies in two. Bradley still thought the assessments were exaggerated, but he left the meeting and phoned his headquarters to give orders that all his divisional commanders were to suspend any forward operations and remain free for employment towards the Ardennes. Next morning, before Bradley left to return to Luxembourg, Eisenhower took the decision to hold Bastogne, and ordered the 101st Airborne Division out of reserve near Reims, under Bradley's command, and up to the town immediately on wheels.

On Tuesday 19 December Eisenhower and his senior SHAEF staff officers drove to Verdun to meet Bradley, Patton, Devers and other commanders. By now Strong's intelligence estimate was that some twenty-five German divisions were involved in the attack. Patton somewhat egotistically thought that the Germans would wheel south to try and catch his Third Army in the rear, but Eisenhower continued to agree with Strong's estimate that Brussels and Antwerp were the strategic objectives. He then fixed the line of the Meuse as the point at which the Germans had to be stopped at all costs, and ordered Patton to attack north to relieve Bastogne, which was by then surrounded. Devers was ordered to stretch his 6th Army Group north along the Rhine to take over part of Patton's front. Eisenhower cautioned Patton not to start his attack until he had assembled sufficient forces to give it full weight against the experienced and heavy German divisions he would be hitting. Patton surprised everybody by saying he could be under way in twenty-four hours.

There had been neither panic nor alarm at Supreme Headquarters in any of this – if anything there was a certain sense of elation that the Germans were pushing major forces into a salient that could be cut off if the American army did its job. By the time Eisenhower and the senior SHAEF staff officers got back to Versailles in the early evening after the Verdun conference, the intelligence reports pouring in for General Strong were increasingly serious. The Germans had pushed ahead rapidly that afternoon (the weather still had not cleared to allow the air forces to get cracking) and the thrust now was cutting off Bradley's communications with his units on the northern side of the attack.

Around midnight Strong and Whiteley jointly went to Eisenhower's dynamic, volatile and truculent Chief of Staff, Lieutenant-General Walter Bedell Smith, and recommended that Bradley's command should be split and the northern flank placed under Montgomery. Strong says they acted 'fully realizing the mistrust of Montgomery among many senior Americans' but feeling that this should not alter the judgement of the situation. Smith lost his temper, swore at 'you goddamned British with a British answer for everything', and even informed the two officers that he was relieving them of their responsibilities and shipping them back to Britain the next morning. But by morning he had cooled down, apologised for losing his temper ('I was so damned mad because I knew you were right'), and asked them to accompany him to Eisenhower, but to keep absolutely silent while he put the recommendation forward because it was important that the proposal come from an American. Eisenhower listened, briefly debated the pros and cons, and then picked up the telephone and asked to be put through to Bradley. He told Bradley what he was about to do, listened to Bradley for a long time, and then finally ended the conversation by saying abruptly: 'Well, Brad, those are my orders'. A few hours later Churchill called from London to urge Eisenhower to consider giving Montgomery control of the northern battle, and for once Eisenhower could tell Churchill that he had already met a British request.

The reaction in Britain was one of almost instant jubilation – Eisenhower's decision was seen as a vindication for all of the British arguments about the need for a single ground commander and a greater concentration of forces instead of fighting on a long line. Montgomery did not help things with a press conference after the battle, which left the impression that the British had bailed out the Americans who did not know how to handle a battle. But as far as handling the battle was concerned, Montgomery had infuriated Eisenhower by delaying for three days a counter-attack, which Eisenhower was demanding and which he believed Montgomery had agreed to produce on 1 January. The feelings of Bradley, Patton and other American commanders about Montgomery by this time had become unprintable.

Nevertheless the Germans had shot their bolt and done Eisenhower the service of breaking what otherwise would have been a long winter stalemate and slogging operation. He now turned back to closing to the Rhine on a broad front. But as soon as the battle of the Bulge was over the battle of the Allies resumed. When Eisenhower moved the US First Army back to Bradley's command (leaving the US Ninth under Montgomery) the British started up all over again about the need for an overall ground commander – or at least an enlarged and enhanced command for Montgomery. Finally Marshall cabled Eisenhower: 'Under no circumstances make any concessions of any kind whatsoever. I am not assuming that you had in mind such a concession. I just wish you to be certain of our attitude. You are doing a grand job, and go on and give them hell.' After that the command argument simply petered out. But Brooke continued to wrangle over the broad front strategy and press for concentrating in a single major assault across the Rhine north of the Ruhr.

In early January, the Combined Chiefs of Staff stopped off at Malta, *en route* to the Yalta meeting of Roosevelt, Churchill and Stalin, to review with Eisenhower's Chief of Staff, Bedell Smith, the SHAEF plans for finishing off the war. Smith emphasised that Eisenhower was now in particular convinced that the broad front strategy was gaining additional strategic benefit from the way the Germans were fighting. Instead of pulling back forces across the Rhine to mount a strong defence in the heart of Germany, Hitler was forcing them to fight right where they were. This therefore offered the Allies the opportunity of chopping up and destroying the remaining bulk of the German army to the west of the Rhine before ever crossing the river.

Through Bedell Smith, Eisenhower again repeatedly and explicitly re-assured Brooke and the British that within this strategy Montgomery would make the major thrust north of the Ruhr and the US Ninth Army and other American forces would remain under his command to do it. In fact, Montgomery planned for employment of twenty-five divisions under his 21st Army Group in the north, but Eisenhower and the SHAEF planners insisted that this be increased to thirty-five divisions. When Montgomery crossed the

Rhine he had more American divisions under his command than British and Canadian. On the record, Eisenhower could scarcely be accused of squeezing Montgomery or holding him back. But at the same time, he made it just as clear to the Combined Chiefs that Bradley would be making a major thrust with American forces through the centre of Germany in the Frankfurt area, and that he intended to take advantage of any other sound opportunities to cross the Rhine as they opened up on his very long front.

Still, Brooke was only partly mollified. Yet curiously he sent a minute to Montgomery at about this same time on operations of the 21st Army Group which, at least by implication, conceded the wisdom of the broad front advance. Pointing out to Montgomery that he was proposing to close to the Rhine in the north only from Arnhem to Dusseldorf, Brooke said:

> Will this be a long enough stretch to enable you to achieve the necessary tactical surprise for the movement across the river to the north of the Ruhr? Would it not probably be desirable first to clear up a further stretch of the west bank of the Rhine, say down to Bonn, if necessary forces can be made available?

Eisenhower was proposing to clear the Rhine not merely from Arnhem to Bonn but all the way down to Basel to obtain maximum tactical surprise for river crossings for all of the armies. As the Allies closed to the Rhine, the loss of prisoners and casualties for the Germans became enormous – 250,000 prisoners taken by Hodges US First Army and Patton's Third Army alone, between Cologne and Mainz, on top of heavy casualties which the Germans had already suffered in the Bulge. When the US 9th Armoured Division in Hodge's army seized a bridge intact across the Rhine at Remagen on March 7, the German army was already a spent force with the end in sight. Had the Brooke strategy prevailed, it would have been difficult to exploit the bridge at Remagen. But when Bradley telephoned Eisenhower with the news, his immediate response was: 'Go ahead and shove five divisions across instantly, Brad.' He then ordered the bridgehead expanded slowly and held on the defensive until Montgomery crossed the Rhine two weeks later – at which point the US forces broke out from Remagen and drove north to link up with Montgomery's Army Group and complete the encirclement of the Ruhr. Meanwhile, Patton had slipped across the river well to the south, below Mainz, one day before Montgomery.

Churchill and Brooke flew out from Britain to watch Montgomery's assault crossing, and crossed the Rhine themselves later in the day. Eisenhower in his memoirs quotes Brooke as turning to him that day and saying: 'Thank God, Ike, you stuck by your plan. You were completely right and I am sorry if my fear of dispersed effort added to your burdens. The German is now licked. Thank God you stuck by your guns.' But Brooke, in his memoirs, comments:

> To the best of my memory, I congratulated him heartily on his success and said that, as matters had turned out, his policy was now the correct one;

that with the Germans in defeated condition no dangers now existed in a dispersal of effort. I am quite certain that I never said to him "You were completely right", as I am still convinced that he was 'completely wrong'.

As the armies raced on across Germany a last controversy flared over Churchill's hopes that the Allies might capture Berlin and 'shake hands with the Russians as far east as possible'. In a flurry of telegrams and conferences Eisenhower again stuck to his plans, taking the simple position that from a military standpoint 'Berlin is no longer a particularly important objective.' His armies were again outrunning their logistic support as they did in the dash across France. At best he could only have pushed spearheads up to Berlin from the Elbe, while the Russians were already within artillery range of the city with a mass of some two million men to encircle it for the final battle of the war. In any case both Churchill and Eisenhower knew that the four-power zones of occupation had long been fixed, and that the allied forces would have to withdraw anyway from any territory that they went on taking to the east of the Elbe.

Still, as with so many other decisions and actions that Eisenhower took in the vast panorama of his wartime responsibilities, the alternatives go on being debated, the 'ifs' and the controversies remain. When Field Marshal Jodl signed the unconditional surrender at SHAEF Advance Headquarters near Reims, Eisenhower said all that he needed to say in his final signal of the war to the Combined Chiefs of Staff in London and Washington: 'The mission of this Allied force was fulfilled at 0241 local time 7 May 1945.'

General of the Army Omar N. Bradley

Forrest C. Pogue

Often called the 'soldiers' general', Omar N. Bradley gained the warm affection of the troops he commanded in North Africa, the Mediterranean, and in north-west Europe. Without Patton's showmanship or MacArthur's theatrical bearing, he gained the respect of his colleagues and his subordinates by his sober dependability, dogged determination, attention to detail, and proper concern for those who served under him. At the Infantry School in Fort Benning, Georgia, and as commander of two divisions before 1944, he showed his great ability as a trainer of troops. As a corps, army and army group commander in combat he proved himself to be one of the great field commanders in the Second World War.

Born in Clark, Missouri, on Lincoln's birthday in 1893, Bradley like his classmate Eisenhower and others of his generation came to West Point because it was a place where a young man with a desire for an education but without the means to finance it could get highly acceptable training without cost. He taught briefly before going to the Military Academy, exhibiting early the ability to teach. His modest bearing and gentle manner suggested less the fiery soldier than the sympathetic mentor eager to instruct the men entrusted to his care.

Seen in the field or at a conference table, Bradley often puzzled his colleagues by his quietness and soft voice. Permitting full discussion and disagreement, he sometimes seemed to be lax in control. Then suddenly he would cut through verbiage and desultory quibbling to seize the central point of a conference and announce a decision. Not one to swear or rant, he was still prompt to reprimand or relieve a commander who was giving less than his best in a crisis or failing to measure up to expectations. He performed these unpleasant tasks with the least possible wounding of pride and the continued respect of those he penalised.

Like a number of his American colleagues in the Second World War, Bradley had not served abroad in the First World War. He owed his steady rise instead to the efficient performance of routine assignments in the early years of his career and the exceptional performance of difficult jobs given him by George C. Marshall.

While assistant commandant in charge of instruction at the Infantry School, Fort Benning, in the period 1927–32, Marshall selected Bradley as one of his picked instructors in a group which included Joseph Stilwell, J. Lawton Collins, Walter Bedell Smith and Matthew Ridgway. In 1929 Bradley caught Marshall's eye by his ability to impart instruction to young officers in a simple, forceful manner. He named him Chief of the Weapons Section, saying that he had found him 'conspicuous for his ability to handle people and his ability to do things carefully and simply'. He praised his ability to strip away the non-essentials and to stage special demonstrations which made crystal clear basic lessons of warfare. Bradley was one of the officers that Marshall early marked down for future command. Several years later he wrote: 'I very much hope we will have an opportunity to serve together again. I can think of nothing more satisfactory to me.'

Bradley was serving on the War Department staff when Marshall became Chief of Staff of the US Army in September 1939. In 1940 he transferred Bradley to the post of Assistant Secretary General Staff under his direct command. Several months later Bradley had an opportunity to go to the United States Military Academy, West Point, as Commandant of Cadets, a post coveted by former cadets. To his surprise Marshall asked a few days later if he would like instead the more important post of Commandant, Infantry School. Bradley eagerly accepted and was promoted soon afterwards from lieutenant-colonel to brigadier-general, receiving his first star before former classmate Dwight D. Eisenhower.

Six months later Marshall began measuring him for another position. Shortly before Christmas 1941 he made him commander of the 82nd Infantry Division, later transformed to airborne status. Bradley impressed Marshall by his training of the unit. In another six months the Chief of Staff asked his protégé to assume command of a National Guard unit, the 28th Division. The unit, which later would have a distinguished record in the Second World War, was beset by problems which had been intensified by having to furnish some of its best men to cadres for newly formed divisions. Marshall made clear that Bradley was in line for corps command but that he would have to serve until he straightened out the division. His placid acceptance of the situation pleased Marshall, who kept him in mind for further advancement. On 12 February, a birthday Bradley shared with Lincoln, the Chief of Staff in his birthday congratulations said that it was fitting that Bradley would soon have his corps. But before that dream was realised another assignment lay ahead.

At the Casablanca Conference in January 1943 General Marshall was disturbed by the fact that Eisenhower had to handle high-level political and strategic duties while dealing constantly with units in the line. Desiring to free him of some of the pressures, the Chief of Staff proposed that he send over an officer who could be used by Eisenhower as his 'eyes and ears' and asked which officer he would like. The Supreme Allied Commander listed some dozen officers, among them General Bradley, as suitable for the post. Marshall at once made Bradley available for the assignment.

General Bradley arrived in Algiers on 24 February, some ten days after German units had smashed through Faid Pass and then through Kasserine Pass to create a dangerous situation for American forces. On the 21st the attack had been contained and on the 23rd the enemy units withdrew. But much remained to be done to restore American morale and fighting stance. Bradley's first task was that of checking on the performance of American weapons and fighting men and giving an appraisal of the leadership of the II Corps commander, US Major-General Lloyd R. Fredendall. Before Bradley could report on the growing loss of confidence in Fredendall by British and American colleagues, Eisenhower had decided on 9 March to relieve the corps commander and replace him by Major-General George S. Patton, Jr, who had commanded the Western Task Force in its invasion of North Africa the previous November.

Shortly after Patton's arrival he asked that Bradley become his deputy commander. The arrangement, approved by Eisenhower, proved tremendously important because it gave Bradley the valuable contact with II Corps officers and men, which he would need when a few weeks later Patton was summoned to higher headquarters to begin planning for the invasion of Sicily – slated for mid-July. Before leaving, Patton asked if his deputy would head a force in that attack. Bradley, assuming II Corps command, promptly agreed. Both men knew that much had to be done in Tunisia before Bradley could take a new role. He saw at once that he must convince his superiors that the American soldier could carry his share of the battle load.

Years later Bradley wrote of General H. L. G. Alexander, Eisenhower's Deputy Commander-in-Chief and Commander-in-Chief of the 18th Army Group which included British First and Eighth Army, the American II Corps and the II French Corps, that he was 'a patient, wise, and fair-minded soldier'. It was he, more than anyone else, he wrote, who 'helped the American field command mature and eventually come of age in the Tunisian campaign'. Bradley, like Eisenhower, would conclude that the experience in North Africa was essential to the later successes in north-west Europe.

On his assumption of authority Bradley was disquieted by Alexander's clear distrust of the battleworthiness of American soldiers and weapons and the fact that his plans for coming battles pinched the American forces out of a fighting role. Bradley had told Patton – who needed no prodding – of his fears and helped urge Eisenhower to provide a larger share in the coming campaign for II Corps. Alexander had agreed to this request before Bradley assumed command of II Corps at midnight on 15 April 1943.

In the less than one month that remained before the defeat of the Axis forces in Tunisia, Bradley worked with the British First Army commander, General K. A. N. Anderson, in co-ordinating the actions of II Corps with the British attack on Tunis. In the advance from Hill 609 towards Mateur and

Bizerta, the American general pushed his tank attack, held firm against Anderson's suggestion that a regiment of Bradley's forces be shifted to support the British advance, and won a change in the proposal that he send his troops around German troops in the hills rather than to advance along the ridge line. Bradley's four divisions, 9th Infantry (under Manton Eddy), 34th Infantry (under Charles Ryder), 1st Infantry (under Terry de la Mesa Allen), and the 1st Armored Division (under Ernest Harmon) pushed north and east in early May – taking Mateur on 3 May and entering Bizerta on 7 May, a few minutes after the British forces had entered Tunis. The Axis forces surrendered two days later. On 13 May Bradley was ordered to Algiers to aid Patton in planning for Sicilian operations.

In the North African fighting Bradley learned much about the weaknesses and inexperience of a number of the American units. He no less than Patton recognised the need of stricter discipline; more than Patton he stressed the importance of proper supply organisation. He worked closely with his division commanders, noting their weaknesses and strengths. With his British colleagues he pursued a policy of understanding, insisting only that American forces be given a proper opportunity to prove their worth, asking that discredited units be given another chance, and demanding that Americans have their proper share of the battle. In this last effort he was elated when General Marshall stressed that precise point in a message to Eisenhower. He entered the Sicilian campaign prepared for a larger role in a more challenging campaign.

Brought back to Algiers before the final mop-up in Tunisia, Bradley worked with Patton's staff (soon to become Seventh Army) to plan for the landings in Sicily, on 10 July. For that invasion his II Corps, with the 1st and 45th divisions, were to land on the south and south-western shore of Sicily, while an infantry division and part of an armoured division landed to his left. On the right Montgomery's Eighth Army was to hit the south-eastern coast and drive for Messina. Patton's forces were to drive northward through the centre of the island to split the enemy forces in half, while auxiliary forces cleared the north-west corner of Sicily. Alexander planned a major thrust by Montgomery which would seize Messina and the eastern sector of the island, opening the way for invasion of the boot of Italy. When his advance stalled Bradley and the other American commanders sought their objectives, Patton threw additional duties on the II Corps and demanded extra-heavy performance from his supply groups. In the early phases it seemed that enemy reaction would prove too much for the invading units but, as Bradley watched, the seasoned troops of 1st Division held. Later, Patton's forces moved into Messina ahead of Montgomery's units. Sicily provided new lessons for the later landings. One of the most massive operations of the war in which units brought from overseas were committed directly into action helped prepare the Americans for the cross-Channel attack with many inexperienced troops.

Bradley's most severe test in the closing days of the campaign was the relief of the commanders of the most experienced American division, the 1st, the famous Red One of the First World War on whose staff Marshall had served as Chief of Operations. Not for lack of fighting skill or determination were Major-General Allen and his deputy, Theodore Roosevelt, Jr, relieved. Bradley in his memoirs told in detail of the developments which led to his action – a decision for which he took full responsibility, although friends of Allen blamed Patton and, sometimes, Eisenhower for the relief. Bradley had become aware in North Africa that Allen sometimes disregarded directives of higher headquarters in order to win his objective. In the period after the victory in Tunisia, he was disturbed when Allen's troops showed their disdain for other units, especially those in the rear areas, by open contempt of the Military Police and by rioting in the streets. He determined before the end of the campaign in Sicily to relieve Allen and he deemed it necessary to remove Roosevelt as well. In one of his most difficult decisions of the war, he removed the two commanders after some of their best fighting. But he did it without prejudice. Marshall, who had picked Allen despite the misgivings of some of his advisers, gave him another division with which he won new plaudits late in the war. Roosevelt, a special favourite of Marshall's since the First World War in the 1st Division, went in on D-Day on Utah Beach and a few weeks later was recommended by Bradley for division command shortly before he died of a heart attack.

The conquest of Sicily was followed by an attack on the toe of Italy and developments which brought negotiations for surrender by representatives of the King of Italy. As the Combined Chiefs of Staff met in Quebec in August 1943 overtures for an armistice as well as preparations for an Allied attack at Salerno were approved. Meanwhile Churchill told Roosevelt that since the Americans would put the larger number of men into the cross-Channel attack in north-west Europe they should appoint the supreme commander. It was understood that this officer would be George C. Marshall, Bradley's long-time supporter. As the attack in Italy developed, Marshall and Eisenhower discussed the proper make-up of the command for the cross-Channel attack. Eisenhower, disturbed lest he be brought back to Washington as Chief of Staff instead of Marshall, still loyally suggested the command arrangements he thought best for Overlord. When, at the end of August 1943, officers in London pressed Marshall to name an army commander for the invasion, he informed Eisenhower: 'My choice had been Bradley . . . Could you relieve Bradley for this command?'

Shortly before the request Eisenhower had told Marshall that Bradley was capable of commanding an army and that he had 'a fine capacity for leadership and a thorough understanding of the requirements of modern battle'. At Marshall's request he said that he was unhappy to lose him but that he was the obvious man for the job. A week later he wrote that he believed Bradley to be the best rounded combat leader I have yet met in our service. While he probably lacks some of the extraordinary and ruthless driving power that Patton can exercise at critical moments, he still has such force and determination that even in this characteristic he is among our best. In all other things he is a jewel to have around . . .

Patton had commanded in North Africa and Sicily but it was Bradley who stood out in Eisenhower's mind. Historians and film makers have made undue importance out of the slapping incident in which Patton was involved as being decisive in the decision to choose Bradley. Marshall had not even known of the slapping incident at the time he agreed to the selection of Bradley. Undoubtedly it was a factor in Eisenhower's thinking. But more important in the minds of Eisenhower and Marshall was the knowledge they had gained over many years – Eisenhower since West Point and Marshall since Fort Benning – that this was a man who could be depended on in a pinch. He never gives his commander a moment of worry, wrote Ike.

Marshall was delighted at Eisenhower's recommendation. Although he withheld judgement for the moment as to the future army group commander – listing Lieutenant-General Jacob L. Devers, then Commanding General, European Theatre of Operations, US Army, and Lieutenant-General Lesley McNair, Commander of the Army Ground Forces, among his senior candidates, he obviously kept Bradley high in the running. More important, Bradley doubled in brass as commander of both headquarters. As the invasion neared it became clear that he would command the army group well as that of First Army. Near the end of 1943 the Third Army commander in the United States, Lieutenant-General Courtney H. Hodges, another Marshall associate, was tagged as deputy to Bradley in the opening phase of the invasion with the understanding that he would command First Army when Bradley took over 12th Army Group.

Bradley was sent to the United Kingdom before Montgomery and Eisenhower arrived. He was familiar with the proposals of the Cossac planners and arrived at the views, pushed by Montgomery and Eisenhower, that the area chosen for invasion be broadened and that an additional beach to the left of the main American invasion on Omaha Beach – that now known as Utah Beach – be added. He insisted that airborne assistance to close the gap between Omaha and Utah Beach in the American sector was essential. Despite the arguments of Air Marshal Sir Trafford Leigh-Mallory that the airborne effort would suffer unacceptable losses, Bradley – backed by Montgomery – won Eisenhower's insistence that the drop be made. Bradley had argued that without air drops he would prefer to give up the Utah Beach assault.

Bradley set up his army group headquarters in Bryanston Square in London. Shortly afterwards, he chose space in Clifton College, Bristol, for First Army headquarters. At least half of his staff included former colleagues in the Mediterranean. Higher headquarters later complained of his staff.

Bradley himself wrote that as a result of its high-handed treatment by the Seventh Army staff in Italy 'First Army was critical, unforgiving, and resentful of all authority but its own.' This attitude would cause problems later when Bradley moved to 12th Army Group, leaving some of the First Army staff members behind. Particularly, there developed a rift between his chief of intelligence at 12th Army Group and at First Army which proved embarrassing during the battle of the Ardennes. Moreover the army group staff, although less touchy, developed problems of its own. War Department observers in Europe during the December fighting reported back to Washington such bitterness over alleged favouritism to Montgomery, that Marshall's deputy, General Handy, declined to send the report to Marshall.

Despite the difficulties between staffs Bradley was aided personally by his own close relationships with Eisenhower, Bedell Smith and other Mediterranean officers who had come to Supreme Headquarters in the United Kingdom. His former associates at First Army continued their personal loyalty to him whatever their quarrel with 12th Army Group. By the same token Bradley benefited from the close relationships he had developed in North Africa and Sicily with Patton and many of his subordinates.

In addition to his request for airborne assistance for the invasion, General Bradley asked for close air support, increased naval backing, and commitment of the Ranger battalions to the west of Omaha Beach. He was criticised later by British advocates of special weapons for his failure to make use of flails and other special techniques. Indeed some writers have blamed all the delays on Omaha Beach on his failure to use these devices. Bradley could rejoin that some of his setbacks occurred because the special DD tanks, which he did accept, sank in the heavy seas off the coast and that his troops on Utah Beach, where enemy defenders were fewer and less well entrenched, went inland without special devices almost without losses.

Bradley's pre D-Day preparations, while not bold, made effective use of careful training – with numerous manoeuvres designed to make his troops combat-ready. In the last days before the attack he grew concerned by the mounting anxiety over heavy casualties in the opening phases of the attack. Some spoke of fifty thousand and even a hundred thousand casualties. Shortly before the final assembly of men in the marshalling areas, he made numerous speeches and published an article in army publications predicting many fewer casualties than expected and pointing to the improvement of medical care which would reduce rates of mortality. He proved to be an accurate prophet.

Deliberately lacking in the colourful displays of Patton and Montgomery, Bradley was less well known than they to the bulk of the twenty divisions in the United Kingdom before D-Day. He wore no distinctive beret or brace of pistols and he was noted neither for his profanity or pieties. But his reputation had preceded him. Ernie Pyle, the soldiers' favourite columnist in North Africa and the Mediterranean, accompanied Bradley for a time and dubbed him 'the Soldiers' General'. Pyle, an unspectacular reporter, had found a kindred spirit in Bradley and had spelled out this homespun set of qualities for his readers. Soldiers late come to the battle area felt safer and a bit more reconciled to battle when they knew they would be under a commander who would weigh their personal welfare in reaching his final conclusions.

Bradley as much as any commander in Europe favoured the fullest use of armour, artillery and air power to minimise losses of the foot soldier. He shared Marshall's high regard for the infantry and believed that everything possible should be done to make more bearable the life of the man in the field and to increase his chances for survival in combat.

For the invasion Eisenhower arranged for Montgomery to serve as initial ground force commander with Bradley as the American army commander under him. It was clearly understood that when a second American army should be brought into France Bradley would become commander of an army group and Eisenhower would assume ground command over Montgomery and Bradley. Both Montgomery and Bradley have made clear that to a great extent Montgomery allowed great freedom to Bradley for his sector. In addition Bradley attached planners from his own staff to Montgomery's staff. At the same time Bradley conferred often with Eisenhower, passing on his own thinking and that of his staff. As a result Bradley was fully represented to Eisenhower. His staff with that of Montgomery made an impact on planning perhaps stronger than that of Eisenhower's own staff.

Although Montgomery in pre D-Day briefings spoke of possible break-outs on his front towards Paris from the area of Caen, it was clear to Bradley and others that Montgomery would likely pull the Germans on to the Caen front as Bradley's forces pushed down from the beaches to St Lô to the base of the Cotentin peninsula. Once that goal was achieved, Third Army would be brought in to press still farther to the south and then turn towards Brest with part of its forces and eastward towards Paris north of the Loire.

Swift-moving activities were inhibited in late June and early July as the hedgerows and bad weather impeded progress. Several regimental and division commanders were relieved as units and officers inexperienced in battle failed to move forward. Some tentative efforts to move south of the St Lô area were checked. Montgomery's effort in the Caen area, preceded by tremendous air preparation, failed to gain the expected dividends. At length Bradley's staff developed a plan, Cobra, which as a part of a larger Allied plan, attempted to break through to the base of the Cotentin peninsula and pave the way for a drive to Brest and to Paris. The plan has been confused with Montgomery's somewhat earlier preparations and, more often, with Patton's spectacular drive in August. But the breakthrough that made the break-out and pursuit possible was made by First Army and especially by Major-General J. Lawton Collins's reinforced VII Corps behind massive air preparations. The three-day attack, beginning on 25 July after a false start on the previous day, stunned the Germans and prepared the way for the combined

American drive of two armies, after Patton's Third Army became active on 1 August. On that day Bradley became commander of the active 12th Army Group, assigning Hodges to command First Army.

In his new role Bradley headed all American ground forces in France for the moment, co-ordinating both the First and Third Army drives. Patton would win headlines for his armoured thrusts towards the Seine so that Bradley's role seemed overcast and Hodges's First Army activities seemed almost non-existent, but it was still Bradley who directed the American ground attack.

In the early phases of the August attack Bradley faced the problem of deciding what emphasis to place on the sweep into Brittany. He agreed with many of his subordinates that one corps was sufficient to drive towards Brest while the remainder of Third Army drove towards Germany. He gave free rein to Patton in his decision to wheel eastward and to drive north of the Loire with little more than the air force to protect his flanks. Perhaps on the basis of radio intercept, Patton confided to his subordinates at an early briefing that the enemy had only a few battalions on their front, but not to tell the reporters.

Bradley had to deal with an ill-advised German decision – prompted by Hitler – to strike from Mortain westward at the American line of communications moving southward near the base of the Cotentin. For a few hours there was danger of a shattering of the American supply line but aggressive American action smashed the German effort and turned the momentary threat into an Allied opportunity to destroy the Germans in Normandy. When the enemy decided at last in desperation to withdraw towards the Seine, Bradley wheeled both his armies northward. At the request of the British Second Army commander he stopped the forces near Argentan short of link-up with General Miles Dempsey's troops south of Falaise. Patton and other Americans later charged Montgomery with demanding a halt which allowed a considerable part of the Germans to escape. Bradley in his memoirs took the responsibility for stopping short, indicating that there were problems of communications to consider and that the enemy did not escape with his vehicles and arms.

Bradley had the task of co-ordinating the First and Third Army attack towards Paris. He had the delicate task of entering Paris after Eisenhower's initial intention of bypassing that city had been proclaimed and of arranging for the honour of entering the city first to be extended to the 2nd French Armoured Division under General Jacques LeClerc while ensuring that American support was at hand to secure the protection of the city. At Eisenhower's request that an American division proceed through the city on the way to battle, Bradley arranged that one of his divisions – one that he had once trained – the 28th – march in battle formation through the city north-eastward where it was soon engaged in battle.

During the drive for the German border Bradley became embroiled tangentially with Montgomery because of the tendency of the press to assign all victories and all advances to Montgomery's troops – even at the time when the main movement was on the American front. Not from Bradley but from the American press came protests to Marshall, who passed the complaints on to Eisenhower with the suggestion that as soon as possible Ike take personal command in the field with Bradley made equal in command authority with Montgomery. On 1 September this change was made. From that point on Bradley became completely equal in authority with his former temporary superior. By this time he commanded a force superior in size to that commanded by Montgomery. Far more important, as Ninth US Army under Lieutenant-General William H. Simpson became operational and as Fifteenth Army, destined for Lieutenant-General Leonard T. Gerow, was put on the boards, he was to be the chief field commander in western Europe ultimately with four of the five American armies under his command as contrasted with one British and one Canadian army under Montgomery's 21st Army Group and one American and one French army under General Devers's 6th Army Group. He would have under him the largest American force ever deployed in the field. Despite this change Bradley and Hodges played second fiddle to Patton in the press until Marshall pressed Eisenhower to do something to play up Courtney Hodges's important role.

Some writers have given the impression that in the pursuit across France Patton masterminded the attack. One might get the impression that Bradley and the First Army had no part in the activities. It was First Army that caught the brunt of the German attack at Mortain and contained it as Patton turned south. It was also First Army that circled northward to help contain the German forces near Falaise and then drive for the Seine. In Patton's attack Bradley helped to represent him to Eisenhower. Newly relieved of his command of First Army, he continued to play an important role in the first days of that army's movements. With Bradley's firm backing that army would send elements into Paris on 25 August and drive northward towards the Siegfried Line, entering Belgium on 1 September, encircling German forces in the Mons Pocket, crossing into Luxembourg on 9 September and entering Germany on 11 September.

The drive towards Germany would bring criticism of Eisenhower from Montgomery and Patton because of the Supreme Commander's selection of a broad rather than a narrow front concept. Although inclined to back an advance on his own front, Bradley did not criticise Montgomery's proposal for a plan to bounce the Rhine – although he was startled to find that Montgomery had advanced such a bold course. In the closing day of August and the early days of September as supply insufficiencies forced Eisenhower to choose between Montgomery's narrow thrust and American advances on a broad front, Bradley loyally backed Eisenhower's decision. Unlike Montgomery and Patton, who later insisted that Eisenhower had prolonged the war by his failure to put all his effort behind one great thrust or the other,

Bradley saw the supply difficulties and the problems that Eisenhower faced as a commander of a coalition. One of his most important contributions as a commander was an understanding of this latter problem at key points of the conflict. Always more aware than Patton of supply problems, he saw the weakness of Patton's claim that he could have gone to Berlin with all-out American support. Aware of possibilities on his own front he was sceptical of some of Montgomery's claims for what he could have gained. Patton's out-rageous diary sometimes called Bradley over-cautious and even weak-kneed because he failed to attack more vigorously Montgomery's demand for a narrow thrust.

When the failure at Arnhem and the string of losses on all fronts brought the great pursuit to a halt, Bradley prepared for a longer war. He ran into a more optimistic view in Washington. Marshall, aware of some new develop-ments, such as that of the proximity fuze, was hopeful that the war might be concluded by the end of the year. In order to explore the ground he flew to Paris in October with War Mobilisation director, James F. Byrnes. Often with Bradley, and sometimes with subordinate commanders, they visited the front. Bradley, glad at the opportunity to discuss with Marshall some of his views, made clear the serious problems the Americans faced. Marshall would recall later the strong arguments presented by Bradley. He returned to the United States convinced that a longer campaign had to be faced and prepared to meet its demands. He was still seeking additional munitions and man-power when the attack came in the Ardennes on 16 December 1944.

Before the Germans struck, Eisenhower had talked with Bradley and Montgomery of possible Allied thrusts against the enemy. Bradley and First Army planners fashioned an attack through the Hurtgen forest. Official his-torians in recent years have criticised this approach, saying that a flank attack would have been better. The area was heavily forested, strongly forti-fied, and in an area with a poor road net. The American commanders argued that other approaches offered no better opportunities. The attack could scarcely have fared worse. Six American divisions showed the scars of the fighting and none had completely refitted when the enemy struck in the Ardennes.

Bradley like most of the Allied commanders had minimised the danger of a German attack in the Ardennes. The rugged terrain and the north-south road net seemed to preclude an armoured attack. It seemed absurd for the Germans to give the Allies what they wanted – an emergence from the defences of the Siegfried Line – so that the Allies could get at them. While the Germans pre-pared in great secrecy, Bradley's forces made plans for a limited attack to the east. In those cases where German preparations were reported, it was assumed that they were preparing to meet the coming American attack.

ULTRA information would normally have been expected to give the Allies some idea of an attack. The Germans had been careful to maintain a high degree of radio silence in their preparatory moves and the Allies as a result had no inkling that the Germans were aiming for Antwerp and hoping to frustrate further Allied attacks for some months.

In meeting the last major enemy challenge Eisenhower faced the fact that his only reserve consisted of his two American airborne divisions and the troops under Montgomery – north of the Bulge. After careful consideration and a meeting of his advisers at Verdun, he turned Patton towards the relief of Bastogne. A short time later he agreed to put all American troops north of the Bulge under Montgomery. Although German troops had cut off direct communication by road between Bradley in Luxembourg and Hodges in the north, Bradley protested that he could still get through to the First Army commander. Eisenhower held to his decision, adding First Army to the US Ninth Army already under Montgomery's command.

The ensuing two weeks were the most difficult that Bradley recalled during the war. Although Patton was under him, his great exploits seemed to belong to him solely rather than to his superior. To the north Montgomery appeared to rule supreme, receiving from Eisenhower and Bedell Smith the authority to relieve the First Army commander – reported by Montgomery to be tired – in case it proved necessary. Supported by Patton to the hilt, Bradley for the only time during the war exploded to Eisenhower. Aware that Montgomery had long wanted to regain control of ground forces and aware that the British were using the Ardennes situation as a means of achieving this goal, Bradley told Eisenhower that he would not serve again under Montgomery and Patton made clear that he supported this resolve.

Eisenhower later recalled this reaction as the worst problem he had faced in the war. The situation was made worse when Montgomery, in an interview which he gave as a means of helping Eisenhower, praised the private American soldier in a way that implied criticism of the higher American command. He not only aroused opposition of the American field commanders concerned but the wrath of General Marshall in the United States. The American Chief of Staff, who backed Bradley as much as ever, directed Eisenhower to resist the effort of the British to establish a ground command. Montgomery saw the message and concluded that there was no point in persisting in the pressure for the command. Churchill, shifting to Alexander, did not give way until March, but the issue had been resolved earlier.

The broader question, which cannot be settled totally, is to what extent Eisenhower's determination to make up to Bradley the slight he had suffered determined certain basic strategy during the remainder of the war. In September Eisenhower had backed Montgomery's thrust to the north-east, giving him the US Ninth Army for some weeks and turning US First Army to his support. Although he left Ninth Army with Montgomery in the drive to the Rhine after the Ardennes attack and during the late March crossing of the Rhine, he made clear that the arrangement was not permanent. After the crossing of the Rhine the Ninth Army would support Bradley's operations. His focus of attack was on Leipzig and the Elbe – aimed at a meeting on the

Elbe with the Russians and a clearing of the areas to the right and left of the river to prevent any effort by the Germans to establish a redoubt, from which the Allies would require weeks of hard fighting to oust them.

Eisenhower spelled out his high regard for Bradley in a message to General Marshall in late March. General Bradley, he declared:

> has never once held back in attempting any maneuver, no matter how bold in conception and never has he paused to regroup when there was opportunity lying on his front. His handling of his army commanders has been superb and his energy, commonsense, tactical skill and complete loyalty have made him a great lieutenant on whom I can always rely with the greatest confidence. I consider Bradley the greatest battle-line commander I have met in this war.

He was reflecting his admiration for 12th Army Group's victories during the month. On 7 March a lieutenant in First Army had led a small group across the bridge at Remagen, which the Germans were supposed to have destroyed before they arrived. The last bridge still standing across the Rhine was open to them and they were soon across, without approval of higher authority. But in a short time Bradley had urged them on and Eisenhower backed the decision. While Montgomery completed a more ambitious plan in the north, Bradley strongly reinforced the bridgehead, crossing in considerable strength before Montgomery's setpiece battle went forth brilliantly in his sector. In the south Patton slipped across the river at Oppenheim before Montgomery attacked and in the south the US Seventh Army was over the river shortly afterwards.

Bradley's thrust gained strength after 4 April when he regained control of Ninth Army, thus commanding four of the five American armies in Europe. Three days earlier armoured units of US Ninth Army, still under Montgomery, had joined with the armour of First Army to encircle the Ruhr. Other elements entered Bavaria in early April and held Munich by the end of the month. On 25 April patrols from the v Corps' 69th Division met Russian troops beyond the Elbe; the first formal link-up occurred at Torgau the following day. Earlier, on 12 April, day of Roosevelt's death, Bradley's forces had crossed the Elbe near Magdeburg with the way seemingly open for a quick drive to Berlin. Churchill, ever fearful of a Russian threat, pressed Eisenhower to take Berlin. Eisenhower, aware of new priorities in the Far East, said that he needed political direction. He added that Bradley had suggested that it would cost a hundred thousand casualties to reach the German capital and clear it of its defenders (a figure indeed reached by the Russians in achieving that goal). He saw no reason to expend these forces when they would have to draw back. In his statement Bradley followed the lead of Marshall and Eisenhower in arguing that the military should leave to the political leaders the conclusions of political policy. It is hard to challenge his view.

Once the decision had been made to drive on a broad front in the centre, there was little at this stage of the war to show the special abilities of Bradley and his subordinates. The need was for constant pressure, speed, and reasonable care for supply columns. In this latter particular Bradley continued to show more careful regard than most of his subordinates.

Bradley later spoke of his *naïveté* in failing to understand the political factors involved. In fact he followed a guideline set by Marshall and Eisenhower and one of which in later years he could not be ashamed.

Overall Bradley must be judged against Montgomery and his American subordinates. He was less cautious than Montgomery save for the Arnhem drive. He was more cautious than Patton, but responsible for the reasonable approach that made Patton's advances possible. He worked closely with Eisenhower and was the honest broker between the French and British and Patton. He made it possible for Patton to perform at his best and arranged the necessary bridge between rival commanders.

Leader of more American troops than any American field commander had led in battle, he managed to wield together four armies and he managed while safeguarding American *amour propre* to work with British and French units to move successfully against the enemy. Always the Missouri country boy, suddenly raised to fame through the chance of war, he reacted effectively to his various challenges to contribute mightily to victory.

Apparently guileless, Bradley knew the value of appearing gullible in certain situations. More than once Patton gloated in his diary that he had outfoxed Bradley and other superiors. Bradley made clear in private asides to confidants that he had already won Eisenhower's acceptance of some of the concessions. The smooth working of the early months owed much to the fact that Eisenhower and Bradley, as former classmates, could speak freely of their mutual problems. In some instances, where Eisenhower would have had to order Patton to accept an unpalatable directive, he was able to win Bradley's assistance in persuading Patton that Allied considerations required an understanding of British interests. Bradley was basically sympathetic with Patton's desire for dashing drives and for flank envelopments. He was equally insistent that supply be carefully established and not improvised in the heat of battle.

As 12th Army Group commander, Bradley became aware of a certain remoteness from battle which he had known as commander of First Army or of II Corps. The progress of battle he now knew from others. His role was to push the army commanders; only occasionally did he actually see the forward units moving as he had in North Africa and Sicily. Yet his influence was felt because Patton knew that he would protect him and defend his case for supplies secure from Montgomery's supposed control of Supreme Commander Eisenhower. In his more generous movements Patton was well aware that Bradley had helped save him in the case of the slappings and that his strong belief in Patton counted with Marshall and Stimson in Washington in 1944.

In most activities Bradley worked as a team member in pressing for strategic decisions. He worked with Eisenhower and Montgomery in insisting on a much larger force in the attack and the build-up, he made an airborne drop on his right flank an essential element of the opening attack. He strongly propounded the enveloping movement to the base of the Cotentin and then eastward along the Loire while First Army aided Montgomery in drawing German strength on to the Caen area.

He helped win for Patton a larger share in the drive for the Rhine in the race across Paris, while allowing First Army a lion's share of resources as it protected Montgomery's flank in his drive for Antwerp and beyond. The British would complain that he shielded Patton in hiding his evasion of strict adherence to Eisenhower's direction that he make only minor advances during a crucial phase of the attack across France. Actually Bradley won many of his points in dealing with Eisenhower by his understanding of the need for team play – a point he had difficulty in explaining to George Patton. Despite Patton's snide entries in his journal, he benefited from Bradley's admonitions to look at the broader picture and to be an Allied member rather than a narrow American fighter intent on his personal pursuits.

There is a question of the extent to which Bradley was mainly responsible for Eisenhower's decision to advance the broad front strategy or of the point at which the 12th Army Group commander loyally carried out the Eisenhower concept. Certainly Bradley made clear to the Supreme Commander in late August that the American army commanders – Hodges and Patton and their corps commanders – would not mildly accept the proposal that they cease their exploitation of a seeming rout of the enemy in order to allocate scarce American resources to support Montgomery's advance on a narrow front. Montgomery's insistence that the advance on the Third Army front prolonged the war overlooks the fact that at the critical point of his attack, Bradley's First Army, which was closely following Montgomery's advance as part of his plan, was receiving most of the gasoline available to Bradley's 12th Army Group. It is ironical that Patton and his close adherents joined Montgomery on the single point of attacking Eisenhower for losing the chance to win the war in September or early October by failure to support a single front. Although Bradley supported some of Patton's drives, he did not share this censure of Eisenhower. He saw the general supply shortages caused by the rapid thrusts across France as the real culprit. He was aware that the optimistic initial forecast of a drive to the Seine in ninety days had been exceeded but that the drive to the German border, estimated at 330 days, had been accomplished in a little more than ninety. This feat was accomplished mainly by over-extending lines of communication and driving men and vehicles rather than by the careful regrouping and steady logistic build-up that had been envisaged in the earlier planning.

One does not find in Bradley, any more than in Marshall or Eisenhower, a great spark of sudden inspiration leading to victory. He influenced the tide of battle by attention to the details that make up military success. He recognised that realisation of one's plans required more than *élan* and a white plume. Fresh troops, tins of gasoline, food for tired warriors, spare parts for worn-out tanks had to be provided. Also it took a watchfulness over subordinates. Even as he believed in resting troops, he believed in encouraging exhausted leaders. It was due in considerable part to his words on behalf of Hodges during a trying time in the Ardennes that that officer was saved from the relief that Montgomery thought might be necessary. Conversely, he was prepared to make reliefs of divisional or corps commanders, almost surgically, if illness or indecision or lack of self-discipline made them unable to perform at their maximum at the point when all their energies and brain were needed.

In sum, Bradley accepted the overall Allied leadership for most part; he favoured vigorous action; he respected his subordinates – backing their plans and interfering at a minimum – and understanding the American soldier as much as any American field commander he favoured the marriage of fire power and tactics, the use of artillery and air, which spared human life and reduced casualties. Once committed to a particular line of approach, he did everything possible to support that advance. He was a general treasured by Marshall, who admired the dash of Patton and Terry Allen, but put his final trust in the sure but steady Bradley.

GENERAL GEORGE S. PATTON

Martin Blumenson

George Smith Patton, Jr, embodied the offensive spirit. He believed fervently in the attack. What he could do better than most commanders was to transmit to his troops his constant and ruthless desire to close with and destroy the enemy.

A professional soldier in the best sense of the term, Patton had mastered the means of waging war in his time. He had a flair for handling large forces, a sixth sense about what the enemy was likely to do, and a capacity for inspiring and leading men. By his victories on the battlefields of North Africa, Sicily, and Europe in the Second World War, he gained fame, the status of a living legend and, after his death, a place in American folklore.

He was an anguished, even tortured, man, exuberant and moody by turns, deeply religious yet profane in his speech, gregarious and solitary, reckless and reflective, rough and sentimental. To the public he presented a flamboyant image of the gentleman warrior, athletic, impeccably attired, witty and imposing. To the press he was always good copy. By his personality too he captured the imagination of the world.

Patton was born at San Gabriel in southern California on 11 November 1885. His father was a lawyer who was district attorney of Los Angeles for a time, a businessman who managed vineyards and wineries, and a politician who ran unsuccessfully in 1916 for the US Senate. He had been brought from Virginia to California by his widowed mother, whose husband, the son of a governor of the state, had commanded a Confederate Army regiment in the Civil War and died of battle wounds in 1864. The first Patton to arrive in the United States had probably come from Scotland and had settled in Fredericksburg in the 1770s.

On his mother's side General Patton was descended from an officer who fought in the War for Independence and later became speaker of the Tennessee House of Representatives. Patton's maternal grandfather was Benjamin Davis Wilson, who travelled overland and reached California in the 1840s. He came into large landholdings through his marriage to the daughter of a wealthy Mexican, founded the orange industry, planted the first great vineyards, gave his name to Mt Wilson, where the observatory now stands, was elected to the state legislature, and was widely respected. Upon the death of his wife, Wilson remarried. A daughter born of this union was General Patton's mother.

The Pattons regarded themselves as aristocratic Virginians and were proud of their lineage, which they traced to George Washington and beyond to the barons of the Magna Carta. The Wilsons were an eminent pioneer family and proud of their early presence in California. The outlook of one side and the energy of the other combined to give Patton his special qualities as a warrior. Cultured, charming and well mannered, Patton was also, as Field-Marshal Haig once said, a 'fire-eater' who longed for the fray.

Adored by his parents, his sister, and a large assortment of relatives, Patton spent a happy childhood on a ranch. He learned to love horses. Probably because he had a mild sort of dyslexia, which impeded his reading and writing, he went to a private school in Pasadena when he was eleven years old, later than most children. He excelled in history. He had already decided to be an army officer.

At the age of eighteen he entered Virginia Military Institute, from which his father and grandfather had graduated. And after one year he received an appointment to the Military Academy at West Point. Because of his deficiency in mathematics he had to repeat his first year. He was then, in sequence, cadet corporal, sergeant and adjutant. He played football, but failed to make the varsity team, became proficient in fencing, and won his letter for athletics in track and field events.

He had already recorded in his notebook his enormous ambition. Believing that he was fated or destined for greatness, he worked hard to make that fate or destiny come true. He drove himself relentlessly to make good, to become important, to merit recognition, to receive applause. To his parents he wrote: 'I have got to, do you understand, got to be great. It is no foolish child dream. It is me as I ever will be . . . I would be willing to live in torture and die tomorrow if for one day I could be really great.' With these sentiments spurring him, he exerted all his energy in the pursuit of excellence, fighting the temptation to relax or be lazy.

Graduating from West Point in 1909, and standing about in the middle of his class, he was commissioned in the cavalry and assigned to Fort Sheridan, Illinois, near Chicago. A year later he married Beatrice Banning Ayer, daughter of a wealthy businessman from Massachusetts. This marriage was exceptional happy and produced two daughters and a son. The incomes from the Patton and Ayer fortunes enabled the future general to have horses for riding, racing and showing, as well as a string of polo ponies. He and his wife were handsome and endowed with charm. Their social connections gave them access to important circles.

The initial turning-point in Patton's career was his transfer in 1911 to Fort Myer, Virginia, near Washington, DC, and close to prominent men in government. He served on occasion as aide-de-camp to Leonard Wood, Army

Chief of Staff, and to Henry L. Stimson, Secretary of War, who would again hold that position during the Second World War. As Patton said, the capital was 'nearer God than elsewhere and the place where all people with aspirations should attempt to dwell'. While he cultivated individuals who could help him advance, he studied and worked hard at his profession. He also began to participate in horse shows, horse racing and polo, explaining to his father-in-law that this activity was 'the best sort of advertising'.

In 1912 Patton was selected to compete in the Olympic Games at Stockholm. He performed in the modern pentathlon, five gruelling events – pistol shooting, 300-metre swim, fencing, steeplechase, cross-country foot race – and finished in fifth place against forty-three competitors. He then travelled to the French cavalry school at Saumur and spent several weeks there to improve his skill in fencing. He also travelled extensively in his automobile through the country over which his army would move thirty-two years later.

The following year Patton returned to Saumur for additional work. His reward was to be named Master of the Sword, the leading expert in the US Army. With this title he was assigned to Fort Riley, Kansas, as instructor in the sword and as a student at the Cavalry School.

When the First World War broke out, Patton thought at once of volunteering for service in the French army. Leonard Wood advised him against this step, saying that he would be needed when the United States became involved in the war. A year later, still chafing under the routine of peacetime service, Patton was transferred to Fort Bliss, Texas, which was under the command of John J. Pershing.

Pancho Villa's raid on Columbus, New Mexico, in 1916 and his killing of several Americans led to the formation of the Punitive Expedition under Pershing, who was to pursue Villa into Mexico. He took Patton as an unofficial and additional aide. Patton performed a variety of duties – as assistant intelligence officer and headquarters commandant, as messenger and liaison officer. He also attained brief fame when he killed three Villistas in a gun battle that had developed out of a corn-purchasing assignment. Patton led fourteen men, travelling in three automobiles, in a surprise descent upon a ranch and discovered the enemy soldiers. It was probably the first motorised action in American army history. He returned to the United States as a first lieutenant early in 1917.

Patton had taken Pershing as his model of a commander. He studied his manner of conducting himself, judging his subordinates, reaching decisions. Like Pershing, he would insist on strict discipline, strong loyalties up and down the chain of command, absolute devotion to duty, complete attention to military courtesy, cleanliness on the part of his troops, and faultless dress. Like Pershing, he was entirely pragmatic in his outlook and practices, and he believed that hard work and meticulous attention to detail would ensure success.

Soon after the United States entered the First World War, Pershing was named Commander-in-Chief Allied Expeditionary Force. Again he took Patton with him as an official aide when he sailed to France with his small advance party. In Paris and later at Chaumont, now a captain, Patton acted in diverse capacities at the AEF headquarters. Offered command of an infantry battalion, Patton chose instead to enter the Tank Corps then being formed. The decision was a gamble, for before the battle of Cambrai in November 1917 tanks were still unproved and unreliable instruments of warfare.

As the first American officer assigned to the Tank Corps, Patton familiarised himself with this new weapon and its employment by visiting British and French tank centres. He then wrote a lengthy report that became the basic American tank document. In it he discussed the construction of tanks, their repair and maintenance, methods of training tankers, and tactical use. The essential doctrine then in force was to have tanks support the infantry and help the foot soldier break the trench, barbed wire and machine-gun defences.

At Langres, early in 1918, Patton established a school for tankers, but he soon moved to the nearby hamlet of Bourg where he had ample grounds for training, exercises and manoeuvres. Using French Renaults, light tanks, Patton directed his school and commanded a growing formation that attained brigade status. While he prepared his men for battle, he also attended and completed the course at the General Staff College at Langres. He was promoted to major, then to lieutenant-colonel.

In the battle of St Mihiel, Patton led his two battalions of tankers, plus an attached French *groupement*, with conspicuous success. His troops were eager to fight, and they fought like veterans. They exhibited the aggressive forward movement against the enemy that was already Patton's trademark.

He then moved his units to take part in the Meuse-Argonne offensive. On the first day of that attack he was wounded while rallying infantrymen and tankers. Hospitalised, he was shortly thereafter promoted to colonel and awarded the Distinguished Service Cross for gallantry in action and the Distinguished Service Medal for proficiency in the training of his tankers.

Returning home early in 1919, Patton was assigned to Fort Meade, Maryland, the tank centre, where he met and became friendly with Dwight D. Eisenhower, who had commanded tankers in training in the United States. The young officers had long discussions on how to develop tanks into a powerful and mobile arm that would not be tied to the slower-moving infantry.

The National Defense Act of 1920, which reorganised the army, put an end to these talks. The law placed the Tank Corps under the infantry and demoted regular officers to lower grades. Reduced to major, and unwilling to enter into the infantry, Patton transferred to his basic arm, the cavalry.

He served at Fort Myer, attended the advanced course at the Cavalry School, and graduated from the Command and General Staff College at Fort Leavenworth, Kansas. He was a staff officer in Boston, in Hawaii, and in

Washington. In 1932 he participated in the action to disperse the Bonus Marchers, veterans who clamoured for immediate payment of a promised emolument for war service. Serving in the office of the Chief of Cavalry, Patton became trapped in the controversy between those who advocated modernisation and motorisation at the expense of the horse, and those who believed in the continuing need for horses, particularly in primitive regions in the world where roads were lacking. He had a foot in both camps. He defended the horse cavalry and the horse artillery, but at the same time kept himself abreast of armoured developments, particularly those espoused by Fuller, Liddell Hart and Guderian.

Graduated from the Army War College, Patton completed his formal military schooling and became eligible for general officer rank. He was promoted to lieutenant-colonel and placed in command of a cavalry regiment in Texas.

In 1939 Patton was again a colonel and in command of Fort Myer. His major responsibility was to stage equitation shows for congressmen and other governmental dignitaries. Not until July 1940, after the surrender of France, did Patton receive an assignment directly related to combat. He was transferred from the cavalry to the newly created Armored Force and sent to Fort Benning, Georgia, to command the armoured brigade of the 2nd Armored Division then being formed.

He was in his fifty-fifth year and at the height of his powers and maturity. All that he had ever done seemed to have prepared him for his coming participation in the Second World War. He had studied military history thoroughly, reading voraciously in the literature of warfare, and he could discourse easily on scale, chain and plate armour, German mercenaries in the Italian wars, Polish and Turkish horsemen, Arabian and Oriental military techniques, and other esoteric subjects. He could compare the heavy cavalry of Belisarius with the modern tank.

He had become an expert in amphibious warfare, having analysed the operations at Gallipoli, having taken part in practice landing exercises at Hawaii, having even predicted the Japanese attack at Pearl Harbor. He had thought long and hard about military equipment, had designed the sabre used by the cavalry, invented a machine-gun sled to give assaulting riflemen more direct fire support, devised a new saddle pack, and worked directly with J. Walter Christie to improve the silhouette, suspension, power and weapons of the tank.

For his own amusement he had restructured the infantry division into triangular shape, thereby anticipating the reorganisation that would take place in 1942. He had earned his licence as an aircraft pilot so that he could better understand air attack and ground defence against it. He had learned navigation and had sailed his yacht from Hawaii to California so that he could better direct armed forces in desert warfare.

In addition he was well known in the army as an officer who was loyal to his superiors, dedicated to his profession, energetic, forceful and competent.

At Fort Benning, Patton soon regained his position as the army's leading tanker. He quickly acceded to command of the 2nd Armored Division and was promoted to brigadier-general and major-general. He trained his men with thoroughness and zeal. So well did he teach them their trade that his men performed in outstanding fashion during the 1941 manoeuvres in Tennessee, Texas-Louisiana and the Carolinas. Early in 1942, with the United States now actively in the war, Patton was appointed to command I Armored Corps, to which were assigned the 1st and 2nd Armored Divisions.

He had demonstrated that he was capable of turning citizen conscripts into skilful soldiers. To the troublesome question never explicitly asked but always in the minds of American leaders, would American drafted men fight? Patton provided an answer – under him they would.

Because of the prospect of sending American troops to fight alongside the British in North Africa and the Middle East, Patton opened a desert training centre in the south-western part of the United States. He processed a series of units through exercises and manoeuvres, all the while testing weapons, equipment, as well as leaders, experimenting with new tactical formations, and training men for the rigours of actual warfare. In July, when the United States and Great Britain decided to execute Operation Torch, an invasion of French North Africa, Patton was selected to head the American forces designated to sail directly from the western hemisphere to landings in Morocco.

At the head of the Western Task Force, his corps headquarters directing the equivalent of two divisions, Patton took his men ashore on 8 November against great difficulties of surf and spirited opposition. Three days later, as he was about to attack Casablanca, the French authorities agreed to a ceasefire.

As the senior officer in French Morocco, Patton somewhat reluctantly settled into the routine of a soldier-diplomat, although he continued to train his men avidly and to hope for a hostile act emerging out of Spanish Morocco.

The fighting continued in Tunisia, where British, French and American units tried vainly to seize Bizerta and Tunis. They encountered considerable German and Italian contingents that had been rushed to the country. In northern Tunisia were elements eventually grouped into a field army under von Arnim. In southern Tunisia, coming from Libya and pursued by Bernard L. Montgomery's Eighth Army, was Erwin Rommel's Italo-German *Panzerarmee*, which had been defeated at El Alamein in Egypt the previous October. After establishing contact, these Axis forces attacked the Allies in February 1943, inflicted a serious defeat on the Americans and French, and, in a series of actions known as the Battle of Kasserine Pass, drove them back about 50 miles. When the situation became stable early in March, Eisenhower, the Allied commander, called Patton from Morocco, gave him temporary command of US II Corps in Tunisia, and charged him with restoring American morale and efficiency.

Eleven days afterwards Patton had so transformed the American combat spirit that his troops advanced vigorously from Kasserine, took Gafsa and El Guettar, and regained the ground lost during the Kasserine Pass battle. They also threatened the flank of Rommel's army, which was defending the Mareth Line against Montgomery. When the Axis forces withdrew to the north, Patton, now a lieutenant-general, turned command of II Corps over to Omar N. Bradley, his deputy, for the final stage of the Tunisian campaign, while Patton returned to Morocco to plan the invasion of Sicily.

This operation had been decided in January at the Casablanca Conference, and on 10 July, with Harold Alexander in command of the Allied ground forces, Montgomery's Eighth Army and Patton's newly activated Seventh Army came ashore. Since Montgomery was scheduled to move up the east coast to Messina, the only real strategic objective on the island, Patton was to perform the distinctly subsidiary role of protecting Montgomery's flank. But Patton requested and received permission to drive for Palermo, which he captured by a daring armoured thrust. Because Montgomery was blocked by strong German defences at Catania, Patton was allowed to head for Messina along the northern shore of Sicily. By pushing his troops ruthlessly, and by staging three small amphibious landings to envelop and outflank successive Axis defensive lines, Patton reached Messina first and thereby brought the campaign to an end.

Winning the race to Messina not only enhanced Patton's reputation; more importantly it gave confidence and pride to the American soldiers who had felt somewhat inferior to the British veterans. It also promoted a new respect for American combat capabilities on the part of Allies and enemy alike.

Montgomery soon crossed the Straits of Messina to start operations on the Italian mainland, a new American army under Mark W. Clark invaded southern Italy at Salerno, and Bradley went to the United Kingdom to organise the American forces that would take part in Overlord, the cross-Channel attack. Patton meanwhile remained in Sicily with nothing to do.

In large part his idleness stemmed from the slapping incidents. Twice while visiting the wounded in field hospitals Patton had encountered soldiers who suffered from combat exhaustion. Believing them to be malingerers, Patton lost his temper, called them cowards and slapped them. His aim, he said later, was to restore their manhood. But the medical authorities objected to this treatment and protested to Eisenhower, who reprimanded Patton privately, ordered him to apologise to all the troops in Sicily, and secured a promise from the press to keep the matter from public knowledge, hoping thereby to prevent an outcry for Patton's relief.

Eisenhower believed that Patton was too valuable in combat to lose; in fact he thought Patton indispensable for Allied victory. But he resolved to advance Patton no further beyond command of a field army. In November, when the public learned of the slapping incidents, some sentiment developed for removing Patton. But Eisenhower retained him after making clear that his loss would be advantageous to the Axis only.

In January 1944 Patton travelled to England to take command of the Third Army, which he trained rigorously for its follow-up role in Overlord. Bradley's First Army, directed by Montgomery's 21st Army Group headquarters, made the American landings in June and secured the American beachhead. Patton's Third Army assembled in the Cotentin in July.

By virtue of Operation Cobra, launched on 25 July to end the agonising static warfare in the hedgerows, Bradley broke through the German defences. Two days later, anticipating the insertion of the Third Army into the battle, he instructed Patton to take charge, unofficially, of VIII Corps and to exploit the penetration towards Avranches, the entrance into Brittany. Bringing armoured divisions into the lead, Patton plunged forward and reached Avranches by the end of the month. On 1 August, when Bradley took command of the 12th US Army Group, leaving the First Army to Courtney Hodges, Patton's army became operational. The situation could not have been more fluid, a condition that could not have been more suitable for Patton's military talents.

He had the mission of turning westward to seize Brittany, particularly the ports of St Malo, Brest, Lorient and Quiberon Bay. But his aggressiveness and speed of movement transformed a local breakthrough into the exhilarating war of movement called the break-out, thereby precipitating a general German withdrawal from Normandy. Eisenhower turned the bulk of the four Allied armies – now consisting of one British, one Canadian and two American – eastward to the Seine. Sending the VIII Corps westward into Brittany, Patton committed XV, later the XX, and still later XII Corps to the east, generally towards the Paris–Orléans gap.

When the Germans turned and attacked through Mortain in an attempt to recapture Avranches, cut off the break-out forces, and reimpose the conditions of static warfare, Patton suggested to Bradley that XV Corps be shifted northward from Le Mans to Alençon, then to Argentan, in order to encircle the Germans at Mortain. Bradley assented, and on 13 August Patton's troops were at Argentan and just across the inter-army group boundary. There Bradley halted further advance and awaited Montgomery's invitation to move into the 21st Army Group zone and north towards Falaise. Believing that the Canadians could move south from Caen to Falaise more quickly, Montgomery issued no invitation. By the time the Canadians reached Falaise three days later, the Germans were starting to escape eastward through the Argentan–Falaise gap.

The Germans were not home free, for Patton had meanwhile persuaded Bradley to let him send part of XV Corps eastward from Argentan to the Seine. Thus when the Germans who streamed out of the Argentan–Falaise pocket before it was closed on 20 August reached the Seine below Paris, they found another enveloping arm of Patton's army pushing them towards the lower reaches of the river, where it was wider and more difficult to cross. At the same time, at Mantes-Gassicourt, 30 miles north-west of Paris, Patton sent an infantry division across the Seine on 19 August, thereby making it impossible for the Germans to use the river to re-establish a defence.

The Allied front was then reordered, and a theatre-wide pursuit of the defeated Germans ensued. While the Canadians worked up the coast, reducing the port cities, the British headed for Brussels and the US First Army struck towards Liège and Luxembourg. Patton was oriented towards the Paris–Orléans gap. With xv Corps transferred to the First Army for the liberation of Paris and viii Corps occupied in Brittany hundreds of miles to the west, Patton sent xx and xii Corps towards Sens, Troyes and Montereau. Slashing forward with armoured divisions in the vanguard and with motorised infantry eliminating bypassed enemy pockets, Patton swept eastward, took Reims and Châlons. At the end of August he was at the Meuse river. Five hundred miles to the rear, viii Corps was battling for Brest.

The marvellous sweep across France in August can be largely attributed to Patton's ardour and skill. He let nothing halt his relentless drive, neither caution nor hesitation. When a corps commander asked how much he should worry about his open flank along the Loire, Patton replied that that depended on how nervous he was.

But the break-out and pursuit had overtaxed the supply system. Since it was impossible to keep the combat elements supplied with gasoline and ammunition, the advance sputtered and died.

Leaving viii Corps at Brest to the newly arrived US Ninth Army head-quarters, and regaining control of xv, Patton, despite supply shortages and worsening weather, moved his units forward in September, crossed the Moselle, and opened operations that resulted in the capture of Nancy and Lunéville. Metz would hold out until November. Hampered by deficiencies in manpower and material, as well as what was by then abominable weather, Patton had to accept what was called the October pause.

He attacked again on 8 November, hoping to cross the Saar, penetrate the Siegfried Line and reach the Rhine. But the terrain and weather, as well as a strong German defence, conspired against him. He had barely reached the Siegfried Line in his sector and begun to reduce the fortifications when the Germans launched their Ardennes counter-offensive against Hodges's First Army on 16 December, and quickly drove a salient or bulge into the American lines.

Three days later, asked how soon he could reorient his army northward to strike the German flank, Patton at first advocated letting the Germans advance even farther so that the three German armies involved could be entirely cut off and destroyed. But realising the enormous gamble that this course of action entailed, he quickly asserted, at a conference called by

Eisenhower at Verdun, that he could attack to the north in forty-eight hours.

This was an astounding declaration, for turning an army from an eastward to a northward movement was an extremely complicated endeavour that required extensive alterations in the use of the road-net and in the flow of the supply system. Yet this is what Patton accomplished with amazing dexterity. On 22 December three corps attacked towards Bastogne in an effort to re-establish contact with American forces, mainly paratroopers, surrounded in the town.

Despite foul weather, Patton's troops drove forward. On 26 December they broke through the besiegers of Bastogne, denied the Germans that important road centre, and demonstrated that the Ardennes counter-offensive had failed to achieve a gain of strategic significance. Although hard fighting would continue for several weeks as the Germans sought to maintain the southern shoulder of the salient in order to prevent their troops from being encircled, the Allied line was restored, the bulge eliminated by the end of January 1945 when the Third and First Armies joined at Houffalize.

The Allied armies then continued towards the Rhine, which Patton's forces reached on 22 March. Without waiting Patton staged a virtually *ad hoc* crossing that night. By then the German military machine was disintegrating, and Patton's Third Army, together with the others, raced across Germany to the Elbe and Mulde rivers and meetings with the Russians.

A controversy developed when Patton sent a small task force of three hundred men to liberate several thousand Allied officers who were prisoners of war, among them his son-in-law, being held at Hammelburg. The task force was encircled and destroyed, and some newspaper reporters accused Patton of having sacrificed American lives to rescue his son-in-law. But the action was justified by Patton on two grounds: he feared that the Germans might massacre the prisoners, and he wished to use the task force as a feint to conceal his main axis of advance – and the episode was quickly forgotten as the end of European hostilities approached.

Now a full and four-star general, Patton conducted the final operation of the war in Europe when he sent a corps into Czechoslovakia to Pilsen. No doubt he could have liberated Prague, but he was prevented from doing so because of the plans for the Allied occupation zones in Germany.

The Third Army occupied and governed part of the American zone called the Eastern Military District, and Patton soon attracted controversial head-lines by disagreeing with the official policies of non-fraternisation, de-Nazification, and dismantling of the economic power of Germany. Discerning the shadows of the coming cold war, Patton favoured rebuilding Germany as a bulwark against the Russians who, he believed, would soon overrun all of Europe. When he said at a press conference that the Nazi party was hardly different from the Republican and Democratic political parties, Eisenhower relieved him of his Third Army command and sent him to the Fifteenth

Army, which had the mission of studying and writing the tactical and log-istical lessons of the campaign in Europe.

On 9 December, a day before he was to depart for leave in the United States and probable retirement, he was injured in an automobile accident. Hospitalised in Heidelberg, he died on 22 December. He was sixty years old. He was famous. He had achieved his fate, his destiny. He had earned the recognition and applause he had sought.

Instantly, Patton attained the character of an American folk hero. The newspapers had already made him a legend, and the two guns that he carried, the impeccable uniform that he wore, the picturesque language that he used, and the outbursts of temper that he displayed were well known. Now he was regarded as a throwback to the cowboy gunslinger type famous in American history and myth, from Daniel Boone through Davy Crockett to Wyatt Earp and Matt Dillon. His posturing and play-acting, which he developed to pro-ject his particular image of the warrior, were accepted as the essential quali-ties of a unique military man whose cussing, ferocity, and ruthlessness, as well as his vast fund of military knowledge, enabled him to propel the Amer-ican ground forces in the European side of the war to victory. Without him, it was widely believed, and with justification, the war would have taken longer to win.

Actually Patton was sensitive and naturally mild. He preferred solitary pursuits such as riding and reading over the team play required, say, in polo and in war. He wrote poetry and short stories, articles and essays, and his language was always original and rich. He was in essence a thoughtful person who studied carefully and worked out diligently his ideas of how to wage war better. He concentrated on the tactical and was always concerned with what was possible and practical. Yet his views encompassed improvements in equipment and weapons, formations and manoeuvres, fire support and the like.

Because he believed that a successful American commander had to embody the qualities of the extroverted 'he-man', as he often said, he sought to hide his quiet and reflective side behind a façade of the violent, outspoken, flam-buoyant fighter, which he specifically cultivated. His profanity in speech, as well as for example his highly polished boots, was designed to create his conception of the leader.

Yet the trappings that he presented to the public and his troops, his appearance as well as his exuberant talk, his air of confidence, as well as his bearing, his supposedly offhand manner of reaching decisions – all were care-fully calculated. His military acts were grounded in his splendid knowledge of history as well as in his meticulous use of his staff. The public Patton was quite different from the private Patton, who was studious and deliberate in his preparations for activity and execution.

What the Patton legend consists of is the personal bravura of Patton the man and the solid successes of Patton the soldier. Through this combination he won the affection of his troops and of the larger public, the respect of his enemies, and his reputation as a military genius.

His achievements made him indispensable to the American ground forces. It is difficult, if not impossible, to imagine who else could have accomplished what he did on several specific occasions. During the training period before the United States entered the war, he set high standards and turned citizen soldiers into fighting troops with such success that his 2nd Armored Division became a model of skill and *esprit*. His amphibious landings near Casablanca were models of efficiency, and the subsequent few days of operations demonstrated the Patton touch, the aggressive movements of confident troops.

In Tunisia no one else could have taken hold in such decisive fashion of the units defeated and demoralised by Kasserine Pass battle. He imbued them with the Patton spirit, and the operations at Gafsa and El Guettar demonstrated the miracle he had inspired. His newly formed Seventh Army in Sicily proved itself the equal of the veteran British Eighth Army mainly because of Patton's ruthless power to drive forward. By reaching Messina first he dissipated the feeling – fashionable in some Allied circles – that American soldiers were of poor quality or, at best, inexperienced.

In Normandy Patton exploded a local breakthrough into a theatre-wide break-out to the German border that liberated all of France north of the Loire. And finally in Luxembourg, perhaps his sublime hour, he was masterful in the manner in which he turned his army against the German Ardennes counter-offensive.

He was called the Green Hornet from a tank suit he designed, Gorgeous Georgie because of his manner of dress, but mainly Old Blood and Guts. They were all said with affection. In their thousands, Americans still say with considerable pride, 'I rolled with Patton'.

Apart from the psychology involved in leading men, he had an immense technical competence, a mastery of weapons and equipment, of tactics and operations, of manoeuvre and logistics. He was intimately acquainted with the field and technical manuals of his time. It is sometimes said reproachfully that his interest in the tactical led him to overlook the importance of the logistical, but the hours he spent on the docks of Casablanca and the careful briefings he required from his supply officers attest to his perspicacity in this area too.

Patton's single manifestation of deficiency as a twentieth-century commander was his attitude towards coalition warfare. No doubt reflecting Pershing's difficulties with his partners – a view expressed as, 'For God's sake, don't have anything to do with allies,' and an outlook stressed in the American military colleges between the wars – Patton was out of step with combined operations. In his private papers, his diary and his letters home he constantly grumbled about the need to subordinate American interests to the Allied cause. Although he refrained from public complaint because he knew that Eisenhower would fire him if he did so, he felt that the British were, as he often wrote, 'pulling our leg'. He resented serving under British command, although he liked Alexander personally and admired Montgomery and others, for it seemed to him that the British were running the show. Furthermore he believed that Eisenhower was more British than the British. What escaped him of course was the close affinity between warfare and international politics, if, indeed, affinity is strong enough. But his temperament too would probably have betrayed him had he had to function in a 'political' post that required the special niceties, tact and forbearance of coalition practice. He preferred to function on the national and operational level where he could be 'military' in the traditional nineteenth-century sense.

Patton gained his military expertise not only from his reading but also from his training activities. He regarded training as a vehicle to attain two ends. First, training accustomed men to obey orders automatically, not merely instantly, but also unquestionably. It also taught men to perform their tasks automatically. Only when soldiers were so proficient in their duties could they function under battlefield conditions. Despite the fear engendered by the proximity of death, despite the presence of confusion, men had to be able to carry out their military functions, and this required both automatic response to orders and automatic performance.

The second end achieved by training, and hardly less important in Patton's view, was the use of unit manoeuvres and exercises to test and experiment with doctrine. While training exercises could demonstrate the soundness of doctrine, they could also become an opportunity to improve doctrine or methodology. When Patton commanded the tank training centre in France in the First World War, he conducted a multitude of exercises and sham battles to examine the then still rudimentary tank tactics. But he also experimented with new techniques. For example, should infantry precede or follow tanks in the attack and at what distances?

Throughout his adult life, during his thirty-five years of active duty, Patton's efficiency reports noted with remarkable consistency his enthusiastic study of and devotion to his profession. It all paid off in the Second World War.

In 1919 he lectured as follows:

We, as officers . . . are not only members of the oldest of honorable professions but are also the modern representatives of the demi-gods and heroes of antiquity.

Back of us stretches a line of men whose acts of valor, of self-sacrifice and of service have been the theme of song and story since long before recorded history began . . .

In the days of chivalry . . . knights-officers were noted as well for courtesy and gentleness of behavior, as for death-defying courage . . . From their acts of courtesy and benevolence was derived the word, now pronounced as one, Gentle Man . . . Let us be gentle. That is, courteous and considerate of the rights of others. Let us be men. That is, fearless and untiring in doing our duty . . .

Our calling is most ancient and like all other old things it has amassed through the ages certain customs and traditions which decorate and enoble it, which render beautiful the otherwise prosaic occupation of being professional men-at-arms: Killers.

In his own life he sought perfection and was never satisfied with his performance. He was always apprehensive that he would be found wanting, not quite up to the standards he demanded of himself. He always feared that he lacked the qualities to reach the goal he dreamed of gaining.

He worked hard for what he wanted. He was exceptionally honest and clearheaded. He tried to be fair to all. He loved beauty in all its manifestations.

What made it possible for Patton to achieve what he wished so ardently was not only his driving will-power. It was also his great good fortune that his lifetime required the kind of military leadership he personified. In this he was lucky. But it was not entirely a matter of luck. When opportunity knocked, he knew how to open the door.

A man of action, he was also a man of culture, knowledge and wit. A man of erudition, he found his highest calling in execution. A throwback to the Teutonic knight, the Saracen, the Crusader, he was one of America's greatest soldiers, one of the world's great captains.

He believed in audacity and speed, and when his superiors unleashed him, his operations followed these precepts. Thoroughly grounded in the means of waging war in his time, he had an intuitive perception, a sixth sense, of enemy capacities and intentions. His predictions – for example, at Salerno, Anzio and the Ardennes – proved remarkably accurate.

Patton quickened the pace of the war, contributed *élan* to the campaigns in which he participated, and inspired his troops, as no one else, with pride, confidence and a desire to win. He was a masterful leader whose personality and exploits captivated not only his contemporaries but also subsequent generations. He was an authentic military genius.

General Carl A. Spaatz

Alfred Goldberg

Of all the great Anglo-American commanders of the Second World War, General Carl A. (Tooey) Spaatz was and remained the most private and the most obscure – by his own choice. A very private man with a positive distaste for personal publicity, he shunned the limelight, discouraged and forbade personal publicity on his behalf, and insisted that his major subordinate commanders – Doolittle, Brereton, Vandenberg, and Twining* – be accorded the publicity build-ups that sometimes seemed to be major functions of the modern war machines.

Only in this publicity war did Spaatz fail to measure up to the demands made on him by his chief military sponsor – General Henry H. (Hap) Arnold, Commanding General of the US Army Air Forces, who was at the same time his greatest admirer. As part of his dream of an independent American air force, Hap Arnold hoped that Tooey Spaatz would become in the public mind the embodiment of American air power in action. For years Arnold waged a campaign to persuade Spaatz to seek public recognition for himself and to use all the considerable resources at his disposal to gain the attention of the Anglo-American public and thereby foster the cause of air power. Only the last consideration – the cause of air power – could appeal to Spaatz, and he did indeed seek to secure recognition for air power's deeds and ideas.

In his heartfelt endeavour Arnold succeeded only partially. Unlike Eisenhower – and MacArthur, Patton, Montgomery, and even Doolittle and Chennault† – Spaatz never became a household name in the United States or in Britain. And yet, by most standards, Spaatz must be accounted the premier air commander and one of the very greatest of all of the military commanders of the Second World War. He fulfilled to the utmost the expectations and hopes of achievement held for him by Arnold, Eisenhower and other

* Lieutenant-General James H. Doolittle, commander of the United States Eighth Air Force, 1944–5, Lieutenant-General Lewis H. Brereton, commander of the United States Ninth Air Force, 1942–4. Lieutenant-General Hoyt S. Vandenberg, commander of the United States Ninth Air Force, 1944–5. Lieutenant-General Nathan F. Twining, commander of the United States Fifteenth Air Force, 1944–5.

† Major-General Claire L. Chennault, commander of the Flying Tigers in Burma and of the United States Fourteenth Air Force in China 1942–5.

sponsors. He attained the pinnacle of his profession because he was extraordinarily well qualified by character, temperament, experience and instinct to be a commander. To put it simply – he had the knack.

Spaatz's professional qualifications as a commander derived from his long and unusually broad and deep experience as an airman. When he arrived in Britain in June 1942 as commander of the fledgling Eighth Air Force, he was just fifty-one years old and a veteran of more than twenty-six years of flying. He had been a contemporary of Eisenhower's at West Point, from which he graduated in 1914, a year ahead of Eisenhówer. After completing his army flying training at San Diego, California, in 1916, Spaatz served as a pilot on the Mexican border with General John J. Pershing's Expeditionary Force, pursuing Pancho Villa.

In the First World War Spaatz commanded a pursuit squadron and organised and commanded the huge American flying school at Issoudoun in France. It was only in response to his own urgent requests that he was granted a brief tour of combat duty in September 1918, during which he shot down three German planes. By the end of the war Spaatz was a thoroughly seasoned flyer and commander, enormously imbued with the spirit of flying and impressed with the potential of military aviation.

In the sometimes dispiriting years between wars, Spaatz commanded pursuit and bomber units, attended advanced service schools, and served in a variety of capacities in the highest echelon of the army air arm, the office of the Chief of Air Corps: Chief of Training and Operations, Chief of Plans, and Assistant Chief of the Air Corps. A pioneer and innovator of new tactics and techniques, he commanded the famous refuelling endurance flight in the *Question Mark* over Los Angeles in 1929. He wrote a series of texts for flying officers, sat on evaluation boards that selected most of the American army military aircraft of the 1920s and 1930s, and planned many of the principal air exercises and manoeuvres, with which he was generally associated as commander or senior staff officer. This was an unusually rich background of experience that few if any other American air officers could match at the beginning of the war.

Spaatz capped this rich experience when he spent four months in France and England, beginning in May 1940, observing the progress of the air war. He witnessed the crucial phase of the Battle of Britain, absorbing information, ideas and lessons that he later put to use. He predicted that the RAF would prevail over the *Luftwaffe*.

Like most great military men, Spaatz was a pragmatist. He began the war with certain firmly held ideas about air warfare and strategy, but when some of them failed to stand the test of experience, he discarded or modified them. About some of his ideas, he changed his mind more than once during the war, for he experienced the uncertainties, fears and pressures that afflict all leaders having to make great decisions. War is the ultimate test of strategic and tactical concepts and doctrines; the successful generals are those who can change or adapt their ideas opportunely to accord with the reality of events. This flexibility and sensitivity is not given to all commanders – Spaatz had it, Bomber Harris* did not.

Since the 1920s Spaatz had held firmly to the notion of air power as a separate military element capable of operating independently of ground and naval forces. A strong supporter of Billy Mitchell† in his fight for autonomy of the air arm, he continued to hold as a tenet the goal of a separate air force. Eventually, after the Second World War, Spaatz presided over the creation of the US Air Force. But at the onset of the Second World War, he insisted that any move for a separate air force was premature and inopportune and should be postponed until after the war; he adhered to this position until the end of the war.

At the same time Spaatz took such administrative and logistical preparatory steps towards independence as could be accommodated within the US Army. And Spaatz resisted and overcame all efforts to make the American air forces in Europe subordinate to or dependent on the British.

Along with the other leaders of the US Army Air Forces, Spaatz believed in strategic bombardment as the prime air mission and in the superiority of the bomber over the fighter. Here too his ideas derived initially from Billy Mitchell and received reinforcement subsequently from the emergence and acceptance in the 1930s of strategic bombardment as the basic doctrine of the US Army Air Corps. Like Arnold, Spaatz favoured giving priority to the war against Germany, influenced in no small measure by the practical consideration that in 1942 it was possible to get at Germany from the air, but not Japan. The American air leaders, encouraged by the British, resolved to test their strategic bombing theory against Germany. Spaatz became the chief protagonist and director of the test.

In the face of British scepticism and disbelief, Spaatz adhered tenaciously to the belief that bombers *en masse* could conduct a daylight strategic campaign against Germany. He and Eaker‡ maintained that four-engine B-17 Flying Fortresses and B-24 Liberators could penetrate Germany and bomb successfully from altitude. In the long run they were proven amply correct, but not before they were compelled to make important modifications in their ideas.

Perhaps the most important change involved the issue of escort fighters. Spaatz's original belief and position in 1942 that massed bombers could extend their operations into Germany in daylight without fighter escort became untenable in the face of the heavy and unacceptable losses sustained

---

* Air Chief Marshal Sir Arthur Harris, Air Officer Commanding-in-Chief RAF Bomber Command, 1942–5

† Brigadier-General William Mitchell, US Air Service, was court-martialled by the US Army in a famous trial in 1925.

‡ Lieutenant-General Ira C. Eaker, commander of the VIII Bomber Command under Spaatz in 1942, commander of the Eighth Air Force in 1943, and commander of the Mediterranean Allied Air Forces, 1944–5.

during operations in 1943 – particularly against Ploesti and Schweinfurt. Fortunately for the American bomber commanders and crews, the great American fighter planes – the P-51 Mustang and the P-47 Thunderbolt – were developed into long-range aircraft in time to reach the United Kingdom in great numbers during the winter and spring of 1944.

Spaatz became an ardent advocate of and exceptionally skilled practitioner in the use of the escort fighters. It was a measure of his flexibility, experience in air war and quickness in exploiting opportunity that he turned the whole air war in western Europe around in a matter of a few months. In December 1943 and January 1944 American bombers hardly dared venture to the borders of Germany, let alone penetrate into the heartland. By early April 1944 American Mustangs and Thunderbolts ruled the air over Germany, and the American bombers went everywhere, striking from their bases in the United Kingdom and Italy. Goering knew that he had lost the air war when American Mustangs appeared over Berlin early in April.

It is to Spaatz's credit that he personally directed the aggressive strategy and tactics in the onslaught of the fighters against the *Luftwaffe*. He insisted that the fighters not be tied to the bombers as escorts, that they surge ahead of the bomber formations, seek out the German fighters in the air and on the ground, and destroy them. This brilliant stroke derived from Spaatz's boldness and his confidence in the strength and quality of his forces. The *Luftwaffe* never recovered from the crippling effects of these great air battles.

The dazzling victories over the Germans in the winter and spring of 1944 led to the air supremacy that Spaatz had always maintained would be required for a successful outcome of the war. As a commander of tactical air forces in the Mediterranean area during 1943 he had found ample confirmation of his firm belief that air supremacy was indispensable to victory in the war. In North Africa, Sicily and Italy, Allied air power achieved superiority over the Germans and Italians, and victory on the ground followed. The unacceptable American bomber losses over Germany in 1943 demonstrated the imperative need for control of the air. No air leader in Europe was more keenly aware of the need or laboured so unceasingly to bring it about as did Spaatz.

All of the problems of military strategy and operations were greatly affected by considerations of command during the entire course of the war. The problems of command proved especially complicated and vexatious in the theatres of war in which Spaatz served. The rivalries, personality conflicts and vested interests that are normally present even when only one national interest is involved were enormously magnified in the theatres where the Anglo-American forces waged coalition warfare against Germany. One of the outstanding British air commanders – Sir John Slessor – who was also one of the most successful in building and maintaining Anglo-American command ties, wrote feelingly afterwards that 'war without allies is bad enough – with allies it is hell'.

Some of the greatest, albeit bloodless, battles of the war were waged within the higher military councils of the Anglo-American coalition. By no means did these battles follow purely national lines – groupings often transcended national barriers, following strategic, service, personal, or other interests. And at the centre of most of these battles – certainly a vital element in them – stood the question of Anglo-American air operations – command arrangements and strategy. On the American air side, Spaatz played the pre-eminent role in both the European and Mediterranean theatres.

During his Overlord (code name for the invasion of France in 1944) period – 1944–5 – Spaatz looked back on his North African experience with nostalgia, considering it the high point of his war experience. This feeling he shared with Tedder, who probably held it even more intensely because of his longer service in North Africa. By comparison with western Europe in 1944–5, the Mediterranean area in 1942–3 seemed to have been relatively simple and uncomplicated. It seemed to Spaatz and Tedder that political considerations had been less important – although not absent – and that there had been a spirit of unity and singlemindedness that was difficult to maintain in western Europe because the theatre was too big, too complicated, too political, too beset with rivalries and command problems. It was the reaction of men who had already achieved great victories and found themselves frustrated in their new setting by conditions and rules that they could not change or manipulate to their satisfaction.

In truth the Mediterranean had not been the near-paradise that Spaatz and Tedder later looked back on so nostalgically. The early days of Anglo-American operations in North Africa had indeed witnessed a great deal of storm and stress between the two partners, particularly over command arrangements and strategic plans. That friction between the two air forces did occur is clear from the testimony of most of the leaders in the theatre, but it never succeeded in obscuring the unity of purpose that prevailed. And indeed the relationship between Britons and Americans at the squadron level was often warmer and more cordial than at the higher levels.

By the end of 1943, when Spaatz left the Mediterranean for Britain, the unbroken chain of Allied military triumphs testified to the success of the coalition command. Spaatz and Tedder went to Britain because Eisenhower wanted as his top air commanders men who were thoroughly schooled in air support of ground armies.

In London, at the beginning of 1944, the war looked vastly different to Spaatz. Operating from the seat of the British government, and especially within the immediate orbit of Winston Churchill, presented grave complications for the American commanders – primarily Eisenhower and Spaatz – who had heretofore been insulated by the thousand miles between them and London.

In Britain were the British ministries and additional British national commands – RAF Bomber Command, Home Command, Air Defence of

Great Britain, and others – all with important interests and claims on resources. The British government did not propose to place these vital forces under the command of Eisenhower or any other foreigner. Accordingly they presented additional complications in working out command arrangements that were already terribly complex. The presence of so many levels of authority on the scene, representing so many diverse interests and outlooks, could not help but exacerbate an already difficult situation.

The problems of command arrangements and strategy for Overlord were intertwined and could not be settled separately. This was because the role of the Allied air forces was central to the whole operation. All agreed that control of the air over the landing beaches and as far into western Europe as possible was indispensable to the success of Overlord. Differences over how to achieve this result and how to organise the air forces to bring it about occasioned one of the greatest debates of the war.

The alignment of interests in the controversy cut across national lines and indeed across service lines. Eisenhower and Tedder regarded the great strategic air forces – the RAF Bomber Command and the US Strategic Air Forces in Europe (USSTAF) – as representing the major complicating factor because they had a mission that was independent of Overlord and all other operations. These bomber fleets, controlled by Harris and Spaatz, had not yet reached their full strength in the spring of 1944, but their commanders and other air leaders regarded the strategic bombing campaign as the best hope for the early defeat of Germany and were disposed to resist efforts to divert their forces to other missions. Churchill and the British Chiefs of Staff opposed placing the heavy bombers under Eisenhower.

The question of bringing the strategic air forces under the effective control of Supreme Commander Eisenhower was not settled until he threatened to ask to be relieved from command if he could not have them at his disposal. Churchill and the Chief of the Air Staff, Sir Charles Portal, backed down and settled for language that did not give Eisenhower command in name, although he could and did exercise it in fact. Here Spaatz, a strong Eisenhower supporter, had raised no command issue – he accepted that Eisenhower had to have the bombers available to him in time of need. And the best way to assure their availability was to own them.

On the other main issue – the air strategy for the overture to Overlord – Spaatz took a strong and consistent position that placed him in opposition to both Eisenhower and Tedder. The central issue concerned the best way to use the heavy bombers to help assure the Allies of air supremacy over the invasion areas in Normandy. There was complete agreement on the need for such control of the air – the question was how best to attain it.

Eisenhower, Tedder and Leigh-Mallory* insisted that the success of the

* Air Chief Marshal Sir Trafford Leigh-Mallory, Commander-in-Chief of the Allied Expeditionary Air Force. Both Harris and Spaatz refused to accept Leigh-Mallory as the overall air commander for Overlord. Accordingly they reported to Tedder instead.

invasion could best be assured by sending the heavy bombers against the transportation systems of northern France and Belgium, thereby isolating the lodgement area. Spaatz argued forcefully and cogently that the German fighters would refuse to take to the air in defence of the transportation targets and that the Nazi fighter squadrons in Germany would survive to fight over the beaches in Normandy. He had no doubts that these same squadrons could be brought to battle by a sustained Allied bomber attack against targets in Germany proper – and especially oil targets. If the *Luftwaffe* had to wage a life and death struggle over Germany in defence of the vital oil targets it would not be able to contest control of the air over Normandy on D-Day.

Spaatz carried the burden of the fight for oil, stating his case with vigour and conviction. His status as a commander demanded that his position on the issue be weighed thoroughly. The British authors of the *Strategic Air Offensive*, Webster and Frankland, wrote that

> . . . Spaatz had been placed in a position which, for an air commander, was unprecedented. Not only did his influence outweigh that of Sir Arthur Harris and . . . Leigh-Mallory . . . but it presently came to rival that of Sir Charles Portal himself. General Spaatz carried with him the long-standing and entire confidence of General Arnold and he brought to England a much more powerful and also a more independent judgment than had ever been exercised by General Eaker. This judgment was to have a profound effect upon the course of the Combined Bomber Offensive.

Spaatz did not prevail against the united opposition of Eisenhower, Tedder and Leigh-Mallory. He accepted the decision to send the bombers against the transportation targets, but he elicited from Eisenhower, perhaps, as has been alleged, by using Eisenhower's own tactic of threatening to ask to be relieved of command, permission to launch his bombers against oil targets in Germany when they could be spared from the transportation campaign and the weather was right.

Events proved Spaatz right, but the fate of the *Luftwaffe* had already been settled before the Eighth Air Force carried out its first attack on an oil target – against Merseburg-Leuna – on 12 May. The *Luftwaffe* had already suffered such serious losses in the great daylight air battles of February, March and April against the Eighth and Fifteenth Air Force that it proved only a negligible factor on D-Day. But the threat of the great American bomber armadas had forced the Germans to keep their fighter units in Germany far from the Atlantic coastal areas. As a result they could muster only part of the fighters still available to them for operations against the beachhead.

The initial attacks on oil targets in Germany in May 1944 proved so promising that Eisenhower widened Spaatz's scope of authority to determine target priorities. The rest of the story is well known. Oil did indeed turn out to be the Achilles' heel of the German war machine and economy. It was *the* central target system, even though Harris continued to dismiss it as another of the 'panacea' target systems that he held in contempt.

The successful attack on German oil was a vindication of Spaatz's strategic insight. In conference with General Marshall, as early as May 1942, before he moved the Eighth Air Force to England, Spaatz pinpointed oil as a crucial target, specifically advocating the destruction of the Rumanian oilfields at Ploesti. He favoured the 1942 and 1943 attacks on Ploesti and oversaw the massive attacks by the Fifteenth Air Force in the spring and summer of 1944 that destroyed the oilfields by the time the Russians captured them in August 1944. The attrition of the oil supply from Ploesti made the synthetic oil plants in Germany all the more indispensable to the Nazis. Spaatz's battle within the Allied command to initiate and pursue the oil attacks and his successful conduct of the campaign represented one of his two greatest achievements of the war.

One of the great issues of the Second World War became known as morale bombing – the attacks on cities and populations for the purpose of weakening or breaking the will of the enemy to resist. The issue over area or morale bombing existed on two planes – one pragmatic, the other moral. Inevitably they interacted.

Under Sir Arthur Harris RAF Bomber Command engaged in area bombing with the enemy's morale as the main objective. Spaatz on the other hand consistently expounded the doctrine and followed the practice of selective and precision bombing, selective in the sense that particular target systems were chosen and attacked – oil, aircraft factories, transportation, the electrical industry. Moreover the American air leaders sought to attain a high order of precision – 'pickle barrel' bombing – in their daylight attacks. But accurate bombing proved most difficult for the bomber crews in face of intensive anti-aircraft fire, German interceptor fighters, and bad weather over the targets. It must be conceded that many of the attacks by the bombers of the Eighth and Fifteenth air forces, especially when bombing by radar through overcast, were no more precise than those of the RAF Lancasters and Halifaxes attacking at night. But the Americans adhered to the principle of selective bombing and insisted on the selection of authentic industrial and military targets as their aiming points.

Spaatz recognised that the spillover effects of 'precision' bombing caused much destruction of civilian lives and property, but he accepted this as inevitable. More than once during the war Spaatz expressed his concern about the verdict of history on the strategic bombing of Germany. He expressed the hope that the strategic bombing campaign against Germany would be seen in perspective and in full context as justifiable acts of war and not immoral and terrorist acts. After the war Spaatz learned that some of his own German relatives had died in the Allied bombing attacks on German cities.

Pragmatist that he was, Spaatz's position against attacking cities as such for morale effects wavered sometimes during the last year of the war as special opportunities to achieve potentially decisive effects appeared to offer themselves. In July 1944, at Spaatz's direction, his deputy for operations, Major-General Frederick L. Anderson, issued an order stating, 'We will not, at any time, direct our efforts toward area bombing.' But at the same time Anderson reaffirmed the policy of radar bombing through the overcast. Had the American bombers been required to confine their attacks to occasions when visual bombing was possible, their operations would have been greatly diminished – perhaps by as much as a third or a half.

In August 1944 Spaatz discussed with his key staff officers, including Anderson, whether to attack German morale all-out, with the morale of the German high command as the ultimate goal. Early in September Eisenhower asked Spaatz to be ready to bomb Berlin at a moment's notice. Spaatz instructed his staff and the commander of the Eighth Air Force, General Doolittle, that they should no longer plan to hit definite military objectives but should be prepared to drop bombs indiscriminately on Berlin when General Eisenhower gave the order. Eisenhower did not issue the order and the attack did not take place. This was the first of several climactic occasions on which Allied leaders gave consideration to mounting tremendous aerial blows against Germany in the hope of achieving a rapid deterioration of the German will to resist.

On subsequent occasions Spaatz found it necessary to issue denials, both public and private, that the strategic bombing operations had taken on the character of morale or terror bombing. In February 1945 he reassured Arnold that the policy of precision bombing remained unchanged, although the great Dresden raid of 16 February had given rise to stories of a change. In the last stages of the war, during March and April, with the number of targets greatly diminished, American daylight attacks tended to take on the character of area bombing, until the strategic air war was declared officially ended on 16 April.

In retrospect it seems likely that if Spaatz had believed that area or morale bombing could have been decisive in a relatively short period of time – weeks rather than months – he might well have put aside his opposition to attacking purely civilian targets and joined Harris. He was prepared to do this in September 1944 at Eisenhower's direction. Later, in July and August 1945, when directing the final act of the great bombing onslaught against Japan by the B-29 Superfortresses from the Marianas, Spaatz accepted unquestioningly the policy of burning out and destroying the Japanese cities. Moreover the American leaders, political and military, accepted the use of the atomic bomb against Japan as the surest way of bringing the war to a quick end and saving the lives of large numbers of American soldiers and sailors. Had the atomic bomb been developed before the end of the war in Europe, it is likely that Spaatz would have favoured its use against Germany as the most effective way of ending resistance quickly.

The whole question of the effectiveness of the Anglo-American strategic bombardment campaign against Germany and its contribution to the defeat of the Nazis has remained at issue through the three decades that have elapsed since the end of the war. Within the past few years two eminent American economists – John K. Galbraith and Walt W. Rostow – both of them target planners or analysts of bombing operations during and after the war, have waged a caustic and inconclusive public debate on the subject. Many military analysts and professional military men have drawn diametrically opposed conclusions about the success or failure of the campaign. Some of them – including J. F. C. Fuller and Walter Millis – argued their cases and reached conclusions without the benefit of careful study and analysis of the subject.

Spaatz of course remained a convinced and forceful advocate of strategic bombardment throughout the war. He frequently expressed to his staff and commanders and in correspondence his belief that the bombing of Germany represented the best use of resources and offered the best hope of bringing about an early collapse of the Germans. Early in the war – 1942 – in a meeting at RAF Bomber Command, Spaatz disagreed with Harris's position that the strategic bomber could bring an end to the war without the Allied ground armies having to invade the Continent. But a year later, in August 1943, he wrote to Robert A. Lovett* from North Africa that he was becoming increasingly convinced that Germany could be forced to its knees by aerial bombardment alone. And in the early months of 1944, when he was fighting against the diversion of his bomber forces from their onslaught against Germany, Spaatz on several occasions expressed his belief that full-scale use of the air forces – including the tactical air forces – for strategic bombing would eliminate the need for the 'highly dangerous Overlord operation'. This was the classic position of strategic bombardment leaders in both the RAF and the USAAF. But Spaatz was willing and ready to modify this position and adapt to changing circumstances. In large part this explains his great effectiveness and influence in the Allied war councils.

Spaatz's appraisals of the effects actually being achieved by the strategic bombers during the war varied somewhat with the fortunes of the bomber forces, but his fundamental faith remained unchanged. He opposed the invasion of North Africa in 1942 because it would diminish the forces available in Britain for the bombing of Germany. He favoured oil over transportation in 1944 and sought to limit the use of his bombers against the V-weapon sites before and after D-Day. Still, when confronted with urgent requirements for use of the B-17s and B-24s against tactical targets, Spaatz yielded, sometimes graciously and sometimes less so, but he made certain that his forces operated with maximum effectiveness.

In truth a very large part of the total bombing effort of the Eighth and Fifteenth air forces during 1944–5 was diverted to a variety of tactical targets.

* Assistant Secretary of War for Air, 1941–5, Secretary of Defense, 1951–3.

Depending on whether the transportation targets in Germany proper are categorised as strategic or tactical targets (and there are grounds for debate), this diversion amounted to 25 to 50 per cent of the total USSTAF daylight bombing effort during 1944–5, and probably a lesser percentage for RAF Bomber Command. Thus the strategic bombing leaders could maintain correctly that because of these diversions they had not been able to use the full weight of their bomber forces in a sustained attack against Germany proper during the last year of the war. From this standpoint therefore, there had not been a full and proper test of their strategic bombing concept.

Retrospectively after the war, Spaatz conceded that it had been proper to give Overlord the highest priority and that the use of the bombers in support of the ground campaign had been correct. Moreover he felt that even if he had been given *carte blanche* in April to attack oil targets, he probably would have mounted only one or two more attacks than actually occurred during the spring and summer of 1944.

On the results achieved by the strategic bombardment of Germany, Spaatz held a more balanced view than many of his fellow air power zealots in the US Army Air Forces. He had been instrumental in bringing about the creation of the US Strategic Bombing Survey, and he subscribed to its main conclusion, 'Airpower was decisive in the war in Europe.' Spaatz's postwar statements on the subject sometimes went beyond this ambiguous declaration, which in reality begged the question of the effectiveness of strategic bombardment. He stated that the record of the war would show that air power had carried out the mission of destroying the enemy's power and will to wage war. Subsequently he qualified this by saying, 'I do not mean that we won the war by bombardment alone – but airpower was a predominant force in the victory.' This relatively modest assessment was consistent with the conclusion of the Strategic Bombing Survey. Moreover, among the many statements that Spaatz made on the subject during almost three decades after the war, this probably comes closer than any to representing his abiding view. It was a view that broadened and gained perspective with the passage of time, bringing a degree of understanding and appreciation of the complexities of the conflict that were not as apparent during the hectic years of the war.

With the end of the war in Europe, Arnold insisted that Spaatz take command of the B-29s attacking Japan from the Marianas and Okinawa. Spaatz's stay in the Pacific was brief but eventful. It was he who received President Truman's order to drop the atomic bombs on Japanese targets and oversaw the attacks against Hiroshima and Nagasaki. On 2 September 1945 Spaatz witnessed the surrender of the Japanese on board the battleship *Missouri* in Tokyo Bay. (He was the only person who was present at both the German and Japanese surrenders.) But the Pacific experience, in spite of these dramatic events, was pure anticlimax for Spaatz, and he so expressed himself in letters to colleagues. He was pleased to return to Washington after less than two months in the Pacific.

Early in 1946, Arnold, worn out by his wartime labours, turned over to Spaatz command of the army air forces and the responsibility for presiding over the creation of the independent US Air Force. It was during the battle for an independent air force – 1946–7 – that Spaatz displayed perhaps the strongest feelings and most impulsive behaviour of his career. The US Navy, because of its reluctance to accept the great changes in the defence structure that were in the making and because of its insistence on maintaining a large naval air arm, aroused Spaatz's ire and elicited some of his strongest expressions of dislike and distrust.

When Spaatz became the first Chief of Staff of the US Air Force on 26 September 1947, he was already discontented with high military office in Washington and found it less and less to his liking. The administrative demands of the office and the difficulties in securing acceptable resolutions of issues displeased and frustrated him. After little more than seven months as Chief of Staff, he retired on 30 April 1948.

For a number of years thereafter Spaatz wrote a column of military comment for a news magazine. His views on air power and its dominant role in the nuclear age remained consistent, but he was also appalled at the thought of nuclear war and came to consider it unthinkable. His death in July 1974 momentarily resurrected public recollection of his dynamic role in the Second World War and a renewed interest in his military career.

Any assessment of Spaatz must begin with the understanding that he was 'his own man'. Neither Marshall, nor Eisenhower, nor Arnold or Portal, not even Churchill, overawed him; he regarded himself unselfconsciously as their peer in the art of making war. Nevertheless he did not have the mental arrogance characteristic of many self-made men. But he had strength and force of character – enough to deal on equal terms with other leaders who were strong and stubborn also. And yet Spaatz was a man of genuine modesty and diffidence. There was a sturdy no-nonsense quality and an unmistakable professionalism about him that could not help but impress. His modesty did not inhibit his capacity to command because he knew his own mind and made free to speak it when necessary.

Unlike some commanders who are puppets in the hands of a clever staff, Spaatz dominated his staff. He was capable of thinking big, and like the other great American military leaders – Marshall, Eisenhower, MacArthur, Nimitz – his mind expanded quickly to the scale of the war. He was not an intellectual, but he was a man of intellect. He was not a visionary, but he was a man of vision.

Although Spaatz sometimes felt cramped and irked by higher authority that subordinated his own preferred strategies and operations, he demonstrated his philosophical patience in his loyal acceptance of that authority – after he had had his say. The day after the decision on oil versus transportation went against him in April 1944 he wrote to Arnold that he believed the 'decision reached was justified based on all factors involved, which are predominantly the absolute necessity to insure the initial success of Overlord'. Spaatz was big enough to know that the overall cause was greater than personal or service ambitions and merged his self-interest successfully into the higher purpose of the war.

He had a knack for picking his men, but it was much more than good fortune. He had known and presumably evaluated most of the key officers of the Army Air Forces before the United States entered the war. His key staff officers he chose personally, and he let them work unfettered. This freed him from burdensome details and gave him time to supervise, make decisions and deal with his fellow members of the high command. He gave his subordinate commanders a free hand, handing over the execution of operations while retaining control. This habit of efficient organisation permitted him to see to it that his plans were carried into effect.

Spaatz commanded the respect of his staff, his commanders, his peers and his superiors. They recognised his outstanding professional competence, but even more were they impressed by his strength, his integrity and his decisiveness. He made decisions. He had confidence in himself and he projected it quietly. Certainly, after the Tunisian campaign in 1943, there were few who could doubt his ability to stay the course. Tedder had had some reservations about Spaatz earlier in 1943, but these disappeared, and in the European Theatre in 1944 Tedder observed how Spaatz grew prodigiously in stature and influence among his peers.

Contemporaries spoke of Spaatz's acute perception and instinct. Robert A. Lovett, a close friend and confidant and an unusually keen and accurate observer, felt that Spaatz had an instinct for strategy and that his instinct generally proved correct. Spaatz himself was not a painstaking or systematic planner, allowing his intuition to guide him to the right decisions. He tended towards boldness in strategy and tactics, possessing the courage to make hard decisions and to live with them once made.

Spaatz had the common touch, identifying naturally with his fighting men and visiting combat crews frequently. He had great concern that his men put their trust in him and their other leaders, insisting that they be told the truth about operations and their effects. Because he felt that misleading information and wrong impressions could be harmful to the morale of the fighting men, Spaatz personally took great pains to correct and set right such lapses. Like Eisenhower, he took a personal interest in the problems of officers and enlisted men, often making extraordinary efforts to bring about a resolution of such problems.

Eisenhower named Spaatz and Omar Bradley as the outstanding generals to serve under him during the war. In 1948 he wrote to Spaatz, 'No man can justly claim a greater share than you in the attainment of victory in Europe.' Arnold considered Spaatz the outstanding airman of the war, and Bradley referred to him as a 'deceptively quiet and brilliant man.' Portal and Tedder held him in the highest esteem as a commander, and Sholto Douglas,* who had come to know him well, wrote that of 'all the relatively unknown military leaders of World War II, Spaatz was probably the greatest'. That he was relatively unknown suited Spaatz, for he had no concern about status and image. His achievements as a commander and a major architect of the Allied air war in the Second World War deserve a full measure of historical recognition. May he be accorded his due.

* Air Chief Marshal Sir Sholto Douglas, who commanded both Fighter Command and Coastal Command during the war.

Lieutenant-General Lord Freyberg

———◆———

Dan Davin

The young Bernard Freyberg who got himself to London in 1914 had been born in Richmond twenty-five years before, but from the age of two brought up in New Zealand. He was over six feet tall, of great physical strength, and tireless in energy. Of modest education, he had qualified and practised as a dentist. His passion was for soldiering and he was already a lieutenant in the New Zealand Territorials. He had come to England to get as quickly as possible into the war he had long foreseen and prepared himself for.

Somehow he met and impressed Winston Churchill and through him became a temporary lieutenant in the RNVR. Soon he had command of A Company in the Hood Battalion of the Royal Naval Division. He served with the division in the Antwerp adventure, Churchill's brainchild, and brought his company back via Dunkirk from the subsequent débâcle, the first of his four evacuations by sea.

Next, the Naval Division was assigned to the Gallipoli campaign, and Freyberg sailed with the Hood Battalion on 28 February 1915. By now he was at home in a brilliant group of officers, mostly from Oxford or Cambridge: among them Arthur Asquith, son of the Prime Minister; Patrick Shaw-Stewart, a Fellow of All Souls; A. P. Herbert; and Rupert Brooke. These young men, and others like them, became his close friends. The brilliance and promise of most of them had only a short time to last. And the first to go was Rupert Brooke, Freyberg's cabin mate. On 23 April he died at Scyros of an infection and was buried the same day. Freyberg helped carry the bier and dig the grave.

The Naval Division was to cover the main landings by a mock landing in the Gulf of Xeros. Freyberg persuaded his superiors to let him do the job of diversion alone: he would swim ashore after dark on 25 April and light a series of flares. The force of his personality and persuasion must have been considerable; for his plan was accepted. Performance matched promise. He did the job successfully and received the DSO.

Before long the Naval Division was itself landed and Freyberg took a full share in the grim Gallipoli fighting. He was severely wounded in the stomach on 25 June, but was back with his battalion, by now its commander, by 19 August. 'I guess he's made of india-rubber,' an Australian nursing sister commented.

After the Dardanelles evacuation in January 1916, Freyberg came back to England. The Naval Division was reformed as the 63rd Division, Freyberg was confirmed in command of the Hood Battalion and left for France in May. From then onwards his career was meteoric. His first major battle was in November on the Somme. In an advance of forty-eight hours he was four times wounded but he refused to be evacuated until the forward positions, taken largely by his inspired leadership, were consolidated. He was awarded the VC.

His wounds kept him in England until March 1917, when he was given command of the 173rd Brigade of the 51st Division. He distinguished himself once more at Bullecourt in May, and in September during the Third Battle of Ypres he received multiple wounds. After a long spell in hospital he was given the 88th Brigade, near Passchendaele. He was in much of the major fighting to follow, including the last battle of Ypres, where he won a bar to his DSO. He ended the war, ardent to the last, with a mad dash to forestall the demolition of a bridge at Lessines before 1100 hours on Armistice Day.

In England, though deprecating heroics, he had become a hero. This, and the friendships he had made, opened to him the doors of great houses and he was esteemed among people of reputation and power. Though the war was over, he had found his *métier* and he decided to remain a soldier. The dizzy opportunities were gone with the battles, but his peacetime career was distinguished. He passed the staff course at Camberley, served in the Grenadier Guards and was thence given command of the Manchester Regiment. In 1931 he was AA & QMG of the Southern Command, an experience invaluable later, and by 1934 he was a major-general. But now came a check. He was to have taken a senior command in India but failed the routine medical examination. He was declared medically unfit, suffering from 'aortic incompetence'. A lesser man might have accepted that his heart had been damaged by the strains of the war and by his two attempts to swim the Channel in 1925 and 1926. Instead he went off and climbed Mount Snowdon.

The medical verdict remained however and he was retired as major-general in 1937. He now began to interest himself in business and industry and became a director with BSA. But with the storm gathering in the world, he had little doubt that Othello's occupation would return.

In 1939 Freyberg was fifty. The war – quite apart from his deep sense of duty – could not have failed to seem an opportunity to a born soldier. He had not been happy about his early retirement, and now it was obvious that a man of his rank and experience was bound to be welcomed back and that the more stringent medical criteria of peacetime would be relaxed.

At the outbreak of war he was indeed given a job: that of GOC Salisbury

Plain Area, a mobilisation appointment. But he wanted something more active and so he offered his services to New Zealand, perhaps thinking that he would find the citizen army of his compatriots congenial and that if he were given its command he could serve the common cause at least as well and help bring his two countries closer together.

He was interviewed in London by Peter Fraser, then the New Zealand Deputy Prime Minister. The interview went well. Fraser consulted Ironside and Gort, who both warmly commended Freyberg. Churchill's hearty approval was also forthcoming and Freyberg was appointed commander of the New Zealand Expeditionary Force. After the decision was announced on 24 November Freyberg spent a brief fortnight in France, flew to Egypt and chose a base near Cairo – neither too far from Cairo nor too near – and went on via Australia to New Zealand where he met the officers whom he was to command and had a session with the War Cabinet.

Before leaving England he had talked with General Godley, who had commanded the New Zealanders in the previous war, and in Australia he had called on General Sir Brudenell White, co-author of the Order in Council (1914) which had served as charter for the GOC of the Australian forces. Freyberg now asked for and got a similar charter from the New Zealand Prime Minister. This document provided that while he would be subordinate to the commander of whatever force his own force was serving in, he was to be the sole judge of special situations where he must himself make decisions about its employment and communicate these decisions direct to the New Zealand government. He was also responsible directly under government for organisation, administration, training, grouping, establishment and composition.

He then sailed with the First Echelon (in effect, the 4th NZ Brigade) to Egypt and set about laying the foundations of the division as he wanted it to be. On Anzac Day 1940 he gave pleasure to the 4th Brigade, as Kippenberger recalls, by praying 'for an early chance to go for the Hun and clearly pointed out to the Almighty that we had been waiting for a long time'. He was to have to wait a good deal longer. The Second Echelon (5th Brigade) was diverted to England and became an essential part of the defences against an invasion that Freyberg hoped for but did not expect. And the Third Echelon (6th Brigade) did not reach Egypt until September. Freyberg had to shuttle between England and Egypt and combat the tendency of the Middle East Command to violate his 'charter' by borrowing units in his absence and treating him 'like a Fifth Columnist' when he demanded them back.

The 5th Brigade reached Egypt at the end of February 1941. Within days the whole division embarked for Greece. Freyberg had his misgivings from the first, but believing his government committed at a level far above him he kept his doubts to himself. These doubts appear in his diary of 2 April: 'The situation is a grave one; we shall be fighting against heavy odds in a plan that has been ill-conceived and one that violates every principle of war.'

There was little he could do except handle his division as well as possible in what began as a forlorn hope and rapidly became a withdrawal that at best could end in evacuation. That the evacuation was so successful was due to the Royal Navy and to the troops and fighting commanders. We get a real glimpse of the essential Freyberg in his refusal to obey Wavell's orders to evacuate himself by air. He would stay with his men to the last and come out with them.

Two of his brigades had been evacuated to Crete. He himself halted there on his way, as he thought, to Egypt where he wanted to reform the division. But Wavell himself had flown from Cairo to Crete, and now, with Churchill's support, ordered Freyberg to take command of the island and hold it against German invasion by sea and air. A very few tanks, obsolete artillery and little of it, virtually no air force and every kind of supply problem, made it a desperate undertaking. Freyberg performed prodigies in the three weeks available and almost succeeded. But the enemy, landing by glider and para-chute on 20 May, gained a foothold at Maleme which, after fierce fighting, gave them an airfield. They could then land men and heavy weapons and this, with their total command of the air, meant certain success. In the ten days of hard fighting that ensued the best that Freyberg and his troops could do was to keep an unbroken front, avoid encirclement, and withdraw to the evacuation beach. Once again the Royal Navy brought salvation.

Back in Egypt an inter-services inquiry exonerated Freyberg from blame and praised him warmly. Wavell told Fraser, now Prime Minister of New Zealand, that Freyberg had produced 'one of the best-trained and disciplined and fittest divisions he had seen and must be given the fullest credit for his performance in Greece and Crete'. And Fraser told Freyberg that in future if he had doubts about any role proposed for the division, he must express them early so that his government could consider them fully.

But there was no word of warmth from his old friend Churchill, an omission that wounded him. Indeed the loss of Crete afflicted him more than any subsequent failure, almost to the point of obsession; and one wonders whether he did not feel deep down that the island ought to have been held and that he was somehow at fault. He was not the man however to let vain regret weaken present action, and he pressed on with reorganising the division for desert operations. By the end of July it was up to strength in men and equipment but the Western Desert Force as a whole, was not ready for a major offensive until November. By then Auchinleck had succeeded Wavell and General Cunningham commanded the Desert Force.

The basic plan was outlined at army headquarters on 6 October. The intention was to destroy the Axis forces and relieve Tobruk: XXX Corps, with most of the tanks and two brigades of the 1st South African Division, was to make an enveloping movement and fight the opening and decisive battle by destroying the enemy armour and going on to relieve Tobruk; XIII Corps –

the New Zealand Division, 4th Indian Division and 1st Army Tank Brigade (heavy infantry tanks) – was to pin the enemy in the frontier area and later advance westwards to a junction with xxx Corps. The 4th Armoured Brigade would be on its left flank and 'in support'.

At this conference Freyberg expressed only those of his doubts that related to his own formation. He told Cunningham, 'I did not agree to go out into the blue against unbeaten armoured formations'; that 4th Armoured Brigade would be in support 'meant nothing to me, as they would be ordered away in a crisis and . . . unless we had tanks under our immediate command we should not be ordered across the wire until the armoured battle had commenced'.

In the actual battle, Operation Crusader, the weaknesses of the plan, and the superior German skill in the combined handling of armour, anti-tank guns and infantry, almost brought disaster. In spite of Freyberg's conviction that a division should fight as a division, his three brigades were drawn in piecemeal and without adequate armoured support. The German armour was not destroyed, 5th Brigade headquarters was overrun, and two New Zealand brigades were also overrun around Sidi Rezegh, the ground that Freyberg had from the beginning maintained would be vital for success.

After Tobruk was finally relieved in December 1941, the New Zealand Division withdrew to reform and rest. Relations between Freyberg and Auchinleck were now strained because of their differing views of how a division that was a separate national entity was to be treated and how far its commander should be consulted, and because they were at odds over the use of brigade groups and armour. So Freyberg was much relieved when the division got orders to go to Syria, away from the desert command.

The division did not take part in active operations again until the summer. By 10 June 1942, when the fall of Bir Hacheim made it clear that the battle round Tobruk was likely to be lost, Freyberg foresaw that the New Zealand Division would be wanted urgently. Leaving warning orders, he flew to Cairo where Auchinleck gave him the expected orders to take the division up to the front as fast as possible and occupy a defensive box at Mersa Matruh. So desperate did the position seem that Freyberg felt there was no time to consult New Zealand.

The division took under eight days to travel the 1200 miles – GHQ had allowed for ten days – and by 25 June was ready for battle. Freyberg however disliked having his mobile force boxed up in Mersa Matruh and so took it south to a strong desert position at Minqar Qaim. Here it helped to delay Rommel's armoured drive towards Egypt on the heels of the beaten Eighth Army. And after being surrounded it broke out in a night battle and withdrew to Alamein, where it took its place in the line that finally checked Rommel.

Freyberg had been wounded, but while he was in hospital the division under Brigadier Inglis played its part well. However two actions, at Ruweisat and El Mireir, confirmed troops and commanders alike in their detestation of brigade group operations where the armour 'supported' the infantry but was not under command. In each of these night actions a New Zealand brigade took its objective, expecting armoured support at first light against counter-attack by tanks. In each the armour failed to appear and the enemy tanks overwhelmed the unprotected infantry.

Auchinleck now abandoned an offensive role for the time being. On 10 August Freyberg came back from hospital, his return a tonic to all. Then Alexander succeeded Auchinleck and Montgomery took over Eighth Army. From now on everything changed and Freyberg used to say later that the arrival of these two men marked the end of his three unhappiest years.

Freyberg met Montgomery on 17 August, explained his 'charter' and expressed his views on brigade groups, the co-ordination of infantry and armour, defensive boxes and similar vexed topics. To his relief Montgomery shared them. Two battles followed, the defensive battle of Alam Halfa and the decisive battle of Alamein. In the first the division's role was to provide a buttress at the southern end of the Alamein line and a threat to Rommel's flank. In the second battle, which began on 23 October, it was one of the four infantry divisions, with armour this time under command, that broke into the enemy's main defences and held out against all counter-attack.

Freyberg was in his element at last, confident of victory. Most of the time he would be up in front with his tactical headquarters (himself in a Stuart tank with a dummy wooden gun). Here he could keep his finger on the pulse of the swaying battle. And whenever he thought an intervention might help the determined use of armour to bring about the breakthrough, he would be on the move from one forward headquarters to another or going back to corps headquarters and keeping in touch with Montgomery. Eventually, after a masterly switch by Montgomery, the breakthrough came. Montgomery's confidence in Freyberg's drive ensured that the New Zealand Division, weakened though it was in tanks and bayonet men, was part of the pursuit force. Freyberg was well in the van, riding on the outside of a tank and happy as a cherub.

After a *coup de main* by the 21st New Zealand Battalion had cleared the Halfaya Pass the New Zealand Division rested at Bardia, its future uncertain. New Zealand was considering whether, like the 9th Australian Division, it should be brought home for the Pacific. Freyberg talked to his brigadiers and found they favoured staying in North Africa. The New Zealand government, warmly applauded by Churchill, decided the division should stay.

Then followed Àgheila, where Freyberg led the New Zealand Division with armour under command in a left hook that just failed to cut off Rommel's retreat. A minor left hook was tried again farther west at Nofilia, but again Rommel got away. From then on pursuit was unremitting, the enemy finding neither position nor time for a real stand, and at last on 23 April 1943 Eighth

Army – Freyberg and his troops among the foremost – entered Tripoli, the goal of three arduous years.

Reinforcements now arrived from New Zealand – the first since October 1941 – and were absorbed. Churchill, too, arrived and the New Zealand Division paraded before him, Freyberg in front. After his speech from the rostrum Churchill descended and embraced his old protégé and friend. Crete was forgotten. Churchill had called Freyberg the 'salamander of the British Empire'. When intelligence confirmed that the salamander was a creature whose element was fire, pleasure in the division was universal.

Now followed the left hook in March, which turned the Mareth Line. With armour under command Freyberg swung wide into the desert and then drove fast and hard through almost impassable country to strike and break into the defences at the Tebaga Gap. Montgomery saw his advantage and switched Horrocks and the 1st Armoured Division to the Tebaga front. The reinforced offensive broke through, Mareth became untenable and Rommel, his front pierced, withdrew beyond Gabes.

The New Zealand Division fought some difficult actions trying to break into the *massif* east of Sousse, notably at Takrouna. But Alexander saw that Tunis was best tackled from the west. The final blow came from First Army, with formations from Eighth Army under command, and the Americans driving on Bizerta. On 13 May the enemy surrendered. The war was over in North Africa, and the New Zealand Division set off, three days later, on its way back to Egypt, a journey of 2000 miles through many grimly familiar battlefields.

Meanwhile there had been further prolonged discussions about the future of the New Zealand Division. There were strong political pressures for using it in the Pacific, the manpower situation in New Zealand was difficult, and the division had already seen hard service. On the other hand Montgomery and Alexander wanted it for Sicily and Italy. A complicating factor was that Fraser and his Cabinet were anxious lest Freyberg's professional career suffer from his loyalty to them and the division. In May the Minister of Defence, Mr Jones, came and canvassed the views of the troops themselves. Meanwhile Roosevelt had told Churchill he hoped the division would stay. In the end a compromise was reached: the division would prepare for a role in Italy – it was too late now for a role in Sicily – but a furlough scheme would provide all veterans with three months' leave in New Zealand.

As for Freyberg himself, he indicated that he would prefer his present command to getting a corps. This was a relief to everyone. For in the minds of many he and the division were as inseparable as the parts of a centaur. 'Campaigning without the General seemed unthinkable,' said Kippenberger, his most obvious successor.

Freyberg was soon hard at work incorporating the reinforcements and the new 4th New Zealand Armoured Brigade into the division's new structure and preparing for the very different battle conditions of Italy. His division in its new form must be second to no other, Allied or German, an engine of war with enormous striking power.

By late autumn 1943 the division was in Italy with Eighth Army on the Sangro, where it was to force a crossing and drive a hole into the Germans' Winter Line in readiness for a breakthrough. The job was duly done but more sanguine hopes were not realised. The paratroops, old enemies from Crete, came into the German line when it began to crumble, and severe winter conditions hampered transport and supply and constricted manoeuvre. Orsogna, after three fierce battles, was still untaken and by the end of December stalemate was recognised.

The division was now switched to the west under US Fifth Army. The Americans, with great gallantry and heavy losses, had broken in but not through, south and north of Cassino. There were political and strategic pressures on Alexander for a further attempt on the redoubtable Cassino position and the task was given to Freyberg as GOC New Zealand Corps, with two other divisions and American armour under command. He rated his chances as at best fifty-fifty. The monastery was massively bombed. Two principal attacks followed. The first failed narrowly when the engineers could not quite finish a road by which tanks were to support the Maori battalion's successful night action. The second assault, more elaborate, was defeated by bad weather, by the difficulties of passage over strongly defended hills and through a town reduced to a heap of rubble, and by the fanatical courage and skill of the paratroops.

By 20 March it was clear that Cassino must wait for the big offensive in May. The New Zealand Corps was dissolved and the division withdrew to a quieter sector. Freyberg was glad the Cassino battles were over: the strain on New Zealand's best manpower and the heavy casualties had worried him and in the last stages he had looked unhappy and been apt to recall Passchendaele. He would be glad when the war was over, he used to say, a fact that seemed to surprise him. He found it harder and harder to bear the continual loss of tried soldiers whom he had come to know and to love. He looked forward ironically to peace when the historians and men who had never known battle would criticise the mistakes of the generals. 'A man can as little write about life till he has seen war', he used to say, 'as a spinster or a bachelor can write about marriage.'

After the May breakthrough, the division engaged in flanking advances and the pursuit north of Rome but struck no serious opposition until July when it took the Lignano feature and made possible the capture of Arezzo. Then it played a conspicuous forcing role in the advance towards Florence. According to General Leese, now GOC Eighth Army, if it had not been for Freyberg and his division, the whole advance of Eighth Army would have had to be halted.

For the final phase Eighth Army moved to the Adriatic. In a reconnaissance

Freyberg had an air accident that kept him in hospital until 16 October. While he was away and after his return the division faced a series of difficult opposed river crossings for which the New Zealand engineers devised efficient new techniques. By 17 December spearheads had reached the Senio. But Alexander now decided to postpone the main offensive till the spring of 1945. It was launched on 9 April and was overwhelming. River after river was crossed in rapid succession. To the cry of 'Whips out' Freyberg raced ahead, preceded only by armoured cars of the 12th Lancers. The Po was crossed on 25 April, the Izonzo was 'gate-crashed', and the division was in Trieste on 2 May, the day the Germans in Italy capitulated.

So for Freyberg the second war ended, like the first, with himself in the lead racing to gain a vital position before the guns fell silent, the tanks halted, the infantry grounded arms, and the politicians began to talk.

What, then, was Freyberg's contribution to the war? In the first place the New Zealand Division as he shaped and led it. True, the human material was excellent. But it was Freyberg who made of that material such a superb instrument of war. He quickly saw that these men did not need the whip, could interpret a hint as an order and, apparently casual, were toughly conscientious. As the war went on men and officers developed confidence in one another, and Freyberg accepted, even encouraged, a relaxation of the outward forms of discipline. Men and officers would call one another by their first names – they had often been friends at home – and orders were likely to take the form of 'What about having the truck ready at first light?' But the truck would be there, its engine ticking over, its tank full, and with time to spare.

Freyberg's confidence in the discipline under the informality enabled him to reply when Montgomery remarked before Alamein that the New Zealanders did not seem to salute officers: 'If you wave to them they'll wave back.' The great victory parade at Tripoli was another sort of reply: when spit and polish were really called for, his division could produce them with the best.

In action, too, Freyberg set a standard of courage and fire below which his men were ashamed of falling. They knew that he would be somewhere ahead or not far behind, that he counted on them and their pride, and that what he asked would be reasonable even if on the further edge of possibility. He assumed that for them as for him it was better to die at the peak of one's effort than to survive one's manhood.

They knew also that he was always cherishing their interests, that he thought nothing too good for them, whether in weapons and equipment in battle or in amenities at the clubs he founded for them behind the lines. He never let his staff come between him and them and he was known to them all by sight. As 'the General' he was a myth, and as 'Tiny' he was a mascot. Troops, since they depend so much on chance, are superstitious and so was he.

His respect for luck, his horror of seeing the new moon through glass, these things were laughed at affectionately, but understood by men who hoped that some of the luck would rub off on them. So he was a mascot. But troops need a myth also. Montgomery had to make himself into one; Freyberg did not have to try. This is one reason why he had the sort of fame in the larger world that belongs usually only to the commanders of armies.

He had, too, the gift of finding or making talented senior officers and getting on with them. These were all formidable, critical men, outspoken and tough, tenacious of their own opinions. Yet they accepted his leadership with confidence and took it gladly for granted that he was 'the General'. He governed such men, and the division, by natural authority. He had that quality of being quietly redoubtable, of presence, dignity, total integrity that can leave the outward forms for those occasions when ritual and panoply are needed to remind a formation of its ultimate unity and pride.

His method of command by frequent informal conferences at which his senior staff could be as outspoken as they pleased, but at which he took the ultimate decisions, worked well, though it cost him more effort than he showed. Nothing in the war, he used to confide later, was so frightening as having to outline your plan, on which so many lives depended, in front of these formidable brigadiers. But the system, like that of the warrior Norman kings, combined democracy with authority and worked its way down to platoon level. New Zealanders are by temperament critical, censorious, alert, independent and above all interested. Given officers who commanded their respect – and this was why Freyberg asked whenever an officer was to be given command over infantry: 'Is he tough enough?' – the men fought the better for knowing all there was to be known about the battle plan.

Once action began Freyberg never let himself be confined to the relative safety of his armoured command vehicle. He was tireless and would turn up at a subordinate headquarters any time of the day or night, wherever the action was. He did not usually interfere. He did not expect his officers to be yes-men and they knew he would listen to any criticism based on fact and sense and experience. Underlying his grim self-control there was a certain impulsiveness and boyish fantasy. His sanguine nature and desire to get moving made him apt to imagine that an intensified bombardment meant that the enemy was 'firing off his dumps' before withdrawal and he was likely to say 'he's gawn' when the enemy was very far from gone. Sometimes in his ardour to get on he ordered some impossible task, but he relied on his commanders to resist him or to interpret his order in the way he would himself have done, confronted by the actual situation.

Given juniors who understood him, this foible did no harm. They shared his passion for speed, for getting forward and keeping the enemy off balance, and his determination was a spur. They knew that he would always realise when progress really was impossible, when the troops had had enough and could give no more. He felt very deeply, for his part, that he commanded the fighting flower of New Zealand's manhood, which, once lost, could never be replaced.

So for five long years he commanded the New Zealand Division, in and out of battle. During these years – some of them, most of them, bringing desperate battles – the men of the division inevitably changed, with deaths and wounds, reinforcements and replacements, furlough and promotions. Yet in the final campaign it was recognisably the same and fought with the same *élan*. And this was largely its general's doing.

What did Freyberg contribute to the war upwards, as it were? As a professional soldier, he scrupulously observed the rules towards his superiors – most of them his juniors in service and even reputation. Yet he did not leave his views in doubt at corps or army headquarters if he saw weaknesses in a plan. His seniors knew that if he expressed firm disagreement they had better think again. Equally, the plan once accepted, he could be counted on absolutely. His test question was: 'If we don't do it will some other division, which cannot refuse, have to?' If the answer was 'Yes', he would feel he must accept, though he might press for modifications. Thus many a major scheme owed something to him in its conception or its development, as well as in its implementation. Even Montgomery, not generous to concede credit, was known to acknowledge help from Freyberg.

His example, too, often fortified his superiors as it did the division. Many a corps commander felt he had to live up to this redoubtable subordinate. And his readiness to acknowledge good work made units from other formations proud to come under his temporary command. He was at great pains to promote good relations, in particular between the armoured units that from time to time came under command and his own men. And this helped to give Eighth Army its special sense of being a unified whole, however various the nationalities within it – British, Indian, Polish, Canadian, South African or Greek.

Nor should the high political level be overlooked. He was a sort of plenipotentiary of the New Zealand government, though answerable to it and very aware also of the problems of the British War Cabinet. Here he had the advantages of the expatriate, an equal understanding of both his countries. His discretion in dealing with the awkward problems of a loyalty both common and divided, his modesty and objectivity about himself and his power to transcend the petty, evoked and met corresponding qualities in his government and resulted in a relationship that was a model of its unusual kind.

Indeed this particular role of his is important for constitutional history, for the history of the relations between the United Kingdom and the Dominions and the United States, at a time of the greatest stress. It was not Freyberg's decision that the New Zealand Division stayed and contributed so much to victory in Africa and Europe; but its success under his command, his government's confidence in him, were a very important factor. Political interests seemed to demand that the New Zealand Division be withdrawn to the Pacific. Because of them, the Australian government, not unreasonably, withdrew its own forces. Yet it may be doubted whether they gained by doing so. For whatever happened the Americans were not only going to defeat the Japanese, but were going to dominate the postwar Pacific with or without their Allies. MacArthur would have no second sun in his sky, when the Rising Sun had set; whereas Churchill was prepared, even eager, to share the glory whatever happened to the power. So Freyberg's name remains famous while that of the Australian Blamey, another great soldier, is forgotten outside Australia and except for historians of war.

It is not easy to sum up the Freyberg behind the myth, the man whose spirit burned within the salamander. Cynthia Asquith's diary provides a sketch of him in 1917 still recognisable to another generation: 'It interests me to see him . . . his, in a way, boyish snub face with its extraordinary, almost grim, determination and feel his ambition and energy and practical ability is working away like machinery all the time inside him. He has the shortest nose almost I have ever seen on a man, great breadth of countenance with very rounded outlines everywhere – his frame gives great impression of strength and almost *expresses* swimming.' And again, 'He gives me the impression of a potentially really great soldier – in the Napoleonic sense rather than the VC hero. He seems to have many of the qualities – lack of humour, chafing ambition, and a kind of admirable ruthlessness and positive self-reliance.'

That 'lack of humour' was probably true of him only when he was intent on his profession – and the man she knew was still young and probably trying to impress her – but she was right to concentrate on that strength, both of physique and of character. The boyish quality remained with him to the end – the emanation of a kind of innocence, of the happy warrior who need not question what he is about. For his character was *au fond* one of innocence even though, as Kippenberger said, 'he's as simple as a child and as cunning as a Maori dog'. The innocence was grounded on certainties, and the simplicity was that of the atom with its latent explosive power.

For Freyberg was certain of his values. He would not have used the word 'honour' – however much disposed to pluck it from the pale-faced moon – but he honoured himself and he honoured men. He had a plain code of conduct and he recognised justice. He was a religious man in an elemental sense as well as in the conventional, since he believed life was difficult and mysterious and men needed faith to get through it safely. 'Must have a religion, must have a religion,' I can recall him saying as he urged a lapsed Catholic – and he had a very Protestant mistrust of Catholicism – to rejoin his faith.

Above all he was loyal and this was one of the things that endeared New Zealand to him – *its* loyalty to the Empire. If someone had asked him, 'Where does loyalty get you?' he probably would not have understood. For him loyalty was not a vehicle but a condition, a state, a virtue; and like other virtues, like happiness the sum of virtues, it was its own reward.

Happiness he was lucky enough to have, and not only in the domestic sense. For what he wanted to do and what he ought to do nearly always coincided and in this sense at least he did not suffer from conflict. He was gifted also in being able to do supremely well what he was called upon to do. It so happened that this was to fight for what he believed to be right. And he was lucky because his were just wars and because his own simple, black and white view of rightness corresponded to the rightness and wrongness of the issues for which his wars were fought.

Again, he was fortunate in being exceptionally fearless. His courage was an endless topic in the division. Kippenberger, himself a byword for bravery, used to say that Freyberg was fearless because he did not know what fear felt like; whereas lesser mortals had to be brave in spite of their acute awareness of fear. This courage he was able to elicit or inspire in others. Costello, his intelligence officer, used to relate how, after a friend of them both was killed, he said, 'I'm sorry about Colin Currie. He was such a nice fellow.' 'He was brave too,' Costello said. 'Courage, my dear Costello, is something I take for granted in all my officers.' Costello felt reproved, guilty because he knew his own fear, but fortified in the knowledge that he would have to go on being brave in order to conceal it.

The annals of the New Zealand Division are full of such anecdotes and typical sayings. 'Shells', he used to aver, 'don't hurt anybody, it's aimed fire you've got to watch out for.' This in spite of the shrapnel wounds with which his body was seamed. But he was protected by his own consuming and passionate interest – war – much though he came to hate all that war stood for. Danger is the necessary condition of battle, and since battle was his element it had to be accepted like the weather. His total preoccupation with the fighting enabled him to transcend the flesh which was the medium of the passion and so he escaped from the self.

But though he was thus free from the weaknesses of other men in battle, this did not make him unmindful of others or less gentle towards their frailer humanity. And as the war went on this gentleness, considerateness, became more marked. All witnesses, of whatever rank, recall his magnanimity, his humaneness, the imaginative generosity he would display in unexpected acts of kindness, his care to avoid hurting the feelings of a subordinate by public rebuke, his habit of tempering criticism by praise, his solicitude for weariness in others.

The ascendancy of his myth might give the impression that he was nothing but a soldier, a Norse saga-hero without the finer sensibility or the finer intelligence. In fact he was sensitive to the graces of living when time served. Not an intellectual, he enjoyed encouraging the intellectuals among his staff to let themselves go. In the first war he had criticised Siegfried Sassoon for seeming to imply that those who did not follow his example and refuse to serve actually liked leading men to their deaths; in the second, he would listen to his intelligence officers expound all manner of heresies and would not turn a hair. His own favourite author was Jane Austen, but he did not mind hearing Proust or Brecht or James Joyce praised, perhaps because he knew he would never read them. And he could be irreverent himself. 'The Auk?' he would say. 'A very good sergeant-major.' Or else, 'Montgomery? The British say that Montgomery is a cad. But I say that if Montgomery is a cad it's a great pity that the British Army doesn't have a few more bounders.'

As a young man he was ambitious; but any man conscious of his own powers strives to get where he can use them effectively and unmolested. In later years however maturity and ambition came to terms. He would look at his great map of the Russian front and would envy the space and forces disposed of by the Russian commanders. But there was resignation in the envy. He knew, when he told the New Zealand government he was happiest commanding their division, that he was putting from him the prospect of commanding a corps or even an army. He no longer wanted such things, or did not want them enough. He had become a New Zealander, the expatriate was at home in the mobile New Zealand that was the division, and the highest command in the gift of his country was already his. Enough that he could go on leading it in battle and in honour.

Marshal Alphonse Juin

Colonel Adolphe Goutard

Alphonse Juin was born on 16 December 1888 in the house of his grandfather, a lighthouse keeper at Cape Rosa near Bône, Algeria. His father was a policeman in Constantine but his parents left him at the cape until he was two years old; every year he went back to spend his holidays in this lonely but enchanting place, which he called 'my fairy kingdom'. He always spoke with the utmost respect of his father, a man of strong character who brought him up with a strict sense of duty, and of his mother who came from Corsica and instilled into him a sense of honour.

In Constantine young Juin went first to the ordinary primary school. Noticing his natural ability however his headmaster obtained for him a scholarship admitting him to the Constantine Lycée at the age of thirteen. After matriculation he joined the 'Corniche', the pre-St Cyr class at the Algiers Lycée.

He was brilliantly successful at the entrance examination for St Cyr in 1909, coming seventh out of nearly four hundred candidates. He emerged in July 1912 as the 'Major', or first of his term, ahead of his classmate Charles de Gaulle. 'When I left Saint-Cyr', he wrote later, 'I was impatient to savour the great passions of life in the field.' Second Lieutenant Juin accordingly applied for posting to the 1st Regiment *Tirailleurs Algériens*, which was on operations in eastern Morocco and it was there that he came under fire for the first time.

In 1913 his battalion formed part of General Gouraud's column on the Ouerrha. Later he recorded:

I first met General Gouraud during a lively engagement which he was conducting in masterly fashion. I can still see him standing imperturbably in front of his standard on a terribly exposed mound. That evening I thought over the lessons to be drawn from the day. Success had been due to clever manoeuvring by Gouraud and his use of covering fire from machine guns and artillery, the value of which he had already discovered. In addition he tried to win over the rebels by a combination of political and military action, invariably humane. It was here that I learnt the sublime qualities which should be the attributes of any true French officer.

In August 1914 General Ditte's Moroccan Brigade landed in France and in it was Lieutenant Juin as platoon commander. It was a tragic moment; the French armies had been beaten on the frontier and were flooding back towards Paris.

By 5 September the Moroccan Brigade, which was in Sixth Army, was well placed to fall upon the flank of von Kluck's army west of the Ourcq, when so ordered by Joffre. Contact was gained with the German IV Reserve Corps, the flanking corps of this army, at 10 am in front of Penchard and the Germans were driven back towards La Thérouanne. It was the beginning of the victory of the Marne. Von Kluck's army withdrew to the Aisne north of Soissons with the Moroccan Brigade on its heels.

Juin had been fighting with his arm in a sling from 6 to 15 September, having been wounded in the left hand by a piece of shrapnel on the sixth but refusing to go to the rear. For this he was awarded the Cross of the Legion of Honour with the following citation: 'An officer outstanding for courage, eye for country and power of decision. Though wounded in the hand, he insisted on remaining in command of his platoon despite his suffering.'

After a period of trench warfare on the Aisne front the Moroccan Brigade was next in action in May 1915 at Mesnil-les-Hurlus in Champagne. Juin says: 'Attacks and counter-attacks follow each other at enormous cost in casualties for insignificant gains of ground. The Regiment is melting away. It is a great pity.' For the man destined to be a general this was an illustration of a mistake not to make.

On 15 May Juin was wounded in the right arm, this time seriously, and was evacuated to Bordeaux hospital. After eight months there he returned to the depot in Rabat in April 1916. He was promoted captain and General Lyautey took him as his aide. After six months however he asked his 'revered master' to release him, saying: 'My bent is solely towards the great passions of fighting.' So he left for the front again, where he was given command of a company of *Tirailleurs Marocains*.

In spring 1917 came the setback of the Chemin des Dames but Captain Juin distinguished himself again and was mentioned in the despatches of the 153rd Division. He was then posted to the staff course, first in Senlis and then in Melun; he did not return to the front until October 1918.

In October 1919 Juin was posted to the Staff College. He says in his memoirs: 'I remember nothing particular about my course. The infantry instructors had nothing to teach us at all. The artillery instructors were the only ones who could teach us their trade but their methods were rigid and the human factor was totally disregarded. Fortunately the offensive spirit of the Army of Africa will save me from this doctrinal sclerosis.'

After two years in a staff post in Tunis, he returned to Morocco, Meknès area, in 1923. In 1925, during the Rif war against Abd-el-Krim, General Noguès, commanding the Northern Fez District, selected Juin as his Chief of Staff. Juin says: 'There was tough fighting from Ouezzan to Taza and it was conducted with consummate mastery by Noguès. This was my best training period.'

In September 1925, when the situation had been restored, General Lyautey was dismissed and replaced by Marshal Pétain. Juin records: 'So the man who had created Morocco was unjustly struck down at the moment when he had won the rubber.' Lyautey was nominated member of the *Conseil Supérieure de la Guerre* (Higher Defence Council) and left for Paris where he was allowed a small staff of three officers. He asked Juin whether he would go with him and the latter accepted 'without a shadow of hesitation'. Lyautey said to him at the time, 'How is it that you are willing to come with me now that I am no longer anything! I don't understand you.' 'That's the way I am,' Juin replied in a voice that spoke volumes for his feelings. Lyautey's gratitude was such that he embraced him. 'The two years which I spent in Paris with Lyautey', writes Juin, 'were of the utmost value to me since I learnt so much from his vigorous mind, from his genius.' Lyautey was no less appreciative of his staff officer, writing to Pierre Lyautey, his nephew: 'Juin is fine. He grasps everything. He is of the stuff of which gentlemen are made. I can see him as a great man.'

Given command of a battalion in 1927 Juin had to leave Lyautey in order to do his period in command in Algeria. Two years later he returned to his beloved Morocco, where he was posted to the military bureau of Lucien Saint, the resident general, the head of which was General Noguès. He, Juin says, was 'for me the same indispensable pilot that he had already been during the Rif war'.

In October 1933 Lieutenant-Colonel Juin was appointed general tactics instructor at the Staff College – where I was one of his pupils. We soon realised that we had an instructor unlike the rest. He smiled impishly and he saluted with his left hand. His method of teaching did not follow the solemn, austere lines of the Staff College. He would discuss any given problem quite frankly with us and would accept our solutions, provided they were logical, without insisting on the 'school solution'. In his memoirs he says: 'At the Staff College people clung rigidly to the continuous front, to formal manoeuvres and limited objectives. No one dared dispense with a slide rule for measuring the fronts and axes of attack, which were never allowed to be more than half the width of the jumping-off position.' This implied that if attacking on a 2000-yard front for instance, the advance might not be deeper than a 1000 yards since this might dislocate the front!

We might have been in favour of the teaching methods of this nonconformist instructor, but this did not apply to those in high places and at the end of his first year as instructor he was sent back to Algeria. On 10 March 1937

General Noguès, commanding the North African theatre of operations, selected Juin as his Chief of Staff. In December 1938 he was promoted brigadier-general.

In December 1939 General Juin took over command of the 15th Motorised Infantry Division in First Army. Throughout the winter he chafed against French inactivity. 'We are not attempting even a diversion against the Siegfried Line', he wrote, 'and it was only hurriedly constructed.' However on 10 May 1940, when the Germans invaded Belgium, First Army moved up to the Dyle. On 14 and 15 May it held the enemy in front of the Gembloux gap. 'But', Juin writes, 'this was only a local success, without effect on a battle which had already been lost strategically.' In fact Ninth Army had given way on the Meuse and German armour was pouring through the gap. The Allied armies had been cut in two and in the north First Army withdrew towards Dunkirk covered by Juin's division. After defending Valenciennes from 19 to 26 May it was surrounded in the suburbs of Lille. It was forced to surrender on 30 May with its ammunition exhausted.

Juin was made Commander of the Legion of Honour and mentioned in army despatches for 'proving himself an incomparable leader and tactician and resisting to the utmost limit of his forces'. Later he noted, 'While a prisoner I thought continuously about the reasons for our defeat. We had made no use at all of the offensive spirit peculiar to our race. I vowed, therefore, that if I managed to emerge from prison one day and was given responsibility for a theatre of operations, I would act solely on the principle of the offensive.'

As it so happened in June 1941 General Weygand, Government Delegate-General in French Africa, persuaded the Germans to release General Juin to assist 'in ensuring the defence of North Africa against all comers'. In the German view 'all comers' meant the British, but in that of Weygand and Juin it meant the Germans and Italians. On his release Juin was given command of all troops in Morocco.

In December 1941 Marshal Pétain, under German pressure, recalled Weygand and abolished the post of delegate-general. Juin was appointed Commander Land Forces North Africa. On arrival in Algiers he told his staff: 'One does not replace General Weygand; one succeeds him. Gentlemen, business will proceed.' 'Business' consisted of preparing the Army of Africa to take the field again; secret mobilisation was organised, equipment concealed, etc. Weygand noted: 'I could not have wished for a better successor to complete my task which was to reconstitute the Army of Africa so that one day it could resume the struggle alongside our allies. Juin carried on everything with such enthusiasm that at the end of a year the army could meet any call that might be made upon it.'

'At the end of a year' meant November 1942. By that time the French could provide five mobile divisions (three in Algeria and two in Morocco) and

a Light Mechanised Brigade, all fully trained. In addition preparations had
been made in the probable area of fighting, secret depots being formed in the
Tunisian mountains. General Pedron says: 'General Juin made no secret of
his intention to oppose any withdrawal by Rommel through south Tunisia
towards Tunis via the coastal plain which is overlooked by the mountain
range.'

The Anglo-American landing of 8 November, of which General Juin knew
nothing beforehand, came like a thunderclap. The Allies were counting upon
General Giraud, who had escaped from Königstein, to welcome them and
ensure that there was no fighting 'against all comers'. Unfortunately he spent
two days in fruitless discussions in the Gibraltar headquarters and landed on
Blida airfield, still in civilian clothes, only on the afternoon of 9 November.
General de Monsabert had been waiting for him on the airfield throughout
the morning of the eighth together with a company from my own battalion
(1st Battalion 9th *Tirailleurs Algériens*).

But by 9 November it was too late. Admiral Darlan, a member of the
Vichy government, happened to be in Algiers at his son's bedside and had
seized power on the 8th 'in the Marshal's name'; he enforced the order for
resistance 'to any invader' in Morocco and the province of Oran. Not until
10 November did Darlan give way to General Juin's pleadings and decide to
conclude a general armistice with General Clark. He issued the following
order: 'Our obligations having been fulfilled and further bloodshed having
become useless, the forces of North Africa are ordered to cease operations
against the Americans and their allies and to observe the strictest neutrality.'
There was no question therefore of resuming the struggle alongside the Allies,
but General Juin's message passing on this order changed everything: 'For-
warded for immediate compliance. Task of troops in Tunisia *vis-à-vis* other
foreign forces unchanged. Make arrangements to resist them and cover communications with Algeria.' 'Other foreign forces' were of course the Germans
who had begun landing at Bizerta and on El Aouina aerodrome in order to
assist Rommel who was in difficulties in Libya.

On the next day, 11 November, however, while the Germans were moving
into unoccupied France, a message arrived from Marshal Pétain disowning
Darlan, replacing him by General Noguès and ordering continuation of the
struggle against 'the American invaders'. On 12 November, when Noguès
arrived from Morocco, Darlan made way for him and prepared to cancel his
armistice of the 10th. He was prevented from doing so by energetic representations from Juin. Faced with this indescribable confusion Juin decided on the
next day, 13 November, to precipitate matters. During a 10 am meeting he
appealed to the patriotism of Noguès and the other leaders and persuaded
them to accept the following solution: Noguès to hand authority back to
Darlan, who would become High Commissioner in North Africa, Giraud to
command all French forces, Juin to command the land forces. This agreement
was ratified at a solemn meeting held at 2 pm in the presence of General

Eisenhower who had hurried over from Gibraltar. 'This time', Juin wrote, 'the Army of Africa is re-entering the war of liberation alongside its allies The conscience of every military man will at once be vastly relieved.'

The Germans however continued to land in Tunisia and the Allies, who had not landed east of Algiers, were still far away. The small French forces in Tunisia under General Barré could not stop the enemy by themselves and so were ordered to withdraw slowly and without fighting in order to gain time and occupy the Medjez-el-Bab position covering the Medjerda valley and the Algiers road.

On 19 November the Germans became impatient. They called upon General Barré to allow them through, and when he refused attacked the Medjez position. They were repulsed, the first Allied reinforcements having had time to arrive. The Tunisian campaign had started.

On 25 November General Juin took over command of the French Army Detachment (the DAF) with headquarters at Laverdure near Souk-Ahras. Its task was to hold the eastern 'dorsale' or ridge overlooking the coastal plain south of the Medjerda while the British advanced in the north towards Tunis and Bizerta. By 10 December they had reached Mateur, just over 20 miles from Bizerta, and Djedeida, some 12 miles from Tunis, but then they were counter-attacked and forced to withdraw.

Meanwhile the French mobile divisions from Constantine, Algiers and Morocco had arrived to occupy the passes over the eastern dorsale and prevent the enemy, now all over the coastal plain, from crossing the ridge. So a front was being formed 'to cover communications with Algeria'. On 18 January however the Germans, who now had some Tiger tanks, broke through at the junction between the eastern and western (or 'Great') dorsales in the area of the Oued-el-Kebir dam; they pushed southwards towards Ousseltia, taking the defences of the eastern dorsale in rear. General Juin accordingly persuaded the Americans to allot him General Robinett's armoured group which he launched from the Great Dorsale against the flank of the German armour. The Germans were driven back northwards and by the 28th the position had been re-established.

This action demonstrated how dependent the French were upon their allies owing to lack of modern equipment. Moreover the American 11 Corps had now arrived to take up position on the right (southern) flank of the French Army Detachment. Considering unified command over the entire front to be essential, General Juin proposed to General Anderson that the French forces be placed under his orders. There would then be three sectors, all with an equal call for support on Allied armoured, anti-tank and anti-aircraft units: in the north a British sector (v Corps under General Allfrey); in the centre a French sector (xix Corps under General Koeltz); in the south an American sector (11 US Corps under General Fredendall reinforced by the Constantine division). This proposal was accepted, and on his return from Morocco where he had been present at the Anfa Conference General Giraud could only give it his blessing, although he had disagreed with it in principle.

At this point however fresh danger threatened from southern Tunisia. Rommel was being driven back from Libya by Montgomery's Eighth Army and he crossed the Tunisian frontier on 26 January; his *Afrika Korps* had just established itself on the Mareth Line – built to prevent an Italian invasion from Libya! Rommel thought that before the arrival of the Eighth Army he had time to strike a major blow northwards with his panzers. On 30 January he seized the Faid Col on the eastern ridge and emerged into the plain between the two ridges. Seeing itself outflanked on the eastern ridge, 11 US Corps abandoned it to withdraw towards Tebessa. The German armour reached Sbeitla by 16 February and Kasserine, at the foot of the Great Dorsale, by the 20th. From Kasserine two routes were available across the ridge and into the northern plain in rear of the Allied front in northern Tunisia – the Thala road and the Tebessa road. Rommel accordingly despatched 10th Panzer Division towards Thala, 25 miles to the north. What was there on this road? At the Chambi Pass above Kasserine was an isolated American battalion and in the outskirts of Thala, commanding the entrance to the pass, a battalion of *Tirailleurs Algériens* (my own battalion) equally isolated and without anti tank weapons.

The unified command, which had fortunately been established, now proved its worth. General Anderson despatched General Nicholson's armoured group along this axis to carry out a delaying action. On the evening of the 21 February the panzers arrived in front of Thala, having brushed aside the American battalion in Chambi and driven back the British armour. The situation seemed to us desperate. At dawn on the 22nd, however General Nicholson launched a counter-attack with a small armoured unit, the Lothian and Border Horse; as he himself admitted, it was only 'bluff' and its prospects of success were 'about zero'. Surprised by this unexpected reaction however the German armour withdrew. On this axis the Germans had lost their opportunity.

Rommel however had sent another armoured column along the other axis, that of Kasserine–Tebessa, defended by 11 US Corps. On the morning of the 22 February General Juin heard that this corps had been ordered to withdraw. He hurried at once to Kouif, General Fredendall's headquarters, to implore him to do no such thing.

> Our conversation took an emotional turn [Juin records]. Fredendall's answer to all my objurgations was that he must carry out the order received. I then showed him on my map that the country between Tebessa and Constantine was good tank country and that the abandonment of Tebessa meant opening the road to Constantine to the panzers. 'Now,' I said to him, 'my wife and children are in Constantine. If you carry out this order, I shall

remove from you the Constantine division in order to defend Tebessa and we will get ourselves killed there.' It was the only way of stirring him. I saw his attitude change and, throwing his arms round my neck, he swore not to abandon Tebessa.

Next morning, to everyone's surprise, armoured patrols sent out in front of Thala and Tebessa found no one. The enemy had decamped and contact had been lost. What had happened? Unable to count on a rapid victory Rommel had recalled his armour southwards to the Mareth Line to face Eighth Army.

All attention then turned to southern Tunisia. The Mareth Line was attacked on 20 March and broken on the 27th; the Germans and Italians retreated north along the coastal plain. By the end of April they were confined to the North-East Tunisian Redoubt, facing Eighth Army on the south and First Army on the west. General Alexander, the army group commander, concentrated against the western face of the redoubt. On 6 May the British advanced on Tunis, which they entered next day, while the Americans reached Bizerta. On 13 May the Axis forces, who had taken refuge on Cape Bon in the hope of embarking there, capitulated. German and Italian prisoners numbered a quarter of a million. The Tunisian campaign was over.

General Juin made a triumphal entry into Tunis. The crowd was massed on the pavements of the Avenue Jules Ferry, and when he appeared at the head of the parade he received, in the words of Pierre Lyautey, 'a delirious welcome such as I have never seen'. After the parade Juin assembled the various authorities and told them in a voice husky with emotion: 'I am happy today, infinitely happy, because I am conscious of having liberated my country.' The American government made him a Grand Commander of the Order of Merit for 'exceptionally meritorious conduct and the vital role played by his forces during the Tunisian campaign, all the credit for which is due to him'.

But there were further tasks ahead of us – in Italy. In September 1943 General Juin was commissioned to form the French Expeditionary Corps. General Carpentier, its Chief of Staff, says: 'The CEF consisted of the traditional Army of Africa with its Tirailleurs, its Goums and its Spahis; it was an élite formation under a renowned and beloved commander.' Juin himself says: 'I adored these men because I had trekked with them in Morocco.' So confidence between the troops and their commander was complete.

On 9 September 1943 US Fifth Army landed with some difficulty at Salerno and advanced north towards Naples. General Clark, its commander, invited Juin to pay him a visit. Juin says: 'We landed at Sorrento on 29 September and were welcomed in his tent by Clark. He told us the story of the Salerno landing when he was within an ace of being thrown back into the sea. On 1 October we followed x British Corps as it advanced. We saw 7th

Armoured Division in close column on the road; the mountainous country prevented it from deploying.'

The Italian peninsula consists of a long mountainous spine crossed by narrow valleys. Movement confined solely to the lower levels meant that any advance was restricted to enclosed ground where the enemy could concentrate his resources. General Carpentier says: 'The essential was to widen the front by attacking through the mountains. It meant "invading the mountains". Only the CEF could do this, relying on the legs of its Tirailleurs or its Goums and the hoofs of its mules.'

On 22 November 2nd Moroccan Infantry Division (2 DIM) landed at Naples. General Juin arrived on the 15th and issued the following order of the day: 'The hour we have been waiting for has struck at last! The battlefields of Italy are open before you and you are called upon to fight at the side of our valiant allies for the liberation of our country. You will give proof of the faith which inspires you. The eyes of suffering France are fixed upon you.'

At this point Fifth Army, working its way along the western slope of the Apennines, was facing the Gustav Line running from the southern spur of the mountains to the sea and using the Garigliano and Rapido rivers as an anti-tank ditch. The position extended from Monte Cairo to the Monti Aurunci mountains (5000 feet and 4600 feet respectively) and effectively blocked the entrance to the Liri valley through which ran the road to Rome. The entrance to this valley, moreover, along which General Clark proposed to launch his armour, was overlooked by a spur of Monte Cairo, Monte Cassino, crowned by its monastery.

When the French arrived Fifth Army still had to capture a number of snow-covered ridges rising to over 3000 feet before it reached the Gustav Line. This was the sector in which 2nd Moroccan Infantry Division went into action on 11 December. By the 15th it had captured Monte Pentano and by the 27th Monte Mainarde. Juin says: 'The good old Moroccan Division! It's trial shot has been a masterpiece. The Americans are open-mouthed. They watch while our tirailleurs sweep away obstacles which have held them up so long. They never tire of singing their praises.'

At the end of December General Juin was reinforced by 3rd Algerian Infantry Division (3 DIA) under the intrepid General de Monsabert. On 3 January 1944 the French Expeditionary Corps, now at a strength of two divisions, took over a sector of Fifth Army front. General Carpentier comments: 'The appearance of General Juin with his five stars might have been embarrassing to General Clark, who was only a corps commander. But he soon captivated the Allied leaders by his modesty and candour. No one was afraid of him. He attracted people.'

The arrival of the French Expeditionary Corps enabled General Clark to resume the offensive. On 3 January he explained his plan to General Juin: on the left British x Corps was to move up to the Garigliano and establish a bridgehead; on the right US ii Corps was to force its way into the Liri valley and open the road to Rome for the armour. Juin comments: 'To imagine that armour could easily drive through to Rome along the narrow passage of the Liri valley implied total disregard of the overriding influence of the terrain.'

The offensive opened on 8 January. Though x Corps reached its objective on the lower Garigliano, US 11 Corps failed against the Liri valley and was pinned to the ground by flanking fire from Monte Cassino. Clearly there was no more to be done here while this bastion stood. On 22 January Clark assigned this task to US 34th Division with the French Expeditionary Corps covering it on the right by capturing the Belvedere. Juin allotted this objective to 3rd Algerian Infantry Division. On 25 January de Monsabert's tirailleurs crossed the Rapido with the water up to their waists and hurled themselves at the Belvedere which they captured in hand-to-hand fighting next day. 'I do not think', Juin writes, 'that there has ever been a more brilliant feat of arms in the annals of the French army.'

But US 34th Division failed against Monte Cassino. General Alexander, the army group commander, accordingly placed at General Clark's disposal the Indian Corps and General Freyberg's New Zealanders. At the preliminary discussion General Juin suggested that Monte Cassino be taken by continuing the outflanking movement already begun with the capture of the Belvedere. General Freyberg however preferred a direct assault preceded by massive air bombing to destroy everything, both the monastery and the village. 'On 15, 16 and 17 February', Juin says, 'I watched the most frightful bombing imaginable. The monastery vanished in a cloud of thick smoke which rose into the sky spreading like a mushroom. But the Indians who had been withdrawn for safety reasons were unable to regain their trenches in time; some had even been occupied by the enemy who had taken cover in them.'

In view of this setback bombing was resumed on 15 March at even greater intensity; hundreds of aircraft in waves dropped 1200 tons of bombs and the artillery expended 200,000 shells. The ground was so churned up as a result that tanks could not operate. The Indian attack on Monte Cassino failed, and though the New Zealanders managed to penetrate into Cassino village they met desperate resistance from German parachute troops who emerged from the cellars and ruins, and they were driven back. Field-Marshal Kesselring says in his memoirs: 'The bombing of the monastery was quite unnecessary . . . Once and for all I wish to establish the fact that the monastery was not occupied as part of our line.'

Faced with these setbacks General Clark summoned General Juin to his headquarters on 21 March to ask whether, in his view, the offensive should be continued at all costs. Juin replied that he thought it better not to go on. After a further fruitless attempt General Alexander decided on 24 March to halt the operation and resume it in April on a fresh basis.

At the end of March the front was reorganised for the offensive. General Alexander, still determined to force his way along the valleys, concentrated his resources. Eighth Army was to work along the Liri valley, supported on its left by Fifth Army; the latter allocated the Ausente valley to the French Expeditionary Corps and the coastal route to US II Corps. General Carpentier says: 'No progress was possible along the narrow coastal strip and our advance along the Ausente was doomed to failure.'

On 1 April General Brann, head of Fifth Army operations section, arrived to explain the plan to General Carpentier, who countered with a plan prepared by General Juin:

> The best objective for the army is the lateral road Itri-Pico beyond the Monti Aurunci; it is the supply route for the Hitler Line. To reach it we shall move along the Monti Aurunci where the enemy is not expecting us. We can perfectly well do this with our tirailleurs and our goums and it will lead to a definite breakthrough. General Brann gazed pensively at the mountain range on my map; there was neither road nor track to be seen. I then took him to General Juin who confirmed the explanation I had given and said that he would despatch a memorandum on the subject.

In this memorandum, dated 4 April, General Juin explained in detail that to reach the Itri–Pico lateral no attempt should be made to outflank the Monti Aurunci via the valleys, which were strongly held, but that the advance should be direct through the mountains. General Clark was attracted by the boldness of this plan and adopted it.

On 24 April General Juin allocated to his divisions the tasks best suited to them. The first essential was to break out of the Garigliano bridgehead and capture Monte Majo (2800 feet) with its spurs, Monte Feuci, Monte Cerasola and Monte Girofano; penetration of this first line was assigned to 2nd Moroccan Infantry Division under General Dody, known as 'the CEF's battering ram'. On its right was 1st Free French Division (1 DFL) under General Brosset, keeping touch with Eighth Army, to which it had belonged in Libya. On the left was the redoubtable 3rd Algerian Infantry Division under General de Monsabert, which was to take the key position of Castelforte and so open the Ausente valley.

Once this first phase was over the Mountain Corps was to make its way into the Aurunci *massif* which was 10 miles deep and rose to heights of 3300 and 4600 feet. The corps consisted of 4th Moroccan Mountain Division (4 DMM) under General Sevez and the Goums ('Group of Moroccan Tabors'); Berber mountaineers under General Guillaume. The corps was to drive across the *massif* and cut the Itri–Pico lateral, which was vital to the enemy. The operation was to start with a surprise night attack without artillery preparation.

The Allied leaders, Alexander, Clark and Maitland Wilson, were all extremely interested in this plan and each in turn paid a visit to Juin's headquarters at Sessa Aurunci. He explained his ideas to all of them, opening his window and saying: 'There's my battlefield.' Looking at the great peaks his visitors shook their heads incredulously.

By the end of April the French divisions had concentrated in the narrow Garigliano bridgehead. D-Day was fixed for 11 May and H-Hour for 11 pm.

At 11 pm on 11 May night turned into day as the artillery opened in support of the start of the attack. The 2nd Moroccan Infantry Division moved off towards Monte Majo but encountered firm defences and was able to capture only Monte Faito, a spur of Monte Majo. Hearing of this setback, on the morning of the 12th General Juin left for Monte Ornito, where he had a good view over the countryside. It was a difficult climb, first in a jeep, then on foot, under mortar fire and along a rough path strewn with the bodies of mules. Juin says: 'On reaching the top I found Colonels Calliès and Molle who made no secret of the fact that it was tough going. The enemy was counter-attacking Monte Faito. I observed, however, that our artillery was very active and that the German reserves were being battered by our four hundred guns. I concluded that the attack should be resumed.'

He returned to his headquarters to issue his orders. General (as he was later) Beaufre, at the time Chief of Staff to 4th Moroccan Mountain Division, says:

> What an initial setback! We were deeply disillusioned. But then arrived General Juin. After we had explained the situation to him, he rapped on the table and said in his hoarse clipped voice: 'It's gone wrong. But they are as tired as we are. We'll start again tomorrow morning after a full-scale artillery preparation and it will go.' This little scene is for me a typical illustration of the leader's role – to get the feel of the battle and revive people's energies. When Juin left, all our anxiety had gone. We issued fresh orders. The order for resumption of the attack was everywhere received with relief. Although checked, we could not let matters rest there.

At 4 am on 13 May the French moved on again. Monte Cerasola, Monte Feuci and Monte Girofano were captured. The enemy was giving ground. Juin had been right; the German reserves had been dissipated on the previous evening. At 1 pm a radio message in clear from General Mackensen, commanding Fourteenth German Army, was intercepted: 'Monte Feuci having been taken, the order for general withdrawal is issued.' At 3 pm Monte Majo fell and an enormous tricolour flag was hoisted on its summit. At 4 pm came a further message from Mackensen: 'Monte Majo having been taken, withdrawal should be accelerated.'

The Ausente valley now being clear, the Mountain Corps could move up into the Aurunci mountains. General Guillaume, commanding the Tabors (the Goums) saw General Juin drive up the track in his jeep, wearing his beret and in high spirits. 'We've got them,' he said. 'Off you go, Guillaume, as fast as you can to Monte Petrella' (4600 feet). General Guillaume says: 'No order was ever so willingly obeyed. The Goums dashed into the rocks. It was Juin who had set them going and we went because he was the well-loved friend of us all. We were like intoxicated youngsters as we set off with him on the path of victory again.' Field-Marshal Kesselring says: 'Thenceforth there was no stopping the French advance. The French units were used to mountain work and could go where they liked.'

On 15 May, after capturing Monte Petrella, the Goums pushed on to Monte Revole (4000 feet). On reaching it they saw in a hollow below them two German battalions disembarking from their trucks and starting to climb the slope. General Guillaume ordered: 'Not a shot from rifle or gun!' They let the Germans climb, and when they were near the top loosed a hellish storm of fire that annihilated the two battalions. The survivors said: 'We would never have believed that you would be on peaks like this.'

On 18 May the Mountain Corps reached its objective, the Itri–Pico road. On its right 1st Free French Division (1 DFL) had reached Pontecorvo on the Liri, 10 miles behind the Gustav Line and Monte Cassino, which was at last abandoned by its defenders. The Liri valley was now open to Eighth Army.

This was victory. Visitors flowed into the Sessa Aurunci headquarters to congratulate General Juin – General de Gaulle from Algiers, General Maitland Wilson, C-in-C Mediterranean, and General Alexander who said: 'Well, I congratulate you. I must admit that I was not confident. Only your divisions could have done it.'

On 22 May 3rd Algerian Infantry Division reached Pico via Esperia. General Juin sent it off with 1st Free French Division to San Giovanni on the Liri behind the Hitler Line, the last obstacle in the valley. When they arrived there on the 25th, the Germans evacuated the entire valley. The road to Rome was open.

Meanwhile on the coast US 11 Corps had joined up with the Anzio bridge-head. There was then a general rush towards Rome, which the Germans evacuated in a hurry, withdrawing northwards by every available route. By 4 June the American corps had reached the city suburbs. That evening General Clark passed word to General Juin that he wished to have him at his side when he made his entry into Rome next day. They were to meet at the Capitol at 10 am.

At 10 am on 5 June Clark took Juin on board his jeep and they made a triumphal entry into the Eternal City. Juin says: 'We were hugged almost to death by the Romans who had come out in crowds to welcome their "liberatori"; the church bells were going full blast.'

General Juin was received in private audience by Pope Pius XII. 'Our talk was a cordial one,' he says. 'His Holiness had heard from the Germans of the decisive part played by the CEF and they had added: "Without these French devils, we should never have lost Rome." His Holiness congratulated me discreetly.' In the great hall the Pope then received a party of French officers, of whom I was one. He told us in French how pleased he was to welcome us and he prayed for God's blessing on us, our families and, he added, 'on your dear country, France'.

On 10 June 3rd Algerian Infantry Division and 1st Free French Division, constituted as a 'pursuit echelon' under General de Larminat, left Rome to rejoin the Allies who had been pursuing northwards. By 30 June this force had fought its way to the Mersa, 6 miles from Sienna. General Juin had urged that, the city being full of art treasures, it should not be attacked direct and so an outflanking movement was organised. The Germans however did not wait and evacuated the town during the night 2–3 July. On the morning of 3 July we entered Sienna to the cheers of the populace, overjoyed that their town had been liberated without damage. They threw flowers at us; my jeep was piled high with them. Next day General Juin reviewed 3rd Algerian Infantry Division on the famous Piazza del Campo.

From Sienna 4th Moroccan Mountain Division and 2nd Moroccan Infantry Division continued the pursuit towards Florence. On 21 July however all French divisions were routed to Naples to embark for Operation Anvil, the landing in southern France. Before departure a parade was held to say farewell to General Juin who was leaving us. After the parade he assembled the officers and said to us: 'You have restored honour to our army and glory to our colours. But your task is not finished. The enemy still occupies France. It is your turn to land and hunt him out.'

However exciting the prospect, we could not help being somewhat disillusioned at being robbed of our victory. The Allied army in Italy was deprived of its impetus and was to lose the French Expeditionary Force just at the moment when General Juin had put forward a Napoleonic plan to strike the enemy in his 'soft underbelly' on the Danube. Pierre Lyautey says: 'What a sublime goal for these troops from Italy, hardened by victory. We should have been ahead of the Russians in the heart of Europe and our unhappy peace would have been very different.' General Chambe says:

> Operations were now to be interminable; we had to force our way through the defences of the Maginot Line which had been turned against us, then the Siegfried Line and finally the Rhine. General Juin, with whom I was at the time, was furious. I can still see him rapping the map of Europe with his wounded hand, saying: 'What! They are stopping an army in full flood when it has only to charge on to cross the Po plain without firing a shot, cross into Venetia, reach Lyublyana and arrive on the Danube; from there it could break into Germany, outflanking all the defences facing west. We should be in Berlin ahead of the Russians. What madness! One should never stop a victorious army.'

The first result of this halt was to save the German armies from annihilation. General Westphal admits: 'After Rome we were threatened with complete collapse. We had no troops worthy of the name in the Po valley. In all probability Kesselring's Army Group would have been destroyed'. The German General Böhmler says:

The Allied victory of Rome was not followed up, to the great benefit of Stalin and Hitler. In the light of 'Anvil' the latter had no need to worry further about the Balkans. So he withdrew the 'Hermann Goering' Panzer Division and two mechanised divisions from Italy and sent them to France. Had 'Anvil' not removed General Alexander's 'spearhead', the CEF, undoubtedly the Union Jack and Stars and Stripes would have been hoisted on the Vienna Ballhausplatz instead of the Hammer and Sickle.

Generals Alexander, Clark and Maitland Wilson made similar representations, urging that victory in Italy be followed up, but the highest authorities insisted that the strategy laid down at Teheran in November 1943 be adhered to. 'At Teheran', Clark says, 'Stalin had urged an invasion of southern France in order to keep us away from the Balkans which were to be the preserve of the Red Army.'

Juin appealed to de Gaulle but he replied that Juin must 'play the game and continue to follow the Allied plan'. He was forbidden to cross the Arno valley. 'There was nothing to do but conform', Juin says, 'and forget my dreams which had led to a Napoleonic concept of invading the Danube valley; it would have taken us quickly to Vienna, Prague and the Elbe. This was the end of all these dreams.'

On 1 August 1944 General Juin handed over command to General de Lattre de Tassigny and the French Expeditionary Corps became the French First Army, later to be the *Armée Rhin et Danube*. It did not reach the Danube until 1945, after a hard winter's campaigning, whereas we could have reached it in late summer 1944, so shortening the war. What casualties and destruction would have been saved!

On 14 August 3rd Algerian Infantry Division embarked at Taranto and we set sail towards the coast of Provençe to liberate our country.

Faced with this great task it was sad no longer to be led by General Juin. I asked General de Monsabert about him and he replied: 'He was a practical man rather than a theorist. In planning his battle on the Garigliano he counted on the fact that the troops from Africa were experts in mountain warfare. But he said to me himself: 'This solution would never have been passed at the Staff College.'''

For General Carpentier, his Chief of Staff, Juin was a 'profoundly human leader who knew how to talk both to commanders and to the humblest tirailleur either in French or in Arabic. He was the "Chief", the "Boss".' Only those who went with him during his tours of the front could realise the affectionate respect in which he was held. When asked what he thought were the qualities of a commander, he replied: 'Radiate confidence and enjoy taking risks.' As we have seen he always radiated something to his men, but he did so also to his allies. General Clark, in his farewell letter on Juin's departure from Italy, said: 'I do not know how to express my sadness at losing, not only the support of four of the best divisions that have ever fought, but also the wise counsel of a good and sincere friend.'

In August 1944 General Juin was appointed Chief of Staff of National Defence. In December 1950 General Eisenhower, Supreme Commander NATO, asked the French government to give him General Juin as Commander-in-Chief Land Forces Central Europe in Fontainebleau and he was there for five years. In May 1952 he was made Marshal of France. In October 1956, seared by the developments that were tearing Algeria, his native country, apart, he withdrew to his tent.

He ultimately died, exhausted, on 27 January 1967 at the age of seventy-nine. His state funeral took place on 1 February. As his coffin was lifted on to a gun-carriage after a service in Notre Dame his companions in arms ranged themselves on either side. There was Field-Marshal Earl Alexander, carrying his baton, bent on escorting his friend to the crypt of the Invalides; there was General Lemnitzer, Supreme Commander Europe. General Clark, unable to be present owing to illness, sent a magnificent wreath of orchids to the Invalides. It was the final tribute paid by our allies to the man who had inspired that magnificent fighting formation, the French Expeditionary Corps in Italy.

For the rest of us, as General Carpentier his Chief of Staff has said: 'We bore, and shall always bear, the honoured mark of its membership.'

INDEX

Figures in bold type indicate entire chapter on the subject.